CHESS EVOLUTION

September 2011

By

Arkadij Naiditsch

Quality Chess
www.qualitychess.co.uk

First edition 2011 by Anuk.doo
with technical assistance from Quality Chess UK Ltd

CHESS EVOLUTION - September 2011

ISBN 978-1-907982-06-4

All sales or enquiries should be directed to Quality Chess UK Ltd,
20 Balvie Road, Milngavie, Glasgow G62 7TA, United Kingdom
Phone +44 141 333 9588
e-mail: info@qualitychess.co.uk
website: www.qualitychess.co.uk

Distributed in US and Canada by SCB Distributors, Gardena, California, US
www.scbdistributors.com

Distributed in Rest of the World by Quality Chess UK Ltd through
Sunrise Handicrafts, Smyczkowa 4/98, 20-844 Lublin, Poland

Responsible editor: Arkadij Naiditsch
Typeset by Jacob Aagaard
Proofreading by Colin McNab
Additional editing by Colin McNab, Andrew Greet & John Shaw
Cover design by Milos Sibinovic
Printed in Poland by Drukarnia Pionier, 31-983 Krakow, ul. Igolomska 12

CONTENTS

Key to symbols used

±	White is slightly better
∓	Black is slightly better
±	White is better
∓	Black is better
+–	White has a decisive advantage
–+	Black has a decisive advantage
=	equality
⯑	with compensation
⇄	with counterplay
∞	unclear
↑	with initiative
→	with an attack
Δ	with the idea
□	only move
?	a weak move
??	a blunder
!	a good move
!!	an excellent move
!?	a move worth considering
?!	a move of doubtful value
#	mate

Editorial Preface

Chess Evolution takes great steps forward!

First the good news and then even more good news!

In early August I received an email from Jacob Aagaard of Quality Chess with a proposal for cooperation between Quality Chess and Chess Evolution. It was a very pleasant surprise. Chess Evolution has been very good in terms of the chess content, but perhaps I could softly say: "not the best at making a nice looking book out of a pgn file". With Quality Chess we gained a partner which is one of the world's leading chess publishers, with a very high level of typesetting and editing.

The Chess Evolution team is very happy about the deal and we are sure that with the professionalism Quality Chess has shown over the years, together we will produce not only fine chess material but also good-looking books which will be available all over the world.

The second piece of good news is that Chess Evolution will be translated into the French language starting from the September issue. CE and Marseille Chess Club are going to work together. Marseille are the current French Team Champions and definitely the most active and expanding chess club in France (at the moment they have almost 900 club members/school pupils). My thanks especially to the "cornerstones" of the club, Laurie Delorme and Yannick Gozzoli.

Now some chess news about the Chess Evolution September 2011 issue:

First, we welcome a new member of CE, GM Nikola Sedlak – a strong attacking player with many interesting ideas who has been a good friend of mine for many years. The endgame section was written this time by GM Konstantin Landa. The puzzle section is by GM Jacob Aagaard.

A new price for Chess Evolution

Chess Evolution is changing slightly its price structure. Instead of the current 36 Euro per book with shipping included, we are changing to 32.99 Euro per book plus 3 Euro shipping costs.

Great bonuses for Chess Evolution half-year and full-year subscribers!

Chess Evolution will now offer half-year and full-year subscribers **Interactive Services**:

➢ A 6-month subscriber will be able to ask 1 question about each issue for free!
➢ A whole-year subscriber can ask 3 questions about each issue for free!

Questions can be asked in many different languages due to our cosmopolitan team: English, German, French, Russian, Dutch, Serbian, Polish... Sorry no Chinese at the moment! More information can be found at www.chess-evolution.com

Chess Evolution is breaking new barriers and producing not only high-class chess analysis but will also give our customers higher quality books and a better service. In keeping with our ambition to stay ahead of the game, Chess Evolution is now the first interactive-service book and we hope our readers will welcome our pioneering efforts.

Overview of Major Events from the Past Two Months

1) Biel Chess Festival 16-29 July 2011

Biel is one of the few serious tournaments in the world that uses the 'football' scoring system of three points for a win and one for a draw. This suits the uncompromising style of Magnus Carlsen, who continued his winning ways. Alexander Morozevich also made a successful return after going almost a year without playing. The Open section was won by Ni Hua with a score of 8½/11.

1. Carlsen 19, **2**. Morozevich 17, **3**. Vachier-Lagrave 12, **4**. Shirov 12, **5**. Caruana 10, **6**. Pelletier 5

2) World Team Chess Championship 17-27 July 2011

Armenia won convincingly with 14 points out of a possible 18. China finished second with 13, followed by Ukraine with 12. The event was a big disappointment for the Russian team, who only managed to take fourth place with 10 points.

Team	Armenia	China	Ukraine	Russia	Hungary	USA	Azerbaijan	India	Israel	Egypt			
Armenia		2½	2	2	2½	2	2	2½	3½	3½	14	22½	1
China	1½		2½	2½	2½	3½	2	3	1½	3½	13	22½	2
Ukraine	2	1½		2	1½	2½	2½	2½	2½	2½	12	19½	3
Russia	2	1½	2		3	3	1	1½	4	3	10	21	4
Hungary	1½	1½	2½	1		2	2½	2	3½	3	10	19½	5
USA	2	½	1½	1	2		2½	3	2½	3½	10	18½	6
Azerbaijan	2	2	1½	3	1½	1½		3	2	2½	9	19	7
India	1½	1	1½	2½	2	1	1		2½	2½	7	15½	8
Israel	½	2½	1½	0	½	1½	2	1½		3	5	13	9
Egypt	½	½	1½	1	1	½	1½	1½	1		0	9	10

3) Dortmund Chess Meeting 21-31 July 2011

Once again Vladimir Kramnik proved himself the King of Dortmund, winning this event for an incredible tenth time. Along the way he took some risks, and showed great fighting spirit in additional to his high level of chess. Le of Vietnam performed solidly to take second place with nine draws and one win.

1. Kramink, 7, **2**. Quang Liem 5½, **3-4**.Ponomariov 5, **4**.Giri 5, **5**.Nakamura 4½, **6**. Meier 3

4) Russian Super Final 7-15 August 2011

Peter Svidler won the prestigious Russian Super Final for an impressive sixth time, despite losing in the last round to Morozevich, who finished in sole second place with 4½/7.

Player	Rating										
Svidler	2739		½	½	1	1	1	0	1	5	1st
Karjakin	2788	½		0	½	1	½	½	1	4	
Grischuk	2746	½	1		1	½	½	0	½	4	3rd
Galkin	2598	0	½	0		½	½	½	0	2	
Timofeev	2665	0	0	½	½		½	0	0	1,5	
Nepomniachtchi	2711	0	½	½	½	½		1	0	3	
Morozevich	2694	1	½	1	½	1	0		½	4,5	2nd
Kramnik	2781	0	0	½	1	1	1	½		4	

Arkadij Naiditsch
September 2011

Contributors

Etienne Bacrot: France, 28 years old, GM 2705, number 43 in the world. Became GM at the age of 14, a record at the time.
Six times French Champion starting from 1999.

Winner of many international events including: 2005: 1st place in Poikovsky, 3rd in Dortmund and 3rd of the World Cup in Khanty-Mansiysk. 2009: 1st in Aeroflot Open, second in Montreal and Antwerp. 2010: First equal in Gibraltar, 3rd in Nanjing and winner of Geneva Open. 2011: First equal in Basel, Geneva (rapid) and Rabat (blitz).

Baadur Jobava: Georgia, 27 years old, GM 2704, number 36 in the world.

Georgian Champion. 2003 and 2007. Gold medal on 4th board the Calvia Olympiad 2004. Silver medal 2010 European Individual Ch. Rijeka, Croatia.

Winner of: 2003 Dubai Open; 2005 Samba Cup, Skanderborg, Denmark; 2006 Aeroflot Open, 2011 Bosna-Open, Sarajevo.

Sebastien Maze: France, 26 years old, GM 2575

Winner of 2008 Rabat blitz tournament, 1st equal in Marseille 2009 and Menton 2009.

Member of the French team in the Olympiad in Dresden 2008.

Was the second of Etienne Bacrot in FIDE Grand Prix Elista 2008, Dortmund 2009 and Nanjing 2010.

Kamil Miton: Poland, 27 years old, GM 2628.

World Junior U12 Champion in 1996. No 2 at the World Junior Champion (U 20).

Twice the winner (2002 and 2005) of one of the world's biggest tournaments, the World Open in Philadelphia, USA.

Arkadij Naiditsch: Germany, 25 years old, GM 2707, number 40 in the world. Became International Master at the age of 13, Grandmaster at 15.

Winner of 2005 Super-tournament in Dortmund and since 2006 the top-rated German player. In 2007 was German Champion and won the Baku Open. In 2010 Arkadij won a match against Efimenko in Mukachevo and was 1st equal in the European Rapid Championship in Warsaw.

Borki Predojevic: Bosnia and Herzegovina, 24 years old, GM 2643. Gained the GM title at the Calvia Olympiad in 2004 when he was 17. Best Elo was 2654 in September 2009. Joined the top 100 in 2007; highest place so far was 68th on the October 2007 list.

Winner of several international open tournaments including: Open Metalis in Bizovac, Croatia in 2006, Zagreb Open, Croatia in 2007, Hit Open in Nova Gorica, Slovenia in 2008, Acropolis Open in Greece 2009. in 2008, Acropolis Open in Greece 2009.

Nikola Sedlak: Serbia, 28 years old, GM 2589

Winner of the 3rd European Union Individual Chess Championship in 2007 and 2009 BH Telecom tournament in Sarajevo.

Ivan Sokolov: 43 years old, GM 2673, number 69 in the world. Best world ranking on the FIDE list of 12th (several times).

Winner of many top GM events of which the most important are: Hastings, Sarajevo, Selfoss, Reykjavik, Hoogeveen, Lost Boys, Staunton Memorial. Yugoslav Champion in 1988 and Dutch Champion in 1995 and 1998. Won team gold with the Dutch team at the 2005 European Championship in Gothenburg.

A

GAME 1

▷ **P. Svidler (2739)**
▶ **V. Kramnik (2781)**
64th Russian Championship, Moscow
Round 1, 08.08.2011 **[A07]**
Annotated by Baadur Jobava

Svidler chose a rare line that Kramnik had faced only once before, in a blitz game. Soon after play diverged from that game, Kramnik sacrificed a piece with 14...e5, which made the position extremely complicated and difficult to understand, even analysing at leisure. Great tension remained until 28...dxe3? turned the game in White's favour, and after Black's final mistake on the very next move, everything was over. All in all, a very interesting game.

1.♘f3 d5 2.g3 ♘f6 3.♗g2 c6 4.d3 ♗g4 5.♘bd2

5.0–0 is the main alternative.

5...♘bd7 6.h3 ♗h5 7.g4 ♗g6 8.♘h4 e6

8...e5 is also common.

9.e3 ♗d6 10.♕e2

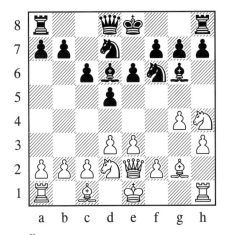

10...♕c7

10...♘b6 11.♘df3 ♘fd7 12.a4 ♗e7 13.♘xg6 hxg6 14.a5 ♘c8± Nguyen Ngoc Truongson – Goldenberg, Beijing (blitz) 2008.

10...a5 11.a4 ♕e7 12.0–0 e5 13.e4 ♘c5 14.exd5!?

14.♘f5?! ♗xf5 15.exf5 g6!∓ Gutierrez Olivares – Almagro Llamas, Spain 2011.

14...♘xd5

14...cxd5 15.♖e1 ♘e6 16.♘df3 0–0 17.♘f5 ♗xf5 18.gxf5 ♘d8 19.♘xe5 ♕xe5 20.♕xe5 ♗xe5 21.♖xe5 ♘c6 22.f4!! ♖ac8 (22...♖fe8 23.♖xe8† ♖xe8 24.♗d2 ♘d4 25.♖e1 ♖xe1† 26.♗xe1 ♘xc2 27.♗xa5+–) 23.c3! ♘xe5 24.fxe5 ♘d7 25.d4±

15.♘c4 0–0∞

11.0–0 0–0–0

A logical continuation of Black's plan. After castling long, the position is very sharp and the game is going to be in style of "who is faster in the attack".

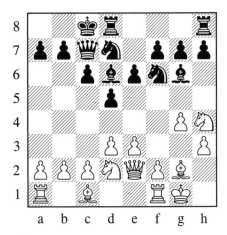

12.♖b1

White immediately prepares an advance of the b-pawn that would shake up Black's structure. It seems to be the best plan for White, because any waste of time can be fatal.

12.f4 h6 13.♘xg6 fxg6 14.♘f3?! e5∓ Morozevich – Kramnik, Moscow (blitz) 2007.

12...♕a5!?

This move is a preparation for an aggressive plan. Firstly, Black stops the immediate movement of the b-pawn; and secondly he is preparing a "super team" of bishop and queen on the b8-h2 diagonal. It seems that Kramnik already saw the upcoming piece sacrifice

13.a3 ♗b8 14.f4 e5

A very brave decision by Kramnik. 14...♕c7!? was also worth a thought.

15.f5 e4

There is no choice: 15...♕c7? 16.e4+–

16.dxe4

16.fxg6? hxg6 17.g5 ♕c7 18.♖f2 ♕h2† 19.♔f1 ♘h5 20.♕g4 ♘g3† 21.♔e1 ♖xh4 22.♕xh4 ♕g1† 23.♗f1 ♘f5 24.♕g4 ♗g3 25.♕e2 ♘h4 26.dxe4 dxe4 27.♘xe4 ♘e5 28.♘xg3 ♕xg3

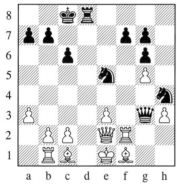

In this beautiful position, it is time for White to resign.

16...♕c7

Another try is:
16...dxe4!? 17.♘xe4 ♘xe4 18.♗xe4 ♕e5 19.♗xc6
    19.♕g2 ♕e7! 20.fxg6 hxg6 21.♘f3 (21.♘xg6 fxg6 22.♗xg6 ♗c7 23.b4 ♘e5 24.♗f5† ♔b8⩲) 21...♕xe4 22.♘g5 ♕xg2† 23.♔xg2 ♘e5∓
19...♕g3† 20.♕g2 bxc6 21.♘f3 ♗xf5 22.gxf5 ♘f6 23.b4 ♖he8
    Black will have to defend a very unpleasant endgame.

17.♖f4!

Svidler's choice is the best one!

After 17.♖d1 we look at three replies:

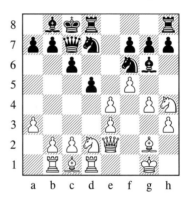

a) 17...dxe4 18.♘f1! ♘e5 19.♗d2 ♕e7 20.♗e1⩲

b) 17...♕h2† 18.♔f1 ♘xe4!
    18...dxe4 19.b4! ♘e5 (19...♗g3?? 20.♘hf3 exf3 21.♘xf3) 20.♗b2⩲
19.♘xe4 dxe4 20.♗d2 ♗g3 21.♗e1 ♗xe1 22.♕xe1 h5 23.fxg6

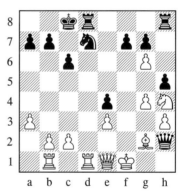

23...♖df8
    23...hxg4 24.♘f5 fxg6 25.♕g3! ♕xg3 26.♘xg3 gxh3 27.♗xe4±
    23...fxg6 24.g5! This is a very cool and strong answer, after which it seems that Black cannot find anything effective. 24...♖hf8† 25.♔e2 ♕e5 26.♖d4! ♕xg5 (26...♕b5† 27.c4 ♕xg5 28.♗xe4 ♖de8 29.♘f3 ♕g2† 30.♕f2 ♕xh3 31.♗xg6 ♖e6 32.♖g1 ♘e5 33.♗e4 c5 34.♖g3

♘g4 35.♕g1 ♕xg3 36.♕xg3 cxd4 37.♔d3 dxe3 38.♗d5+–) 27.♖bd1 ♘f6 28.♖xd8†
♖xd8 29.♖xd8† ♔xd8 30.♔d1 ♘d5 31.♗xe4 ♘xe3† 32.♔e2+–

23...♖hf8 24.♔e2! hxg4 25.♖h1 ♕e5 26.♗xe4 f5 27.♗xc6 bxc6 28.♕xc6† ♕c7 29.♕xc7† ♔xc7 30.♖d5+–

24.♖xd7!

24.g5?! f6! 25.gxf6 ♖xf6† 26.♔e2 ♘e5 27.♕g1 ♕g3 28.♕e1 ♕h2=

24...♔xd7 25.♕b4 fxg6† 26.♔e2 ♔c8 27.♖h1 ♕g3 28.♕e1 ♕d6 29.♖xe4 ♖f6 30.♗d3

Bringing the king to the queenside, White stands better.

c) 17...h5! 18.exd5
18.g5? ♘xe4 19.♘f1 ♗h7∓

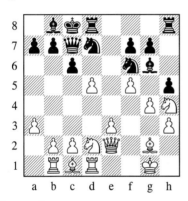

Here we have two options:

c1) 18...♘xd5 19.c4 hxg4 20.cxd5 gxh3
20...♖xh4 21.hxg4 ♗h7 22.d6 ♖xd6 23.♘f3 ♕g3 24.♘xh4 ♕xh4 25.e4± White is slowly defending against the attack, letting him escape an exchange up.
21.♗f3
21.d6 ♕xd6 22.♘df3 ♕f6 23.fxg6 hxg2 24.♕f2 fxg6 25.e4 ♖df8 26.♕xg2 ♖xh4 27.♗g5 ♕xf3 28.♕xf3 ♖xf3 29.♗xh4 g5 30.♔g2 ♖b3 31.♗f2 ♘f6 32.♖e1 ♗e5 33.♖e3 ♖xb2 34.♖xb2 ♗xb2 35.♖b3=
21...♗h5 22.♘f1!
22.♗xh5? ♖xh5! 23.♕xh5 ♕h2† 24.♔f1

♗g3 25.♘e4 ♘f6 26.♘xg3 ♘xh5 27.♘xh5 ♖h8–+

22.dxc6 ♕xc6! 23.♕c4 ♘e5! 24.♕xc6† bxc6 25.♖f1 ♗g4 26.♗xg4 ♘xg4 27.♘df3 ♖d3∓
22.♘e4 cxd5 23.♖xd5 ♘f6! 24.♖c5 ♘xe4 25.♖xc7† ♗xc7

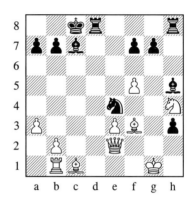

Although a queen up, White is lost.
22...♘f6 23.e4 ♗xf3 24.♘xf3 ♖he8 25.♘g5 ♖xd5 26.♖xd5 ♘xd5 27.♕f3

Black has insufficient compensation for the piece.

c2) 18...hxg4! 19.dxc6 bxc6 20.♕a6† ♕b7 21.♕xb7† ♔xb7 22.fxg6 ♖xh4 23.hxg4 ♘e5 24.g5 ♘fg4 With the activity of his pieces, Black can face the future with confidence.

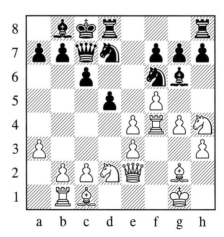

17...♖de8
17...dxe4 18.♘xe4 ♕b6 19.♕f2 ♗xf4

20.exf4 ♘xe4 21.♗xe4 ♖de8 22.♕xb6 axb6 23.♗d3 ♖e1† 24.♔f2 ♖h1 25.♘f3+– This line can never satisfy Black.

18.fxg6 hxg6 19.♘hf3 ♕b6 20.e5! ♘xe5 21.♘xe5

21.♖b4!? ♕c7 22.♘xe5 ♕xe5 23.♘f3 ♕c7 24.♗d2 ♘e4 25.c4 d4 26.exd4 ♘g3 27.♕d3 ♘e2† 28.♔f2 ♕g3† 29.♔f1 and it seems that White is doing well. But of course it would be almost unreal to find such a defence at the board.

21...♗xe5

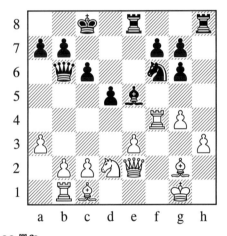

22.♖f3

White could also consider:
22.♖f1 ♗d4 23.♘e4! ♘xe4 24.exd4 ♘g3
24...♘c3 25.bxc3 ♖xe2 (25...♕xb1 26.♕f2 f6 27.♗h6+–) 26.♖xb6 axb6 27.♖xf7 ♖e1† 28.♖f1 ♖he8 (28...♖e2 29.♗g5 ♖xc2 30.♖f3 ♖e8 31.♗f1 b5 32.♗h4±) 29.♗d2 ♖1e2 30.♖d1+–
25.♕f2 ♘xf1 26.♗xf1 ♖e4 27.♗f4 ♕xd4 28.♕xd4 ♖xd4 29.♗e5±

22...♘h7 23.c4

23.♖f1! ♗d4 (23...♘g5 24.♘f3 ♘xh3† 25.♗xh3 ♖xh3 26.♘xe5 ♖xe5 27.♔g2 ♖h8 28.♖xf7 ♕d8 29.♕f2 ♖e4 30.♕g3 ♖h4 31.♖c7†! ♕xc7 32.♕xh4 ♕d7 33.♔h3+–)

24.♘f3 ♗xe3† 25.♗xe3 ♖xe3 26.♕f2 By giving up the second pawn White has clarified the position, and holds a decisive advantage.

23...♘g5 24.cxd5 cxd5 25.♘f1 ♔b8 26.b4 d4

26...f5 27.gxf5 ♘xf3† 28.♕xf3±

27.♗d2 ♖e7

27...d3 28.♕xd3 ♘xf3† 29.♗xf3 ♖xh3 30.♔g2 ♖hh8 31.♖c1 ♖e7 White's advantage is only symbolic, because Black has rook and pawn for two minor pieces and the white kingside is seriously shaky.

28.♖c1

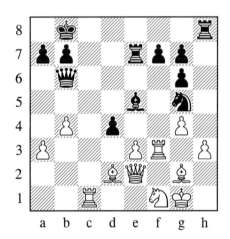

28...dxe3?

Probably the decisive mistake. Kramnik fails to maintain the tension (maybe because of time trouble), but simplifying the situation is clearly in White's favour.

After 28...♕d6! followed by advancing the d-pawn, the position would remain very unclear.

29.♗xe3 ♗d4?

29...♘xf3† 30.♕xf3 ♕f6 would have been the last chance to keep the game alive. For the remainder of the game, no more comments are needed.

30.罝g3+– 臭xe3† 31.包xe3 罝he8 32.罝c3 a6
33.豐f2 f6

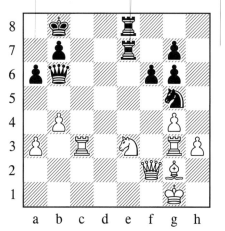

34.包c2 豐xf2† 35.壹xf2 罝e2† 36.壹f1 罝d2
37.罝gd3 罝ee2 38.罝xd2 罝xd2 39.包e3 包e6
40.包c4 罝d1† 41.壹f2 包f4 42.臭f3 罝a1
43.h4 g5 44.h5
1–0

GAME 2
▷ **V. Gashimov (2760)**
▶ **Wang Yue (2709)**
8th World Team Championship, Ningbo
Round 1 – 17.07.2011 [A28]
Annotated by Borki Predojevic

The English Opening continues to grow in
popularity at the highest level. Gashimov
chose 4.a3!?, deviating from the main line since
his opponent, Wang Yue, has achieved good
results there. On move 11 Black employed a
novelty in 11...罝ae8!?N. This did not alter the
fundamental character of the position, but it
prevented one of White's main ideas, namely
the 包g5-e4 manoeuvre, which Potkin had
utilized against Wang Yue in a previous game
after 11...罝ad8.

White chose a different knight manoeuvre
with 包h4-f5-e3-d5 (after e4) and after 19
moves he had the better position although
Black's position remained solid. But shortly
after he committed a strategic mistake in 22.f4?

(22.c4! would have kept some advantage), after
which Black took over the initiative and won
the game in nice style.

The 4.a3!? sideline is likely to be tested
more in the future, which is why I analysed
alternatives for both sides, including 7.dxc3!?
and 9...b6, which may be of interest to readers
who play either side of this line.

1.c4 包f6 2.包c3 e5 3.包f3 包c6 4.a3!?
The idea behind this rare move is to play
a reversed Sicilian, while avoiding variations
such as 4.g3 臭b4, which is the main line.
Other options include 4.e3 and 4.e4!?.

4...d5
4...g6 is a popular alternative. Still, after
5.g3 White gets a comfortable version of a
reversed Closed Sicilian (or reversed Dragon
after 5...d5) as Black's early ...包f6 has blocked
his f-pawn.

5.cxd5 包xd5

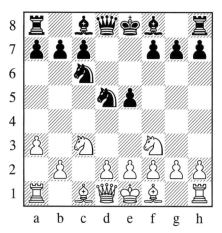

6.豐c2
This is the most flexible move, and the main
line according to theory. White plays a reversed
Taimanov and waits before deciding whether
to push his e-pawn one or two squares.

After 6.e4 Black should play 6...包f4 7.d4

(7.d3 ♘e6 8.♗e2 ♘ed4 9.♗e3 ♗c5= leads to a comfortable position for Black) 7...exd4 8.♗xf4 dxc3 9.♕xd8† (9.bxc3 ♕xd1† 10.♖xd1 [10.♔xd1 ♗c5∓] 10...♗xa3 11.♖xc7 ♔e7↑) 9...♘xd8 10.bxc3 ♘e6 11.♗g3 ♗c5= with a nice position.

6...♘xc3!

The best reply.

6...♗e7

This is the main alternative, but it is slightly less accurate.

7.e3 0–0

White has several options here, including:

8.b4

8.♗b5 does not give any advantage, despite the fact that White enjoys an extra tempo over the normal Sicilian position. Black equalizes with: 8...♘xc3 9.bxc3 ♕d5 10.♗d3 f5 11.e4 ♕f7 12.exf5 ♗xf5 13.♗xf5 ♕xf5 14.♕xf5 ♖xf5 15.d3 ♗c5 16.♖f1 ♖af8= Jaracz – Naiditsch, Bundesliga 2011.

However, the strongest continuation is: 8.♘xd5! ♕xd5 9.♗d3± For further information on this line I would advise the reader to check the game Roiz – Rasmussen, Bundesliga 2009/2010, which can be found in *Mega Database 2011* with instructive comments by GM Roiz.

8...♘xc3 9.dxc3

Now Black can equalize with the calm move:

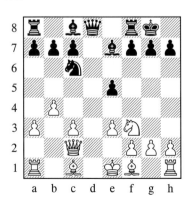

a b c d e f g h

9...a6!

9...♗f6 looks unnatural and White obtains the advantage with simple play: 10.♗d3 g6 11.0–0 ♗g7 12.e4 ♗g4 (12...a5 13.♗e3) 13.♘d2 a5 (13...♗h6 14.♘c4 ♗xc1 15.♖axc1±) 14.b5 ♘b8 15.h3 ♗e6 16.♗c4 ♖e8 17.♖d1 ♘d7 18.a4 ♗f8 19.♗xe6 ♖xe6 20.♘c4± Franco Ocampos – G. Garcia, Cienfuegos 1991.

10.e4

10.♗b2 f5 11.c4 e4 12.♘e5 ♘xe5 13.♗xe5 c5!?⇄

10...♕d6 11.♗e2 ♕g6⇄

Black has a promising position, for instance:

12.h4

12.0–0 ♗h3 13.♘e1 ♗g5=

12...♗g4 13.h5 ♕e6 14.♕a2 ♕xa2 15.♖xa2 a5 16.♖c2 axb4 17.axb4 ♖a1 18.♘d2 ♗e6 19.♗c4 ♗xc4 20.♘xc4 ♗xb4!∓

Black got the upper hand in Jobava – Rublevsky, Khanty-Mansiysk (1) 2005.

7.bxc3

7.dxc3!?

This capture is a serious alternative. Black should respond with:

7...a5

Preventing b4.

8.e4 ♗d6

I propose a new move here:

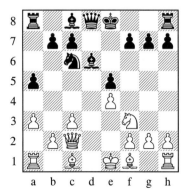

a b c d e f g h

9.♗g5!?N

9.♗c4 appears less promising: 9...0–0
10.♗g5 ♕e8 11.0–0 ♗e6 12.♘d2 ♗xc4
13.♘xc4 ♕e6 14.♘e3 (14.♕e2 a4 15.♖ad1
♘a5 16.♘xd6 cxd6 17.♖d5 ♖fc8 18.♖fd1
♘c4 19.♗e3 ♖ab8=) This position occurred
in Zvjaginsev – Lima, Tripoli (1) 2004, and
now Black should have played 14...f6N
15.♗h4 a4 with a good game.
9...f6 10.♗e3 ♗e6
10...♕e7 11.♗c4 ♗e6 12.♘d2 0–0 13.0–0
♘d8 14.b4±
11.♘d2 0–0 12.♗c4 ♗xc4 13.♘xc4 a4 14.b4!
White has the better chances, as taking
en passant would expose Black to a double
attack.

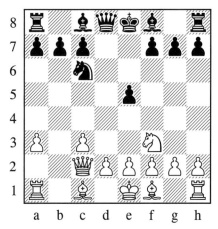

7...♗d6 8.g3

8.e4 0–0 9.♗e2 ♕e7 10.0–0 b6 11.d4 ♗g4
12.♗g5 f6 13.♗e3 ♔h8 14.h3 ♗d7 gave Black
good play in Bauer – Karpov, Ajaccio (blitz)
2007.

8...♕e7

By creating the positional threat of ...e4,
Black practically forces his opponent's next
move.

Another option is:
8...0–0 9.♗g2 ♖e8 10.d3
Just as in the game, White is obliged to play
this move in order to stop ...e4.

10...♘a5 11.0–0 c5
With the potential positional threat of ...c4.
12.c4±
This move is typical in similar Sicilian
positions with reversed colours. Now White's
main plan will be to transfer his knight to
d5, usually via d2-e4(b1)-c3.

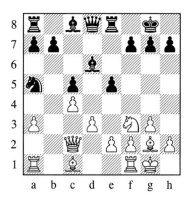

12...♘c6
Another game continued 12...♗d7 13.♘d2
♘c6 14.e3 ♗f8 15.♘e4 ♗f5 16.♗b2 ♕d7
17.♖fd1 ♖ad8 18.♖d2 ♗h3 19.♗h1 ♕f5
20.♘c3 White is finally in a position to
realise his ambition. 20...♖e6 21.♘d5 ♖h6
22.♗e4 ♕h5 23.♕d1 (23.f4!?) 23...♗g4
24.f3 ♗c8 25.g4 ♕g5 26.♖g2± White kept
the better chances in M. Gurevich – Gordon,
Gibraltar 2009.

13.e3
White should prevent the knight jump to d4.
13.♗b2 ♗g4 14.h3 ♗h5 15.e3 ♗c7 16.♖fd1
f5 17.♗c3 ♕e7 18.♕b2 ♗b6 19.♖d2± was
slightly better for White in Schlosser –
Babula, Bundesliga 2007/2008.
However, Black has an improvement in
13...♘d4! 14.♘xd4 exd4 with equal chances.
13...♗f5 14.♘d2 ♕d7 15.♘e4 ♗f8 16.♗b2
♖ad8 17.♖ad1±
White continues preparing to occupy the
d5-square. The position is not dynamic, which
counts in White's favour.

9.d3

Worse is 9.♗g2?! e4 10.♘d4 ♘xd4 11.cxd4 ♗f5 when Black has a nice game, for instance 12.0–0 0–0 13.f3 exf3 14.♕xf5 fxg2 15.♖f2∓ as in Gelfand – Karjakin, Moscow (blitz) 2008.

9...0–0

The main line is:

9...b6 10.♗g2 ♗b7

Here Black offers some opposition on the long diagonal.

11.0–0

Here we will look at two high-level games to see how the play might develop.

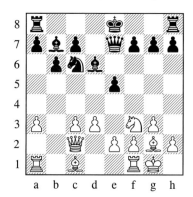

a) 11...♘a5 12.c4

12.a4 does not make much sense, and after 12...0–0 13.♘d2 ♗xg2 14.♔xg2 ♕e6 15.♕a2 ♕d7 16.♔g1 ♕c6 17.c4 ♖ad8 18.♘b3 ♘xb3 19.♕xb3 ♗c5∓ Black was better in Kovalyov – Kritz, Conegliano 2008.

12.e4!? is possible though.

After the text move we will follow a game of the legendary Viktor Korchnoi.

12...0–0

12...e4 13.♘h4 0–0 14.♗d2 reaches the same position.

13.♗d2 e4

13...♘c6 14.♗c3 ♖fe8 15.e3 ♖ab8 16.♕b2 ♘d8 17.d4 e4 18.♘d2 f5 19.a4 keeps a slight plus for White.

14.♘h4 exd3 15.exd3 ♗xg2 16.♔xg2 ♘c6

16...♕d7 17.♗xa5 bxa5 18.d4 ♖fe8

19.♘f3±

17.♗c3 ♗e5

17...♕d7 18.d4 ♘e7 is better option for Black, reaching a position which resembles a Petroff.

18.♖fe1 ♕f6 19.♗xe5 ♘xe5

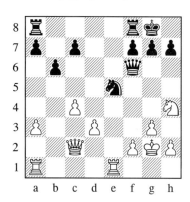

20.d4!

A beautiful pawn sacrifice!

20...♕c6† 21.♔g1 ♕xc4 22.♕e4 ♘g6 23.♘f5 ♕e6

23...♕a4 24.h4↑ looks very promising for White.

24.♕f3 ♕f6

24...♕d7 25.h4!

25.♖ac1 c5 26.♘h6† ♔h8 27.♕xf6 gxf6 28.dxc5 bxc5 29.♖xc5±

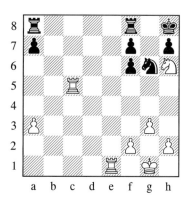

White is already much better and Black does not have many moves available. The game continued:

29...♘e5 30.♖d1 ♖ad8 31.♖xd8 ♖xd8 32.f4

Rd1† 33.♔g2 ♘d3 34.Rc8† ♔g7 35.♘f5†
♔g6 36.♘e7† ♔h5

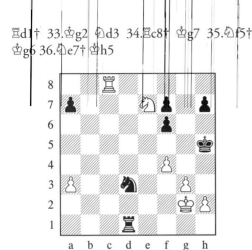

Now in the game Korchnoi – Rublevsky,
Russia 2008. White missed the winning
continuation:

37.Rg8! Rd2† 38.♔f3 ♘e1† 39.♔e3 Rxh2
40.♘d5+–

The black king is caught in a mating net.

b) 11...0–0

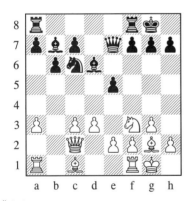

12.♘h4!?

An interesting plan. Several other moves
deserve consideration:

12.d4 e4 13.♘d2 f5 14.♘c4 ♕e6 and
12.♘g5 h6 13.♘e4 ♘a5 both give Black
promising play.

The more typical 12.e4 ♘a5 13.♘h4 can be
met by 13...g6 14.♗h6 Rfe8∞ with an unclear
game. In one game White continued with
the suspicious 15.Rae1?! and after 15...Rad8

16.♔h1 ♗a6∓ Black was better and went on
to win in M. Gurevich – Gupta, Chalkida
(op) 2009.

The plan with 12.c4 works less well here than
it did after 11...♘a5 in variation 'a' above.
Black should react with a central strategy and
play 12...f5 13.♗b2 ♔h8 14.e3 Rae8 when
his position is quite satisfactory. The following
game was quite instructive: 15.d4 e4 16.♘d2
♘d8! 17.♘b3 ♘e6 A strong and thematic
knight manoeuvre. 18.a4 ♕f7 19.Rfe1

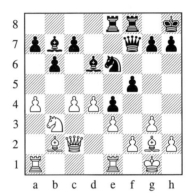

19...f4! 20.d5?! fxg3 21.fxg3 ♘g5 22.♘d4
♗c8∓ Kovalyov – Cornette, Montreal 2008.

12...f5

I also analysed 12...♕e6 13.e4 with two
possibilities for Black:

a) 13...♘e7 14.d4 ♕c4 15.Re1 Rad8 (15...exd4
16.e5) 16.♗f1 ♕e6 17.♗b2 Rfe8 18.a4 a5
19.♗b5! c6 20.♗d3±

b) 13...g6 14.♗e3 (It is too early for 14.f4?!
exf4 15.gxf4 [15.♗xf4 ♗xf4 16.gxf4 ♕f6!]
15...♕g4 16.♕f2 ♗a6 17.h3 ♕e6 18.e5 ♗c5
19.♗e3 ♗xe3 20.♕xe3 Rad8 21.Rfd1 f6
22.d4 ♘e7 when Black has the initiative.)
14...♘a5 15.f4 exf4 16.gxf4 ♕g4 17.♕f2
♘b3 18.Rad1 ♗xa3 19.h3 ♕h5 20.f5∞
White has a promising initiative.

13.e4

13.♕a4?! is objectively not a good move,
although it does set a trap so Black should
be careful:

a) The tricky point is revealed after 13...♘a5?

14.♗xb7 ♘xb7 15.♘xf5! ♖xf5 16.♕e4 ♖af8 17.♕xb7± Rotstein – Karpatchev, Kerkyra 2009.

b) The superior 13...♕e8!N highlights the fact that the queen on a4 is misplaced. Here is my analysis: 14.♗d5† (14.g4?! is well met by 14...♔h8! intending ...♘d4; 14.e4 fxe4 15.♗xe4 ♘a5 16.♕xe8 ♖axe8∓ looks good for Black thanks to the misplaced knight on h4.) 14...♔h8 15.e4 This seems like a principled approach, but it brings nothing but trouble to White. 15...f4! (better than 15...fxe4?! 16.♕xe4 ♖b8 17.♘f3 ♘a5 18.♗xb7 ♘xb7 19.♗e3±) 16.♘f5 ♖d8 17.d4 (17.♘xd6 ♖xd6 18.gxf4 exf4 19.f3 ♗c8→) 17...fxg3 18.hxg3 exd4 19.cxd4 ♖xf5! 20.exf5 ♗xg3 21.fxg3 ♖xd5 22.♗f4 ♖xd4 23.♖ae1 ♕h5 Black has a strong attack.

13...fxe4

Another possibility is 13...f4 14.♘f5 ♕f7 15.gxf4 exf4 16.♕a2 with double-edged play.

14.♗xe4 ♘a5 15.♗xb7 ♘xb7 16.♗b2 ♕e6 17.♖ae1∞

The position is unclear and holds chances for both sides.

10.♗g2 ♗d7 11.0–0

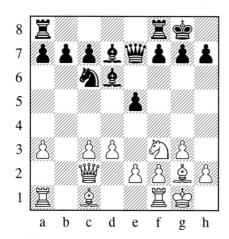

11...♖ae8!?N

With this new and quite logical move Black prepares active central play with ...f5 and ...e4. He also prevents the thematic ♘g5-e4 manoeuvre.

A previous Wang Yue game continued:
11...♖ad8 12.♘g5!? h6
  12...f5 13.♗d5† ♔h8 14.♕a2 f4 15.♘f7† ♖xf7 16.♗xf7 ♗h3 17.♗d5!?±
13.♘e4 b6 14.a4 ♘a5 15.c4
  Another idea was: 15.f4 exf4 (15...♗c6 16.♘xd6 cxd6 17.e4 f6 18.c4 ♘b7 19.♗e3 f5 20.exf5 ♗xg2 21.♕xg2 ♖xf5 22.g4 ♖f7 23.♕d5±) 16.♘xd6 cxd6 17.♖xf4 f5!∞
15...♗b4
  15...c5 16.♘c3 ♘c6 17.♕b2±
16.♘c3 ♗xc3 17.♕xc3 ♖fe8 18.♗a3
  18.♗d2 ♗c6=
18...♕e6 19.♗d5 ♕g4

20.♗f3

Better was 20.♖fe1!? when Black has to find a beautiful idea in the critical line: 20...♗c6 21.♗b4 ♗xd5 22.cxd5 ♖xd5 23.e4 Now the key idea is 23...♖d4 (23...♖d7 24.♗xa5 bxa5 25.♕xa5 c6 26.♕a6 ♕f3 27.♖e3 ♕f6 28.♖c1 ♖c7 29.♖ee1±) 24.♗xa5 c5!!⇄ with equal chances. (Instead 24...bxa5 25.♕xa5± would give White some advantage.)

20...♕g6=

Here White lost the thread and chose:
21.♗b4? ♘c6 22.♖fe1 ♘d4 23.♗g2 a5 24.♗a3 ♗xa4 25.♗e7 ♖xe7 26.♖xa4 ♕f6∓

Black won a pawn and the game in Potkin – Wang Yue, Ningbo 2010.

Another reasonable line is:
11...♘a5 12.♘d2
> 12.♘g5!? and 12.d4!? both deserve attention.
12...c5
> 12...♗c6 13.♘e4 (13.e4 is met by 13...♗c5 14.♗b2 ♕d7! intending ...♗a4 and ...♖ad8) 13...♕d7 14.♖a2 ♔h8 15.a4 b6 16.♘xd6 cxd6 17.♗d5 ♗xd5 18.♕xd5 ♕c6 19.♕xc6 ♘xc6 20.c4 ♖ad8 ½–½ Kovacs – Ruck, Oberwart 2001. In the final position White has a small advantage. His plan is connected with pressure on queenside and the a4-a5 break.
13.♘e4
> 13.c4!? f5 (13...♘c6 14.♘b1 ♘d4 15.♕b2 ♗c6 16.♘c3±) 14.♘b1± was a different and possibly better way to continue the game.
13...f5 14.♘xd6 ♕xd6 15.f4 ♖ae8 16.fxe5 ♕xe5 17.♖f2 ♗c6 18.♗xc6 ♘xc6 19.♕b3† ♖f7 20.g4∞
Vaganian – Chernin, USSR 1988.

Finally, another game continued: 11...b6 12.♘d2 f5 13.♘c4 ♖ae8 14.a4 f4 15.a5 ♗c5 16.axb6 axb6 17.♘d2 ♕f7 18.♘e4 ♗e7 19.♕a2± White obtained a Sicilian-type endgame with firm control over the e4-square, Wahls – Werle, Germany 2003.

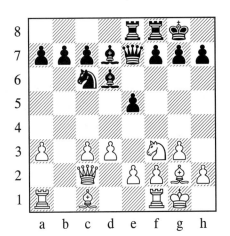

12.e4
This looks logical in view of the position of the black rooks.
> One of the points of Black's last move is that 12.♘g5?! runs into the strong response: 12...f5! 13.♕b3† ♔h8 14.♗d5 ♘d8!∓ The f7-square has been defended successfully, White's pieces are misplaced and Black is ready to come forwards with ...h6 followed by ...♘e6.

12.♘d2!?
> This is a more reasonable alternative. White wants to put the knight on c4 or e4.
12...♘a5
> Covering the c4-square.
> In the event of 12...b6 13.♘c4 (13.♘e4 f5 14.♘xd6 cxd6 15.♗d2 ♖c8 is double-edged) 13...♗c5 14.a4 f5 15.a5 ♔h8 16.axb6 axb6 17.e3± White keeps a slight edge.
13.♘e4
> 13.a4 f5 14.♘b3 ♘c6 15.a5∞
13...♗c6 14.c4 b6 15.♗d2
> Now if Black wishes to obtain counterplay he must venture a risky pawn capture.

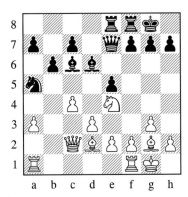

15...♗xa3!?
> 15...♘b7 16.♘f6†! ♕xf6 17.♗xc6± gives White an obvious advantage.
16.c5 ♗xe4 17.♗xe4 ♗xc5
> 17...♕xc5? 18.♕a4 ♗b2 19.♗b4+−
18.♗xa5
> 18.♗xh7† ♔xh7 19.d4† ♔g8 20.dxc5 ♘b7 21.♖xa7 ♘xc5 22.♗e3 ♖a8 23.♖fa1 ♖xa7

24.♖xa7 ♖c8 25.♗xc5 ♕xc5 26.♕xc5 bxc5=
18...bxa5 19.♖xh7† ♔h8!

19...♔xh7 20.d4† e4 21.dxc5±
20.♗f5∞

The position holds chances for both sides.

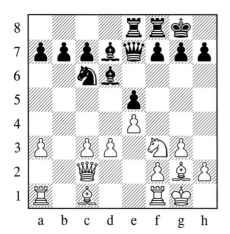

12...♘a5 13.♘h4 b6 14.♘f5 ♕f6 15.♘e3!
The correct decision.

After 15.♘xd6 ♕xd6 Black has no problems.
For instance, after 16.d4?! exd4 17.♖d1 there
is 17...♗e6 18.♖xd4 (18.♖b1 ♕c5∓) 18...♕c5∓
and soon the c4-square will be occupied by one
of Black's minor pieces.

15...♗e6 16.♗b2 ♗c5 17.♕e2
17.♘d5 can be met by 17...♕d8, and after
18.d4 ♗d6 19.♘e3 ♘c4 20.♗c1 c6 21.a4∞ the
position is unclear. White's central pawns look
impressive, but Black controls the c4-square
and his pawn structure is healthier.

17...♖d8 18.♘d5
18.f4? meets with a beautiful refutation:
18...♖xd3!! 19.♕xd3 ♗c4 20.♕d2 ♗xf1
21.♔xf1 ♘b3 22.♕e2 ♘xa1 23.♗g4 (23.♗xa1
exf4 24.♘g4 ♕g5 25.h4 ♕d8–+) 23...♕e6
24.♗xa1 exf4 25.gxf4 f5∓

18.♖ad1?! is also unimpressive: 18...♗xe3
19.♕xe3 (19.fxe3 ♕e7∓) 19...♘b3 20.♖d2

♕d6 21.♗c1 ♕c6! (21...♗a4 22.f4 ♘b3 23.fxe5
♕d7↑) 22.♗b2 ♕d7 23.♗c1 ♗a4∓ White has
a tough time with ...♘b3 coming next.

18...♗xd5
Black has no other choice.

19.exd5±
White's two bishops give him slightly better
chances. The position is not dynamic and
Black has a nice blockade, but his position is
a bit passive.

19...♗d6
19...♖de8!? was another idea, delaying the
bishop retreat and contemplating ...c6 if the
right opportunity presents itself.

20.♖ae1 ♘b3 21.♕d1 ♘c5

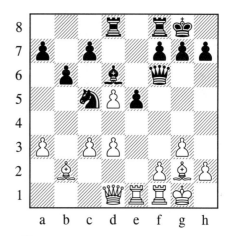

22.f4?
Gashimov's move is connected with the
occupation of the e5-square, which looks like
a tempting and 'human' idea. Nevertheless it
is a mistake.

It was time to open another diagonal with
22.c4! ♕g6 23.♖e3 f6 24.♖fe1 ♖fe8 25.h4
♕f7 26.h5±. In this case White has a pleasant
advantage. The plan is ♗h3 followed by
breaking with d4 at an opportune moment.

22...exf4 23.d4 ♘d7 24.gxf4

24.♗c1 ♖fe8 25.a4 ♕g6∓

24...♕h4 25.♖e5

Finally, White achieves what he wanted, but Black is under no obligation to take the rook. 25.♕f3 ♖fe8 26.♖e5 b5! is also good for Black.

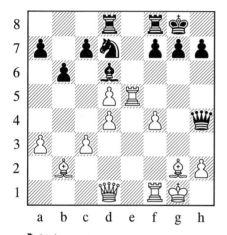

25...♘f6!↑

Targeting the weaknesses in the enemy position, namely the d5-pawn and the kingside.

26.♕e1

Played to prevent the plan of ...♗xe5 and ...♘xd5, but this move leads to a difficult endgame and is a clear admission of failure.

A more consistent follow-up to White's previous play would have been 26.c4!? ♗xe5 27.dxe5 ♘g4 with two possibilities:

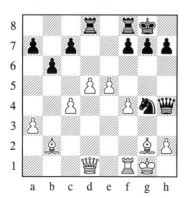

a) 28.h3!? ♘e3 29.♕f3 ♘xf1 30.♗xf1 should eventually be winning for Black, but White's powerful bishops and central pawns give him some practical compensation for being two exchanges down.

b) 28.♖f3 ♕xh2† 29.♔f1 ♕h5 30.♔g1 ♘e3 31.♕e2 ♘f5 Once again Black is objectively better and quite possibly winning, but White is still very much in the game.

26...♕xe1 27.♖exe1

27.♖fxe1 ♗xe5 28.fxe5 ♘xd5–+

27...♖fe8 28.♗c1

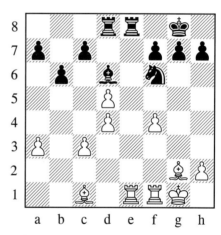

28...b5!

An excellent move. Now c4 is impossible and the d5-pawn becomes a serious weakness.

29.♗d2?

A huge mistake, giving up an important pawn for no good reason. Better was 29.♗f3 although 29...♗f8! 30.♖xe8 ♖xe8 31.♖f2 ♖d8 wins the d5-pawn. The best White can do is 32.c4 bxc4 33.♖c2 ♘xd5 34.♖xc4 when his bishop pair and active rook give him chances to save the game.

29...♗xa3∓ 30.♖b1

30.♖a1 is met by 30...b4! when Black is

winning. Perhaps this simple point is what Gashimov overlooked on the previous move.

30...a6 31.♗f3

Once again 31.♖a1 is strongly met by 31...b4!.

31...♘xd5 32.♖b3 ♗f8 33.♖a1 ♘b6 34.♖xa6 ♘c4 35.♖a2 b4!−+

Destroying White's centre.

36.♖c2 ♘xd2

The transition to an opposite-coloured bishop endgame only makes Black's job easier, as all White's pawns are on dark squares. The rest is easy.

37.♖xd2 bxc3 38.♖e2 ♖xe2 39.♗xe2 ♖xd4 40.♖xc3 ♗d6 41.♖b3 ♖xf4 42.♖b8† ♗f8 43.♖c8 c5
0−1

GAME 3
▷ **I. Nepomniachtchi (2711)**
▶ **Z. Efimenko (2706)**
8th World Team Championship, Ningbo
Round 6, 23.07.2011 **[A29]**
Annotated by Borki Predojevic

This game is a typical example of the English Opening. Black opted for a scheme called the reversed Rossolimo. In my opinion, Efimenko's 6...♖e8 was already imprecise and the problem with this move is White's strong option of 8.♘h4!. Black answered with 8...d6 when Nepomniachtchi employed the novelty 9.f3!? (however the alternative 9.d3 looks better). As my analysis shows, this was not a serious improvement, but Black was unable to find the best answer. He played 9...♘xd5?! and after a few moves White gained the advantage and had pressure throughout the game. Both opponents were making mistakes, but finally Black was able to hold a draw after a long and stubborn defence. The right move for Black

was 9...e3! which is critical for the evaluation of this line.

1.c4 ♘f6 2.♘c3 e5 3.♘f3 ♘c6 4.g3

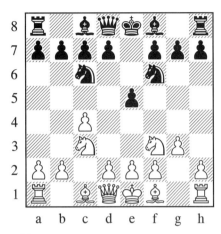

4...♗b4

Nowadays a popular alternative is:
4...♘d4
Black uses the fact that White has played g2-g3 to simplify the position immediately. Also, exchanging the c6-knight creates the new idea of ...c6 and ...d5. White usually plays:
5.♗g2
And after:
5...♘xf3† 6.♗xf3 ♗c5
An interesting way to start a concrete fight is:
7.e3!?
7.0–0 is the main move.
Here Black usually plays:
7...0–0
There are alternatives:
a) An interesting way to continue is: 7...♗b4!? 8.♕b3 ♕e7 (8...♗xc3 9.♕xc3±) 9.0–0 0–0 10.d3∞
b) 7...♕e7?! is suspicious. After 8.0–0 (intending d2-d4) 8...e4 9.♗g2 0–0 10.d3 exd3 11.♕xd3± White has the better position.
8.d4 exd4 9.exd4 ♖e8† 10.♗e3 ♗f8

After 10...♗b4 as in McNab – Stark, Hereford 2006, White should play the normal: 11.0–0 ♗xc3 (11...d6 12.♕b3 ♗xc3 13.♕xc3± planning d5 and ♗d4) 12.bxc3 d6 13.♖e1 h6 14.g4!?↑ White's position is preferable.

11.0–0±

White is better thanks to his superior development and space advantage.

11...d6 12.♖e1 c6 13.d5! c5 14.h4 ♗f5?! 15.g4 ♗c8 16.g5 ♘d7 17.♗f4 ♘e5 18.♗xe5 dxe5 19.♗g4 f5 20.gxf6 gxf6 21.♗xc8 ♕xc8 22.♘e4 ♖e7 23.♕h5±

White had a nearly-winning position and eventually won in A. Zhigalko – Escobar Forero, Khanty-Mansiysk (ol) 2010.

5.♗g2 0–0 6.0–0

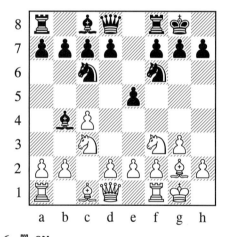

6...♖e8?!

I do not think this is Black's best option. He decides to wait before taking on c3, but after the next move he will not be able to take at all. My evaluation of 6...♖e8 as dubious is perhaps too rigid, but Black is passive in all the lines which I analysed in this game.

The alternative is:
6...♗xc3 7.bxc3
7.dxc3 is also possible.
7...e4 8.♘g5

8.♘d4!? ♖e8 9.d3 is another option for White.
8...♖e8 9.f3
Now Black reacts with:
9...e3!?
This move became popular after the well-known game Kasparov – Karpov, Seville (2) 1987. The main line goes:
10.d3 d5 11.♕b3 ♘a5 12.♕a3 c6 13.cxd5 cxd5 14.f4∞
With an unclear game.

6...e4 7.♘g5 ♗xc3 8.bxc3 leads to the same position as after 6...♗xc3.

7.♘d5 e4

Black does not want to retreat his bishop from b4.

After 7...♗f8 8.d3 h6 9.e4 d6 10.h3 ♘xd5 11.cxd5 ♘e7 12.d4 exd4 13.♘xd4 c6 14.dxc6 ♘xc6 15.♘b5 ♗e6 16.♘c3 ♖c8 17.b3 ♗e7 18.♗b2 ♗f6 19.♖b1 ♕a5 20.♘e2 ♗xb2 21.♖xb2 ♖ed8 22.♘f4± White was better in Damljanovic – Drenchev, Branko Vukmanovic Memorial (op) 2011.

7...♗c5 8.d3 ♘xd5 9.cxd5 ♘d4 10.♘d2 d6 11.e3 ♘f5 12.♘c4± also looks better for White. His idea is to play on the queenside with ♗d2, b4, a4, ♘a5 and attack the c7-square with ♕c2 and ♖fc1.

7...♘xd5 8.cxd5 ♘d4 9.♘xd4 exd4 10.e3 dxe3 11.dxe3 d6 12.♗d2± is an edge for White. In the future he will create pressure along the c-file. Black's counterplay is limited so he is doomed to a long passive defence.

8.♘h4!

This is a rare move after 7...e4 but it transposes to a line which arises after a more solid set-up for White: 1.c4 e5 2.♘c3 ♘f6 3.g3 ♘c6 4.♗g2 ♗b4 5.♘d5 0–0 6.♘f3!? e4 7.♘h4 ♖e8.
The main alternative is 8.♘e1.

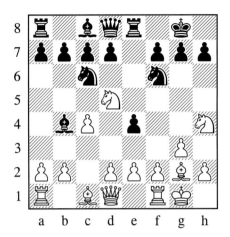

8...d6

The most common move here is:

8...♗c5

We will follow the game Vitiugov – Volkov, Russia 2008. White played the strong:

9.e3! d6

Wrong is 9...g5? 10.♘f5 d6 as in Marin – Fressinet, Plovdiv 2007, because White has the nice 11.♘fe7†! ♖xe7 12.♘xf6† ♔g7 13.♘xe4+– with a winning position.

10.f3!

A typical break; White opens the f-file and his plan is very simple.

10...♘xd5 11.cxd5 exf3 12.♘xf3 ♘b8 13.♘h4 ♘d7 14.b3 ♗b6 15.♗b2±

White is much better. His pieces are very active which gives him good chances for a kingside attack, while Black's bishops are out of play.

8...♗f8

This line was analysed in Marin's book *The English Opening: Volume One* where he gives the following line as best for White:

9.d3 ♘xd5

9...exd3 10.♕xd3 ♘e5 11.♕c2 c6 12.♘xf6† ♕xf6 13.b3! d6 14.♗b2 ♕h6 15.♖ad1± Petrosian – Liebert, Siegen (ol) 1970.

10.cxd5 exd3 11.♕xd3 ♘e5 12.♕c2 c5 13.f4 ♘g6 14.♘f3 d6 15.e4 ♗g4 16.f5 ♗xf3

16...♘h8 17.♘e1 ♗h5 18.h3 f6 19.♘d3

(with the idea ♘f4-g6) 19...g5□ 20.b3± Black is very passive, Vaganian – Taimanov, Baku 1977.

17.fxg6 ♗h5 18.gxf7† ♗xf7 19.b3 b5 20.♗b2±

Marin

9.f3!?N

A novelty by Ian. Objectively, this is not an improvement, but it leads to a very complicated position. In fact, on the very next move Black lost his way.

Previously played was:

9.d3

This is promising for White.

9...exd3

9...♘xd5 10.cxd5 exd3 11.♕xd3 – 9...exd3

10.♕xd3 ♘e5

10...♘xd5 11.cxd5 ♘e5 12.♕c2±

11.♕c2 ♘xd5

11...♗c5 12.b3 c6 13.♘xf6† ♕xf6 14.♗b2±

12.cxd5 ♗c5

The key move for White is:

13.b3!

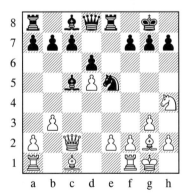

Black has a few alternatives here and I chose as the main line:

13...♗d7

Black has been able to hold this position in practice.

13...♕e7 14.♗b2 a5 15.a3 ♘g6 16.♘xg6 hxg6 17.e4± leads to a better position for White, Lautier – Karpov, Dortmund 1993.

13...♘g6 14.♘f3 ♘e5 15.♘xe5 ♖xe5
16.♗b2 ♖e8 17.e4±
14.♗b2 a5

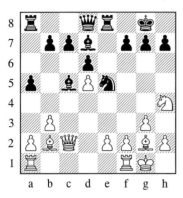

And here I suggest the novelty 15.a3N±/= as
a better option for White. The idea is to stop
Black's plan of ...a5-a4.

Instead after 15.♖ad1 a4 16.♗d4 axb3
17.axb3 ♗xd4 18.♖xd4 ♕f6 19.♖b4 (Black
is OK after 19.♖fd1 ♖ec8⇄ or 19.♕xc7N g5
20.f4 ♘g6 21.♖c4 gxh4 22.♕xd7 ♖xe2⇄)
19...c5! 20.dxc6 bxc6 21.♖f4 ♕e7 22.♘f5
♗xf5 23.♕xf5 ♖ab8 24.♕c2 d5 Black was fine
in Izoria – Mchedlishvili, Tbilisi 2001.

9.♘xb4!? ♘xb4 10.d3 h6 11.dxe4 ♘xe4
12.♗e3 is slightly better for White according to
Lautier. The final position should be checked.
A possible plan for Black is to play ...a5, ...♗d7
and ...♗c6, similarly to some lines of the Bogo-
Indian (1.d4 ♘f6 2.c4 e6 3.♘f3 ♗b4†).

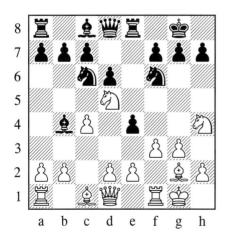

9...♘xd5?!

A typical decision, but it does not bring
anything good for Black.

A similar type of position would arise after:
9...exf3 10.♘xf3 ♗g4 11.e3
   The inadvisable 11.d4 would give Black
the chance for a nice tactic with 11...♘xd5
12.cxd5 ♗xf3 13.♖xf3 ♘d4!. After 14.♖f2
c5 15.e3 ♘b5⇄ 16.♕f1 ♕b6 17.a3 ♗a5
18.♖xf7 ♖f8 19.♖f4 ♘c7∞ the position is
unclear.
   11.♘xb4 ♘xb4 12.d3 also looks interesting.
11...♘xd5 12.cxd5 ♘e5 13.♕c2 ♕e7 14.a3
♘xf3† 15.♗xf3 ♗xf3 16.♖xf3 ♗c5 17.b4 ♗b6
18.♗b2↑
   White has the initiative.

Black missed a very nice tactical idea. He
should play:
9...e3!

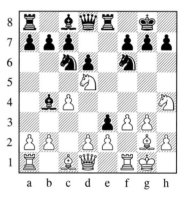

The idea behind this move is connected with
the h4-knight not having any safe squares.
Now, Black has the serious threat of ...g5.

White has a few options to consider:

a) 10.♘xb4 ♘xb4 11.f4
   11.♕b3 a5 12.a3 ♘c6↑
11...♘d3!
   White is in trouble.
12.dxe3

12.♗f3 gives Black the opportunity to play the nice: 12...♘f2! 13.♕b3 (13.♖xf2 exf2† 14.♔xf2 ♗g4∓) 13...exd2 14.♖xf2 dxc1=♕† 15.♖xc1 ♘g4 16.♗xg4 ♗xg4∓ And again White has problems.

12...♘xc1 13.♕xc1 ♕e7 14.♗f3 ♕xe3† 15.♕xe3 ♖xe3∓

This leads to a small advantage for Black.

b) 10.♘xe3 This saves the knight (since 10...g5 can be met by 11.♘hf5) but Black has strong compensation after 10...♗c5. White's knights are on bad squares and Black's last move renews the threat of ...g5. Also, Black has the strong idea of ...d5 to increase the pressure on White's position.

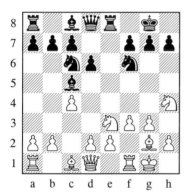

b1) After 11.f4 Black has 11...♘g4 12.♗f3 ♘xe3 13.dxe3 ♕e7 14.♘g2 (14.♔h1 ♗xe3 15.♗xe3 ♕xe3 16.♘g2 ♕c5† is simply better for Black) 14...♗f5 15.♗d2 a5!⩲ With great compensation, as the e4-square is completely controlled by Black.

b2) 11.♔h1 ♗xe3 12.dxe3 g5 13.♘f5 ♗xf5 14.e4 Black should now give back the piece with: 14...♘xe4! (14...♗e6 15.♗xg5⩲ would give White some compensation) 15.fxe4 ♗g6† And after the complications Black's structure is superior.

b3) 11.♕c2 ♘d4

The unnatural 11...♕d7?! is dubious. White can play: 12.f4 ♘g4 13.♔h1! (13.♗f3

♘d4⩲) 13...♘xe3 14.dxe3 ♗xe3 (14...♕e7?! 15.e4) 15.♗xe3 ♖xe3 16.♗f3 And thanks to the queen on d7, White has time to play ♘g2 and e2-e4. 16...♕e8 (16...♘d4? 17.♕d2; 16...♖e8 17.♕c3 ♕e7 18.e4 ♗h3 19.♖fe1±) 17.♘g2 ♖e7 18.♖ad1 ♗h3 19.e4 ♖d8 20.♖fe1 f5 (20...♘b4 21.♕d2 ♗xg2† 22.♔xg2 c5 23.e5±) 21.♘h4↑ White's position is preferable.

12.♕d3

12.♕d1? g5−+

12...d5

12...g5?! 13.b4! gxh4 14.bxc5 dxc5 15.g4 h5 16.♗a3∞

13.♔h1

13.f4 ♗g4 14.♖e1 ♘xe2† 15.♖xe2 ♗xe2 16.♕xe2 d4 17.♗xb7 dxe3∓

13.b4 dxc4 14.♕xc4 ♗b6⩱∞

13...dxc4 14.♕xc4 ♗b6⩱∞/∓

Black has huge compensation and his position is much better.

c) 10.dxe3! g5

10...♗c5 11.♔h1 g5 12.♘f5 transposes to 10...g5.

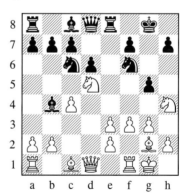

11.♘f5!

This looks like the most precise move. White wants to play e3-e4 while the knight is still on d5 with the idea of forcing Black to take on d5.

11.e4? is bad since Black has 11...♗c5† 12.♔h1 gxh4 13.♗g5 ♘xd5! 14.♗xd8

♘e3 15.♕b3 and now 15...h3!–+ destroys White.

On 11.♘xb4 ♘xb4 12.♘f5 ♗xf5 13.e4 Black has the interesting 13...♘xe4!?. After 14.fxe4 ♗xe4 15.♗xe4 ♖xe4 White can force a draw with 16.a3 ♘c6 17.♕d5 ♖xe2 18.♕xf7† ♔h8 19.♕h5 ♕e8 20.♖f7 ♖e1† 21.♔f2 ♖e2† 22.♔g1 ♖e1†= with a repetition of moves.

11...♗xf5 12.e4

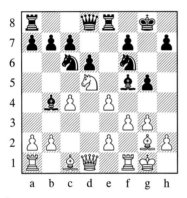

12...♗g6!?

With this move Black parries the idea of ♘xb4 and ♗xg5.

On 12...♗c5† 13.♔h1 ♗e6 14.♗xg5 Black has to take with: 14...♘xd5 (Worse is 14...♗xd5 15.cxd5 ♘e5 when White has a nice game after: 16.♖c1 ♘g6 [16...♘ed7 17.♗h3 ♔g7 18.♕d2⩲] 17.♗h3 a5 18.♗f5 ♔g7 19.♕d2⩲ With huge compensation.) 15.♗xd8 ♘e3 16.♕d2 ♖axd8 17.♖fc1 The position is unclear. A possible continuation is: 17...♘d4 18.♖ab1 ♘xc4 19.♕g5† ♔h8 20.♗h3 ♗e3□ 21.f4 ♗xc1 22.♕f6† ♔g8 23.♕g5† ♔f8 24.♕h6† ♔g8= With a draw. 12...♗e6?! 13.♘xb4 (13.♗xg5 ♘xd5 14.♗xd8 ♘e3 15.♕c1 ♖axd8↑ is a better version for Black than in the previous line.) 13...♘xb4 14.♗xg5 ♘c6 15.♕d2 ♔g7 16.f4 ♕e7 (16...h6 17.♗h4; 16...♗xc4 17.♕c3 ♗e6 18.e5±) 17.b4!±

13.♗xg5

After 13.♘xb4 ♘xb4 14.♗xg5 ♕e7 15.♕d2

♘c6 Black wants to play ...♕e6 or ...♕e5 with the idea of ...♘d7 while the white centre is immobilized because the g6-bishop controls e4. 16.♗h3 (16.b4 ♕e6!∓ planning ...♘d7 and f6) 16...a5∓ Planning ...♕e5 (the immediate 16...♕e5 allows 17.b4!?).

13...♘xd5

13...♗c5† 14.♔h1 ♘xd5 15.♗xd8 ♘e3 16.♗xc7 ♘xd1 17.♖fxd1 transposes below.

14.♗xd8 ♘e3

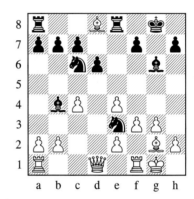

15.♗xc7!?

This is White's extra opportunity after 12...♗g6. If the bishop was on e6 this idea would not work (the pawn on c4 would be hanging in that case).

After 15.♕b3 ♖axd8⩲ Black has good compensation and his bishop on g6 looks good (especially after ...f5 at the right moment).

15...♘xd1 16.♖fxd1

It may look like the position is better for White, but Black has a clever idea:

16...♗c5†

16...♖e6 17.♗h3 ♖f6 18.♖d5 ♗c5† 19.♔h1↑ Planning ♖ad1, while the f6-rook and d6-pawn are both problems.

17.♔h1 ♗e3!

Despite the fact that White will take a fourth pawn, the e3-bishop paralyses the white pieces.

17...f5 18.exf5 ♗xf5 19.e4 ♗e6 20.b3 ♗d4 21.♖ab1 ♔f7 22.♗xd6±

18.♖d3

18.♗h3 f5 19.♗xf5 ♗xf5 20.exf5 ♖ac8 21.♗xd6 ♘d4 22.b3 ♘xf5↑

18...♗d4 19.♖b1 f5 20.exf5 ♗f7!∞

The position is very complicated.

10.cxd5 exf3

10...♘d4 11.e3 ♘xf3† 12.♘xf3 exf3 13.♕xf3 f6 14.♕e2 ♗d7 15.b3± is similar to the game.

11.♘xf3 ♘e5

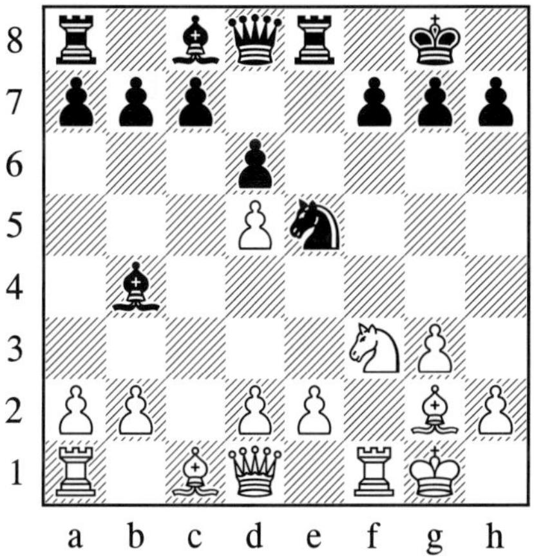

12.♕c2⩲

White has achieved a very promising position, even if it may not look so good at first sight. White's main idea is to play b2-b3 and ♗b2. If ...♗c5 then White will play e2-e3 and thanks to the pawn on d2 Black's dark-squared bishop will be out of play.

12...♗c5†

After the active 12...♘xf3† 13.♗xf3 ♗h3 14.♖f2 ♕d7 White can still continue with his plan: 15.♕c4 ♗c5 16.e3 ♖e7 (16...a5 17.b3 b5 18.♕h4↑) 17.b4!? Gaining more space (17.b3 is also possible). 17...♗b6 18.a4 a5 19.b5 ♗f5 20.♗b2 f6 21.♖af1± White is improving his position while Black has to wait.

13.e3 ♗b6 14.b3 ♗g4 15.♗b2

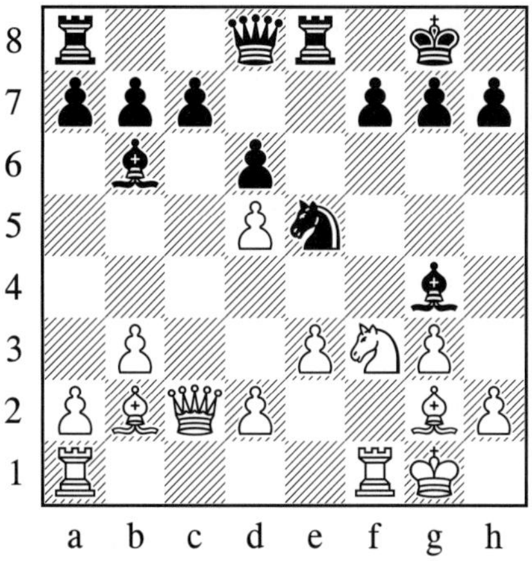

15...♘xf3†

A debatable decision. Black will exchange two pieces on f3, but this will not solve the problem of his dark-squared bishop.

Poor was 15...♕d7? 16.♘g5!.

The best option for Black was:

15...f6!

This move looks strange because Black is weakening the e6-square, but the main idea is to keep the knight active on e5. Also, Black prepares the manoeuvre ...♗h5-g6-f7 and the other idea is ...♕d7 with ...♖ac8 and ...c7-c6.

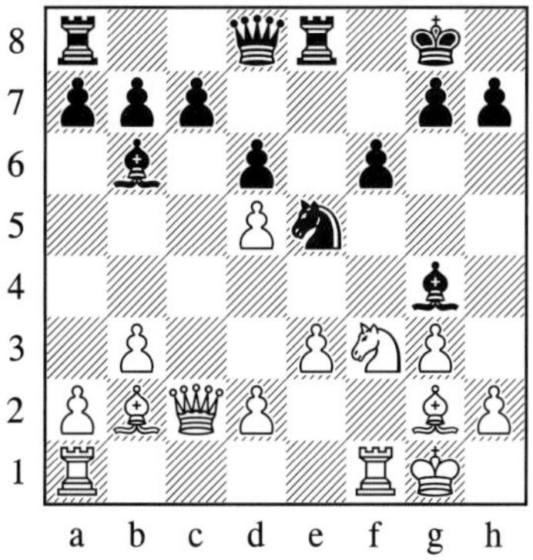

Now logical is:

16.♘d4

16.♘xe5 dxe5⇄ Black plans ...♗h5-f7 targeting d5.

16...♕d7 17.♖f4 ♗h5 18.♗e4 ♗g6 19.♘f5
19.♖af1 ♗xe4 20.♖xe4 ♗xd4 21.♗xd4 c5
22.dxc6 ♕xc6 23.♕xc6 ♘xc6=
19...♖ac8
Simply preparing ...c7-c6.
20.♖af1 c6 21.♗c3 ♔h8 22.b4 ♖f8 23.a3±
White retains some pressure, but Black's
position is very solid.

16.♗xf3 ♗xf3 17.♖xf3 ♕g5 18.♖af1 f6

Of course not: 18...♕xd5? 19.♖xf7 ♕xf7
20.♖xf7 ♔xf7 21.♕f5† ♔e7 (21...♔g8
22.♕d7+–) 22.♗xg7+–

19.♕c4

White has improved his position, while
Black still has huge problems connected with
the b6-bishop.

19...♖f8 20.♖f4 ♖ae8 21.♖g4 ♕h6

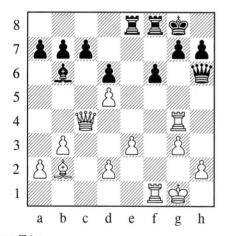

22.♖f5?

A tactical mistake. First White should play
22.♔g2±/± when Black's position remains
critical.

22...a5?

Black missed his chance.

After the strong 22...♖xe3! 23.dxe3 ♕xe3†
24.♔g2 ♕d2† 25.♔h3 ♗g1! White has to

force a draw with: 26.♖xg7† (26.♖e4 ♕xh2†
27.♔g4 g6–+) 26...♔xg7 27.♗xf6† (27.♗c3
♕h6† 28.♕h4 ♕xh4†29.♔xh4 c6∓) 27...♖xf6
28.♕xc7† ♔g6 29.♖xf6† ♔xf6 30.♕xd6†=
With perpetual check.

23.♔g2± ♖f7 24.♖h4 ♕g6 25.♕f4?!

Better was: 25.♖fh5! ♖fe7 (25...h6 26.♖xh6!)
26.♖xh7 ♕xh7 27.♖xh7 ♔xh7 28.♗c3 ♖e4
29.♕b5± Black is in big trouble.

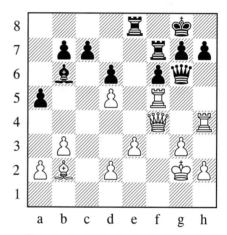

25...♖e5!

Efimenko uses his chance. This move does
not solve all Black's problems, but it's the most
stubborn defence.

26.♖hh5

Interesting was: 26.e4!? ♖xf5 27.exf5
♕g5 28.♗c3 ♕xf4 (if 28...♖e7 then White
has 29.♕f3! with the strong threat of ♖h5)
29.♖xf4 ♖e7 (29...c6 30.dxc6 bxc6 31.♖a4 ♖a7
32.♖c4! ♖c7 33.♖e4 ♔f7 34.♖e6±/± White
has pressure.) 30.♔f1 ♔f8 31.♖a4± White will
take the a5-pawn, but the rook endgame looks
drawish.

26...♖xf5

The alternative was 26...♖e8!? to avoid
exchanges and keep the white rook on h5 where
it looks misplaced. For example: 27.♕f3 (after
27.e4 ♖fe7 28.d3 a4 29.b4 Black has 29...a3

30.♗c3 ♖f8! with the idea ...♕e8-a4 and Black has counterplay) 27...fe7 28.♖h4 Now Black has 28...♗xe3! 29.♗xf6 gxf6 30.♖xf6 ♕g7 31.dxe3 ♖xe3 32.♕f5 ♖3e5= with equality.

27.♖xf5 ♖e7 28.g4! ♕e8?!

Black should insert 28...h6! 29.h4 and only then play 29...♕e8. Now on 30.g5 Black again has a sac on e3: 30...♗xe3! 31.dxe3 ♖e4 32.♕f3 (32.♕f2?! hxg5 33.hxg5 ♖g4† 34.♔f1 ♕e4↑) 32...♖xe3 33.♕g4 ♖e4 34.♖f4 ♖xf4 35.♕xf4 ♕e2† 36.♕f2 ♕g4†= With a draw.

29.g5

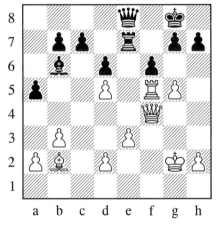

29...fxg5

Wrong is 29...♖e4? 30.♕f3 ♗xe3 31.gxf6 ♕g6† 32.♔h3 ♕h6† 33.♖h5 ♕f4, as White has 34.f7†! ♕xf7 35.♖f5 ♕e8 36.dxe3 ♖xe3 37.♖f8† ♕xf8 38.♕xe3 ♕f5† 39.♔g3 ♕g6† 40.♔h4+− with a winning position.

This was the last moment for: 29...♗xe3! 30.dxe3 ♖e4! It looks like White doesn't have anything better than 31.♕g3 ♖xe3 32.♖f3 and then: 32...♖e2† 33.♖f2 ♕e4† 34.♕f3 ♖xf2† 35.♔xf2 ♕c2† 36.♕e2 ♕f5† 37.♔e3 ♕xg5† 38.♔d4 ♔f8⇄ In the final position Black has three pawns for a bishop and enough counterplay.

30.♖xg5 ♖f7 31.♕g4 ♕d7 32.♕xd7 ♖xd7 33.♗c3

Black has exchanged a lot of pieces, but even so in this endgame he is under pressure.

33...♖f7 34.♖g4 ♔f8 35.b4

35.♖a4 ♖f5 36.♗xa5 ♖xd5 37.♗c3±/± was a reasonable alternative since White's rook will penetrate to the 8th rank.

35...axb4 36.♖xb4 ♔e8!

The best defence; Black will protect his queenside with his king.

37.a4 ♔d7 38.♖b2 ♔c8 39.d4

This move again shows Black's main problem – the dark-squared bishop.

39...g6 40.h3 ♖f5 41.a5 ♗a7 42.e4 ♖f4 43.♖e2 ♔d7 44.♗d2 ♖f8 45.♗e3 ♖e8 46.♗f2

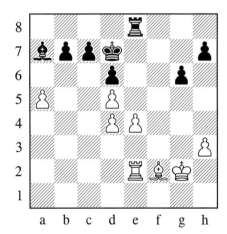

46...b6!

Black doesn't want to play passive moves anymore. This active move came just in time and shows one of the many skills of GM Efimenko – strong and stubborn defence.

The other possibility was 46...g5, but after 47.♔f3 h5 48.♔e3± White has good chances of playing for a win.

47.a6 b5 48.♖b2

The last try was 48.e5!? dxe5 49.dxe5 ♗xf2 50.♔xf2, but after the strong 50...♖a8! 51.♖a2 b4 52.♔e3 b3 53.♖b2 ♖xa6 54.♖xb3 ♖a5!= Black can hold the position.

48...♖xe4= 49.♔f3 ♖e8 50.♖xb5 ♗b6 51.♖b3

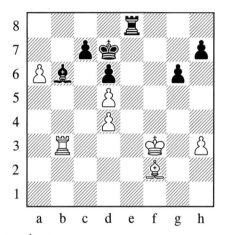

51...♔c8!

The black king comes to a7. White has lost all his advantage, but even if Black reached his "dream position" he still could not win the game.

**52.♗e3 ♔b8 53.♖a3 ♔a7 54.h4 ♖f8†
55.♔e4 ♖f1 56.♖a4 ♖h1 57.♗f2 ♖f1 58.♗e3 ♖h1 59.♗f2 ♖f1**

Neither side can improve his position.

½–½

GAME 4
▷ **V. Kramnik (2781)**
▶ **I. Nepomniachtchi (2711)**
64th Russian Championship, Moscow
Round 4, 11.08.2011 [A30]
Annotated by Borki Predojevic

The English Opening was very popular in the 2011 Russian Championship, and in the fourth round Kramnik chose it against Nepomniachtchi. Ian decided to play 6...g6!?

– an interesting line that has been employed by Grischuk. Kramnik already had some experience in the line, and he played the novelty 7.♗e2, then continued with the logical 9.b3. Here Nepomniachtchi made the first mistake with 9...exd4?. Instead, he could have played the strong 9...♘e7! when Kramnik would have faced some problems with his knight on e5. But after 9...exd4? Kramnik obtained a positional advantage and strong pressure. The game became very interesting when Kramnik sacrificed the exchange with 25.♘d5!?. Immediately after taking the exchange, Black blundered with 26...♗b7? (after the correct 26...♕d6! White would have had sufficient compensation, but no advantage), which gave White the chance for 27.♕b4!. Then Black's position was bad, but not lost. But his final mistake of 36...♗a8? let White win another pawn, and in due course the game.

However, my assessment is that 6...g6!? is playable and that 9...♘e7!N is the right answer to Kramnik's 9.b3.

1.c4 c5 2.♘f3 ♘c6 3.e3!?

An interesting move order, instead of the more popular 3.♘c3.

After the standard 3...♘f6 4.g3, it is likely that Nepomniachtchi had prepared the line which he subsequently played in Round 6 against Svidler; that encounter is also analysed in this issue of Chess Evolution (see Game 6).

On 3...e5 White can transpose into our main game with 4.e3, while another option is 4.g3 g6 5.♗g2 ♗g7 6.0–0, going into one of the main lines of the English Opening.

3...e5

After 3...♘f6 4.d4 cxd4 5.exd4 d5 6.♘c3 the game transposes into the Panov Variation of the Caro-Kann.

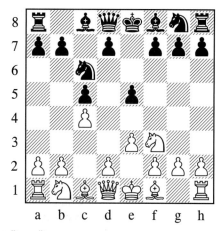

4.♘c3 ♞f6 5.d4

Kramnik originally prepared this line for his match against Grischuk in Kazan 2011. He played it twice in that match, but was unable to win either game.

For players who wish to avoid the concrete lines after 5.d4, I would suggest the calm move 5.♗e2. After 5...d5 6.d4 exd4 7.exd4, theory offers 7...♗e6 as the main move. White can now go into a well-known endgame: 8.cxd5 ♘xd5 9.0–0 ♗e7 10.dxc5 ♘xc3 11.bxc3 ♗xc5 12.♘g5±/= White takes the bishop pair and keeps some chances for a win, although the evaluation of the position is quite close to equal.

5...e4

This is the most flexible move order.

After 5...exd4 6.exd4 d5 I found an old game by Portisch who reacted with 7.♗g5 (7.♗e2 leads to the position mentioned in the previous note, and is also a decent option for White) 7...♗e7 8.dxc5 d4 9.♗xf6 ♗xf6 10.♘d5 0–0 11.♗d3 ♖e8† 12.♔f1∞ Portisch – Radulov, Indonesia 1983.

The main line is 5...cxd4 6.exd4 e4, but after 7.♘e5 Black has to choose between 7...♗b4 or 7...♗d6. Here 7...g6?! doesn't look sound,

since the c1-bishop can be developed along the c1-h6 diagonal. After 8.♗e2 ♗g7 9.0–0 0–0 10.♗f4± White doesn't have to waste time on b2-b3 (as he does in our main game).

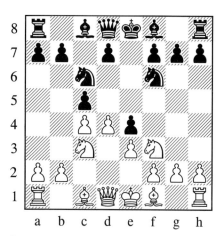

6.♘e5

This is the best reply.

According to theory, 6.♘g5 cxd4 7.exd4 ♗b4⇄ is fine for Black.

6.♘d2 doesn't look good. Again, Black's reply is 6...cxd4 7.exd4 ♗b4⇄ with a good game.

6.d5 exf3 7.dxc6 fxg2 8.cxd7† ♗xd7 9.♗xg2 ♕c7 looks okay for Black.

6...g6!?

This move was introduced by Grischuk in a rapid game in the aforementioned Kramnik – Grischuk match.

The main line is:
6...cxd4 7.exd4

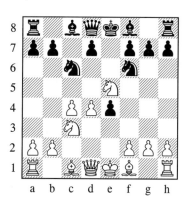

7...♗b4

This is by far the most popular move here, but Black has also played 7...♗d6 8.c5! and now:

a) 8...♘xe5? is a huge mistake: 9.cxd6 ♘g6 10.h4! ♕a5 11.h5 ♘f8 12.d5+– a6 13.♕d4 h6 14.b4 ♕d8 15.♕e5† 1–0 Shengelia – Grover, Dubai 2010.

b) 8...♗c7?! 9.♘c4 d5 10.cxd6 ♗xd6 11.d5 gives the initiative to White.

c) 8...♗b8 9.♘c4 d5 10.cxd6 0–0 11.♗f4 ♘a5 12.♘e3 ♗xd6 13.♗xd6 ♕xd6 14.d5 After a few forced moves, White has achieved a very pleasant position. His knight on e3 is strong and the d-pawn is well protected, while the black knight on a5 is not in the best of positions. Black tried to solve his problems with 14...♕e5 15.♗e2 ♖d8 16.♕d2 ♘c6, but after 17.♖d1 ♘e7 18.♕d4 ♕xd4 19.♖xd4 ♘f5 20.♘xf5 ♗xf5 21.♔d2 ♘e8 22.g4±/± White had strong pressure in the endgame, Kramnik – Grischuk, Kazan (2) 2011.

8.♗e2 ♕a5 9.♘xc6 dxc6 10.0–0

An interesting pawn sacrifice; Black does best to decline it and continue normally.

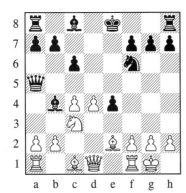

10...0–0

Here is a recent example in which Black snatched the pawn: 10...♗xc3 11.bxc3 ♕xc3 12.♖b1 ♕a5 (12...0–0 13.♖b3 ♕a5 14.♖g3∞) 13.♗d2 ♕c7 14.♗b4 b6 15.♕a4 ♘d7 16.♖fe1∞ Black is facing strong pressure. The game continued 16...f5 17.♗h5†! g6

18.♗d1 ♔f7 19.c5 and Black failed to survive the attack in Miton – Jakubowski, Warsaw 2011.

11.♗d2 ♖e8 12.a3 ♗xc3 13.♗xc3 ♕g5 14.♗d2!

White has usually played 14. ♕c1 here, but that can be met by 14...e3!?.

14...♕g6 15.♕b3 h5 16.♖fe1 h4 17.h3?

This is a huge mistake. Better was 17.♖ad1 h3 18.♕g3!? ♔h7 19.♗f4 and White has some initiative. The situation on the kingside is under control, and he can prepare to break in the centre with d4-d5.

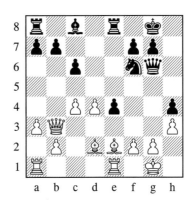

17...e3! 18.♗xe3

18.♗d3 exf2† 19.♔xf2 ♕g3† 20.♔f1 (20.♔g1 ♗xh3–+) 20...♗f5 21.♗c2 ♘e4!–+ 18...♗xh3 19.♗f1 ♗xg2 20.♗xg2 h3 21.♗g5 ♕xg5 22.♕xh3 ♘h5 23.d5 cxd5 24.cxd5 ♘f4 25.♕g3 ♕f6†

Black was clearly better in Potkin – Alekseev, Russia 2011.

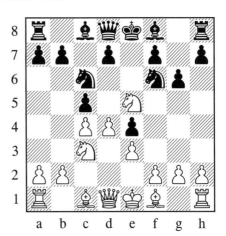

7.♗e2N

This natural move is a novelty. In the rapid game Kramnik played:

7.♖b1 h5

On 7...♗g7 White can reply 8.♘xc6 dxc6 9.dxc5±, and thanks to the rook on b1 he will be able to defend his extra pawn with b2-b4.

However, Black can quite possibly improve with 7...♗d6!? and now:

a) 8.♘g4 ♘xg4 9.♕xg4 0–0 10.dxc5 ♗xc5 11.♕xe4 ♖e8 12.♕f4 (12.♕d3 d5! 13.♕xd5 ♕e7∞ intending ...♗f5) 12...d5!? 13.cxd5 ♘b4 Black has reasonable compensation for the sacrificed pawns.

b) 8.f4 exf3 9.♘xf3 0–0 10.♗e2 ♖e8 11.0–0 b6 leads to an unclear position.

8.♗e2 ♕e7 9.b3

9.f4 cxd4 10.exd4 d6 11.♘xc6 bxc6∞

9...cxd4 10.exd4 d6 11.♘xc6 bxc6 12.♗g5 ♗f5 13.0–0

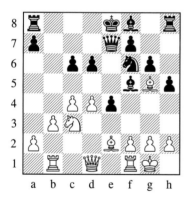

White had the advantage in Kramnik – Grischuk, Kazan (7 – rapid) 2011.

7...♗g7 8.0–0

8.♘xc6 dxc6 9.dxc5 ♕a5=

8...0–0 9.b3

This move looks natural, but there is a nice tactical idea for Black.

9.♘a4 cxd4 10.exd4 ♘e7 11.c5 d6 12.♘c4 b5

13.cxb6 d5 14.b7 ♗xb7 15.♘e5 leads to an unclear game.

9.♘xc6 is not best, since Black can take with the d-pawn: 9...dxc6 10.dxc5 ♕a5 11.♘a4 ♖d8 12.♕c2 ♗g4⇄ and Black has a good game.

9...cxd4?

A serious mistake by Nepomniachtchi.

9...♖e8 10.♗b2

10.♘xc6 dxc6 11.dxc5 ♘d7 12.♗b2 ♘xc5 13.♕xd8 ♖xd8 14.♖ad1 ♗e6 is at least equal for Black.

10...cxd4 11.exd4 d6

11...♘xe5 12.dxe5 ♖xe5 13.♕d2 gives White good compensation.

12.♘xc6 bxc6

Compared with the game, White's dark-squared bishop is less actively placed.

13.d5

13.♕d2 d5⇄

White can consider 13.♗c1!? in order to develop bishop on the c1-h6 diagonal, but clearly the loss of time with the bishop means that Black obtains an improved version of the position in the game.

13...c5 14.♕d2 ♘d7⇄

Black should be satisfied with the outcome of the opening. Continuing with ...f5 offers him a good game.

The best reply was:

9...♘e7!N

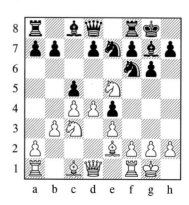

Black's idea is simple: ...d6. It is obvious that the knight on e5 is in danger. It would be very interesting to know Kramnik's opinion of this position.

10.dxc5!?

With this risky move White sacrifices his knight, but the position remains unclear.

The more normal 10.♗b2 d6 11.♘g4 ♘xg4 12.♗xg4 ♗xg4 13.♕xg4 cxd4 14.exd4 d5! 15.♖ad1 ♖e8 is very good for Black.

10.♘g4 ♘xg4 11.♗xg4 d5! looks slightly better for Black.

10.h3 d6 11.♘g4 ♘e8 followed by ...f5, offers Black the better prospects.

10...♘e8!

The knight can also go forward: 10...♘h5 11.♗xh5 ♗xe5 (Worse is 11...gxh5 12.♕xh5 d6 13.♖d1 ♗xe5 14.♗b2 ♘c6 15.cxd6 f5 16.♖d2 and with three pawns for the bishop, a strong d-pawn and a possible attack on the black king, White has the advantage.) 12.♗d2 gxh5 13.♕xh5 f5 14.♘xe4! ♕e8! (14...♗xa1? 15.♘g5 ♖f6 16.♕xh7† ♔f8 17.♖xa1 gives White a devastating attack) 15.♕xe8 ♖xe8 White now has a couple of interesting options:

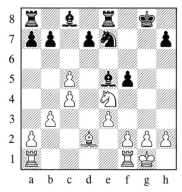

a) 16.♗c3!? ♗xh2† 17.♔xh2 fxe4 White has just two pawns for the knight, but the position remains very unclear. White has an active plan available, while Black still needs to spend time completing his development. 18.♖h1! (18.♖ad1 b6) 18...b6 19.♔g1 bxc5

20.♖h5 ♖b8 (20...a5 21.♖xc5 a4 22.b4⩱ looks rather nice for White) 21.♖g5† ♔f7 (21...♘g6 22.♖d1 ♖b6 23.♖xc5⩲) The position remains unclear, but if anyone is better it should be Black.

b) 16.♘d6 ♗xd6 17.cxd6 ♘c6 18.♗c3 b6 19.♖ad1 ♔f7 20.♖d5 ♔g6 21.g4!? (21.h4 h5∞) 21...fxg4 22.f4 ♖xe3 23.♖g5† ♔f7 24.♖f5† ♔g6 25.♖g5† and the position is equal.

11.♘xf7 ♖xf7

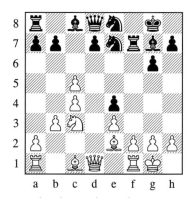

It is very hard to evaluate this position. White has some compensation for the sacrificed piece, but objectively Black should have the better chances.

12.♗b2

12.♕c2 d6! 13.cxd6 ♕xd6 14.♘xe4 ♕c6 15.♘c3 b5 16.♗b2 b4 17.♘d1 ♗b7 18.f3 ♕c5∓

12...b6

12...d6?! 13.cxd6 ♕xd6 14.♕xd6 ♘xd6 15.c5∞ followed by ♗c4.

13.cxb6 axb6 14.♕c2 ♗b7

Black stands slightly better.

10.exd4 ♖e8 11.♗f4 d6 12.♘xc6 bxc6 13.♖c1±/±

As a consequence of 9...cxd4? White has succeeded in developing his pieces to their best positions. His plan is very simple – advancing the queenside pawns. Black's counterplay should be connected to threats against the white king, since Black has the pawn majority on the kingside. This counterplay is limited thanks to the good positioning of White's pieces, the bishop on f4 being especially strong. All these facts tell us that White has the better prospects.

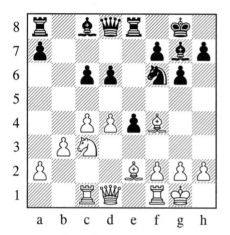

13...d5 14.♕d2 ♗a6

With this move, Black gives up the idea of organizing any kind of kingside attack. This will allow White to increase his advantage with simple moves.

15.♖fd1 ♖c8 16.h3

Prophylaxis. White secures the position of his dark-squared on the h2-b8 diagonal. He also makes space for king in case Black creates any threats on the first rank in the future. 16.♘a4 was possible too.

16...dxc4

Black decides to change the type of position.

16...♗f8 17.♘a4 ♗a3 18.♖b1± doesn't help Black.

17.bxc4 ♘d7 18.♘a4

White is better, but he needs to make a break in order to increase the pressure on Black's position. This break is likely to involve d4-d5, when White may create a strong passed pawn.

18...♗f8

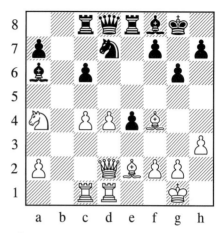

19.♗f1!?

White slowly prepares d4-d5. It is not so easy to find a useful move for Black.

It is too soon break with 19.d5?. Black then has 19...cxd5 20.cxd5 ♖xc1 21.♖xc1 ♗xe2 22.♕xe2 ♘f6! 23.♖d1 ♕d7⇄ and White has lost all his advantage.

19...h5 20.♕c3

With this move, White reveals a new motif: ♘c5. If White manages to play it, then after forced exchanges on c5 he will get the d6-square for his bishop and the possibility of attacking the a6-bishop with ♕a3.

20...♕f6

Black's problems are not solved by: 20...♗g7

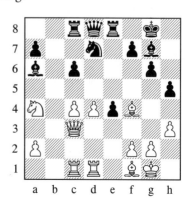

21.♕a3!

Targeting the a6-bishop.

21...♕a5 22.♗d2

Less precise is 22.♖c3 ♕f5 23.♗d6 c5! 24.♘xc5 ♘xc5 25.♗xc5 (25.dxc5 ♗xc3 26.♕xc3 ♗b7∞) 25...♖xc5 26.dxc5 ♗xc3 27.♕xc3 ♕xc5 28.♕f6, when Black has 28...e3! with counterplay.

22...♕f5 23.♗e3 ♕a5

Black has nothing better.

24.♖c3 ♖b8 25.♘c5 ♕xa3 26.♖xa3 ♘xc5 27.dxc5 ♗c8 28.♖xa7±

Black's position is critical.

21.♗e3 c5

Black is aiming to change the pawn structure.

22.♕a5!?

White could create a protected passed pawn with 22.d5. After 22...♕d6 23.♖b1 f5 24.♕a5 White retains pressure.

22...cxd4 23.♗xd4 ♕c6 24.♘c3 ♗h6?!

A weird move. More normal is 24...♗c5, in order to exchange a pair of bishops and take control of the c5-square. After 25.♘d5 ♗b7 (25...♗xd4 26.♖xd4 ♘c5 27.♖d2±) 26.♖b1 ♕a6 (26...♗a8 27.♗xc5 ♕xc5 28.♖b5±) 27.♕d2 ♗xd5 28.cxd5 ♕d6 29.♗b5± White keeps the better chances.

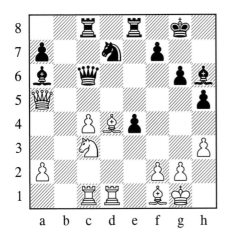

25.♘d5!?

A very brave and intuitive decision. Kramnik decides to sacrifice the exchange, even though it is by no means obligatory. White could safely play 25.♖c2 ♖e6 26.♘d5 ♘c5 27.♕c3±/± and the bishop on h6 would be out of play.

25...♗xc1

Black is practically forced to take on c1, since otherwise White would activate his rook with ♖c3.

26.♖xc1⩱

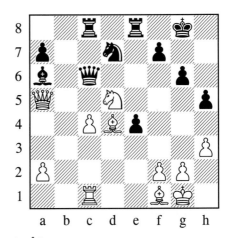

26...♗b7?

Immediately after taking the exchange, Black blunders.

After 26...♖e6 27.♕a3 ♘c5 28.♗a1!∞ White will create threats on the a1-h8 diagonal.

The best defence was:

26...♕d6!

Maybe both players missed this opportunity for Black.

27.♕a4!?

After 27.♗xa7? ♗b7∓ Black has several threats, such as ...♗xd5 or ...♕a6.

27.♗b2 doesn't bring White anything: 27...♘e5 28.♗a3 ♕e6 29.♘e7† (29.♗b2 ♗b7∓) 29...♖xe7 30.♗xe7 ♕xe7 31.♕xa6

♕c5 and the position looks better for Black. With the text, White threatens ♕xd7.

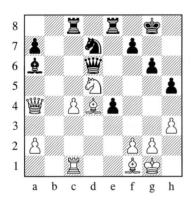

27...♖e6

27...♘e5 is best met by 28.♕b3! (intending c4-c5) and now:

a) 28...♖b8 29.♕e3 ♗b7 30.♗c5 (30.♖d1 ♗xd5 31.♖xa7 ♖bd8 32.cxd5 ♘d3∞) 30...♕d8 31.♖d1 ♗xd5 32.♖xd5 ♕c8 33.♗d4 The position is unclear, with White having good compensation for the exchange.

b) 28...♖ed8 29.♕b2 ♘xc4 30.♗xc4 ♖xc4 31.♘f6† ♔f8 32.♘h7† ♔e8 (32...♔g8 33.♘f6†=) 33.♘f6† ♔e7 34.♖xc4 ♗xc4 35.♕b7† ♔f8 (35...♖d7 36.♕xe4†=) 36.♘h7† with a level position.

28.♕b3 ♘b6

28...♔h7 29.♕e3⩲

29.♗b2 ♘xd5 30.cxd5 ♖xc1

30...♖ee8 31.♖xc8 ♗xc8 32.♕c3⩲

31.♗xc1 ♖f6□ 32.♗b2 ♗xf1 33.♗xf6 ♕xf6 34.♔xf1 ♔g7 35.♔e2 ♕d4=

The position is equal. Following 26...♕d6! I have not been able to find any advantage for White, but of course the computer was helping me to find all the defensive moves for Black. In a practical game it would have been a very difficult task for Black to defend with such precision.

27.♕b4!⩲

Black solved his problems with the a6-bishop, but now he cannot prevent ♘e7.

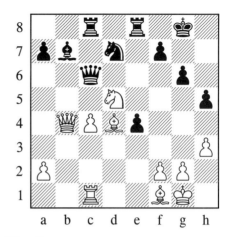

27...a5

The best reply. After 27...♔h7 28.♘e7 ♕c7 29.♘xc8 ♗xc8 30.c5 White has regained the exchange, and the strong passed pawn and bishop pair give him a clear advantage.

28.♘e7† ♔f8 29.♘xg6† ♔g8 30.♘e7† ♔f8 31.♘g6† ♔g8 32.♘e7† ♔f8 33.♘xc6† axb4 34.♘xb4

After a repetition of moves, White decides to play on. This is the correct decision, as Black faces considerable problems.

34...♘c5 35.♖b1 ♖ed8 36.♘c2

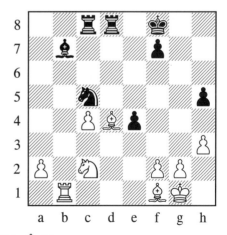

36...♗a8?

The decisive mistake. Now Black loses another pawn, and the game is over.

36...♘e6 was clearly better, although after 37.♗f6 ♖d2 (37...♖d7 38.♖b5!) 38.♘e3 ♗c6 39.a3± White is still on top.

37.♖b5+– ♘d3 38.♖xh5 ♔e8

On 38...♖xc4 comes 39.♗f6! and Black loses a whole rook.

39.♗b6 ♖d6 40.c5

White has a bishop and three pawns for the rook, along with a strong attack on the black king. He has both a positional and material advantage, and Black could have resigned here.

40...♖d5 41.♖h6 ♖g5

41...♘xc5 42.♖h8† ♔d7 43.♗b5† ♗c6 44.♖xc8 ♔xc8 45.♗xc6+– nets White more material.

42.♘d4 ♖g6 43.♖h5 ♔e7 44.a4

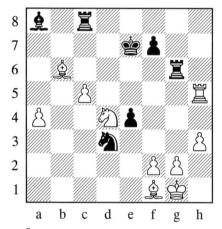

44...♘f4

Black is trying to create some chances, but this doesn't help.

45.♖e5† ♔f8 46.g3 ♘d3 47.♖h5 ♔g8 48.a5 ♖e8 49.a6 ♖e5 50.♖xe5 ♘xe5 51.♗b5 e3 52.a7 ♔f8 53.♗c7

After 53...♘f3† 54.♘xf3 ♗xf3 55.c6 Black can't stop the a-pawn promoting.

1–0

GAME 5

▷ **V. Kramnik (2781)**
▶ **A. Timofeev (2665)**
64th Russian Championship, Moscow
Round 2, 09.08.2011 **[A35]**
Annotated by Borki Predojevic

In the following game we will see a Reversed Maroczy setup in the English Opening. After a few standard moves on both sides, White chose the most dynamic approach with 8.a3, using his extra tempo to prepare b4. Black responded with 8...♗e7 9.b4 0–0, at which point White chose the positional line with 10.bxc5. Black recaptured on c5 with his bishop, but more interesting was 10...♗f5!? with the idea of ...♘e6 and ♘xc5. After 14.d3 White was better, but Black helped him a lot with the mistakes 14...♘b5? and 15...♘c7?!. Kramnik went on to increase his advantage with a fine positional performance, culminating in a nice attack and exchange sacrifice 33.♖xf7!.

The 8.a3 line is likely to remain popular and this game shows that there are still a lot of positions requiring investigation.

1.♘f3 c5 2.c4 ♘f6 3.♘c3 ♘c6 4.g3 d5 5.cxd5 ♘xd5 6.♗g2 ♘c7 7.0–0 e5

Black established the Reversed Maroczy. His pawns on c5 and e5 Black give him a good deal of space in the centre and control over the d4 square. On the other hand, White has a lead in development and has various ways to put his extra tempo to use.

8.a3

Preparing b4 is the most dynamic approach, and is the recommendation of GM Marin in the third of his *Grandmaster Repertoire* books on the English Opening.

8...♗e7

Black simply develops without trying to prevent his opponent's plan.

The most popular move has been 8...f6, after which 9.e3 is the main line, preparing d4. Here Black played an interesting novelty 9...♕d3!?N in the game Svidler – Nepomniachtchi, Russia (ch) 2011, which is also analysed in this issue of *Chess Evolution* on page 48.

Another idea for Black is 8...♖b8!?, when Marin suggests 9.♖b1 f6 10.d3 intending ♗e3, when the latent pressure against the a7-pawn will renew the possibility of b4.

9.b4

In the equivalent variation from the Accelerated Dragon with reversed colours, Black normally has to work extremely hard to execute this pawn break. This is one reversed opening in which the extra tempo really makes a significant difference.

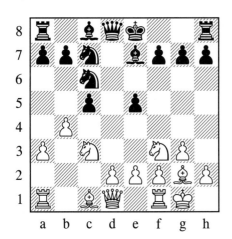

9...0–0

9...f6?! 10.bxc5 ♗xc5 11.♕b3! is troublesome for Black, as shown by Marin.

A more concrete line is 9...cxb4 10.axb4 f6 (10...♗xb4? 11.♘xe5 ♘xe5 12.♕a4† ♘c6 13.♗xc6† bxc6 14.♕xb4±) 11.b5 ♘d4 12.♖b1 with promising play for White. One game continued 12...♗d7 13.b6 axb6 14.♖xb6 ♖a7 15.e3 ♘cb5!? 16.♘d5 ♗c5 17.exd4 ♗xb6 18.dxe5 0–0 19.exf6⩲ Sunye Neto – Machado,

Brazil 1995. Further details of this and other variations can be found in Marin's book.

10.bxc5

Kramnik opts for a straightforward positional move, exchanging a wing pawn for a more central one.

Marin recommends a different variation on the same theme:

10.b5 ♘d4 11.♘xc5

This time White wins the e5-pawn in return for the one on b5, but it seems to me that this approach is less dangerous for Black.

11...♗f6

Marin mainly focuses on 11...♘dxb5, when White does indeed have good chances for an advantage.

12.f4

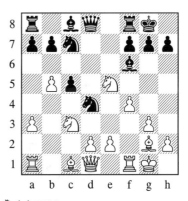

12...♘dxb5!?N

This is my suggested improvement over 12...♗xe5 13.fxe5 ♗g4 14.a4! ♘xe2† 15.♘xe2 ♗xe2 16.♕xe2 ♕d4† 17.♕e3 ♕xa1 18.♗a3 ♕a2, Cu. Hansen – Mueller, Germany 2006, at which point Marin points out the line 19.♗xb7!N ♖ad8 20.♗xc5 ♖fe8 21.d4 ♕xa4 22.♗c6 with a clear advantage for White.

13.♘xb5 ♘xb5 14.♖b1

14.♗b2 ♘d6 15.♕c1 c4 16.a4 ♗f5∞

After the text move White has some pressure on queenside, but Black should be able to deal with it.

14...♘d6

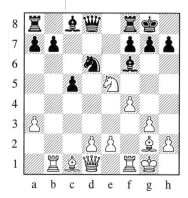

15.♗b2

15.♕c2 ♗f5 16.d3 (16.e4 ♘xe4!) 16...c4! 17.♘xc4 (17.e4 cxd3 18.♕xd3 ♗e6⇄ is promising for Black, who threatens both ...♗xe5 and ...♘c4.) 17...♖c8 18.e4 ♗xe4! 19.♗xe4 ♘xe4 20.dxe4 ♕d4† 21.♕f2 ♖xc4 22.e5 ♕e4 (intending ...♖c2) 23.♗d2 ♗e7 looks pleasant for Black.

15...♗f5 16.d3 ♖c8

White position is slightly more active, but Black is solid enough and can gradually prepare ...f6.

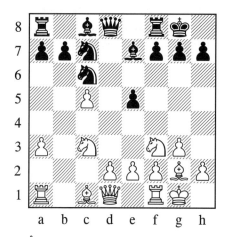

10...♗xc5

A natural move, but the idea of arranging to recapture on c5 with a knight also deserved serious consideration. There are a number of ways in which Black might attempt this.

10...♘a6 is one idea, but after 11.e3 ♕d3 12.♘e1 ♕c4 (12...♕g6 13.d4 ♖d8 14.♘d5‡; 12...♕d8 13.f4! exf4 14.d4 fxg3 15.hxg3↑) 13.♘d5 ♗xc5 14.♖b1!± White has some pressure thanks to his better-coordinated pieces. In particular Black's queen is misplaced and might be in some danger with d3 coming next.

10...♘e6

This move has been tested in two games. The following response looks quite promising:

11.d3!?N

11.e3 is also decent.

11...♖e8

11...♘xc5 is well met by 12.♘xe5! ♘xe5 13.d4. The point is that after 13...♘c4 14.dxc5 ♗f6 White has a second pseudo-sacrifice in 15.♖a2! ♗xc3 16.♖c2 ♕f6 17.♕d3± regaining the piece while keeping an extra pawn.

12.♖b1

12.♗b2 ♘xc5 is equal.

12...f6

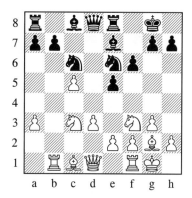

13.e3

Another promising direction is 13.♘d2 ♘xc5 14.♘de4 ♔h8 15.♘xc5 ♗xc5 16.♕a4 with some initiative.

13...♗xc5

13...♘xc5 14.d4! is strong.

14.♗b2±

White's position remains slightly better, as the knight on e6 is less than ideally placed.

White can look to break in the centre with d4 in the near future.

10...♗f5!?

The computer advocates this developing move as Black's best option. The idea is to play ...♘e6 a move later when it will not block the bishop on c8.

11.d3

If 11.♗b2 ♘e6 12.e4 ♗g4 Black obtains a firm grip on the d4-square.

11...♘e6 12.♖b1

12.♗e3 ♘xc5 should be roughly equal.

12...♘xc5

12...♖b8 13.♗e3 ♗xc5 14.♘h4! ♗xe3 15.♘xf5 ♗b6 16.♘d5 ♗c5 17.a4± works out well for White.

13.♗e3 ♕d7 14.♘d2 ♗e6 15.♘c4 f6=

Black can be satisfied with the outcome of the opening.

11.♗b2 ♖e8

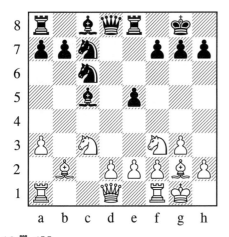

12.♖c1N

This natural move is a novelty. White discourages the bishop from retreating to b6, as it could be targeted by ♘a4.

12.♘e4 gives Black the option of 12...♗b6 as occurred in the following game: 13.d3 ♗g4 14.♖c1

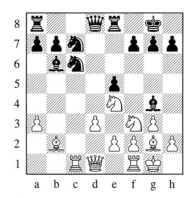

At this point Black should have played 14...f6! with a solid position. Instead he chose 14...♖c8? allowing the crushing 15.♖xc6! bxc6 16.♘xe5 ♗d7 17.♘d6 ♖b8 18.♘xe8 ♗xe8 19.♕c2 when White was winning, Adamski – Wiech, Warsaw 1992.

12...♗f8

Now 12...♗b6 can be met by 13.d3 (also 13.♘a4!? e4 14.♘e1 ♘d5 15.d3↑ favours White) 13...♗f5 14.♘a4± with a small but long-term advantage to White.

13.♘e4!

Transferring the knight to c5 is a thematic plan in the English, and the equivalent manoeuvre is a frequent occurrence in the Dragon positions that can arise with reversed colours. White also sets up the possibility of an exchange sacrifice on c6, as occurred in the Adamski – Wiech game noted above.

13.e3 was less good, and after 13...♗f5 14.d4 exd4 15.exd4 (15.♘xd4 ♘xd4 16.exd4 ♕d7=) 15...♘d5= Black is okay.

There was nothing much wrong with 13.d3 intending ♘e4 next, but Kramnik's move is more accurate as there is no special reason to move the d-pawn just yet.

13...♖b8

It would have been risky for Black to take immediate action in the centre:

13...f5 14.♘c5

But not 14.♕b3†? ♗e6 15.♕xb7 fxe4 16.♕xc6 exf3 17.♗xf3 ♘d5∓ when White has insufficient compensation for a piece.

14...e4

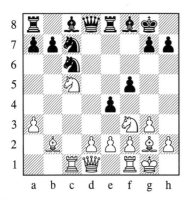

15.♘h4!

15.♘e1could be met by 15...♕d5! with the idea of 16.♘ed3? ♕a2!.

15...♘e6 16.♘b3!

Avoiding the knight exchange, which would only have aided Black's development. Now the f5-pawn is hanging, meanwhile White plans to open the position with d3.

16...g6

Protecting the pawn, but weakening the kingside.

16...♘f4 leads to complications favouring the first player: 17.gxf4 ♕xh4 18.♘c5 ♕xf4 19.♕b3† ♔h8 20.♕f7 ♖d8 21.♘xe4! ♕h6 22.♘f6 ♗xa3 23.♗xa3 ♕xf6 24.♕xf6 gxf6 25.♖fd1∞ White has massive positional compensation for a mere pawn.

17.d3 exd3

17...e3 18.f4! gives White the upper hand.

18.exd3

The isolated d-pawn is largely irrelevant, but Black's lack of development and exposed kingside makes his position tricky.

18...a5!?

18...♗h6?! is strongly met by 19.♖e1! ♗d7 (19...♗xc1? 20.♕xc1±) 20.♗d5 with a strong initiative for White.

19.♖e1

19.d4!? is another promising possibility. 19...a4 20.♘d2 ♕xd3 21.♗f1 ♕d6 22.♘c4 ♕c5

22...♕xd1 23.♖cxd1 ♗c5 24.♘d6 ♖d8 25.♘xc8 ♖xd1 26.♖xd1 ♖xc8 27.♘f3∞

23.♘f3∞

White has fine compensation for a pawn. Here is a sample continuation:

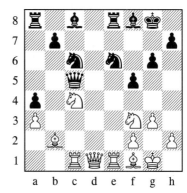

23...♖d8 24.♕e2 ♘cd4 25.♘xd4 ♘xd4 26.♗xd4 ♖xd4 27.♕a2!+−

Black's king is too weak.

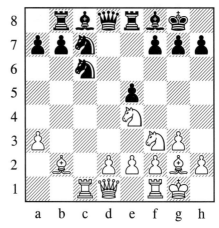

14.d3±

White has a slightly better position, thanks to his more active pieces and pressure in the centre and on the queenside.

14...♘b5?

A serious mistake. Black wants to take control over the d4-square but he should have been more concerned with stabilizing his position and getting his pieces properly coordinated.

Better was 14...f6, for instance 15.♕c2 (15.♕a4 ♗d7∞; 15.♘c5 ♘e6⇄) 15...♗e6 16.d4! exd4 17.♖fd1 ♕e7 18.♘xd4± and White keeps a modest advantage.

15.♘fg5!

Unusually for this opening, Black has some problems with the f7-square.

15...♘c7?!

Not the best reaction.

More stubborn would have been:
15...♕e7 16.e3!
  The tempting 16.a4 is less convincing. Black has two options:
  a) 16...♘bd4?! 17.e3 ♘e6 gives White the opportunity for a spectacular move:

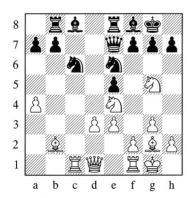

18.♗a3!! ♕c7 (18...♕xa3 19.♕h5 ♘xg5 20.♘xg5 h6 21.♕xf7† ♔h8 22.♗d5+−) 19.♗xf8 ♖xf8 20.♘xe6 ♗xe6 21.♘c5± and White is clearly on top.
  b) However, Black can improve with 16...♘c7! 17.♕b3 ♗g4! (17...♗e6? 18.♘xe6 ♘xe6 19.e3±) 18.e3 h6 19.♗a3 ♕d7 20.♗xf8 ♖xf8 21.♘c5 ♕e7 22.♘xb7 ♗c8 23.♗xc6 hxg5 24.♖b1 ♘e6∞ when the position is

rather unclear. White may have won a pawn but his knight on b7 is in the danger zone.
16...h6 17.♕b3! hxg5
  After 17...a6 18.a4 hxg5 19.axb5 axb5 20.♕xb5± the evaluation is similar.
18.♕xb5±
White has a pleasant advantage.

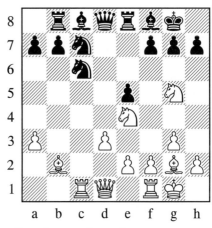

16.♕b3 ♗e6 17.♘xe6 ♘xe6 18.e3±

Black's inaccuracies have left him in an unpleasant situation, as White's unopposed light-squared bishop is tremendously powerful.

18...♕a5

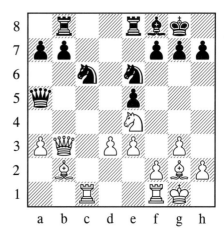

19.♖c4

Kramnik goes for the positional approach, doubling his rooks. Another interpretation

of the position would have been 19.f4!? exf4
20.gxf4 ♘c5 21.♘xc5 ♗xc5 22.d4 ♗b6
23.♗d5± with a large advantage.

19...♖ed8 20.♖fc1 ♕b6 21.♕c2

21.♕xb6?! axb6 would be unhelpful to
White, as his a3- and d3-pawns would become
vulnerable.

21...♘a5 22.♖c3 ♖d7 23.♘d2!

The knight has done its job on e4, so Kramnik
sets about finding a new home for it. Black's
position is tough and he has no counterplay
whatsoever.

23...♖bd8 24.♘f3 ♖d5

24...♘c6 can be met by 25.♖b1! when Black
faces similar problems as in the game. Play
might continue 25...♕a6 (or 25...♗d6 26.♖c4!
♕a5 27.♗c3 ♕c7 28.♕b2± with d4 to follow)
26.♗f1 ♗d6 27.♘d2± with a large advantage.

25.♗a1 ♕a6 26.♖b1 ♘c6

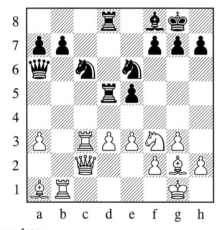

27.♗f1!+−

Suddenly it transpires that Black is lost. All
his pieces are badly placed and he has no good
defence against d4.

27...♗xa3

27...♖5d7 28.d4 ♕a5 29.♖b5 ♕c7 30.♘xe5
is winning for White.

28.d4 ♕a5 29.♖xb7 ♗c5!

Timofeev finds the best chance to survive.

29...♘cxd4 30.exd4 exd4 31.♖cb3+− is
hopeless for Black.

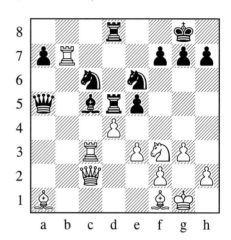

30.♖xc5?!

30.♖c4!

This was the strongest continuation, although
this judgement relies upon the accurate
assessment of the following long line:

30...♕a6!

The only chance. Instead after 30...♕xa1?
31.♖a4! Black loses his queen.

31.♕b1 ♘a5

Here White needs to find a strong move:

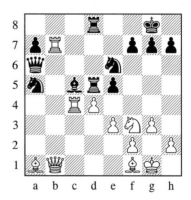

32.♖b5! ♘xc4

32...exd4 33.♖cxc5 ♘xc5 34.♗xd4 ♘ab3
35.♖xb3 ♕d6 36.♖a3+−

33.♗xc4 ♗xd4!? 34.♗xd5 ♗xa1 35.♗xe6 fxe6

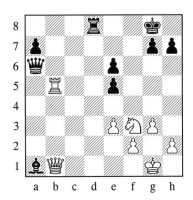

36.♖b8!

Maybe this is move which Kramnik either overlooked, or failed to evaluate properly in his calculations.

36...♖xb8 37.♕xb8† ♔f7 38.♘g5† ♔g6

38...♔e7 39.♕c7† ♔f6 40.♕f7† ♔xg5 41.♕xg7† ♔f5 42.f3! leads directly to mate.

39.h4 ♕a4 40.♕g8+–

Black is unable to save the game.

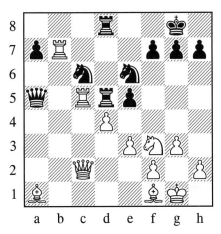

30...♖xc5?

More resistance would have been offered by: 30...♘xc5! 31.dxc5 ♕xa1 32.♕f5! (32.♘g5 g6 33.♘xf7 ♖d1=) 32...♖f8 33.♘g5 g6 34.♕h3 h5 35.♖xf7! It looks like White is crashing through, but Black's resources are not yet exhausted...

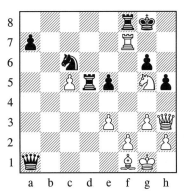

35...♘d8! (or 35...♖xf7 36.♕e6 ♖dd7 [36...♘d8? 37.♕xd5+–] 37.♘xf7 ♖xf7 38.♕xg6† ♔f8 39.♕h6† ♔g8 40.♕xc6 and White should win) 36.♖xf8† ♔xf8 37.♕c8 ♖d1 38.♔g2 ♕a2± Black's position remains precarious, but he still has some chances to save the game.

31.dxc5 ♕xa1 32.♕f5 ♖f8

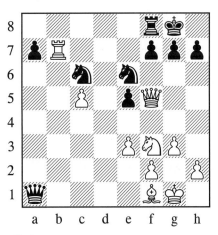

33.♖xf7!

The final touch, after which Black is lost.

33...♖xf7 34.♕xe6 e4 35.♕xe4

35.♘g5 ♕f6 36.♗c4 ♕xe6 37.♗xe6 ♘d8 38.c6! was also winning, but the text move was enough to force Black's resignation. He has no good defence, as 35...♕f6 36.♗c4 is hopeless for him.

1–0

GAME 6

▷ **P. Svidler (2739)**

▶ **I. Nepomniachtchi (2711)**

64th Russian Championship, Moscow
Round 6, 14.08.2011 **[A35]**
Annotated by Borki Predojevic

The Reversed Maroczy appeared for the first time in the 2011 Russian Championship in Round 2; this game from Round 6 was the second game in the same variation of the English Opening. White again chose the same line, 8.a3, but in this game Black did not follow Timofeev's idea from the 2nd round (8...♗e7) and instead played the main line with 8...f6. After 9.e3, which is White's best reply, Black played an interesting novelty, 9...♕d3!?N. It seems that this is perfectly playable for Black. Svidler as White played a very good game and eventually won, but Black's play can be improved. There are possibilities (such as 10...♕a6!?, 11...♗d7 or 15...h5!) which lead to unclear play. My conclusion is that 9...♕d3!?N should be played more in the future, since it looks more solid than the main line.

1.♘f3 c5 2.c4 ♘c6 3.♘c3 ♘f6 4.g3 d5 5.cxd5 ♘xd5 6.♗g2 ♘c7 7.0–0 e5 8.a3

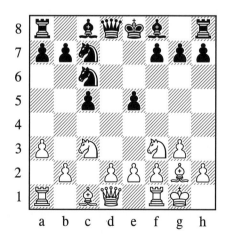

8...f6

The main line. Black stops the idea of b2-b4, since after Black takes twice on b4 there are no

tricks with ♘xe5 and ♕a4† (since the f6-pawn protects e5). On the other hand, with his last move Black weakened his light squares and the a2-g8 diagonal.

8...♗e7 was played in the Russian Championship a few rounds earlier. After 9.b4 0–0 10.bxc5 Kramnik later won against Timofeev. This game is also analysed in this issue of *Chess Evolution* (see page 40).

To appreciate the ideas in this game it is important to mention the move 8...♕d7, which was first played by Korchnoi. Here White has to play actively with 9.♖b1 f6 10.e3! in order to push with b4 or d4. After 10...♗e7 11.b4 cxb4 12.axb4 ♘xb4 13.d4 White has good compensation according to Marin.

9.e3

This is best. White has a lead in development and he wants to open the position with d2-d4.

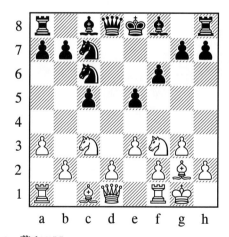

9...♕d3!?N

A typical Nepomniachtchi move, which is a novelty in this position. Usually, Black does not prevent d2-d4 and instead continues developing. Other lines were analysed in the book *The English Opening: Volume Three* by Mihail Marin, so we will give some variations he mentioned.

9...♘e6?! looks dubious. After 10.♘h4! g6 11.f4 exf4 12.gxf4 f5 13.♘f3 ♗g7 14.b4! 0–0 (14...cxb4 15.axb4 ♘xb4 16.♕a4† ♘c6 17.♗a3± Marin) 15.♕b3 ♔h8 16.♗b2± White is better, Gamundi – Magem Badals, Andorra 1997.

9...♗g4 10.h3 ♗e6, with the idea of winning a tempo with ...♕d7, is met by: 11.d4 exd4 12.exd4 cxd4 13.♘e2 d3 14.♘f4 ♗c4 15.b3! A novelty Marin gave in his book. 15...♗a6 16.♖a2 ♗e7 17.♖d2 0–0 18.♘xd3± White keeps the better chances.

The main line is:
9...♗e7 10.d4 cxd4 11.exd4 exd4
   11...♘xd4 12.♘xd4 exd4 13.♘e2 ♘e6 14.♕b3↑
12.♘e2⩲
   Now Black has two options: 12...♘e6 or 12...d3. In both lines the position remains complicated, but it seems White has good chances of seizing an advantage. In recent games, players with Black have chosen the former line:
12...♘e6 13.b4 d3 14.♘f4 ♘xf4 15.♗xf4

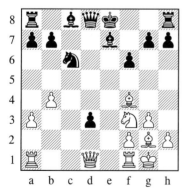

But the players with Black were unable to equalize. The two moves played were a) 15...♗e6? and b) 15...0–0:

a) 15...♗e6?
   A novelty, but not a good one.
16.♖e1 ♗f7

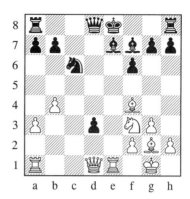

And here White could play:
17.b5!N
   In the game White played the less precise 17.♖e3?! but he still had the advantage after: 17...0–0 18.♖xd3 ♕b6 19.♗e3 ♕b5 20.♘d4 ♘xd4 21.♖xd4 ♖fd8 22.a4! ♕e8 (22...♕xb4 23.♖xb4 ♖xd1† 24.♖xd1 ♗xb4 25.♗xb7 ♖b8 26.♗xa7 ♖xb7 27.♖d8† ♗f8 28.♗c5±/±) 23.♗xb7 ♖ab8 24.♗d5 a6 25.♗xf7† ♕xf7 26.♖xd8† ♖xd8 27.♕e2± Arnaudov – Timman, Dieren 2011.
17...♘e5
   17...♘a5 loses to the neat 18.♗d2! while 17...♘b8? fails to 18.♘g5+–.
18.♗xe5 fxe5 19.♘xe5+–
   Black's position is horrible.

b) 15...0–0 16.b5 ♘a5
   After 16...♘e5 17.♕b3† ♔h8 18.♖ad1 ♗g4 19.♗xe5 fxe5 20.♖xd3± White was better in Lobron – Smejkal, Bundesliga 1995.
17.♖c1 ♗d6

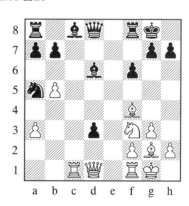

18.♗d2?!

This is a novelty compared to Marin's analysis. Marin gives 18.♗e3! (planning ♖c3xd3) 18...♗xa3 19.♖a1 ♗e7 20.♕a4 b6 21.♘d4 ♗d7 22.♖fd1! with the final evaluation that White has very good compensation for the sacrificed pawn.

18...a6 19.♖c3 ♗c7?

This mistake gives White a clear advantage. Correct was 19...axb5! 20.♖xd3 ♘c4 21.♗b4 ♖a6 22.♖e1 ♕c7⇄ which gives Black counterplay.

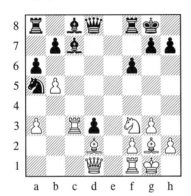

20.♕b1! axb5 21.♖xd3 ♕e8 22.♖e1 ♕h5 23.♘d4

White dominates all over the board; Black's position is critical.

23...♗d7 24.♖e7 ♖ad8 25.♗f3 ♕g6 26.♗e4! f5 27.♗d5† ♔h8 28.♘xb5+−

White soon won in Delchev – Nikolov, Bulgaria (ch) 2011.

10.♘e1

The best reaction. After 10.♘h4 ♗e6 11.♗e4 ♕d7 Black has no problems. For example, 12.♕h5† ♕f7 13.♕f3 ♖d8!? 14.♗xc6† bxc6 15.♕xc6† ♕d7 16.♕xd7† ♔xd7∞ gives Black good compensation.

10...♕g6

This was not inevitable, as Black also had other options.

10...♕d7

If we compare this position with the 8...♕d7 variation, we will see the white knight is on e1 and not on f3. This can be important since now White's idea of ♖b1 and b2-b4 doesn't work as it does after 8...♕d7. Still White can play:

11.♘c2 ♗e7 12.b4 0–0

12...cxb4 13.axb4 ♘xb4 14.♘xb4 ♗xb4 15.♕b3∞/± leads to a better position for White.

13.bxc5 ♗xc5

And now White has a strong reply:

14.d4

14.♘b4!?

14...exd4 15.♘a4 ♗e7 16.♘xd4± White has the initiative and an advantage.

10...♕a6!?

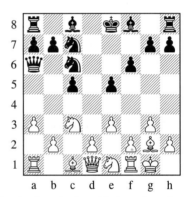

This looks a little odd, but the white pieces are not on the best squares and cannot attack the black queen. Most logical seems:

11.♘c2

11.f4 ♗e6 12.♗xc6† ♕xc6 13.fxe5 ♗e7 14.exf6 ♗xf6∞ gives Black good compensation.

11...♗f5

11...♗e7 12.d4 0–0 13.d5± looks better for White.

12.d4 cxd4 13.exd4 ♗xc2 14.♕xc2 ♘xd4 15.♕e4 0–0–0 16.♗e3∞

White has compensation for the sacrificed pawn, but I am not sure if it is enough for an advantage.

11.d3

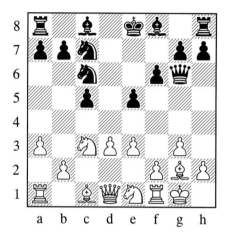

11...♗e6!?

An interesting approach.

More natural was:
11...♗d7
 White can play:
12.♖b1!
  12.♘f3 0–0–0 (12...♗e7 13.d4!) 13.b4 cxb4 14.axb4 ♗xb4 15.♕c2∞ is another possibility.
12...♗e7
  12...0–0–0?! 13.b4 cxb4 14.axb4 ♘xb4 15.♗a3→
13.♗d2
  13.b4 cxb4 14.axb4 ♘xb4 15.♗xb7 ♖b8 16.♗e4 ♕f7 looks OK for Black.
13...♕f7
  13...0–0? 14.♕b3†±
14.b4 cxb4 15.axb4↑
 The position is complicated, but White has good chances of achieving an advantage.

If 11...♗e7 then White can play 12.♖b1 0–0 13.b4 cxb4 14.axb4 a6 15.b5 axb5 16.♘xb5∞ with an unclear position.

12.♕a4 ♗d7

  After 12...♕f7 13.♗xc6† bxc6 14.♕xc6† ♕d7 15.♕xd7† ♔xd7 16.f4± White would

have an extra pawn, but Black's compensation also deserves respect.

13.♘b5

 This logical move is debatable. White exchanges one piece and it looks like he has the advantage, but the analysis shows this is not so clear.

A serious alternative is 13.♗d2!?. White continues with his development and also prepares a later b2-b4. Black can answer with the prophylactic 13...♕f7. (After 13...♗e7 14.♘b5 ♘xb5 15.♕xb5 ♖b8 16.♕c4↑ White has a better version of the game position.) 14.f4 exf4 (14...♗e7 15.fxe5 ♘xe5 16.♕c2±) 15.♕xf4 ♘e6 16.♕h4 ♗e7 17.♘d5 0–0⇄ The position is unclear; White controls the d5-square, but Black's position is solid.

13...♘xb5 14.♕xb5 ♖b8 15.♕c4

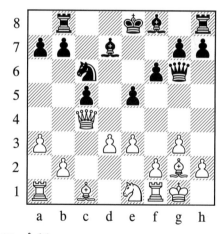

15...♗d6

 This is natural, but Black could play a more interesting idea.

The best move was:
15...h5!
  With the idea of organizing counterplay on the kingside. If Black manages to play ...h5-h4 then his rook will be good on the h-file.

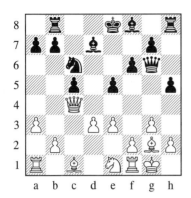

The most logical attempt is:

16.b4

16.♗e4 f5 17.♗d5 b5 is messy but Black seems fine.

16.♘f3 ♕f7 17.♘h4 ♕xc4 18.dxc4 ♗e6 19.♗d5 ♗xd5 20.cxd5 ♘a5 looks OK for Black.

Now Black can parry with:

16...♕g4 17.♕b3

17.♗e4 f5! 18.♗xc6 bxc6 19.♕c3 ♗d6 20.bxc5 ♗c7∞ offers Black good compensation.

17.f4?! h4!

17...cxb4

17...h4 18.♗f3 ♕h3 19.♗g2 ♕f5 20.♗d2 hxg3 21.fxg3 ♕h5 22.♘f3∞

18.♗f3 ♕h3 19.♗g2 ♕g4=

Black has no problems equalizing.

16.b4

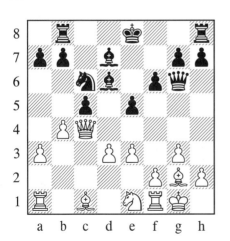

16...cxb4?!

This is a mistake. The correct idea was:

16...♕g4!

Now White has the chance to play:

17.f4

17.bxc5 ♕xc4 18.dxc4 ♗xc5 19.♘d3 ♗d6, planning ...♔e7, is at least equal for Black.

17...cxb4

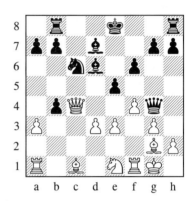

18.d4!

This wasn't so strong with the black pawn on h5, but now it gives more attacking chances.

18.axb4 ♖c8∞ leads to an unclear game.

18...exf4 19.exf4⩲

White has good compensation for the sacrificed pawn.

17.axb4↑ ♔e7

This doesn't look good, but White was better anyway.

After 17...♘xb4 18.♗d2 ♘c6 19.♘c2 ♖c8 20.♕b3⩲ White would have a strong initiative as compensation for the sacrificed pawn.

Now it is too late for 17...♕g4. The simple 18.b5 ♘d8 19.♖xa7 ♖c8 20.♕d5! ♗c5 (20...♗e7 21.♗d2 ♖c5 22.♕a2 ♖xb5 23.d4!) 21.♖a1 ♗xb5 22.f4 gives White the initiative.

17...♗xb4 18.♘c2 ♗e7 19.♗a3⩲ secures White very good attacking chances.

18.b5 ♘b4 19.♕b3!

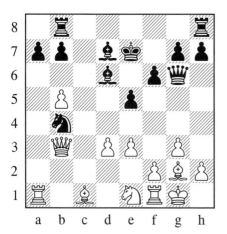

Suddenly, the knight on b4 is in danger; Black's response looks natural.

19...♗e6 20.♕b1 ♕e8 21.♖xa7 ♕xb5 22.♗d2

After a few forced moves, Black saved his knight. However, his problems are not over, as he is now pinned on the b-file.

22...♕b6 23.♖a3 ♗c5

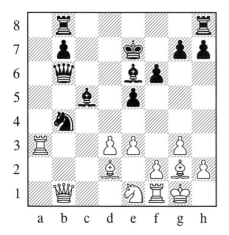

24.d4!±

The correct way; White opens the position as the black king is not safe in the centre.

24...exd4 25.exd4 ♘a6□ 26.♕xb6 ♗xb6 27.♗f4 ♗c7

Worse is 27...♗c4?! 28.♘d3± with ♖e1† next.

28.♘d3

Black has managed to exchange queens, but his position remains critical.

28...♗xf4?!

More stubborn was 28...g5!. Here White can play: 29.♖e1 (29.♗xc7 ♘xc7 30.♘c5 ♗d5 31.♗xd5 ♘xd5 32.♖a7± also leads to an advantage) 29...gxf4 30.d5 fxg3 31.hxg3 ♖hd8 32.♖xe6† ♔f7 33.♖b3± It is clear that White has the advantage, but Black's position is still defendable.

29.♘xf4 ♗c8

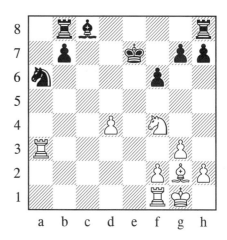

30.♖e1†?!

An inaccuracy, which allows Black chances of saving the game.

The best move was: 30.♖b1! ♘c7 (After 30...b5 31.♖e1† Black is unable to play 31...♔d6 since White has 32.♖xa6† ♗xa6 33.♖e6† ♔d7 34.♖xa6+– with a winning position.) 31.♖e3† Now Black is obliged to play 31...♔d8 and after 32.♖b6!+– all White's pieces are dominant and he should win.

30...♔d6 31.♖ae3

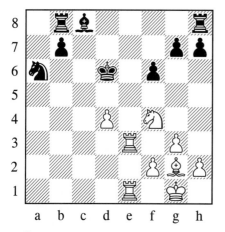

31...♘b4?

Too optimistic. Better was: 31...♘c7! 32.♖e7 (32.♘h5 ♖g8) 32...♖g8 33.♘h5 ♘e6 34.♖f7 b5!±/± This would give Black good practical chances of survival.

32.♖b1! ♘c6 33.♖c3+–

Finally, all White's pieces are on the right squares; Black can no longer hold the position.

33...♗f5 34.♖b6 ♔c7

34...♔e7 35.d5 ♘e5 36.♖c7† ♗d7 37.d6† ♔d8 38.♖bxb7 ♖xb7 39.♖xb7+– is agony for Black.

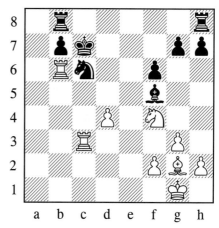

35.♖b5!

White wins a piece and everything is clear.

35...♗d7 36.d5 ♖he8 37.h4 ♖e5 38.♖b2 ♖c8 39.♘d3 ♖ee8 40.dxc6 ♗xc6 41.♘b4

Black resigned.

1–0

B

GAME 7

▷ **J. Hector (2568)**
▶ **D. Fridman (2659)**
Politiken Cup, Helsingor
Round 5, 02.08.2011 [B12]
Annotated by Nikola Sedlak

GM Jonny Hector is known as a very interesting player who always seeks dynamic and active positions. A few years ago Alexander Morozevich played 3.f3 against the Caro-Kann; now it has returned to fashion and is considered dangerous for Black. The main problems Black had in this game were due to bad pre-game preparation and ignorance of the game Polivanov – Yevseev, Voronezh 2011, where White played the strong novelty 10.♗c4 after which Black has great difficulties.

1.e4 c6 2.d4 d5 3.f3 ♕b6 4.♘c3 dxe4 5.fxe4 e5 6.♘f3 exd4 7.♘xd4

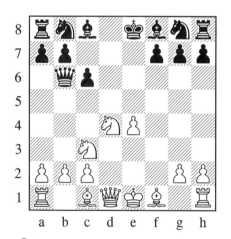

7...♘f6

This is a little-explored position and instead of the text move Black has also tried:
7...♗c5 8.♘a4 ♕a5† 9.c3 ♗e7 10.b4 ♕e5 11.♗d3 ♘f6

11...♗xb4 12.0–0 ♗xc3 (If Black plays something slow then he will be in trouble due to White's rapid development. For example: 12...♗e7 13.♗f4 ♕a5 14.e5 b5

15.e6+–) 13.♘f3 ♕a5 14.♘xc3 ♕xc3 Here White has a few possible ways to fight for a serious advantage: 15.♗f4 (15.♗e3 ♘f6 16.♗d4 ♕b4 17.♕c1 with a lot of threats such as ♗c5, e5 and ♕g5; 15.♖b1 ♕c5† 16.♔h1 ♘d7 17.♕b3±) 15...♘f6 16.♗d6± And probably next e5.
12.0–0 0–0 13.♗f4 ♕h5

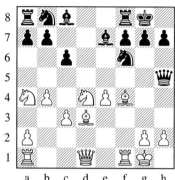

14.♕e1

A better choice was: 14.♗e2 ♗g4 (14...♕g6 15.♘f5±) 15.♗xg4 ♕xg4 16.♘f5±
14...♖e8 15.♕g3 ♘bd7 16.e5 ♘d5 17.♘f5 ♗f8 18.♗h6 g6 19.♗xf8 ♘xf8 20.♘d6 ♖e7 21.♖ae1 b6 22.♘e4 ♕h6 23.♘b2 b5 24.♗c2 ♗e6 25.♗b3 a5 26.bxa5 ♖xa5 27.♘d3 ♔h8 28.♘dc5 ♖aa7 29.♘d6 ♕g7 30.♕f2 ♖a8 31.♕d4 ♘c7 32.♕h4 g5 33.♕d4 ♘g6 34.♘xe6 ♘xe6 35.♕b6

1–0 Vitiugov – Janjgava, Sevan 2006.

8.e5 ♘g4 9.e6 ♗xe6

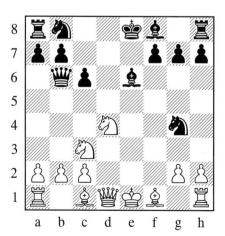

10.♗c4‼ ♗xc4 11.♕xg4

A fantastic idea; Black faces a serious attack.

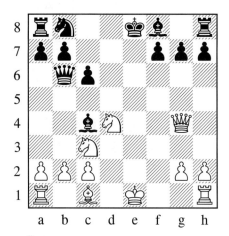

11...♘d7?

After this logical move Black loses by force.
11...♘a6! was the only move after which Black
can defend his position with computer moves.
Here White can try:
12.♕e4† ♔d7

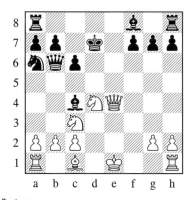

13.♘de2

13.♕f5†? ♗e6 14.♘xe6 ♖e8 15.♗g5
(15.♕xf7† ♖e7 16.♕f5 ♖xe6† 17.♔d1 ♗d6
18.♗d2 ♖f8 19.♕g4 g6∓) 15...♖xe6† 16.♘e2
♗b4† 17.c3 ♔c8 18.0–0–0 (18.cxb4 ♕xb4†
19.♔f2 ♘c5 20.♖hd1 ♘e4† 21.♔g1 ♕b6†
22.♔f1 g6 23.♕f4 ♕b5 24.♗h4 g5 25.a4
♘g3† 26.♕xg3 ♕xe2† 27.♔g1 gxh4–+)
18...♕c5 19.♘d4 ♕xf5 20.♘xf5 ♗c5
21.♖he1 ♖xe1 22.♖xe1 f6 23.♗f4 g6∓

13...♗xe2 14.♗e3
14.♕f5†? is still a mistake: 14...♔e8 15.♗xe2
(15.♕e5† ♗e7 16.♕xg7 ♔d7 17.♘xe2 ♘b4
18.g4† ♔e8 19.♕e4 f5! 20.♕c4 [20.♕xf5
♖f8 21.♕h5† ♔d8 22.♔d1 ♕f2∓] 20...♕c5
21.♕xc5 ♗xc5 22.♔d2 ♖g8 23.g3 ♖g4∓)
15...♕c5 16.♕e4† ♕e7 17.♗e3 ♕xe4†
18.♘xe4 ♘b4∓

14...♗c5 15.♗xc5 ♘xc5
After 15...♕xc5 16.♘xe2 ♖ad8 17.0–0–0†
♔c7 White has just enough compensation
to level the game.

16.♕xe2 ♕xb2 17.0–0 ♖af8
17...♕xc3? 18.♖xf7† ♔c8 19.♕g4† ♔d8
20.♖d1† ♔e8 21.♖f2+–

18.♕e5
18.♕c4 ♕a3 19.♖xf7† ♖xf7 20.♕xf7† ♔c8
21.♕xg7 ♖d8⇄

18...♕b6 19.♔h1
19.♖ab1 ♘d3† 20.♖xb6 ♘xe5 21.♖xb7†
♔e6 22.♘e4 ♘d5 23.♘g5 ♖b8 24.♖xa7
♖a8 25.♖e7 f6 26.♖d1† ♔c4 27.♘e4 ♖xa2
28.♖xg7 ♖xc2=

19...♕c8 20.♖ab1 ♘d7 21.♕xg7 ♕c5 22.♘e4
♕e5 23.♕xe5 ♘xe5 24.♘d6† ♔c7 25.♘xb7
♖b8 26.♘a5 ♖xb1 27.♖xb1 ♖d8=

12.♗d2 ♘c7

12...c5?! 13.♕e4† ♗e6 14.♘xe6 ♕xe6

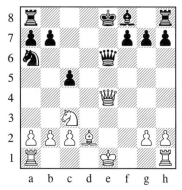

15.♕xe6†! (15.0–0–0 allows Black to
equalize with accurate play: 15...♕xe4
16.♘xe4 0–0–0 17.♘g5 ♖d7 18.♗f4 f6

19.罝xd7 含xd7 [19...fxg5? 20.罝hd1 gxf4
21.罝d8† 含c7 22.罝1d7† 含c6 23.罝f7+–]
20.公f7 罝g8 21.罝d1† 含e8 22.公d8 g5
23.奠g3 罝g7 24.公e6 罝g8 25.公d8=)
15...fxe6 16.0–0–0 奠e7 17.罝he1 含f7
18.罝e2 罝ad8 19.罝f1†! (if 19.罝de1 then
Black can defend with: 19...公c7 20.奠f4 罝d7
21.罝f2 公d5 22.公xd5 罝xd5 23.奠e5† 含g6)
19...奠f6 20.公e4 含e7 21.罝fe1 e5 22.奠g5
含e6 23.罝f2 罝hf8 24.奠xf6 gxf6 25.罝ef1±

13.0–0–0 奠e6

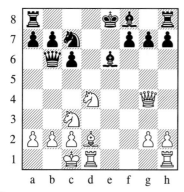

14.公xe6!

14.罝he1 is only level: 14...0–0–0 15.公xe6
公xe6 16.公e4 g6 17.奠c3 罝xd1† 18.含xd1
奠b4 19.奠xh8 豐d8† 20.含e2 f5 21.豐g3
奠xe1 22.豐e5 豐d5 23.公d6† 含d7 24.豐xd5
cxd5 25.公xf5 奠b4 26.公d4 奠c5=
14...公xe6 15.罝hf1±

12.豐e4†+–

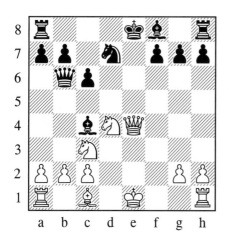

12...含d8

Black is lost no matter what he plays; he
finally varies from the aforementioned game A.
Polivanov – D. Yevseev, Voronezh 2011, which
continued 12...奠e7 13.公f5! 豐c5 14.奠g5
奠e6 15.公xg7† 含d8 reaching the following
position:

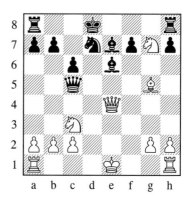

White played the reasonable 16.公xe6† but
even better was 16.奠xe7†!. Now 16...含xe7? is
hopeless and after 17.公xe6 fxe6 18.豐h4† 含e8
19.0–0–0+– Black can resign. So he would
have to play 16...豐xe7, but then the simple
17.0–0+– should win easily enough.

13.奠g5† f6 14.0–0–0 fxg5

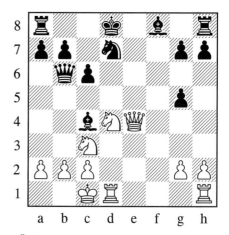

15.公f3?!

Not the best! An easy win was possible
with:

15.♘e6†! ♗xe6 16.♕xe6 ♕c7 17.♖d3 ♗d6
18.♖hd1 ♖e8 19.♕f7 ♖e7

    19...♗e7 20.♔b1+– Just to avoid ...♕f4
check; the next move would likely be ♕f5.
20.♕g8† ♖e8 21.♕xg7 ♗e7

    21...♖e7 22.♕g8† ♖e8 23.♕xg5† ♔c8
24.♖xd6+–

22.♕xh7 ♔c8 23.♖xd7 ♕xd7 24.♖xd7 ♔xd7
25.♘e4 ♔e6 26.♕g6† ♔d7 27.♘xg5+–

15...♔c7

Black had two other options to look at:

15...♕c5 16.♘e5

    16.♖d4 ♕e7 17.♖xc4 ♕xe4 18.♘xe4 h6
19.♖d1 ♔c7 20.♘d4 ♖e8 21.♘b5† ♔b8
22.♖xd7 cxb5 23.♖cc7 ♖xe4 24.♖xb7† ♔c8
25.♖bc7† ♔b8=

16...♗e6

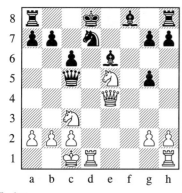

17.♖xd7†

    17.♘xd7 ♗xd7 18.♕e6 ♕e7 19.♖xd7†
♕xd7 20.♖d1 ♕xd1† 21.♔xd1 ♔c7=

17...♗xd7 18.♖d1 ♔e8!

    18...♔c8? loses after 19.♘xd7 ♕e7 20.♕g4
♔c7 21.♕g3†+–. For example: 21...♔c8
22.♕h3 g4 (22...♔c7 23.♘c5 ♕xc5
24.♕d7† ♔b6 25.♘a4† ♔a6 26.♘xc5†)
23.♕xg4 ♕e3† 24.♔b1 ♔c7 25.♕c4

19.♖xd7!

    19.♘xd7† ♕e7 20.♘e5 ♖d8 21.♖e1 ♖d6
22.♕e3 b6 23.♘e4 ♖e6 24.♘xg5 ♖xe5
25.♕xe5 ♕xe5 26.♖xe5† ♗e7= 19.♘g6†??
♗e7 20.♘xh8 ♕f5–+

19...♗e7 20.♖xb7 ♖d8

    20...♔c8? 21.♕f5 ♕e3† 22.♔d1 ♖d8†
23.♖d7+–

21.♕xc6† ♕xc6 22.♘xc6 ♖d7 23.♖b8† ♗d8
24.b4 ♖f8 25.♘e4±

White goes for the win. Black is in a kind of
stalemate; all White's pieces are working well
and the pawns on the queenside are fast.

15...♗a3 16.bxa3 ♕c5

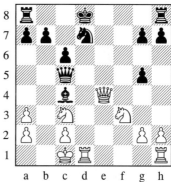

17.♕d4! After the exchange of queens the
attack is still strong enough to win material:
17...♕xd4 18.♖xd4 ♗d5 19.♘xd5 cxd5
20.♖xd5 ♔c7 21.♖hd1 ♘f6 22.♖c5† ♔b6
23.♖xg5±

16.♕xc4 ♕c5 17.♕d3 .♘f6?

    The last chance to stay in the game was
17...♗d6. White keeps an advantage after:
18.♘d4 (18.♖he1 ♖ad8 19.♘d4 ♖he8
20.♘db5† cxb5 21.♖xe8 ♖xe8 22.♘xb5† ♔c6
23.♕xd6† ♕xd6 24.♖xd6† ♔xb5 25.♖xd7
♖e1† 26.♔d2 ♖g1 27.g3 ♔c6 28.♖xg7 ♖g2†
29.♔d3 ♖xh2 30.♖xg5±) 18...♖ae8 19.♘db5†
cxb5 20.♘xb5† ♔b8 21.♕xd6† ♕xd6
22.♘xd6 ♖e2 23.♖he1 ♖xe1 24.♖xe1 ♔c7
25.♘b5† ♔c6 26.♘d4† ♔d5 27.♖e7 ♘c5
28.♘f3 g4 29.♘d2 ♖g8 30.b4 ♔d6 31.♖f7
♘d7 32.♘e4† ♔e6 33.♘g5† ♔d6 34.♘xh7
b5 35.♘g5±

18.♘d4!+– ♕e5 19.♖he1 ♕xh2 20.♘e6† ♔b6

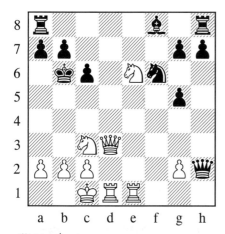

21.♕d4† ♔a6

There is no defence. For example: 21...c5 22.♘a4† ♔c6 23.♘axc5+–

22.♕c4† ♔b6 23.♘a4† ♔a5 24.♘ac5 b5 25.♘b3† ♔b6 26.♕d4† ♔a6 27.♘bc5† ♗xc5 28.♘xc5† ♔b6 29.♘d3† ♔c7 30.♖e7† ♔c8 31.♕c5 ♕xg2 32.♕d6
1–0

GAME 8
▷ **A. Grischuk (2746)**
▶ **A. Galkin (2598)**
  64th Russian Championship, Moscow
  Round 6, 14.08.2011 **[B12]**
  Annotated by Kamil Miton

In this game Grischuk chose to meet the Caro-Kann with 3.e5 followed by ♘f3 and ♗e2, one of the most topical systems at White's disposal. Galkin opted for a rare setup involving an early ...♘h6. Black's opening was not too bad, but he failed to generate any counterplay, which could have been achieved by means of either 7...c5 or 12...f6. Once he missed these, he never really got into the game and Grischuk was able to build up a winning position without taking any risks.

1.e4 c6 2.d4 d5 3.e5 ♗f5 4.♘f3 e6 5.♗e2 ♗e7

Galkin had played this rare move a few times before and obtained a good score, so he decided repeat it again. The main moves are 5...c5 and 5...♘e7.

6.0–0

One of Galkin's recent games continued 6.♘bd2 ♘h6 7.♘b3 0–0 8.♗xh6 gxh6 9.♗d3 ♗g6 10.♕d2 ♔g7 11.h4 ♘d7 12.0–0–0 a5 13.♔b1 a4 14.♘c1 a3 15.b3 ♕a5 16.♕xa5 ♖xa5 17.h5 ♗xd3 18.♘xd3 b6= Inarkiev – Galkin, Taganrog 2011.

6...♘h6

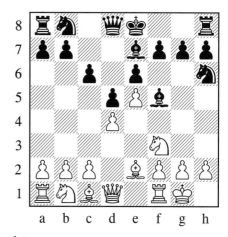

7.b3

A typical idea for such positions. Since Black has decided to postpone the standard ...c5 break, White decided to take some space on the queenside for himself. Of course the immediate 7.c4?! would be a mistake, as after 7...dxc4 Black obtains a fine square on d5 for a knight.

7.c3 0–0 8.♗xh6 gxh6 9.♕d2 ♔g7 10.♕e3 ♕b6 11.♘bd2 ♘d7 12.♗d3 ♗g6 13.b4 a5 14.a3 axb4 15.axb4 ♕c7 16.h4 b6 17.g4 c5⇄ Sjugirov – Galkin, Novokuznetsk 2008.

7...0–0

Galkin repeats the move he played two years before. Apart from that, the database contains no other games from this position, making it a fertile area for investigation.

7...c5!?N

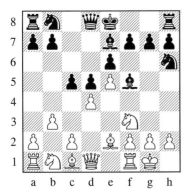

This thematic move was a serious alternative, not least because this is realistically Black's last opportunity to play it. Black's bishop on e7 and knight on h6 may not be ideally placed in the resulting position, but on the other hand the same could be said about White's pawn on b3. There have been no games from this position, so I decided to analyse the various possibilities in some detail. White has two main responses, which we will consider in turn.

a) 8.dxc5 ♘c6 Black makes a useful developing move rather than move his bishop for a second time. Now White has four main ideas:

a1) 9.b4?! is unimpressive: 9...♘xb4 10.♗b5† ♘c6 11.♘d4 0–0 12.♗xc6 bxc6 13.♗xh6 gxh6 14.♘xf5 exf5∞ In this murky position Black's chances are no worse.

a2) 9.c4 leads to unclear consequences: 9...dxc4 10.♘a3 ♕xd1 11.♖xd1 cxb3 12.♘b5 0–0 13.♘d6 ♗c2 14.♖d2 a5 15.axb3 ♗xb3 16.♘xb7 ♗d5 17.♘d6∞

a3) 9.♗xh6 gxh6 10.♕d2
  10.♘d4 should be met by: 10...♘xd4 (10...♗g6 is less good: 11.♘xc6 bxc6 12.♕d4

♗xc2 13.♘d2 0–0 14.b4 a5 15.a3 ♗g6 16.♘b3 axb4 17.axb4 ♕c7 18.f4±) 11.♕xd4 ♕c7 12.b4 b6! Black has to activate his dark-squared bishop quickly, before White can consolidate with ♘d2 and f4. 13.♘c3 bxc5 14.♘b5 ♕b6 15.bxc5 ♗xc5 16.♘d6† ♗xd6 17.♕a4† ♔f8 18.♖ab1 ♕c7 19.exd6 ♕xd6 20.♗d3 ♗g6 21.♖fe1 e5∞

10...♗xc5

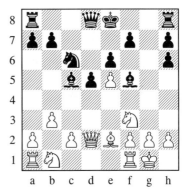

11.♕xh6
Picking up a pawn, but Black has promising compensation thanks to his control over the dark squares.

11...♕c7
Other possibilities include:
  11...♗xc2 12.♕g7 ♖f8 13.♖c1 ♗d4 14.♘xd4 ♘xd4 15.♘c3 (15.♖xc2 ♖c8!) 15...a6 16.♕g4 ♕b6 17.♗f1 ♗f5 18.♕f4 ♘c2 19.♖xc2 ♗xc2 20.♕a4† ♔d8 21.♖c1↑
  11...♗f8!? 12.♕f4 ♗xc2 13.♗b5 ♗g6 14.♘d4 ♖c8 15.♖c1 ♕d7∞
12.♘c3

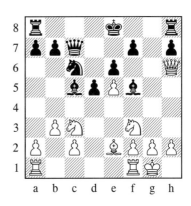

12...♖g8

12...a6?? 13.♘xd5! exd5 14.♕f6+-

13.♘b5 ♕b8 14.c4

14.♗d3 ♘xe5 15.♘xe5 ♕xe5 16.♗xf5 ♕xf5 17.♘c7† ♔d7 18.♘xa8 ♖xg2† leads to a draw by perpetual.

14...dxc4 15.♕f4 ♖g4 16.♕d2 ♔f8 17.♖ac1

The position remains highly unclear.

a4) **9.♗e3 ♘g4**

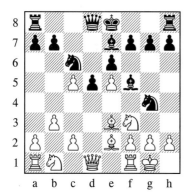

10.♗d4

Worse is 10.♗f4? g5 11.♗g3 (11.♗c1 ♘gxe5 12.♘xe5 ♘xe5 13.♗b2 ♗f6∓) 11...h5! when Black has already seized the initiative. After 12.♘d4 (12.h3? h4 13.hxg4 hxg3 14.gxf5 ♗xc5-+) 12...♗xc5 13.♘xc6 bxc6 14.♘c3 h4 15.♗xg4 hxg3 16.hxg3 ♗xg4 17.♕xg4 f5∓ Black is at least slightly better.

10...♕c7 11.♘c3 a6 12.♘a4 0-0!

12...♘gxe5 allows White to obtain two pieces for a rook: 13.♘xe5 ♘xe5 14.g4! ♗e4 15.f3 ♗g6 16.f4 ♘c6 17.f5 ♘xd4 18.♕xd4 ♗f6 19.♕f2 ♗xa1 20.♖xa1 0-0 21.fxg6 fxg6 22.♕e3±

13.♗b2 ♗e4=

Black is doing fine. White's extra pawn on c5 is not doing much, his pieces are badly placed and the e5-pawn is weak.

b) 8.c4

This is White's other serious idea.

8...dxc4

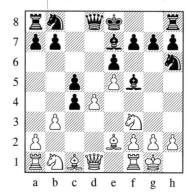

Once again we must consider a number of possible continuations.

b1) 9.bxc4 cxd4 10.♘xd4 ♘c6! 11.♘xc6 bxc6 is fine for Black.

b2) 9.♗xc4 cxd4 10.♘xd4 (10.♗xh6 gxh6 11.♕xd4 ♘c6 12.♕e3 ♕b6 13.♕xh6 0-0-0∞) 10...♗g6 11.♘c3 0-0 12.♗e3 ♘f5 13.♘xf5 ♗xf5 14.♕e2 ♘c6 The position is balanced.

b3) 9.♗xh6 gxh6 10.♘c3

10.bxc4!? cxd4 11.♘xd4 ♗g6 12.♗f3 ♕b6 13.c5!? ♗xc5 14.♕a4† is interesting.

10...cxd4

10...♘c6?! is risky, and 11.d5 exd5 12.♘xd5 cxb3 13.♕xb3 0-0 14.♖ad1 ♗e6 15.♖fe1 gives White a promising initiative.

11.♘xd4

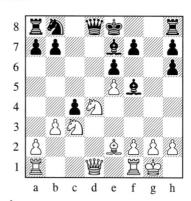

11...♗g6

11...♗d3 12.♗xd3 ♕xd4 13.♗e4 ♕xd1 14.♖fxd1 ♘c6 15.♗xc6† bxc6 16.bxc4±

12.♗f3 a6 13.♗xb7 ♖a7 14.♗c6† ♘xc6 15.♘xc6 ♕xd1 16.♖fxd1 ♖c7 17.♘xe7 ♔xe7=

The complications have subsided and the resulting endgame is balanced.

b4) 9.♘c3

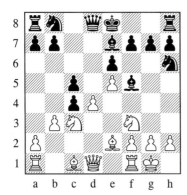

With this flexible move White keeps the option of ♗xh6 in reserve. Now it is Black who must make a choice.

a) 9...cxb3?! 10.♕xb3 hands White the initiative.

b) 9...♕a5 10.♗xh6 ♕xc3

10...gxh6 11.♖c1 cxd4 (11...♘c6 12.d5±) 12.♘xd4 ♕xe5 13.♖e1 ♕f6 14.♘cb5 0–0 15.♘xf5 ♕xf5 16.♘c7±

11.♖c1 ♕b2 12.♗xg7 ♖g8 13.♗f6 ♗xf6 14.exf6 ♘c6 15.♖xc4 0–0–0 16.♖xc5 ♔b8 17.g3

17.♖xc6 bxc6 18.♘e5 ♗e4 19.f3 ♖xd4∞

17...♘xd4 18.♘xd4 ♖xd4 19.♕a1 ♖d2 20.♕xb2 ♖xb2 21.♗h5 ♗g6 22.♗xg6 ♖xg6 23.♖fc1 a6 24.♖1c2

Black is not out of the woods in this endgame as his h-pawn is weak.

c) 9...cxd4 10.♘xd4 ♘c6

10...♗d3 11.♗xd3 ♕xd4 12.♗e4 ♕xc3 13.♗d2 ♕xe5 14.♗xb7 c3 15.♗xh6 gxh6 16.♗xa8 0–0 17.♖e1±

11.♘xc6

11.♗xh6? ♕xd4 is no good for White.

After 11.♘cb5 ♘xd4 12.♘xd4 ♗g6 13.♗xc4 0–0 14.♗xh6 gxh6 15.♕d2 ♕b6 Black's two bishops and active pieces are at least as important as his damaged kingside structure.

11...bxc6 12.♗xc4 ♕a5

Black seems to have enough dynamic play to compensate for his split queenside pawns. My main line continues as follows:

13.♕e1 ♘g4 14.♗f4 g5 15.♗g3 h5 16.h3 ♘h6

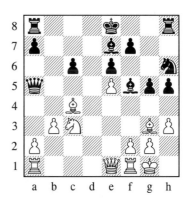

17.♘e4 ♕xe1 18.♖fxe1 ♗xe4 19.♖xe4 ♘f5 20.♗h2 0–0–0

The position remains double-edged, but Black should not be in trouble as the bishop on h2 is badly placed.

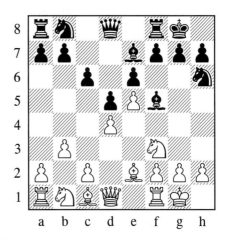

8.c4

Once this move has appeared on the board, it will be hard for Black to arrange ...c5, as after the reply cxd5 he will have to choose between two unattractive options. If he takes back with the pawn then his d5-pawn could become weak, and if he takes with the queen then White will get some advantage with ♘c3 followed by d5.

8...♗g6

Now the knight may come to f5 at any moment, so Grischuk decides to eliminate it.

9.♗xh6 gxh6 10.♘c3 ♘d7

Worse is: 10...♕a5? 11.♕d2 ♗b4 12.♖fc1! It is important to use this rook, as the other one will be needed to support a3. 12...♗a3 (12...♔g7 13.a3±) 13.♕xh6! ♗xc1 (13...♗b2 14.h4 ♕a3 15.h5 ♗xc1 16.♖xc1 ♗xh5 17.cxd5 cxd5 18.♘h2 ♗g6 19.♘b5 ♕b2 20.♘g4+–) 14.♖xc1 ♘d7 15.h4 Black's king is in trouble.

11.♕d2 ♔g7

Up to this point the players had been following a previous game of Galkin's, but now Grischuk unveils an improvement.

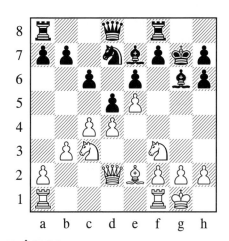

12.♗d3!N

White's plan is simple and logical: he wants to transfer knight the knight from c3 to f4 or g3, where it will help to develop threats against the black king.

The aforementioned game continued 12.♖fe1 a6 13.♗f1 ♕a5 14.a3 ♖ae8 15.b4 ♕c7 16.♖ac1 ♕b8 17.♖e3 dxc4 18.♗xc4 ♘b6 19.♗b3 ♖d8 20.♘e4 ♘d5 21.♗xd5 ♖xd5∞ and Black eventually prevailed in Pushkarev – Galkin, Ulan Ude 2009.

12...a6?!

Instead of this slow move, Black should have begun searching for counterplay.

The attempted tactical solution 12...dxc4?! 13.bxc4 ♘xe5 does not work, as after 14.♘xe5 ♕xd4 15.♘xg6 hxg6 16.♘e2 Black does not have enough for the piece.

12...a5!?

Considering that Black plays this in the game anyway, it was worth considering it immediately. Let us see if White can exploit the weakened b5-square.

13.cxd5

In fact it would be better for White to improve his position with 13.♖fe1!± before committing himself on either flank.

13...cxd5 14.♘b5

It turns out that this is not such a big achievement for White, so perhaps he should prefer 14.♘e2!?, although in that case Black would have an improved version of the game.

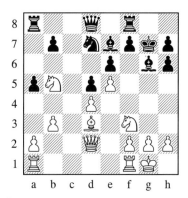

14...♘b8!

A typical way to improve the knight in such positions.

15.a3 ♘c6 16.♖fc1 ♕b6∞

Black is doing enough to keep his opponent occupied on the queenside, and he always has the option of ...♘a7 to eliminate the intruder on b5.

Although the above line is interesting, Black's best option would have been:

12...f6!

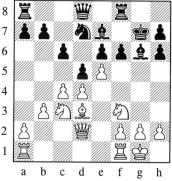

An absolutely thematic move for the 3.e5 Caro-Kann, as well as the French Defence of course. Black undermines the enemy centre and increases the scope of both his rook and dark-squared bishop. This was Black's last opportunity to play it before the white knight makes its way over to the kingside.

I analysed two responses for White:

a) 13.cxd5?!

Opening a queenside file seems to help Black more than White.

13...cxd5 14.exf6†

Fighting for the e5-square leads nowhere special for White: 14.♗b5 fxe5 (14...♗h5!? 15.♗xd7 ♕xd7 16.exf6† ♗xf6 17.♘e5 ♗xe5 18.dxe5 ♗g6 19.♘e2 ♖ac8 20.♘d4±) 15.♗xd7 exd4! 16.♗xe6 dxc3 17.♕xc3† ♗f6 18.♘d4 ♕b6∓

Also after 14.♖fe1 fxe5 15.♘xe5 ♘xe5 16.♖xe5 ♗g5 17.♕e2 ♗f6 Black is doing well.

14...♖xf6 15.♗b5

Both 15.♘h4 ♖c8 16.♘e2 e5∞ and 15.♘e2 ♗d6 16.♕e3 ♕b6 are quite satisfactory for Black.

15...♗h5

15...♖xf3!? is a typical idea from French structures, and is rather a tempting proposition here too. 16.gxf3 ♗d6 17.♗xd7 ♕xd7 18.♘e2 ♖f8↑ Black has good compensation.

16.♘e1

White hopes to exchange on d7 and then take control over the e5-square with after ♘d3 and a rook to the e-file.

16...♘b8!∞

An excellent reply. Black intends to play ...a6 followed by ...♘c6 with a promising position.

b) 13.exf6†

Keeping the c-pawns on the board looks like a better bet for White.

13...♖xf6 14.♘e2

Also possible is: 14.♖fe1 ♗d6 15.♗xg6 hxg6 16.♕d3 A prophylactic move, directed against the sacrifice on f3. 16...♕f8 17.♖e2 ♕f7 18.♖ae1 ♖f8∞

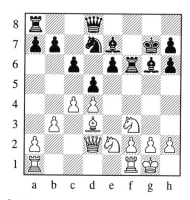

14...♗d6!

Taking control over the f4- and e5-squares. Note that after cxd5 Black might be tempted to recapture with the e-pawn.

15.♕e3

Intending to clamp down on the enemy

position with ♘e5 and f4.

Another idea is 15.♘h4 when Black should play 15...e5!∞ before White can set up the desired central clamp.

15...♕c7 16.♗xg6

16.g3 ♖af8 17.♘h4 e5⇄ gives Black a good game.

16...hxg6 17.c5 ♗f8

17...♗f4!? should be met by 18.♕c3.

Now the battle revolves around whether Black will be able to free his position with ...e5.

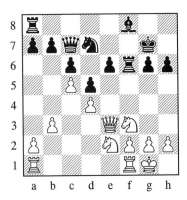

18.♖ae1!

The immediate 18.♘c1?! allows 18...b6! 19.b4 a5 when Black successfully undermines the c5-pawn.

18.b4 is met by: 18...♖e8 19.♖ae1 e5! 20.♘xe5 ♘xe5 21.f4 ♘f3† 22.♕xf3 ♔g8⯑ The d4-pawn is weak and White does not have time to transfer a knight to e5, so Black has reasonable compensation.

18...♖e8 19.♘c1!

Now this move works well.

19...b6 20.b4 a5 21.a3

White keeps his queenside together without leaving the rook on a1 vulnerable.

21...♔h7 22.♘d3 axb4 23.axb4 bxc5 24.bxc5 ♗g7 25.♖e2 ♖f5 26.♖fe1± White has successfully prevented ...e5. The e6-pawn is weak and Black has little counterplay.

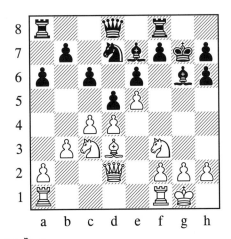

13.♘e2

13.♖fe1 was also promising, for instance 13...dxc4!? 14.bxc4 b5 15.♗xg6! (15.c5 ♗xd3 16.♕xd3 ♘xc5 17.♕d2 ♘d7 18.♘e4⯑) 15...hxg6 16.c5± and White's knight will come to d6.

13...a5 14.♕e3 a4 15.c5

Taking more space and preventing any queenside counterplay.

15...axb3 16.axb3 b6 17.b4 ♕c7 18.♘f4 ♕b7 19.h4 ♖xa1 20.♖xa1 ♖a8

Exchanging pieces is generally a wise policy for the side with less space, but it does not solve his problems here.

21.♕c1 ♘f8

Here is another nice line: 21...♖a7 22.♕b1 ♕a8 23.♖xa7 ♕xa7

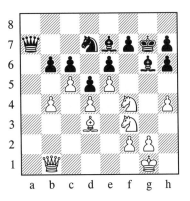

24.b5! White can afford to destabilize his mighty pawn centre as the text move wins by force. 24...♞b8 25.♗xg6! hxg6 26.h5 g5 27.♞xe6†+–

22.♖a3

A standard idea, preparing to put the queen behind the rook on order to take control of the open file.

22...bxc5 23.bxc5

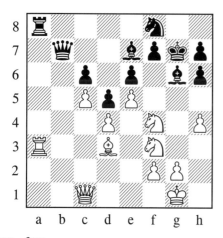

23...f5?!

Black's position was already unpleasant, but giving himself an extra weakness on e6 was hardly the way to improve it.

It is worth considering the winning plan in the event that Black does nothing and waits. Here is a line I analysed:

23...♗d8

White's general policy should be to stretch the defence by focusing on two or more weaknesses, but before doing that he should tidy up his king's position.

24.g3 ♖xa3 25.♕xa3 ♞d7 26.♔g2

These kinds of tiny improving moves are not only objectively useful, they also have a practical advantage as they tend to wear down the opponent. When you have such a dominating position there is no need to rush.

26...♞f8

Black continues to wait. The c6-pawn is weak, but it is not easy for White to attack it. Black's kingside also looks a bit vulnerable, but how can White make progress there?

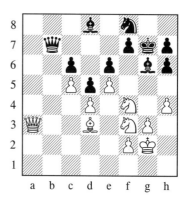

27.♞h2!

The knight is heading for g4, in order to provoke the h6-pawn into advancing.

The direct attack on the c6-pawn is less convincing: 27.♕a4 ♞d7 28.♞e1 ♞b8 29.♞c2 ♞d7 30.♞b4 ♞b8 It is not easy to increase the pressure.

27...♞d7

27...f6 does not help, as after 28.exf6† ♗xf6 29.♗xg6 hxg6 30.♕e3 h5 31.♞f3 ♕f7 32.♕e2 Black will not be able to defend all three weaknesses on c6, e6 and g6.

28.♞g4 h5

Black does not have much choice, as ♕c1 was too strong a threat.

29.♞h2 ♞f8 30.♞f3±

Now in addition to c6, the h5-pawn is a permanent weakness, and it is doubtful that Black will be able to defend both of them.

24.g3 ♗d8 25.♕a1 ♖xa3 26.♕xa3 ♗e8 27.♔g2 ♔g8 28.♞e1!

The knight is heading for d3. From here it will constantly threaten ♞b4, while also supporting the f4-knight should Black try to exchange it with ...♞g6.

28...♗f7 29.♗e2 ♘g6 30.♘ed3 ♘xf4†
31.♘xf4 ♔f8 32.♗h5 ♗g8 33.♘d3 ♗f7
34.♗xf7 ♔xf7 35.♘f4 ♗e7

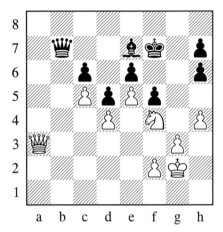

Black has weak pawns on c6, e6 and h6, as
well as invasion squares on a6 and a8 which
need to be defended. Grischuk conducts a
simple yet elegant dance with his queen in
order to break the defence.

36.♕a4 ♗d8 37.♕d1 ♕d7 38.♕a4 ♕b7
39.♕d1 ♕d7 40.♕h5† ♔g7 41.♕e2 ♔f7

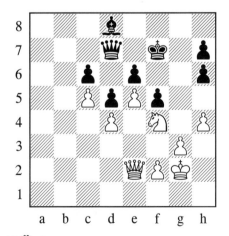

42.♕a6
   Mission accomplished. Now Black loses the
c6-pawn.

42...♔e7 43.♘d3 ♕c7 44.♘b4 ♔d7 45.♕a8

♗e7 46.♘a6 ♕c8 47.♕a7† ♔e8 48.♕b8
♔d7 49.♕b6 ♗d8 50.♘b8†
1–0

GAME 9

▷ S. Karjakin (2788)
▶ A. Morozevich (2694)
64th Russian Championship, Moscow
Round 1, 08.08.2011 [B12]
Annotated by Kamil Miton

Here we see another 3.e5 Caro-Kann with
♘f3 and ♗e2. Morozevich played 6...♘e7,
eschewing the more popular 6...♕b6 and
6...cxd4. It looks like Karjakin either had no
new ideas against this line, or could not recall
them having been taken by surprise. His
plan of 8.c3?! and 9.♘d4 was too slow, and
Morozevich equalized effortlessly. Instead of
Karjakin's plan, the analysis shows that the
more active 8.♘c3 and 8.♘d4 both create
difficult problems for Black to solve.

1.e4 c6 2.d4 d5 3.e5 ♗f5 4.♘f3 e6 5.♗e2 c5 6.♗e3 ♘e7

   6...cxd4 and 6...♕b6 are the main lines, and
subjects for a separate discussion.

7.dxc5

   7.0–0 is sometimes played, but the text is
more dangerous.

7...♘d7

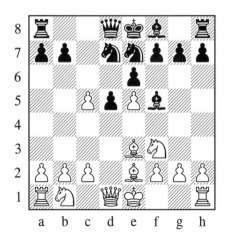

8.c3?!

This move is too slow and passive. White has a number of other ideas: he can aim to protect the c5-pawn, or open the centre with c4. In some cases he can give up the e5-pawn with the intention of developing a quick attack with f4 and g4. There are many different ways of approaching the position, and we will look at each of the main ones in turn.

8.0–0 ♘c6 9.c4 is a decent option, which transposes to a theoretical position usually reached via the move order 5...♘e7 6.0–0 c5 7.dxc5 ♘ec6 8.♗e3 ♘d7 9.c4. My intention is to focus on independent possibilities associated with the move order used in the present game, so I will not say anything more about this line here.

8.♘a3 ♘c6 9.c4 ♗xc5 10.cxd5 exd5 11.♗xc5 ♘xc5 12.♘b5 0–0 13.0–0 ♗e4 is fine for Black, as the pawn on e5 is weaker than the one on d5.

8.b4!? ♘c6 9.♘d4

This line is aggressive and ambitious, but Black should be okay.

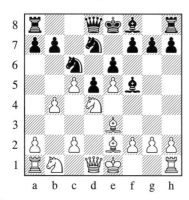

9...♘xb4

9...♘g6?! is inadvisable: 10.♘xc6 bxc6 11.0–0 ♘xe5 (11...a5 12.b5↑) 12.f4 ♘d7 (12...♘c4 13.♗xc4 dxc4 14.♕e2 ♗e7 15.♘a3 c3 16.♘c4 0–0 17.♘e5 ♗e4

18.♖fd1±) 13.c4! dxc4 (13...♗e7 14.cxd5 cxd5 15.♘c3±) 14.♘a3 a5 (14...c3 15.♗f3 ♖c8 16.♕a4 a5 17.♗xc6 axb4 18.♘c4 ♗c2 19.♕b5+–) 15.♘xc4 axb4 16.♗f3 ♖a6 (16...♖c8 17.♘b6±) 17.♕e2↑ White has strong pressure with ♖d1 coming next.

10.♘xf5 exf5 11.♘c3

After 11.c3 ♘c6 12.♕xd5 ♘xc5 (12...♘dxe5 13.♕b3 f4 14.♗xf4 ♘d3† 15.♗xd3 ♕xd3 16.♕xb7 ♕e4† 17.♔f1 ♕d3† 18.♔e1=) 13.♕c4 ♘xe5 14.♕b5† ♘ed7 15.♘d2 ♗e7 16.0–0 0–0 Black has no problems.

11...♗xc5 12.♗xc5 ♘xc5 13.♗b5† ♘c6 14.♕xd5 ♕xd5 15.♘xd5 ♖c8=

Black is okay in the endgame.

8.c4

Opening the centre immediately fails to unlock Black's defences.

8...dxc4 9.♘a3

9.♘bd2 c3 10.♘c4 ♘d5 11.bxc3 ♘xc5=

9...c3!

A typical reaction.

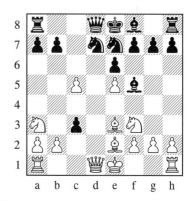

10.bxc3

10.♗g5?! does not work: 10...cxb2! 11.♘c4 (11.♘b5 ♕a5† 12.♗d2 ♕xb5 13.♗xb5 ♗c2 14.♖b1 ♗xd1 15.♔xd1 ♘c6 16.♖xb2 ♗xc5∓) 11...♘d5 12.♗xd8 ♘c3! Black will regain his material and keep a better position. 13.♕xd7† ♔xd7 14.♘xb2 ♖xd8∓

10...♘d5 11.♘b5 ♘xe3 12.fxe3 ♗xc5

13.♘d6† ♗xd6 14.exd6 0–0 15.0–0 ♕b6
16.♕d4 ♖ac8=

Black has no reason to be worried.

8.♘bd2 ♘c6 9.♘b3

This time White defends the c5-pawn, so
Black should target the one on e5 instead.

9...♗g4

9...♘xc5?? is obviously no good: 10.♘xc5
♗xc5 11.♗xc5 ♕a5† 12.b4+–

9...♘dxe5? 10.♘xe5 ♘xe5 11.♗b5† ♘c6
12.♘d4± also turns out badly for Black.

The simplest way to solve his opening
problems looks to be 9...♗e4!= targeting the
e5-pawn. Nevertheless the text move makes
an interesting topic for analysis.

10.♘fd4

10.0–0 should be met by 10...♗e7.

10...♗xe2 11.♕xe2

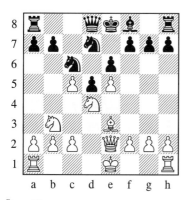

11...♘cxe5!

11...♘dxe5 12.f4 ♘c4 13.♘xc6 bxc6
14.♗d4 ♕h4† 15.g3 ♕h6 16.0–0±

12.f4

12.0–0–0 does not achieve much either:
12...♘c4 13.♖he1 (13.♗f4 ♕f6) 13...♗xc5
14.♘xc5 ♘xc5 15.♘f5 ♕f6 16.♘d6† ♘xd6
17.♗xc5 ♘c4 18.c3 ♖d8∓

There is always the option of playing safe
with 12.0–0, but the best White can hope
for here is equality and the move is hardly
consistent with his previous dynamic play.

12...♘c4 13.f5

13.0–0–0 ♗xc5 14.f5 0–0 15.fxe6 fxe6∓

13...e5 14.♘f3

14.0–0–0 exd4 (14...♘xc5   15.♘b5±)
15.♗xd4† ♕e7 16.♖he1 ♕xe2 17.♖xe2†
♔d8 18.♗c3 b5! 19.♖xd5 ♔c7 leaves White
with insufficient compensation.

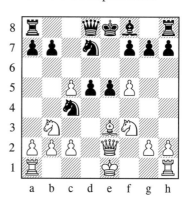

14...e4!

14...♗e7 is a bit too slow: 15.0–0–0 ♘f6
16.♗g5 h6 17.♗h4 e4 18.♘fd2 ♘xd2
19.♖xd2 0–0 20.♖hd1 ♕c7 21.♗xf6 ♗xf6
22.♖xd5±

15.♗d4 ♗e7 16.♘fd2 ♘xd2 17.♕xd2 0–0
18.♗c3 ♕c7 19.♕xd5 ♖ad8 20.0–0 ♘xc5

Black is at least equal.

More interesting is:

8.♘c3!? ♘c6

8...a6 9.0–0 ♘c6 10.♘a4±

9.♘b5

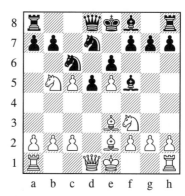

Now Black must make an important
choice.

a) 9...♘dxe5?!

This looks excessively risky.

10.♘xe5 ♘xe5 11.♘d4

Aside from this logical move, White has two tempting alternatives:

11.♗f4 f6 12.♘d4 ♗xc5 13.♘xf5 exf5 14.♗b5† ♔f7 15.0-0⩲⩱

11.0-0 ♘c6 (11...a6 12.♘d4 ♗g6 13.f4 ♘c6 14.f5 ♘xd4 15.♕xd4 ♗xf5 16.♖xf5 exf5 17.♖e1±) 12.c4! (12.♗f4 e5 13.c4 d4 is not so convincing) 12...dxc4 13.♗xc4 a6 14.♘d6† ♗xd6 15.cxd6 0-0 16.♕d2±

11...♗g6 12.♗b5† ♘d7

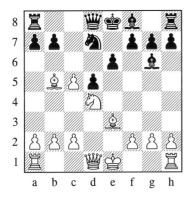

13.0-0

The tempting 13.c6 is not altogether clear: 13...bxc6 14.♘xc6 ♕c7 15.c4 a6 16.♗a4 dxc4 17.♕d4 ♘c5 (17... ♗d3!?) 18.♖xc4 ♘xa4 19.♕xa4 ♕b7 Black is okay as there are no truly damaging discovered checks.

13...a6

13...♕c7 14.♕g4 ♗e7 15.h4!↑

14.♗a4 ♗xc5 15.♘xe6 fxe6 16.♖xd7† ♕xd7 17.♗xc5 ♖c8 18.♕d4 ♗xc2 19.♖ac1 ♗f5 20.♖fe1

Black has an extra pawn, but White's compensation in view of better bishop and safer king is more than enough for material disadvantage.

b) 9...♘xc5

This has been played in a few games.

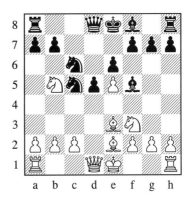

10.0-0

I consider this the most promising direction for White.

10.♘fd4!? is another possibility which led to a rich struggle in the following game: 10...♗e4 (10...♗g6!?) 11.0-0 a6 12.♘d6† ♗xd6 13.exd6 ♕xd6 14.♘xc6 bxc6 15.f3 ♗g6 16.♕d4 ♘d7 17.♕xg7 ♕e5 18.♕xe5 ♘xe5 19.♗d4 f6 20.b3 ♘d7 21.♗b2 c5 22.♗d3 ♗xd3 23.cxd3 ♔f7 24.♖ac1 ♖hc8 ½-½ Ehlvest – Khalifman, Parnu 1996.

10...♗e7

10...♗e4 11.c4 ♗xf3 12.♗xf3 dxc4 13.♗g5 ♕d7 14.♖xd7† ♔xd7 15.♖fd1† ♔c8 16.♖ac1±

10...♘d7 11.♘fd4 (or 11.c4!? dxc4 12.♗g5 f6 [12...♕b6 13.♗xc4] 13.exf6 gxf6 14.♘fd4 ♘xd4 15.♘xd4 ♘e5 16.♗e3) 11...♗g6 12.c4 dxc4 13.♘xc6 bxc6 14.♘d6† ♗xd6 15.♕xd6 ♕e7 16.♕xc6 0-0 17.♕xc4 ♘xe5 18.♕c3 ♘d7 19.♖ac1±

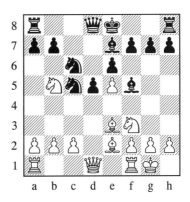

11.c4

Or 11.♘fd4, when we are left with two choices for Black:

a) 11...♘xd4 12.♘xd4 ♗g6!? (12...♗e4 13.♗b5† ♘d7 14.♕g4 ♗g6 15.f4↑ Weiss – Bokar, e-mail 2001) 13.f4 0–0 14.f5 exf5 15.♘xf5 ♗xf5 16.♖xf5 ♘e6 17.c3 ♖c8 and Black is okay.

b) 11...♗g6 12.♘d6† ♗xd6 13.exd6 ♘e4 14.c4 ♘xd6 15.cxd5 exd5 16.♘xc6 bxc6 17.♖c1 ♕d7 18.♕a4 0–0 19.♕xc6 ♕xc6 20.♖xc6 ♘c4 21.♗d4 ♖fe8 Black is marginally worse, but he should have enough activity to hold the ending.

11...dxc4 12.♗xc4

12.♕c1 ♗d3 13.♖xd3 (13.♗xc5 ♗xe2 14.♗xe7 ♕xe7 15.♘d6† ♔f8 16.♕f4 ♗xf1 17.♖xf1 ♖d8 18.♖d1 f6∓) 13...♘xd3 14.♕xc4 0–0 is fine for Black, as 15.♖ad1? can be met by 15...♘xb2∓.

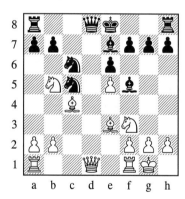

This position has not yet been reached in practice, but I consider it critical for the assessment of 9...♘xc5. I analysed two main possibilities for Black, but it seems that neither of them brings him to full equality.

b1) 12...♗g4 13.b4

13.♘d6†!? is also interesting: 13...♗xd6 14.exd6 ♘e4 15.♗f4 (15.h3? ♘xd6) 15...0–0 16.♖e1 ♗xf3 17.♕xf3 (17.gxf3? ♘xf2!) 17...♘xd6 18.♖ad1 e5 19.♗e3 ♕c7 (19...♘d4 20.♗xd4 exd4 21.♗b3± The

bishop is much stronger than the knight.) 20.♗d5⊞

13...♘d7

13...♘e4 14.♕c2 ♗f5 15.♖fd1 ♕c8 16.♘fd4±

13...♘xd1 14.♖fxd1 ♘a6 15.a3 ♗xf3 16.gxf3 ♘xe5 17.♗e2±

14.♘d6† ♗xd6 15.exd6 0–0

15...♘b6 16.♗e2 0–0 17.b5 ♘b4 18.♗c5 ♘4d5 19.d7±

16.♖c1

16.a3 is less convincing: 16...♗xf3 17.♕xf3 ♘ce5 18.♕f4 ♘xc4 19.♕xc4 ♘f6 20.♖fd1 ♘d5 21.♖xd5 exd5 22.♕xd5 ♕d7 White has sufficient compensation for the exchange, but no real advantage.

16...♘xb4

16...♘de5?! does not work: 17.♗e2 ♗xf3 18.♗xf3 ♘xf3† 19.♕xf3 ♘xb4 20.♕xb7 ♘d5 21.d7 ♘xe3 22.fxe3 ♕b6 23.♕xa8 ♖xa8 24.♖c8† ♕d8 25.♖xa8 ♕xa8 26.♖c1+–

16...♘b6!? is interesting though, for instance: 17.♗a6!? ♕d7 18.b5 ♘a5 19.♖c7 ♗xf3 20.gxf3 ♕e8 21.♗xb7 ♘xb7 22.♖xb7 ♕xb5 23.d7 ♖fd8 24.♕d6 ♕f5 Black maintains the balance.

17.h3!

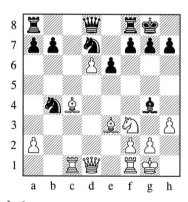

17...♗xf3

17...♗h5 18.g4 ♗g6 19.♕b3 ♘c6 20.♕xb7 ♘a5 21.♕a6 ♘xc4 22.♕xc4 ♘b6 23.♗xb6 axb6 24.♖fd1 ♖a5 25.♕b4±

18.♕xf3 ♘c6

18...♘b6 19.♕g3 ♘xc4 20.♖xc4 ♘d5
21.♗h6 ♕f6 22.♗xg7 ♕xg7 23.♖g4+–)
19.♕g3 ♘de5 20.♖fd1 ♘xc4 21.♖xc4 ♕d7
22.♗h6 f5 23.♗f4∞

White's active pieces and strong d-pawn give him good compensation. The whole line is rather tricky and double-edged, but overall I consider it more dangerous for Black.

b2) 12...0–0

This leads to an altogether different type of struggle.

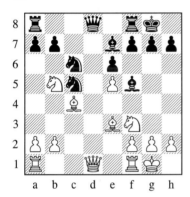

13.♘bd4

This time 13.♘d6 leads nowhere: 13...♗xd6
14.exd6 ♘e4 15.♗f4 ♕f6=

13...♗e4

13...♘xd4 14.♘xd4 ♕c7 (14...♗e4? 15.b4!
♘d7 16.♘xe6!+–; 14...♗g6 15.♖c1 a5
16.f4±) 15.b4 ♘e4 16.♖c1 ♕xe5 17.g4
♗g6 18.f4 ♕d6 19.f5 ♗g5 20.♗xg5 ♘xg5
21.fxg6 ♖fd8 22.gxf7† ♔f8 23.♘xe6† ♘xe6
24.♕xd6† ♖xd6 25.♖ce1±

14.♘xc6 bxc6

14...♗xc6?! leads to trouble: 15.♘d4 ♗d5?!
Consistent, but bad. (15...♕c7 16.♘xc6
♕xc6 17.♖c1±) 16.♗xd5 ♕xd5? (16...exd5
17.♘f5±) 17.♘f5!+–

15.♕e2

15.♘d4 ♕c7 (15...♗d5 16.b4) 16.f4 ♖fd8
17.♕e2 a5 18.f5 (18.♖ad1) 18...♕xe5
19.fxe6 ♖xd4 (19...fxe6 20.♖ad1∞) 20.♗f4
♕f6 21.♗e3 ♕e5=

I believe this position to be better for White. Black has potential weak pawns on c6 and a7, and the knight on c5 is in the wrong position.

15...♘d7

15...♕c7 should be met by 16.♗d4, and 15...♗d5 by 16.♘d4.

**16.♖fd1 ♗xf3 17.gxf3 ♕c7 18.f4 ♘b6
19.♖ac1**

The weakness of the c6-pawn is more significant than White's doubled f-pawns.

c) 9...♗xc5!N

This untested move looks like the most convincing way to solve Black's opening problems.

10.♗xc5 ♘xc5 11.♘d6† ♔f8 12.0–0

The pawn structure arising after 12.♘xf5 exf5 is quite playable for Black, for instance 13.♕c1 (13.♕d2!? ♘e4 14.♕e3; 13.0–0 g6 14.b4 [14.♕d2 ♗g7 15.♖ad1 ♕b6 16.♕xd5 ♖hd8 17.♕c4 ♖xd1 18.♗xd1 ♘e4∞] 14...♘e6 15.c3 ♔g7=) 13...g6 14.♕h6† ♔g8 15.0–0 and now 15...♕b6 looks correct, rather than 15...♕e7 16.♖ad1 ♖d8 17.♗b5 ♘xe5 18.♘xe5 ♕xe5 19.♖fe1 when White keeps a slight edge.

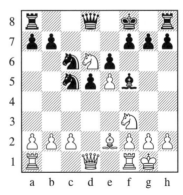

In this position it looks sensible for Black to move his bishop, and there are three possible squares.

c1) 12...♗g6?! looks like the weakest of the three. After 13.b4 (13.c4 ♘xe5 14.b4)

13...♘e4 (13...♘xb4 14.♖b1 a5 15.a3 ♘c6 16.♘xb7 ♕xb7 17.♖xb7 ♗e4 18.c4) 14.♘xb7 (14.c4 ♘xd6 15.exd6 ♕xd6 16.cxd5 exd5) 14...♕c7 15.♘d6 White has good chances to obtain the advantage.

c2) 12...♗e4 13.b4

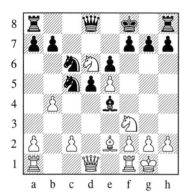

13...♘d7

13...♘a4 14.♕e1±

13...♘xb4 14.♕d4 ♕a5 15.♕e3! ♘xc2 16.♕f4 ♕c7 17.♖ac1 b6 18.♕d2±

14.c4 ♗xf3

14...♘dxe5 15.♘xb7 ♕c7 16.♘xe5 ♕xe5 17.♘c5 ♖d8 is playable, but still worse for Black.

15.♗xf3 ♘cxe5

15...♘dxe5 16.♘xb7 ♕f6 (16...♕b6 17.cxd5 exd5 18.♗xd5 ♕xb7 19.♖b1±) 17.cxd5 ♘xf3† 18.♕xf3 ♕xf3 19.gxf3 exd5 20.b5 ♘d4 (20...♘e7 21.♖fc1±) 21.♖fd1 ♘xf3† 22.♔g2 ♘h4† 23.♔f1±

In this position White has a nice sacrifice:

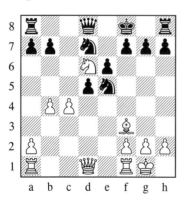

16.♗xd5!

Stronger than 16.c5.

16...exd5 17.♕xd5 ♕f6 18.♖ad1 g5 19.c5∞

Black's knights are not doing much in this position. White will soon take a second pawn on b7, after which his queenside pawns will cause Black plenty of problems.

c3) 12...♗g4!

This seems to be the most reliable move.

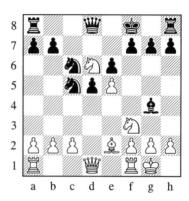

13.b4

The main alternative is: 13.♘d4!? ♗xe2 (13...♘xe5 is also reasonable for Black, for instance: 14.♗xf7? [14.♘xb7 ♘xb7 15.♗xg4 ♕f6 16.♗e2 g6=] 14...♗xe2 15.♘xd8 ♗xd1 16.♘8xe6† ♘xe6 17.♘xe6† ♔e7 18.♘c7 ♗xc2∓) 14.♕xe2 ♘xd4 15.♕e3 White regains the piece but gets no advantage:

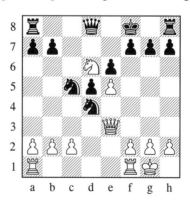

15...♘e4! 16.♘xe4 ♘f5 17.♕a3† ♕e7 18.♘d6 ♖d8 19.♕xa7 ♘xd6 20.exd6 ♖xd6

21.c4 g6 The position is equal.

After 13.b4 Black should react with:

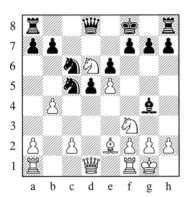

13...♘e4!

The passive 13...♘d7 enables White to seize the initiative: 14.c4! dxc4 15.♘xc4 ♗xf3 16.♗xf3 ♘dxe5 17.♘xe5 ♕xd1 18.♖fxd1 ♘xe5 19.♗xb7 ♖b8 20.♖ac1 g5 21.♖c7 ♔g7 22.♖e1 ♖hd8 23.h4 ♖d7 24.♖xd7 ♘xd7 25.♗c6 ♘f8 26.b5 gxh4 27.♖e4±

14.♘xe4 dxe4 15.♘d2 h5 16.♘xe4

In the event of 16.h3 Black has the strong 16...♗xh3! intending ...♕g5† and ...♖ad8.

16...♕xd1 17.♖xd1 ♘xe5=

Black has no problems in this endgame.

However, there is one final possibility on move 8 which is arguably the most dangerous for Black to face.

8.♘d4!

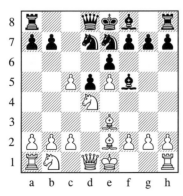

Black has three main responses:

a) 8...♘xe5?! is risky: 9.♗f4 ♘5c6 10.♘b5 ♘g6

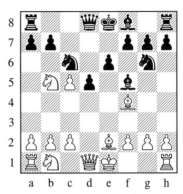

11.♗d6! (The tempting 11.♘c7† fails to achieve anything after 11...♔d7 12.♗g3 ♖c8 13.♘xd5 ♔e8 14.♘e3 ♕xd1† 15.♖xd1 ♗xc5= when Black is okay.) 11...♗xd6 12.♘xd6† ♔f8 13.♕d2 b6 14.♘xf5 exf5 15.cxb6 ♕xb6 16.0–0 White has the initiative.

b) 8...♘xc5 9.0–0 a6

9...♗g6 10.♘d2 reaches line 'c' below.

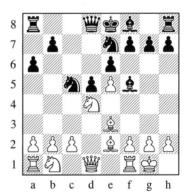

10.g4!?

It is logical to go for a quick attack, as Black is several moves away from kingside castling and his light-squared bishop is a target.

10.♘d2 is the solid option, and after 10...♗g6 11.♘2b3 ♘a4 12.♖b1 White's superior development gives him slightly better chances, although Black's position remains solid.

10...♗g6 11.f4 ♕d7

Black could consider 11...h5!? 12.f5 hxg4 13.fxg6 ♘xg6 with some compensation for the piece.

12.♘c3 ♘e4

12...♖d8 13.f5 exf5 14.gxf5 ♗xf5 15.♘cb5! axb5 16.♗xb5 ♘c6 17.♘xf5 ♘e6 18.c3±

Now the critical line continues:

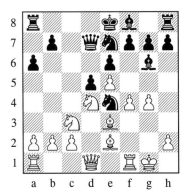

13.f5! exf5 14.gxf5 ♘xc3 15.bxc3 ♗xf5 16.♘xf5 ♘xf5 17.♗g4 g6 18.♗d4 ♖g8 19.♔h1

The position is unclear but more dangerous for Black.

c) Now we come to Black's final option against 8.♘d4.

8...♗g6

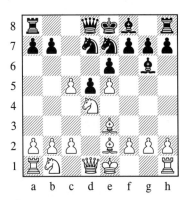

9.0–0 ♘xc5

I checked some other moves as well:
9...a6 10.b4 ♘xe5 11.c3 ♘7c6 12.♘d2 ♗e7 13.f4 ♘d7 14.♘2b3±

9...♘c6 does not quite equalize: 10.c4! dxc4 (10...♘xd4 11.♗xd4 dxc4 12.♘a3 ♗xc5 13.♘xc4 0–0 14.♖c1±) 11.♘xc6 bxc6 12.♕a4 ♕c7 13.♕xc4 ♘xe5 14.♕c3 ♗e7 15.♗d4 f6 16.♘d2 0–0 17.f4±

9...♘xe5

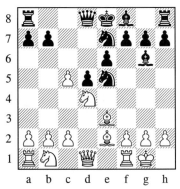

10.h4! ♘5c6 (10...h6 destabilizes the bishop on g6, allowing White to reveal the point behind his last move: 11.♗f4! ♘7c6 12.♗xe5 ♘xe5 13.♗b5† ♘d7 14.♕e2! With the nasty threat of ♘xe6) 11.h5 ♘xd4 12.♗xd4 ♗f5 13.g4!? ♘c6 14.♗b5 ♕g5 15.f3 h6 (15...♕f4?! 16.♗f2 ♗xc5 17.♔g2 ♗d6 18.♖h1±; 15...e5!?) 16.♕e2 ♗h7 17.♗xc6† bxc6 18.♕a6 ♔d8! Black is surviving but his position looks suspicious.

10.♘d2 ♘c6

10...♘d7? 11.c4! is excellent for White.
Perhaps 10...a6!? could be considered.

11.♘2b3

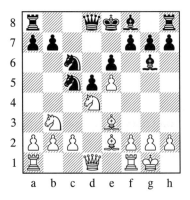

11...♘xb3

11...♘d7 12.f4 ♗e7 13.f5 ♗xf5 14.♘xf5 exf5 15.♕xd5 ♘dxe5 16.♕xd8† ♖xd8 17.♖xf5 White has the advantage of the two bishops.

12.axb3 ♘xe5

12...♗e7 13.♗b5 ♕c7 (13...♕d7 14.♖a6!±) 14.c4 dxc4 15.bxc4 0–0 16.♗xc6 bxc6 17.♖a6↑ Black has weak pawns on c6 and a7.

13.f4 ♘c6 14.f5 exf5 15.♘xf5 d4 16.♗d2

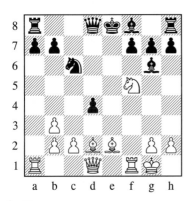

16...♗xf5

Otherwise it will be hard for Black to get castled.

16...d3?! 17.♗xd3 ♗c5† does not work: 18.♔h1 0–0 19.♗c3 ♗xf5 20.♖xf5 ♗d4 21.♕h5! g6 22.♕h6±

17.♖xf5 ♗d6 18.♗d3 0–0 19.♕h5 g6 20.♕h6 White's attack is dangerous, but perhaps Black can survive as follows.

20...♕c7!?

Intending to put the knight on e5, for instance:

21.♖h5 f5 22.♗c4† ♔h8 23.♕xg6 ♗xh2† 24.♔h1 ♘e5⇄

8...♘c6 9.♘d4

The combination of White's last two moves does not make a good impression. Black will regain his pawn and quickly finish development, and he does not even have to worry about the exchange on f5.

A bit more challenging would have been:

9.b4!?

This is the most principled way for White to try and justify his previous move, although it should not lead to any advantage against correct defence. White keeps his pawn majority on the queenside while Black gets the advantage in the centre.

9...♘dxe5

Black can also consider 9...a5!? in order to disrupt White's queenside chain. Play might continue: 10.♘d4 axb4 (10...♗g6!?) 11.cxb4 ♘xb4 12.♘xf5 exf5 13.0–0

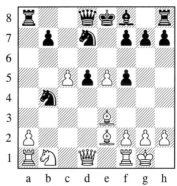

13...d4! (13...♗xc5 14.e6 fxe6 15.♗xc5 ♘xc5 16.♕d4 ♕a5 17.♖c1 b6 18.♕xg7 0–0–0 19.♘d2±) 14.♗xd4 ♗xc5 15.♗xc5 ♘xc5 16.♗b5† ♘c6 17.♕c2 ♕b6 Black seems to be holding his own, for instance: 18.♗xc6† ♕xc6 19.♘d2 0–0 20.♕xf5 ♕d5 21.♘f3 ♖xa2 22.♘g5 g6 23.♕h3 h5= Black has no problems.

10.♘xe5 ♘xe5 11.0–0 ♗e7

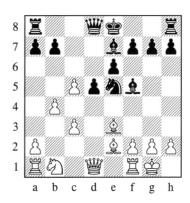

12.g4!?

The most principled approach, but Black has sufficient resources.

12...♗g6

12...♗xb1 13.♖xb1 0–0 14.f4 ♘c6 15.♕d2±

13.f4 ♘c4 14.♗d4 ♕d7 15.♗xg7

White can also consider: 15.♘d2 ♘xd2 16.♕xd2 0–0 17.♗d3 ♗xd3 18.♕xd3 a5 19.f5∞

15...♖g8 16.♗d4 ♗f5

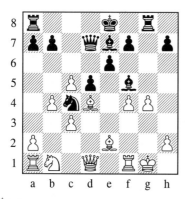

17.♔h1

17.h3 is met by 17...h5 when White's king is weak.

17...♗e4† 18.♗f3 e5 19.fxe5 ♕xg4 20.a4

Intending ♖a2 with a solid defence, but Black can force a draw in brilliant style:

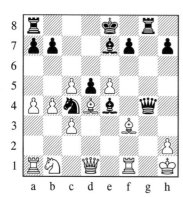

**20...♕g2†!! 21.♗xg2 ♗xg2† 22.♔g1 ♗h4!
23.♖f4**

White has nothing better.

23...♗h3† 24.♔h1 ♗g2†=

The game ends in perpetual check.

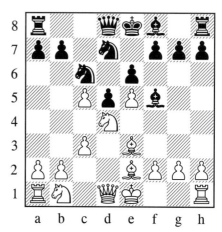

9...♗xc5!?

The normal-looking 9...♗g6 is also fine: 10.♘xc6 (after 10.b4 ♘dxe5 11.f4 ♘c4 the d3-square is weak) 10...bxc6 11.b4 ♘xe5 12.f4 ♘c4 13.♗xc4 dxc4 14.♕xd8† ♖xd8 15.♘d2 ♗d3= Black has a good position.

10.0–0 0–0

10...♗g6 also offers Black a good game, but Morozevich prefers not to lose time.

11.♘xf5 exf5 12.♕xd5 ♗xe3 13.e6

13.fxe3 ♘dxe5 14.♕xd8 ♖axd8 15.♖xf5 ♖fe8⩱

13...♕b6

Black has more than one way to maintain the balance, but the game continuation looks like the most direct of them.

**14.♕xd7 ♕xb2 15.exf7† ♔h8 16.fxe3 ♕xe2
17.♕xb7 ♘e5 18.♘a3 ♕xe3† 19.♔h1
♘g4 20.♕f3 ♕e5 21.♕f4 ♖xf7 22.h3 ♕xf4
23.♖xf4 ♘e3**

Both sides have played logically over the last ten moves, and the position remains balanced, although it is White who has to be slightly more careful due to his weak c-pawn.

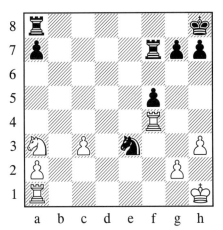

24.♖e1 ♘d5 25.♖f3 g6 26.♖e5 ♘f6 27.♘b5
♖d7 28.♘d4 ♘e4 29.♖a5 ♖b8 30.♔h2 ♖b1
31.h4

White has to be active in order to keep a balanced position.

31...♖c1 32.h5 ♔g7 33.♖a6 ♖xc3 34.♘e6†
♔h6 35.hxg6 hxg6 36.♖xc3 ♘xc3 37.♘f8

Black has won a pawn, but material is limited and White's pieces are active enough for him to hold the position.

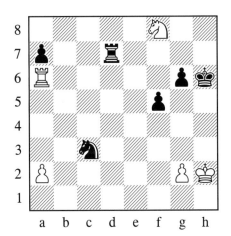

37...♖g7 38.♖a3 ♖c7 39.♖a6 ♖g7

39...♘e4 40.♖xg6† ♔h5 41.♖a6 ♖f7 42.♘e6 is equal. The white knight returns to the defence.

40.♖a3 ♖c7 41.♖a6
½–½

GAME 10

▷ D. Navara (2722)
▶ V. Laznicka (2681)

Match in Novy Bor, Czech Republic
Game 4, 2011 **[B12]**
Annotated by Kamil Miton

This was a theoretically significant game in one of the main lines of the topical ♘f3 and ♗e2 system. The same variation occurred twice in the match between these two players, and White failed to obtain any advantage on either occasion. The key moment came at move 17 when, having sacrificed a pawn in pursuit of the initiative, White should have tried either 17.g3!? or 17.h3!?N, a couple of unspectacular moves which nevertheless give White chances to fight for a long-term advantage. In the game Black had no problems at all, although White always kept enough compensation to maintain the balance.

1.e4 c6 2.d4 d5 3.e5 ♗f5 4.♘f3 e6 5.♗e2
c5 6.♗e3 cxd4 7.♘xd4 ♘e7 8.♘d2 ♘bc6
9.♘2f3

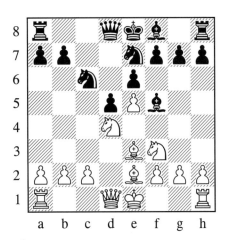

9...♗e4

The other main line is 9...♗g4 10.0–0 when there are two main branches:

a) 10...♘xd4 11.♕xd4 ♗xf3 12.♗xf3 ♕c7

12...♘c6? 13.♕f4 ♗e7 14.c4±
12...♘f5 13.♕a4† ♕d7 14.♕xd7† ♔xd7
15.c4 ♘xe3 16.fxe3 ♗c5 17.cxd5 ♗xe3†
18.♔h1±

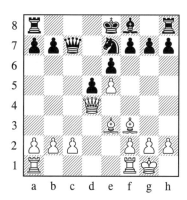

13.c4

White needs to get his light-squared bishop working, and opening the centre also highlights Black's lag in development.

Also promising is: 13.♕a4† ♕c6 14.♕b3 ♘g6 15.c4 ♘xe5 16.cxd5 ♘xf3† 17.gxf3 ♕xd5 18.♕xd5 exd5 19.♖fd1 b6 20.♖xd5 ♖d8 21.♖b5± White's active pieces enable him to exert pressure with a4-a5, and the doubled pawns are unimportant.

13...♘f5 14.♕f4 dxc4

14...♘xe3 15.fxe3 dxc4 16.♗h5 g6 17.♕f6 ♖g8 18.♗d1 a6 19.♖c1 ♗g7 20.♖xc4 ♗xf6 21.♖xc7 ♗xe5 22.♖cxf7 0–0–0 23.♗g4±

15.♖ac1 ♖c8 16.b3

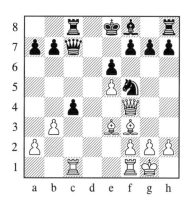

16...c3

16...♘xe3? 17.fxe3 ♗c5 18.♖xc4 0–0 19.♖fc1 ♕b6 20.♔f2 a5 21.a3+–
16...b5 17.bxc4 b4 (17...bxc4 18.♖b1→) 18.c5 ♗e7 (18...♘xe3? 19.fxe3 ♗xc5 20.♗c6†+–) 19.c6 0–0 20.♖fd1 ♖fd8 21.♖xd8† ♖xd8 22.♗e4 ♘xe3 23.♕xe3± Black faces an unpleasant defence against the mighty pawn on c6.

17.♕a4†

Also interesting is 17.♖xc3!? ♕xc3 18.♖c1 ♕xc1† 19.♗xc1↑ when Black is slightly ahead in material but lags in development.

17...♕d7 18.♕xd7† ♔xd7 19.♖fd1† ♔e8 20.♗xa7 ♗b4 21.♖c2±

White should be able to round up the strong c-pawn, using his a-pawn as a decoy if necessary, and his bishop pair could become a powerful force later in the endgame.

b) 10...♘g6!?

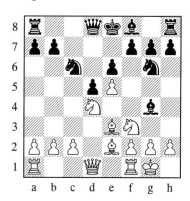

Unblocking the bishop while targeting the e5-pawn. Here I analysed two continuations for White.

b1) 11.♖c1!?

This interesting move is yet to be tested. The idea is to prepare c4 with a view to recapturing with the rook.

11...♗xf3

11...♗e7 12.c4 dxc4 13.♘xc6 ♕xd1 14.♗xd1 bxc6 15.♖xc4 ♗xf3 16.♗xf3 ♘xe5 17.♗xc6† ♘xc6 18.♖xc6±

12.♘xf3 ♗e7

12...♘gxe5 13.♘xe5 ♘xe5 14.♗b5† ♘c6 15.c4±

13.c4

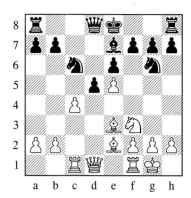

13...dxc4

13...0–0 14.cxd5 (14.♕b3 d4 15.♖fd1 ♗c5 16.♕xb7 ♕b6 17.♕xb6 axb6 18.♘xd4 ♘xd4 19.♗xd4 ♗xd4 20.♖xd4 ♖xa2 21.♖d2 ♘xe5 22.f4 ♘c6=) 14...♕xd5 15.♕xd5 exd5 16.♖fd1 ♖fd8 17.♖c2 ♖ac8 (17...♘gxe5 18.♘xe5 ♘xe5 19.♖c7 ♗f6 20.♖xb7 ♘c4 21.♗c1±) 18.♖cd2 ♘gxe5 19.♘xe5 ♘xe5 20.♖xd5 ♖xd5 21.♖xd5± White has a typical advantage based on his bishop pair, while the black knight lacks a stable base in the centre.

14.♖xc4

Compared with the main game, the rook on c4 leads to some differences in the play, but it does not yield any objective advantage to White.

14...0–0

14...♘gxe5 15.♘xe5 ♘xe5 16.♕a4† ♘c6 17.♖d1 ♕c8 18.♗f3±

Black can try to win the e5-pawn directly, although this entails some risk: 14...♕b8 15.♕b3 0–0 16.♖e4! ♖d8 (16...♘gxe5 17.♘xe5 ♘xe5 18.♗f4 ♗d6 19.♖d1 ♗c7 20.♕g3 f6 21.♕b3±) 17.♕c3 ♖d5 (17...♖c8!?) 18.♗c4 ♖a5 (18...♘cxe5 19.♗xd5 ♘xf3† 20.gxf3 exd5 21.♖a4 ♘h4 22.♔h1±) 19.♖c1 ♘gxe5 20.♘xe5 ♖xe5

21.♗f4 ♗d6 22.♗xe5 ♗xe5 23.♕b3 ♗xh2† 24.♔h1↑ In material terms Black is doing fine with two pawns for the exchange, but his poor coordination swings the balance in White's favour.

15.♕c2 ♕b8

Attacking the e5-pawn is typical idea for Black in this structure, so this queen move often features in his plans at some point. Alternatives include:

15...♘b4 16.♕e4 ♘d5 17.♖d1±

15...♘gxe5 16.♘xe5 ♘xe5 17.♖d1 ♗d6 18.♖cd4 ♕c7 19.♕xc7 ♗xc7 20.♖b4 b6 21.f4∞

16.♖d1 ♖d8

16...♘gxe5 17.♘xe5 ♘xe5 18.♗f4 ♗d6 19.♖c3 ♘f3† 20.♗xf3 ♗xf4 21.g3 ♗e5 22.♖b3 ♕c7 23.♕xc7 ♗xc7 24.♖xb7 ♗b6 25.♖xb6 axb6 26.♗xa8 ♖xa8 27.a3±

17.♖xd8† ♗xd8 18.♗d3 ♘cxe5 19.♘xe5 ♕xe5 20.g3 ♗b6 21.♗xb6 axb6 22.♖c7 ♕d6=

White can regain his pawn for equality, but it is tough for him to aspire to anything greater.

b2) 11.c4 dxc4

11...♗xf3 12.♘xf3 transposes to Navara – Laznicka. Alternatively White may consider 12.♗xf3!? ♘gxe5 13.cxd5 ♘xf3† 14.♕xf3 ♕xd5 15.♕xd5 exd5 16.♖fd1 with promising compensation.

12.♕a4 ♕a5

A logical move, intending to exchange the active White queen.

12...♗xf3 13.♗xf3 ♘gxe5 14.♗xc6† ♘xc6 (14...bxc6 15.f4 ♘d7 16.f5 e5 17.♘e6 ♕c8 18.♘xf8 ♔xf8 19.♕xc4→) 15.♖fd1 ♕a5 16.♕xc4 ♖c8 17.♘xe6! fxe6 18.♕xe6† ♘e7 19.♕d7† ♔f7 20.♕xb7 White has a promising attack for the sacrificed piece.

13.♕xc4

13.♕xa5 ♘xa5 14.♖fc1 ♗c5 15.♗xc4 ♘xc4 16.♖xc4 ♗xf3 17.♖xc5 ♗d5 18.f4 ♔d7=

13...♗xf3

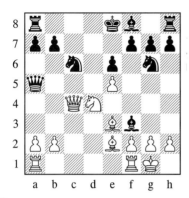

14.♘xf3

14.♗xf3 ♘cxe5 15.♕b5† (15.♕e2 ♘xf3†
16.♕xf3 ♕a6 17.a4 ♗e7 18.♘b5 ♖c8
19.♘xa7∞) 15...♕xb5 16.♘xb5 ♘xf3†
17.gxf3 ♖d8∞

14...♗e7

14...♘gxe5 15.♘xe5 ♕xe5 16.♗f3 ♖c8
17.♗d4 ♕f4 18.♕c3 ♖c7 19.♗xg7 ♖g8
20.♕f6 ♕xf6 21.♗xf6=

15.♕b5 ♕c7

15...0–0!? could be considered.

16.♘d4

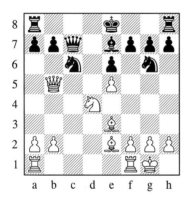

16...0–0

16...♘gxe5!? leads to extremely complex
play: 17.f4 a6 (17...♘d7 18.♖ac1 ♖c8 19.f5
e5 20.♘e6 (△20.♘xc6! bxc6 21.♕a4 0–0
22.♗a6±) 20...fxe6 21.♗h5† g6 (21...♔f8
22.fxe6† ♘f6 23.♖xf6† ♗xf6 24.♗c5†
♘e7 25.♗xe7† ♔xe7 26.♕b4†+−) 22.fxg6
hxg6 23.♗xg6† ♔d8∞) 18.♕a4 ♗c5
19.b4!? An interesting suggestion from

the computer. (also possible is: 19.♔h1
♘d7 20.♘xc6) 19...♗a7 20.fxe5 ♕xe5
21.♘xc6 ♕xe3† 22.♔h1 0–0 23.♘e7†
♔h8 24.♗f3 ♖ae8 25.♖ae1 (25.♕d7 ♗b8
26.♗xb7 ♖d8 27.♕a4 ♕e5 28.g3 ♕c7
29.♗xa6 ♕xe7∞) 25...♕d3 26.♗xb7 ♖xe7
27.♕xa6∞

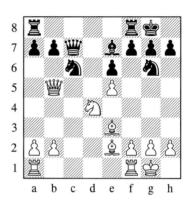

17.f4

17.♖ac1 ♖ac8 18.♘xc6 bxc6 19.♕a4 ♕xe5
20.b3 ♗g5 21.♖c5 ♕b2 22.♖xg5 ♕xe2
23.♖a5 ♖fd8⇄

17...♘xd4 18.♗xd4 a6 19.♕b6 ♖ac8 20.♕xc7
♖xc7 21.♖ad1 ♖d8 22.♗e3 ♖c2 23.♖xd8†
♗xd8 24.♖d1 ♗a5 25.♖c1 ♖xc1† 26.♗xc1
♘e7 27.♔f2 ♘d5 28.♔f3 ♔f8 29.♔e4 ♔e7
30.a3±

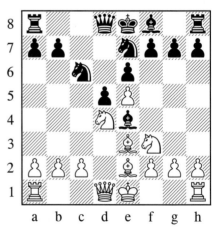

10.0–0 ♗xf3

10...♘g6?!

This natural move does not equalize against accurate play.

11.♘xc6

11.c4 ♗e7 is okay for Black, as the attempt to play actively with 12.♘xc6 bxc6 13.♘d4 soon backfires: 13...dxc4 14.♕a4 ♘xe5 15.f4 ♗c5 16.♖fd1 ♘d7∓

11...bxc6 12.♘g5!

12.♘d4 ♘xe5 13.f3 ♗g6 14.f4 ♘d7 15.f5 (15.c4 ♗c5∞) 15...♗xf5 16.♖xf5 exf5 17.♘xc6 ♕c7 18.♕xd5 ♗d6 19.♖d1 ♗xh2† 20.♔h1 ♘f6 21.♕xf5 0–0 22.♗f3 ♖fe8∞

12...♗e7

12...♘xe5 13.♕d4±

13.♘xe4 dxe4 14.♕d4 ♕xd4 15.♗xd4

From this position the weak pawns on a7, c6 and e4 should ensure White of some advantage.

15...0–0

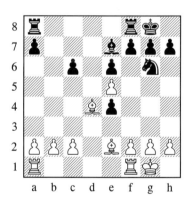

16.♖fe1

16.g3 ♖fd8 17.♖fd1 f6 (17...♖d5 18.c4 ♖xe5 19.♗xe5 ♘xe5 20.♔g2±; Perhaps Black should consider 17...♗b4!? intending ...♗a5-b6) 18.exf6 ♗xf6 19.♗e3 ♗xb2 20.♖ab1 ♖xd1† 21.♗xd1 ♗a3 22.♖b7±

16...♖fd8 17.♖ad1 ♗b4 18.c3 ♗a5 19.♗g4!

19.♗a6 ♗c7 20.♗b7 ♖ab8 21.♗xc6 ♖xb2=

19...c5 20.♗xc5 ♘xe5 21.♗e2 ♗b6 22.♗e7 ♖xd1 23.♖xd1±

11.♘xf3

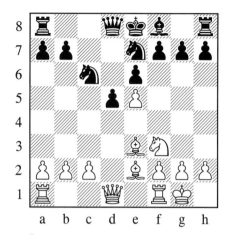

11...♘g6

Less purposeful is:

11...♘f5?! 12.♗f4 ♗e7

12...h6 13.♗d3 g5 14.♗d2 ♗g7 15.♗xf5 exf5 16.♗c3 0–0 17.♕d3±

13.♗d3 ♘h4 14.♘xh4 ♗xh4 15.♕g4 g6

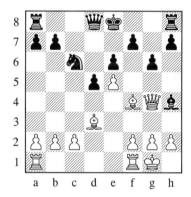

16.c4!

An important improvement over a game of mine where White got nowhere: 16.♗h6 ♗e7 17.♖fe1 ♗f8 18.♗xf8 ♔xf8 19.c4 dxc4 20.♕xc4 ♔g7 21.♗e4 ♖c8 22.♗xc6 ½–½ Kritz – Miton, Lubbock 2008.

16...dxc4

16...h5 17.♕f3 g5 18.cxd5±

16...♗e7 17.♖ad1 d4 18.♗e4 ♕b6 19.♗xc6† bxc6 20.♗h6 c5 21.♖d3±

17.♗xc4 h5

17...0–0 18.♖ad1 h5 19.♕f3 ♕e7 20.♖d6 ♗g5 21.♖fd1±

18.♕f3 0–0
    18...♗e7 19.♖fd1 ♕b6 20.♕e4±
19.♖ad1 ♕a5
    19...♕e7 is possible, although the bishop on
    h4 would be uncomfortably placed.
20.♕e4 ♖fe8 21.♗d2 ♕d8 22.♗c1 ♗e7 23.♕f4
g5 24.♕e3 ♕b4 25.♗d3 g4 26.♕h6
    1–0 Volokitin – Ruck, Budva 2009.

Another possible setup is:
11...g6!? 12.♗f4!
    12.c4?! ♗g7 13.cxd5 ♘xd5 14.♗c5 ♗f8
    15.♕c1 ♖c8 16.♗xf8 ♘d4 17.♕d1 ♘xe2†
    18.♕xe2 ♔xf8 19.♖ac1 ♔g7 20.h4 ♕b6=
    Kamsky – Topalov, Sofia 2009.
12...♗g7 13.♗d3 0–0 14.c3 a6 15.♕e2

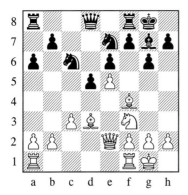

Compared with the Kamsky – Topalov game,
White's position is much more position.
The g7-bishop is of little use, apart from
defending the kingside. Black can try play
by b5 and transferring a knight to c4, but
what next? White's plan on the other hand is
simple: h4-h5 to attack the kingside, as well
as centralizing the rooks of course.
15...♕c7 16.h4 ♘c8 17.h5 ♘b6 18.♖fe1 ♘d7
19.♗g3 b5 20.♕e3 b4 21.♖ac1 ♕b7 22.c4
♘b6 23.c5 ♘a4 24.♖e2±
    Jakovenko – Magem Badals, Clichy 2009.

12.c4
This move is often a key part of White's
plans.

12...dxc4 13.♗xc4
    13.♕xd8† ♖xd8 14.♗xc4 a6 15.♗b6 ♖c8
    16.♖ac1 ♘gxe5 17.♘xe5 ♘xe5 18.♗b5† ♘c6
    19.♗xc6† ♖xc6 20.♖xc6 bxc6 21.♖c1 ♗d6
    22.♖xc6 ♔d7=

13...♕c7

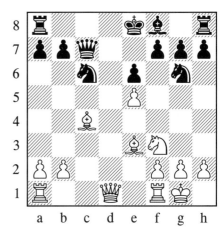

14.♖c1
14.♗b5
    Navara played this move in the first game of
    the same match, but got no advantage.
14...♗e7 15.♕a4
    15.♘d4 ♘gxe5 (15...0–0!? 16.♗xc6 bxc6 17.f4
    ♕b6 intending ...♗c5, ...♘e7 and ...♖d8)
    16.♗f4 (16.f4 a6 17.♗a4 ♘c4∞) 16...0–0
    17.♗xc6 bxc6 18.♖c1 c5 19.♖e1 ♗f6 20.♘c2
    ♖ad8 21.♕h5 ♖d5 22.♘b4 ♖d4 23.♗xe5 ♗xe5
    24.♖xe5 ♖xb4 25.♖exc5 ♕d8 26.b3=
15...0–0 16.♗xc6 bxc6 17.♕e4 ♖ab8 18.♗d4
♖fd8 19.♗c3 ♖d5 20.h4 h6 21.♖ae1 ♖bd8
22.h5 ♘f8=
    Navara – Laznicka, Novy Bor (1) 2011.

14...♗e7
    14...♘gxe5 is less good due to 15.♘xe5
    ♕xe5 16.♕b3 ♕c7 17.♗f4 ♗d6 (17...♕b6
    18.♕g3 ♕xb2 19.♖b1 ♕d4 20.♗e2±) 18.♗xd6
    ♕xd6 19.♕xb7 ♖b8 20.♕a6 ♖b6 21.♕a4
    0–0 22.♖fd1± when Black might have some
    problems with the a7-pawn.

15.♕b3 0–0 16.♗d3

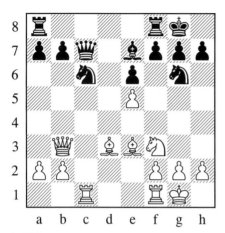

16...♕b8

16...♖fd8 17.♖fe1!?

17.g3 ♕b8 (17...♖ac8 18.♗xa7 ♘gxe5 19.♘xe5 ♕xe5 20.♗b6±) 18.♗e4 (18.♖fd1 transposes to 17.g3 ♖fd8 17.♖fd1 in the note to White's 17th move in the main game.) 18...♘gxe5 19.♘xe5 ♕xe5 20.♗xh7† ♔xh7 21.♕xb7 ♖ac8 22.♖xc6 ♖xc6 23.♕xc6 ♕xb2 24.a4 a5 25.♖c1 ♖d5=

17...♖d7

17...♕b8!? deserves attention: 18.♗e4 ♘gxe5 19.♘xe5 ♕xe5 20.♗xc6 bxc6 21.♗b6 ♕xe1† 22.♖xe1 axb6 23.a3± White can press here, but Black has good chances to make a draw.

18.♖ed1 ♕b8

18...♖ad8 might be the lesser evil although White still keeps an edge: 19.♗xa7 ♘f4 20.♗b6 ♕b8 21.♗f1 ♖xd1 22.♖xd1 ♖xd1 23.♕xd1 ♘xe5 24.♘xe5 ♕xe5 25.g3±

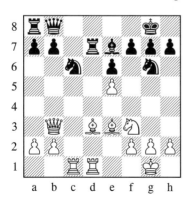

19.♗e4!±

Usually, in this kind of position, White should keep the light-squared bishop because it is a very strong piece. Instead 19.♗xg6?! ♖xd1† 20.♕xd1 (or 20.♖xd1 hxg6 21.♖d7 b6 intending ...♕c8 next) 20...hxg6 21.♕d7 ♕c8 is only equal.

17.♖fd1?!

This automatic developing move lacks any real bite. This is the prime time for White to search for an improvement, and the second and third of the following lines deserve particular attention.

17.♗e4 ♘gxe5 18.♗f4

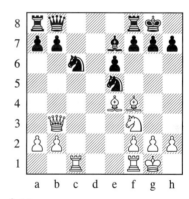

18...♗d6

18...♘xf3†?! is riskier: 19.♕xf3 e5 (Weakening the light squares, but 19...♕c8 20.♖c3→ was not ideal for Black either.) 20.♗e3 ♕d6 21.♗xc6 bxc6 22.♖xc6 ♕b4 23.♖c7 e4 24.♕f5 ♗d6 25.♖d7 ♖ad8 26.♖xa7 ♗b8 27.♖a5 ♕xb2 28.♕xe4±

19.♗xe5 ♗xe5 20.♗xc6 bxc6 21.♕xb8 ♗xb8 22.♖xc6 ♖d8 23.g3 ♗d6 24.♖d1 ♗e7 25.♖xd8† ♗xd8

The position is roughly level.

17.g3!? ♘gxe5

17...♖d8 18.♖fd1 ♘gxe5 19.♘xe5 ♘xe5 20.♗e4 (20.♗f4 g5 21.♗xe5 ♕xe5 22.♕xb7 ♗c5=) 20...♖xd1† 21.♕xd1⩲ Compared with the 17.h3 line there are some differences, for instance if ...f5 comes then White can retreat the bishop to g2.

18.♘xe5 ♘xe5 19.♗f4 ♗d6

19...♘f3† 20.♔g2 e5 21.♗e3 ♘d4 22.♗xd4 exd4 23.♖fe1±

20.♗e4 ♘c6 21.♗xh7† ♔xh7

21...♔h8 22.♗xd6 ♕xd6 23.♕xb7 ♘d4 24.♗d3 ♖ab8 25.♕g2 ♔g8 26.f4±

22.♕d3† ♔g8 23.♗xd6 ♖d8 24.♖fd1±

17.h3!?

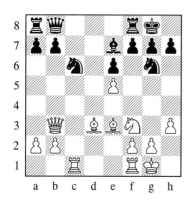

17...♖d8

17...♘gxe5 18.♘xe5 ♘xe5 19.♗e4 White can immediately put the bishop on its best diagonal as the g4-square is under control. 19...♘c6 20.♖fd1 ♖d8 (20...♕c7 21.♕c2 h6 22.♗xc6 bxc6 23.♕xc6 ♕xc6 24.♖xc6±) 21.♖xd8† ♘xd8 22.♕b5 ♘c6

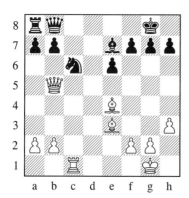

23.♖xc6! a6 24.♕c4 bxc6 25.♕xc6 ♖a7 26.♗xa7 ♕xa7 27.♕e8† ♗f8 28.♗xh7†

♔xh7 29.♕xf8 ♕c7 30.♕b4±

18.♖fd1

18.♗e4? ♘gxe5 19.♗f4 ♘xf3† 20.♕xf3 ♘d4∓;

18.♗xg6?! White should keep this strong bishop! 18...hxg6 19.♖fd1 ♖xd1† (19...♕c7 20.♘d4 ♖ac8 21.♘xc6 bxc6 22.♕c3±; 19...♘xe5 20.♖xd8† ♗xd8 21.♘xe5 ♕xe5 22.♕xb7 ♖b8 23.♕xa7 ♖xb2 24.♕d7 ♗f6 25.a4±) 20.♖xd1 ♕c7 21.♖c1 ♕d7 22.♖d1 ♕c7=

18...♘gxe5 19.♘xe5 ♘xe5 20.♗e4

White has fine compensation; his bishops are powerful, the b7-pawn is weak and Black's queenside pieces are clumsily placed. Black's main goal will be to return the pawn to equalize the position.

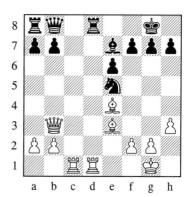

20...♖xd1†

20...♘c6? 21.♖xd8† ♗xd8 22.♕a4 ♗b6 23.♖xc6 ♗xe3 24.fxe3 ♕e8 25.♖c4 b5 26.♗xa8! bxa4 27.♗b7+−

21.♕xd1

21.♖xd1 is also promising: 21...♕c7 22.♖c1 (22.♗f4?! g5! 23.♗g3 ♖d8 24.♖xd8† ♗xd8 25.♗xb7 ♕c1† 26.♔h2 ♗b6 Black's pieces are becoming active and White has to be careful. He can maintain the balance as follows: 22.♕xb7 ♕xb7 23.♗xb7 ♖b8 24.♗e4 ♖xb2 25.♗d4 ♖e2 [25...♖b4=] 26.♗b1 ♘c6 27.♗a1 ♗c5 28.♖c1 ♗b6 29.♖xc6 ♖e1† 30.♔h2 f6=) 22...♘c6 23.♕c2 g6 24.♗xc6 bxc6 25.♕xc6 ♕xc6 26.♖xc6 a5 27.♔f1±

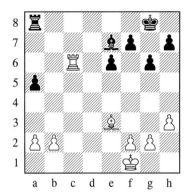

This kind of endgame should be tenable but a bit unpleasant for Black. His a-pawn could become a target, White has chances to create a passed pawn on the queenside, and his king is a bit more active too.

21...♗d8

21...f5!? Normally such a move would be very risky due to the weakening of the e6-pawn, but Black wants to solve the problem of the b7-pawn by driving the bishop away from the h1-a8 diagonal.

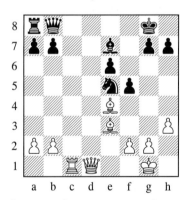

22.♗c2 (22.♗b1 b5 23.a4 ♘c4 24.♗a2 ♘xe3 25.♗xe6† ♔h8 26.♕f3 ♕d8 27.axb5 f4 28.fxe3 fxe3=) 22...♕d6 23.♕e2 (23.♗b3 ♕xd1† 24.♖xd1 ♔f7 25.f4 ♘c6 26.♖d7 b6∞) 23...♖c8 (After 23...♘c6 24.♗b3 ♕e5 25.f4 ♕e4 26.♖c4 ♕b1† 27.♔h2 ♗f6 28.♖c2 Black's queen is misplaced and the e6-pawn remains weak.) 24.♖e1 a5!? 25.♗b3 ♗f6 26.♗d4 (26.♗d2 ♖a8 27.a3±) 26...a4! This is the reason for Black's 24th move. 27.♗xe5

♗xe5 28.♗xa4± Black is still not out of the woods as the e6-pawn is a problem.

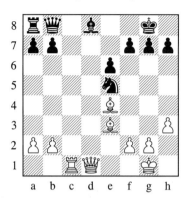

22.♗f4

22.f4 ♘c6 23.♕d7 ♗b6 24.♗xb6 axb6 25.♗xc6 bxc6 26.♖xc6 g6 27.♖c7 ♕f8 28.♕c6 ♕c5† 29.♕xc5 bxc5 30.a3 ♖b8=
22.♕b3 ♗b6 23.♗xb6 (23.♗f4 ♗xf2† 24.♔h1 ♕d6 25.♕xb7 ♖f8 26.♗xh7† ♔xh7 27.♕e4† ♔g8 28.♗xe5 ♕d5=) 23...axb6 24.♕xb6 ♖xa2 25.♗xb7 ♖xb2!= White must play accurately to avoid being left a pawn down.

22...♗c7

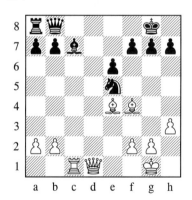

23.b4!?

Directed against ...♘c6.

23.♗xh7† ♔xh7 24.♕c2† ♔g8 25.♕xc7 ♘d3 26.♕xb8† ♖xb8 27.♗xb8 ♘xc1 28.♗xa7 ♘xa2=

23...f5

23...♘f3† 24.♕xf3 ♗f4 25.♖c4 ♕e5 26.♗d3 ♕e1† 27.♗f1 ♗d6 28.♕xb7 ♖d8

29.a3 ♕e5 30.g3 ♗b8 31.h4±
24.♗c2 ♕d8
24...♘f7 25.♗xc7 ♕xc7 26.♗xf5 ♕b6
27.♗g4 ♘e5 28.♖c3!±
25.♕e1 ♘f3† 26.gxf3 ♗xf4 27.♕xe6† ♔h8
28.♖d1 ♕f6 29.♕xf6 gxf6 30.♖d7±

Black is still under some pressure although he should ultimately be able to hold the position.

17...♘gxe5 18.♘xe5 ♘xe5

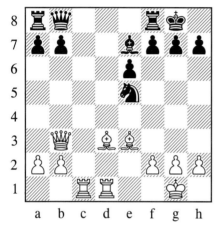

19.h3

19.♗e4 is met by 19...♘g4!, which explains why 17.h3!? was an improvement.

19.♗e2

This move is playable, but the bishop really belongs on e4.

19...♖d8 20.♗f4 ♖xd1† 21.♖xd1 ♗d6 22.♕g3
22.♔f1 ♕c7 (22...♘c4? 23.♖xd6 ♘xd6
24.♕d1±) 23.♕a4 (23.♕g3 ♖c8) 23...♖d8
(23...f6 24.♕b3 ♖e8) 24.♕xa7 ♘c6 25.♗xd6
♖xd6 26.♕a8† ♖d8 27.♖xd8† ♘xd8 28.g3=
22...♘f3† 23.♕xf3 ♗xf4 24.♖d7 ♗xh2†
24...♕c8? 25.♖xb7 ♕c1† 26.♔f1 ♖f8
27.♖xa7 ♗xh2† 28.♔xh2 ♕xf1 29.a4±
25.♔f1 ♕e8 26.♖xb7 ♗e5 27.♗b5 ♕f8
28.♖xf7 ♕c5 29.♕xa8† ♔xf7 30.♕e8† ♔f6=

19...♘xd3

After this Black should be fine.

20.♖xd3 ♖d8 21.♖xd8† ♗xd8 22.♕b5 ♗c7

22...♗b6?! is inaccurate: 23.♗xb6 axb6
24.♕d7 g6 25.♖c7 ♕f8 26.♖xb7 ♖d8 27.♕c6
♖d1† 28.♔h2 ♕d6† 29.♖xd6 ♖xd6 30.b4±
White's rook is ideally placed.

23.♕d7

White's active pieces give him enough compensation, but it is hard to improve his position in a way that will cause problems for Black. 23.♖d1 is met by 23...a6 24.♕d7 ♕d8.

23...♗h2† 24.♔f1 ♗d6 25.a4 h6 26.♖c4

26.a5 b6 27.a6 ♕d8 28.♕b7 was another idea.

26...b6 27.b4 ♕d8 28.♕xd8† ♖xd8 29.a5 ♖b8 30.♖d4 ♖d8

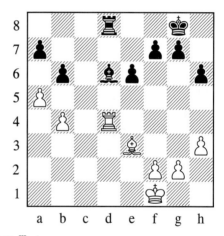

31.♖c4

31.♗f4 ♗c7 32.♖xd8† ♗xd8 33.a6 ♔f8
34.♗b8 ♔e8 35.♗xa7? ♗c7∓ turns out badly for White as his bishop is trapped.

31...♖b8 32.♖d4 ♖d8

32...♗c7!? could have been considered as a winning attempt, although White should be active enough to draw.

33.♖c4
½–½

GAME 11

▷ **P. Leko (2717)**
▶ **M. Roiz (2669)**
8th World Team Championship, Ningbo
Round 5, 21.07.2011 **[B12]**
Annotated by Arkadij Naiditsch

This is an interesting and important game in the popular 3.e5 line against the Caro-Kann. Peter has shown in many previous games that he is very well prepared in this opening. In my opinion, Black managed to equalize in this game, but White has an interesting improvement with 14.♘d6!?N. Very important for the current line is the evaluation of the position after 11...d3!? when it is hard to say if White has anything.

1.e4 c6 2.d4 d5 3.e5 ♗f5 4.♘f3 e6 5.♗e2 ♘e7 6.0–0 c5 7.c4 ♘bc6 8.♘a3

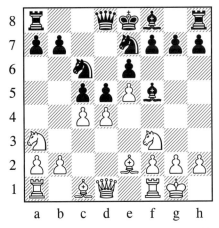

This is a very important position for the evaluation of this line. Black now has a few continuations, but the move played in the game is definitely the most critical.

8...a6
The alternative is:
8...dxc4
This move was popular until the end of 2010 then suddenly it went out of fashion, by in

the following games Black was doing fine. Let's see if we can find something new for White.
9.♘xc4 ♘d5 10.♗g5
10.♕b3
10...♕d7 11.♖c1 h6 12.♗e3 b5 13.♘a3 a6 14.dxc5 ♗e7!?
14...♘xe3 15.♕xd7† ♔xd7 16.fxe3±
15.♘c2 ♘xe3 16.♘xe3
16.♕xd7† ♔xd7 17.♘xe3 ♗g6 18.♘c2 ♔c7 19.♘cd4 ♘xd4 20.♘xd4 ♖ad8=
16...♗e4

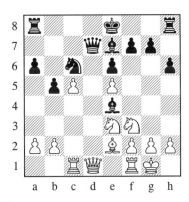

17.a4
After 17.♕e1!? somehow Black should be OK, but it is not easy to find a clear way to equalize. Black always seems to be slightly worse. 17...0–0 18.b4 ♕c7 19.♕c3 a5 20.a3 axb4 21.axb4 ♖a2 22.♘d2 ♕xe5 23.♕xe5 ♘xe5 24.♘xe4 ♖xe2 25.♖b1 ♖b8 26.♖fd1±
17...♕b7 18.axb5 axb5

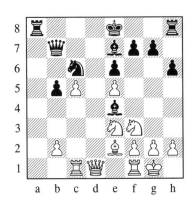

a) 19.♗d3 ♗xd3 20.♕xd3 0–0= In this kind of position, which is typical for the line, Black has no problems.

b) 19.♕b3

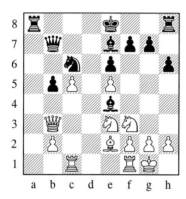

b1) 19...♖b8 20.♕c3 ♕c7

20...b4 21.♕c4 ♘a5 22.♕a2 ♖a8 (22...♘c6 23.♘d2) 23.♕a4† ♘c6 24.♕b5 ♕xb5 25.♗xb5 ♔d7 26.♘d2 (26.♖fd1† ♔c7 27.♘d4 ♖hd8=) 26...♗g6 27.♘b3 ♔c7 28.♗xc6 ♔xc6 29.♘d4† ♔c7 30.♖fd1+–

21.b4

21.♘d4 b4 22.♕c4 Motylev – Riazantsev, Poikovsky 2010. 22...♕xe5 23.♘b3! (23.♖fd1 ♘xd4 24.♖xd4 ♗c6=) 23...♖c8! Black's position looks very dangerous, but he seems to be holding. (23...♗d5 24.♘xd5 exd5 25.♕a6 0–0 26.♗b5 ♘d8 27.♗d7±; 23...0–0 24.f4 ♕xb2 25.♘d1 ♕a2 26.♕xe4 ♕xb3 27.♕xc6 ♕a3 [27...♖fc8 28.♕f3 ♕xf3 29.♖xf3 ♗xc5† 30.♔f1±] 28.♖b1 ♖fc8 29.♕e4 ♗xc5† 30.♔h1±) 24.f4 ♕xb2 Here we have a typical computer position where White has many continuations; a good moment to turn on a chess engine and do some mouse-clicking. 25.♖f2 (25.♕xe4 ♕xe2 26.♖f2 ♕h5 27.f5 0–0 28.fxe6 ♕e5 29.exf7† ♖xf7 30.♕c4 ♖cf8 31.♘g4 ♕c7=) 25...♗d5 26.♘xd5 exd5 27.♕xd5 ♕f6 28.♗a6 ♖c7 29.♕e4 0–0=

21...♗xf3 22.♗xf3 ♘xe5 23.♗e4 0–0 24.f4 ♘c6 25.♗xc6 ♕xc6 26.♘g4±

b2) 19...0–0! 20.♕xb5

The text move is tempting but White should instead choose 20.♖fd1 ♕c7⯹.

20...♕xb5 21.♗xb5 ♗xf3 22.gxf3 ♘xe5

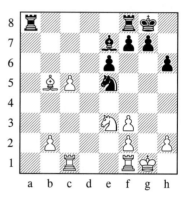

It is hard to believe, but Black seems to be fine here:

23.c6

23.♗e2 ♘c6!

23.f4 ♘f3† 24.♔g2 ♘d2 25.♗d7 ♘xf1 26.♔xf1 ♖fd8 27.c6 g6 28.♘g4 ♗d6 29.c7 ♖xd7 30.♘f6† ♔g7 31.♘xd7 ♖c8 32.b4 ♗xf4 33.♖c4 ♖xc7 34.♖xc7 ♗xc7 35.b5 (35.h3 f5 36.b5 ♔f7 37.b6 ♔e7) 35...♗xh2 36.b6 f5 37.b7 g5 38.♔g2 ♗d6 39.b8=♕ ♗xb8 40.♘xb8 ♔g6∓

23...♘xf3† 24.♔g2 ♘d4 25.♗d3 ♖fc8 26.b4 ♖xc6 27.♖xc6 ♘xc6 28.♗e4 ♖c8 29.b5 ♘e5 30.b6 f5 31.b7 ♖b8 32.♖c1 ♔f7 33.♖c8 ♗d6∓

c) 19.♘d2!?

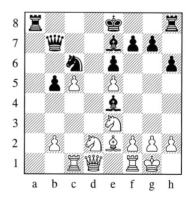

A nice idea of Cheparinov in his game against Bologan from the 2009 World Cup.

19...♖d8N

This novelty is logical and clearly the only critical reply.

19...♗g6?! 20.f3 (20.♗h5 ♘xe5 21.c6 ♕c7 22.♗xg6 ♘xg6 23.♕b3 0–0 24.♘f3 ♕b6=) 20...♖d8 21.♖a1! 0–0 22.♕c1±

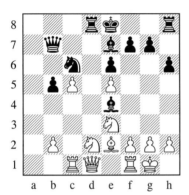

20.♘xe4!?

An interesting queen sacrifice, which definitely needs a practical test.

20.♕e1 ♘d4 21.♘xe4 ♕xe4=

20...♖xd1 21.♖fxd1 ♘xe5

21...0–0 22.♘d6 ♕a7 23.b4!↑

22.c6 ♕c7

22...♘xc6 23.♗f3

23.♘c3! 0–0 24.♘xb5 ♕b6 25.c7 ♖c8 26.♘c4

26.g3!?

26...♕xb5 27.♘d6 ♘f3† 28.♗xf3 ♗xd6 29.♖xd6 ♕xb2 30.♖dc6±

9.dxc5 d4 10.♕a4 ♘g6

Instead 10...d3 11.♖d1 ♘g6 is just a transposition to the 11...d3 line considered below.

11.♖d1 ♗xc5

A vital alternative is:
11...d3!?

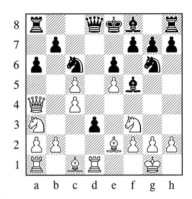

12.♗e3

12.b4!?N leads to a very dynamic and concrete position where Black seems to be holding. 12...♗e7 13.♗xd3 (13.♕b3 ♘gxe5 14.♘xe5 ♘xe5 15.♗b2 ♗f6 16.♖ac1 ♕c7 [16...♕c8 17.♗f1] 17.♗xe5 ♗xe5 18.♗xd3 ♗xh2† 19.♔h1 ♗g4 20.f3 ♗h5∓) 13...♗xd3 14.♕b3 ♘gxe5 15.♘xe5 ♘xe5 16.♗f4 ♕d4 17.♗xe5 ♕xe5 18.♕xd3 0–0 19.♘c2 a5 20.a3 ♖fd8 21.♕b3 axb4 22.axb4 ♖xa1 23.♖xa1 ♖d2 24.♖f1 ♗g5= Black clearly has enough compensation for a pawn.

12...♕d7!?

A strong move by Riazantsev, who is a big specialist in this line.

12...♗e7 13.♘c2 0–0 14.♗xd3 ♗xd3 15.♘ce1 ♘cxe5 16.♘xe5 ♘xe5 17.♘xd3 ♘xd3 18.♕a3± S. Zhigalko – Bologan, Russia 2011.

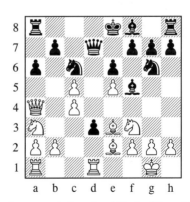

a) After 13.g4 ♗xg4 14.♖xd3 ♕c8 Black is fine.

b) 13.b4!? &d8!

13...&e7 14.&xd3 (14.&e1 &gxe5 15.b5 &d4 16.&xd4 &xd4 17.bxa6† Now 17...&c6= was level in Edouard – Riazantsev, France 2011, but instead Black should play: 17...&d7!? 18.&xd7† &xd7 19.&xd3 &xd3 20.&xd3 &xc5∓; 14.b5 &cxe5 15.&xe5 &xe5 16.f4 &c8!) 14...&xd3 15.&e1 &gxe5 16.b5 (16.f4 &g4 17.&xd3 &c8↑) 16...&d4 17.&xd4 &xd4 18.bxa6† (18.&xd3 0–0) 18...&d7 19.&xd7† &xd7 (19...&xd7?? 20.axb7 &xa3 21.c6+–) 20.&xd3 &xd3 21.&xd3† &c6 22.axb7 &a4=

14.b5 &cxe5 15.&xe5 &xe5 16.f4 axb5 17.cxb5 &c8∞

The position is a total mess and needs many hours of analysis. My feeling is that White should be better.

c) 13.&c2 0–0–0!? 14.&ce1

14.&b4 &gxe5 15.&xe5 &xe5 16.c6 &xc6 17.&xd3 &d4 18.&xd7† &xd7=

14...&cxe5 15.&b3∞

This seems to be a critical position for the line and it requires practical tests.

12.b4!?

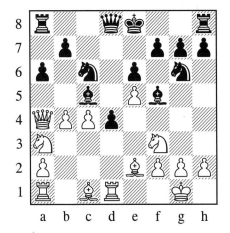

12...&a7

We must also analyse the capture: 12...&xb4

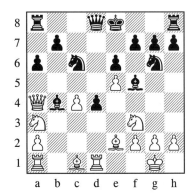

a) 13.&xd4 &a5 14.&xa5 &xa5 15.&xf5 exf5 16.&c2

16.&b1 &c5

16...&c5

16...&c3 17.&b1 f4 18.&d3 &xe5 seems to have been agreed drawn here in Motylev – Zhou, Aeroflot 2011, but White has the advantage: 19.&d5 &c3 20.&b2 &xb2 21.&xb2 &c6 (21...f3 22.&xf3 &xc4 23.&xb7 0–0 24.g3 with a much better endgame for White) 22.&xb7 0–0 23.&b4±

17.&d5 b6 18.&e3 &xe3 19.&xe3 &f4 20.&d2±

b) 13.g4!? A pretty and unusual tactical blow. 13...b5! 14.cxb5 axb5 15.&xb5 &e4 16.&xd4 (16.&xd4 &d5) 16...&a5 17.&xc6 (17.&xe6 &xd1† 18.&xd1 &xb5 19.&c7† &d7 20.&axb5 &cxe5 White has a slight advantage, but it should be a draw.) 17...&xd1† 18.&xd1 &xb5 19.&xb5 &xc6 20.&b1±

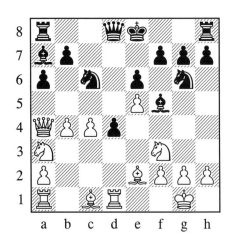

13.c5

White's main idea now is to play against Black's bad bishop on a7.

13...0–0 14.♘c4

Black can defend against the alternative: 14.♗g5 ♕d5

14...♕c7 15.♘xd4 ♘xd4 16.♖xd4 a5 (16...♕xe5 17.♕d1!±) 17.♘b5 (17.♗e3 axb4 18.♘b5 ♕xc5 19.♘xa7 ♖xa7 20.♕xb4 ♕xe5=) 17...♕xe5 18.♗e3 ♗b8 19.g3±

15.♗c4

15.♘c4 h6 (15...♘gxe5 16.♘cxe5 ♘xe5 17.♘xd4±) 16.♘d6! (16.♗e3 d3) 16...d3 17.♘xf5 exf5 18.♗xd3 ♘gxe5 19.♗xa6 (19.♘xe5 ♕xe5 20.♗d2 ♖fd8) 19...♘xf3† 20.gxf3 ♕xf3 21.♗xb7 ♕g4† 22.♔h1 ♕f3† 23.♔g1=

15...♕e4 16.♗d3 ♕d5=

14...♗e4

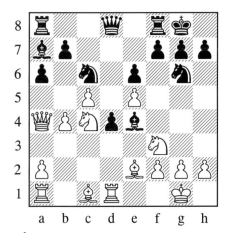

15.♗e3

A very natural move, but maybe not the best: 15.♘d6!? ♗xf3 16.♗xf3 ♘gxe5 17.♗e4 ♕h4 (17...f5 18.♗xc6 ♘xc6 19.♗b2±) 18.g3 ♕h3 19.♖d2! White seems to be better.

15...d3 16.♘e1

16.♕b3 ♗b8 17.♗xd3 ♗xf3 18.gxf3 ♕h4 19.♗xg6 hxg6 20.f4 ♕g4† 21.♔h1= (21.♔f1? g5)

16.♘b2 ♗xf3 17.♗xf3 ♘gxe5 18.♗xc6 ♘xc6 19.♖xd3 ♕h4 20.♖d7 ♗b8 21.h3 ♗e5 22.♕b3 ♖fd8 23.♖xb7 ♘d4 24.♕c4 ♘f3† 25.gxf3 ♕xh3 26.f4 ♗xb2 27.♖e1 ♕g4† 28.♔f1 ♕h3†=

16...♕d5

16...♗d5 17.♗xd3 ♕h4 18.g3 ♕g4 19.f3 ♗xf3 20.♘xf3 ♕xf3 21.♖f1 ♕g4 22.♔g2 ♖fd8 23.h3 ♘h4†=

16...♘gxe5 17.♘xe5 ♘xe5 18.♘xd3 ♕f6 19.♘xe5 ♕xe5 20.♖ac1 ♗b8 21.g3 ♕f5 22.♕b3 ♗e5 23.♗d3 ♖fd8 24.♗e4 ♕xe4 25.♗g5 White has a minimal edge.

17.♘d6

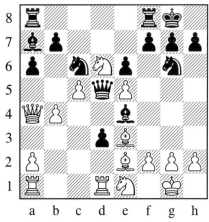

17...♘gxe5?

Black could equalize with accurate play: 17...♘cxe5 18.♘xe4 ♕xe4 19.♘xd3 ♘h4 20.♘f4 (20.♘e1 ♘f5 21.♗d3 ♘xd3 22.♖xd3 a5 23.a3 ♕e5 24.♕d1 ♗b8 25.♘f3 ♕e4=; 20.♗f1 ♘ef3† 21.gxf3 ♘xf3† 22.♔h1 ♘h4†=) 20...g5 21.♖d4 ♕c6 22.♕xc6 ♘xc6 23.♘h5 ♘xd4 24.♗xd4 ♖fd8 25.♘f6† ♔g7 26.♗c3 a5 27.b5 ♖ac8 28.♘d7† ♔g8 29.♘f6† ♔g7=

18.♘xe4 ♕xe4 19.♘xd3± ♘xd3 20.♗xd3 ♕xb4 21.♕c2

21.♕xb4 ♘xb4 22.♗e4 ♘d5 23.♗xd5 exd5 24.♖xd5 ♖fd8 25.♖ad1 ♖xd5 26.♖xd5 ♔f8=

21...♕h4 22.g3 ♕h5 23.♖ab1 ♖ab8 24.♗e2

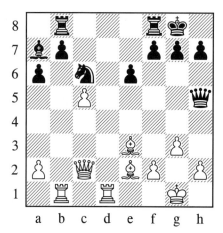

24...♕e5?

The final mistake. 24...♕g6 25.♕xg6 hxg6 26.♖d7 ♖fc8 27.♗f4! (27.♖bxb7 ♖xb7 28.♖xb7 ♗xc5 29.♗xc5 ♘a5 30.♖b6 ♖xc5 31.♗xa6 ♔f8 After a little suffering, Black should reach a draw.) 27...e5 28.♗e3 ♘d4 29.♗c4 ♗xc5 30.♗xf7† ♔h7 31.♖dxb7 ♖xb7 32.♖xb7±

25.♖d7+− ♖fd8 26.♖xd8† ♖xd8 27.♖xb7

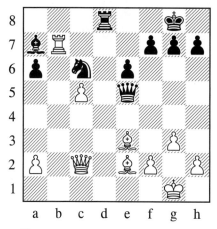

27...♖b8

27...♕d5 28.♕d3!! ♕xd3 29.♗xd3 ♖xd3 30.♖c7+−

28.♗xa6 ♘b4 29.♕a4 ♘d5 30.♕d4
1–0

GAME 12
▷ **I. Nepomniachtchi (2711)**
▶ **J. Polgar (2699)**
8th World Team Championship, Ningbo
Round 2, 18.07.2011 **[B60]**
Annotated by Borki Predojevic

In the following game we will check out a line in which the fight starts after sixteen moves that are more or less obligatory for both sides. I shall give an explanation of which move order is most precise (an example is that 13...♔b8, as played in the game, gives White a chance for 14.♖f3!? – and so 13...♗e7 is more precise). On the 16th move Black chose to play the most popular plan with 16...♖c8. White answered with 17.♕e1, and after 17...♘b4 he repeated moves and then tried 19.a3. Both 17.♕e1 and 19.a3 are not the most precise. Better is 17.♖d3!, which gives White a small but long-term advantage. In reply to 19.a3 Black missed 19...♘a5!, which would have solved any problems. After that, White was better, but the imprecise 21.♖h3?! gave another opportunity to Black in the shape of 21...d5!. Black missed this chance too, and it was then clear that White was on top. The middlegame was played very well by White, and the game finished with a strong attack on the black king and a nice win for White.

Summing up, my view is that the set-up which arises after sixteen moves in this line of the Richter-Rauzer gives the better prospects to White.

1.e4 c5 2.♘f3 d6 3.d4 cxd4 4.♘xd4 ♘f6 5.♘c3 ♘c6 6.♗g5 ♕b6 7.♘b3 e6 8.♗xf6 gxf6 9.♕d2

The main line. Another possibility is 9.♗e2, with the idea of castling kingside.

9...a6 10.f4 ♗d7 11.♗e2 h5 12.♖f1

A transposition to the game would occur after 12.0–0–0 0–0–0 13.♖hf1 (or 13.♔b1 ♔b8 14.♖hf1).

12...0–0–0 13.0–0–0 ♔b8

13...♗e7 looks more precise, preparing ...♖dg8 to attack the g2-pawn. After 14.♖f3 ♖dg8 15.♗f1 ♔b8 16.♔b1 we would arrive at the same position as in the game.

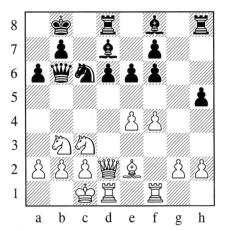

14.♔b1

Thanks to Black's inaccurate 13th move, White can immediately start manoeuvring his rook to h3 with 14.♖f3!, while avoiding having to retreat his bishop to f1 to defend the g2-pawn. Black has several options:

a) 14...♘e5

This move is superficially attractive...
15.♖h3 h4 16.♔b1 ♘g6
...but the black knight ends up in a questionable position on g6.
17.♖d3 ♗c8
17...♕f2 18.♖xd6 ♗xd6 19.♕xd6† ♔a7 20.♕c7±
18.♘a4 ♕c6

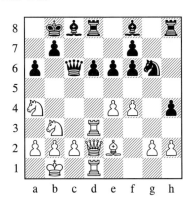

This was Lahno – Korbut, Dagomys 2008.
White should now play:
19.♖d4!N
White has strong pressure on the queenside, with ideas such as ♘a5, ♖c4 or ♕a5.
19...d5 20.f5!
20.exd5 ♖xd5 21.♗f3 ♖xd4 22.♕xd4 e5 23.fxe5 fxe5 24.♗xc6 exd4 25.♗f3 d3!⇄
20...e5 21.exd5 ♕e8 22.♖c4 ♗xf5 23.♘bc5+–
White has a decisive attack.

b) 14...♗e7 15.♖h3 h4 (15...♖dg8?! 16.♗xh5) 16.♕e1 ♖dg8 17.♗f3 By defending the g2-pawn in this way White keeps the g4-square under control and thus prevents ...♖g4. Black now loses the h4-pawn. On 17...♕d8 White can play the calm 18.♔b1 and Black is still not able to defend the h4-pawn: 18...♕f8 19.♖xh4 ♖xh4 20.♕xh4 ♖h8 21.♕g3 f5 22.h3 fxe4 23.♘xe4±

c) Black's best try is:
14...h4

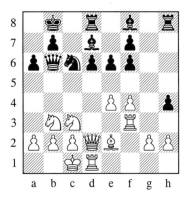

The idea behind this move is to hinder the direct ♖h3 and ♕e1 that White can play against other moves.
15.♕e1!
With this accurate move order, White will reach the same position as in line 'b'.
On 15.♖h3?! Black has the strong 15...♕f2! with a good game, because White is forced to exchange queens.

15.♔b1 ♗e7 16.♕e1 ♖dg8 17.♗f1 leads to the position which occurs after 16...h4 17.♕e1 in the note to Black's 16th move.

15...♗e7 16.♖h3 ♖dg8 17.♗f3

White has the advantage. He has found the time to put his bishop on f3, and h4 is hanging.

14...♗e7

There are two main alternatives:

14...♗c8

This has the idea of saving the e7-square for the knight, but it looks too passive. White continues with the typical:

15.♖f3

Again Black is not able to play ...♖dg8 in time to force White to reply ♗f1.

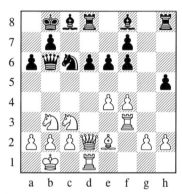

15...♗h6

15...h4 16.♕e1 ♗e7 17.♖h3 ♖hg8 18.♗f3! Black is losing h-pawn. 18...f5. 19.♘d5 (very interesting, though the simpler 19.exf5 d5 20.g4 hxg3 21.hxg3± also looks better for White) 19...exd5 20.exd5 ♗f6 21.dxc6 bxc6 22.c4 White went on to win the game in fine style in Chirila – Moldovan, Eforie Nord 2009.

16.♕e1 ♘e7 17.g3 f5 18.exf5 ♘xf5 19.♘a4 ♕a7 20.♘a5!

White has a dangerous attack.

20...d5 21.♖b3 ♖d6 22.c4 dxc4 23.♖xd6 cxb3 24.♖b6+–

White soon won in Groszpeter – Lupulescu, Hungary 2007.

14...♘a5

Going for the exchange of knights is a typical plan, but in my opinion this manoeuvre is too early and it gives White an opportunity to carry out the standard plan of attacking the h-pawn without having to lose a tempo with ♗f1 to defend the g2-pawn.

15.♖f3

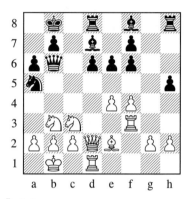

15...♘xb3

After the dubious 15...♗e7?! 16.♖h3 ♘xb3 17.axb3 Black can't defend the h-pawn. 17...h4 (17...♕c5 18.♗xh5 ♖xh5 19.b4!) 18.♕e1 ♗c6 19.♖xh4 ♕c5 20.♖xh8 ♖xh8 21.♕g3 (also possible is 21.h3 ♕e3 22.f5!±) 21...b5 22.♕g7 ♖f8 23.♗f3 a5 24.♘e2 a4 25.♘d4 ♗d7 26.♗g4 axb3 27.♘xb3 ♕e3 28.f5± White was a clear pawn up in Van der Weide – N. Guliyev, Vienna 2006.

16.axb3

Here Black has tried lots of moves, but none of them is satisfactory.

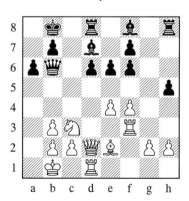

16...♗c6

16...♕c5 17.♖h3 ♗c6 18.♗xh5! ♖h7 19.g4 ♗e7 20.♖d3± and White was a pawn up in Firman – Miroshnichenko, Sochi 2005.

16...h4 17.♕e1 White is ready to play ♖h3 next. In Manik – P. Hoffmann, Litomysl 2009, Black tried 17...♗h6 18.♕xh4 ♗g7 19.♕g4 ♗h6 20.♖fd3 ♗c6, but here simply 21.f5± gives White a clear advantage.

16...♕a5?! leaves Black in big trouble after the strong: 17.♕d4! ♖g8 (17...♗e7? 18.b4 ♕c7 19.♘d5 exd5 20.♖c3 dxe4 [20...♗c6 21.exd5+–] 21.♖xc7 ♔xc7 22.♕xe4 ♖de8 23.♗f3 1–0 Gonzalez Vidal – Ruiz, Santa Clara 2007) 18.b4 ♕c7 19.♘d5! exd5 20.♖c3 ♗c6 21.exd5 f5 22.♕f2 ♗g7 23.♖c4 ♖ge8 24.♗f3 ♖e7 25.♖d3 ♖de8 26.dxc6 b5 27.♖cd4 ♗xd4 28.♕xd4± White was on top in Smirin – Melia, Athens 2008.

17.♖h3!N

Worse is 17.f5 ♗e7 18.♗c4 ♗xe4 19.♘xe4 d5 20.♕d4 dxe4 21.♕xb6 ♖xd1† 22.♔a2 ♖d6 23.♕e3 exf3∞ and Black had counterplay in Fier – Matnadze, Sabadell 2010.

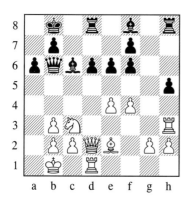

17...h4 18.♕e1 ♗e7 19.♖xh4±

White has won a pawn. Black does not have full compensation, but he has the bishop pair and a solid set-up which is hard to break down.

15.♖f3 ♖dg8

15...h4 is met by 16.♕e1! followed by ♖h3.

16.♗f1

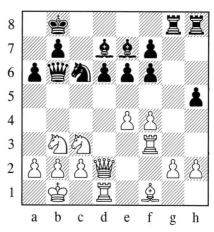

This is the starting position in the line with ...♕b6. This universal type of position can come from both the Richter-Rauzer and Najdorf variations of the Sicilian Defence. I believe that both opponents were aiming for this position. Black has several plans here. On the other hand, White's plan is clear: firstly, to organize pressure on the kingside by attacking the h-pawn; secondly, to improve his position on the queenside, for example with a2-a3 and ♘a4-b6; thirdly, at the right moment to attack the black king, when the white rook on the third rank will be the key to a successful attack.

16...♖c8

This is the most common move, with the principal aim of starting action on the queenside. This includes the idea of sacrificing the h-pawn for counterplay in the centre and on the queenside. Black also has other plans here:

16...h4 17.♖d3!?

This is a natural idea when the black rook has left the d-file.

17.♕e1 ♖h5! gives Black good counterplay. His main idea is to push ...f5.

17...♕c7

17...♗e8?! looks dubious. After 18.a3 ♖h5 19.♕e1 ♕c7 20.♗e2 ♖hh8 21.♗f3 ♗d7 22.♕f2 ♖d8 Sethuraman – Debashish, Vung Tau 2008, White could get a serious advantage with 23.♘a4! ♘e5 24.♖c3 ♘c4 25.♘d2 ♗xa4 26.♘xc4 ♗c6 27.♘b6!± and Black cannot defend against ♘d5.

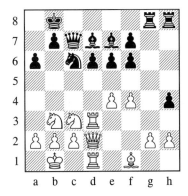

18.♕e1

This is usually the best square for the queen. White is preparing an attack with ♘d5 and is also keeping an eye on the h4-pawn.

18.♕f2 ♘a5? (18...b5! intending ...♕a7, was the right answer) 19.e5! ♘xb3 20.exd6 ♗xd6 21.♖xd6 ♘c5 22.♕d4 ♗c8 23.♕xf6+– led to a win for White in Korneev – Kolev, Lorca 2004, but it is obvious that Black's 18th move was a big mistake.

18...♖h5

On 18...♕b6 White improves his position with 19.a3±

This position occurred in G. Guseinov – Ibrahimov, Abu Dhabi 2005, and here White should react with:

19.♗e2 ♖h7 20.♗f3±

White has improved the position of his bishop, while Black has not made any gains.

16...♖g4?!

This looks premature. White can continue with his plan:

17.a3 ♗c8 18.♘a4

18...♕c7

I would generally prefer 18...♕a7 in order to hold the g1-a7 diagonal, although here White has: 19.♖d3 ♖d8 (19...b5 20.♘c3, with the ideas a3-a4 or ♖e1 and ♘d5, gives White an advantage) 20.g3! This move is usually not good, but here Black pieces are misplaced and White has the concrete idea of playing ♘a5. 20...♖gg8 21.♘a5 ♘xa5 22.♕xa5 ♗d7 23.♖c3 ♗c6 The only way to stop White's threat. 24.♖xc6! bxc6 25.♘b6 White now intends ♖d3-b3, so Black may try running with his king. 25...♔c7 26.♘d5† ♔d7 27.♗xa6 ♔e8 28.♘b4 ♖b8 29.♘xc6 ♕b6 30.♕c3± White has a clear advantage.

19.♕f2

White's idea is simple – he wants to play ♘b6 and ♘xc8. After that, the plan with g3, ♗h3 and f5 would give a clear advantage to White, thanks to the strong pressure on the light squares.

19...b5 20.♘c3 ♕a7 21.♕e1

White provoked ...b5, and now he is ready to start an attack on the black king.

21...♖hg8

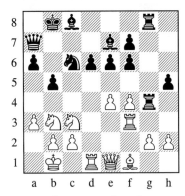

22.a4! b4 23.♘a2 a5 24.♗b5 ♗b7

White now won with a nice trick:

25.♗xc6 ♗xc6 26.♘xa5! ♕xa5 27.♘xb4 ♔b7□ 28.♖b3+–

Alekseev – Kiselev, Tula 2002.

16...♗c8 is dubious: 17.a3 h4 18.♖d3± White

can carry out a similar plan as in the line after 16...h4.

17.♕e1

17.a3 transposes into game at move 19.

Nepomniachtchi has played this position with the black pieces too, but without success: 17.♘a4 ♕a7 18.a3 ♔a8 19.♘c3 ♕b6 20.♘a4 ♕a7 21.♖h3 ♖cg8 22.♕e2!? h4 23.♘c3 ♗c8 24.♕d2 ♕b6 25.♕e1 ♖g4 26.♖f3 ♗f8?! 27.♘a4 ♕a7?

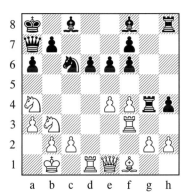

28.♘a5! ♗d7 29.♖b3 b5 30.♗xb5 ♘xa5 31.♕xa5 ♗xb5 32.c4 ♖h5 33.f5 ♖xe4 34.cxb5 ♖xf5 35.♖c1

1–0 Sjugirov – Nepomniachtchi, Dagomys 2009. This game is a typical example of the hard positional fight which can occur in this line.

17.♖d3!

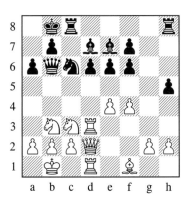

This is a serious alternative and I believe it to be the best move. As Gofshtein has pointed out, White is putting pressure on d-file, while preparing an attack on the h-pawn with ♕e2 and ♖h3. It is important to note that with his last move White has prevented the idea of ...♘a5.

17...♖cd8

17...♖c7 weakens the defence of the kingside. After 18.♖h3! ♖cc8 (18...♘a5 19.♗e2 h4 20.♕e1 ♖g8 21.♗f1) 19.♕e2 h4 20.♕e1± White won the h-pawn in Yudasin – Paschall, New York 2003.

17...♘a5? is a tactical mistake. In Dembo – Fuchs, Rijeka 2010, White missed: 18.♘d5!N exd5 (18...♘xb3 19.♖xb3+–) 19.♘xa5 ♗a4 20.b3 (20.♖c1!? dxe4 21.♖d4±) 20...dxe4 21.♖d4 ♗c6 22.♘xc6† ♕xc6 23.♖c4 ♕d7 24.♖xe4± White will bring his bishop to d5 with a clear advantage.

18.a3±

White has won a couple of tempos, as the moves ♖d3 and a3 were in his plans anyway.

17...♘b4! 18.♕d2

On 18.a3? Black wins pawn with 18...♘xc2! 19.♔xc2 ♗a4∓.

18...♘c6 19.a3

White believes the position is in his favour, and wants to play on.

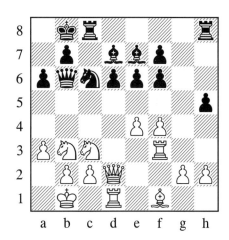

19...罝c7?!N

This waiting move is a novelty, but it is not the best option for Black.

The previously played 19...公a5! is correct. Carrying out this manoeuvre at the right moment solves Black's problems. There is no better option for White than 20.公xa5 (20.公d5 exd5 21.公xa5 fails to the strong 21...鼻d8!∓) 20...豐xa5, when the exchange of knights has improved Black's position.

On 19...h4 White can play 20.罝d3±.

20.公a2!?±

An interesting idea of Nepomniachtchi's. He stops ...公a5, while also discouraging the advance of Black's queenside pawns.

He could stop ...公a5 with the typical 20.公a4, but this is not best because after 20...豐a7∞ with the idea of ...b5, the rook on c7 is well placed, as it can be activated along the 7th rank.

20...h4

This move could be questioned since the pawn on h4 can be easily attacked by 豐e1 and 罝h3. On the other hand, this is a typical response and it is very hard to give a clear evaluation as to whether this move is useful or not.

21.罝h3?!

An imprecise move. 21.豐e1± was safer.

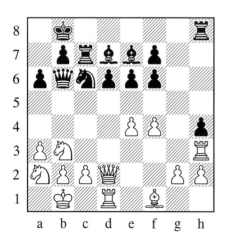

21...罝cc8?

A serious mistake, which calls into question the idea of 19...罝c7.

The computer immediately gives a dynamic idea: 21...d5! 22.exd5 exd5 Black's structure is destroyed, but thanks to the knight being on a2 White doesn't have pressure on the centre. 23.公c3 This is best. (23.罝e3 鼻e6! gives the initiative to Black as ...d4 cannot be stopped. For example 24.公ac1 d4 25.罝ee1 罝d8 and the white pieces are really passive.) 23...鼻xh3 24.公xd5 豐a7 25.gxh3 (25.公xc7 鼻g4∓) 25...罝d7 26.鼻g2 White has sufficient compensation, but no advantage.

22.豐e1 豐c7 23.豐f2 查a8 24.公c3±

In the last few moves, White has improved his position. Meanwhile Black has played ...查a8, ...罝c8 and ...豐c7 – all passive moves. Black now has serious problems with the h4-pawn.

24...公a5

We have already discussed this idea, but here it comes too late.

25.公c1!?

An interesting approach. White does not hurry to take on h4. For him, the positional advantage is more important.

The alternative 25.罝xh4 公xb3 26.cxb3 f5 27.罝xh8 罝xh8 28.exf5 罝xh2 29.b4± would lead to a better position for White, but without any positional pressure.

25...罝h5

After 25...公c4 26.鼻xc4 豐xc4 27.罝xh4 罝xh4 28.豐xh4± White has a positional and material advantage.

Nor does the active 25...f5 solve Black's problems: 26.exf5 d5 27.fxe6 fxe6 28.f5 罝hf8 29.罝f3±

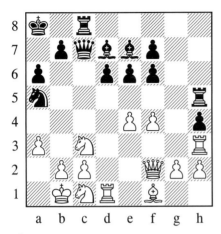

26.♘1a2

Again, White chooses not to take on h4. He believes in his strategy of making improvements on the queenside.

The normal 26.♖xh4 ♖xh4 27.♕xh4 ♕b6 28.♔a2± was also good.

26...♖ch8

Finally, Black is able to defend the h4-pawn, but this doesn't help much. While the black rooks are defending the h4-pawn, White's pieces gradually start the attack on the black king.

27.♗e2 ♖5h7 28.♘b4 ♗e8 29.f5!

This is a good positional move, since Black pieces are very far from the e5-square. Blocking the fifth rank keeps the black rooks out of play.

29...♕c5 30.♕f1 ♘c6?

A tactical mistake, but Black had already been positionally outplayed.

After 30...♗d7 White has the strong 31.♘cd5! exd5 32.♖c3 ♕b6 33.♘xd5 ♕d8 34.♗xa6!± with a huge attack. All White's pieces are going into the attack – next will come ♖d4.

30...♕c8 was the best defence, although White is much better and he can even continue with

the awkward 31.♘ca2!?± followed by ♖c3 and a sacrifice on a6 in the near future.

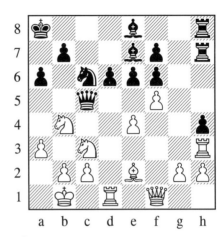

31.♗xa6!+–

This move destroys Black's defences.

31...bxa6 32.♘xa6 ♕a5 33.♘b5!

The key move. White has a devastating attack and Black is simply lost. The game continued with almost forced moves.

33...♗d8 34.♖b3 ♗b6

On 34...h3 the simplest is 35.g3+–.

35.♘xd6

35.♖xd6 ♔b7 36.♘bc7 wins too.

35...♘e5

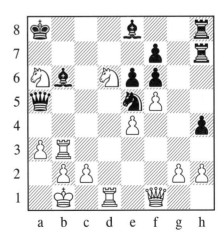

36.♘xe8 ♖xe8 37.♖d6 ♔a7 38.♖dxb6 ♕xb6
39.♖xb6 ♔xb6 40.a4 ♖c8 41.♕b5†
1–0

GAME 13
▷ F. Caruana (2711)
▶ M. Vachier Lagrave (2722)
Accentus GM Tournament, Biel
Round 1, 18.07.2011 [B96]
Annotated by Arkadij Naiditsch

An interesting game in the fashionable 6.♗g5
Najdorf line with 7...h6 and then 8...♕b6,
which was brought to prominence mainly by
Anand's seconds, especially Wojtaszek. In reply
Caruana tried the simple but perhaps very
strong 9.a3!?. In the game White gained a huge
advantage and Black only managed to survive
due to a miracle. It seems to be difficult for
Black to equalize, so I think we will see many
games in the very near future with 9.a3. Even
maybe from me. :)

**1.e4 c5 2.♘f3 d6 3.d4 cxd4 4.♘xd4 ♘f6
5.♘c3 a6 6.♗g5 e6 7.f4 h6 8.♗h4 ♕b6
9.a3!?**

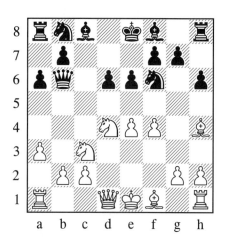

This is definitely a move for lazy people
and those who have had enough of analysing
the forcing and complicated 9.e5 lines. And
actually, why not just protect the pawn on
b2!? The move a2-a3 can useful for White

in many future lines and Black has to prove
that he gained something by playing ...♕b6.
Of course a2-a3 would not make any sense in
the position after 7...♕b6 8.a3?! ♘c6 as White
has no ♗f2 resource, as he does with the moves
7...h6 8.♗h4 included.

9...♘bd7
If 9...♘c6 10.♗f2 ♕c7 11.♕d3 then we can
see that the move a2-a3 is useful for White,
while Black gained absolutely nothing by
playing ...♕b6-c7.

10.♗c4 g5
This is a typical move for this kind of
structure and probably the best way to make
some sense of the move 8...♕b6, but whether
it helps Black is another question.

A natural alternative is:
10...♗e7 11.♗f2 ♕c7

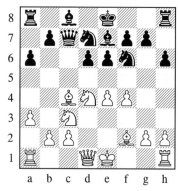

Now there are two main continuations: the
simple and strong a) 12.♕e2!? and the complex
sacrifice b) 12.♗xe6!?:

a) 12.♕e2!? ♘b6 (12...b5 13.♗xe6 fxe6
14.♘xe6 ♕b7 15.♘xg7† ♔f7 16.♘f5±)
13.♗b3 White is clearly better.

b) The sacrifice is promising but very
complicated:
12.♗xe6 fxe6 13.♘xe6 ♕c4 14.♘xg7† ♔f7
15.♘f5 ♘xe4

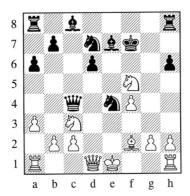

We need a further split between a1) 16.♕h5† and a2) 16.♕g4!.

b1) 16.♕h5†

This natural move seems to be good enough only for a draw.

16...♔f8

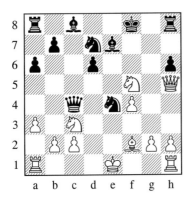

17.♕g6

17.♘xe7 ♘xc3 18.♘g6† ♔g8 19.♘xh8 ♕e6† 20.♔f1 ♕c4† 21.♔e1 ♕e6†=

17.♘e3? ♕c6 18.♘xe4 ♕xe4 19.0–0–0 ♘f6 20.♕a5 ♗d7 21.♖he1 ♖c8∓

17...♗f6 18.0–0–0 ♗xc3

18...♘xf2? 19.♘d5 ♕a2 20.c3!+−

19.♘xd6

19.bxc3 ♕g8! 20.♘h4 ♕xg6 21.♘xg6† ♔g7 22.♗d4† ♔xg6 23.♗xh8 ♘dc5∓

19...♕a2

19...♘xd6 20.♕xd6† ♔f7 21.bxc3→

20.♕e8† ♔g7 21.♘f5† ♔h7 22.♖xd7† ♗xd7 23.♕xd7† ♔g8 24.♘e7† ♔f8 25.♘g6† ♔g8=

b2) 16.♕g4!

White can gain a clear advantage, but only after some long sharp lines.

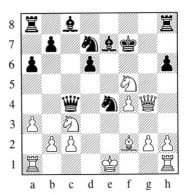

16...♖h7

16...♗f6 17.0–0–0! Of course we need a computer to figure all this out. 17...♗xc3 (17...♘xf2 18.♘xd6† ♔f8 19.♕f5 ♕g8 20.♖he1 ♔g7 21.♘xc8 ♘xd1 22.♕xd7† ♕f7 23.♕xf7† ♔xf7 24.♘d6† ♔g6 25.♘xd1± 3 pawns is more than enough for the exchange.) 18.bxc3 ♖h7 19.♘xd6† ♘xd6 20.♖xd6

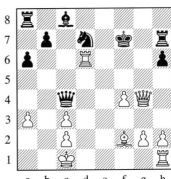

20...♘f8 (20...♘f6 21.♖xf6† ♔xf6 22.♗d4† ♔f7 23.♕h5† ♔f8 24.♕g6 ♖e7 25.♕xh6† ♔e8 26.♕h8† ♔d7 27.♖d1 ♔c7 28.♗e5† ♖xe5 29.♕xe5† ♔b6 30.h4!?+−) 21.♕h5† ♔g8 22.♗d4 ♕f7 23.♕f3 ♗e6 24.♖e1! This is even stronger than the direct alternative. (24.♕g3†!? ♖g7 25.♗xg7 ♕xg7 26.♕xg7† ♔xg7 27.♖e1 is also quite strong.) 24...♕f5 25.g4 ♕f7 26.f5+−

17.♘xe7

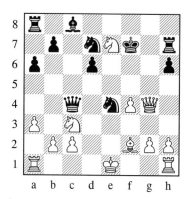

17...♔xe7

17...♖g7 18.♕f5† ♘df6 19.♘xc8 (or 19.♘xe4 should transpose) 19...♖xc8 20.♘xe4 ♕xe4† 21.♕xe4 ♘xe4 22.0-0 ♖xc2 23.♖ac1 ♖d2 24.g3± For once Black almost had the initiative, but now it's over and White's extra pawn is the significant point.

18.♕g6 ♘ef6

If 18...♘df6 then 19.♗h4!+– is even stronger than it is in the main line.

19.♗h4 ♕f7

19...♖f7 20.♖d1! ♔f8 21.♕xh6† ♔g8 22.♖xd6±

20.♕d3→

Black is unlikely to survive the attack.

11.♗f2 ♕c7

The French Super-GM shows good nerves and pretends not to be afraid of the sacrifice on e6; this is easy to explain – Black has no choice.

11...♘c5

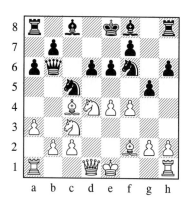

12.♕f3! g4 (12...gxf4 13.0-0! White's threat is now b2-b4. 13...♕c7 14.♕xf4 ♘xe4 15.♘xe4 ♘xe4 16.♗xe6 fxe6 17.♕xe4±) 13.♕e3 ♕xb2 14.0-0↑

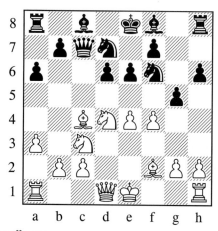

12.♕e2?!

White clearly saw the sacrifice on e6, but probably evaluated it wrongly.

12.♗xe6!

This seems to bring White the advantage. I am quite confident this will very soon be tested over the board.

12...fxe6 13.♘xe6 ♕c4 14.♘xf8 ♖xf8

14...♘xf8 15.♕xd6 ♕e6 16.0-0-0-0+–

15.♕xd6

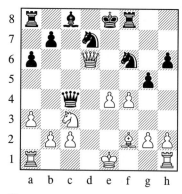

15...a5!

The only move to stay in the game. 15...♕c6 16.♕d4 gxf4 17.e5 ♘g4 18.0-0-0 ♘dxe5 19.♖he1+–

15...♘g4 16.♘d5!

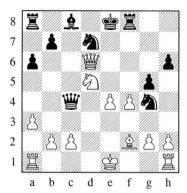

16...♔f7 (16...♖f7 17.♘c7† ♔d8 18.♘e6†
♔e8 19.♗d4+–; 16...♕xe4† 17.♔d2 ♔f7
18.♖ae1 ♘gf6 19.♘xf6 ♘xf6 20.♕c7†+–)
17.♕e7† ♔g8 18.b3! ♕xc2 19.♗d4 ♘de5
20.0-0 ♕xe4 21.♗xe5 ♘xe5 22.♕xe5 ♕xe5
23.fxe5±

16.0-0-0 ♖a6 17.♕d2 gxf4 18.♖he1

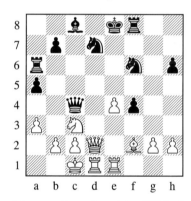

In this complicated position White has great
compensation for the piece. Defending this
position would be very hard for Black.

18...♖e6
18...♘g4 19.e5 ♖e6 20.♘e4, ♕a2? 21.♘d6†
♔d8 22.♕xa5† b6 23.♗h4†+–
19.♗d4 ♘g4 20.♘d5 b6 21.♔b1→

12...♘b6
Not 12...gxf4? due to: 13.♗xe6 fxe6
14.♘xe6 ♕b8 (14...♕a5 15.0-0+–) 15.♗h4
♖g8 16.♘d5 ♔f7 17.0-0! ♔xe6 18.♖xf4 With
a deadly attack.

13.♗b3 gxf4 14.0-0-0

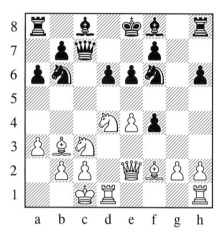

We have reached a very interesting position.
Black is a pawn up, but all White's pieces
are very active and the black knight on b6 is
clearly not a thing of beauty. White needs to
do something fast so that Black is not allowed
to complete his development.

14...♗e7
If 14...♗d7 then 15.g3! is an amazingly
strong computer move! 15...fxg3 16.♗xg3
Black cannot defend properly against the
threat of e4-e5.

15.♖he1!

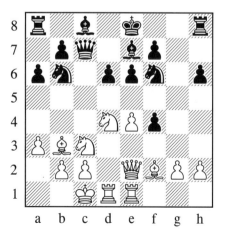

15...♖g8

Black is in trouble:

15...♗d7   16.♘f5!   exf5   17.exf5   ♘c8
18.♗d4+–

15...e5 16.♘f5 ♗xf5 17.exf5 is clearly better for White.

15...♘bd7   16.♗xe6   fxe6   17.♘xe6   ♕b8
18.♗h4 ♘e5 19.♗xf6 f3 (19...♗xf6 20.♕h5†
♘f7 21.e5!+–) 20.gxf3 ♗xf6 21.♘d5 ♗g5†
(21...♗xe6 22.♘xf6† ♔f7 23.f4+–) 22.♘xg5
hxg5 23.♕d2+–

16.g3↑ fxg3 17.♗xg3

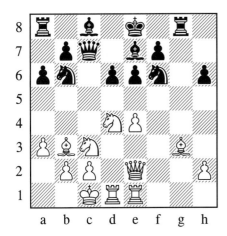

17...e5

An ugly move to have to make, but there was nothing better: 17...♘g4 18.♘f5! As in many other lines, this move destroys Black's defence. 18...♘e5 (18...exf5 19.exf5 ♘e5 20.♕h5! ♖g7 21.♘e4+–) 19.♘xe7 ♕xe7 20.♖d4 With a crushing advantage.

18.♘f5 ♗xf5 19.exf5+– ♖g7

Black is urgently trying to castle long.

20.♔b1

Interesting was 20.♗f2!? keeping the black king in the centre. 20...♘bd7 (20...0-0-0

21.♗xf7!±) 21.♖g1 ♖xg1 22.♖xg1 ♕c6
23.♗h4↑

20...0-0-0 21.♗f2 ♖d7?!

A blunder or perhaps Maxime evaluated his position as much worse and just wanted to search for practical chances in a bad position but with opposite-coloured bishops.
If 21...♘bd7 then White has a strong attach after: 22.♘d5 ♘xd5 23.♗xd5 ♘f6 24.♗h1→

22.♗xb6 ♕xb6 23.♗xf7 ♔b8 24.♗b3

White has a comfortable advantage, but it is still not easy to win.

24...♖c7 25.♖d3 ♖g5 26.♖f1 h5 27.h3

White doesn't want to hurry with the exchange of knights, but I think it needed to be done sooner or later, so maybe now would be a good moment for: 27.♘d5 ♘xd5 28.♗xd5±

27...♖g1 28.♖xg1 ♕xg1† 29.♔a2 ♕g5 30.♕f3 h4

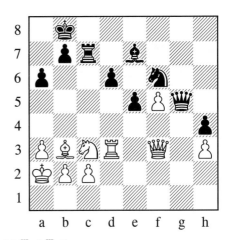

31.♖e3 ♖c5

31...♖c6 was a better move even though the position would remain very unpleasant to defend.

32.♘e4

Finally White decided to exchange knights.

32...♘xe4 33.♖xe4

White's idea is to combine threats against Black's king with the prospect of pushing the f-pawn forward.

33...♗f6 34.♖b4! ♕g7

34...♖b5 35.♖xb5 axb5 36.♕d3+–

35.♕d3 ♕d7

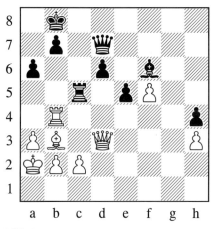

36.♖b6?

Why not just take on a6!? The only explanation is time trouble, so the next few moves should not be judged too harshly: 36.♕xa6 e4 37.♖xb7†! (37.♗e6 ♕c7 38.c3+–) 37...♕xb7 38.♕xd6† ♕c7 39.♕xf6+– White is totally winning.

36...♖c6 37.♖b4 ♕c7 38.♕d5 ♔a7 39.♖g4 ♕c8 40.♕e4 d5

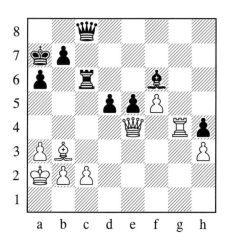

41.♕xd5??

A shocking move. Maybe White was not sure if he had actually made 40 moves... To give away the passed pawn on f5 is a bad decision, especially when you spot the forced win: 41.♗xd5 ♖xc2 42.♕e3†! ♕c5 43.♕b3+–

41...♕xf5 42.c3?!

42.♕d2± would keep the last sliver of White's advantage.

42...♕f2 43.♕f7 e4 44.♖g7 ♕b6 45.♖g2 e3

And now only Black could fight for the advantage, but a draw was agreed.

½–½

GAME 14
▷ **I. Nepomniachtchi (2711)**
▶ **S. Mamedyarov (2765)**
8th World Team Championship, Ningbo
Round 4, 20.07.2011 **[C02]**
Annotated by Arkadij Naiditsch

Black chooses the relatively rare 6...f6!? against the Advance French, which in my opinion is interesting and at least deserves attention and further practical testing. White reacted poorly with 8.dxe5?!, instead of the clearly superior 8.♘xe5, and soon got into trouble. But later Black made a few inaccurate moves which enabled his opponent to equalize.

1.e4 e6 2.d4 d5 3.e5 c5 4.c3 ♘c6 5.♘f3 ♗d7 6.♗e2

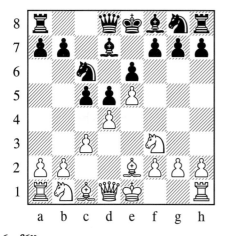

6...f6!?

If White is given time to develop his pieces while keeping his strong pawn centre, then he will have good chances for an opening advantage. Here are two recent examples where Black played more slowly and failed to equalize in the opening:

6...♘ge7 7.♘a3 cxd4 8.cxd4 ♘f5 9.♘c2 ♘b4 10.♘xb4 ♗xb4† 11.♔f1 ♗e7 12.g3± Jakovenko – Ponkratov, Russia 2011.

6...♖c8 7.0–0 cxd4 8.cxd4 ♘ge7 9.a3 ♘f5 10.b4 ♕b6 11.♗b2 h5 12.♔h1 ♗e7 13.♘c3 g5 14.♘a4 ♕d8 15.♘c5± Adams – Polzin, Bundesliga 2010.

7.0–0 fxe5 8.dxe5?!

Clearly the wrong choice. White was probably surprised by his opponent's opening choice and tried to steer the game into 'unknown waters', but the knight on f3 is definitely not a hero and should have been exchanged off.

More logical would have been: 8.♘xe5 ♘xe5 9.dxe5 ♕c7

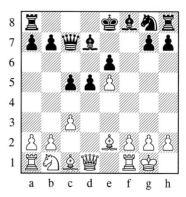

10.c4! It is important to disrupt Black's smooth wall of central pawns. (10.♖e1 0–0–0 11.♘d2 h6 12.♗g4 ♘e7 13.c4 ♔b8 14.cxd5 ♘xd5 15.♘c4 ♗c6∞) 10...d4 (10...♗c6 11.cxd5 exd5 12.♗g4) 11.♗d3 0–0–0 12.f4 ♘e7 13.♘d2 ♘c6 14.♘e4 ♗e7 15.a3±

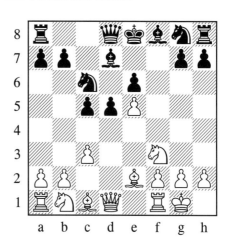

8...♘h6!?

Creative and strong play by Black.

9.c4

9.b4!? cxb4 10.c4 d4 transposes to 10.b4!? in the following note.

9...d4 10.♗xh6?!

Swapping off this important bishop was not a wise decision. The doubled h-pawns are not a big problem for Black, and the exchange on h6 also creates an ideal square for the black bishop on g7.

10.♖e1 is playable but a little slow, and Black soon obtains a good position after completing development: 10...♘f7 11.♘bd2 ♗e7 12.♘e4 0–0 13.♗f4 ♕c7 14.♗g3 ♘h6 15.♘d6 ♘f5 16.♘xf5 ♖xf5 17.♗d3 ♖f7 18.a3∞

As we will see in the game, White's position is strategically dangerous, and it will not take much for him to slip into serious difficulties. In such situations the best practical strategy is often to play for complications, which could have been achieved by the following remarkable idea:
10.b4!?

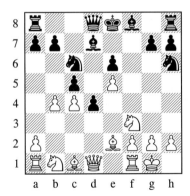

10...cxb4
10...♘xb4? 11.♗xh6 gxh6 12.♘xd4! cxd4
13.♗h5† ♔e7 14.♕xd4±
11.♘bd2

Keeping the position complicated.
11.♘xd4?! ♘xd4 12.♕xd4 ♗c6∓ is worse.
11...♗e7 12.♘b3 ♘f5 13.♘bxd4 ♘fxd4
14.♘xd4 ♘xe5 15.♗h5† ♘g6
15...g6 16.♖e1 ♘c6 17.♘xc6 ♗xc6
18.♕g4!↑
16.♖e1∞
White should have just enough compensation in this position, although Black's position remains fully playable.

10...gxh6

Now White must worry about the simple plan of ...♗g7, ...0–0 and ...♕c7 followed by taking on e5 with a winning position.

11.♘fd2!?

White decides to give up the e5-pawn immediately in the hope of exploiting his lead in development before Black can get organized.

11...♘xe5 12.♗h5† ♘g6 13.♘e4 ♕e7!

Black responds strongly. The plan is to put the queen on g7 and bishop on e7, followed by castling when everything will be rosy for him.

14.b4!

The best practical chance, searching for activity before Black completes his regrouping.

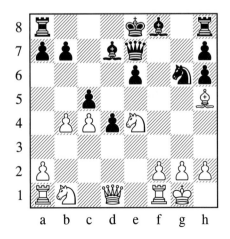

14...cxb4

It would be too much to call this move an objective mistake, but it seems to have been the first step along a path where it became difficult to increase Black's advantage. Perhaps Mamedyarov became overconfident after a supremely successful opening which already yielded him an almost winning position.

14...♕g7 was a reasonable alternative: 15.bxc5 0–0–0 16.♘bd2 ♗c6 17.♕g4 ♔b8 18.♖ab1 e5 19.g3 ♖g8∓

I believe the best practical decision would have been 14...♗c6!?, for instance 15.♘xc5 ♕g5 16.♗f3 ♗xc5 17.bxc5 0–0 18.♗xc6 bxc6 19.g3 ♕xc5 and Black has a clear advantage.

15.c5

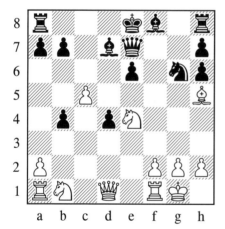

15...♕g7

The most logical and solid move. Black has no reason to allow his king to come under attack in the centre.

15...♗c6?!
   This would have given White unnecessary attacking chances:
16.♘d6†
   White should certainly take the opportunity to prevent his opponent from castling.

16.♘bd2? ♕g7 17.♕g4 0–0–0 18.a3 b3 19.♘xb3 d3 20.♕xe6† ♔b8∓
The preliminary 16.♗xg6†?! does not make much sense: 16...hxg6 17.♘d6† ♔d7 18.♘d2 ♗g7 19.♖e1 ♖af8 20.♘2e4 ♕h4 21.a3 ♗e5 22.g3 ♕h5 23.♕xh5 gxh5 24.axb4∓
16...♔d7 17.♗f3

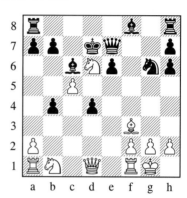

17...♖g8

Some other moves are possible, but in each case White remains very much in the game:
17...e5 18.♘d2 ♘f4 19.♘xb7 ♖g8 20.g3 ♕e6 21.♔h1 ♗xf3† 22.♕xf3 ♘h3 23.♘a5 ♖c8∞
17...♕g7 18.♘xb7 ♖c8 19.♗xc6† ♖xc6 20.♕a4 ♘f4 21.g3 ♘e2† 22.♔g2 ♕e5 23.♘a5 ♕xc5∞
17...♕f6 18.♘d2 ♗xd6 19.cxd6 ♖ac8 20.♗xc6† ♖xc6 21.♕a4 a6 22.♕xb4 b6 23.♘e4 ♕g7 24.g3∞
18.♕xd4 ♗g7 19.♕xb4 ♗xf3 20.gxf3 ♕g5† 21.♔h1 ♖ab8
Both kings are vulnerable, and the game turns out to be balanced.
22.♖d1 ♕f4 23.♘f5† ♔e8 24.♕xf4 ♘xf4 25.♘xg7† ♖xg7 26.♘c3 ♖d8=

16.a3!

A nice idea to stay in the game! White not only improves his position on the queenside by opening lines and/or capturing the pawn on b4, but also prepares to swing his rook from a3 to g3 to attack Black's king in the future.

16...♗e7!

Another good practical decision from Mamedyarov, who has so far been doing everything right. Instead 16...bxa3?! 17.♘xa3 ♗e7 18.♕b3↑ gives White promising counterplay.

17.axb4 0–0 18.♖a3 ♔h8?!

Better was 18...♗c6 19.♖e1 a5!∓. Black's extra pawn, bishop pair and kingside attacking chances should add up to a winning advantage.

19.♖e1 e5 20.♘bd2∓

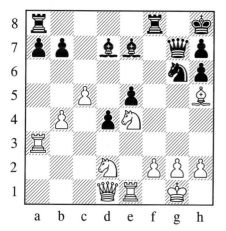

Black's position is still better, but White has managed to stabilize and coordinate his pieces, and the superb knight on e4 gives him reasonable hopes for a brighter future.

20...♗e6 21.♗xg6! hxg6 22.♕a1 ♗d5 23.♖xa7 ♖ac8

23...♖xa7 24.♕xa7 ♕f7 would have preserved a marginal edge for Black.

24.♕a4! g5

Realising that his advantage has evaporated, Black invites the following move repetition.

25.♕d7 ♖cd8 26.♕c7 ♖c8 27.♕d7 ♖cd8 28.♕c7 ♖c8

½–½

GAME 15

▷ **T. Gharamian (2670)**
▶ **Ni Hua (2662)**
Biel Open
Round 7, 25.07.2011 **[C11]**
Annotated by Sebastian Maze

In a French Defence, Gharamian went for a rare line with 11.♘b3. On move 15, Ni Hua played a novelty with 15...a5 which looks risky for Black. The Frenchman playing White reacted badly and had to defend a difficult position. Later Ni Hua missed some good chances. Instead of the mistake 19.♗xc4, I think 19.a4 gives White a good position. In the game, White suffered a lot but finally managed to draw.

1.e4 e6

It's quite difficult to prepare against the Chinese player. He can play many openings, and he plays all of them very fast.

2.d4 d5 3.♘c3 ♘f6 4.e5 ♘fd7 5.f4

The French player chose the line with 5.f4, which is an interesting system against the French Defence. In my opinion, it's more strategic than the 4.♗g5 system.

5...c5 6.♘f3 ♘c6 7.♗e3 cxd4 8.♘xd4 ♗c5 9.♕d2 0–0 10.0–0–0 a6

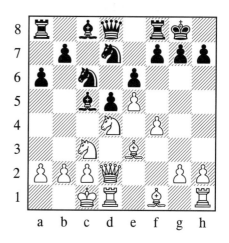

For the moment, we have a well-known position with a lot of theory. Now, it's the first critical moment for Gharamian. He has many choices.

11.♘b3

Tigran Gharamian chose a secondary line that is not so well known; he wanted to surprise his opponent. One of the ideas of this move is to avoid all the lines with ...♗xd4 or ...♘xd4. White wants to keep his knight and control the c5-, a5- and d4-squares.

11.h4 is the main move, as played by Kasparov, Kramnik and Anand.

11.♕f2 ♗xd4 12.♗xd4 b5 13.♗e3 b4 14.♘a4 a5∞ Jakovenko – Ni Hua, Russia-China Match, Taiyuan 2006.

11...♗b4

11...b6 is also playable, but in my opinion it looks weird to play a plan with ...b6 because it is just too slow. 12.h4 ♗b7 13.♖h3 ♖c8 14.a3± Najer – Buhmann, Mainz (rapid) 2008.

12.♗d3 b5 13.g4

13.♖hf1 ♘b6 14.a3 ♗e7 15.♘d4 with a complicated position, Anand – Morozevich, San Luis World Championship Tournament 2005.

13...♘a5 14.♗d4 ♘c4 15.♕f2

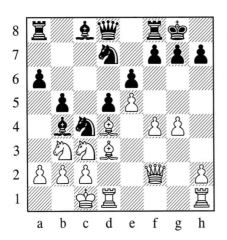

15...a5N

This is the novelty. It looks more direct and faster than 15...♖b8. Black is putting White under pressure, but the b5-pawn will be hanging.

Previously played was: 15...♖b8 16.g5 ♖e8 17.♕h4 ♘f8 18.♖hg1 g6 19.♕f2 a5 With chances for both sides in T. Kosintseva – Xu Yuhua, China-Russia Match, Sochi 2009.

16.a3 ♗e7

Not 16...♗xc3? 17.♗xc3 ♕c7 18.♖hg1 ♖e8 19.♖g3 with a strong attack. Without the dark-squared bishop, Black is paralysed. For example: 19...b4 20.axb4 axb4 21.♗xb4 ♘f8 22.♗xf8 ♖xf8 23.♖h3±

17.♘xb5□

Of course, White had no choice as otherwise his king's defences would be destroyed by ...b5-b4.

17...♗a6 18.♘c3 ♕c7

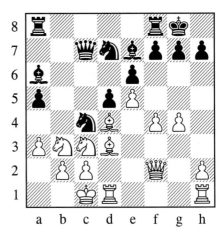

19.♗xc4?!

Why give up this strong bishop? This move is a significant strategic mistake. White's position was good; Black had no threats for the moment, so it was important to keep the bishop for the attack against the black king.

19.a4

This simple move gives White a good edge and secures some space on the queenside.

19...Rfc8 20.Rhg1 Nb8

Or 20...Bb4 21.Rg3 g6 (21...Nxb2 22.Bxh7† Kxh7 23.Rh3† Kg8 24.Qh4±) 22.Bf1 followed by Rh3 and Qh4.

21.g5 Nc6 22.Bxh7†! Kxh7 23.g6† fxg6 24.Qg2 Bf8 25.Qxg6† Kg8 26.Qxe6† Qf7 27.Qxf7† Kxf7 28.Nxd5±

19...Bxc4 20.Nd2 Rab8?

It's the turn of Ni Hua to make a strategic mistake! The best idea was to save this bishop, which is powerful on the a6-f1 diagonal.

20...Ba6 21.f5 Rab8 22.f6 Bc5 23.fxg7 Rfc8 24.Rhf1 Bxf1 25.Rxf1 Kxg7 26.Bxc5 Nxc5 27.Qf6† Kg8 28.Qg5† Kf8 29.Qh6† Kg8= It is a draw by perpetual check.

21.Nxc4 Qxc4 22.Qe2?

Too slow... White needs to put some pressure on the black king.

22.f5

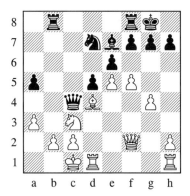

22...Qc7 (22...Bc5 23.Bxc5 Nxc5 24.Qd4 Qxd4 25.Rxd4 Rb7 26.Rhd1 Rc8 27.h4± White has a pleasant advantage in this endgame.) 23.a4 Rb4 24.Rhf1 Bc5 25.Nb5 Bxd4 26.Rxd4 Qxe5 27.Rxb4 axb4 28.Kb1± The position is rather unclear, but it looks easier to play for White.

22...Qc6

The evaluation is changing with every move! Now Black has the advantage and Gharamian will have to defend accurately to stay in the game.

23.Rd3 Rfc8∓ 24.Rf1 Bc5 25.Nd1 Qb5

Step by step, the Chinese player prepares his attack, putting his pieces on the perfect squares.

26.Rf2 Qc4 27.Qe3 Qa2

A very pleasing manoeuvre; the queen comes to a2 via c6-b5-c4! Now White has big problems.

28.Kd2 Nb6

The immediate 28...Bxd4! would have gained a huge advantage: 29.Rxd4 Qb1 30.c3 Nb6∓

29.Ke1

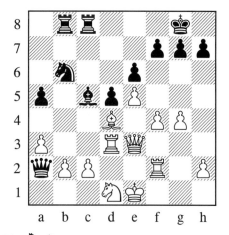

29...Nc4?

After such a fine strategic attack, Ni Hua missed the ultimate finesse – putting his queen on b1.

29...Bxd4! 30.Rxd4
   30.Qxd4 Rc4 31.Qe3 Re4–+
30...Qb1!

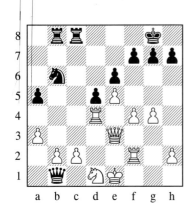

The point! The b1-square is crucial for the black queen, putting pressure on the c2-pawn and also against the king.

31.b3

31.f5 tries to find some counterplay but it's far too slow. 31...♖xc2 32.♕d3 (32.f6 ♖xf2 33.♔xf2 ♘c4 34.♕g5 ♕g6–+ And it's over; Black's pieces are so well placed.) 32...♖c1 33.♕f3 ♖c7 34.♕d3 ♕c1 It's close to zugzwang; there are just no ideas for White and ...♘c4 is coming. 35.♕d2 ♕xd2† 36.♖fxd2 ♘c4 37.♖e2 ♖b3∓

31.c3 ♘c4 32.♕e2 ♘xb2–+

31...♘d7 32.a4

32.♖dd2 ♘c5 33.♕d4 ♘e4∓

32...♖xc2 33.♖xc2 ♕xc2 34.♖d3 ♖c8∓

30.♕c1

Controlling the first rank.

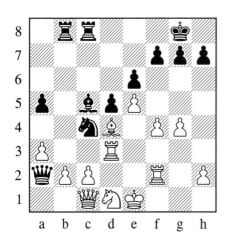

30...♗e7

30...♗xa3?! is a little premature. But I suspect that Black missed this idea during the game, because over the next three moves he didn't play this sacrifice. 31.♖xa3 ♘xa3 32.bxa3 ♖b1 33.♕d2 ♕xa3 34.f5 a4 35.♕a5 With a complicated position.

31.g5?

Gharamian missed the idea too! He had to protect the a3-pawn with 31.♖ff3.

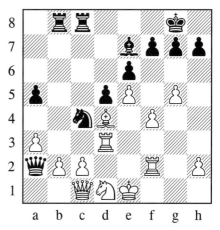

31...g6?

31...♗xa3! would work very well! 32.♖xa3 ♘xa3 33.bxa3 ♖b1 34.♕d2 ♕xa3 35.c3 a4 36.♕a2 ♕b3 37.♕xb3 axb3 38.♖b2 ♖xb2 39.♘xb2 ♖a8∓ With a pleasant endgame for Black with no risk. And it's not so easy for White to coordinate his pieces.

32.♖e2 a4

Of course the sacrifice still worked.

33.♔f2 ♖b7 34.h4 h5 35.♔g2 ♔h7

35...♗c5 was a logical move to exchange bishops and eliminate a protector of the b2-pawn. 36.♖f2 (36.♗c3?? ♗xa3–+) 36...♗xd4 37.♖xd4 ♘xb2∓

36.♖f2 ♖cb8 37.♖df3 ♔g8 38.♖d3

38.f5 is a computer move. 38...exf5 (38...gxf5

39.♕f4 and ♖g3 is coming. It could be dangerous for Black if the knight reached f4.) 39.♖e2 ♘xb2 40.♗xb2 ♖xb2 41.♘xb2 ♖xb2 42.e6 d4 43.exf7† ♔xf7 44.♕d1 ♗c5 Black is OK despite being an exchange down.

38...♗f8 39.♖df3 ♖c8 40.♖d3 ♖cb8

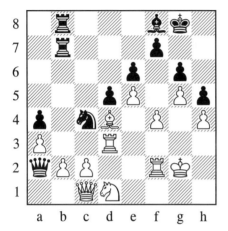

Now the position is about equal; both sides seem to lack a really constructive plan.

41.♖df3 ♖c8 42.♖c3 ♖bc7 43.b4

Gharamian tries to create some play! Now maybe White's position looks better, and Black has to be careful.

43...♗e7 44.♖cf3 ♗f8

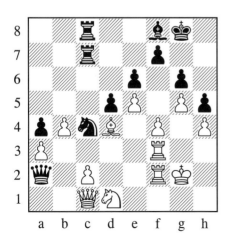

Finally, the French player was happy with a draw! He didn't want to continue the game with this small plus. After 45.♕a1 ♕xa1 46.♗xa1 ♖b7 47.♗d4 ♔g7 48.♖c3 ♖bb8 49.♘e3 ♘xe3† 50.♖xe3 ♖c4 Black should be able to hold the position.
½–½

GAME 16
▷ **I. Nepomniachtchi (2711)**
▶ **A. Onischuk (2675)**
8th World Team Championship, Ningbo
Round 1, 17.07.2011 **[C45]**
Annotated by Borki Predojevic

The Scotch Opening is one of the sharpest openings after 1...e5. Recently it has been played a few times by Ian Nepomniachtchi and this game is one more instance. In the main line he opted for 9.b3!?, a move which hasn't been played so much in the last few years. Black followed the main line by playing 9...a5 (I also look at the moves 9...g6 and 9...♕e6). The first real surprise was White's choice of the rare 11.♕e3!?. Black did not play precisely, and after 14.♗e2!N and 16.0–0 he was faced with problems.

Despite the fact that White won this game in fine style, the line with 11.♕e3!? should not be dangerous for Black. He can obtain a decent position by playing 13...♕b4!†, 14...♕b4† or even 15...♗e7. Against 13...♕b4!† I analyse the new move 14.♔d1!N, but even this improvement does not promise White any advantage.

1.e4 e5 2.♘f3 ♘c6 3.d4 exd4 4.♘xd4 ♘f6 5.♘xc6 bxc6 6.e5 ♕e7 7.♕e2 ♘d5 8.c4 ♘b6

This is the most flexible continuation. The other popular move is 8...♗a6.

9.b3!?

In the last few years move this move has rarely been played at the highest level. For some time 9.♘c3 has been the main line here, but 9...♗b7 has become a popular reply this year, and up to now White hasn't found a way to get an advantage.

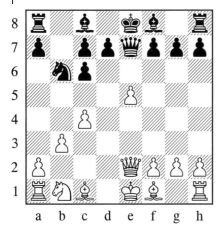

9...a5
The main option.

A typical move for the Scotch is:
9...g6!? 10.♗b2 ♗g7 11.g3
White goes for the double fianchetto.
11.♘d2 0–0 12.0–0–0 is another idea, but I don't think this is a good plan for White in this concrete position. After 12...a5 Black's attack is faster.
11...0–0

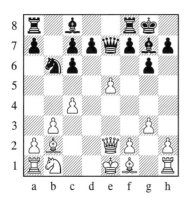

12.♘d2
12.♗g2 is less precise. The correct reply is: 12...♖e8! 13.0–0 ♗xe5 14.♘c3 ♗b7

(14...♗xc3 15.♕xe7 ♖xe7 16.♗xc3 a5 17.a4 is good for White; 14...♗a6 15.♖ae1 ♕f8 16.♘e4 gives White a powerful attack) 15.♖ae1 d6 16.♕d2 ♕f8 17.f4 ♗g7 18.♘e4 ♗xb2 19.♕xb2 ♘d7 The position is rather unclear, but I slightly prefer Black.
12...♖e8
12...d6 13.♗g2 ♗b7 14.0–0 dxe5 15.a4⩲
13.f4 d6
13...f6 14.exf6 ♕f7 15.fxg7 ♖xe2†
16.♗xe2±
14.♗g2 dxe5

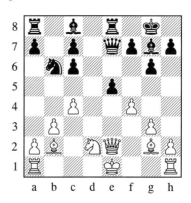

15.0–0
15.0–0–0!? is another option.
15...♘d7 16.f5 ♘f6 17.fxg6 hxg6 18.♖ae1
White has reasonable compensation. I think the idea with 9...g6 is interesting and deserves to be played more in the future.

9...♕e6 10.♗b2 a5

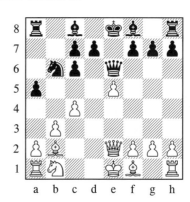

Here White can play Vallejo's idea:

11.♕c2! ♗b4† 12.♘d2 a4 13.♗d3 ♕h6

13...axb3 14.axb3 ♖xa1† 15.♗xa1 d6 16.0–0 dxe5 is met by 17.♘f3 f6 18.♗xh7! f5 19.♗xe5 ♖xh7 20.♗xc7 ♘a8 21.♗f4! with a strong attack for White.

14.♖d1 axb3 15.axb3 ♖a2 16.0–0 0–0

16...♗a3 17.♗xa3 ♖xc2 18.♗xc2±

17.♕b1 ♖a5 18.♘f3 d5

This was Vallejo Pons – Leko, Linares 2004. Now White should play:

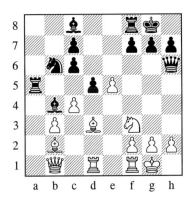

19.exd6!N cxd6

19...♗xd6 doesn't work. White has 20.♗c1 ♕h5 21.b4 ♖f5 (on 21...♗g4 22.♗xh7† ♔h8 23.♖xd6 ♗xf3 24.bxa5 ♕g4, White has 25.♖g6! with a winning position) 22.c5 ♖xf3 23.cxd6 ♖f6 24.dxc7 ♘d5 25.b5 ♘c3 26.♕b3! ♘xd1 27.♖xd1 cxb5 28.♗a3+– The c-pawn will decide the game.

20.♘d4

White has a clear advantage. Black must avoid:

20...♖h5?! 21.♗c1 ♕f6 22.♗e2! ♖h4 23.♘xc6+–

10.♗b2 a4 11.♕e3!?

This rare move was probably a surprise for Onischuk. White is preparing ♗d3 and 0–0.

The main line goes:

11.♘d2 axb3 12.axb3 ♖xa1† 13.♗xa1 ♕a3 14.♕d1 ♗b4 15.♗d3 ♕a5 16.♔e2 d6!

According to theory, this is fine for Black. Worse is 16...0–0 17.♕c2 d6 18.♗d4!, when White threatens ♖a1. After 18...♗xd2 19.♕xd2 ♕a3 20.♕b2 ♕xb2† 21.♗xb2 dxe5 22.♖a1 ♗d7 23.♖a7 ♖c8 24.♗c3± White had a strong initiative in S. Zhigalko – Cs. Balogh, Aix-les-Bains 2011.

17.♘f3

17.♕c2 dxe5 18.♗b2∞

17...♗g4 18.h3 ♗xf3† 19.♔xf3 dxe5∞

11...axb3

On 11...♕e6 it is possible to play 12.♗e2!? ♗b4† 13.♘d2± followed by 0–0.

11...♕b4†?! 12.♗c3 ♕c5 13.♕xc5 ♗xc5 14.♗d3±

11...d5!? 12.♗e2!N

12.♗d3 ♕c5! leads to a decent position for Black: 13.♗d4 (after 13.♕g3 axb3 14.axb3 ♖xa1 15.♗xa1 ♕a5† 16.♗c3 ♗b4 Black has the initiative) 13...♕a5† 14.♔e2 c5 15.♗c3 ♕a6 16.cxd5 (16.♕g3 d4 17.♗b2 g6 18.♖e1 ♗g7 19.♔f1 0–0 20.♘d2 ♕a5 is okay for bBlack) 16...♘xd5 17.♕e4 ♕b7⇄ Black has a good game. His next move could be ...g6 intending ...♗f5.

12...axb3 13.axb3 ♖xa1 14.♗xa1

We have transposed into the game.

12.axb3 ♖xa1 13.♗xa1

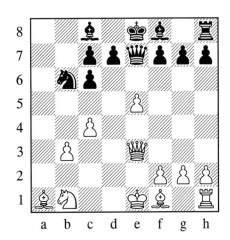

13...d5!?

In my opinion this natural move is not best. Black should play:

13...♕b4†!

Probably Nepomniachtchi had analysed this position and prepared a new move:

14.♔d1!N

White will aim to finish his development with ♘d2, ♔c2 and ♗d3. However, Black should not be unhappy with the position.

Practice has seen the weak 14.♕c3? ♘a4! 15.♕xb4 ♗xb4† 16.♔d1 ♘c5 17.♔c2 d6 and Black was clearly better in Shandrina – S. Vajda, Szeged 2006.

After 14.♘d2 ♕a3! 15.♗c3 ♗c5 Black is better.

14...♗c5

The manoeuvre 14...♘a4 15.♔c2 ♘c5 is not so strong now. After 16.♘d2 ♗e7 17.♗c3 ♕b7 18.f4 0–0 (18...d6 19.exd6 cxd6 20.♗xg7 ♗f5† 21.♔c1 ♖g8 22.♗f6 ♘e6 23.♗b2± should be better for White) 19.f5 White has secured his king and taken space on the kingside, and his position is preferable.

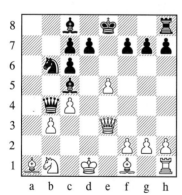

15.♕g3

The pawn sacrifice with 15.♕c3 ♕xc3 (15...0–0 16.♕xb4 ♗xb4 17.♘d3 d6 18.♔c2 ♘d7 19.exd6 cxd6 20.♗c3 ♗c5∞) 16.♘xc3 ♗xf2 17.♘e4 ♗h4 18.♔c2 0–0 19.♗d3 looks interesting. White has compensation, but only enough for equality.

15...0–0 16.♔c2

16.♘d2 ♕a3 17.♗c3 ♗b4! would be okay for Black.

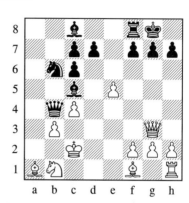

16...♕e1!

This is Black's best option.

16...♕a5?! 17.♗c3 ♗b4 18.♗d3 ♗xc3 (18...♗a6 19.e6!) 19.♘xc3±

16...d5 17.exd6 ♗f5† 18.♗d3 ♗xd3† 19.♕xd3 ♖a8 (19...♗xd6 20.♕d4 f6 21.♗c3 ♕c5 22.♕xc5 ♗xc5 23.f3 is slightly better for White) 20.♕c3 ♕xc3† 21.♘xc3 cxd6 (21...♗xd6 22.♗b2 gives White a small advantage thanks to his better structure) 22.♘e4 ♗b4 (after 22...♖a2† 23.♔b1 ♖e2 24.♘xc5 dxc5 25.♖d1 f5! 26.♗c3! ♖xf2 27.♗a5 ♘xc4 28.bxc4 ♖xg2 29.♖d2 the endgame is better for White) 23.♗c3 ♗xc3 24.♔xc3 White has a small plus.

17.f4 ♗f2 18.♕d3 d5 19.♗c3 ♕e3 20.♕xe3

20.g3?! ♕c5∓

20...♗xe3 21.♘d2 ♗c5

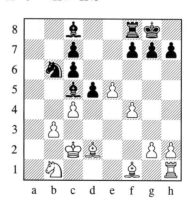

Black has a nice game. For example, 22.cxd5 is strongly met by 22...♘xd5! 23.♗d3 ♗e6 24.♖c1 ♖b8 and White has problems with the knight on b1.

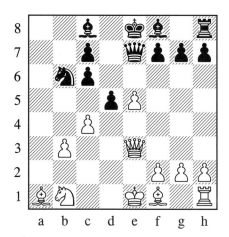

14.♗e2!N

A strong and natural novelty. White continues with his development, while Black has problems developing his kingside.

14.exd6 ♕xe3† 15.fxe3 cxd6 led to an equal game in Gillen – Berry, Toulon 1993.

14...♕c5

An alternative was:
14...♕b4† 15.♘d2
  15.♕c3? dxc4
15...dxc4 16.bxc4 ♕a3
  16...♕c5 17.♕c3 0–0 18.0–0±
17.♕xa3 ♗xa3
  In the endgame Black hopes to use the b4-square for bishop and to attack on the c4-pawn.
18.♗d3 ♔e7 19.♔e2 c5 20.♘f1 g6 21.♘e3
  White has secured his c-pawn, but Black still keeps good chances for equality.
21...♗b7 22.♖b1 ♗b4 23.f4 ♖a8 24.♗b2
  24.♗c2 h5 25.g3 ♖a2⇄
24...♘a4⇄

15.♕c3!

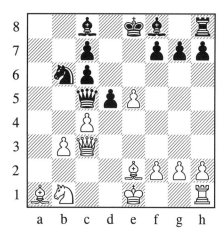

15...♕b4?!

This is a critical moment, and the move played is a strategic mistake. Black loses important time for his development and also the exchange of queens doesn't help him here.

More natural was:
15...♗e7 16.0–0 0–0 17.♖c1
  17.♘d2 ♗f5 18.♘f3 dxc4 19.♘d4 ♗g6 20.bxc4 ♖a8⇄ gives Black good play.
  Black now has to decide how to react to White's obvious threat of 18.cxd5. Fortunately he has a really beautiful resource:
17...♗f5 18.cxd5 ♖a8!!⇄
  This is the key move. Black threatens ...♖xa1, so White cannot take on c5.
19.g4
  19.d6 ♕xc3 20.♘xc3 cxd6 21.exd6 ♗xd6 22.♗f3 ♗a3 23.♖e1 ♖c8=
19...♗g6 20.d6 ♕xc3 21.♘xc3 cxd6 22.exd6 ♗xd6 23.♗f3 ♗a3 24.♖e1 ♖c8
  Black is very close to equality.

16.0–0± ♕xc3 17.♗xc3 ♗e6 18.♘d2 ♗e7 19.f4!?

White is trying to use his lead in development. This is not the most precise plan, but it's a very brave decision by Nepomniachtchi.

Another option was the calm 19.♖a1 ♔d7 20.♗d3 g6 21.♔f1± with a slight plus for White thanks to his better structure.

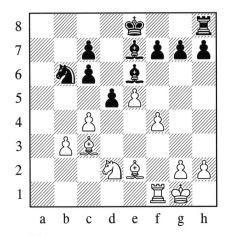

19...f5?!

A dubious move. Black wants to stop the advance of the white kingside pawns, but this gives White the chance to open the centre and activate his pieces.

The right continuation was 19...♗c5†! 20.♔h1 0–0 21.f5 ♗c8 22.g4 ♖e8⇄ and Black has counterplay. 23.♘f3 (23.cxd5?! cxd5 [23...♘xd5 24.♗b2± intending ♘c4] 24.♘f3 ♗b7 gives Black the initiative) 23...dxc4 24.bxc4 ♗a6 25.♗a5 ♖a8 26.♔g2 ♘xc4 27.♗xc4 ♗xc4 28.♖c1 ♖xa5 29.♖xc4= The game will end as a draw.

19...0–0 20.f5 ♗c5† 21.♔h1 ♗d7 22.g4 ♖a8 23.♖a1± looks better for White.

20.exf6! gxf6 21.♖e1 ♔d7

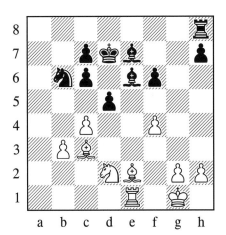

22.♗d3±/±

After having opened the centre, White's pieces are now attacking the black kingside weaknesses. It is very hard for Black to find any counterplay.

22...h5

On 22...h6 White can play 23.♖a1±/±.

23.♗d4!?

I like this move. White threats c4-c5 and if Black plays ...c5 himself, the white bishop will switch to the h4-d8 diagonal.

23.♗g6!?± also gives White a reasonable advantage.

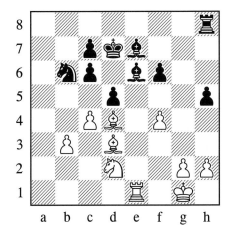

23...c5 24.♗f2 d4

This turns out in White's favour and increases his advantage.

More stubborn was 24...dxc4! 25.bxc4 ♖a8. Here White has several options, one of them being 26.f5 ♗f7 27.♗h4 ♖a3 28.♗e2 ♔d8 29.♘e4 with advantage to White.

25.♗h4 ♖f8 26.♘e4±

Finally, the position is clear. White has a huge advantage. His main threat is to attack the black pawns on f6 and h5. The black knight is out of game.

26...♘c8

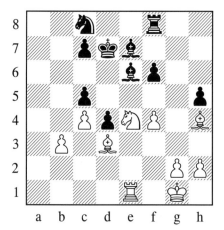

27.♗c2! ♘a7

After this move White will win the h5-pawn.

27...♔c6 would avoid losing the pawn, but after 28.♘g3 ♗f7 29.♗d1 ♖h8± Black is very passive.

28.♘g3 ♘c6 29.♘xh5 f5

29...♘b4 30.♗e4 ♗g4 31.♘g7 ♗d8 32.h3 is also bad for Black.

30.♗xe7 ♘xe7

31.♘g7! ♗g8 32.h4+–

White has won the pawn, and along with his material advantage he is also positionally superior.

**32...♖f7 33.♘e6 ♔d6 34.b4! cxb4 35.c5†
♔d7 36.♘xd4 ♖f8 37.♖d1**

Black resigned here. 37...♗d5 38.♔f2 doesn't give him any chances.

1–0

GAME 17
▷ **S. Karjakin (2788)**
▶ **V. Kramnik (2781)**
64th Russian Championship, Moscow
Round 3, 10.08.2011 [C67]
Annotated by Borki Predojevic

The Berlin variation of the Ruy Lopez is very popular at the highest level. This game was played between Karjakin, who is an expert on the Berlin with White and Kramnik who is an expert on the black side. The game went into the main line, where Black decided to play the 10...b6 line which became popular at the start of this year. Karjakin had prepared the novelty 11.a4!?N. His idea was to provoke a blockade on the queenside before he started his play on the kingside. After 11...a5 White opted for the dynamic 12.g4 and 13.♘g5. Kramnik chose 13...♗e8 as his defence, but the alternative 13...♔e8 also deserves attention.

In a very interesting and typical game for the Berlin, White was preparing the f5-break, while Black played normal plans for positions where his king goes to c8. Black's position was fine until he made a mistake with 23...♗c8? (instead 23...♗c6! would have given him a good game). After that, White was better and he found a clever way to increase his advantage with the strong pawn sacrifice 30.e6!. In mutual time-trouble both players played a few imprecise moves, but after 39...c6? Kramnik was unable to hold the position.

The 10...b6!? line is playable for Black and I

am sure there will be more high-level games in this variation.

1.e4 e5 2.♘f3 ♘c6 3.♗b5 ♘f6

This is the Berlin Defence, one of the most popular variations of the Ruy Lopez. It became popular after the 2000 Kasparov – Kramnik match in London. Kasparov was unable to win a single game as White in this variation which is the main reason why many people use the "Berlin wall" as an alias for this defence. Today, this defence can be played in many different ways with both colours.

4.0–0 ♘xe4 5.d4 ♘d6 6.♗xc6 dxc6 7.dxe5 ♘f5 8.♕xd8† ♔xd8 9.♘c3

9...♗d7

With this move Black prepares a plan connected with ...♔c8, ...b7-b6 and ...♔b7. Besides the game move, Black has a few alternatives and one of them is 9...♘e7, which delays the decision about where the king will go.

10.h3

Practice has shown that this is White's most useful move. In almost every position White needs this move and the main advantage is that he still has not decided which set-up he will choose (with b3 and ♗b2 or ♗f4 and ♖ad1).

If 10.b3 then Black can immediately play 10...♔c8, without fearing 11.g4?! ♘e7 12.♘g5?! when the g4-pawn is hanging and 12...♗xg4∓ leads to a better position for Black.

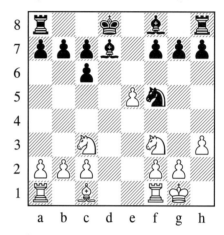

10...b6

Lately, this line was played twice by Magnus Carlsen. Black's idea remains the same: he prepares to transfer the king with ...♔c8-b7, but this move order is more precise than the alternative 10...♔c8.

10...♔c8

Now the best option for White is 11.g4 ♘e7 12.♘g5↑ and according to theory, White has the better prospects. For many years theory considered 10...h6 to be essential, with next ...♔c8 and possibly ...b7-b6 and ...♔b7. However the most common plan with White is:

11.b3

In the last game between the same opponents, Kramnik tried:

11...c5

11...♔c8 12.♗b2 b6 13.♖ad1 ♘e7 14.♖d2 c5 15.♖fd1 ♗e6 is another line which is popular at the highest level.

Now Kramnik faced another interesting novelty:

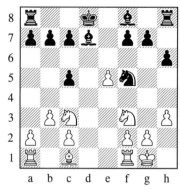

12.♘d5!?N c6 13.♘f4 g5 14.♗b2

14.♘h5 was also possible.

14...♖g8

Interesting is 14...gxf4!? 15.e6 ♗g7 16.♗xg7 ♘xg7 17.exd7 ♔xd7 18.♘e5† ♔e7 and Black's king will be safe in the centre. After 19.♖fe1 ♘e6 20.♘d3 ♔f6 21.♖e4 ♖hg8 22.♔f1 f3 23.g3⩲ the position looks unclear, but Black has to be more careful in order to avoid trouble.

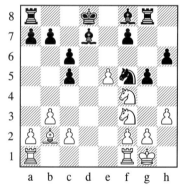

15.e6! ♗xe6

15...fxe6 16.♘h5 ♗e7 17.♖ad1↑

16.♖ad1† ♔c7 17.♘xe6† fxe6 18.g4 ♗g7 19.♗xg7 ♘xg7 20.♘e5⩲

White had strong compensation in Karjakin – Kramnik, Monaco (blindfold) 2011; Black was unable to save the game.

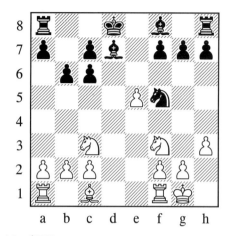

11.a4!?N

A typical plan is:

11.b3 ♔c8 12.♗b2

This gives Black a better position than in the variation after 10...h6. Here he is not obliged to play ...h6 and he can continue with:

12...h5

Black should not have any problems. His set-up is better as the b2-bishop looks passive, since White does not have time to create pressure in the centre (by doubling rooks on the d-line) or on the kingside. 12...♗e7 13.g4 ♘h4 14.♘xh4 ♗xh4 15.♖ad1 h5 16.f3 hxg4 17.hxg4 c5 also looks OK for Black.

In this position, White continued with:

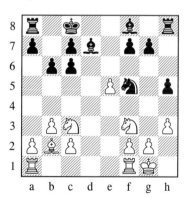

13.g3

With the idea of preventing ideas with ...h5-h4, which would neutralize White's extra pawn on the kingside.

13.♘e4 ♗e7 14.♘fg5 would not give White an initiative. After the calm 14...♗e8 15.♖ad1 ♖h6!⇄ Black stops White's threats and prepares ...♖g6. Black has a nice game.

13...♗e7 14.♖ad1 a5 15.a4 ♖e8

Black already had a good position. The game continued:

16.♖d3?! c5 17.♘d5 c4! 18.♖c3 ♗c5 19.♔h2
19.♖xc4 ♗c6 20.♖d1 ♖d8∓

19...♗c6 20.bxc4 ♗xa4 21.♖a1 ♗c6

Black had a huge advantage in Smeets – Carlsen, Wijk aan Zee 2011.

A central strategy with the set-up 11.♗f4 ♔c8 12.♖ad1 does not lead to any advantage for White. After the normal 12...h6 Black transposes to a position from the 10...h6 line, but with the big difference that White has not been able to use the plan with b2-b3 and ♗b2, which is the most dangerous after 10...h6. One top game continued: 13.♗h2 a5 14.g4 The only active plan in this set-up. 14...♘e7 15.♘d4 h5! 16.e6 fxe6 17.♖fe1 hxg4 18.hxg4 ♖h6 19.g5 ♖h5 20.♘xe6 ♗xe6 21.♖xe6 ♖xg5† 22.♔f1 ♖f5† White was fighting for a draw in Vachier Lagrave – Carlsen, Wijk aan Zee 2011.

11.♖d1

In two games Black reacted with:

11...♔c8

An alternative is 11...♗e7N.

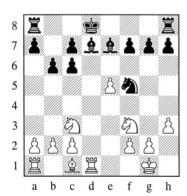

12.♘g5 ♗xg5 13.♗xg5† ♔c8 White took his opponent's dark-squared bishop, however now Black is able to play ...c5 with a good game. 14.g4 looks like the best option for White, but after 14...h6 15.♗f4 (15.e6 fxe6 16.♗f4 ♘e7 17.♗e5 ♖g8 is OK for Black) 15...♘e7⇄ Black should be satisfied with his position; he will play ...h5 plus ...c5 and ...♗c6.

The critical move now is:

12.g4

12.♖d3 is imprecise. Now Black has the nice idea 12...h6 13.b3 ♘e7 and White is unable to occupy the d-file in time since 14.♗b2 is met by the logical 14...♗f5!. After 15.♖d2 c5 16.♘e2 ♘g6 (16...♔b7 was another option. On 17.♘g3 ♗e6 18.♘h5 Black can play 18...g5∞ with the idea of putting the knight on c6.) 17.♘g3 ♗e6 18.♘h5 ♖g8 19.c4 ♗e7 20.♘h2 (If 20.g4 then Black can react by playing 20...♔b7 21.♗g2 a6∞ with the idea ...b5.) 20...♗g5! 21.♖e2 ♔b7 Black had a fine position in Bromberger – Cs.Balogh, Austria (tch) 2011.

12...♘e7 13.♘g5

Now Black played a move which is not so typical for the Berlin.

13...f5!

An alternative is 13...♗e8 14.f4 h5 15.♔g2 ♘d5∞.

14.e6 ♗e8

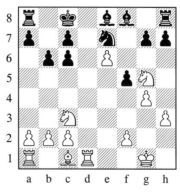

Now there is a split:

a) 15.♔g2

Black should react with:

15...h6 16.♘f3

If 16.♘f7?! then 16...♗xf7 17.exf7 g5! intending ...♖h7.

16...fxg4

16...g5 is also good.

17.hxg4 g5

The position looks good for Black; White's pawn on e6 is blocked and soon it will be a target for the black pieces.

18.b3 ♗g7 19.♗b2 c5

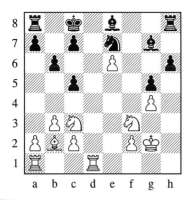

20.♖d3

Worse is: 20.♖e1 ♗c6 21.♔g3 (21.♘d5 ♘xd5 22.♗xg7 ♖h7 23.♗e5 ♔b7∓) 21...♖f8 22.♘d2 (22.♖e3?? ♖xf3† 23.♖xf3 ♗e5† 24.♔g2 ♘g6–+) 22...h5! 23.gxh5 (On 23.f3 h4† 24.♔h3 ♔b7 25.♘a4 Black has the nice 25...♖ad8! 26.♗xg7 [26.♖ad1 ♗xb2 27.♘xb2 ♗xf3 28.♘xf3 ♖xf3† 29.♔h2 ♖xd1 30.♖xd1 ♖e3–+ is also lost for White.] 26...♖xd2 27.♗xf8 ♘g6–+) 23...♘f4 24.f3 ♘f5† Black has a strong attack.

20...♘g6

20...h5!?

21.♔g3 ♘f4 22.♖e3 ♗g6

White can hold the e-pawn with:

23.♘a4 ♗xb2 24.♘xb2

But this doesn't solve his problems after:

24...♗xc2 25.e7 ♔b7 26.♘e1

26.♘e5?! ♖ae8 27.♖c1 ♗g6–+

26.♖c1 ♗g6∓

26...♗h7! 27.♘g2

This looks like White's best, but after:

27...♘d5 28.♖e5 ♘b4 29.♖h1 ♘c6 30.♖e6 ♘d4

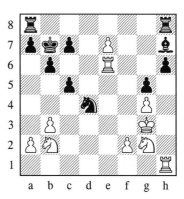

31.♖ee1

31.♖exh6 is met by: 31...♗e4!! 32.f3 (32.♖1h5 ♖xh6 33.♖xh6 ♘e2† 34.♔h3 ♖e8–+ and White is losing the e-pawn) 32...♖xh6 33.♖xh6 ♗xf3–+ The e-pawn will soon drop.

31...♗g6 32.f4 gxf4† 33.♘xf4 ♗f7∓/∓

Black is on top.

b) 15.♖d3 leads to an equal game after: 15...h6 16.♘f7 (16.♘f3 g5∞) 16...♗xf7 17.exf7 fxg4 18.♗f4 g5 19.♗h2 ♖h7 20.♖ad1 ♘d5 21.♘xd5 cxd5 22.♖xd5 ♖xf7 23.hxg4 ♗c5=

c) White can play the concrete:

15.♘f7 ♗xf7 16.exf7

But Black holds with a strong reply:

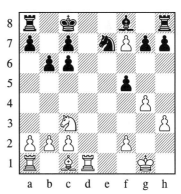

16...♘g6! 17.gxf5 ♘h4 18.♘e4 ♗e7 19.♖d3
♖f8 20.♗f4

20.♗g5 ♗xg5 21.♘xg5 h6 22.♘e6 ♖xf7=

20...♘xf5 21.♖ad1

Intending ♖d7.

21...a5

Now White found an interesting idea with:

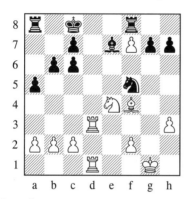

22.♘g3! ♘d6

22...♖xf7 23.♘xf5 ♖xf5 24.♗xc7 b5
25.♗b6∞

23.♗xd6 cxd6 24.♖f3

But it was just enough for a draw after:
24...d5 25.♖e1 ♗f6 26.♖xf6! gxf6 27.♖e7 ♔d8
28.♘f5 ♖c8 29.♖b7 ♖c7 30.♖b8† ♖c8 31.♖b7
♖c7 32.♖b8†

½–½ Navara – Hammer, Wijk aan Zee
2011.

In one game, White played:
11.g4 ♘e7 12.♘g5 ♔e8

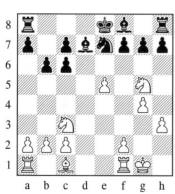

13.♗d2

Critical was: 13.f4 ♘d5 (13...h5 14.f5 hxg4
15.hxg4 ♖h4 16.♖f4 ♘d5 17.♘xd5 cxd5
18.♗e3 c5 19.♖e1 ♗c6 20.♘f3 ♖h8 21.c3∞)
14.♘xd5 cxd5 15.f5 h6 16.♘f3 c5 17.c3 h5
18.♗f4 ♖d8∞ With an unclear game.

13...♖d8!N

After the text move Black shouldn't have any
problems.

In the game Black played: 13...h5 14.f3 f6
(14...♘g6 15.♖ae1 ♖d8 16.e6 ♗xe6 17.♘xe6
fxe6 18.♖xe6† ♔f7 19.♖e2 ♗b4⇄ leads to
a good game for Black. White's kingside
pawns are immobile, while all Black's pieces
in the area are active.) 15.exf6 gxf6 16.♘ge4
♗g7 After 17.♖ae1 ♔f7 18.♘e2!↑, intending
♘f4, White was better in Negi – Hammer,
Dubai (op) 2011.

14.♖ad1 h6 15.♘ge4 h5 16.f3 ♘g6 17.♖fe1
♗c8 18.♔g2 hxg4 19.hxg4 ♗e7 20.♘f6† ♔f8
21.♘h5 c5↑

And next ...♗b7 looks nice for Black. White
is unable to advance his f-pawn and his
e-pawn remains weak.

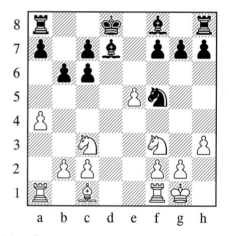

11...a5

A logical reaction, but we will also check the
alternatives:

11...♔c8

White would continue with:

12.a5

The main problem for Black is that ...♔b7 would be met by a5-a6 when the rook on a8 would be out of the game for a long time, while Black has no clear way to win the a6-pawn.

12.♘g5 is not dangerous due to 12...f6⇄.

12.♖d1 a5 13.g4 ♘e7 14.♘g5 f5!∞ leads to a similar position as in the game Navara – Hammer, Wijk aan Zee 2011. The difference is two inserted moves (a4 for White and ...a5 for Black) and this should favour Black since in the abovementioned game after a few concrete moves Black was obliged to play 21...a5, which gave an important tempo to White who then had time to equalize.

12...♗b4

This logical move is met by a strong idea:

13.axb6

13.a6 ♗xc3 14.bxc3 c5⇄

13.♘e4 ♗e6 14.c3 ♗e7 15.♗g5 ♗d5 16.♖fe1 ♗xg5 17.♘fxg5 ♔d7∞

13...cxb6

13...♗xc3? 14.♖xa7!

14.♘a4! ♔b7 15.g4!

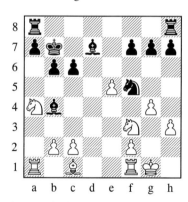

And now Black is obliged to play:

15...♘e7!

15...♘h6 16.♖d1 ♗e6 17.♘d4 ♗d5 18.♗d2 ♗xd2 19.♖xd2± is clearly better for White; the knight is very bad on h6.

16.♖d1 ♗e6 17.c3 b5□ 18.cxb4 bxa4 19.♘d4 ♗d5

White has a lot of moves but best is:

20.♖xa4 h5 21.♘f5!

If 21.g5?! then Black would have good chances to survive by playing 21...♖hd8 22.♖a3 ♗e6 23.♔g2 ♖d5⇄. For example, 24.♖dd3 ♘g6 25.f4 ♖ad8 26.♘xe6 fxe6 27.♖xd5 ♘h4† 28.♔f2 cxd5 29.♔e2 a6⇄ is good for Black.

21...♘g6 22.♘d6† ♔b8 23.♖xd5 cxd5 24.♘xf7 ♖c8 25.♗g5±

With advantage to White.

11...h6 12.a5 ♗b4 is again met by 13.axb6! cxb6 14.♘a4 ♔c7 15.g4!↑ with strong pressure and an advantage for White.

12.g4 ♘e7 13.♘g5

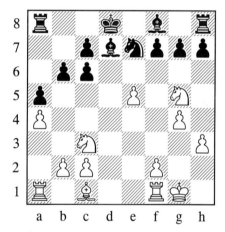

13...♗e8!?

It is very hard to evaluate this move. It is a normal defensive move in the Berlin, but in this position it looks passive. Now White can easily play f2-f4 and there is no pressure on his pawns.

An alternative was:

13...♔e8

Now the position is different from Negi – Hammer, Dubai (op) 2011 – a4 and ...a5 are inserted. White can continue with the typical:

14.f4

On 14.e6 Black has: 14...fxe6! (14...♗xe6 15.♗f4 ♖c8 16.♖fe1 ♗d5 17.♖ad1⩱) 15.♖e1 ♘d5 16.♘xd5 cxd5 17.♘xe6 ♗xe6 18.♖xe6† ♔d7 19.♖e5 c6⇄ With a good game.

14.♔g2?! is slow. 14...h5 15.f3 (15.♔g3?! f6!↑) 15...♘g6 16.♖e1 ♗e7↑ Black is doing well.

The critical position arises after:

14...h5

14...♘d5 15.♘xd5 cxd5 16.f5 h6 17.♘f3 c5 18.c3 h5 19.♗f4 hxg4 20.hxg4 ♗e7 21.♔g2↑

15.f5☐ hxg4 16.hxg4 ♖h4 17.♖f4

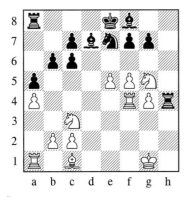

17...♘d5

17...g6?! is met by 18.e6 fxe6 19.fxe6 ♗c8 20.♗e3 ♘d5 21.♘xd5 cxd5 22.♘f3 ♖h7 23.♖f6 ♖g7 24.♘d4 ♗e7 25.g5! ♗a6 26.♔f2± intending ♖h1.

18.♘xd5 cxd5

After a few forced moves we reach a position which looks interesting, despite the fact that there are not so many pieces on the board. A normal continuation would be:

19.♗e3 c5 20.♖e1 ♗c6 21.♘f3

21.c3!? is interesting,. The idea is to keep the knight on g5 as long as possible.

21...♖h6 22.c3∞

The final position should be examined more. Black has the bishop pair, but all White's pieces are active and his kingside pawns control a lot of space.

14.f4

The break with 14.e6 is not best. 14...f6 15.♖d1† ♔c8 16.♘f3 (16.♘f7 ♗xf7 17.exf7 ♘g6 18.♘e2 ♘e5 19.♘d4 ♘xf7 20.♘xc6 h5!↑) 16...c5⇄ Black will slowly improve his pieces and the e6-pawn will later be weak.

14...h6 15.♘f3

Now the threat is f4-f5. Instead 15.♘ge4 ♔c8 16.f5 c5⇄ intending ...♘c6 would leave the e5-pawn without strong defence. Also the d4-square would be controlled by Black.

15...g6 16.b3 ♔c8 17.♗b2 ♗g7 18.♘e4

A typical manoeuvre: the knight goes to g3 and after that the threat of f4-f5 is renewed.

White could play 18.♖ad1, but then Black can reply 18...♔b7 19.♘e4 c5 20.♘g3 c4!. White will have pressure on the kingside, but Black has also achieved something – he has destroyed White's queenside pawn structure.

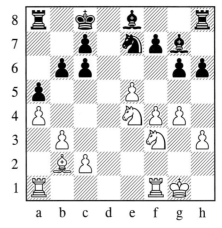

18...c5

This is a typical reaction, but Black also had other options.

Interesting was:
18...♘d5!?

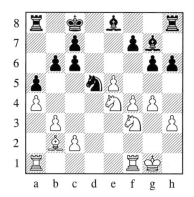

19.♘h4

White can sacrifice a pawn with 19.f5 gxf5 20.gxf5 ♖g8 21.♔h2 ♘e3 22.♖f2 ♘xf5 23.♖g1 when he has compensation. Black has to play 23...♘e7 24.♖fg2 ♘g6 in order to cover the g-line. 25.h4 h5 26.♖g5 ♖h8 27.♘g3 c5 28.♖xh5 (28.♘xh5 ♗h6 29.e6 ♗xg5 30.♗xh8 ♗e7∓) 28...♗c6 29.♖xh8† ♗xh8 30.♖f1 ♗xf3 31.♖xf3 ♘xh4 32.♖xf7 ♘g6⇄ Black has no problems.

19.♘h2 c5 20.f5 gxf5 21.♖xf5 (21.gxf5 ♘e3! and next ...♗c6 and ...♖g8) 21...♘e7 22.♖f2 h5∞ This leads to an unclear game.

Here the point is that Black has:

19...h5!

White is forced to play:

20.g5 ♘e3 21.♖f2 ♗d7 22.♔h2

Black has blockaded the white majority, but White still has some pressure after:

22...♖d8 23.♖e1 ♘f5 24.♘xf5 ♗xf5 25.♘g3 ♗d7

25...♔b7 26.♘xf5 gxf5 27.♔g3±
26.h4↑

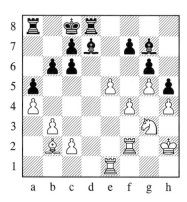

White keeps the initiative. His main threat is clear – break with f5 – but Black is unable to stop it. For example:

26...♗g4

26...♗f5 27.♘xf5 gxf5 28.g6 fxg6 29.♖g1± 27.f5 ♔b7 28.♗a1 ♗f8 29.e6! ♗c5 30.♖g2 fxe6 31.fxg6±

19.♘g3 ♖g8

Of course Black has to stop f5.

After 19...♗c6 20.f5 gxf5 21.gxf5 ♘d5 22.f6 ♗f8 23.e6! ♗d6 24.♘e5 fxe6 25.♖ae1± White dominates since his passed pawn will reach the seventh rank.

20.♔h2 ♗d7

Once again 20...♘d5 doesn't solve Black's worries. After 21.f5 ♘e3 22.♖f2 gxf5 23.gxf5 ♗d7 24.♘h4± White's central pawns remain stable and Black has serious problems.

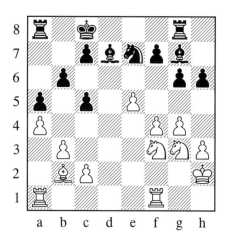

21.c4

With this move White blockades the queenside, which is a good decision since all of his pieces will be included in the plan of pushing f4-f5. It is worth saying that the blockade with c4 is not good in every position. If Black became active, say his bishop came to the h7-b1 diagonal, White would have a serious problem with his weakness – the pawn on b3. Here, it is very hard to believe that Black will be able to attack the b3-pawn, so White's decision is good.

21...♔b7 22.♖ad1 ♖ad8 23.♖d3

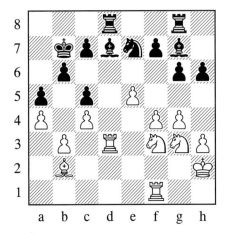

23...♗c8?

This looks passive. Black's idea is to save the c6-square for his knight while from c8 the bishop can control the f5-break. The main weakness of this plan is its lack of active play. White can slowly improve his pieces, while Black has to wait.

More concrete was: 23...♗c6! 24.♖fd1 ♖xd3 25.♖xd3

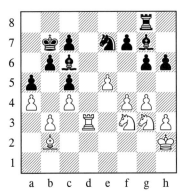

Black has two options.

The simple 25...♗xf3 26.♖xf3 ♖d8 looks good

for Black. After 27.♘e4 ♖d1 28.♗c3 ♘c6⇄ Black will prepare an invasion with ...♘d4. Meanwhile, White cannot push f5...

More dynamic is: 25...h5!? 26.♗c3 (26.♔g2 hxg4 27.hxg4 ♗c8 28.♔f2 ♗d7∞ also leads to a good game for Black) 26...♗h6 27.g5 ♗g7 28.♘h4 Now after 28...♔c8 29.f5 (29.♖d1 ♖d8 30.♖xd8† ♔xd8 intending ...♗d7) 29...gxf5 30.♘hxf5 ♘xf5 31.♘xf5 ♗f8∓ Black has the possibility of organizing an attack on the b3-pawn. In my opinion, the position is already slightly better for Black.

24.♖fd1 ♖xd3 25.♖xd3 ♖e8 26.♘e4 ♘c6 27.♔g3±

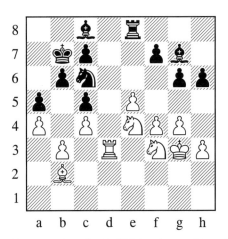

Due to 23...♗c8? White has achieved a dream position. Black is not able to create any counterplay on the queenside, while White can slowly prepare the f5-break or some other active plan on the kingside.

27...♔b8

With this move Black prepares ...♗b7. If instead 27...♖d8 then 28.♖xd8 ♘xd8 29.♘h4± intending f5.

28.♗c3

This is a typical move; on c3 the bishop is protected and controls the b4-square.

28...罝d8 29.罝xd8 ♞xd8

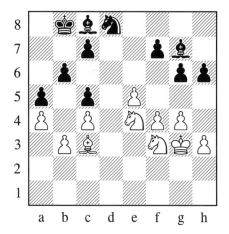

30.e6!

I gave this move an exclamation mark because it is a typical idea in many variations of the Berlin, but it is rarely seen after a lot of exchanges. Positionally, White is still better and now with this neat sacrifice he invades Black's position. One more time Kramnik's knight comes to the g7-square – the same as in the game Karjakin – Kramnik, Monaco (blindfold) 2011.

White could instead continue with:
30.♞h4!?

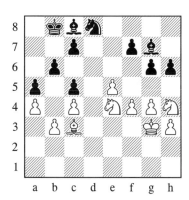

30...♝b7
30...♞e6 31.f5 ♞g5 32.♞f2! gxf5 33.♞xf5 ♝f8 34.h4 ♞e6 35.h5± is simply better for White.

30...♝f8 31.f5 ♝c7 would give White the chance for an attractive sacrifice: 32.♞xg6! fxg6 33.fxg6 ♝f8 34.♚h4± Black has big problems.
31.♚f3 ♞e6 32.♚e3±
Black feels no relief after:
32...g5 33.fxg5 hxg5 34.♞f5!
   34.♞f3 ♝f8 35.♞f6 ♚c8 36.♝d2 ♝e7 37.♚e2 ♝xf6 38.exf6 ♚d7 39.♞xg5 ♞xg5 40.♝xg5 ♝e4⇄
34...♝f8 35.♝d2 ♚c8 36.♝d3 ♝xe4† 37.♚xe4 ♚d7 38.♚e3 ♚e8 39.♞g3 ♝e7 40.♚d5! ♚d7 41.♞h5±
   And next will be ♞f6 with the idea of ♚e4-f5.

30...♞xe6 31.♝xg7 ♞xg7

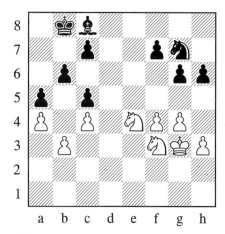

32.♞e5?
This is an error; White underestimates Black's possibilities.

32.♞f6!
   The idea is to prevent the move ...f7-f5.
32...h5
   32...♞e6 33.♞e5 ♞d4 34.♞xf7 ♞xb3 35.♞xh6 ♝e6 36.f5 gxf5 37.♞xf5 ♝xc4 38.h4! b5 39.♞e3 ♝d3 40.♞d7† ♚b7 41.♞e5 ♝e2 42.axb5 a4 43.♞5c4 This is in White's favour.
   32...♝e6 33.♞e5 ♚c8 34.♞g8 h5 35.♞h6!±

33.♘e5 ♗e6

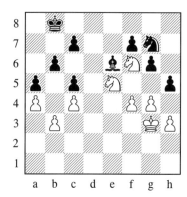

The white king joins the attack with:
34.♔h4! hxg4 35.hxg4 ♔c8 36.♔g5 ♘d8
37.♘c6† ♔c8 38.♔h6

Black is not able to hold the position after:
38...♘e8 39.♘xe8 ♗xg4 40.♘e7† ♔b7

40...♔d8 41.♘d5 ♗d1 42.♘exc7 ♗xb3
43.♔g7 ♗xa4 44.♘xb6 ♗c2 45.♘cd5 a4
46.♘e3 ♗b3 47.♘xa4 ♗xa4 48.♔xf7+–
41.♘d5± ♗d1 42.♘exc7 ♗xb3 43.♘b5 ♔c6
44.♘a3+–

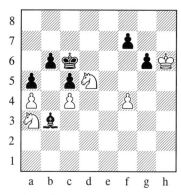

32...f5!⇄ 33.♘f6 g5

An alternative was: 33...fxg4 34.hxg4
h5 35.f5 (35.♘xg6 hxg4 intending ...♗f5)
35...hxg4 (35...♘xf5† 36.gxf5 ♗xf5 37.♘f3 c6
38.♔f4 ♔c7⇄ was another option for Black)
36.fxg6 ♗f5 37.♘d5 ♗c2 38.♔xg4 ♗xb3 This
leads to a draw after: 39.♘c3 ♔c8 40.♔g5
♔d8 41.♔f6 ♘e8† 42.♔f7 ♘d6† 43.♔f8
♘e8!=

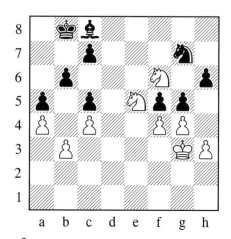

34.♘c6†

34.♘h5! was more tempting. Black should
react with: 34...gxf4† (34...fxg4 35.♘xg7
gxf4† 36.♔xf4 gxh3 37.♘f3± looks better for
White, as the black king will not be able to get
into the game for a long time.) 35.♔xf4 ♘xh5†
36.gxh5 ♗e6 37.♘c6† ♔a8! 38.♘e7 ♗f7
39.♘g6 c6 40.♔xf5 b5⇄ Black's counterplay
is in time.

**34...♔b7 35.♘d8† ♔b8 36.♘c6† ♔b7
37.♘d8† ♔b8 38.fxg5**

White decides to play for a win. This is risky,
as Black has nice defensive ideas.

38...hxg5 39.♘h7

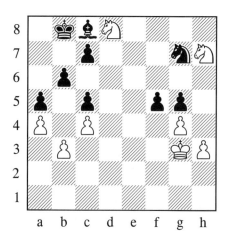

39...c6?

Probably the last few moves were played in mutual time-trouble. Black's last move is a serious mistake and after it Black cannot hold the position.

The right idea was: 39...fxg4 40.hxg4

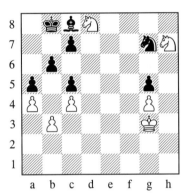

40...♘f5†!! 41.gxf5 ♗xf5 42.♘xg5 ♗c2 Now White is fighting for a draw. After 43.♘c6† ♚c8 44.♘e7† ♚d7 45.♘d5 ♗xb3 46.♘c3 ♗xc4 47.♚f4∓/= Black has a small advantage, but probably it is not enough for a win.

40.♘xg5± ♚c7 41.♘df7

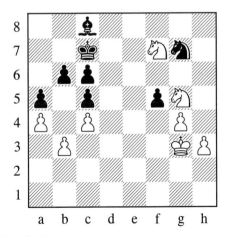

41...b5?!

Again, Black's best chance was a sacrifice with: 41...fxg4 42.hxg4 ♘f5†! 43.gxf5 ♗xf5

However, here White has 44.♘f3 b5 45.♘d2 bxa4 46.bxa4 ♗c2 47.♚f4 ♗xa4 48.♘b1!±/+− and Black has little chance of surviving.

42.♚f4 fxg4 43.hxg4 ♘e6† 44.♘xe6† ♗xe6 45.♘e5+−

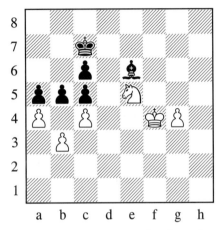

After a few mistakes by both sides, White was winning easily. Kramnik fought for another fifteen moves, but he couldn't avoid his second loss in a row against Karjakin.

45...♚d6 46.g5 bxa4 47.bxa4 ♚e7
    47...♚g8 48.♚f5+−

48.♘xc6† ♚d6 49.♘xa5 ♚c7 50.♚e5 ♗g8 51.♘b3 ♗xc4 52.♘xc5

Black could have resigned here, but he continued with:

52...♚b6 53.♘e4 ♗b3 54.♘c3 ♗c2 55.♚f6 ♚c5 56.g6 ♚b4 57.g7 ♗b3 58.♘e4 ♗g8 59.♚e7

Kramnik finally resigned. A possible finish was: 59...♚xa4 60.♚f8 ♗c4 (60...♗h7 61.♘g5+−) 61.♘g5 ♚b4 62.♘f7+−
1−0

GAME 18
▷ **V. Ivanchuk (2768)**
▶ **P. Leko (2717)**
8th World Team Championship, Ningbo
Round 4, 20.07.2011 **[C89]**
Annotated by Nikola Sedlak

This meeting between two top-class players featured a major theoretical battle. Leko turned out to be better prepared, and the position should have been heading for a draw when Ivanchuk overestimated his chances on move 30 and slid into a bad endgame which the Hungarian grandmaster eventually converted, although both players made some technical errors along the way. The game was an interesting and theoretically important one, especially for Marshall Attack fans.

1.e4 e5 2.♘f3 ♘c6 3.♗b5 a6 4.♗a4 ♘f6 5.0–0 ♗e7 6.♖e1 b5 7.♗b3 0–0 8.c3 d5 9.exd5 ♘xd5 10.♘xe5 ♘xe5 11.♖xe5 c6 12.d4 ♗d6 13.♖e1 ♕h4 14.g3 ♕h3 15.♕e2 ♗g4 16.♕f1 ♕h5 17.♘d2

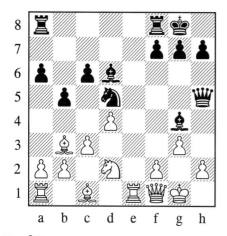

17...f5!?
This move is typical for the Marshall Attack in general, but it has been quite rare in this particular position. Black has also tried:
17...♘f4?!
This tempting move is not quite sound.

18.gxf4 ♗xf4

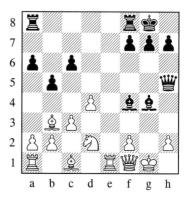

19.h4!
19.♕g2 ♗h3 20.♕xc6 ♗xh2† 21.♔h1 ♗f4 22.♔g1 ♕g5† 23.♔h1 ♕h5=
19...♕xh4 20.♕g2 ♖ae8
After 20...♗h3 21.♘f3 ♕h5 22.♗xf4 ♗xg2 23.♔xg2± White's three well-coordinated pieces are stronger than Black's queen.
21.♖xe8 ♖xe8 22.♘f1 ♗h3 23.♕xc6 ♗h2† 24.♔h1 ♖c8 25.♕b7 ♗c7 26.♔g1 ♕g4† 27.♘g3 ♗xg3 28.fxg3 ♕xg3† 29.♔h1 ♗g4 30.♕xf7† ♔h8 31.♗d5 ♕e1† 32.♔h2 ♖e8 33.♗g5 ♕e2† 34.♗g2 ♗h5 35.♕f4 ♕xb2 36.♖e1 ♕xa2 37.♖xe8† ♗xe8 38.d5
1–0 So – Megaranto, Olongapo City 2010.

17...♖ae8 has been the most popular choice. 18.f3 f5!? 19.fxg4 fxg4 20.♖xe8 ♕xe8 21.♕g2 ♕e3† 22.♔h1 ♖f2 23.♕g1 ♗xg3 24.♕xg3 The position looks almost lost for Black, but he manages to stay alive with the help of some strange tactics.

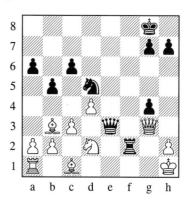

24...♕e2! 25.♕g1 (25.a4 ♔f8 26.♗xd5 cxd5
27.axb5 ♖f1†! 28.♘xf1 ♕xf1† 29.♕g1 ♕f3†
30.♕g2 ♕d1†=) 25...♔h8 26.♗d1 ♖xh2†
27.♕xh2 ♕e1† ½–½ So – Gupta, Wijk aan
Zee 2009.

18.c4

18.f3 ♗h3 (18...♖ae8!? transposes to So
– Gupta as referenced above.) 19.♕f2 ♖ae8
looks very unclear.

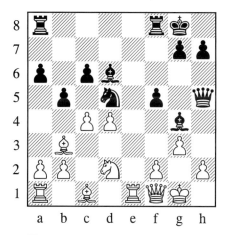

18...f4!N

A nice idea, improving over 18...♗h3 and
18...bxc4, both of which had been played in
obscure games several years prior.

19.cxd5 c5!

It was essential to follow up Black's previous
move correctly. It seems amazing that Black
can sacrifice a piece and then calmly move a
pawn on the queenside, but it important to
stop White from taking a free pawn on c6,
which would also liberate his bishop on b3.
Leko is undoubtedly one of the biggest experts
on the Marshall Attack, and he proved it again
with this fantastic piece of preparation.

19...fxg3? is feeble, and after 20.dxc6† ♔h8
21.hxg3 ♗xg3 22.fxg3 ♖xf1† 23.♖xf1 White
is just winning.

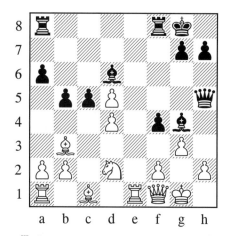

20.♖e4

We have reached a critical moment in the
game, where White has numerous possibilities.

One of the simple tactical points behind Black's
idea is that 20.dxc5?? fxg3 21.hxg3 ♗xc5! wins
for him.

20.♖e5 does not lead anywhere special for
White: 20...♗xe5 21.dxe5 c4 22.♗c2

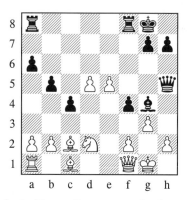

22...fxg3 The safest move, leading to an
equal endgame. (If Black wants to keep the
game complex he may try: 22...♖ae8 23.♘e4
fxg3 24.♘xg3 ♕xe5 25.♗e3 ♕xd5 26.♖e1∞)
23.hxg3 ♕xe5 24.f4 ♕xd5 25.♕g2 ♕h5
26.♘f1 ♖fe8 27.♗e3 ♗f3 28.♕h2 ♕xh2†
29.♘xh2! ♖xe3 30.♘xf3 ♖e2 31.♖c1 ♖ae8
32.♘e5 ♖d8 33.♘f3 ♖de8=

20.♕g2

This is an important alternative, but it seems that White has no more than a draw.

20...♖ae8

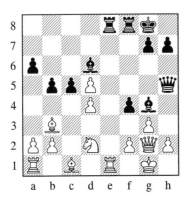

Now White has a variety of options.

a) 21.♖xe8? ♖xe8 22.f3 ♖e1† 23.♔f2 ♗h3 24.♕xh3 ♕xh3 25.♔xe1 fxg3 26.hxg3 ♗xg3† 27.♔e2 c4–+

b) 21.♖e4 might be the safest way for White to bail out to a draw: 21...fxg3 22.hxg3 ♖xe4 23.♘xe4 ♗f3 24.♗d1 ♗xg2 25.♗xh5 ♗xe4 26.♗e3 c4 27.f4 g6 28.♗g4 ♗xd5 29.♔f2 ♔f7 30.♗f3 ♔e6 31.♗g4† ♔f6 32.♗f3=

c) 21.♖e6 c4!

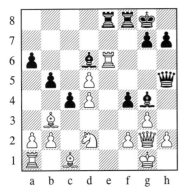

22.♗c2

22.♘xc4 bxc4 23.♗xf4 cxb3 24.♖xd6 bxa2↑

22...♗xe6 23.dxe6 ♖xe6 24.♗e4

24.♘e4 f3 25.♕f1 ♖fe8 26.♗e3 ♖xe4 27.♗xe4 ♖xe4 28.a4 ♖e8 29.axb5 axb5 30.♖a6 ♕d5 31.♕h3 ♖d8∓

24...f3! 25.g4 ♕e8 26.♗xf3 ♖e1† 27.♘f1 ♔h8∓

White is almost stalemated.

d) 21.♖f1?!

Ambitious, but the position turns out to be more dangerous for White.

21...♗h3 22.♗d1 ♕h6 23.♕h1

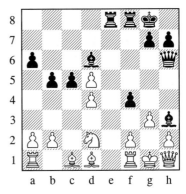

23...♕g6!

An important move, after which White cannot prevent the sacrifice on g3.

23...♗xf1 24.♘xf1 ♕f6 25.♕g2 ♕xd4 26.♗f3 ♖e1 27.♗xf4 (27.♗e3 ♖xf1† 28.♖xf1 fxe3 29.fxe3 ♕xe3† 30.♔h1 (30.♕f2?? ♖xf3–+)) 27...♖xa1 28.♗xd6 ♖xf1† 29.♕xf1 ♖xf3 30.♕e2 ♖xf2 31.♕xf2 ♕d1† 32.♕f1

♕d4† 33.♕f2 ♕d1†=

23...♕f6!? is also promising, for instance:
24.♕f3 ♗xf1 25.♘xf1 ♕xd4 26.g4 ♖e1
27.♗c2 c4 28.♖b1 ♖fe8 29.♗e3 ♖xf1†
30.♖xf1 fxe3 31.fxe3 ♕xe3† 32.♔g2∓
24.♗f3 ♗xf1 25.♔xf1 fxg3 26.hxg3 ♗xg3

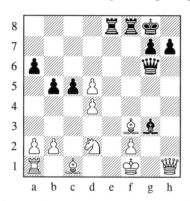

We are facing a crazy position which is impossible to analyse without the help of our metal friend!

27.dxc5

Others are no better:

27.♘e4 ♖xe4 28.♗xe4 ♖xf2† 29.♔g1 ♕g4
30.♗e3 ♗h4† 31.♔g2 ♖f3 32.d6 ♖xe3
33.♖f1 ♖e1 34.♖xe1 ♕xd4+–+

27.♕h3 ♗xf2! 28.♔xf2 ♕d3 29.♔g2 ♖e2†
30.♔h1 (30.♗xe2 ♕xe2† 31.♔h1 ♕e1†
32.♔h2 ♖f2† 33.♔g2 ♕e2 34.♕xf2 ♕xf2†
35.♔h1 ♕xd4–+
27...♕d3† 28.♔g2 ♗f4

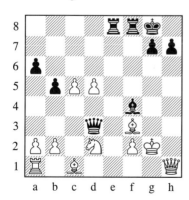

Now my main line continues:

29.♘e4 ♗xc1 30.♕d1 ♕xd1 31.♗xd1 ♗xb2
32.♖b1 ♖xe4 33.♖xb2 ♔f7 34.d6 ♔e8 35.♗f3
♖c4 36.c6 ♖d4 37.♖e2† ♔d8 38.♖e6 ♔c8
39.♗e4 g6 40.♔g3 ♖d8 41.f3 ♖4xd6 42.♖e7
♖d2 43.♖xh7 ♖xa2 44.♖a7 b4–+

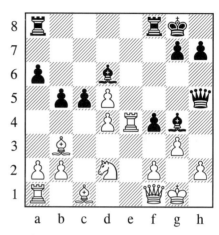

20...c4!

This gives rise to a long and forcing line resulting in a perpetual check. Leko probably prepared it all at home.

**21.♗c2 fxg3 22.hxg3 ♗xg3 23.fxg3 ♖xf1†
24.♘xf1 ♕h3 25.♖e3**

25.♖f4 ♖e8 26.♗e3 ♖xe3 27.♘xe3 ♕xg3†
28.♘g2 ♗f3 29.♖xf3 ♕xf3∓

**25...♖f8 26.♗d2 ♗f3 27.♖xf3 ♖xf3 28.♗e4
♖xg3† 29.♘xg3 ♕xg3†**

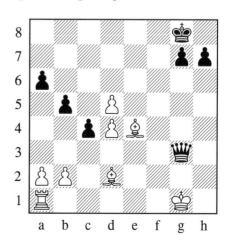

30.♗g2?

A bad decision. White had an easy draw with 30.♔f1 ♕h3† 31.♔e2 ♕h2† 32.♔e3 ♕h6† 33.♔e2 ♕h2†= but it looks like Ivanchuk overestimated his position and tried to play for a win.

30...♕d3 31.♗e1

31.♗c3 b4 32.♗xb4 ♕xd4† 33.♔h1 ♕xb2 34.♖d1 ♕xb4 35.d6 ♕a4 36.♖d5 ♕d7 37.♔h2 g5 38.♖xg5† ♔f7 39.♖d5 c3 40.♗h3 ♕c6 41.♗g2 ♕c4 42.d7 ♕h4† 43.♗h3 ♕f4†–+

31...♕xd4† 32.♗f2 ♕xb2 33.♖f1 ♕d2 34.♗c5

We have reached an unusual type of endgame which is far from easy for a human player to evaluate over the board. Computer analysis confirms that Black has a big advantage though.

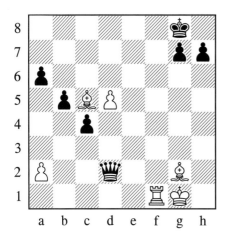

34...g6?

Black should have made more space for his king with 34...h5! 35.♖f8† ♔h7 36.♗e4† g6 37.♖e8 c3 38.♖e7† ♔h6 39.♖e6 h4 40.♖xg6† ♔h5–+.

35.♖f8† ♔g7 36.♖f2 ♕d1† 37.♖f1 ♕d2 38.♔h2?

Once again Ivanchuk becomes too optimistic and tries to play for a win without justification.

Of course White should have continued with: 38.♖f2 ♕e1† 39.♖f1

Black is not forced to repeat the position, but avoiding it brings him no more than a draw, for instance:

39...♕e5 40.♗f8†

40.♖d1? allows Black to win in style: 40...c3! 41.♗d4 ♕xd4† 42.♖xd4 c2 43.d6 c1=♕† 44.♔h2 ♕h6† 45.♔h3 ♕g5 46.♖d1 ♕f4† 47.♔g2 ♕e4† 48.♔f2 ♕c2† 49.♔e1 ♕c3† 50.♔e2 ♕xh3 51.d7 ♕g4† 52.♔e1 ♕h4†–+

40...♔h8 41.d6

Or 41.♗h6 ♕d4† 42.♖f2 c3 43.d6 c2 44.♗f1 g5! 45.♗xg5 ♕g4† 46.♖g2 ♕xg5 47.♖xg5 c1=♕ 48.♖d5 ♕e3† 49.♔h2 ♕f4† 50.♔g1 and White just holds.

41...h5 42.♗e7 ♕d4† 43.♖f2 ♔h7 44.♗c6 c3 45.d7 c2 46.♗a3 ♕d1† 47.♔g2 ♕g4†=

38...c3 39.♖f2 ♕e1 40.♗d4† ♔h6 41.♗h3

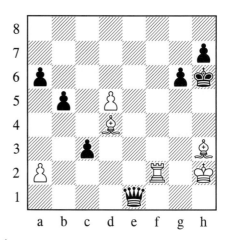

41...c2!
0–1

White resigned in view of 42.♖xc2 ♕e4 when he loses a bishop, leaving Black with an easy technical conversion.

D

GAME 19

▷ **Yu Yangyi (2672)**
▶ **C. Balogh (2643)**
8th World Team Championship, Ningbo
Round 9, 26.07.2011 **[D10]**
Annotated by Sebastian Maze

What a game!! Both players quickly headed for a crazy position where anything was possible. Balogh chose a rare line in the Slav with 3...dxc4 before developing the g8-knight, and then played a logical novelty with 9...♞xe4. After this, Yu Yangyi found a nice plan and achieved a completely winning position, but then he missed the fantastic 23.d5. The Hungarian player managed to escape from the strong attack against his king, and step by step he gained the advantage. He finally succeeded in winning this crazy game!

1.d4 d5 2.c4 c6 3.♘c3 dxc4

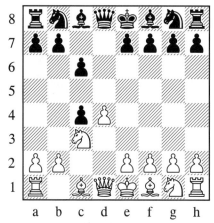

Balogh decides to take the pawn before developing his knight to f6. This is quite an interesting line to avoid big theory in the Slav.

4.e3

4.e4 b5 5.a4 b4 6.♘a2 ♘f6 7.e5 ♘d5 8.♗xc4 e6 is a popular line.

4.a4 can be met with the aggressive 4...e5, while 4...♘f6 is also an option.

4...b5 5.a4

5.♘xb5? cxb5 6.♕f3 ♕c7 7.♕xa8 ♗b7 8.♕xa7 e5 9.♗xc4 bxc4 10.♕a4† ♘d7∓

5...b4

For his first five moves, Balogh has moved only pawns!

6.♘e4

After 6.♘a2 e6 7.♗xc4 ♘f6 8.♘f3 ♘bd7 we have returned to a typical Slav structure with the knight on a2. White's plan will be to bring the knight to b3 and then put a rook on c1.

6...♕d5

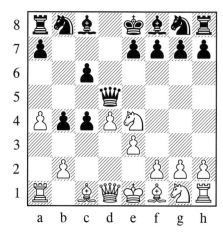

7.♘g3

The other main line is quieter and more positional:
7.♘d2 c3!?
7...♗a6 8.♕c2 ♘f6 9.♘xc4 ♘bd7 10.♘f3 c5 11.b3 cxd4 12.♘xd4±
8.bxc3 bxc3 9.♘b1
9.♘c4 and 9.♘df3 are also playable.
9...♕a5 10.♕c2 ♘a6 11.♗a3 e5
11...♘b4 12.♗xb4 ♕xb4 13.♘xc3±
12.♗xf8 ♔xf8 13.♗xa6 ♗xa6 14.dxe5 ♖b8
15.♘xc3 ♕xe5 16.♘ge2
16.♘f3 ♕c5 17.♕d2 ♘f6 18.♖c1 ♕e7
19.♘d4 ♕d6 20.f3=
16...♗xe2 17.♔xe2 ♘f6=
Giri – Holzke, Wijk aan Zee 2009.

7...♘f6 8.♗e2 ♗a6 9.e4

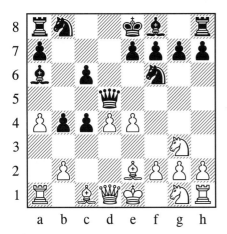

9...♘xe4N

A logical novelty; Balogh doesn't want to allow White a strong centre.

9...♕a5?! 10.♘f3 e6 11.0–0 ♘bd7 12.♗g5 h6 13.♗xf6 ♘xf6 14.♖c1± Shabalov – Krush, US Championship 2010.

10.♗f3 f5 11.♘1e2

Yu Yangyi is two pawns down, but he aims to develop all his pieces and put pressure on the black king.

11...g6

11...c3 12.bxc3 ♗xe2 13.♘xe2 bxc3 14.0–0 ♘d7 15.♗xe4 ♕xe4 16.♘xc3± Black's structure is terrible, with c6 and f5 both weak. After ♖e1 and ♕b3, White's advantage may take on significant proportions.

12.♘f4 ♕f7 13.♘xe4

It's important to keep the light-squared bishop, as it will play a crucial role in this game.

13...fxe4 14.♗g4

A nice finesse. Yu Yangyi doesn't care about the pawn, his attention is focused on the e6-square.

14...h5 15.♗e6 ♕f6 16.♗h3

A good manoeuvre, aimed against ...g5.

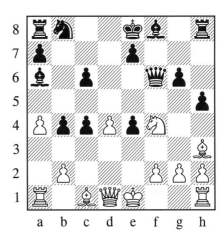

16...c3

The game has reached a messy position, Black is two pawns up, but his king is vulnerable in the centre.

16...g5!

Even after the ♗e6-h3 manoeuvre, this advance was playable and is in fact quite strong. From my point of view, it would be impossible to play this move – only computers can play like this! There are too many tactics and with just two hours on the clock, your head is liable to explode!

17.♘xh5 ♕f7 18.♘g3

18.♗g4 ♘d7 19.♘g3 ♕d5 20.♗e3 ♗g7 21.♘h5 ♔f8 22.♘xg7 ♔xg7 23.♗xd7 ♕xd7 24.♗xg5∞

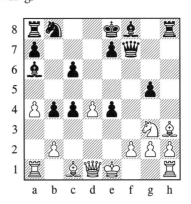

18...℟xh3! 19.gxh3 c5!

A second fantastic move to open up the position!

20.♘xe4 cxd4 21.0–0! ♘c6 22.℟e1 e5∞

White is an exchange up, but his king is really weak and the black bishop will be dangerous on b7. So let's agree with our metal friend, and call it unclear!

17.♘e6

Taking the pawn is weaker:

17.bxc3?! ♗c4

A crucial square for the bishop, preventing both ♘e6 and 0–0.

17...g5? 18.♘xh5 ♕f7 19.♘g3 ℟xh3 20.gxh3 ♗d3 21.f3 ♕c4 22.♘xe4 ♘d7 23.♔f2 ♗g7 24.℟e1±

18.cxb4

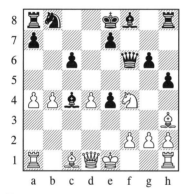

18...♕f7

18...e5 is another wild computer line: 19.dxe5 ♗xb4† 20.♗d2 ♕xf4 21.♗xb4 e3 22.♕f3 exf2† 23.♔xf2 ♕d4† 24.♕e3 ♕b2† 25.♗d2 ℟f8† 26.♔g3 g5 and the computer says equal! This position is just unbelievable, with all the pieces in crazy places!

19.♘e2 ♗g7 20.0–0 0–0 21.℟a3

21.♕c2 ♗d3 22.♕b2 ♘a6 23.♗e3 ♗xe2 24.♕xe2 ♘xb4∓

21...♘a6

The position is complicated, but Black looks okay and may even be slightly better.

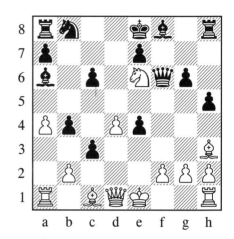

17...cxb2

Black had a crazy alternative:

17...♗d3 18.♘c7† ♔d8 19.♗g5! ♕f7

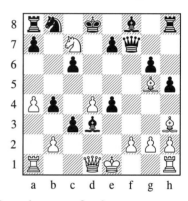

The only square for the queen.

20.♘e6† ♔e8 21.bxc3 ♘a6 22.cxb4 ♗c4

22...♘xb4 23.♕b3 ♘c2† 24.♔d1 ♕xf2

What a position! Both sides are attacking like mad! Who will mate first?

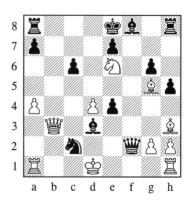

25.♖a2! The point! Now Black is lost. 25...♕e2† 26.♔c1 e3 27.♖xc2 ♗xc2 28.♕xc2 ♕xc2† 29.♔xc2+–

23.d5! ♗g7

23...♗xd5 24.♕d4 ♗xe6 25.♗xe6 ♕xe6 26.♕xh8±

24.♖c1 ♗xd5 25.♘xg7† ♕xg7 26.♕d2±

18.♗xb2 e3 19.♕f3

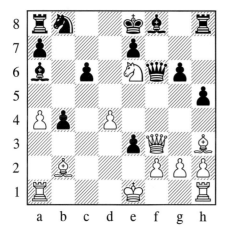

19...g5

19...♕xf3 20.gxf3 ♗c8 21.fxe3

As I see it, White's position is lovely. The bishops are radiating power, the rooks will arrive on the open files and the black king is weak.

21...♗h6 22.d5± ♖g8 23.♘c7† ♔d8 24.♗xc8 ♔xc7 25.♗e6

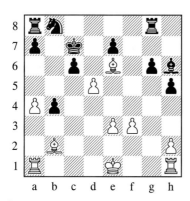

25...♗g7

25...♘a6 26.♗e5† ♔b6 27.a5† ♔b5 28.♗h3!± with the idea of ♗f1†.

26.♗xg8 ♗xb2 27.♖b1

27.♖d1 ♘d7 (27...♘a6 28.♗f7 c5 29.♖g1 ♖f8 30.♖xg6 ♘b8 31.♗e6 ♖xf3 32.♗e2 ♖f8 33.♖h6±) 28.dxc6 ♘c5 29.♗c4 ♗f6 30.a5∞

27...♗c3† 28.♔e2 ♘a6 29.♗f7

The b-pawn gives Black some compensation for the exchange, but with a few accurate moves White should be able to win this position.

20.♘c7† ♔d8 21.♘e6† ♔e8 22.♗f5

Yu Yangyi is not here to make a quick draw; that is not the Chinese style! He is looking for action!

22...♗c8?

Balogh didn't see the idea with d4-d5. During a tactical game like this, it's difficult to calculate everything, and sometimes we miss out on great moves. But this ...♗c8 is not logical, because it's very passive and now all Black's pieces except the queen are back "home".

22...g4

This is the best move by far.

23.♕f4 ♗h6

24.d5 ♗xf4

24...♕xb2?? 25.♗g6† ♔d7 26.♕c7#

25.♗xf6 exf6 26.♘xf4 ♔d8!

26...cxd5 27.♖c1 b3 28.fxe3 is slightly worse for Black.

27.罝d1

27.fxe3 奧c8 28.奧xc8 當xc8 29.罝c1 a5 30.罝f1 罝a6 31.ㄠe6 ㄠd7 32.罝xc6† 罝xc6 33.dxc6 ㄠe5 34.當e2 ㄠxc6 35.罝xf6=

27...奧c4 28.dxc6† 當c7 29.罝d4 奧f7 30.fxe3 罝d8 31.罝xb4 ㄠxc6=

Black should be fine.

23.ㄠc7†?

Sadly, Yu Yangyi missed the super move that would have destroyed the black position. He decided to take the a8-rook, but in fact this was the decisive mistake.

23.d5!!

What a great move; White sacrifices the b2-bishop in order to open all the lines around the black king.

23...豳xb2 24.奧g6† 當d7 25.0–0

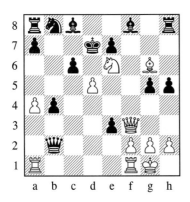

Now White's king is safe and his rooks will arrive in the centre. "Fire on the board" is coming soon...

25...exf2† 26.當h1 當d6

26...豳f6 27.dxc6† 當xe6 28.豳e4† 豳e5 29.奧f7† 當xf7 30.豳xe5+−

27.dxc6 奧xe6 28.豳g3† 豳e5 29.罝ad1† 奧d5

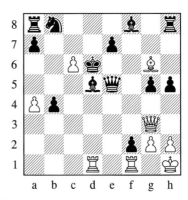

30.罝xd5†

And boom! Another great sacrifice to bring the king right to the centre of the board!

30...當xd5 31.罝d1† 豳d4

31...當e6 32.豳b3† 當f6 33.豳f7#

32.罝xd4† 當xd4 33.豳xf2† 當d5 34.c7 ㄠc6 35.豳c2 罝h6 36.奧e4† 當e5 37.奧xc6 罝c8 38.奧d7 罝xc7 39.豳xc7†+−

23...當d8

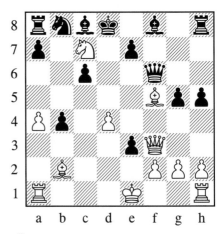

24.ㄠxa8

24.♘e6† ♗xe6 25.♗xe6 exf2† 26.♔xf2 ♗g7 27.♕xf6 ♗xf6 28.♖ac1 ♔c7 29.♖c4 a5∓ Black should easily win this endgame with two extra pawns.

24.d5?? Now this is no longer working! 24...♕xb2 25.0–0 exf2† 26.♔h1 ♔xc7 Black is two pieces up, and White has no real play. 27.♕g3† e5 28.dxe6† ♗d6–+

24...♕xf5 25.♕xe3
25.♕xf5 ♗xf5 26.fxe3 ♔c8 27.d5 ♖g8 28.0–0 ♗e4 29.dxc6 ♘xc6 30.♖ac1 ♔b7 31.♖fd1 ♖g6 (31...♔xa8? 32.♖c4± was the last trick) 32.♖c4 ♖e6 33.a5 ♔xa8 34.a6 ♔b8∓

25...♕d5∓

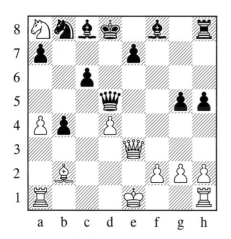

Suddenly White's position has become unpleasant. Black has huge compensation for the exchange.

26.♖c1 e6 27.♖c5
The Chinese player tries to find some play with this "positional sacrifice". But the road to the equality is too long, and there is little chance for White to survive.

After 27.0–0 ♗b7 28.f4 ♗xa8 29.fxg5 ♖g8 Black's position is delicious; the a8-bishop will soon shine after the move ...c5, his king is safe

on d8, and there is just no counterplay for White with such a bad bishop on b2.

27.h4 ♖g8 28.hxg5 ♖xg5–+

27...♗xc5 28.dxc5 ♖f8 29.0–0 ♗a6 30.♕g3

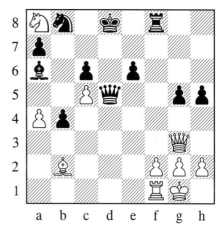

30...♖f4
30...e5 31.♕xg5† ♔c8 32.♖e1 ♘d7 was winning immediately.

31.♗f6† ♔c8 32.♘c7 ♔xc7 33.♗xg5 ♗xf1 34.♗xf4† ♔b7 35.f3
35.♗xb8 ♕xg2† 36.♕xg2 ♗xg2 37.♗f4 ♗f3 38.♔f1 ♔a6 39.♗c7 b3 40.♗e5 ♔a5 41.♔e1 ♔xa4 42.♔d2 ♔a3 43.♔c1 ♔a2 and Black will win the a-pawn.

35...♗c4–+ 36.♕g7† ♕d7 37.♕h8 ♘a6

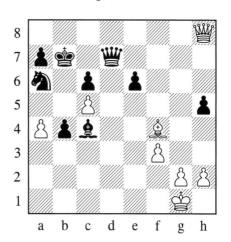

The Hungarian player is a piece up, and the game is essentially over.

38.♗d6 ♘xc5 39.♕b8† ♔a6 40.♕xb4 ♕xd6 41.♕xc4† ♔b7 42.♕b4† ♔c8 43.h4 e5 44.♕e1 ♕d4† 45.♔h1 ♕f4 46.♕f2 ♘d3 47.♕xa7 ♕xh4† 48.♔g1 ♕d4†
0–1

GAME 20
▷ **P. Harikrishna (2669)**
▶ **D. Jakovenko (2736)**
FIDE World Cup 2011, Khanty-Mansiysk
Round 2, Game 1, 31.08.2011 **[D16]**
Annotated by Arkadij Naiditsch

This game developed into a thematic struggle in an IQP position. After obtaining a better position from the opening, Harikrishna miscalculates and opts for the forcing 16.♗h6, which leads to a draw at best, instead of the superior 16.a5 which would have given White clearly better chances. Later on in a worse endgame White failed to offer much resistance and lost almost without a fight.

1.d4 d5 2.c4 c6 3.♘f3 ♘f6 4.♘c3 dxc4 5.a4 e6 6.e3 c5 7.♗xc4 ♘c6 8.0–0 cxd4 9.exd4 ♗e7 10.♕e2 0–0 11.♖d1

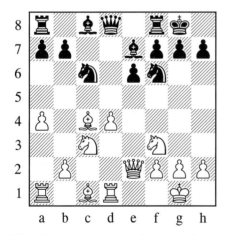

The players have reached a typical position with an isolated d-pawn. White will attempt to develop an initiative based on breaking with d5, and/or attacking on the kingside. Black's plan is to blockade on the d5-square using his knights, and to exchange as many pieces as possible, especially minor pieces. Having provoked the early a2-a4, he might use the b4-square as an outpost for a knight where it helps to control d5.

The same position can be reached via the Queen's Gambit Accepted, except for the position of the black pawn on a7 instead of a6, which could potentially benefit either side.

11...♘d5
The main alternative is:
11...♘b4 12.♘e5 ♗d7 13.a5 ♖c8!?
  13...♗c6 14.a6 ♖c8 (14...♕b6 15.♘xf7 ♖xf7 16.♕xe6±) 15.axb7 ♗xb7 16.♖xa7 ♕b6 17.♖a3±
  13...a6 14.♗g5 ♗c6 15.♘xc6 bxc6± The weaknesses on a6 and c6 give White some advantage. 16.♗f4 ♘bd5 17.♗d2 ♕c8 18.♘a4 ♘d7 19.♗e1 ♕b7 20.g3 ♖fb8 21.♖d3 ♗f6 22.♖b3 ♕c8 23.♖xb8 ♘xb8 24.♗xd5 cxd5 25.♘b6 ♕b7 26.♘xa8 ♕xa8 27.♖c1 ♘c6 28.♕c2 ♘a7 29.♕c5 h6 30.♗d2 ♔h7 31.♗e3 1–0 Kacheishvili – Kuzubov, Dubai 2005.

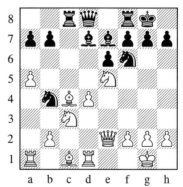

14.♗g5
  14.d5 exd5 15.♘xd5 ♘bxd5 16.♗xd5 ♘xd5 17.♖xd5 ♖c5 (17...♗g4 18.♕b5 ♕xd5 19.♕xd5 ♖cd8 20.♕b3 ♖d1† 21.♕xd1 ♗xd1 22.♗e3 ♗e2 23.♗xa7 ♖c8=) 18.♖xc5

♗xc5 19.♗g5 ♕xg5 20.♘xd7 ♖d8=
14.a6 bxa6 15.♗xa6 ♘xa6 16.♖xa6 ♖c7
(16...♕c7 17.♗g5±) 17.♗f4 ♗c8 18.♖c6
♖b7∞

14...♘fd5
14...♗c6 15.a6±
14...h6 15.♗f4±

15.♘xd5 exd5
15...♘xd5!? 16.♗xd5 exd5 17.♘xd7 ♖e8
18.♕b5 ♗xg5 19.♘c5 b6=

16.♘xd7
16.♗xe7 ♕xe7 17.♘xd7 ♕xd7 18.♗b5 ♕d6
19.♖ac1=

16...♗xg5 17.♗b5 ♖e8 18.♘e5 ♖e6 19.♖a4∞

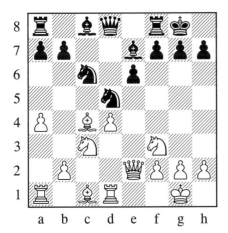

12.♗b3

This is always a useful prophylactic move.
White retreats the bishop out of harm's way
and reminds Black that his own light-squared
bishop is not so easy to develop.

12.♘e5 is not especially promising at this
stage: 12...♘xc3 13.bxc3 ♘xe5 14.dxe5 ♕c7
15.♕e4 ♗d7 16.♗d3 g6 17.h4 ♖fd8∞

12.♕e4!?

This is a more interesting move, intending to
transfer the queen to a more purposeful square
on the kingside. Black has two main replies.

a) 12...♘cb4 13.♘e5

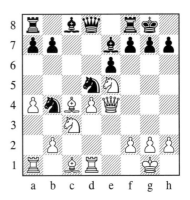

13...b6

Black has some other possibilities as well:
13...♔h8 14.♗d3!? Normally it would be
unthinkable for White to exchange this
bishop for a knight, but here it makes for
an interesting way to mobilize the white
pieces. 14...♘xd3 15.♖xd3 f5 16.♕e2 ♔g8
17.♘xd5 ♕xd5 18.♕h5 f4 (18...♗d7 19.♖h3
h6 20.♗xh6 ♗e8 21.♘g6 ♗f6 22.♗e3 ♗xg6
23.♕xg6±) 19.♗xf4 ♖xf4 20.♕e8† ♗f8
21.♖c1 b5 22.♖xc8 ♖xc8 23.♕xc8 ♖e4
24.♘f3 bxa4 25.♕c2±
13...♗f6 14.♗d2 b6 (14...a5!?) 15.♘xd5
(White could consider 15.♘b5 a5 16.♖a3!, a
nice way of mobilizing the rook for attacking
duties) 15...exd5 16.♕f3 ♘c2 17.♘xf7 ♖xf7
18.♗xd5 ♘xa1 19.♗xf7† ♔xf7 20.♕xa8
♘b3 21.♕xa7† ♕d7 22.♕xb6 ♘xd4 23.♖e1
♕xa4 24.♕c7†∞

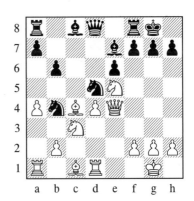

14.♘c6! ♘xc6

14...♘xc3 15.♘xe7† ♕xe7 16.bxc3 ♗b7

17.♕e2 ♘d5 18.♗xd5 ♗xd5 19.c4 ♗b7
20.♗a3 ♕g5 21.f4 ♕xf4 22.♗xf8 ♖xf8
23.a5±

15.♘xd5 ♗b7

After 15...exd5!? 16.♗xd5 ♗g4 17.f3 ♗d7
18.♗xc6 ♗xc6 19.♕xc6 ♗d6 Black has some
compensation for the missing pawn although
White should be better.

16.♘xe7†

16.♗d3!? g6 17.♘xe7† ♕xe7 18.d5 exd5
19.♕f4∞

16...♕xe7

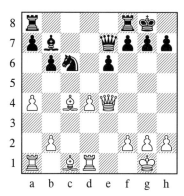

17.d5! exd5 18.♗xd5 ♕xe4 19.♗xe4 ♘a5
20.♗xb7 ♘xb7 21.♗e3±

White has a risk-free endgame advantage, as
his bishop is stronger than Black's knight.

b) 12...♘f6 13.♕h4

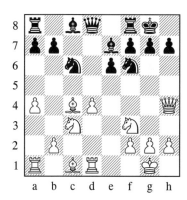

From here Black has two main lines.

b1) 13...♘d5 14.♕h3

Alternatives lead nowhere:

14.♕g4 e5 15.♕h5 ♘f6 16.♕h4 exd4
17.♘b5 ♗g4=

14.♕g3 ♗d6 15.♕h3 e5 16.♕h5 ♘f6
17.♕h4 ♗g4 18.dxe5 ♘xe5 19.♘xe5 ♗xd1
20.♘xf7 ♖xf7 21.♗xf7† ♔xf7 22.♕c4† ♔f8
23.♘xd1 ♗xh2† 24.♔xh2 ♕xd1 25.♗e3
♕d5 26.♕f4 ♖c8 27.♗xa7 ♖c4 28.♕b8†
♔f7∞

14...e5

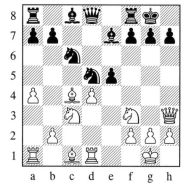

15.♕g3 ♘xc3 16.bxc3

16.♗h6 ♗f6 17.bxc3 exd4 18.cxd4 ♗f5
19.♘e5 ♖c8 is okay for Black.

16...exd4

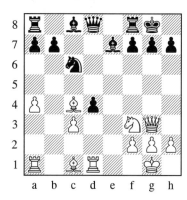

17.cxd4↑

Better than 17.♘xd4 ♘xd4 (or 17...♗h4
18.♕f4 ♕f6) 18.♖xd4 ♕b6 19.♗e3 ♕g6
20.♕xg6 hxg6 21.♗d5 ♗f6 22.♖dd1 ♗xc3
23.♖ab1 a5 with equality.

17...♗d6

17...♗f5 18.d5 ♗f6 19.♗g5 ♘a5 20.♗d3
♗xd3 21.♖xd3 ♗xg5 22.♘xg5±
18.♗f4 ♗xf4 19.♕xf4 ♕f6 20.♕xf6 gxf6 21.d5
♘a5 22.♗e2±

b2) 13...♘b4 14.♗g5 h6

This is the only move to have been tested,
but it carries certain risks as White always
has the possibility of a sacrifice on h6.

14...♘fd5 15.♘xd5 ♘xd5 16.♗xd5 ♗xg5
17.♘xg5 h6 18.♗f3 hxg5 19.♕g3±

14...b6!? It looks logical for Black to prepare
to put his bishop on b7 where it will help
to control d5. 15.d5 (15.♘e5 is met by
15...♗b7 intending ...♘fd5 to exchange
some minor pieces; 15.♗xf6 ♗xf6 16.♕e4
♖b8 17.d5 ♗b7 18.dxe6 ♗xe4 19.exf7†
♔h8 20.♖xd8 ♖bxd8 21.♘xe4∞) 15...exd5
16.♘e4 ♗f5 17.♘xf6† ♗xf6 18.♗xf6 ♕xf6
19.♕xf6 gxf6 20.♗xd5 ♖ad8= Black's active
pieces make up for his damaged kingside
structure.

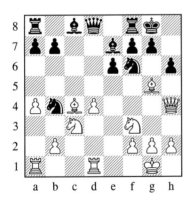

After the provocative text move, there are a
number of ideas to consider.

b21) 15.♘e4 ♘fd5! 16.♗xe7 ♕xe7=

b22) 15.♗d2

This has been White's choice in both games
to have reached this position thus far.
15...b6

15...♗d7?! 16.♘e5 ♗c6 17.♗xh6! gxh6
18.♕xh6 ♘h7 19.♗d3 ♘xd3 20.♖xd3 ♗g5
21.♕h5 ♕f6 22.♖g3 ♔h8 23.♘xc6 ♕h6
24.♕xh6 ♗xh6 25.♘e5 ♖ad8 26.♖d1+−
Kulaots – Jakovenko, Khanty-Mansiysk (ol)
2010.

16.♘e5 ♗b7

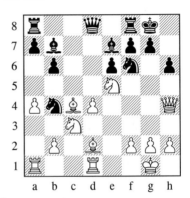

17.♗xh6!

It was impossible for White to resist the
temptation any longer!

17...gxh6 18.♕xh6 ♘h7 19.♗d3

19.♘xf7 ♖xf7 20.♕xe6 ♕e8 21.♖e1 ♔f8
22.♘e4 ♗f6 23.♘xf6 ♕xe6 24.♘xh7† ♖xh7
25.♖xe6 ♖c8∞

19...♘xd3 20.♖xd3 ♗g5 21.♕h5 ♕f6

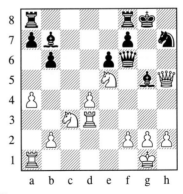

22.♖h3

22.♖g3 ♔h8 23.♘d7 ♕h6 24.♕xh6 ♗xh6
25.♘xf8 ♘xf8∞

22...♕g7 23.♖g3 ♖fd8

23...f6!? 24.♘g6 ♕f7 25.♖h3 (25.h4 ♔g7
26.♘f4 ♕xh5 27.♘xh5† ♔h6 28.hxg5†

♔xh5 29.g6 ♘g5 30.f4 ♔xg6 31.fxg5 fxg5
32.♖e1 ♗d5 33.♖e5 ♖f5=) 25...f5 (25...♖fd8
26.f4 ♖xd4 27.fxg5 ♖d2 28.♖g3 fxg5 29.♖f1
♕g7 30.h4↑) 26.♘xf8 ♖xf8 27.♕xf7† ♖xf7
28.♖e1 ♘f8∞

23...♖ad8 24.♖d1 ♖xd4 25.♖xd4 ♕xe5
26.♘e2 ♗a6 27.f4 ♕xe2 28.♕xe2 ♗xe2
29.fxg5 ♖c8∞

24.♘f3

24.h4 ♖xd4 25.♘f3 ♖d3 26.a5 ♖ad8 27.axb6
axb6 28.hxg5 ♘f8 29.♖a7 ♖8d7∞

24...♗xf3 25.♕xf3 ♕h6 26.♘e4 ♔f8 27.♖h3
♕g6 28.♖g3 ♕h6 29.♖h3 ♕g7 30.♖g3 ♕h6
½-½ Grischuk – Karjakin, Nice (rapid)
2010.

b23) There is an obvious question as to
what happens if White sacrifices on h6
immediately.
15.♗xh6!?N gxh6 16.♕xh6

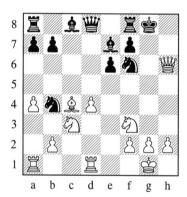

16...♘h7!

This is normally the right defensive plan after
the sacrifice on h6. Alternatives are worse:
16...♕c7? 17.♘e5 ♘h7 18.♘e4+–
16...♘fd5? 17.♘e4 ♖e8 18.♖a3+–
16...♖e8 Black's idea is ...♗f8-g7, but he
does not get the time for it. 17.♕g5† ♔h7
18.♕h4†! (18.d5 exd5 19.♖d4 ♘g4 20.♕h5†
♔h6) 18...♔g7 19.♕g3† ♔f8 20.♘e5 ♗d6
21.♕f4→
16...♘g4 17.♕h5 ♘f6 (17...f5 18.♕g6†
♔h8 19.♘e5 ♖f6 20.♘f7† ♖xf7 21.♕xf7

♕f8 22.♗xe6 ♕xf7 23.♗xf7±) 18.♕g5†
♔h7 (18...♔h8 19.♘e5 ♘h7 20.♕h5±)
19.♗d3† ♘xd3 20.♖xd3 ♖g8 21.♕h4† ♔g7
22.♘e5 ♔f8 23.♖f3 ♖g7 (23...♔e8 24.♘e4
♘xe4 25.♕h5 ♘g5 26.♖xf7 ♕c7 27.h4+–)
24.♕h8† ♘g8 25.♘xf7 ♖xf7 26.♖g3 ♗g5
27.♘e4+–

17.♕h5

17.d5?! is premature: 17...exd5 (17...♘xd5
18.♖d4 ♔h8) 18.♘xd5 ♘xd5 19.♖xd5 ♕b6
black queen is coming to help 20.♕h5 ♕xb2
21.♖e1 ♗e6 22.♖b5 ♕g7 23.♗xe6 fxe6
24.♖xe6 ♗f6∓

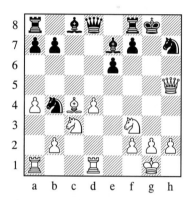

At this point we have lots of moves to
analyse. We will start by briefly considering
some inferior options, before moving onto the
two most important moves of 17...♕e8!? and
17...♘d5.

i) 17...♕c7 18.♘e5 ♗f6 19.♖d3 ♗xe5 20.♖h3
   f5 21.dxe5 ♔h8 22.♘b5→
ii) 17...♗g5? 18.♘e4+–
iii) 17...♗f6? 18.♘a2+–
iv) 17...f5 18.d5→
v) 17...♔h8 18.♘e5±
vi) 17...♔g7 18.♘e5 ♘d5 (18...♗g5 19.♖a3
   ♕f6 20.♘e4 ♕h6 21.♕e2 ♘d5 22.♖g3†;
   18...♕e8 19.♗b5 ♘c6 20.♖d3+–) 19.♗xd5
   exd5 20.♖d3 ♗h4 21.f4→
vii) 17...♗d7 18.d5 exd5 (18...♔h8!?) 19.♘xd5
   ♘xd5 20.♖xd5 ♕c8 21.♖d4 ♗f5 22.♖e1 ♗f6
   23.♖f4+–

b231) The first really important option is:
17...♕e8!?

Preparing ...f5 or ...f6.

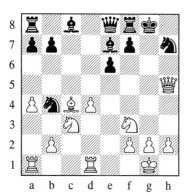

18.d5

Other options are:

18.♘e5 is met by 18...f6.

18.♗b5 ♗d7 (18...♘c6 19.d5+–) 19.♗xd7 ♕xd7 20.♘e5 (20.d5 exd5 21.♘xd5 ♘xd5 22.♖xd5 ♕c6∓) 20...♕e8 21.♘b5 f6 22.♕g4† ♘g5 23.♘c7 ♕c8 24.♘xa8 (24.f4 fxe5 25.fxg5 ♖f4 26.♕h3 ♕xc7 27.♕xe6† ♔f8∓) 24...fxe5 25.♖ac1 ♕xa8 26.dxe5 ♘d5∞

18.♘b5!? f6 (18...♗d8 19.♕g4† ♔h8 20.♘e5 ♕e7 21.♖a3 ♕h4 22.♕xh4 ♗xh4 23.♘d6 ♔g7 24.f4↑; 18...♕d8 19.♘e5 ♘d5 20.♗xd5 exd5 21.♖d3 ♗h4 and now 22.f4!→ prevents ...♕g5) 19.♕h6 ♕d8 20.d5 exd5 21.♘c3 dxc4 (21...♗e6 22.♘d4) 22.♖xd8 ♗xd8 23.♘b5±

18...exd5 19.♘xd5 ♘xd5 20.♖xd5

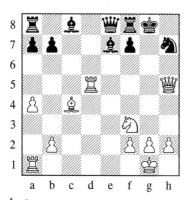

20...♗e6

20...♕c6 21.♘e5 ♕f6 22.♖d3 ♗f5 23.♖g3† ♔h8 24.♘xf7† ♖xf7 25.♕xf7 ♕xf7 26.♗xf7 ♗f6 27.♗g6±
21.♗b5 ♕c8 22.♖e1 ♖d8 23.♗d3 ♘f8 24.♖g5† ♗xg5 25.♕xg5† ♔h8 26.♕h4† ♔g8=

b232) And now for the other main option:
17...♘d5

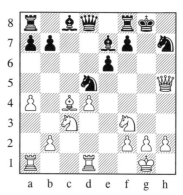

18.♘e5

18.♘xd5 exd5 19.♗d3 f5 20.♕g6† ♔h8 21.♘e5 ♗d6 22.♘f7† ♖xf7 23.♕xf7 ♕g8 24.♕h5 ♕g4=

18...♘df6

18...♗d6 19.♖d3 ♘f4 20.♖g3† ♔h8 21.♕g4 ♕g5 22.♕xg5 ♘xg5 23.♖xg5 f6 24.♘g6† ♔g7 25.♘xf8† fxg5 26.g3 ♔xf8 27.gxf4 ♗xf4 28.♖e1±

19.♕h6 ♘e8 20.f4 ♘d6

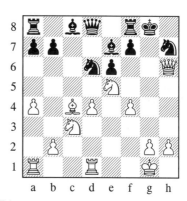

21.♖d3

21.♗d3 f5∞

21...♘f5 22.♕h5 ♘g7 23.♕h6 ♘f5=

It is tough to draw any firm conclusions from the above, as there are so many sharp and unclear positions. It seems to me that even if Black's position proves strong enough to withstand the weakening caused by 14...h6, the suggested alternative 14...b6 seems like a much more reliable path to a safe position.

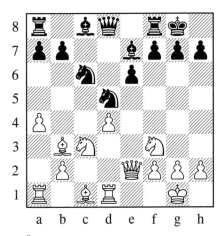

12...②cb4

Black has tried some other moves here too:

12...②a5? 13.♗a2 ②b4 Black plays to eliminate the light-squared bishop at any cost, but he wastes too much time.

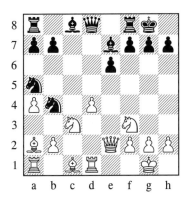

14.d5! Thematic and strong. 14...②xa2 15.♖xa2 ♗f6 16.dxe6 ♕e7 17.②d5 ♕xe6 18.b4 ②c6 19.b5 ②e5 20.②c7 ②xf3† 21.gxf3 ♕xe2 22.♖xe2 ♗e6 23.②xa8 ♖xa8 24.♗b2+– Kramnik – Shirov, Bilbao 2010.

12...♖e8 13.h4!?
Creating some extra options on the kingside, such as putting a piece on g5.
13.a5?! is unimpressive: 13...②xa5 14.♗xd5 exd5 15.♕b5 b6 16.②xd5 ♗b7 17.②xe7† ♖xe7 18.d5 ♖d7∓

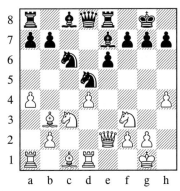

13...②a5
13...♗f8 14.♗c2 (White should consider 14.h5!? ♗d7 15.h6 g6 16.♗g5 f6 [16...♕b6 17.♗c4 ②a5 18.♗xd5 exd5 19.②e5↑] 17.②xd5 exd5 18.♗xd5† ♔h8 19.♗e3 [19.②e5 ②xe5 20.dxe5 fxg5 21.♗xb7 ♕e7 22.♗xa8 ♖xa8∞] 19...♗xh6 20.②e5 fxe5 21.♗xh6 exd4 22.♕d2 and Black's king is in big danger.) 14...②cb4

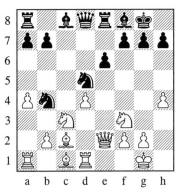

15.♗b1 (15.♗xh7†!? leads to a draw: 15...♔xh7 16.②g5† ♔g8 17.♕h5 ②f6 18.♕xf7† ♔h8 19.②ce4 ②bd5 20.♗f4 ♕d7 21.♕g6 ♖e7 22.②d6 ②xf4 23.②df7† ♔g8 24.②h6† ♔h8=) 15...h6 (15...b6!? 16.②g5 g6 17.h5 ♗a6 18.♕f3 ♕f6 19.♕h3 ♕g7) 16.②e5

♕xh4 17.♕f3 f5 18.♘xd5 ♘xd5 19.♗xf5 exf5 20.♕xd5† ♗e6 21.♕xb7 ♖ad8⇄

14.♗c2 ♘b4

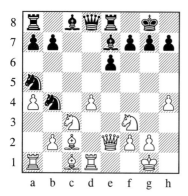

15.♗g5

15.d5!? resembles the Kramnik – Shirov game noted above, and although the evaluation is less clear-cut, White seems to have good prospects. 15...exd5 (15...♘xd5 16.♘g5!→; 15...♘xc2? 16.dxe6 ♘xa1 17.♖xd8 ♗xd8 18.exf7† ♔xf7 19.♘g5† ♗xg5 20.♕h5† ♔f8 21.♗xg5 ♗e6 22.♕xh7±) 16.♘xd5 ♘xd5 (16...♗d6 17.♘f6† gxf6 18.♖xd6 ♖xe2 19.♖xd8† ♔g7 20.♗d1±) 17.♕e4 f5 18.♕xd5† ♕xd5 19.♖xd5 ♘c6 (19... b6 20.♗d2±) 20.♗xf5 ♗xf5 21.♖xf5 ♖ad8 22.♗e3 ♗f6 23.♖b1±

15...h6 16.♗xe7 ♕xe7 17.♕e4 f5 18.♕e2 b6 19.♖e1 ♗a6∞

Gelfand – Shirov, Moscow 2010.

12...b6?!

This offers White several promising options.

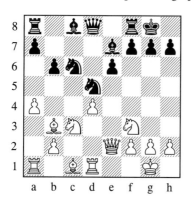

13.♘xd5

Another idea is 13.h4!? ♘a5 14.♗a2 ♘b4 15.d5 (or 15.♗b1 ♗b7 16.♘g5) with some initiative.

13.♕e4 is also quite dangerous: 13...♘xc3 14.bxc3 (14.♕xc6 ♘e2† 15.♔h1 ♘xc1 16.♖axc1 ♖b8 17.d5 ♗b7 18.♕b5 a6 19.♕d3 exd5 20.♗xd5 ♗xd5 21.♕xd5 ♕xd5 22.♖xd5=) 14...♗b7 15.♕g4 (15.♗c2 g6 16.♗h6 ♖e8 17.♕f4 ♕d6=; 15.d5 ♘a5 16.♗a2 [16.♗c2?! g6 17.♗h6 ♖e8 18.♕f4 ♗d6∓] 16...exd5 17.♗xd5 ♗xd5 18.♖xd5 ♕c7 19.♗f4 ♕c4 20.♖d4 ♕e6=) 15...♘a5 16.♗a2 (16.♗h6 ♗f6 17.♗c2 ♖c8 18.♕h3 ♗xf3 19.♗f4 g6 20.♕xf3 ♗g5∓) 16...♖c8 17.♖d3 ♘c4 18.♗h6 ♗f6 19.♗xc4 ♖xc4 20.♘d2 ♖xc3 21.♖xc3 ♕xd4 22.♕xd4 ♗xd4 23.♗xg7 ♗xg7 24.♖g3 ♖c8⇄

13...exd5

Exchanging to this pawn structure usually results in either equality, or a slightly better position for White. The ...b7-b6 move does not help Black at all, so in this particular case White's chances are higher.

14.♘e5

14.♗f4 ♗e6 15.♖ac1 ♖c8 16.♕b5 is another way.

14...♘xe5

14...♘b4!? could be considered to prevent ♗c2 and ♖d3.

15.dxe5 ♗e6

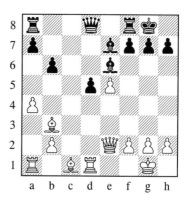

16.♗e3!

Completing development and intending to set up a solid blockade of the d-pawn. Attempting to win the pawn outright leads to unclear consequences:

16.♕f3 d4 17.♗xe6 (17.♗c2 ♖c8 18.♗e4 f5 19.exf6 ♖xf6 20.♕h5 h6) 17...fxe6 18.♕g4 ♕d5 19.♖xd4 ♕xe5 20.♖e4 ♕d5 21.♕xe6† ♕xe6 22.♖xe6 ♖ad8 23.♔f1 ♗f6⩲⩱

16.♕d3 ♗c5 17.♗e3 (17.♗xd5 ♗xd5 18.♕xd5 ♕xd5 19.♖xd5 ♖fd8 20.♖xd8† ♖xd8 21.♗f4 h6) 17...d4 (17...♖c8 18.♗xc5 ♖xc5 19.♕e3 ♕c7 20.♖d4 h6 21.♖ad1 ♖d8 22.h3 a5 23.f4) 18.♗xe6 (18.♗c2 ♕h4 19.♗xd4 ♖ad8 20.g3 ♕h5 21.♕c3 ♖d5 22.♗e4 ♗xd4 23.♖xd4 ♖xe5=) 18...dxe3 19.♗xf7† ♔h8 20.♕xd8 ♖axd8 21.e6 e2 22.♖e1 ♖d2 23.♖ac1 g6 24.♖xc5 bxc5 25.e7 ♔g7 26.exf8=♕† ♔xf8 27.♗b3 c4 White is worse and must fight for a draw.

16...♖c8 17.♖d3 ♕c7 18.♗d4 ♖fd8 19.♖ad1 ♗f5 20.♖g3 ♗f8 21.♗c3±

12...♗f6!?

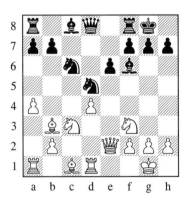

This time Black borrows a manoeuvre from the Panov-Botvinnik Attack, namely ...♘ce7 intending ...b6 and ...♗b7. From e7 the knight can help to protect the kingside, compared to b4 where it looks nice but will not necessarily exert much of an influence on the game.

13.♕e4 ♘ce7 14.♗c2

14.♘e5 ♗d7 15.♗xd5 ♘xd5 16.♘xd5 exd5 17.♕xd5 ♗xa4=

14...g6

14...♘g6 15.h4 ♗xh4 16.♘xh4 ♘xc3 17.bxc3 ♕xh4 18.♕xh4 ♘xh4 19.♖b1 ♘f5 20.♗f4∞

15.h4

15.♗h6 ♖e8 16.♘e5 ♘f5⇄

15...♗d7 16.h5 ♗c6 17.♕g4∞

13.♘e5 ♗d7 14.♕g4 ♘f6 15.♕g3 ♗e8

Once again Black has some other options.

15...♗c6 16.♗h6 ♘e8 17.♖ac1 ♔h8 18.♘xc6 bxc6 19.♗f4 ♘d6 20.♗e5 ♘f5 21.♕h3 ♕b6 22.♘e4 ♖ad8 23.♕g3± Kasimdzhanov – Perez Garcia, Lugo 2009.

15...♖e8

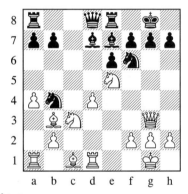

16.♗h6

16.d5 exd5 17.♘xd5 ♘fxd5 18.♗xd5 ♘xd5 19.♖xd5 ♗h4=

16...♗f8

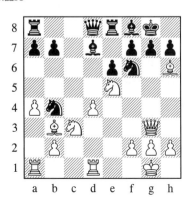

17.d5! exd5 18.♘xd5 ♘bxd5 19.♗xd5 ♘xd5
   19...♖xe5 20.♕xe5 gxh6 21.♗xb7 ♕b8
   (21...♖b8 22.♗c6 ♖b6 23.♕g3† ♗g7
   24.♗xd7 ♘xd7 25.♕d3 ♖b7 26.♖ac1±)
   22.♕xf6 ♕xb7 23.♖d3 ♗g4 24.♖g3 h5
   25.♕f3 ♖c8 26.h3 ♗d6 27.hxg4 ♗xg3
   28.♕xg3 ♕xg4 29.♕e3± Black's king is
   weak.
20.♖xd5 ♕f6
   20...♕e7 21.♖xd7 ♕xe5 22.♕xe5 ♖xe5
   23.♗e3 ♖e7 24.♖ad1±
21.♘xd7 ♕xh6 22.♘xf8 ♖xf8 23.♖d6 ♕h5
24.♖d7±

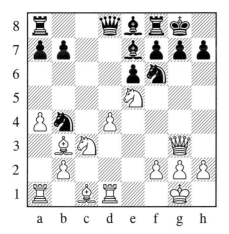

16.♗h6?!

This tempting move leads to complications where Black is holding his own. White should instead choose a different way to fight for an advantage.

After 16.♗g5?! ♘h5 17.♗xe7 ♕xe7 18.♕f3 ♘f6 the bishop exchange has benefitted Black.

16.a5!

This subtle move was the right way to play.
16...♔h8
   The following lines illustrate Black's problems:
   16...♖c8? 17.♗h6 ♘h5 18.♕g4 f5 19.♗xe6†
   ♔h8 20.♗xf5 Now the black rook is hanging.
   20...♖xf5 21.♕xf5 gxh6 22.d5+−

16...a6?! 17.♘c4! Aiming at the weakened b6-square. 17...♘bd5 18.♘xd5 ♘xd5 19.♗h6 ♗f6 20.♗c2±
17.♗g5 ♖c8
   17...♘h5 18.♗xe7 ♕xe7 19.♕e3 ♘f6 20.d5±
18.♕f3
   18.d5 ♘fxd5 19.♗xe7 ♕xe7 20.♗xd5 ♘xd5 21.♘xd5 exd5 22.♕e3 ♔g8=
   18...♗c6 19.♘xc6 bxc6 20.g3±

16...♘h5 17.♕h3
   17.♕g4?! f5 18.♗xe6† ♔h8 19.♗xf5 gxh6∓

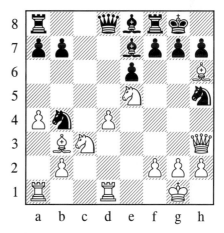

17...f6

The alternative was:
17...♘f6 18.♗g5
   18.d5!? is interesting but only leads to a draw: 18...♘fxd5 19.♕g3 ♗f6 20.♘e4 ♗xe5 21.♕xe5 gxh6 22.♗xd5 ♘xd5 23.♖xd5 exd5 24.♘f6† ♔h8 25.♕f5 ♗g7 26.♘h5† ♔h8 27.♘f6=
18...♗c6
   18...♘fd5 19.♘xd5 ♘xd5 20.♗xd5 ♗xg5 (20...exd5 21.♗xe7 ♕xe7 22.♕b3 ♗c6 23.♖e1± White has a small but safe advantage.) 21.♗xb7 ♖b8 22.♗e4 f5 23.♗c2 ♖xb2 24.♗b3 ♕b6 25.♗c4 The e6-pawn is weak.
   18...♖c8 19.d5 exd5 (19...♘bxd5 20.♗xd5?! [White should prefer 20.♘xd5 which will

transpose to 19...exd5] 20...exd5 21.♗xf6
♗xf6 22.♘xd5 ♖c5 23.♘d7 ♗xd7 24.♕xd7
♕xd7 25.♘xf6† gxf6 26.♖xd7 ♖fc8=)
20.♗xf6 ♗xf6 21.♘xd5 ♘xd5 22.♖xd5 ♕c7
23.♘d7 ♗xb2 24.♖ad1 ♗xd7 25.♖xd7↑
Black is under pressure and the b7- and f7-
pawns are both likely to fall.

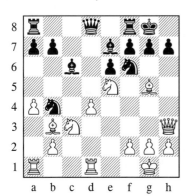

19.♘xf7!?

Another typical motif, but it brings White
no more than equality here.
19.a5 ♘fd5 20.♗d2 ♖c8∞
Perhaps White can consider 19.♘xc6 bxc6
20.a5 ♖b8 21.♗c4 ♘fd5 22.♗d2, hoping to
make something of the two bishops.
19...♖xf7 20.♗xe6 ♕e8 21.♗xf6 ♗xf6 22.d5
♗d7 23.♘e4 ♘xd5 24.♗xf7† ♕xf7 25.♘xf6†
♘xf6
White should be okay in this position, but
Black certainly has no problems.

18.♕xe6†

18.♘c4 gxh6 19.d5 f5 20.dxe6 ♕b8 21.♘d6
♗xd6 22.e7† ♔h8 23.exf8=♕† ♗xf8 24.♕xf5
♕f4∞

**18...♔h8 19.♗e3 fxe5 20.dxe5 ♕c7 21.♘b5
♗xb5 22.axb5 ♘f4**

Since White's slight inaccuracy both sides
have played logically and consistently, but now
White goes astray.

23.b6?!

White could have maintained the balance
with: 23.♗xf4 ♖xf4 24.g3 (24.♖d7?! ♕c5
25.♖f1 ♖e8 26.g3 ♖ff8∓) 24...♖ff8 25.♖d7
♕c5 26.♕xe7 ♕xf2† 27.♔h1 ♕f3† 28.♔g1=

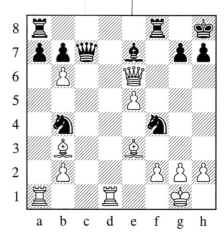

23...♘xe6 24.bxc7 ♘c5 25.♗xc5 ♗xc5

White has two strong pawns and a great
light-squared bishop, yet he is still struggling
to demonstrate full compensation.

26.♖ac1?!

White could have obtained good drawing
chances with 26.e6!, for instance 26...♘c6
27.♖ac1 ♗xf2† 28.♔h1 ♘e7 (28...♗b6
29.♖xc6 bxc6 30.e7 ♖fe8 31.♖d8 ♗xc7
32.♖xa8 ♖xa8 33.♗f7=) 29.♖d7 ♗h4 30.g3
♗f6 31.♖f1 threatening to take on f6 and e7,
and after 31...♖ae8 32.♔g2 it is hard for either
side to improve their positions.

**26...♗xf2† 27.♔h1 ♗e3 28.♖c3 ♗d4
29.c8=♕ ♖axc8 30.♖xc8 ♖xc8 31.♖xd4
♘c6**

Black could have won a pawn in another
way: 31...♖c1† 32.♗d1 (After 32.♖d1?! ♖xd1†
33.♗xd1 ♘d3 34.♗f3 b6 the endgame with no
rooks is virtually hopeless for White) 32...♘c6
33.♖d2 ♔g8 34.e6 ♔f8 35.♔g1 ♔e7 36.♔f2
♔xe6∓

32.♖c4

White will inevitably lose a pawn, but with little material left on the board his rook and bishop should offer him good chances to hold the position against Black's rook and knight.

Another idea was 32.罩d5!?

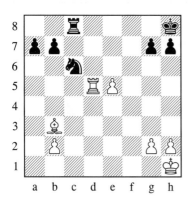

32...勾xe5 (32...罩e8 33.h3 罩xe5 34.罩d6 g6 35.皀d5 罩e1† 36.查h2 罩d1 37.罩d7 勾e5 38.罩d8† 查g7 39.罩g8† 查f6 40.皀xb7=) 33.h3 勾c6 34.罩d7 with decent drawing chances.

32...罩e8 33.h3

33.皀a4 罩xe5 34.查g1 罩e6∓

33...罩xe5 34.罩f4?!

34.皀a4 罩e6 (34...勾e7 35.罩c7=) 35.b4 罩d6 The idea is ...罩d4 36.罩e4 查g8 37.罩e8† 查f7 38.罩c8 勾d8∓

34...h5! 35.罩f7 勾e7∓

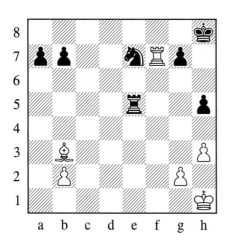

Jakovenko has found an excellent arrangement for his pieces. The rook and knight stand perfectly, and Black can now focus on improving his pawns and king.

36.罩f8† 查h7 37.罩d8 a5 38.皀c2† g6 39.皀d3 b5 40.罩b8 b4 41.罩b6 查g7 42.查g1 罩d5 43.皀e4 罩d4 44.皀f3 罩d2 45.罩b5 罩xb2 46.罩xa5

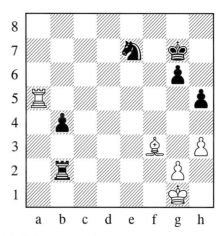

46...h4!–+

Great technical play by Jakovenko. White has failed to offer much resistance and Black has achieved everything he wanted. With his last move he fixes the enemy kingside pawns and sets up potential mating nets involving a knight on g3.

47.罩a6 查h6 48.皀e4 查g5 49.罩b6 勾f5 50.皀d3 b3 51.查h2 勾e3 52.罩xg6† 查f4

The g6-pawn was not really important, and Jakovenko is more concerned with improving his pieces, including the king.

53.罩g8 罩d2 54.皀h7 b2 55.罩f8† 查g5 56.罩g8† 查h6 57.皀e4 勾f1† 58.查g1 勾g3

The bishop runs out of squares and the game is over.

59.皀g6 罩d6 60.罩b8 罩d1† 61.查f2 罩d2† 0–1

GAME 21
▷ **A. Morozevich (2694)**
▶ **A. Timofeev (2665)**
64th Russian Championship, Moscow
Round 4, 11.08.2011 **[D20]**
Annotated by Kamil Miton

In this game Morozevich reminds us of the important idea of 11.e6. In my opinion, Black should hold the position, but during a practical game without good preparation, it is easy to allow White the initiative. Timofeev quickly blundered, but as we know, he was in poor form during this tournament. The end of the game was played in time trouble.

1.d4 d5 2.c4 dxc4 3.e4 ♘f6 4.e5 ♘d5 5.♗xc4 ♘b6 6.♗d3

6.♗b3 is the alternative: 6...♘c6 7.♘e2 ♗f5 8.♘bc3 e6 9.a3 Aimed against ...♘b4-d5. 9...♕d7 10.0–0 ♗e7 Black prepares short castling. The other plan is to go for ...0–0–0, ...f6 and ...h5-h4. 11.♗e3 0–0 12.♗c2!? ♗xc2 13.♕xc2

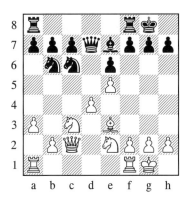

This was Miton – Markowski, Warsaw 2004. I recommend this game as a good example of how to play this structure. Our intuition may tell us that without any weaknesses and with control over the d5-square, Black should not have any problems, but it is difficult to find a good plan for Black. On the other hand, White's plan is very simple: to slowly develop

an attack against the black king with ♘e4, ♖d1-d3, ♘g3-♘h5 etc.

6...♘c6 7.♘e2 ♗g4 8.f3 ♗e6 9.♘bc3 ♗c4

9...♕d7 10.♘e4 ♗d5 11.♘c5 ♕c8 12.a3 e6 13.♕c2 ♗xc5 14.♕xc5 ♕d7∞

10.♗xc4 ♘xc4

11.e6

The idea of this move is to cause Black some problems with his development, and then to start playing very actively with moves such as ♕b3 and ♘f4.

The alternatives are:

11.d5 ♘6xe5 12.0–0 (12.b3 is also possible) 12...e6 13.f4 ♗c5† 14.♔h1 ♘d7 15.dxe6 fxe6 16.♕b3 ♘d6 17.♕xe6† ♕e7 18.♕xe7† ♔xe7 19.♘d5† ♔f7 20.♘xc7 ♖ac8 21.♘d5 ♖he8⯰

White can try pushing his e-pawn a move later: 11.♕b3 ♘b6 12.e6 (12.♗e3 e6 13.0–0 ♘b4 14.♘f4 Fighting for the d5-square. 14...♗e7 15.a3 ♘4d5 16.♘fxd5 ♘xd5 17.♘xd5 ♕xd5 18.♕xd5 exd5 19.f4 f5! This typical reaction ensures that Black is fine.) 12...fxe6 13.♗e3 (13.♕xe6 ♕d7=) 13...♕d7 14.0–0 g6 15.♖fd1 ♘a5 16.♕b4 ♘c6 17.♕b3 ♘a5 18.♕b4 ♘c6 19.♕b5 a6 20.♕b3 ♘a5 21.♕b4 ♘c6 22.♕b3 ♘a5 23.♕b4 ♘c6 24.♕b3

½–½ Mamedyarov – Bacrot, Wijk aan Zee 2006.

11.0–0 e6 12.a3!? White sometimes plays this move to prevent the logical ...♘b4, after which both black knights may be able to control the very important d5-square. 12...♕d7 13.♕b3 ♘b6 14.♖d1 ♗e7 15.♗e3 (15.d5 ♘xe5 16.♘f4 0–0 17.dxe6 ♕c6= followed by ...♕c4) 15...0–0 16.♕c2 ♖ad8= Comparing this with my game against Markowski, it is better for White when his pawn is still on f2, enabling the potential rook transfer ♖d3-g3(or h3).

11...fxe6 12.0–0

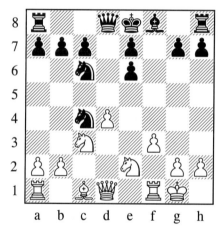

12...♘b6

At this point Black has two other natural options:

12...g6

Black intends to continue his development with ...♗g7.

13.♕b3 ♘b6 14.♕xe6

14.♖d1!? looks very interesting: 14...♗g7 15.♕xe6 (15.d5 exd5 16.♘xd5 ♗d4† 17.♘xd4 ♕xd5 18.♕xd5 ♘xd5 19.♘xc6 bxc6=) 15...♕d6 16.♕e4 Black does not have time to set up a blockade on the d5-square. 16...0–0–0 17.d5± White will next transfer his knight to e6, with good prospects.

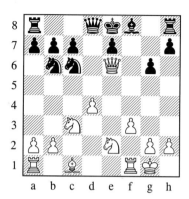

14...♘xd4

14...♕d7 is worse: 15.♕xd7† ♔xd7 16.d5 Otherwise Black will play ...♘b4 or ...e6, and blockade on d5. 16...♘b4 17.♖d1 e6 18.dxe6† ♔xe6 19.♘e4 ♘4d5 20.a4! Black's pieces are totally uncoordinated.

15.♘xd4

15.♕e5 ♘xe2† 16.♘xe2 ♖g8 17.♘f4 ♕d6 18.♕b5† c6 19.♕b3 ♘d5 20.♘xd5 cxd5 21.♗e3 ♗g7 22.♖ad1 ♖d8 23.♗xa7 ♔f7=

15...♕xd4†

Having taken a pawn, Black will now look for an opportunity to exchange queens.

16.♗e3 ♕f6 17.♕b3

17.♕e4 0–0–0 18.♘b5 ♗g7 19.♖ac1 ♖d7 20.♘xa7† ♔b8 21.♘b5 ♕e5 22.♕xe5 ♗xe5=

17...♕f7

17...♗g7 18.♘b5 0–0–0 19.♘xa7† ♔b8 20.♘b5 ♕xb2 21.♗xb6 cxb6 22.♕a4 ♗d4† 23.♔h1 ♕xa1 24.♖xa1 ♗xa1 25.f4 and White has the initiative.

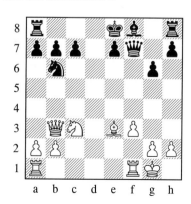

18.♘b5 ♛xb3 19.♘xc7† ♔f7

19...♔d7 20.axb3 ♔xc7 21.♖fc1† ♔d7 22.♗xb6 e5 23.♖c7† ♔e6 24.♖xa7 ♖xa7 25.♗xa7±

20.axb3 ♖c8 21.♗d4

On 21.♖fc1 ♗g7 22.♖xa7 ♗xb2 23.♖d1 ♖xc7 24.♗xb6 ♖c2 25.b4 ♖b8 Black should hold the position. For example: 26.♖d7 ♖c1† 27.♔f2 ♖c2† 28.♔g3 ♗e5† 29.♔h3 ♗d6 leads to an equal position.

After 21.♘b5 ♘d5 22.♗d4 e5 23.♗xe5 ♗c5† 24.♔h1 ♖he8 Black has a pleasant game. His much better king position gives Black compensation for the pawn.

21...♗g7 22.♗xg7 ♔xg7 23.♘e6† ♔f6 24.♖fe1

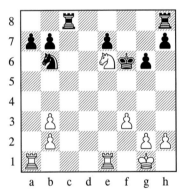

24...♖c6

24...a6 25.♖ad1 ♖c6? 26.♘d8+−

25.♘d4 ♖d6 26.♘b5 ♖d2=

Black should have enough counterplay.

12...♛d7

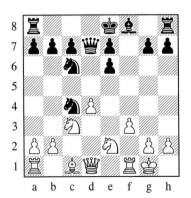

Another typical reaction. Black prepares to castle long, while defending the e6-pawn.

13.♘e4

13.♛b3 ♘b6 14.♖d1 (14.♘e4 ♘xd4 15.♘xd4 ♛xd4† 16.♗e3 ♛c4 17.♛a3 ♛a4 18.♛d3 Of course, White keeps the queens on the board. 18...♖d8 19.♛e2 ♛c4 20.♛f2 White has a good initiative in return for the pawns) 14...0–0–0 15.♘e4 (15.a4 a5) 15...g6 (15...♛d5!? transposes to the line reached after 13.♘e4) 16.♘c5 (16.♗f4 ♛d5 17.♘g5 ♗h6 18.♘xe6 ♛xb3 19.axb3 ♗xf4 20.♘2xf4 ♖d6 21.d5 ♘b4=; 16.♘g5 ♗g7 17.♘xe6 [17.♘f7 e5!⇆] 17...♘a5 18.♛e3 ♘d5 19.♛e4 ♘f6 20.♘c5 ♘xe4 21.♘xd7 ♖xd7 22.fxe4 c5 and Black takes the initiative) 16...♛d5 17.♘xe6 ♖d6 18.♘2f4 ♛xb3 19.axb3 ♗h6= Black has exchanged queens and developed his bishop, thereby solving all his problems.

13...0–0–0 14.♛b3

14.b3?! ♘b6 15.♘g5 ♖g8 (15...♘xd4? 16.♗b2 is slightly better for White, since Black can't exchange queens) 16.♛d3 g6 17.♛e4 ♘d5 18.♘xe6 ♘f6 19.♛e3 ♘d5=

14.♘g5 ♘xd4 15.♘xd4 ♛xd4† 16.♛xd4 ♖xd4 17.♘xe6 ♖d7 White has compensation for the pawn, because the knight on e6 hinders the development of the black kingside. However, Black should cope with this problem easily enough; possible plans are to play ...♖g8 and ...g6, or ...♘b6, ...c6 and ...♘d5. Meanwhile White may try b3 and ♗b2, or f4-f5.

14...♛d5

14...♘4a5 15.♛a4 ♘xd4 16.♛xa5 ♘xe2† 17.♔h1 ♛d4 (17...a6!? ♛b5) 18.♛e1 (18.♗d2 ♖d5 19.♛a3 ♘g3†! 20.♘xg3 ♛xd2 21.b4∞) 18...♛c4 19.b3±

15.♖d1

15.♘f4 ♘xd4 (15...♛xd4† 16.♔h1 e5 17.♘e6 ♛d3∞) 16.♘xd5 ♘xb3 17.axb3 exd5 18.bxc4 dxe4 19.♖xa7 ♔b8 20.♗e3 ♖d3 21.♖fa1 ♔c8∞

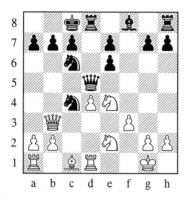

15...♘b6!

The position looks very unclear.

15...g6?! 16.♘4c3! (16.♘f4 ♘xd4! is fine for Black; after 16.♘g5 Black can sacrifice the exchange to obtain active pieces with 16...♗g7 17.♘f7 ♘xd4 18.♘xd4 ♗xd4† 19.♔h1 ♖hf8 20.♘xd8 ♖xd8∞) 16...♘4a5 17.♕c2 Black has to be careful with the knight on a5. 17...♕f5 18.♘e4 ♗g7 19.♗e3 ♘b4 20.♕a4 ♘ac6 21.♖ac1±

16.♘g5 ♕xb3 17.axb3 ♖g8

Black is happy to give a pawn back.

18.♘xh7

18.♘xe6 ♖d6 19.♘c5 g6=

18...g6 19.♘g5 e5∞

Black shouldn't have any problems.

13.♘e4

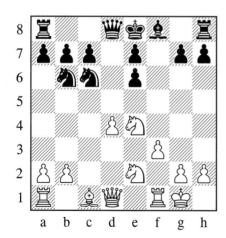

13...g6

In a previous game Black played:
13...♕d5 14.♗e3

14.a4!? is a very interesting idea. Having the pawns on a4 and a5 may make an important difference when Black castles long. 14...a5 (14...0–0–0 15.a5 ♘c4 16.♖a4 ♘4xa5 17.♗d2 ♕b5 18.♗xa5 ♘xa5 19.♘f4 gives White the initiative) 15.♗e3 g5 16.♖c1 ♗g7 17.♘xg5 ♘c4 18.♘f4 ♕xg5 19.♖xc4 0–0–0 20.♖xc6 (20.♖c5 ♕xc5 21.dxc5 ♖xd1 22.♖xd1 ♗xb2 23.♘xe6=) 20...bxc6 21.♕d3 Here we see an effect of the earlier moves with the a-pawns, as Black does not have ...♕b5 available. 21...♕f5 22.♕a6† ♔d7 23.♖c1 ♔e8 24.♕xc6† ♔f7 25.g4 White has a strong attack.

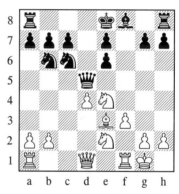

After 14.♗e3 Black has two options:

a) 14...g5!?

Black wants to prevent ♘f4, and also quickly activate his bishop.

15.♖c1!?

15.♘xg5 ♗h6 16.f4 ♘c4 17.♗f2 ♗xg5 18.♘c3 ♕f5 19.fxg5 ♕xg5 20.♕e2 ♖g8 21.g3 ♘b6∞; 15.♗xg5 0–0–0 16.♗e3 e5 17.dxe5 ♕xe5 18.♕b3 ♗g7=

15...♗g7

15...0–0–0   16.♖c5   ♕xa2   (16...♕d7 17.♕b3↑) 17.♘2c3 ♕xb2 (17...♕a6 may be safer) 18.♖f2 ♕b4 19.♖b5 ♕c4 (19...♖xd4? 20.♕c1 ♕c4 21.♖c5 ♕b4 22.♗xd4 ♕xd4 23.♘b5 ♕a4 24.♖xc6 bxc6 25.♕xc6 ♕d1†

26.♖f1 ♕d7 27.♘xa7† ♔d8 28.♕c2±)
20.♖c5 ♕b4 21.♕c1! The black queen is in
some danger.

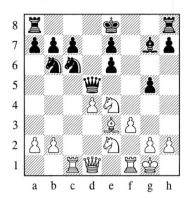

16.♘xg5

After 16.♖c5 ♕d7 White has no time for
17.♕b3, because the d4-pawn would be
hanging.
16...♘c4 17.♘f4 ♕xg5 18.♖xc4 0–0–0
19.♖xc6

19.♕a4 ♖d6 20.♖c5 ♕h4∞

19...bxc6

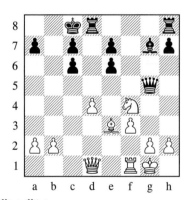

20.♕e2 ♕b5

Black may be able to get away with 20...♗h6
21.♕a6† ♔d7, but it looks dangerous.
21.♕xb5 cxb5 22.♘xe6 ♗f6

22...♖dg8 23.f4⊠

23.♘xd8 ♖xd8 24.♖d1 c5 25.♖c1 c4 26.b3
♗xd4 27.♔f2 ♗xe3†

27...♗b2 28.♖c2 c3 29.♗xa7 ♖d5 30.a3!±

28.♔xe3 ♖d3† 29.♔e2 ♖d4 30.bxc4 bxc4
31.♔e3 e5=

Or 31...♖d3† 32.♔f4 c3 33.♔e4 ♖d2
34.♖xc3† ♔b7=.

b) 14...0–0–0?

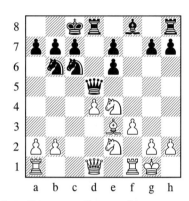

15.♘f4 ♕f5 16.g4 ♕f7 17.♕b3

The black position is very bad.

17...♖d5

17...♘xd4 18.♗xd4 ♖xd4 19.♘xe6 ♖d5
20.♘4c5 g6 21.♖ad1 ♖xd1 22.♖xd1 ♗g7
23.♕d3+–

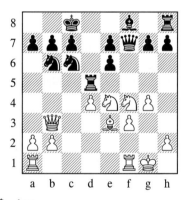

18.♘xd5?!

This mistake allows Black to comfortably
complete her development.

The right move was 18.♖ac1!±.

18...exd5 19.♘g3 g6 20.♔h1 h5 21.gxh5 gxh5
22.♕d3 e6 23.b3 ♗d6 24.♘e2 ♔b8∓

Zhao Xue – Ushenina, Krasnoturinsk 2007.

An idea that should be tested is 13...e5 14.dxe5
♕xd1 15.♖xd1 e6. Black has given back the
pawn, but improved his pawn structure.

14.♘c5

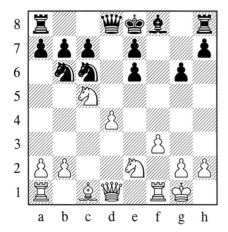

14...♕d6?

This is a huge mistake. In many positions it is normal that if one of the players has sacrificed material (here a pawn) for the initiative, then his opponent may give back the material to stop the initiative and obtain some counterplay. But in this case, White regains the pawn with tempo.

14...♔f7!? is interesting. Compared to the game, the e6-pawn will be protected.

The most typical reaction is:
14...♕d5 15.♗e3
    15.♘f4 ♕xd4† 16.♕xd4 ♘xd4 17.♘fxe6 ♘xe6 18.♘xe6 ♘d5=
    15.♘xb7 ♗g7 16.♗e3 0–0∞

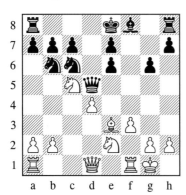

15...0–0–0
    15...e5 16.♘c3 (16.♘xb7 exd4 17.♗xd4 ♘xd4 18.♕xd4 e5 19.♕xd5 ♘xd5 20.♖fd1 ♘e3 21.♖d3 ♖b8 22.♖xe3 ♖xb7 23.♖xe5† ♔f7 24.♖b1 ♗g7=) 16...♕c4 17.dxe5 ♗h6 18.♗f2 (18.f4!?) 18...♖d8 19.♕b3 (19.♕b1 is also worth considering) 19...♖d2 20.♘xb7 ♕xb3 21.axb3 ♖xb2 22.♘c5 0–0 The position is unclear, with both sides having a lot of potential weaknesses.
16.♘f4 ♕f5
Here White has several choices, but none gives him any real advantage.
17.♕b3
    17.♘fxe6 ♖d6 18.♕b3 ♘a5 (or 18...♕d5) 19.♕c3 ♖xe6 20.♘xe6 ♕xe6 21.d5 ♘xd5 22.♕xh8 ♕xe3† 23.♔h1 ♕f4 24.♕xh7∞
    17.g4 ♕f7 18.♕b3 ♖xd4 19.♘fxe6 ♖b4 20.♕c3 ♖g8∞
17...♗h6 18.♘fxe6 ♗xe3† 19.♕xe3 ♖d6 20.♖ac1 ♘d5 21.♕e2 ♘d8 22.♖fe1 ♘xe6 23.♘xe6 ♔b8

The position is roughly equal. The d5-knight and the e7-pawn are no worse than the e6-knight and the d4-pawn.

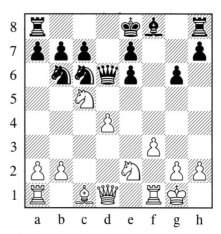

15.♘xb7±
Naturally White takes the pawn.
    15.♗f4 e5 16.♘xb7 ♕d5 17.dxe5 ♖b8 18.♖c1 ♖xb7 19.♕xd5 ♘xd5 20.♖xc6 ♖xb2 21.♖d1 ♔d7 22.♖c4 e6 23.♘c3 c6=

15...♕d5 16.♗e3 ♗g7 17.♘f4 ♕f5 18.♖c1 ♘xd4 19.♗xd4 ♗xd4† 20.♕xd4 e5 21.♕b4 ♕xf4

21...exf4 22.♖xc7 0–0 23.♖xe7 ♖f7 24.♕xf7† ♕xf7 25.♖xf7 ♔xf7 26.♖d1±

22.♕b5†

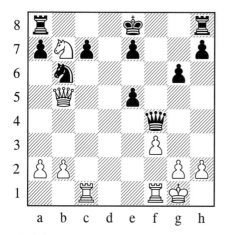

Black has too many weak pawns.

22...c6 23.♕xc6† ♔f7 24.♘c5 ♕d4† 25.♔h1 ♕d5 26.♕xd5† ♘xd5

White clearly has the better structure, the doubled pawns being weak. On the other hand, the black king is much better placed, and so White is obliged to play a lot of technical moves in order to get winning chances.

27.♘d3

27.♖fe1 was another option.

27...♔f6 28.♖c6†

After 28.♖fe1 ♖hc8 29.♘xe5 ♖xc1 30.♘d7† ♔f7 31.♖xc1 ♘b4⇄ 32.a3 ♘d3 it turns out that the white knight is badly placed on d7.

28...e6 29.♖e1

29.♖fc1 was possible. The main idea is to prevent ...♖c8, and to carry out the manoeuvre ♘c5-e4 followed by b3 or ♖a6.

29...♖hc8 30.♖a6

White improves his position: the rook on a6 is excellent placed.

30...♖c2 31.h4

31.♖xe5? ♘f4

31...♖c4 32.♖e4 ♖d4 33.♘c5 ♘f4 34.♖xd4 exd4 35.g3 ♖c8

Since both players were in time trouble, Timofeev was probably looking for some practical counterplay.

36.b4

If White accepts the knight sacrifice, Black activates his king and rook, but it is not enough: 36.♘e4† ♔e5 37.gxf4† ♔xf4 38.♔g2 ♖c2† 39.♘f2 ♖xb2 40.♖xe6 ♖xa2 41.♖e4† ♔f5 42.♔g3+–

36...♘d5

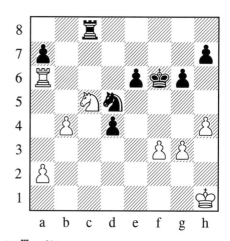

37.♖xe6†?

This is a blunder.

After 37.a3 White is winning, but Morozevich probably didn't have enough time to calculate the variations if Black sacrifices the exchange: 37...♔f5 (37...d3 38.♖xe6† ♔f5 39.♖e4+–) 38.♖xa7 (38.♔g1 is also good enough) 38...♖xc5 39.bxc5 d3

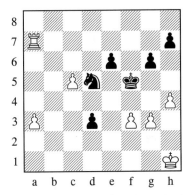

40.♖a4! If it were not for this, Black would win. But now it goes the other way. 40...e5 41.g4† ♔e6 42.♖a6† ♔e7 43.♖d6+–

37...♔f7 38.♖a6 ♘xb4 39.♖xa7†

It appears that Black lost on time here. In the final position he has obtained serious drawing chances.

1–0

GAME 22

▷ **E. Bacrot (2710)**
▶ **R. Edouard (2587)**
86th French Championship, Caen
Round 9, 23.08.2011 **[D27]**
Annotated by Etienne Bacrot & Arkadij Naiditsch

Black's choice of 11...♗d7?! is not the best solution in the position. Black should stick to the more common 11...♘a5 with very unclear play. White chose the wrong reply with 12.♖ad1 – instead 12.♖fe1! would have given him a clear advantage. After a few mistakes on both sides, Black couldn't stand the pressure and blundered with 23...♗c5??.

Overall, an interesting fighting game, but less interesting theoretically: 11...♗d7?! is simply a "do-not-play-again" move.

1.d4 d5 2.c4 dxc4 3.♘f3 ♘f6 4.e3 e6 5.♗xc4 c5 6.0–0 a6 7.♗b3 ♘c6 8.♘c3 cxd4 9.exd4 ♗e7 10.♗g5 0–0 11.♕d2 ♗d7?!

11...♘a5 is the main move in the position.

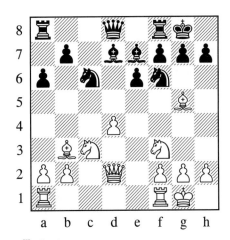

12.♖ad1?!

Not the best! The right move was:
12.♖fe1!

This is clearly the main move here.

12...♖c8

If Black wants to try the same idea as in the game, then now a surprise awaits him: 12...♘a5 13.♗c2 ♘c4 14.♕e2 ♘xb2?? Compared to the game, there is no white rook on d1 under attack. 15.♗c1!+– Black's knight is trapped.

13.♖ad1 ♘a5 14.d5 ♘xb3 15.axb3 h6 16.♗xh6 gxh6 17.d6±

Caruana – Istratescu, Switzerland 2010.

12...♘a5 13.♗c2 ♘c4 14.♕e2

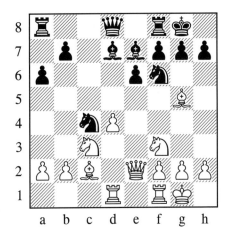

A critical moment of the game.

14...罝c8?!

Black didn't use his chance and continued with schematic play.

14...②xb2! was possible after which Black is at least equal.

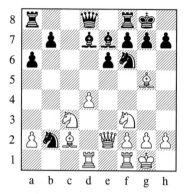

a) 15.罝c1 ②c6
  15...b5 16.②xf6 ②xf6 17.②e4 b4! 18.②xa8
(18.②b1 ②a4 19.②xa8 豐xa8 [19...②b5
20.豐d2 豐xa8 21.豐xb4 ②xf1 22.②xf1 豐e8
23.②bd2 豐b5† 24.豐xb5 axb5 25.②e4±]
20.豐c2 a5 21.罝fe1 豐d5∓; 18.豐xb2 bxc3
19.罝xc3 罝b8 20.豐c2 g6 21.罝c1 豐b6∓)
18...bxc3 19.②e4 ②b5 20.豐e3 ②xf1 21.②xf1
②a4 22.豐d3 g6 23.豐xa6 ②b2 24.罝xc3
②xd4 25.罝c2 ②f6 26.g3=
  15...罝c8 16.②e5 罝xc3 17.②xf6 罝xc2
(17...②xf6 18.②xh7† ②xh7 19.罝xc3 ②g8
20.罝h3 ②xe5 21.dxe5 ②a4 22.豐h5 f5
23.exf6 豐xf6 24.豐h7† ②f7 25.罝f3+−)
18.豐xc2 ②xf6 19.豐xb2 ②b5 20.罝fe1
豐d6± The bishop pair promises Black good
compensation, but White is the only one
who can play for the advantage.
16.罝b1 豐a5 17.②xf6 ②xf6 18.②e4 ②a4
  18...②b5 19.②xf6† gxf6 20.②e4 f5 21.豐f4
②xf1 22.豐g5† ②h8 23.豐f6† ②g8 24.②g5
豐c7 25.豐h6 f6 26.②xe6 豐e7 27.②xf8
②d3

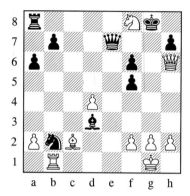

28.②xh7! A very beautiful tactic. 28...②xc2
(28...豐xh7 29.豐d2 ②xc2 30.豐xc2+−)
29.②xf6† ②f7 30.②d5 豐e4 31.豐f6† ②e8
(31...②g8 32.②e7† 豐xe7 33.豐xe7 ②xb1
34.d5+−) 32.豐h8† ②f7 33.豐h7† ②f8 34.②f6!
豐xd4 (34...豐e6 35.②d7† ②e8 36.②c5 豐e7
37.豐g8† 豐f8 38.罝e1† ②e4 39.豐b3+−)
35.豐h8† ②f7 36.豐xa8! ②xb1 37.豐e8†
②g7 (37...②xf6 38.豐h8†+−) 38.豐e7† ②g6
39.豐h7† ②g5 40.豐g7† ②f4 41.豐g3#
19.②xf6† gxf6 20.②e5
  20.豐e3 ②g7 21.②e5 fxe5 22.豐g5† ②h8
23.豐f6† ②g8 24.豐g5†=
  20.②xh7† ②xh7 21.②e5 fxe5 22.豐h5† ②g8
23.豐g5† ②h7 24.豐h4†=
20...fxe5 21.②xh7†

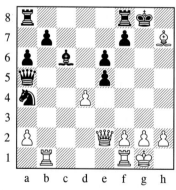

21...②g7 22.豐g4† ②xh7 23.豐h5† ②g8
24.豐g5† ②h7 25.豐h5†=

b) 15.罝b1 罝c8 16.罝xb2 罝xc3 17.罝c1 ②d5
18.②xe7 豐xe7 19.罝xb7 罝fc8∓

c) 15.♗xf6 ♗xf6 16.♗xh7† ♔xh7 17.♕xb2
♗c6 18.♘e5 ♗xe5 19.dxe5 ♕g5 20.f4 ♕f5∓

d) 15.♗xh7†

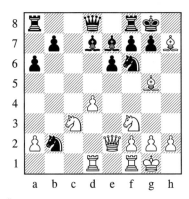

15...♘xh7!

15...♔xh7 16.♕xb2 ♗c6 17.♘e5 ♔g8
18.♖d3± White has good attacking chances
on the kingside.

16.♗xe7 ♘xd1

16...♕xe7 17.♕xb2 ♖ac8 18.d5 (18.♘e5
♘f6 19.♖fe1 ♗c6 20.♘xc6 bxc6=) 18...♕c5
19.♘e4 ♕c2 20.♕e5 ♕xa2 21.dxe6 ♗xe6
(21...♕xe6 22.♘d6 ♕xe5 23.♘xe5 ♖c7
24.♖c1 ♖xc1 25.♖xc1 ♘f6 26.♘xd7 ♘xd7
27.♖c7 ♘f6 28.♘xb7=) 22.♘d6 ♖cd8
23.♖d2 ♕a3 24.♘h4!⩲
17.♗xd8 ♘xc3 18.♕d2

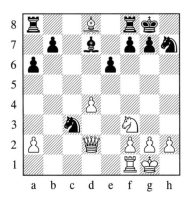

18...♘e2† 19.♕xe2 ♗b5 20.♕e4 ♗xf1
21.♔xf1 ♖fxd8 22.♕xb7 ♖db8 23.♕c6 ♖c8
24.♕a4 ♖c1† 25.♔e2=

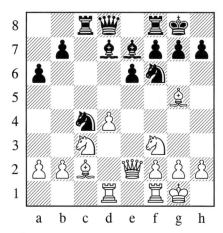

15.♗b3!

The best decision. Black can't defend against
the logical d4-d5! which is usually crushing in
such structures.

15.♗d3 ♘b6 16.♘e5 ♗c6 17.♖fe1 leads to a
typically unclear IQP position.

15...b5

15...♘a5 16.d5 exd5 17.♗xd5±.

15...♘b6 16.♘e5± ♗c6 17.♘xc6 ♖xc6
(17...bxc6 18.♕xa6±) 18.♗xf6 ♗xf6 19.d5 exd5
20.♘xd5 ♘xd5 21.♗xd5 ♖d6 22.♗xb7 White
is a clear pawn up and has a big advantage, but
Black still has some chances to fight for a draw
due to the opposite-coloured bishops.

15...♘d6 16.d5 exd5 17.♘xd5 ♘xd5 18.♖xd5
♗xg5 19.♘xg5 ♗b5 20.♕d2 ♗xf1 21.♖xd6
♕xd6 22.♕xd6 ♖c1

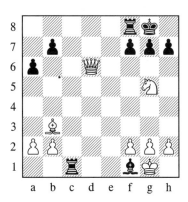

23.♗xf7†!+– ♖xf7 24.♕d8† ♖f8 25.♕d5†
♔h8 26.♘f7† ♔g8 27.♘h6† ♔h8 28.♕g8†
♖xg8 29.♘f7#

15...♗b5 16.a4 ♘a5 17.axb5 ♘xb3 18.d5
exd5 19.bxa6 bxa6 20.♗xf6 ♗xf6 21.♘xd5 a5
22.♖fe1±

16.♘e5 ♘b6

16...♕c7 17.♗xc4 bxc4 18.d5 exd5 19.♗xf6
♗xf6 20.♘xd7 ♕xd7 21.♘xd5±

17.♖fe1 h6

It may look as though Black is creating a
weakness, but it was not easy to find a good
move in this position.

17...b4

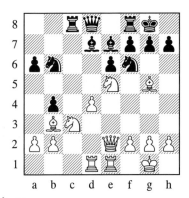

18.♗xf6

18.d5!? exd5 19.♘xd7 (19.♘xd5 ♘bxd5
20.♗xd5 ♘xd5 21.♖xd5 ♗xg5 22.♘xd7 h6
23.h4 ♗xh4 24.g3 ♗g5 25.f4 ♗f6 26.♕xa6
♖e8 27.♘xf6† ♕xf6 28.♖xe8† ♖xe8 29.♕xf6
gxf6 30.♔f2 ♖a8 31.♖d4 ♖xa2 32.♖xb4 h5
White has a slightly better endgame, but
Black can draw with correct play.) 19...♕xd7
20.♕xe7 ♕xe7 21.♖xe7 bxc3 22.bxc3 ♖xc3
23.♖a7 ♖a8 24.♖xa8† ♘xa8 25.♗xf6 gxf6
26.♖xd5 With a much better endgame.
18...♗xf6 19.♘xd7 ♕xd7 20.♘e4 ♗e7
20...♗xd4 21.♘g5 e5 22.♕e4 g6 23.♕h4 h5
24.♖xe5 ♗xe5 25.♖xd7 ♘xd7 26.g4±
21.♕xa6±

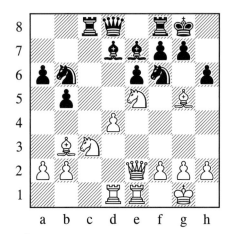

18.♗xh6?!

This looks very pretty but it gives Black
chances. White had better possibilities:

18.♗h4 b4 19.d5 exd5 (19...♘fxd5 20.♘xd5
♘xd5 21.♘xd7 ♗xh4 22.♘xf8 ♕xf8 23.♗xd5
exd5 24.♖xd5+–) 20.♗xf6 ♗xf6 21.♘xd5
♘xd5 22.♗xd5 ♗xe5 23.♕xe5 ♖e8 24.♕f4
♖xe1† 25.♖xe1 ♕f8 26.h4±

18.♗xf6! ♗xf6 19.♕e4

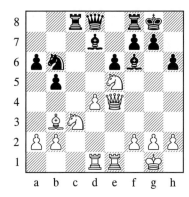

With the simple and almost deadly threat of
♗c2.
19...♗xe5
19...b4 20.♗c2 g6 21.♘xg6 fxg6 22.♕xg6†
♗g7 23.♕h7† ♔f7 24.♗g6†+–
19...♕e7 20.♕b7 ♗xe5 21.dxe5 ♕c5 22.♘e4
♕c7 23.♕xc7 ♖xc7 24.♘d6±
20.dxe5 ♘c4 21.♗c2 g6 22.♗b3±

22.♕f4 ♕g5 (22...♔g7 23.♘e4 ♘xb2 24.♖d2 ♕a5 [24...♘c4 25.♕f6† ♔g8 26.♕xd8 ♖fxd8 27.♘f6† ♔g7 28.♖xd7 ♖xd7 29.♘xd7 ♘xe5 30.♘xe5 ♖xc2 31.♖a1 ♔f6 32.♘g4† ♔g5 33.♘e3 ♖b2 34.a3±] 25.♖e3! ♖xc2 If Black doesn't sacrifice the exchange, then next will be g4 with ♖h3 and Black cannot defend. 26.♖xc2 ♘c4 27.♖ec3 ♗c6 28.♕f6† ♔g8 29.♘d6 ♗d5 30.h4 Note that 22...♘xb2 23.♘e4 ♔g7 24.♖d2 transposes to 22...♔g7.) 23.♕xg5 hxg5 24.♖xd7 ♘xb2 25.♖b1 ♘c4 26.♘e4 ♘a3 27.♖b3! ♖xc2 (27...♘xc2 28.♖h3+–) 28.h4!+–

The idea is that after:
22...♘xb2

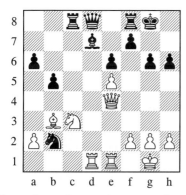

23.♗xe6! ♗xe6 24.♖xd8 ♖fxd8 25.♕h4!±

18.♗f4!? is also interesting with the idea ♖d3 followed by ♗xh6 or a breakthrough with d4-d5. Sometimes the threat is stronger than its execution :) – a famous chess rule! 18...b4 Not best, but what else can Black do?! (18...♗b4 19.♖d3 with a strong attack)

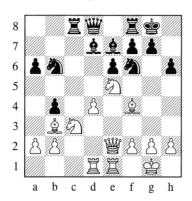

19.d5! A killing move. 19...exd5 20.♘xd5 ♘bxd5 21.♗xd5+– Black is losing material.

18...gxh6 19.♖d3

19.d5 exd5∞ 20.♘xd7 ♕xd7 21.♕xe7 ♕xe7 22.♖xe7 ♖fd8 23.♖a7 ♘c4 with serious counterplay for Black.

19...♔h8

19...♘c4 20.♗c2 ♔h8 21.♖g3 with a strong attack.

20.♕d2

20.d5 exd5 (20...b4 21.dxe6+–) 21.♘xd7 ♘bxd7 22.♕xe7 ♕xe7 23.♖xe7 ♘c5 24.♖d1 ♘xb3 25.axb3 b4 26.♘e2 ♖c2 27.♘d4 ♖xb2 28.f3 White has compensation.

20...♘g8 21.d5

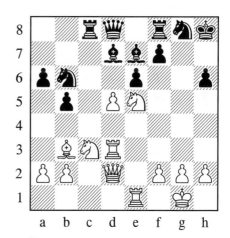

21...♘c4!?
The best defence!

21...b4?! 22.dxe6
    22.♘e4 exd5 23.♗xd5 ♗b5∓
22...bxc3 23.bxc3 fxe6 24.♗xe6
    After 24.♘xd7 ♗g5! 25.♘xf8 ♗xd2 26.♖xd8 ♖xd8 27.♘g6† ♔g7 28.♖xe6 ♘f6 29.♘e5 ♖e8 the position is about equal.
24...♗xe6 25.♘g6† ♔g7 26.♖xe6 ♘c5 27.♘xf8 ♕xf8∞ 28.♖f3 ♕d8 29.♖g3† ♔f7 30.♕e2

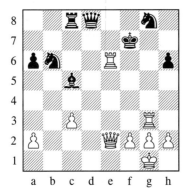

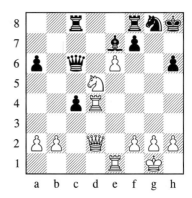

A funny position. Black has three minor pieces for just one white rook, but Black is probably lost! Don't ask me why, turn on your engines!

30...♗e7 31.♖xg8 ♔xg8 32.♖xe7+−

This line would of course be very hard to calculate during the game.

22.♗xc4 bxc4 23.♖d4

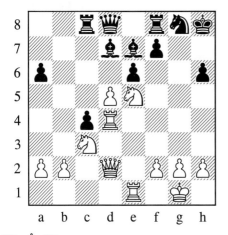

23...♗c5??

Black's first big mistake and also his last.

Black should have played:

23...♕e8! 24.♘xd7
  24.♘xc4⩲ ♗b5 25.d6 ♗g5 26.f4 ♗h4 27.g3 ♖xc4∓
24...♕xd7 25.dxe6 ♕c6∞ 26.♘d5

26...c3!

With the idea of preventing White from playing ♕c3.

27.bxc3 ♗g5 28.f4 ♗h4 29.g3 fxe6! 30.♘b4 ♕b7

Now, if White takes with 31.gxh4? then after 31...♘f6 it is very strange, but now Black is simply mating White!

31.♖d7∞

24.dxe6! ♗xd4 25.♕xd4

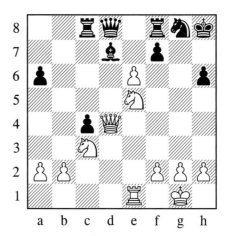

25...♕f6 26.exd7 ♖cd8 27.♖e3 ♘e7 28.♖f3 ♘c6

28...♘f5 29.♕e4 ♕g5 30.h4!+−

29.♘xf7† ♖xf7 30.♕xf6†
1−0

GAME 23

▷ **H. Melkumyan (2600)**
▶ **S. Zhigalko (2689)**

Lake Sevan GM Tournament, Martuni
Round 9, 30.07.2011 **[D31]**
Annotated by Sebastian Maze

In the well-known 4.e4 pawn sacrifice line against the Semi-Slav, Melkumyan tried a new idea with 12.f3. I have to say that it's an interesting novelty, which puts a lot of pressure on Black. After analysing, I think that Black should be OK after 12...♕g6. In the game, Zhigalko went for the mistaken 12...♕f5 and after 13.♖d1 Black's position is very bad. But the Armenian player instead chose 13.0–0–0 when the position was unclear. After some inaccurate moves from White, Zhigalko took the lead in the game but one more time he blundered with 27...♖a8. This time, Melkumyan didn't miss his chance and won the game in a pleasant endgame.

1.d4 d5 2.c4 e6 3.♘c3 c6

Zhigalko chose a very tactical and theoretical move order to try to reach the Semi-Slav.

4.e4 dxe4 5.♘xe4 ♗b4† 6.♗d2

6.♘c3?! is too quiet to fight for an advantage. 6...e5 or 6...c5 are good alternatives for Black.

6...♕xd4 7.♗xb4 ♕xe4† 8.♗e2

The Marshall Gambit is a very sharp variation, and it's tough to play this kind of position with Black, because you need to be focused on every move – the first mistake could lose immediately.

8...♘a6

8.♘d7 and 8...c5 are the old lines of this variation.

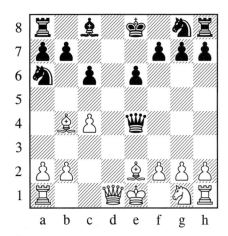

9.♗a5

9.♗d6 is the other main move, for example: 9...♕xg2 10.♕d2 ♘f6 11.♗f3 ♕g6 12.0–0–0∞ Gustafsson – Pavasovic, Mitropa Cup, Rogaska Slatina 2009.

9.♗c3 is also possible.

9...b6

9...♗d7 and 9...f6 10.♘f3 b6 11.♘d2 ♕f4 12.♗h5†± are Black's other options.

10.♕d6 ♗d7

10...bxa5 11.♖d1 f6 12.f3 ♕e3 13.♕xc6† ♔f7 14.♕xa8 ♘e7∞ *Chess Evolution May 2011*: Naiditsch – Buhmann, European Championship, Aix-les-Bains 2011.

11.♗c3 f6

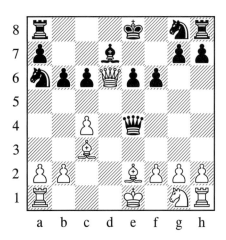

12.f3N

This is a novelty by the Armenian player. It looks logical and it puts the question to the black queen. 12.♘f3 is the main move: 12...♘e7 13.0–0–0 ♕xe2 14.♖xd7† ♔f7 15.♖he1 ♕xc4= Vitiugov – Romanov, Moscow 2009.

12...♕f5?!

Not the best square for the queen; in some variations the queen looks in danger on f5.

12...♕g6

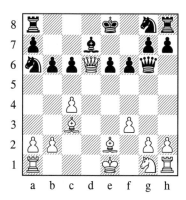

This is the right move.
13.♖d1
   13.g4 h5 14.0–0–0 0–0–0 15.♘h3 hxg4 16.♘f2 gxf3 17.♗xf3 ♘c5∓
13...0–0–0
   13...♖d8?! 14.♔f2 ♕f5 15.b4 ♘e7 16.♗d3 ♕h5 17.♘e2 e5 18.♗e4↑
14.♕a3 ♔b7
   14...♕xg2 15.♕xa6† ♔b8 16.♗d4 ♕xh1 17.♗xb6+–
15.♔f2
   After 15.c5 ♘c7 16.♔f2 ♕f7 17.♗c4 ♘e7 18.♘e2 ♘b5 Black should be fine.
15...♕h5
   15...c5 16.♗d3 f5 17.♘h3 ♘e7 18.♗e2 ♕h6 19.♖he1⩱
16.f4
   16.b4 ♘e7 17.f4 ♕f5 18.♗f3 ♕xf4 19.♗d2 ♕c7 20.♘e2 e5∓

16...♕c5† 17.♕xc5 ♘xc5 18.♗f3 ♘e7 19.b4 ♘a4 20.♗a1 ♘g6 21.♘e2 e5 22.h4 exf4 23.h5 ♘e5 24.♘xf4∞

Black is maybe slightly better and this position looks as though it holds no risks for Black.

Now White missed his first chance:

13.0–0–0

More precise was:
13.♖d1!

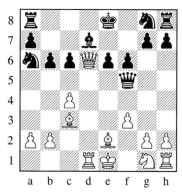

The king is better placed in the centre after the line with 16.b4.
13...e5
   13...0–0–0 14.♕a3 ♔b7 15.♘h3 ♕c5 16.b4 ♕e7 17.0–0 ♘h6 18.♘f2±
14.♘h3 ♘h6
   14...♕e6 15.♕a3 ♘c5 16.b4 ♘b7 17.f4 e4 18.♘g5 ♕e7 19.0–0 ♗f5 (19...fxg5 20.♗h5†+–) 20.♕a4±
15.♕a3 ♘c5 16.b4 ♘b7 17.c5 bxc5 18.♘f2 0–0 19.♗c4† ♘f7 20.bxc5±

The black pieces are not coordinated at all, while White's pieces are shining!

13...e5 14.♘h3 ♘h6 15.f4?!

Trying to open lines to profit from the central position of the black king.

This time 15.♕a3 doesn't give White an edge, but in my opinion it was better than the game. 15...♘c5 16.g4 (16.b4 ♘b7 17.c5 bxc5 18.g4 ♕g6 19.♕a6 ♘d8 Compared to the line with 13.♖d1, the king is not safe on c1.)

16...♕e6 17.♘f2 ♘f7 18.♔b1 a5 19.♘d3∞
The position is not clear at all.

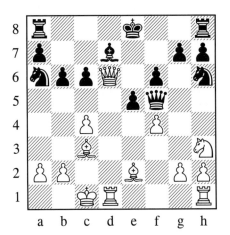

15...♘c5?!

Better was: 15...♘f7 16.g4 (16.♕a3 ♘c5
17.fxe5 ♘xe5 18.♗xe5 ♕xe5 19.♖he1 0–0–0
20.♗f3 ♕c7∓) 16...♘xd6 17.gxf5 ♘f7 18.fxe5
♘xe5 19.♖hf1 ♘c5 20.♘g5∞

16.fxe5 ♘f7 17.♕c7

17.♕d2 ♘e4 18.♕e3 ♘xc3 19.exf6† ♕e5
20.♕xc3 ♕xc3† 21.bxc3 gxf6=

17...♖c8 18.♕xa7 ♘xe5 19.♖hf1

19.♗xe5 ♕xe5 20.♖he1 0–0 21.♖xd7 ♘xd7
22.♕xd7 ♖cd8 23.♕xc6=

19...♕e4 20.♗xe5 ♕xe5 21.♘f4 ♕e3†
22.♖d2 0–0 23.♖f3 ♕e7

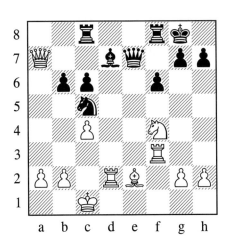

24.♕xb6?

For the cost of the b6-pawn, Black manages
to castle and achieve compensation.

24.b4 was preferable: 24...♕e5 25.♖xd7 ♕a1†
26.♔c2 ♘xd7 27.♖xd7 ♕xa2† 28.♔c1 ♕a1†
29.♔c2 ♖a8 30.♕e6† ♖f7 31.♕xc6 ♖a2†
32.♔d3 ♕b1† 33.♔e3 ♕g1† 34.♔d3=

24...♗f5 25.♘d3 ♗xd3 26.♗xd3 ♖fd8?!

Stronger was 26...♕e1†! 27.♖d1 ♕e5 28.♖h3
g6 29.♕b4 ♖a8∓ with pressure on the a- and
b-files.

27.♖e2 ♕d6 28.♗c2 ♖a8?

This move looks logical, but Melkumyan
finds a way to gain an edge.

28...♖e8 was the right move and leaves Black
close to equality. 29.♖d2 ♖e1† 30.♗d1 ♕e7
31.a4 (31.b4 ♘e4 32.♖e3 ♕e5 33.♖d8† ♖xd8
34.♕xd8† ♔f7 35.♕d7† ♔g6 36.♕g4†=)
31...♖e5 32.♖f1! (32.a5 ♕e8 33.♔b1 ♖b8
34.♕c7 ♖c8=) 32...♘e4 33.♖d4 ♕e8∞

28...♖b8 29.♕a5 ♕xh2 30.b3 ♕g1† 31.♕e1
♕d4 32.♔b1 ♘a4 33.♕c1±

28...♕xh2 29.♕a5 ♕h6† 30.♔b1 ♕h1†
31.♕e1 ♕xe1† 32.♖xe1 ♖d2 33.b4±

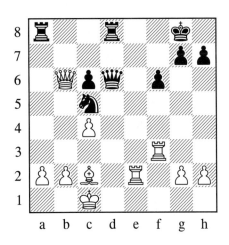

29.b4!± ♘d7 30.♕e3 ♘e5
Definitely not: 30...♕xb4??

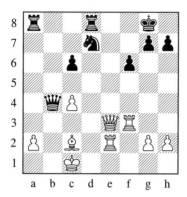

31.♗xh7†!
This is the move Zhigalko may have missed when he played 28.♖a8.
31...♔h8
31...♔xh7 32.♖h3† ♔g6 33.♕e4† ♔f7 34.♕e6† ♔g6 35.♖g3† ♔h7 36.♕f7 and mate is coming!
32.♗c2 ♘f8
32...♘e5 33.♕e4 ♔g8 34.♕h7† ♔f8 35.♕h8† ♔f7 36.♕h5† ♔f8 37.♕xe5+−
33.♖h3† ♔g8 34.c5+−

31.c5

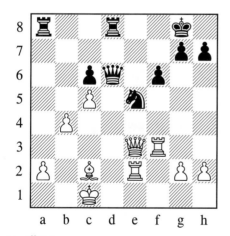

31...♕d4
Also possible was:
31...♕b8

But White still has a good advantage.
32.♕b3† ♔h8 33.♖h3
With a strong attack against the black king.
33...h6 34.a3
34.♕e6 ♕xb4 35.♖xh6† gxh6 36.♕xf6† ♔g8 37.♗b3† ♔d5 38.♕xe5 ♕xc5† 39.♔b2 ♔h7 40.♕e4† ♔g7 41.♗xd5 cxd5 42.♕e5† ♔h7 43.♕e7† ♕xe7 44.♖xe7†±
34...♖d4 35.♕e6 ♕f8 36.♕f5 g6 37.♕e6±

32.♕xd4 ♖xd4 33.♖b3
Now White has a safe advantage in this ending with an extra pawn.

33...g6
33...♖xa2 34.♗xh7† ♔xh7 35.♖xa2+−

34.a3 ♘c4?!
After this move White exchanges a pair of rooks and wins easily. 34...♔f7 was more tenacious: 35.♖e4 ♖xe4 36.♗xe4 f5 37.♗f3 ♔e6 38.♔b2 g5 39.♖e3±

35.♖e4 ♖xe4 36.♗xe4+− ♘e5 37.♔c2
37.b5! was stronger: 37...f5 38.♗xc6 ♘xc6 39.bxc6 ♔f7 40.♔b2 ♔e6 41.♖d3 White wins by force. 41...♖c8 42.♖d6† ♔e5 43.a4 g5 44.a5 g4 45.a6+−

37...f5 38.♗f3 ♔f7 39.♖e3 ♘c4 40.♖c3 ♘e5 41.♔b3 g5 42.b5 g4 43.♗xc6 ♘xc6 44.bxc6 ♔e7 45.♖d3

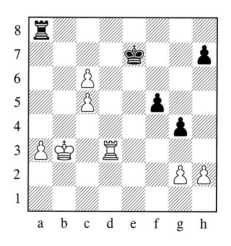

Black's position is hopeless.

**45...f4 46.♖d4 ♖b8† 47.♔c4 ♖f8 48.c7 f3
49.gxf3 gxf3 50.♖d8 ♖f4† 51.♔d5 ♖f5†
52.♔e4 f2 53.c8=♕ ♖f4† 54.♔e5**
1–0

GAME 24
▷ **A. Morozevich (2694)**
▶ **A. Grischuk (2746)**
64th Russian Championship
Round 2, 09.08.2011 **[D31]**
Annotated by Baadur Jobava

In the opening, Morozevich tried a rare but interesting continuation, 7.h3. His opponent replied with the concrete 8...♕b6. At move 17 Grischuk avoided the principled 17...♕c3 and faced positional pressure. 25.h5? instead of 25.♖h3! let slip a lot of White's advantage. Then 27.♕h4? should have lost for White, but with 32...a5?? Black placed a big 0 on all his earlier efforts in the game.

**1.d4 d5 2.c4 e6 3.♘c3 ♗e7 4.cxd5 exd5
5.♗f4 c6**

5...♘f6 is another main line.

6.e3

6.♕c2 is also common.

6...♗f5 7.h3

This move is not as popular as 7.g4 or 7.♘ge2. The first time 7.h3 was used, as far as I know, was in the game Bronstein – Darga, Amsterdam 1964.

7...♘d7

7...♘f6 8.g4 ♗e6 9.♗d3 ♘bd7 10.♘f3 ♘b6 11.♕c2 is what happened in the aforementioned game.

8.♘f3

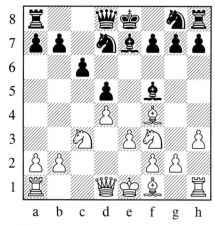

8...♕b6N

With this move Grischuk starts concrete play. He is trying to provoke the white queen into moving to d2, to gain a tempo with the manoeuvre ...♘f6-e4. But Morozevich has reserved a different place for his queen...

8...♘b6 9.♗e2 (9.g4!? ♗e6 10.♗d3 ♘f6 11.♕c2) 9...♘f6 10.0-0 0-0 Dao Thien Hai – Miranovic, Hungary 1995.

9.♕e2!?

9.♕d2 ♘gf6 10.g4 ♘e4 11.♕c2 ♗g6 12.♗d3 ♘d6 By playing 8...♕b6, Black was probably trying to reach something similar to this position.

9...♘gf6

An interesting way to save the light-squared bishop was: 9...h6!? 10.g4 ♗h7 11.♗g2 ♘gf6 But this would also have a minus side: White gains a target in the h6-pawn. If Black castles short, he will always have to remember that g4-g5 would open up his king.

10.g4 ♗g6 11.♘h4

Weaker is 11.♗g2?! ♘e4.

11...♕a5

11...♘e4 12.♘xg6 ♘xc3 13.bxc3 hxg6 14.♗g2±

12.♗g2 ♘e4 13.♘xg6 ♘xc3 14.♕d2

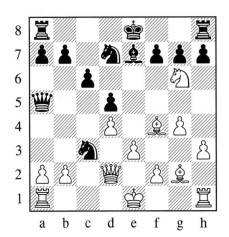

14...hxg6

Also interesting was:
14...♗b4!? 15.a3!

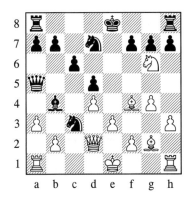

15...hxg6

15...♘b5 16.♕xb4 (16.axb4 ♕xa1† 17.♔e2
♘xd4† 18.♕xd4 ♕a6† 19.♔f3 hxg6
20.♕xg7 0–0–0∓) 16...♕xb4† 17.axb4 hxg6
White has a much better endgame.

16.0–0 ♘e4 17.♕xb4 ♕xb4 18.axb4 g5
19.♗h2 ♔e7

Black's idea is to close the position as much
as possible. It is well known that in closed
positions the bishop pair is much weaker than
in open ones. Because of that, the following
set-up would make sense: ...♘b6, ...a6, ...♔d7,
...♘d6 and ...f6. Of course, White would not
stand around and wait, but it seems that Black's
position generally has no direct weaknesses.

15.bxc3 ♘b6 16.0–0 ♘c4 17.♕e2!?

If 17.♕d3 then 17...♗d6!. Take away from
White the advantage of the bishop pair!

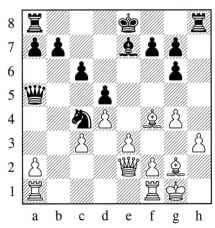

This is the most critical position of the
game! Grischuk had two choices: the one he
played in the game and of course taking on c3,
which required exact calculation. Probably he
overrated White chances, or didn't find enough
resources for himself – so he chose the modest
17...0–0.

17...0–0?!

After taking:
17...♕xc3!
Black was probably afraid of:
18.e4
18.♖ab1 ♕d2! 19.♕f3 g5 20.♗g3 ♘b6
21.e4 0–0=
18...♕xd4

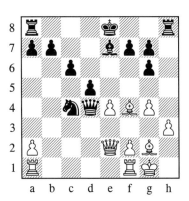

19.罝fe1

19.罝ad1 豎b2! 20.豎xb2 (20.罝fe1 豎xe2 21.罝xe2 d4 22.罝xd4 ♘b6∓; 20.豎d3 豎f6 21.♗c1 ♘b6 22.exd5 ♘xd5 23.♗xd5 cxd5 24.豎xd5 0–0 25.豎xb7 ♗c5=) 20...♘xb2 21.exd5 (21.罝b1 ♘d3 22.♗e3 d4! 23.♗xd4 0–0–0 24.♗xg7 罝h7 25.♗a1 ♘f4∓) 21...♘xd1 22.dxc6 0–0 23.cxb7 罝ad8 24.b8=豎 罝xb8 25.♗xb8 罝xb8 26.罝xd1 罝b2 In such a position, Anatoly Evgenievich would have played for a win!

19...0–0 20.罝ad1 豎f6 21.exd5 豎xf4 22.豎xe7 cxd5 23.♗xd5 ♘d6=

And it seems that everything is all right.

18.e4! ♗d6 19.e5 ♗a3

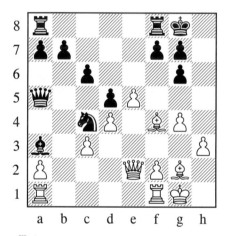

20.罝ab1!

White doesn't want to lose time protecting the c3-pawn and, as we will soon discover, the opened third rank will play a positive role for White.

20...豎xc3

Black has no choice except to suffer a pawn up! Actually, the upcoming play is one-sided – White is attacking and Black is watching.

21.罝fd1 b5 22.罝b3 豎a5 23.g5 罝fe8 24.h4 ♗f8

It is difficult to suggest anything better.

Grischuk, seeing the breakthrough on the h-file, brings over the bishop to protect the kingside.

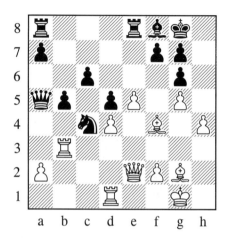

25.h5?

Better was: 25.罝h3 ♘d6 26.h5 ♘f5 27.hxg6 fxg6 28.豎c2 With advantage to White. Morozevich probably didn't want to give Black the possibility of bringing his knight into their defence.

25...gxh5 26.豎xh5 g6 27.豎h4?

27.豎e2 was the only move.

27...豎xa2 28.罝h3 ♗g7 29.豎h7† ♔f8 30.罝f3 豎e2 31.罝dd3 罝e6 32.♗g3

After 32.♗h3 罝ae8 33.♗xe6 罝xe6 Black simply has a winning position.

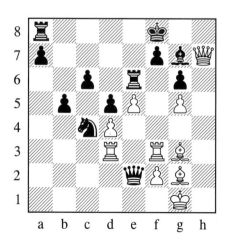

32...a5??

Probably Grischuk was (as so often) in deep time trouble. Otherwise, it would be difficult to explain such a big mistake.

Correct was 32...♘d2! 33.♖fe3 ♕d1† 34.♔h2 a5–+.

33.♗f1+– ♕e4

33...♕c2 34.♖xf7† ♔xf7 35.♖f3†+–

34.♖f4

34.♖f6 ♕g4 (34...a4 35.f3 ♕f5 36.♖xf5 gxf5 37.♗e1 c5 38.f4 a3 39.dxc5 a2 40.♗c3 a1=♕ 41.♗xa1 ♖xa1 42.♔f2+–) 35.♖df3 ♖a7 36.♗h3+–

34...♕xf4 35.♗xf4 a4 36.♖d1 a3 37.♗xc4 dxc4

37...bxc4 38.♗d2 c5 39.♕h1!+–

38.♗d2

38.d5 cxd5 39.♗d2 ♖a4 40.♗e3 ♖c6 41.♕h1! a2 42.♕xd5 a1=♕ 43.♕d8#

38...♖a4

The last chance was: 38...c5 39.f4 a2 40.♖a1 b4 41.♕h1! ♖ee8 42.♕d5 b3 (42...c3 43.♕xc5† ♔g8 44.♕xb4 cxd2 45.♕xd2+–) 43.♕xc5† ♔g8 44.♗c3 ♖ab8 But of course it is clear that White would probably win anyway.

39.♗e3 ♖e7 40.d5 a2 41.d6 ♖d7 42.♗d4 b4

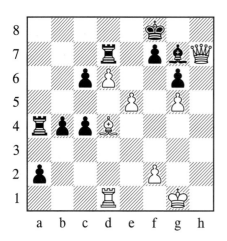

43.♕xg7†

Boevik!

1–0

GAME 25
▷ **S. Mamedyarov (2765)**
▶ **G. Sargissian (2663)**
8th World Team Championship, Ningbo
Round 8, 25.07.2011 **[D35]**
Annotated by Ivan Sokolov

7.g4!? is an interesting idea of Mamedyarov in the increasingly popular line with 6.a3!?. In the search for an improvement, Black should in my opinion look closer at 7...c5!? and 10...c5!?.

1.d4 d5 2.c4 e6 3.♘c3 ♗e7 4.♗f4 ♘f6 5.e3 0–0

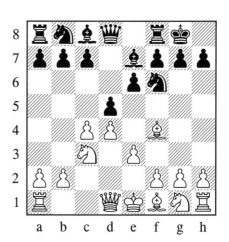

6.a3!?

The idea behind this move is to avoid the 6.♘f3 ♘bd7-line, where White is having problems fighting for an advantage at the minute.

6...b6

6...c5 7.dxc5 ♗xc5 8.♘f3 ♘c6 would transpose to the main line after 6.♘f3 c5.

If Black looks for the 6...♘bd7 line, with 6...♘bd7, White probably has an easy way to

get an opening advantage with: 7.♘b5 ♘e8
The only move which does not lose material.
8.♘f3 c5 9.cxd5 exd5 10.dxc5 ♘xc5 11.♗e2±

7.g4!?N

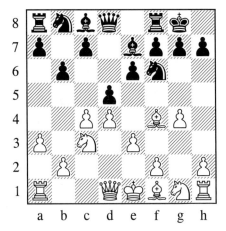

I am quite sure we will see this idea in more games in the recent future.

7...♗b7

A classic recipe against flank attacks is a counterattack in the centre, so it is very logical to analyse the following line:
7...c5!?

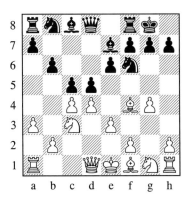

Here we have a few options. The most promising seems to be c) 8.g5.

a) 8.dxc5 bxc5 9.♗g2 ♗b7 10.♘ge2 (10.g5
♘e4 11.♘xe4 dxe4 12.♕xd8 ♖xd8 13.♘e2

transposing to line c) 10...♘bd7 11.cxd5
♘b6∞

b) 8.♗g2 cxd4 9.exd4
  9.♕xd4? ♘c6 10.♕d1 (10.♕d2 ♘a5
11.cxd5 ♘b3 12.♕d1 ♘xa1 13.d6 ♗xd6
14.♗xd6 ♗a6 15.♗xf8 ♕xd1† 16.♔xd1
♖d8† 17.♔c1 ♔xf8∓) 10...e5 11.cxd5?
exf4 12.dxc6 fxe3 13.♕xd8 exf2† 14.♔xf2
♘xg4†–+
9...♗b7
  9...♗a6 10.g5 ♘e8 (10...♘fd7 11.cxd5
♗xg5 12.dxe6 ♗xf4 13.exf7† ♖xf7 14.♗xa8
♘f6 15.♘ge2 ♗d6 16.♕d2±) 11.cxd5 ♗xg5
12.dxe6 ♗xf4 13.exf7† ♖xf7 14.♗xa8 ♘c7
15.♗e4 ♘d7 16.♘ge2±
10.h4

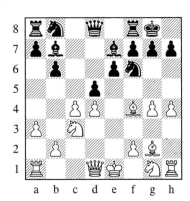

10...♕c8
  10...♕d7 11.g5 ♘e4 12.♘xe4 dxe4 13.♘e2
b5 (13...♘c6 14.d5 ♘a5 15.d6 ♗d8 16.♖c1
♖c8 17.b3 e3 18.0-0 ♗xg2 19.♔xg2 exf2
20.♖xf2 f6∞) 14.c5 ♘c6 (14...f5 15.gxf6
♗xf6⇄) 15.♗xe4! ♘xd4 16.♕xd4 ♕xd4
17.♘xd4 ♗xe4 18.f3 ♖fd8 (18...♗xc5?
blunders a piece: 19.♘b3 ♗xf3 20.♖h3 ♗g2
21.♖g3) 19.♘xb5 ♗xf3 20.♖h3±
11.g5 ♘e4 12.♘xe4 dxe4 13.♕c2 ♘d7
14.♘e2 b5 15.♗xe4
  15.c5 e5
  15.b3 bxc4 16.bxc4 e5 (16...e3 is also good)
17.dxe5 e3 18.f3 ♘b6 19.♖b1 (19.♖c1
♗xa3) 19...♗a6

15...♗xe4 16.♕xe4 ♕xc4 17.♖c1 ♘c5!
18.♖xc4 ♘xe4

Black has a fine position; if anybody is better
here, it is not White.

8.g5

Forcing a queen swap and hoping to prove
that White is better in the ending.
8...♘e4 9.♘xe4 dxe4 10.dxc5 bxc5 11.♕xd8
♖xd8 12.♗g2 ♗b7 13.♘e2 ♘d7∞ 14.♘c3 e5
15.♗g3 ♘b6 16.♗xe4

16.b3 ♖d3

16...♗xe4 17.♘xe4 ♘xc4

18.♔e2!

The only way for White to fight for a small
advantage.
18.0–0?! ♘xb2 19.♗xe5 ♘d3
18.♖b1?! ♖ab8
18.b3 ♘a5 19.♖b1 c4! 20.b4 ♘b3 21.♗xe5
a5 and Black gets his pawn back.
18...♖ab8
18...♘xb2 19.♖hc1
19.b4! cxb4 20.axb4 ♗xb4 21.♖xa7±

8.♗g2 ♘bd7

Black can also try 8...c5 9.dxc5 bxc5, when
White can either play 10.♘ge2!?, or 10.g5
♘e4 11.♘xe4 dxe4 12.♕xd8 transposing to
line c above.

9.h4

Mamedyarov ensures that once he pushes

g4-g5, the pawn will be defended and not just
hanging there.

9...♘e4

Black has no easy solutions: 9...♕c8 10.cxd5
♘xd5 11.♘xd5 ♗xd5 12.♗xd5 exd5 13.g5±

10.♘ge2

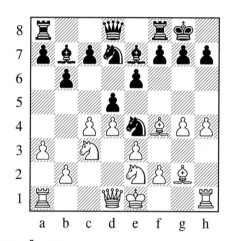

10...♘xc3?!

Black is by no means forced to release the
central tension.

It looks more logical to play 10...c5!?
11.cxd5 exd5 12.g5 cxd4 13.exd4 ♖c8 with
a complicated game. (13...♖e8?! 14.♘b5 ♖c8
15.♘xa7 ♖a8 16.♘b5 ♗a6 17.♗xe4 [17.♘c7
♗xe2 18.♕xe2 ♗b4† 19.♔d1 ♘c3†] 17...♗xb5
18.♗d3±) Now if White plays 14.0–0, Black
gets excellent counterplay with 14...f6.

11.♘xc3 c5 12.g5 b5

12...cxd4 13.exd4 ♖e8 14.0–0 ♘f8 15.♖e1
♖c8 16.cxd5 exd5 17.♕g4±

13.cxd5 b4

13...♘b6 14.dxc5 ♗xc5 15.♖c1±

14.axb4

14.dxc5? bxc3 15.c6 cxb2 16.♖b1 ♗a6!
17.cxd7 ♕xd7↑

14...cxb4 15.♘b5

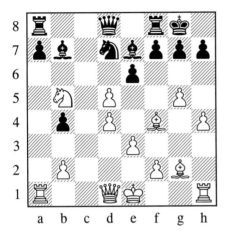

15...♕b6?

A crucial mistake. Black's position is far from easy. The only way to stay in the game was probably:

15...♘b6! 16.♗c7

16.♘c7 ♘xd5 17.♘xa8 ♘xe3 18.fxe3 ♗xg2 with compensation for the exchange.

16...♕c8

16...♕d7? 17.dxe6 ♕xb5 18.♗xb7†‑

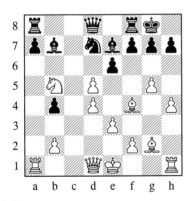

17.♗d6

17.d6 ♗xg2 18.dxe7 ♗xh1 19.exf8=♕† ♕xf8 is not clear, but maybe still White's most ambitious try!?

17...♕d7 18.♗xe7 ♕xe7 19.d6 ♕d7 20.♗xb7 ♕xb7∞

The white pawn on d6 is going to fall and Black is no worse.

15...♗xd5? loses a pawn to 16.♗xd5 exd5 17.♘c7.

16.♘c7

Also good for White was 16.♕a4 ♖fc8 (16...♗xd5 17.♗xd5 exd5 18.♘c7+-) 17.♘xa7 ♖d8 18.♕a5, when he is a healthy pawn up.

16...♖ac8 17.0–0 e5

Black tries to mess things up, though this does not work out to his benefit here. In a couple of moves the position is clarified and White has obtained a winning advantage.

17...♖xc7 18.♗xc7 ♕xc7 19.♖xa7 with threats such as ♖xb7 and dxe6, or immediately dxe6 or d6, also secures White a winning advantage.

18.dxe5 ♖xc7 19.d6 ♗xg2 20.♔xg2 ♗xd6

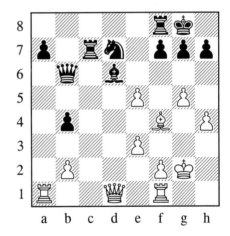

21.exd6

White is a healthy pawn up, far advanced and well placed on d6! On top of this he is simply better. The game should simply be over, but now Mamedyarov starts to make mistakes and Black gets some chances.

21...♖c5 22.♖c1

22.e4! looks simple and strong.

22...♖xc1 23.♕xc1 ♕b7+ 24.f3 ♖c8 25.♕d2

a5 26.♖a1 ♕b5 27.b3 ♖c3 28.♕a2 h5 29.♔g3
♖c5 30.♕d2 ♖c3 31.♖c1 ♖xb3 32.♖c8+ ♔h7
33.♕c2+ ♕d3 34.♕xd3+ ♖xd3 35.♖c7 ♘b6
36.♗e5!

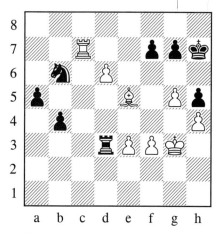

36...♔g6?

The last mistake. 36...♖d5 37.f4 ♔g8! was
the only way to stay in the game.

37.♗d4

Now Black loses his knight.

**37...b3 38.♖b7 ♘d7 39.♖xd7 a4 40.♖b7
a3 41.d7 ♖xd4 42.exd4 a2 43.d8=♕ a1=♕
44.♕b6+ ♔h7 45.d5**
1–0

GAME 26
▷ **E. L'Ami (2611)**
▶ **I. Sokolov (2645)**
Dutch Championship, Boxtel
Round 8, 04.07.2011 [**D36**]
Annotated by Ivan Sokolov

White's 14.♘f4? in the opening was definitely
not a good idea. However, questions also
remain as to whether White should hurry to
push his g-pawn in this opening, and the best
square for his king's knight. This opening line
is not played so often nowadays, but it requires
subtle handling and I have mentioned some

important games which could be of interest to
reader wishing to delve deeper.

**1.d4 ♘f6 2.c4 e6 3.♘c3 d5 4.cxd5 exd5
5.♗g5 ♗e7 6.e3 c6 7.♕c2 ♘bd7**

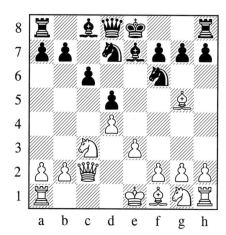

8.♗d3

Another interesting plan for White is to
postpone the development of this bishop, so
that if he subsequently establishes a knight
on e5 and Black threatens to exchange it, the
knight might drop back to the d3-square.
Here is a relevant example: 8.♘f3 ♘h5 9.♗xe7
♕xe7 10.h3 ♘b6 11.0–0–0 g6 12.g4 ♘g7
13.♘e5 f6 14.♘d3 ♗e6

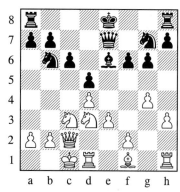

15.♖e1 This looks a bit too timid. White
is still not really threatening e4, and if he is
going to prepare it with f3 anyway then the
rook move may not be needed. (More to the

point was 15.f3!? 0–0–0 16.♗g2 with ♕f2 and e4 to follow.) 15...0–0–0 16.♘a4 ♘xa4 17.♕xa4 ♔b8 18.♗e2 ♗f7= The game was soon drawn in Topalov – I. Sokolov, Sarajevo 2000.

8...♘h5

This is one of the oldest lines of the QGD Exchange Variation. It is more subtle than it may appear, and requires accurate treatment by both sides.

9.♗xe7 ♕xe7

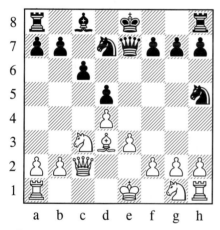

10.♘ge2

Another option for White is to castle immediately and keep the destiny of the g1-knight a mystery for the time being.

The following game of Bareev is a good example for White to follow.
10.0–0–0 g6
Another interesting game continued: 10...♘b6 11.h3 g6 12.♔b1 ♘g7 13.g4 ♗d7 (Wrong would have been 13...h5? due to 14.♘f3 ♗e6 15.♘e5 when the g6-pawn is no longer defended, and after 15...♘d7 16.f4 it is hard for Black to kick the knight away from e5.) 14.♘f3 0–0–0 15.♘e5 ♔b8 16.♖c1

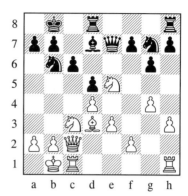

16...♗c8 (other ideas included 16...♘e8!? with ...♘d6 and ...f6 to follow, or the immediate 16...f6 17.♘xd7† ♕xd7) 17.♘a4 f6 18.♘f3 ♘xa4 19.♕xa4 ♘e6?! (Black could have obtained excellent counterplay with 19...g5! followed by ...h5) 20.♖c3! A standard way for White to develop his queenside initiative in this line. 20...♖d6?! 21.♖hc1 b6 22.b4 ♗d7?! 23.♘e5!± ♖c8 24.♗a6 ♖c7 25.♘xc6† White won a pawn and soon the game in Salov – Andersson, Szirak 1987.
11.♔b1 ♘b6 12.♘ge2 ♗d7 13.♔a1 ♘g7

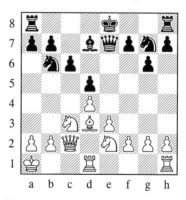

14.h4!?
An interesting plan. White has no problem exchanging bishops and instead tries to obtain other positional advantages, beginning with a well-placed knight on f4.
14...♗f5 15.♘f4 0–0–0 16.♘a4!
This knight exchange helps White by removing an important defender on the queenside.

16...♘xa4 17.♕xa4 ♔b8 18.g3 h6 19.♕c2

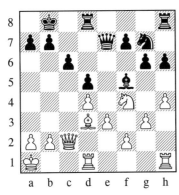

19...♗e4?

A bad decision, allowing White to transform the pawn structure.

20.♗xe4 dxe4 21.d5!

Black must have underestimated this move.

21...g5 22.hxg5 hxg5 23.♖xh8 ♖xh8 24.♘e2 cxd5 25.♘c3 ♖c8 26.♖xd5±

Black has a difficult task defending his pawns in the centre and on the kingside, Bareev – Van der Sterren, Munich 1994.

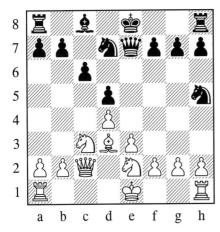

10...♘b6

I would like to present an extremely instructive game from 23 years ago. White was the 13th World Champion and in my opinion the greatest player of all time, and Black was a top-level grandmaster who was one of the biggest experts on the black side of this variation.

10...g6 11.0–0–0 ♘b6 12.♘g3!?

Preventing the plan of ...♗f5. Compared with the main game, White leaves his kingside pawns at home in order to avoid giving the opponent a target for counterplay.

12...♘g7

Exchanging does not solve Black's problems either, since in the resulting pawn structure the presence of light-squared bishops clearly favours White: 12...♘xg3 13.hxg3 h5 14.♔b1 ♗e6 15.♖c1 ♔f8 16.♘e2 ♔g7 17.♘f4 ♕f6 18.f3± Goldin – Vescovi, Buenos Aires 2003.

13.♔b1 ♗d7 14.♖c1 0–0–0

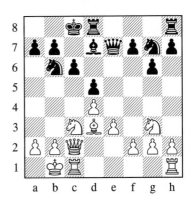

15.♘a4!

Once again White exchanges knights in order to clear space to attack the enemy king.

15...♘xa4 16.♕xa4 ♔b8 17.♖c3

White follows the standard attacking plan of doubling the rooks.

17...b6

Black would normally prefer to avoid such moves, but he has to clear some space to organize his defensive position.

18.♗a6 ♘e6 19.♖hc1 ♖he8 20.♕b3 ♕d6 21.♘f1!

The knight has done its job and it is time for it to search for a more active role.

21...♔a8

The immediate 21...♘c7 looks better.

22.♘d2 ♘c7

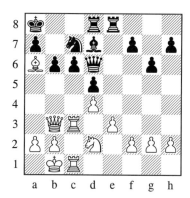

23.♗f1!

The bishop will be ideally placed on g2.

23...♘e6 24.g3 ♖c8 25.♗g2 ♖c7 26.h4

Black is under serious pressure and has no counterplay whatsoever.

26...♖d8 27.♘f3 ♗c8 28.♕a4

Black is forced to compromise his pawn structure further.

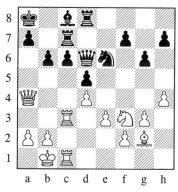

28...c5 29.♘g5! ♘xg5 30.hxg5 ♗b7 31.dxc5 bxc5 32.♕f4 ♕xf4 33.gxf4±

Black soon lost a pawn and the game in Kasparov – Andersson, Reykjavik 1988.

11.h3

11.0–0–0 would transpose to one of the lines analysed above. By the way, short castling is hardly ever dangerous to Black in this line.

11...g6 12.0–0–0 ♘g7 13.g4

This pawn push may appear "active" for White, but in reality it provides Black with an attractive target for counterplay.

13...♗d7

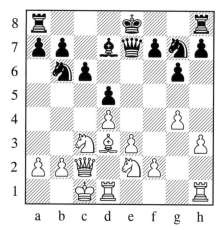

14.♘f4?

Provoking ...g5, but Black is more than happy to play this move!

14...g5 15.♘fe2 h5!

Black has easy play and White is already slightly worse.

16.♘g3 0–0–0 17.♘f5 ♗xf5 18.gxf5

Also after 18.♗xf5† ♔b8 19.♗d3 ♖h6 Black is better, with ...♖dh8 coming next.

18...♘e8 19.♖he1 g4 20.hxg4 hxg4 21.♘e2

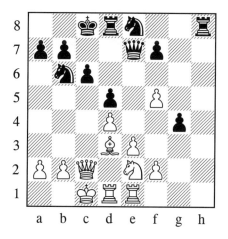

21...♘f6

Another possibility was 21...♖h2 22.♘g3 ♘d6 23.♖h1 ♖dh8 24.♖xh2 ♖xh2 25.♖h1 ♖h3 when Black has pressure and it is not easy for White to release the tension, since 26.♗f1? falls to 26...♖xg3.

22.♖h1 ♖h3

Black's advantage is not huge, but White is under pressure and his position is unpleasant to defend. He was also beginning to run short of time.

23.♖dg1 ♖dh8 24.♕d1 c5!?

White is busy solving problems on the kingside, so it makes sense to switch to the other flank. 24...♘c4 was a good alternative.

25.dxc5 ♕xc5† 26.♔b1 ♘c4 27.♘f4 ♖h2

27...♖xh1 is premature, as after 28.♖xh1 ♘d2† 29.♔a1 ♖xh1 30.♕xh1 g3 31.fxg3 ♕xe3 32.a3 White should draw.

28.♖xh2 ♖xh2 29.♕e1 ♘e5!

29...♘e4

This is playable, but ultimately less promising. 30.♗xe4 dxe4

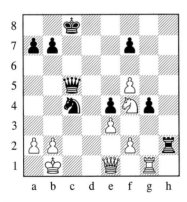

31.a3

White must avoid 31.♖xg4? due to 31...♘xe3! 32.♖g8† ♔c7 33.a3 ♕c2† 34.♔a1 ♕d1† 35.♕xd1 ♘xd1 36.♖g7 ♖xf2 37.♖xf7† ♔d6 and Black wins.

31...♕b5

This tempting move does not achieve anything so Black should prefer 31...a6 or 31...b5, although White has good drawing chances in either case.

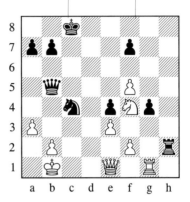

32.♕c3!

White is fine. 32...♖xf2 is met by 33.♖c1.

30.♕e2 ♔b8 31.♖c1 ♕d6 32.♕c2 ♘c6

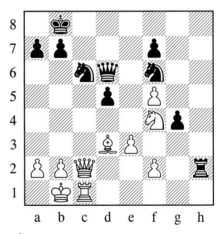

33.♗f1!

A good defensive move.

33...g3 34.♗g2 ♘g4

This move looks tempting, but objectively stronger would have been 34...gxf2 35.♕xf2 ♕e5 36.♕g3 ♖h8∓ when Black maintains some pressure.

35.fxg3?

A crucial mistake. White had a strong defence in 35.♕e2! ♘xf2

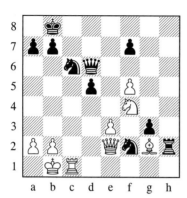

36.♕f3! ♘e4 37.♕g4= winning back the pawn with a safe position.

35...♘xe3∓ 36.♕f2 ♕e5 37.♔a1 ♘xg2
37...d4 38.♕g1 ♖h6 is also strong.

38.♘xg2 d4

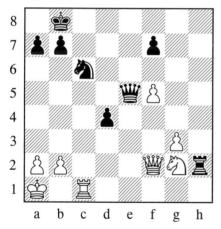

39.♖g1?!
Losing quickly, but other moves also fail to help, for instance: 39.a3 d3 40.♖d1 ♘d4 41.♖xd3 ♖h1† 42.♔a2 ♘e2−+

39...d3 40.♖d1
Or 40.g4 ♘d4.

40...♕e2
0–1

GAME 27
▷ **A. Giri (2701)**
▶ **R. Ponomariov (2764)**
39th Dortmund GM Tournament
Round 7, 28.07.2011 **[D37]**
Annotated by Sebastian Maze

In a fashionable Queen's Gambit line, Giri played a new idea with 15.♕c2. A good try! Ponomariov reacted badly and chose a line that offers White a better endgame. Instead, analysis suggests the simple 16...♘e6 would equalize immediately. In the game, after a long defence a pawn down, the Ukrainian player blundered another pawn on move 50 and lost soon after.

1.d4 ♘f6 2.c4 e6 3.♘f3 d5 4.♘c3 ♗e7 5.♗f4 0–0 6.e3
6.♖c1 c5 7.dxc5 ♗xc5 8.e3 ♘c6 9.a3 d4∞ Grischuk – Gelfand, Kazan (3.1) 2011.

6...♘bd7
6...c5 was the main move, but it is becoming less popular. 7.dxc5 ♗xc5 8.♕c2 (8.a3 is also possible) 8...♘c6 This reaches a well-known position with many top level games.

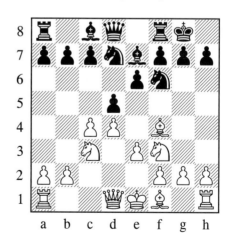

7.a3
Giri avoids the famous line from the Candidates matches with 7.c5, where all the

games finished in draws. For example: 7.c5 ♘h5 8.b4 ♘xf4 9.exf4 c6 10.♗d3 b6 11.0–0! a5= Grischuk – Kramnik, Kazan (rapid 2.6) 2011.

7...c5

7...c6 is passive but playable.

8.cxd5 ♘xd5 9.♘xd5 exd5 10.dxc5 ♘xc5

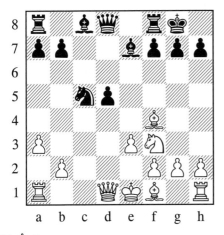

11.♗e5

A logical move to gain total control of the d4-square. Ponomariov decided to play a position with an isolated pawn, so now he has to play very actively to avoid having a difficult game.

11.♗e2 ♗f6 12.♗e5 ♗xe5 13.♘xe5 ♗e6 14.♘f3 ♕b6 15.♕d4 ♖fc8 16.0–0 ♘b3= Kramnik – Radjabov, Kazan (1.4) 2011.

11...♗g4

11...♗f6 12.♗xf6 ♕xf6 13.♕d4 ♕xd4 14.♘xd4 ♗d7 15.♗e2 ♘e6 16.♘f5 ♖fd8 17.0–0–0 ♔f8 Black has good chances to draw. Now after 18.♖xd5? ♖ac8† 19.♔b1 ♘c7 the f5-knight is lost, so instead White played 18.♔b1= in Mamedyarov – Onischuk, Bursa 2010.

12.♗e2 ♗xf3

Black made this exchange to avoid facing a strong white knight on d4.

12...♘e6 is an interesting alternative. 13.0–0 ♗f6 14.♗xf6 ♕xf6 15.♗xd5 ♕xb2 16.♖a2 ♕b6 White might try: 17.♕c4!?N (17.♕e4 ♗h5 18.♕h4 ♗g6 Shulman – Bhat, US Championship 2010) 17...♗h5 18.♖c1 This should give White a small advantage, as his pieces are better placed.

13.♗xf3 ♗f6 14.♗xf6 ♕xf6

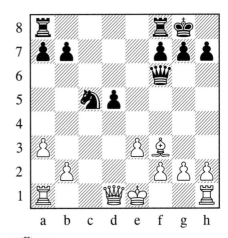

15.♕c2N

An interesting novelty by Giri. He simply wants to move the queen from the d-file and take the d5-pawn with the bishop.

15.0–0 was played in Mamedyarov – Kramnik, Dortmund 2010. 15...♖fd8 16.♖c1 ♘e6 17.♕b3 d4 18.♕xb7 ♖ab8 19.♕xa7 ♖xb2 20.♕a6 g6 White is a pawn up but Black's pieces are very active; Kramnik later drew easily.

15...♖ac8

15...♘e4 was also playable. 16.♖d1 (16.♗xe4 dxe4 17.♕xe4 ♕xb2 18.0–0 b6=) 16...♖ac8 17.♕b3 ♘c5 18.♕b4 ♕a6 19.♗e2 ♕e6 20.0–0 ♖fd8 21.♖d4 This position may look quite balanced, but in fact it is not easy for Black to equalize. Soon ♖fd1 will be played and White will put pressure on the central pawn. Black will have to work hard for a draw.

16.♗xd5

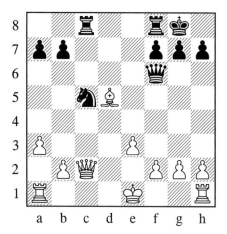

16...♖fd8?

This key mistake leaves Black a pawn down permanently. Maybe the Ukrainian player forgot that the queen can hide on a2.

16...♘e6

This was the only way to claim equality.

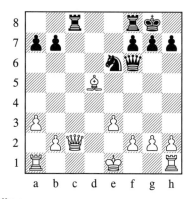

17.♕b3

17.♕e2?! allows Black a pleasant choice between 17...♘f4= and the even stronger 17...♘d4! when White struggles to hold on to equality.

17.♕d2 ♖fd8 18.0–0 ♘c7 19.e4 ♘xd5 20.exd5 ♖c5 Winning back the pawn.

21.♖fd1 g6 22.d6 ♖c6 23.d7 ♖c7 24.♕e2 ♔g7 (24...♖dxd7?? 25.♖xd7 ♖xd7 26.♕e8†+–) 25.♖ac1 ♖dxd7=

17...♘c5 18.♕c4 ♕xb2 19.0–0 b5 20.♕b4 ♕e5 21.♖fd1 ♖fd8 22.e4 a6 23.♖ac1 ♘d3

A nice trick which leads to an equal position.

24.♖xc8 ♖xc8 25.♗xf7† ♔xf7 26.♕b3† ♖c4 27.♕xd3 ♖xe4=

17.♖d1± ♕e5 18.♕c4

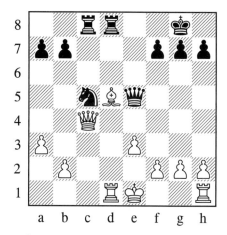

18...b5

18...♘e6 19.♕b3 ♖d6 20.0–0 ♖b6 21.♕a4 ♖xb2 22.♕xa7 h5 23.h3± White has a pleasant advantage.

19.♕a2

A clever finesse! The queen is well placed, protecting the bishop and no longer under pressure from the black rooks.

19...♖d7 20.0–0 ♘a4 21.♗b3 ♖dc7 22.♖d4 ♘b6 23.♖fd1 g6

The advantage is now significant. White's rooks are well placed and the queen and the bishop are putting pressure on the f7-pawn. Black faces a hard fight to try to save this position.

24.♕b1 ♔g7 25.g3 ♘c4 26.♔g2 ♕f6

27.♗xc4 bxc4

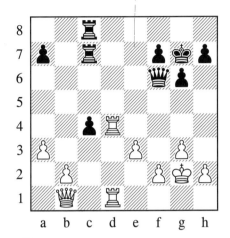

28.♕e4

28.♖d6 ♕e5 29.♖1d5 ♕e8 30.h4 c3 31.♕c2 ♖c6 32.♖d7 gives White a good advantage.

28...♖e7 29.♕d5 c3 30.bxc3 ♖xc3

For Black it is quite good news to exchange this pawn and also later the queen.

31.♖f4 ♕c6 32.♕xc6 ♖xc6 33.♖dd4

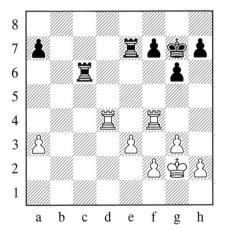

Now we have a rook endgame. In my opinion, Black has good chances to draw; the extra pawn being on the kingside makes it easier for Black to defend.

33...♖c2 34.♖d5 h5 35.♖a5 ♖b7 36.h3

♖a2 37.♖fa4 ♖bb2 38.♖f4 ♖b7 39.g4 hxg4 40.hxg4 ♖c7 41.♔g3 ♖b2 42.g5 ♖b1 43.♔g2 ♖b2 44.♖fa4 ♖cc2 45.♖f4 ♖b7 46.♔g3 ♖c1 47.♖d4 ♖b2 48.♖f4 ♖b7

The position is very close to being a draw, as White has no plan to make progress.

49.♖d4 ♖b2 50.f3

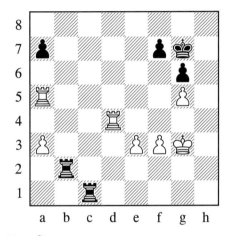

50...a6?

It is difficult to understand this move! Ponomariov has defended well, and in my opinion he was managing to hold the position.

50...♖c7 51.♖da4 ♖bb7 52.♔f4 ♖d7 53.e4 ♖d3 54.♖d5 ♖c3 55.♖b4 ♖b6 56.♖xb6 axb6 This position will be a draw after the exchange of pawns on the queenside.

51.♖xa6 ♖b5 52.f4 ♖b3 53.♖e4 ♖cc3 54.a4 ♖xe3† 55.♖xe3 ♖xe3†

I guess Ponomariov thought that he would be able to hold this position, but unfortunately it is lost by force.

56.♔f2 ♖a3 57.♖a7 ♔f8 58.a5 ♔e8 59.a6 ♔f8 60.♔e2 ♔e8

60...♔g7 61.♔d2 ♖a4 62.♔c3 The king is coming. 62...♖xf4 63.♖b7 ♖a4 64.a7+–

61.♖a8†

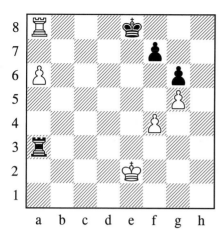

61...♔d7

61...♔e7 62.a7 ♖a4 63.f5! gxf5 64.g6 Wonderful! White sacrifices two pawns to open the 7th rank. 64...fxg6 65.♖h8 ♖xa7 66.♖h7†+–

62.a7 ♔c6 63.♖c8† ♔b7 64.♖f8

Giri will take the f7- and g6-pawns and win easily.

1–0

GAME 28

▷ **A. Morozevich (2694)**

▶ **F. Caruana (2711)**

Accentus GM Tournament, Biel
Round 9, 28.07.2011 **[D43]**
Annotated by Sebastian Maze

In the Moscow Variation, Morozevich went for the line with 9.♘e5 and introduced the interesting novelty 13.♕f4. Two moves later he played the nice 15.♔e2! In my opinion, 15...♕f6 looks a better reply than Caruana's 15...♕e5. As the game progressed, Caruana blundered with 21...fxe4, but the Russian player missed the opportunity to take advantage with 22.♖hd1. Instead he played 22.♖xe6 and the position remained complicated. Finally, after some inaccurate moves from Morozevich, Caruana obtained a good position and managed to win.

1.d4 d5 2.c4 c6 3.♘f3 ♘f6 4.♘c3 e6 5.♗g5 h6 6.♗h4 dxc4 7.e4 g5

The Botvinnik Variation with 7...b5 is the principal alternative here.

8.♗g3 b5 9.♘e5

Morozevich doesn't play the usual 9.♗e2.

9...♗b7 10.h4 g4

This move is a positional sacrifice. Black gives back the pawn in order to open the g-file, and also to avoid the possibility of the h-file being opened for the h1-rook. 10...♖g8 is an alternative.

11.♘xg4 ♘xg4 12.♕xg4 ♕xd4 13.♕f4N

13.♖d1 is the usual move, for example: 13...♕f6 14.a4 h5 15.♕g5 ♕xg5 16.hxg5∞ Van Wely – Smeets, Dutch Championship 2010.

13...♗b4

The logical reply.

14.♖d1 ♗xc3† 15.♔e2!

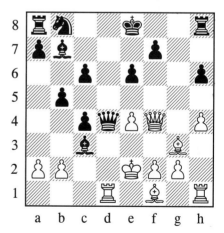

Moro's style! We shall see that theoretically Black has no problems, but he has to play the best moves, and it's not easy to find them over the board.

15.bxc3 ♕xc3† 16.♖d2 ♕c1† 17.♔e2 ♘d7
18.♕c7 ♖d8 19.♗e5 c3 20.♖d3 ♕c2† 21.♔e3
♕c1† 22.♔e2 ♕c2†=

15...♕e5?!

Even if this move is not really a mistake, it puts Black under some pressure.

15...♕f6 16.bxc3 (16.♕c7 ♗xb2 17.♕xb7 0–0 18.♕xa8 c3 19.♗d6 c2 20.♗xf8 cxd1=♕† 21.♔xd1 ♕d4† 22.♔c2 ♕c3† 23.♔d1 ♕d4† and it finishes in a draw by perpetual check) 16...♕xf4 17.♗xf4 ♘d7 18.♗d6 ♘b6 19.♗e5 ♖g8 20.h5 c5 21.f3 ♖d8 22.♖xd8† ♔xd8 23.♗f4 ♖h8 24.♗d6∞ Black's position looks okay, although it is still very complicated. There is one difference compared to the game, White having a pawn on c3 rather than b2. This seems to be a plus for Black, because the pawn can be attacked more easily.

16.♕xe5 ♗xe5 17.♗xe5 ♖h7

Let's evaluate this position. Black has a pawn more, but his pieces are still "at home". Also, White has the bishop pair, and the dark squares around the black king are weak. In my opinion, White's position is pleasant, and Caruana will have to play precisely to stay in the game.

18.♔e3 ♘d7 19.♗g3 0–0–0 20.♗e2

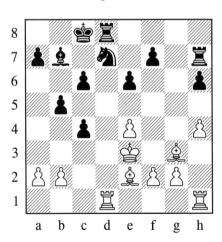

20...f5

A good reaction by Caruana; he wants to open files and take advantage of the central position of the white king.

21.♖d6 fxe4?

21...c5 22.♖hd1 ♗xe4 23.♖xe6 ♘b6 24.♖xd8† ♔xd8 25.f3 ♗b1∞

22.♖xe6

The Russian player takes the pawn too soon.

It was better to first play: 22.♖hd1! h5 23.♖xe6 ♘c5 24.♖e5 ♘d3 25.♖xh5 ♖xh5 26.♗xh5± White, with his strong bishop pair and passed h-pawn, shouldn't have too much trouble winning.

22...♘c5 23.♖g6 h5 24.♖g5 ♖d5 25.♖d1

Caruana is now right back in the game. White has to be prudent, because Black's queenside pawn majority could become really dangerous.

25.b3!? cxb3 (25...c3 26.♖xd5 cxd5 27.♗xb5 a6 28.♗e2 ♘e6 29.♗e5 ♖d7 30.♗d4±) 26.axb3 ♘xb3 27.♖b1 ♘d4 28.♖xd5 ♘xe2 29.♖f5 ♘xg3 30.fxg3 ♔c7 31.♖bf1 ♗c8 32.♖f7† ♖xf7 33.♖xf7† ♔d6 34.♖xa7 ♔d5=

25...♘d3 26.b3 ♗a6

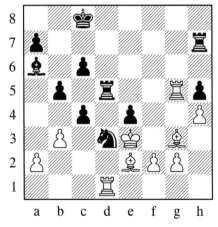

27.bxc4?!

White should have preferred: 27.♖g8†
♔d7 28.♖a8 ♗b7 29.♖xa7 ♔e6 30.bxc4 bxc4
31.♖a4±

27...bxc4 28.♖d2

28.♖b1 ♔d7 29.♗d1 ♘c5 30.♗c2 ♖f7
31.a3∞

28...♔b7

Now Black is slightly better, and White must
play carefully.

29.♖g8

29.♖c2 ♔b6 30.a3 ♘e1 (30...♖b5 31.a4
♖b3 32.♔xe4 ♘b4 33.♖xc4 ♖e7† 34.♗e5
♖b2 35.♔f3 ♗xc4 36.♗xc4 ♖c2 37.♗b3
♖d2 38.♗c4=) 31.♖b2† ♔c5 32.♗e5 ♘xg2†
33.♔xe4 ♖e7∓

29...♔b6∓ 30.♖c2?

A blunder. After 30.♖b8† ♔c5 31.♖b1 ♗b5∓
he would only be a little worse.

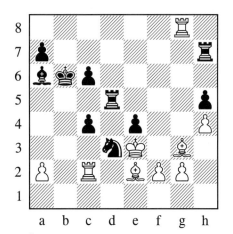

30...♘e1!

Morozevich had forgotten about this
tricky double attack. White's position is now
completely lost.

**31.♖c1 ♘xg2† 32.♔xe4 ♖e7† 33.♔f3
♘xh4†∓**

The point! With this key move, Black goes
two pawns up.

34.♗xh4 ♖f5† 35.♔g2 ♖xe2

White's position is now hopeless.

36.a4 ♖b2?!

36...♔c5 was more precise: 37.♖g7 ♖a2
38.♖xa7 ♖xa4–+

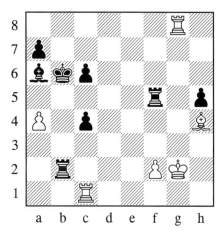

37.♖b8†?

Morozevich misses a final resource: 37.♗d8†!
♔b7 (37...♔c5? 38.♗e7† ♔d5 39.♖d8† ♔e6
40.♗h4 Suddenly the black king is in trouble
and White is back in the game!) 38.♖g7† ♔a8
39.♗h4 ♖b8∓ Black is still better, but it will be
not so easy to win the game.

**37...♔b7 38.♖xc4 c5† 39.♔h2 ♖b1 40.f4
♖d5 41.♖d8 ♖bd1 42.♖xd5 ♗xd5**

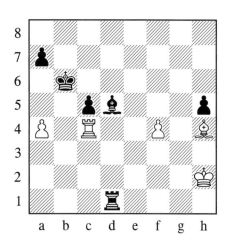

Game over! The Italian player will push his c-pawn and take the a4-pawn.

43.Ĕc3 c4 44. Åf6 Êc5 45.Êg3 Êb4 46.Ĕc2 a5 47.f5 Ĕf1
0–1

GAME 29
▷ **R. Ponomariov (2764)**
▶ **A. Giri (2701)**
39th Dortmund GM Tournament
Round 2, 22.07.2011 **[D46]**
Annotated by Kamil Miton

Ponomariov decided to play the less popular line 11.Ĕd1 (11.a3 is the main line) after which Giri chose a logical plan based on ...b4 and ...c5. In my opinion, he had good chances to equalize at a few points (including the very interesting idea 16...♕a8), but he allowed White to transfer his knight to the queenside too easily and ran into trouble.

1.Ĉf3 d5 2.c4 c6 3.e3 Ĉf6 4.Ĉc3 e6 5.d4 Ĉbd7 6.♕c2 Åd6 7.Åd3 0–0 8.0–0 dxc4 9.Åxc4 b5 10.Åd3 Åb7 11.Ĕd1

The main line is 11.a3. Now Black has a few plans: 11...a6 (11...a5, as played by Shirov, was analysed in July's issue of *Chess Evolution*. Another alternative is 11...♕e7 with the idea of later playing ...e5.) 12.b4 a5 13.Ĕb1 axb4 14.axb4 ♕e7 15.e4 e5 16.Ĉe2 With many complications.

11...b4!?

Black wants to push ...c6-c5 at any cost. If this plan is achieved without any problems then Black will have a nice game.

12.Ĉa4

12.Ĉe4 is not dangerous: 12...Ĉxe4 13.Åxe4 Ĉf6 (13...f5 14.Åd3 c5 15.e4∞) 14.b3 (14.Åd3 c5 15.dxc5 Ĕc8 16.♕e2 Ĕxc5 transposes to the game; 14.Ĉd2 ♕c7=) 14...Ĉxe4 15.♕xe4 ♕e7 16.Åb2 c5= The position is roughly equal.

12...c5 13.dxc5 Ĕc8

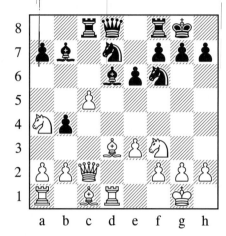

14.♕e2

It's too early for quick attacks: 14.Åxh7†? Ĉxh7 15.Ĕxd6 Åxf3 16.gxf3 ♕g5† 17.Êf1 Ĉxc5∓ and 14.Ĉg5? Åxh2† 15.Êxh2 Ĉg4† 16.Êg1 ♕xg5 17.Åxh7† Êh8 18.Ĕxd7 Åc6∓ does not work.

14...Ĉxc5

An alternative is:
14...Åb8!?

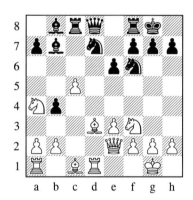

This looks very strange but maybe this idea is playable. It seems that the best answer is:
15.b3
15.Åa6 Åxa6 16.♕xa6 Ĉxc5=
15.a3 b3 16.Ĉd4 ♕c7 17.f4 Ĉxc5 18.Ĉxc5 ♕xc5 19.Ĉxb3 ♕b6 20.Ĉd4 e5↑
15.Åd2 Åxf3 (15...♕a5 16.b3 Ĉxc5

17.♘xc5 ♕xc5 18.♖ac1 ♗xf3 19.♕xf3 ♕d6
20.♖xc8 ♖xc8 21.♗e1 ♕xh2† 22.♔f1 a5∞)
16.gxf3 ♕a5 17.b3 ♘xc5 18.♘xc5 ♕xc5
19.f4 e5 20.♖ac1 ♕e7∞
15.e4 ♕a5 16.b3 ♘xc5 17.♘xc5 ♕xc5
18.♗b2 ♖fd8∞

15...♕c7 16.e4

16.♗b2 ♗xf3 17.♕xf3 ♕xh2† 18.♔f1 ♘xc5
19.♘xc5 ♖xc5 20.♔e2 ♕h5=

16...♘xc5 17.♘xc5 ♕xc5 18.♗b2 ♖fd8
19.♖ac1

And after:

19...♕b6

19...♕a5!?∞

20.♖xc8 ♖xc8 21.♘e5±

White's knight comes to the c4-square.

15.♘xc5 ♖xc5 16.♗d2

16.e4? ♘xe4 17.♗xe4 ♗xe4 18.♖xd6 ♗xf3
19.♕d2 ♖d5 20.♖xd5 ♗xd5 21.♕xb4 ♕f6∓

16...a5

A typical reaction, but Black also had other
interesting moves.

16...♕a8!?N

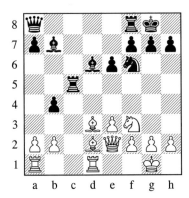

In my opinion, a very strong idea! Black
doesn't give White the chance to gain more
space with the natural e3-e4. Note that the
pawn on b4 is not hanging.

17.e4

17.♗xb4? ♗xf3–+

17.a3 bxa3 18.bxa3 ♖h5 19.♖ab1 (19.h3?
♖xh3∓) 19...♖d8=

17.♖e1? ♗xf3 18.gxf3 ♖g5† 19.♔h1 ♖h5–+

17.♘e1 a5=

17.♗a6 ♗d5

17.h3 ♖fc8 18.a3 bxa3 19.bxa3 a5=

17...♗xe4

17...♘xe4 18.♗e3±

17...♖h5 18.♖e1 a5 19.h3 White is slightly
better because after e3-e4 he will take more
space, and the rook on h5 is out of play.

17...a5 18.♗e3 ♖cc8 19.♘d2 ♕b8 20.g3
This transposes to the 17...♕a8 line analysed
below.

18.♗xe4 ♕xe4

18...♘xe4 19.♗xb4 ♖d5 20.♖xd5 ♕xd5
(20...exd5 21.♗xd6 ♘xd6 22.♖d1±) 21.♖d1
♕c6 22.♗xd6 ♘xd6 23.♘e5 ♕c7 Black
needs to make a few more accurate moves
to equalize.

19.♕xe4 ♘xe4 20.♗xb4 ♖c6

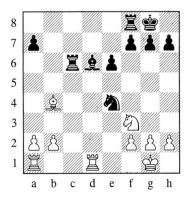

White can't really press in this endgame.

21.♖d4

21.♗xd6 ♖xd6 22.♖xd6 ♘xd6 23.♖d1 ♖d8
24.♘e5 ♘b7 25.♖xd8† ♘xd8=

21...♗xb4

21...♖fc8 22.♗xd6 ♖c1† 23.♘e1 ♘xd6
24.♖xc1 ♖xc1 25.♔f1 ♖c6 26.♘d3 ♔f8=

22.♖xb4 ♘f6 23.♖b7 ♖fc8 24.g3 ♖6c7

24...♖b6 25.♖xa7 ♖xb2 26.a4 ♘e4 27.a5
♘xf2 28.a6 ♘h3† 29.♔h1 ♘f2† 30.♔g2↑

25.♖xc7 ♖xc7 26.♖d1 ♘d5=

17.e4 ♕b8

If instead:

17...♕a8

Then best is:

18.♗e3

This is standard and the best plan in this type of position. White will transfer the knight to c4 (a very solid square) and reduce the b7-bishop's scope with f2-f3. After that, he will try to attack Black's weak pawns on the queenside.

18.a3 bxa3 19.b4 ♖h5 20.♖xa3 ♘xe4 21.♗xe4 ♗xe4 22.♖xa5 ♖xa5 23.bxa5=

18...♖cc8

After 18...♖h5?! 19.h3 Black's rook on h5 looks strange. 19...♗xe4 (19...g6 20.♘d2 ♗e5 21.f3 ♗xb2 22.♖ab1 ♗e5 23.♘c4 ♘d7 24.♘xe5 ♘xe5 25.♗b5±; 19...♖d8 20.♘d2±) 20.♗xe4 ♘xe4 Now White has the strong reply 21.♘g5±. Black's position is critical.

19.♘d2

White follows his idea.

19...♕b8

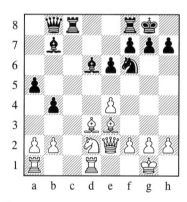

20.g3

20.h3 ♗h2† 21.♔h1 ♗e5 would give Black counterplay. 22.♘c4 ♘xe4 23.♘b6 ♖c7 24.♗xe4 ♗xe4 25.♘d7 ♗xg2† 26.♔xg2 ♕b7† 27.f3 ♖xd7 28.♗c5 ♗f6 29.♖xd7 ♕xd7 30.♗xf8 ♔xf8 31.♖d1 ♕c8∞ Black is not worse.

20...♗e5

20...♖fd8 21.f3 ♗e5 22.♘b3 a4 23.♘c5 a3 24.♘xb7 axb2 25.♖ab1 ♕xb7 26.♗a6 ♖xd1† 27.♖xd1 ♕c7 28.♗xc8 ♕xc8 29.♕c4±

21.♘c4

A tactical approach. The alternative is: 21.♖ab1 ♖fd8 22.f3!± (but not 22.♘c4? ♖xd3!)

21...♘xe4

21...♗xe4 22.♗xe4 ♘xe4 23.♘b6±

22.♘b6 ♖cd8 23.♗xe4 ♗xe4 24.♘d7 ♖xd7 25.♖xd7 ♗c6

25...♗d5 26.♗a7 ♕e8 27.♖xd5 exd5 28.♗c5±

26.♖a7 ♗b5 27.♕f3 ♗xb2 28.♖b1 ♗f6 29.♖xa5±

White has a slight material advantage.

18.h3

Now the most important point for Black is to avoid letting White transfer his knight to c4.

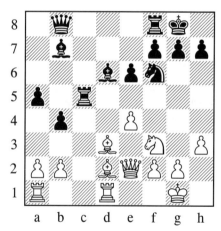

18...♗f4?!

This exchange will not help Black, and he loses important time with this manoeuvre.

The most active-looking move is:

18...♘h5

White's correct response is:

19.♗e3

19.g3?! weakens the h1-a8 diagonal:

19...♘f6 20.♗e3 ♖h5 (20...♖cc8 21.♘d2 ♗xg3) 21.h4 ♘xe4 22.♘d2 ♘xd2 23.♕xh5 ♘f3† 24.♔f1 f5∓

19.♕e1 ♘f4 20.♗f1 f5↑

19...♘f4 20.♕d2 ♖cc8

20...♖d8 21.♗a6 (21.♗xc5 ♗xc5 22.♕c2 ♘xh3† 23.♔f1 ♘xf2 24.♕xc5 ♘xd3 25.♕xa5 ♗xe4∓) 21...♗c7 22.♕e1 ♗xa6 23.♖xd8† ♕xd8 24.♗xc5 ♕f6∞ 25.♕e3 ♕xb2 26.♗d4 ♘e2† 27.♔h1 ♕c2∞

21.♗a6! ♗xa6 22.♕xd6 ♘e2† 23.♔h1 ♗b5 24.a4 bxa3 25.♕xa3 a4 26.♖d6 ♖c6 27.e5±

White is better; the black knight on e2 is not safe.

18...♖cc8

This was a better move for Black; now White doesn't have ♗e3 and ♘d2 with tempo.

19.♗g5

19.a3 bxa3 (19...♖fd8) 20.bxa3 ♗c5 21.♖ab1 (21.♗xa5 ♕a8 22.e5 ♕xa5 23.exf6 gxf6 24.♖ab1=) 21...♕a8 22.♘g5 (22.e5 ♘e4 23.♖xb7 ♗xf2† 24.♔h2 ♗g3† 25.♔g1=) 22...h6 23.e5 ♘d7 24.♘e4 (24.♗h7† ♔h8 25.♗e4 ♗c6) 24...♘xe5 25.♗xh6 ♖fd8 26.♘xc5 (26.♕b2 ♗xe4 27.♕xe5 ♗d4 28.♕xe4 ♕xe4 29.♗xe4 gxh6=) 26...♖xc5 27.♗f4 ♘xd3 28.♖xd3 ♖xd3 29.♕xd3 ♗e4 30.♕d6 ♖c8 31.♖b8=

19...♖fd8

19...h6 20.♗xf6 gxf6 21.♘d2 ♗c5 22.♘c4 ♕c7 23.♖ac1±

20.♘d2?!

This is the move White wants to play, but Black is ready for it. Of course there are safer alternatives:

20.♗a6 ♗xa6 21.♕xa6 ♗e5 22.♖xd8† ♖xd8 23.♕xa5 ♗xb2 24.♖b1 ♗c3 25.e5 ♖d5 26.♕a6 ♘d7=

20.♖ac1 ♖xc1 21.♖xc1 ♗f4 22.♗xf4 ♕xf4=

20...♗e5 21.♘c4

21.♖ab1 h6 22.♗xf6 ♗xf6 23.♘c4 ♗a6∓ 24.♘xa5?? ♖xd3 25.♖xd3 ♕b5–+

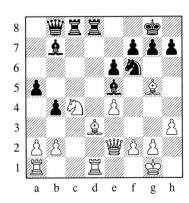

21...♖xd3

A very important trick.

22.♕xd3 ♗a6↑

Another option that looks better than the game is:

18...♖d8 19.a3

19.♗e3 ♖cc8 20.♘d2 ♗e5 21.♘c4 ♖xd3 reaches the same position as the 18...♖cc8 line.

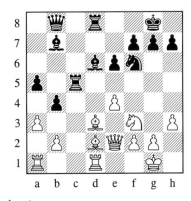

19...bxa3

19...♖cc8 20.axb4 ♗xb4 21.♗g5 (21.♗xb4 axb4 22.♕e3 h6 23.♘d2) 21...h6 22.♗h4 (22.♗xf6 gxf6 23.♕e3 ♔g7 24.e5 f5 25.♘d4 ♖d5∞) 22...♖xd3 (22...♘d7 23.♗g3 ♕a7 24.e5 ♘d5 25.♘d4 planning ♘b5-d6) 23.♕xd3 (23.♖xd3 ♗a6=) 23...♘xe4 24.♖ac1 ♗c5 (24...♖xc1 25.♖xc1 g5 26.♗g3 ♘xg3 27.fxg3 ♕xg3 28.♕d8† ♔g7 29.♕d4†=) 25.♘d2 ♘xd2 26.♕xd2 g5

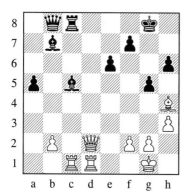

27.♖c3 gxh4 28.♕xh6 ♗d5 (28...♕e5
29.♕xh4 ♗b6 30.♖b3±) 29.♕xh4 ♕xb2
30.♖dd3 ♗xf2† 31.♕xf2 ♕xc3 32.♖xc3
♖xc3=

20.♖xa3 ♗f8 21.♗xa5

21.♖xa5 ♘xe4 22.♗xe4 ♗xe4 23.♖xc5 ♗xf3
24.♕xf3 ♗xc5 25.♗c3 ♖xd1† 26.♕xd1=
21.♖da1±

21...♖xd3 22.♕xd3

22.♖dxd3 ♖c1† 23.♘e1 ♗xa3 24.bxa3 ♖c8
25.e5 ♘d5∞

22...♗xe4 23.♕e3 ♕xb2

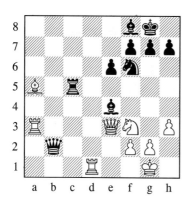

24.♖b3 ♕c2 25.♖d8 ♖xa5 26.♖bb8 ♖a1†
27.♘e1 g6 28.♖xf8† ♔g7 29.♖g8† ♘xg8
30.♕d4† ♘f6 31.♕xa1±

Black's position is worse, but it is not so easy
for White to convert his advantage into a win.

19.a3!±

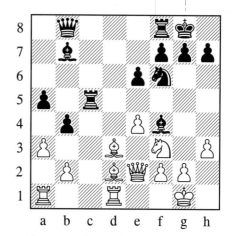

19...♗xd2 20.♘xd2 ♗a8

20...bxa3 21.♖xa3 ♖d8 22.♘b3 ♖cc8
(22...♖g5 23.♘xa5 ♗a8 24.♘c4± ♘xe4
25.♖xa8) 23.♖da1± Putting pressure on a5.

21.♕e3

21.♘b3 ♖e5 22.f4 (22.f3) 22...♖xe4 23.♗xe4
♘xe4 24.axb4 ♕xb4 25.♘xa5 ♗d5∞ This
would offer Black good compensation.

21...♖c7

Both 21...♖fc8 22.♘b3 ♖5c7 23.a4 and
21...♖cc8 were possible but still leave Black
worse.

22.a4

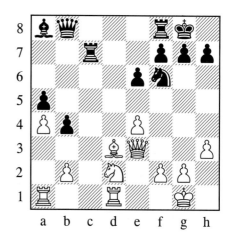

White has a clear advantage because the a5-pawn is very weak. Black should try to create some active counterplay, but this is not an easy task.

22...♗c6

Another option is:

22...♖d8

This looks natural since the rook was passive on f8. A normal reaction is:

23.♘b3 ♖cd7 24.♖d2

White keeps some pressure.

24.♘xa5? is met by a nice trick: 24...♗xe4 25.♗e2 ♖xd1† 26.♖xd1 ♖xd1† 27.♗xd1 ♗xg2! Black has an extra pawn.

24.f3 ♕e5 (24...♕g3!? 25.♘c5 ♖d4 26.♗e2 ♖xd1† 27.♖xd1 ♖xd1† 28.♗xd1 ♗c6) 25.♖dc1! ♘d5 (25...♕xb2 26.♗b5±) 26.♕c5 f5 27.♗b5 ♖c7 28.♕d4 ♖xc1† 29.♖xc1 ♕xd4† 30.♘xd4 ♘f4 31.exf5 ♖xd4 32.♖c8† ♔f7 33.♖xa8 exf5 34.♔f2±

A possible forcing line is: 24.♘c5 ♖d4 25.e5 ♘e4 26.♘b3 ♖4d7 27.♘xa5 ♕xe7 28.♘c4 ♕c5 29.♕xc5 ♘xc5 30.♗e2 ♖xd1† 31.♖xd1 ♖xd1† 32.♗xd1 ♔f8 However, this shouldn't cause Black serious problems.

24...h6

24...♕e5 25.♖c1±

24...♗c6 25.♘c5 ♖d4 26.e5 ♘e4 27.♘b3 ♘xd2 28.♘xd4 ♖xd4 29.♕xd4 ♘b3 30.♕h4+−

24...e5 25.♖c1

25.♖c1 g5 26.♘c5

26.g3

26...♖d4 27.f3 ♕e5 28.♘b3 ♖4d6 29.♗f1

29.♖c5 ♕f4 30.♕xf4 gxf4 31.♖xa5 ♗xe4⇄

29...♖xd2 30.♘xd2 ♕xb2 31.♘c4 ♕a2 32.h4→

Black has gained a material advantage, but his king is unsafe; White has good attacking chances.

23.♘b3 ♕a7 24.♕xa7 ♖xa7 25.f3±

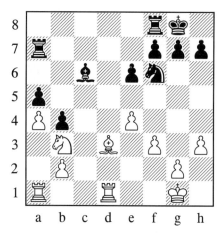

25...♖d8?!

Dubious; Black probably didn't calculate correctly all the consequences of White's next move.

Better was the more passive 25...♖b8. After the simple: 26.♔f2 (26.♖dc1 ♗e8 27.♖c5 ♘d7 28.♖xa5 ♖xa5 29.♘xa5 ♘c5 30.♗b5 ♗xb5 31.axb5 ♖xb5 32.♘c4 ♖b8 33.♔f2±) 26...♔f8 (26...♘d7 27.♘d4) 27.♔e3 ♔e7 28.♖dc1± White has the advantage.

26.♗b5± ♖xd1† 27.♖xd1 ♗xb5 28.axb5 ♔f8 29.♘c5 ♖a8 30.b6 ♔e7 31.b7 ♖b8 32.e5 ♘d5 33.♖a1 ♔d8 34.♖xa5

The only way to stop ♖a8 is 34...♘c7, but after that move Black's pieces can hardly move. Practically all his pieces, including his king, would be immobilized. This is the reason he resigned.

1–0

GAME 30

▷ **M. Carlsen (2821)**
▶ **A. Shirov (2714)**

Accentus GM Tournament, Biel
Round 2, 19.07.2011 **[D48]**
Annotated by Ivan Sokolov

In some ways, this is a strange sort of a game. Carlsen goes for 13.♘d4 – this move has not been popular, probably as a result of defeats suffered by Kasparov and Gelfand, but I feel that its unpopularity is undeserved. Shirov answers with 13...e5, as played in Gelfand – Dreev, but Carlsen improves on Gelfand's play with 16.g3! and gets a clear advantage. Carlson's 16.g3! and his subsequent moves are the first choices of various computer engines (which asks a question about Shirov's opening preparation). I would expect future discussions to focus on Kramnik's 13...♘c5. However, White has a number of promising options here too – please see my suggestions in the analyses below.

1.♘f3 d5 2.d4 ♘f6 3.c4 c6 4.♘c3 e6 5.e3 ♘bd7 6.♗d3 dxc4 7.♗xc4 b5 8.♗d3 ♗b7 9.0–0 a6 10.e4 c5 11.d5 c4 12.♗c2 ♕c7

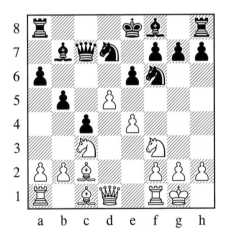

13.♘d4

This line will surely increase in popularity soon. Bringing the knight to d4 is a logical move, but up to now the line has not found many followers, most likely due to the fact that two great experts, Kasparov and Gelfand, have each suffered terrible defeats on the white side.

A recent attempt in this line was:
13.dxe6 fxe6 14.♘e2!?

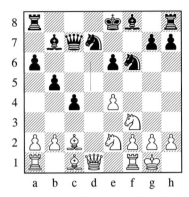

This new idea of Eljanov has been played in just a few games, and definitely deserves further investigation. I have given some lines to explore.

14...e5

14...♖d8 15.♘ed4 ♘c5 16.e5 ♗xf3 17.♕xf3 ♖xd4 18.exf6 gxf6 19.♗e3 ♖h4 20.g3 ♖g8 21.♕xf6 ♗e7 22.♕f3 ♕b7 23.♕xb7 ♘xb7 24.a4 b4 25.♖ac1± Evdokimov – Gorkavij, Armavir 2011.

14...♘xe4 15.♘f4 (15.♗xe4 ♘xe4 16.♘f4 ♘dc5 [16...♕b6 17.♕c2 ♘df6 18.♖e1] 17.♖e1↑ [17.♘xe6 ♕d7!]) 15...♘c5 16.♗xe4 (16.♘xe6 ♕d7; 16.♖e1 ♖d8) 16...♘fxe4 17.♖e1⩲

14...♘xe4 15.♘ed4 (15.♘f4 ♘dc5 16.♖e1 ♖d8 17.♕e2 ♕f7) 15...♘dc5 16.b4 cxb3 17.axb3 e5 18.b4 ♘c3 19.♕e1 ♘5e4 20.♗xe4 (20.♘e6 ♕c4) 20...♘xe4∞ (20...♗xe4? 21.♖a3 ♗xb4 22.♖xc3+–)

14...♘c5!? 15.♘f4 (15.e5 ♗xf3 16.exf6 ♗h5 [or 16...♖d8!?]) 15...♕b6 16.e5 ♗xf3 17.exf6 ♖d8 (17...♗h5 18.♗e5 gxf6 19.♗xf6 ♖g8 20.♗xh7 ♖xg2† 21.♔xg2 ♕b7† 22.f3 ♕xh7 with ...♘d3 to follow) 18.♕e1 ♗e4∞ (or 18...♗b7)

15.♘g3 ♗c5 16.b3! c3 17.a3 b4
17...0–0!? 18.b4 ♗a7 19.♘g5 ♖ae8 20.♗b3† ♔h8 21.♕e2 ♗d4 and Black will get some compensation for the exchange.

18.♘g5 ♕c6 19.axb4 ♗xb4 20.♗a3
20.♘f5 g6 (20...0–0?! 21.♖a4) 21.♘h6±

20...♗xa3 21.♖xa3 h6 22.♘f3 0–0 23.b4 ♕c7 24.♕b1 ♖ac8 25.♘e2 ♔h8 26.♖xc3 ♕b6 27.♖xc8 ♖xc8 28.♗d3±

White went on to win in Eljanov – Gelfand, Moscow 2010.

13...e5

This does not seem to solve Black's opening problems, and I would suspect that in future games the attention will focus on 13...♘c5, which was Kramnik's choice (in his famous win against Kasparov).

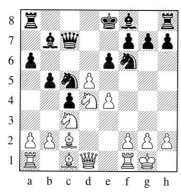

We shall have to wait for another Carlsen game in order to find out what he had prepared. However, White has many interesting options at his disposal – please take a look at my sample analyses:

a) 14.♗g5 0–0–0
   14...♗e7!? 15.b4 (15.f4? b4) 15...cxb3
   16.axb3
15.b4!
   15.♗xf6 gxf6 16.b4 cxb3 17.♗xb3 ♔b8
   18.♖c1 ♗d6 19.♕h5?! (19.g3) 19...♗f4
   20.♘cxb5 ♕b6 21.♘c6† ♗xc6 22.dxc6
   ♘xb3 23.♖b1 axb5 24.♖xb3 ♗e5 25.♖fb1
   ♕xc6 26.♖xb5† ♔c8–+ Chernin – Topalov,
   Budapest 1993.
15...cxb3 16.axb3± b4
   16...♔b8? 17.b4 ♘cd7 18.♘cxb5! axb5
   19.♗e3! ♘e5 20.♘xb5 ♕c4 21.♗a7† ♔c8
   22.♖c1+–

17.♘a4 exd5

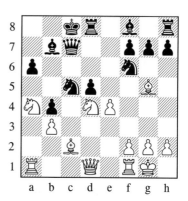

18.e5!
   18.♕f3 dxe4 (18...♘xa4 19.e5 ♘c5 20.exf6
   g6± Hoi – Schandorff, Denmark 1996)
   19.♕f5† ♔b8 20.♗f4 ♗d6 21.♗xd6 ♖xd6
   22.♘xc5 ♖d5 23.♕xd5 ♘xd5 24.♘xb7 ♔xb7
   25.♗xe4 ♕e5 26.♖fe1 ♕xd4 27.♖ad1∓
18...♕xe5

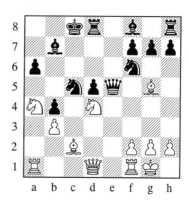

19.♗h4!
   19.♕d2 ♗d6 20.♘f3 ♕e6 21.♘xc5 ♗xc5
   22.♖fc1 ♔b8 23.♗d3 ♕b6 and now:
   a) 24.♗f4† ♔a8 (24...♗d6!? 25.♗e3 d4
   26.♘xd4 ♗xh2† 27.♔xh2 ♖xd4) 25.♕e2
   ♖he8 26.♗xa6 ♖xe2 27.♗xe2† ♕a7 28.♖xa7†
   ♗xa7 29.♖a1 d4 30.♘xd4 ♘d5 (30...♖xd4
   31.♗e3 ♔b8 32.♖xa7) 31.♗d2 ♔b8=
   b) 24.♖xc5 ♕xc5 25.♗f4† ♔a8 26.♗xa6
   ♗xa6 27.♕e2 (27.♕d3 ♖d7 28.♖xa6†
   ♖a7 29.♗e3 d4 30.♖xa7† ♕xa7 31.♗xd4
   ♖d8 32.♕c4 ♖xd4) 27...♖d7 28.♖xa6†

♔b7 (28...♖a7? 29.♗e3 d4 30.♗xd4 ♕c1†
31.♘e1+–) 29.♘e5 ♖e7 30.♔f1 ♖c8 31.♗e3
d4 32.♗xd4 ♕xd4 33.♕b5† ♔c7 34.♕a5†
♔b7 35.♕b5† ♔c7=
19...♘xa4 20.♗f5†
    20.♗g3±
20...♔b8 21.♗g3±

b) 14.b4 cxb3 15.axb3 b4 16.♘a4 ♘cxe4!
17.♗xe4 ♘xe4 18.dxe6 ♗d6 19.exf7† ♕xf7
20.f3 ♕h5 21.g3

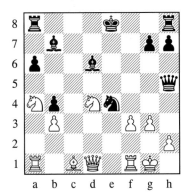

21...0–0
    21...♘xg3   22.♖e1†?   (22.hxg3!   0–0
    [22...♗xg3   23.♕e2†]   23.♖a2)   22...♔f7
    23.hxg3 ♗xg3 24.♖a2 ♖ad8∓ Baramidze –
    Braun, Saarbruecken 2009.
22.fxe4 ♕h3 23.♘f3
    23.♕e2! White moves his queen away from
    the possible d-file pin. 23...♗xe4 24.♗f4±
    23.♖a2 ♗xe4 24.♖e1 ♖ae8⯗
23...♕xg3 24.♘c5 ♖xf3 25.♖xf3 ♕xh2†
26.♔f1

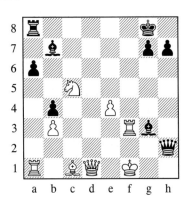

26...♗c6! 27.♗g5 ♗b5† 28.♘d3 ♖e8–+
Kasparov – Kramnik, Dos Hermanas 1996.

c) 14.♕e2 and Black has four options:

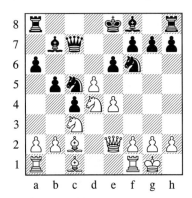

c1) 14...♗d6 15.f4!

c2) 14...♗e7 15.dxe6 ♘xe6
    15...fxe6?   16.e5±   ♘d5   17.♕h5†   ♔d7
    18.♘xe6! ♘xe6 19.♘xd5 ♗xd5 20.♖d1 ♔c6
    21.♖xd5 ♔xd5? 22.♕f3† ♔xe5 23.♗e3 ♖hf8
    24.♕e4†+–

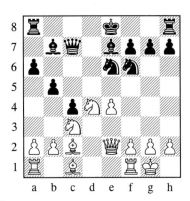

16.♘f5!
    16.♘xe6 fxe6 17.e5 ♕c6 18.f4 ♘d5 19.♕h5†
    g6! 20.♗xg6† hxg6 21.♕xh8† ♔d7 22.♕h3
    ♗c5† (22...♖h8 23.♕xh8 ♘xc3 24.♕h3+–)
    23.♔h1 ♘e7 Black threatens ...♖h8 and has
    decent compensation. (Instead 23...♘xc3
    24.bxc3 ♖h8 can be met by 25.♕g4 ♕e4
    26.a4.)
16...♖d8 17.♗e3±

c3) 14...0–0–0 15.b4 ♘d3 16.♗xd3 cxd3
17.♕xd3 exd5

17...♗xb4 18.♘ce2 ♕c4 19.♕f3±

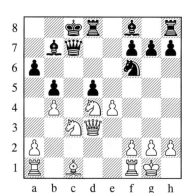

18.e5 ♕xe5

18...♘e4 19.♘ce2 ♗xb4 20.♗f4→

19.♘ce2 ♗d6 20.♗f4 ♕e4 21.♕g3 ♗xf4
22.♘xf4 ♕e5

22...♕xd4?? 23.♖ac1† ♔d7 24.♖c7† ♔xc7
25.♘e6†

23.♖fe1 ♘e4 24.♕e3 ♕f6 25.♖ac1† ♔b8
26.f3 ♖he8

26...♘d6 27.♘c6†+–

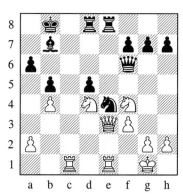

27.♘h5! ♕g6 28.fxe4 ♖xe4 29.♕f2 ♕xh5

29...♖xe1† 30.♖xe1 ♕xh5 31.♘c6†! ♗xc6
32.♕b6† ♗b7 33.♖xd8† ♔a7 34.♕d6+–

30.♘c6† ♗xc6 31.♕b6† ♗b7 32.♕xd8† ♔a7
33.♖xe4 dxe4 34.♕d4†+–

Mulyar – Veech, Philadelphia 2011.

c4) 14...♖d8 15.♗g5 ♗e7

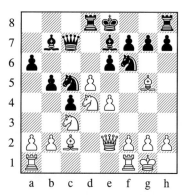

16.♖ae1 (16.♖fe1 0–0 17.♗xf6 ♗xf6 18.e5
♗g5 19.d6 [19.♘f3 ♗h6 20.d6 ♕b6±]
19...♕b6 20.♕g4 ♗h6 21.♖ad1±) 16...0–0
17.♗xf6 gxf6± (17...♗xf6 18.e5 ♗g5 19.d6
♕b6 20.♖d1±)

d) 14.♕f3!? ♗d6 15.♕h3 b4

15...0–0 16.♗g5

15...♗e5   16.♗e3 exd5 17.exd5 ♘xd5
18.♖fe1∞ The black king is stuck in
the middle and White has obvious
compensation. However, Black panics and
loses instantly. 18...♘xe3? 19.♕xe3 f6 20.f4
0–0–0 21.fxe5 fxe5 22.♕xe5 ♕xe5 23.♖xe5
♖xd4 24.♖xc5†+– Moskalenko – Ljukin,
Marganets 1999.

16.♘a4 ♘cxe4 17.dxe6 0–0 18.f3 ♗e5

18...♘c5 19.♗g5 fxe6 20.♔h1↑

19.♗e3 ♘g5 20.exf7† ♖xf7 21.♕h4 ♖d8
22.♘f5 ♘e6 23.♗b6 ♕b8 24.♗xd8 ♘xd8
25.♖ad1+– ♗d5 26.♘e3 ♕a7 27.♕f2+–
Tkachiev – Handoko, Jakarta 1996.

14.♘f5 g6 15.♘h6!

Definitely the best. The white knight on h6
will seriously disrupt Black's development.

15.♘e3 ♗c5 16.♕f3 0–0∞ Anand – Van Wely,
Monte Carlo 2005.

15...♘h5

15...♘g8?!   16.♘xg8 ♖xg8 17.♕f3 ♗d6
18.b3! b4 19.♘d1 a5 This positional sacrifice,

aiming to keep control of the dark squares on the queenside, will not provide Black with enough compensation. (19...c3 20.a3 a5 21.♘e3±) 20.bxc4 ♘c5 21.a3± Szmetan – Morovic Fernandez, Buenos Aires 1992.

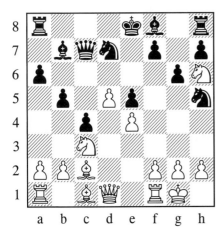

16.g3!

Strangely enough, this simple, logical move is a blockbuster novelty here. Black is already in serious trouble.

One previous top class encounter finished with a brilliant black victory: 16.♕f3 ♘f4 17.♘xf7 ♔xf7 18.g3 g5 19.gxf4 gxf4 20.♕h5† ♔e7 21.♕h4† ♔f7 Since the white king is also vulnerable, it would probably have been wise for White to take the draw by repetition here. 22.♗d1 ♖g8† 23.♔h1 ♘f6 24.♗h5† ♖g6 25.♗xg6† hxg6 26.♖g1 ♗e7 27.♕h6 ♖g8 28.f3 b4 29.♘e2

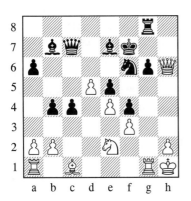

29...♘xd5!! 30.exd5 ♗xd5 Black's attack triumphed in Gelfand – Dreev, Tilburg 1993.

It is strange that a top theoretician and hard worker like Gelfand did not revisit this line and come up with 16.g3!.

16...♗c5 17.♕f3 ♖f8 18.♗d2 ♗d4

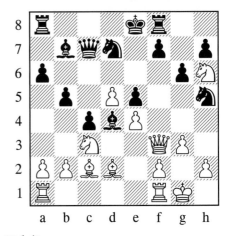

19.b4!

If Black does not take this pawn, White will play a2-a4 next. Black's main problem here is the terrible position of his king, and therefore his inability to coordinate his pieces.

19...cxb3 20.♗xb3 ♕d6 21.♖ac1 ♘g7 22.a4

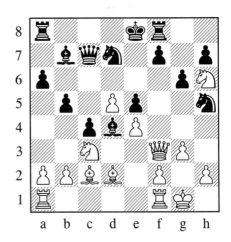

22...f5

Black looks for active counterplay. However, he does not have nearly enough to create any serious threats, and as mentioned above, his badly placed king is playing a significant role.

22...b4 23.♘e2 ♗c5 24.a5! f5 25.♗g5 ♖c8

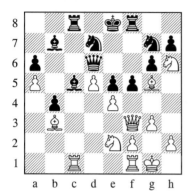

26.♘f4! ♘f6 (26...exf4 27.gxf4 ♕b8 28.exf5 ♖xf5 29.♖fe1† ♔f8 30.♖xc5+−) 27.♘d3 fxe4 28.♘xc5 exf3 29.♘xb7+−

23.axb5 f4 24.♘e2 ♗b6 25.bxa6 ♗xa6

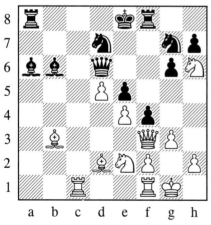

26.♗c4

26.g4 is also winning: 26...♗d8 27.♖c6 ♕a3 28.♖b1 ♗g5 (28...♖b8 29.♗c1 ♕a5 [29...♗xe2 30.♕xe2] 30.♘c3 ♗g5 31.♗d2 ♗xh6 32.♕h3) 29.d6 ♔d8 30.♘c3 ♗xh6 31.♕h3 ♗g5 32.♕xh7+−

26...g5

26...fxg3 27.♕xg3 ♘h5 28.♕h3 ♗xc4 29.♖xc4 ♖a2 30.♗b4 ♕f6 31.♖c8†+−

27.♗xa6 ♖xa6 28.♖c8†

28.♖c6+−

28...♗d8 29.♘f5 ♘xf5 30.exf5 ♘f6

30...♖xf5 31.♘c3+−

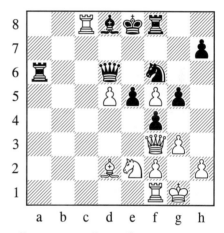

31.♕d3 ♖a7 32.♕b5† ♕d7

32...♔f7 33.♗b4+−

33.♖xd8†

Now 33...♔d8 34.♕b8† ♔e7 35.♗b4† leads to mate.

1–0

GAME 31
▷ L. Aronian (2805)
▶ P. Harikrishna (2669)
8th World Team Championship, Ningbo
Round 6, 23.07.2011 **[D56]**
Annotated by Kamil Miton

I have heard some players opine that if you have a problem choosing an opening, you can always depend on a solid Queen's Gambit Declined. Black's position is reliable and White has had a hard time achieving much advantage against it. My intuition tells me that my good friend Harikrishna, who normally prefers very active chess, was unsure of what to play against Aronian and the aforementioned thought process led him to try the QGD. Unfortunately for him Levon had a surprise in store, and the practical problems proved too much for him to handle over the board. White's amazing tenth move provides a modern twist on a classical variation, and opens all kinds of doors for creative investigation.

1.d4 ♘f6 2.c4 e6 3.♘f3 d5 4.♘c3 ♗e7 5.♗g5 h6 6.♗h4 0–0 7.e3 ♘e4 8.♗xe7 ♕xe7 9.♖c1 c6

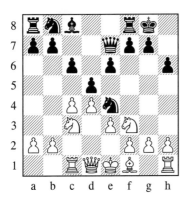

10.h4!?

A remarkable idea from one of the most original players in the world. White wants to take some space on the kingside.

The normal continuation is 10.♗d3 ♘xc3 11.♖xc3 dxc4 when Black will fight for the centre with ...e5 or ...c5. The latest games in this variation show that White has a hard time achieving anything, and the drawing percentage has been high. See for instance the game Radjabov – Kramnik, Candidates Match (3) 2011.

10...♘d7

The other main possibility was:
10...♘xc3 11.♖xc3
 11.bxc3!?
 11...♘d7

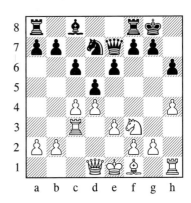

12.g4!

White simply continues with his plan.
12...c5
 12...♘f6? 13.g5 ♘e4 14.gxh6 ♘xc3 15.bxc3 gxh6 16.♘e5→
13.g5 h5 14.♗g2 dxc4
 14...cxd4 15.♕xd4 dxc4 16.♕xc4 ♘b6 17.♕c5±
 14...b6!?
15.dxc5
 15.0–0 b5 16.♘e5 ♘xe5 17.♗xa8 ♖d8 18.♕xh5 cxd4 19.exd4 ♖xd4 20.g6 ♘xg6 21.♕xb5 e5↑
 15.♖xc4 b5
15...♘xc5 16.♘e5

Now it is important for Black to choose the right path.

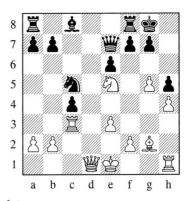

16...♗d7!
 16...♖d8 17.♕xh5 ♘d3† 18.♘xd3 cxd3 19.0–0 e5 20.♖d1 ♗f5 21.e4 ♗e6 22.g6±
17.♕xh5

17.g6 ♘d3† 18.♖xd3 cxd3 19.gxf7† ♖xf7
20.♘xf7 ♕xf7 21.♕xd3=
17...♘d3† 18.♘xd3 cxd3 19.♗e4 g6 20.♕h6
20.♕d1 is met by 20...♗b5.

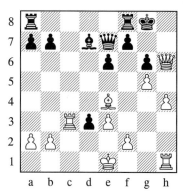

20...♕b4! 21.h5
It seems that this sharp position is destined
to end in a draw.
21...♕xb2
   21...d2† is equally effective: 22.♔xd2 ♗b5
23.♔c1 ♖fc8 24.hxg6 ♖xc3† 25.bxc3 ♕xc3†
26.♔b1 ♕b4†=
22.♖xd3 ♗b5 23.hxg6 ♕c1† 24.♔e2 ♕b2†
   White cannot escape the checks, for
instance:
25.♔f3 fxg6† 26.♔g4 ♕e2† 27.♔g3 ♕xf2†
28.♔g4 ♕e2†=

11.g4!
   White seems to be flouting the established
principles of opening play, but the space-
gaining plan is justified by the slight weakness
of the black kingside caused by the earlier
...h7-h6.

11...e5
   Black is playing logically and trying to obtain
counterplay in the centre.

After 11...b5?! 12.cxb5 cxb5 13.g5 h5 14.♗xb5
♖b8 15.a4 a6 16.♗xd7 ♗xd7 17.♘e5± White
has a good position.

11...f5!? is an interesting move which deserves
attention.

11...c5!?

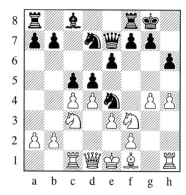

   Along with the game continuation, this
looks like one of the most natural ways to
counterattack in the centre. White has three
main replies.

a) 12.cxd5 ♘xc3 13.♖xc3 (13.bxc3 exd5 14.g5
h5 looks roughly balanced.) 13...exd5 14.dxc5
(14.g5 h5 transposes to line 'c2' below)
14...♘xc5   15.♕xd5   ♗xg4   (15...♘a4!?↑)
16.♕xc5 ♕xc5 17.♖xc5 ♗xf3=

b) 12.dxc5 ♘dxc5 13.cxd5

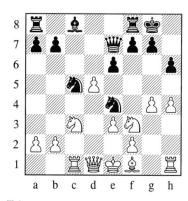

13...♖d8!
   13...♘xc3 14.d6!±
14.g5 h5
   14...♘xc3!?   15.♖xc3   ♘e4   16.♖d3   exd5

17.gxh6 ♗g4 18.♗e2 ♕b4† 19.♘d2 ♗xe2
20.♔xe2 ♘c5 21.♖d4 ♕b5† 22.♔f3 ♘e6
23.♖g4 d4 24.e4 g6∞
15.♘xe4 ♘xe4 16.♕d4 exd5

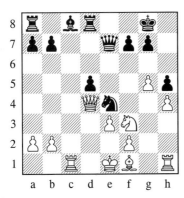

17.♗g2
  17.♗d3 ♗g4 18.♘e5 ♖ac8 19.♖xc8 ♖xc8
  20.♗xe4 dxe4 21.0–0 ♗f5=
  17.♗e2!?
17...♗g4 18.♘e5
  18.0–0 can be met by 18...♕e6 intending
  ...♗h3.
18...♖e8 19.♘xg4
  19.f4 ♖ac8 20.♖xc8 ♖xc8 21.0–0 ♘g3 22.♖e1
  ♗e6 23.♗xd5 ♖c1 24.♔f2 ♖xe1 25.♔xe1
  ♘f5 26.♕d2 ♗xd5 27.♕xd5 ♘xe3=
19...hxg4

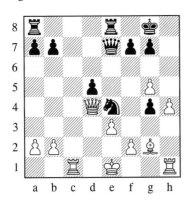

20.g6
  20.0–0 ♖ad8 21.♗xe4 dxe4 22.♕xa7 ♖d2
  23.♕b6 ♖ed8∞
20...♖ad8 21.gxf7† ♕xf7 22.0–0 a6∞

c) 12.g5 h5
  12...♘xc3 will lead to one of the lines given
below, as Black will have to play ...h5 anyway.
  12...cxd4?! 13.♕xd4 ♘xc3 14.gxh6 (14.♖xc3
  h5 15.cxd5 exd5 16.♗d3±) 14...e5 15.♕xc3
  d4 16.♕d2 ♘c5 17.hxg7 ♖d8 18.e4 ♕f6
  19.♕g5±

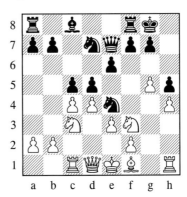

We have reached a final branching point,
with five(!) options for White.

c1) 13.dxc5 ♘xc3 14.♖xc3 ♘xc5 15.cxd5 exd5
16.♕xd5 ♗g4 17.♕xc5 ♕e4 18.♗e2 ♗xf3
19.♖c4 ♕b1† 20.♖c1 ♕e4=

c2) 13.cxd5 ♘xc3 14.♖xc3 exd5

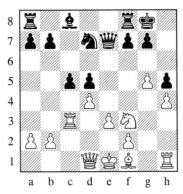

15.♗g2
  15.dxc5 ♘xc5 16.♕xd5 ♘a4 gives Black
reasonable compensation.
  15.♗b5 a6 16.♗xd7 ♗xd7 17.♘e5 cxd4
  18.♕xd4 ♗f5 19.0–0 (19.♕xd5 ♖fd8

20.♘c6 bxc6 21.♕xf5 ♖ab8 22.0–0 ♖b4)
19...♖fe8=

15...c4

15...b6 16.0–0 ♗b7 17.♘e1! g6 18.♘d3±

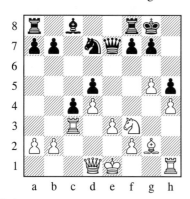

16.♘d2

16.0–0 b5 17.♘d2 ♘b6 18.♕xh5 ♗f5
19.♕f3 ♗d3 20.♖xd3 cxd3 21.♕f5∞

16...♘b6 17.♕xh5 ♗f5

Black has decent compensation as White's
rook and knight are both misplaced. Black's
ideas include ...♕b4 and ...♗d3.

18.♕d1

18.0–0 ♕b4 [18...♘a4 19.♗xd5 ♘xc3
20.bxc3 ♕d7 21.♘e4! ♕xd5 22.♘f6† gxf6
23.gxf6+–] 19.e4 ♗g6 20.♕d1 ♕xb2∞

18...♗d3

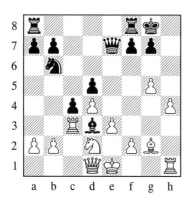

19.♖xd3!?

After 19.♗f1 ♗f5 it is not clear how White
should develop his kingside.

19...cxd3 20.♘b3

The position is unclear.

c3) 13.♗d3 ♘xc3 14.bxc3

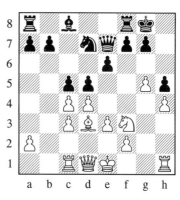

14...e5!?

14...dxc4 15.♗xc4 b6 16.g6! fxg6 17.♘g5
♖f6 18.f4 ♗b7 19.0–0↑

15.♘xe5 ♘xe5 16.dxe5 dxc4 17.♗xc4 ♕xe5

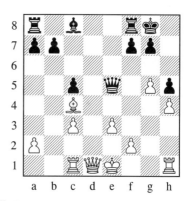

18.♕xh5

18.♕d5 ♕e7 19.g6 ♗e6 20.♕xh5 fxg6
21.♕e5 ♖f6=

18...♕e4 19.g6 ♕xh1† 20.♔e2 ♗g4† 21.♕xg4
♕xc1 22.♕f5 ♕b2† 23.♔f1 ♕b6 24.gxf7†
♔h8 25.♗e6 g6 26.♕xg6

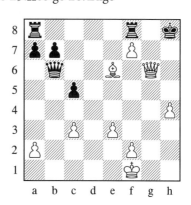

26...♖xf7! 27.♕xf7 ♕b1† 28.♔g2 ♕h7
29.♕xh7† ♔xh7 30.e4±

White's chances are slightly higher in this double-edged endgame.

c4) 13.♗g2

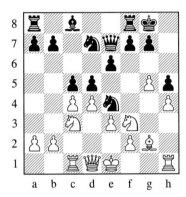

13...♘xc3 14.bxc3 ♘b6

A logical move, after which White will have to play very precisely in order to create any problems for his opponent. Some other moves also deserve attention:

14...b6 15.cxd5 exd5 16.♘d2±
14...♖d8 15.cxd5 exd5 16.♘d2±
14...dxc4 15.♘d2 e5 16.d5±
14...g6!? seems logical: 15.cxd5 exd5 16.c4 dxc4 17.♖xc4 b5∞

15.cxd5!?

15.♘d2 e5! 16.dxc5 (16.cxd5 exd4 17.cxd4 cxd4 18.♕b3 dxe3 19.fxe3 ♗g4 20.0-0 ♕e5=) 16...♘xc4 17.♘xc4 dxc4 18.♕xh5 ♗f5 19.♗d5 ♖ad8 20.e4 ♖xd5 21.exd5 ♕xc5↑ Black has fine compensation.

15.♘e5 looks logical, but after 15...g6 (15...♘xc4? 16.♘xc4 dxc4 17.♕xh5 cxd4 18.exd4 ♖d8 19.♗e4 g6 20.♕h6 ♕f8 21.♕xf8† ♔xf8 22.h5 gxh5 23.♖xh5±) 16.♕b3 ♘xc4 17.♘xc4 dxc4 18.♕xc4 ♗d7 19.♕xc5 ♕xc5 20.dxc5 ♖ac8 21.♗xb7 ♖xc5⩲ Black should have enough counterplay for equality.

15...exd5 16.♘e5 ♗f5

16...g6!? could be considered.

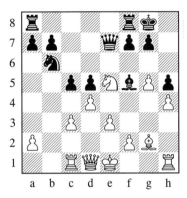

17.0-0!

17.♕xh5 cxd4 18.cxd4 (18.exd4 ♘c4 19.0-0 ♘xe5 20.dxe5 ♕xe5 21.♖fe1 ♕f4 22.♕f3 ♕xf3 23.♗xf3 ♗e6=) 18...♕b4† 19.♔f1 (Or 19.♔e2 ♖ae8 intending ...♖xg4 and ...♗g4.) 19...♖ac8 20.♖e1 ♖c2↑

17...g6 18.a4 ♖ad8 19.a5 ♘c4 20.♘xc4 dxc4 21.e4±

c5) 13.♘xe4 dxe4 14.♘d2

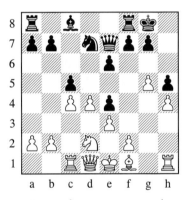

Yet again we have an extremely complex position with numerous possibilities.

c51) 14...f5 15.♕xh5

15.gxf6 ♘xf6 16.dxc5 ♗d7∓
15.♘b3!?
15.dxc5 ♘xc5? This could lead to an amazing line which eventually turns out in White's favour. (The right path is: 15...g6! 16.♘b3 ♘e5 17.♕d6 ♘f3† 18.♔e2 ♕g7∞) 16.♕xh5 ♖d8 17.g6 ♕f6 18.b4 ♘a6 19.a3 ♕b2

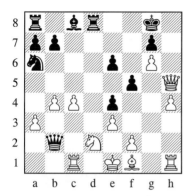

20.♖c2 ♕xc2 21.♕h7† ♔f8 22.♕h8†
♔e7 23.♕xg7† ♔d6 24.♕d4† ♔e7
25.♕xd8† ♔xd8 26.g7 ♕c1† 27.♔e2 ♕xa3
28.g8=♕† ♔c7 29.♕g7† ♗d7 30.♕e5† ♔c8
31.♖g1+−

15...cxd4

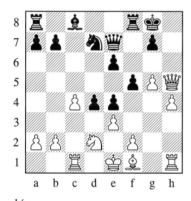

16.exd4

Also interesting is: 16.c5!? dxe3 (16...d3
17.f3) 17.fxe3 ♖d8 18.♗c4→

16...♖d8 17.c5

17.♕e2 ♘b8 (17...♘f8 18.♕e3±) 18.g6
♕f6 19.♕h5 ♘c6 20.♕h7† (20.d5 ♕xb2
21.♘b3 ♘b4 22.♖h3) 20...♔f8 21.h5 ♘xd4
22.h6 ♗d7∞

17...b6

Or 17...♘f8 18.♗c4 ♖xd4 19.♘b3 ♖d8
20.g6 ♕f6 21.♖g1± intending ♖g5 and
♖xf5.

18.c6

18.b4 ♘f8 19.♗c4 bxc5 20.bxc5 ♖xd4
21.♘b3 ♖d8 22.0–0 ♗b7 23.♖fd1 e3

24.fxe3? ♕c7∓

18...♘f8 19.♘b3 a5 20.a4 ♕b4† 21.♖c3 ♕xa4
22.♕e2! ♗a6 23.♕xa6 ♖xa6 24.♗xa6 ♕b4
25.c7 ♖e8 26.0–0 a4 27.♘a1 ♕xb2 28.c8=♕
♖xc8 29.♖xc8 b5 30.♘c2±

c52) 14...cxd4

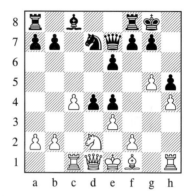

This seems like Black's most reliable answer.
White can choose between taking on e4 or
d4.

c521) 15.♘xe4 f5!

15...dxe3? 16.fxe3 ♘c5 17.♘f6†!+−
15...♘e5 16.c5 dxe3 17.♕xh5 exf2† 18.♔xf2
♗d7 19.♖g1↑
15...e5 16.♕xh5 ♕b4† 17.♔d1! is less
clear-cut, but White's king looks to be the
safer:

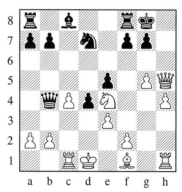

17...♕xb2 (17...dxe3 18.♔c2 b5 19.♔b1
♗b7 20.♗d3±) 18.♗d3 ♕a3 19.♔e2→

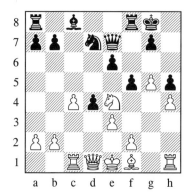

16.gxf6 ♘xf6 17.♕xd4 ♘xe4 18.♕xe4 ♕b4†
19.♖c3 ♕xb2 20.♕c2 ♕xc2 21.♖xc2 ♗d7=

c522) 15.exd4 e5!

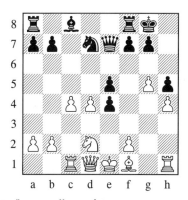

16.d5 ♘c5 17.♕xh5 ♗f5
   17...a5 18.♘b3 ♘xb3 (18...♘d3† 19.♗xd3
exd3 20.♕f3 e4 21.♕f4±) 19.axb3 ♕b4†
20.♖c3 a4 21.♗g2 ♗f5 22.0–0 a3 23.♕e2 a2
24.♖a1±
18.b4
   18.♖c3 b5!↑
18...♘d3† 19.♗xd3 exd3 20.♕f3 g6
   20...♗h7 21.♕g4 ♕xb4 (21...e4!?) 22.h5
♕d6 23.♖g1± White is better as the bishop
on h7 is a problem.
21.♕g3 a5
   21...♕xb4 22.h5→
22.b5 ♕a3 23.♖b1 ♕c3 24.h5 e4∞

It is hard to give a concise summary of the
above analysis. Generally the positions are

richly unbalanced and there is clearly a great
deal of scope for analysis and practical testing
in the above variations.

Let's return to the game after Harikrishna's
11...e5, which also leads to highly complex
play.

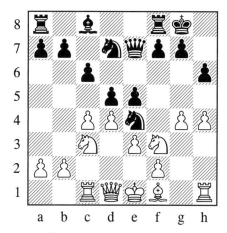

12.cxd5 ♘xc3 13.♖xc3 cxd5
   Wrong is 13...♘f6? 14.d6! ♕xd6 15.♘xe5
when White is clearly better.

14.g5
   14.♘xe5 ♘xe5 15.dxe5 ♕xe5 should lead to
equality: 16.g5 ♖e8 17.gxh6 d4 18.♖d3 dxe3
19.♖xe3 ♕a5† 20.♕d2 ♖xe3† 21.fxe3 ♕xd2†
22.♔xd2 gxh6=

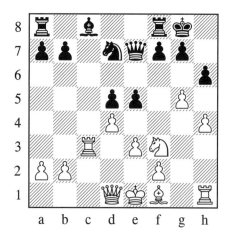

14...h5

14...e4 15.♘d2 hxg5 16.♕h5 g4 17.♕xd5±

14...hxg5!?

This move is risky-looking, but nonetheless playable and interesting.

15.hxg5

15.♘xg5 ♘f6=

15.♘xe5 ♘xe5 16.dxe5 g4 17.♕xd5 ♗f5=

15...e4

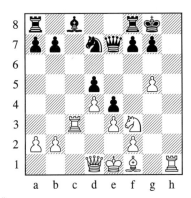

16.♘e5

Wrong is 16.♖c7? since there is no convincing follow-up after 16...exf3, for instance 17.♗d3 ♖e8 18.♕xf3 ♕d6 19.♕h5 ♔f8 20.♖c2 ♔e7 and Black is clearly better.

16.♕c2?! is also unimpressive: 16...g6 17.♘g1 ♕xg5 18.♘h3 ♕h4 19.♗g2 ♘f6 20.♘f4 ♕g5∓

16...♕xg5

16...♘xe5?! 17.♕h5 is too risky for Black, even if 17...f6 does stave off the immediate mate.

17.♖xc8

17.♖h5 ♕e7 18.♘xd7 ♗xd7 (18...♕xd7!?) 19.♖xd5 ♖fc8 20.♖e5 ♕h4 is okay for Black.

17...♖axc8 18.♘xd7 ♖fd8 19.♘c5

The knight is heading for c3, where it will block the open c-file and attack the potentially weak pawn on d5.

19...♖d6

I analysed this position with my friend, grandmaster Marcin Dziuba from Poland.

Black's main goal will be to create counterplay on the c-file. White will counter this plan by putting his knight on c3, where it also helps to attack the d5-pawn. In the medium term, White will look to transfer his bishop to b3. Marcin and I concluded that White's position is slightly more pleasant.

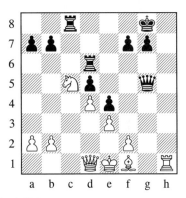

20.♘a4 ♕d8!?

The queen switches to the opposite flank in order to assist with Black's counterplay. Alternatives are less challenging:

20...♖dc6 21.♘c3 g6 22.♕b3± The d5-pawn is weak.

20...a6 21.♘c3 g6 22.♕d2 b5 23.a3 ♔g7 24.♗e2 ♕g2 25.♖f1 ♖h8 26.♗d1 ♖h1 27.♕e2± The bishop will soon complete its journey to b3.

20...♖h6 21.♖xh6 ♕xh6 22.♘c3 ♖d8 23.♕b3 ♕c6 24.♗b5! ♕d6 25.♗a4 Again White will completed the desired bishop manoeuvre shortly.

21.♘c3 ♕a5

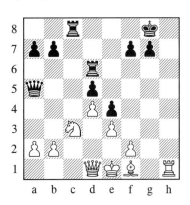

22.♕b3!±

White keeps some advantage. Instead 22.♕d2 enables Black to obtain decent counterplay with 22...♖b6 23.a3 (or 23.♗e2 ♕b4 24.♘d1 ♕xd2† 25.♔xd2 g6 and Black should be okay as White cannot organize his queenside in the desired manner) 23...♖xb2 24.♕xb2 ♖xc3 25.♕b4 ♕xa3 26.♕xa3 ♖xa3 with three pawns for a bishop and mutual chances.

15.♗b5 exd4?!

After this move the balance swings in White's favour.

15...e4!?

This would have been the more active and principled way for Black to continue the game.

16.♗xd7

After 16.♘d2 ♘b6 17.♕xh5 a6 18.♗f1 ♗d7 White has an extra pawn, but Black has good prospects on the queenside with ideas like ...♖c8, ...♕b4 and ...♘a4 on the agenda.

16...exf3

16...♗xd7 17.♘e5 ♗f5 18.♕xh5±

17.♗xc8 ♖axc8

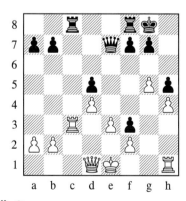

18.♕xf3

18.♖xc8 ♖xc8 19.♕xf3 ♕b4† 20.♔f1 ♕xb2 21.♕xd5 ♖c1† 22.♔g2 ♖xh1 23.♔xh1 ♕xf2=

18...♖xc3 19.bxc3 ♕e6

Slightly surprisingly, Black seems to have

fully adequate compensation. White already has one extra pawn and might even take another on h5, but his vulnerable king and pawn weaknesses on c3 and h4 give Black plenty of opportunities to cause problems.

20.0–0

20.♔d2!? is interesting but 20...g6 21.♖b1 ♕c6 22.♕f6 ♕d7 seems okay for Black, whose next job will be to activate his rook.

20.♕xh5 ♕e4 21.♖h3

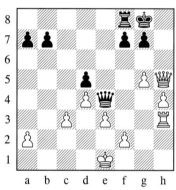

21...♖c8 (after 21...♕b1† 22.♕d1 ♕xa2 23.h5 a5 24.h6 a4 25.♕d3 White's attack is dangerous) 22.♔d2 ♕b1 (22...b5 23.g6 fxg6 24.♕e5±) 23.♕d1 ♕xa2† (23...♕xd1† 24.♔xd1 ♖xc3 25.♖f3 g6 26.♖f6 ♖a3 27.♖d6 ♖xa2 28.♖xd5 ♖xf2 29.♖d8† ♔g7 30.d5) 24.♕c2 ♕a1 25.h5 b5 26.h6 b4 27.hxg7 bxc3† 28.♔e2 ♕b2 29.♔d1 ♕a1†=

20...♖e8!

Black wants to put the rook on e4, targeting the pawn on h4 as well as the white king.

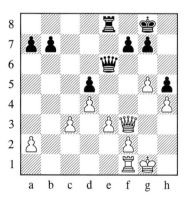

21.♖b1

21.♕xh5 ♖h3 22.g6 ♖e4 23.gxf7† ♔f8 24.♕h8† ♔xf7 25.♕h5† ♔f8=

21...♕d7 22.♕xh5

22.c4 ♖e4 23.♔f1 ♖xh4 24.♖b5 dxc4 25.g6 fxg6 26.♖xb7 ♕e6 27.♖xa7 ♔h7∞

22...♖e4 23.♔f1 ♖xe3 24.fxe3 ♕f5† 25.♔g2 ♕xb1=

16.♕xd4±

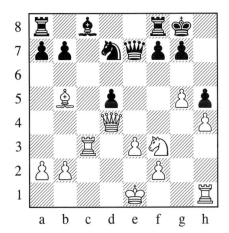

The two pawn exchanges have resulted a more static central structure. Black's weak d5-pawn is a problem, and he will have a hard time generating any counterplay against the white king, despite the unusual kingside structure.

16...♕e4

Black decides to change the central structure, but White keeps some advantage anyway. 16...♘b6 17.♗d3± is also pleasant for him.

17.♕xe4! dxe4 18.♘d2 ♘e5 19.♘xe4 ♗e6 20.f4!

White continues to play energetically.

20...♗d5

The best practical chance, but it is not good enough.

21.fxe5 ♗xe4 22.0–0

White's doubled e-pawns are not a real problem, as his pieces are tremendously active.

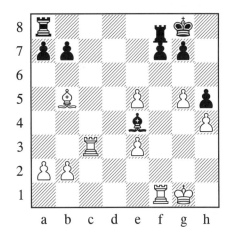

22...♗d5 23.♗d7 ♖fd8 24.♖c7 a5 25.a4+–

White dominates the board, and the rest is simple for a player of Aronian's calibre.

25...♖a6 26.♖f4 ♖f8 27.♖d4 ♗c6 28.e6

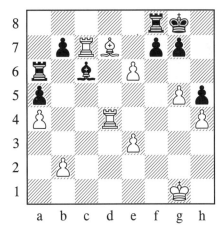

Not only eliminating one of the doubled pawns, but also exposing the black king. Black could have resigned here, but Harikrishna plays on for a few more moves.

28...fxe6 29.♗xe6† ♔h8 30.♗f7 ♖b6 31.b3 ♗f3 32.g6 ♖c6 33.♖xc6 bxc6 34.e4 ♗e2 35.e5
1–0

GAME 32

▷ **A. Morozevich (2694)**

▶ **M. Carlsen (2821)**

Accentus GM Tournament, Biel

Round 3, 20.07.2011 **[D80]**

Annotated by Borki Predojevic

After his win in the first round against Pelletier, Carlsen again chose the Grünfeld Defence with Black. Maybe this was a surprise for Morozevich and he chose to deviate very early from the main line by playing 5.♘xe4!?. Carlsen reacted with the usual plan for Black and did not have any problems after the opening. The line as a whole is not dangerous for Black and he could even try other plans, for example 11...a6!?.

The middlegame was interesting with nice positional moves by both players. Then with 21...a5!? Carlsen opened the position. The game became extremely complicated and after a few imprecise moves by both sides, it finished in perpetual check.

1.d4 ♘f6 2.c4 g6 3.♘c3 d5 4.♗g5 ♘e4

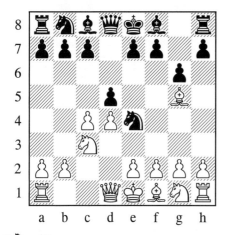

5.♘xe4!?

An interesting choice by Morozevich. This move has never been played at the top level.

5...dxe4 6.♕d2 ♗g7 7.e3 c5

This is the best way to continue.

8.d5 ♘d7

If instead:

8...♕b6

White can try:

9.♖b1

9.0–0–0 ♘d7 10.♘e2 ♘e5 11.♘c3∞ is another possibility.

9...♘d7 10.♘e2 ♘e5 11.♘c3 h6 12.♗h4 g5 13.♗g3 ♗f5 14.♗e2 0–0

This was played in Golod – Fercec, Rijeka 2010. Here White could play:

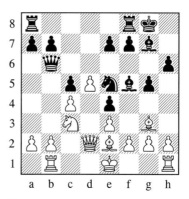

15.h4N

15.0–0 ♕g6⇄

15...g4

Dubious is 15...♕g6 16.hxg5 hxg5. After the strong 17.♗xe5! ♗xe5 18.g4 ♗d7 19.♕c2 f5 20.gxf5 ♗xf5 21.♔d2±

15...♗g6 16.hxg5 hxg5 17.♔f1 ♕b4 18.d6!?

16.h5! ♕b4

Now White can play:

17.0–0

17.a3 ♕b3 18.♕d1 ♕xd1† 19.♔xd1± also looks better for White.

17...♘xc4 18.♕c2 e6 19.dxe6 fxe6

19...♗xe6 20.♖fc1 ♖ad8 21.a3 ♕a5 22.♘xe4 b5 23.♗h4↑ gives White the better prospects.

20.a3! ♘xa3 21.bxa3 ♕xc3 22.♕xc3 ♗xc3 23.♖fc1↑

White has a strong initiative for the sacrificed pawns.

9.♘e2 ♘e5 10.♘c3 f5

10...h6 11.♗h4 f5 12.♗e2∞ would be less precise, as now Black will not have ...♘f7 with tempo.

11.♗e2

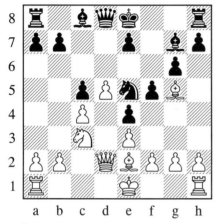

11...♘f7

After 11...0–0?! White has the neat 12.d6! ♕xd6 13.♘d5 and Black will lose the e7-pawn. 13...♕d7 (13...♕a6 14.♘c7 ♕c6 15.♘xa8 ♗e6 16.♗xe7 ♖xa8 17.♖c1±) 14.♗xe7 ♖e8 15.♗xc5 b6?! (stronger was 15...b5 16.♗d4±) 16.♗d4± White was better in Meynard – Schoucair, Saint Affrique 2005.

As I wrote above, I do not recommend that Black play:
11...h6 12.♗h4

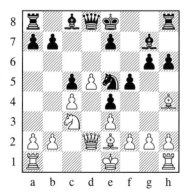

Bangiev now suggests:

12...♕b6!?

As the best move in his analysis for *ChessBase Magazine* 38/1994. Black's idea is to castle long after ...♗d7. Another idea is ...♕b4.
12...0–0 13.f3 exf3 14.gxf3↑
12...♗d7 13.f3 exf3 14.gxf3 g5 15.♗g3↑ White can play f4 or h4.

13.f3
13.♗g3 0–0
13.0–0 g5 14.♗g3 h5 15.h4 gxh4 16.♗xh4 ♗d7∞ looks good for Black. He can prepare an attack on the kingside. Now White has an interesting pawn sacrifice: 17.d6 ♕xd6 18.♕xd6 exd6 19.♖fd1 ♘f7 20.♘d5 ♖b8 21.♖ab1 Intending 21...♖h6 22.b4⩲ with compensation.

13...exf3 14.gxf3 g5 15.♗g3
15.♗f2 ♗d7 16.0–0–0 0–0–0⇄
15...♗d7 16.f4 ♘f7

This leads to unclear play according to Bangiev.

12.♗h4

The natural retreat. Less logical is: 12.♗f4 e5 13.♗g3 (13.dxe6 ♕xd2† 14.♔xd2 ♗xe6⇄) 13...♘d6⇄ Black has a good game.

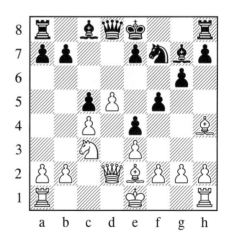

12...0–0 13.f3

With this move White opens the centre; the white king's future will be on the queenside after 0–0–0.

13.0–0 is not so good. Now Black doesn't have a knight on e5, which gives him the opportunity to play 13...g5 14.♗g3 e5! and Black will blockade on d6. I don't see a clear plan for White. 15.f3 exf3 16.♗xf3 ♘d6 17.♗e2 ♗d7↑ looks better for Black.

13...exf3 14.gxf3

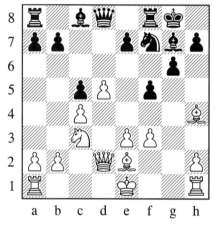

14...♛d6!?

Carlsen wants to push ...e7-e5. Black could play a waiting move:
14...a6!?
   Black waits to see how White will organize his attack and prepares ...b7-b5 in case White chooses to castle long.

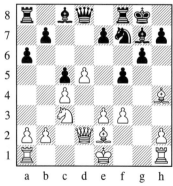

The best reply for White is:
15.♗f2!
   15.0–0–0 ♘d6 16.a4 ♗d7 17.♗g5 b5∓

15.e4 ♘d6∓
15.♗g3 e5 16.h4 ♘d6 17.h5 g5 18.h6 ♗f6 19.♖g1 ♔h8↑ This is a better version for Black than in the game since he has a blockade on d6 and his next ideas are ...♗d7 and ...b5.
15...♗d7 16.h4
   16.e4 ♘d6 17.h4 (17.♗xc5 ♛c7 18.♗f2 fxe4↑) 17...b5↑
16...b5 17.h5 g5
   With an unclear game.

Another interesting idea is 14...♗f6!?.

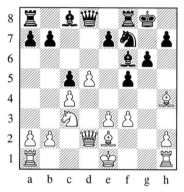

After 15.♗xf6 (15.♗g3 e5 would give Black the possibility to block the d-pawn with ...♘d6. After 16.h4 ♘d6 17.h5 g5 18.♖g1 ♔h8 19.0–0–0 ♗d7∞ the position is unclear, but here Black can push ...b5 very easily and his pieces are better placed than in the game.) 15...exf6 16.0–0–0 ♘d6 The position is very interesting. Black has a lot of pawns around his king, so White's attacking chances are limited. On the other hand, White is better developed and he has to try a break (in the centre or the kingside). 17.h4 ♗d7 18.e4 fxe4 19.♘xe4 ♘xe4 20.fxe4 ♛e7 21.♗f3 ♛e5 22.♖hg1∞/± White may indeed be a little better, but Black has chances connected with ...♖ab8 and ...b5.

14.g5?! 15.♗g3 e5 is not so good for Black. After 16.h4↑ White has good prospects of organizing an attack on the kingside.

15.♗g3

On 15.0–0–0 Black can react with 15...♗d7. (If 15...e5 then White has 16.♘b5 ♕d7 17.d6!; 15...a6 16.♗g3 e5 17.dxe6 ♕xd2† 18.♖xd2 ♗xe6 19.♖hd1 ♘e5 20.♘d5 ♖f7 21.♘b6 ♖e8 22.♔c2∞) 16.♗g3 ♕a6! 17.h4 ♘d6 18.♕d3 (18.♗xd6 exd6 19.h5 g5 20.h6 ♗f6↑) 18...b5! This leads to a promising attack for Black.

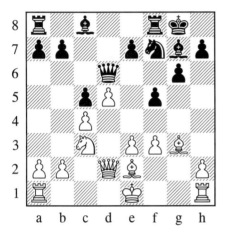

15...e5!∞

The key move. Now White's threats on the kingside are not dangerous. Advancing with h4-h5 can always be met by ...g6-g5. White must castle long (castling short would be a positional surrender) but then he will be faced with ...a6 and ...b5.

16.0–0–0 ♗d7 17.♔b1 a6 18.e4 f4

Black has to keep the position blocked. With 18.e4 White gave up on the idea of attacking on the kingside. Now he will create pressure on the c-pawn after Black's standard move ...b7-b5.

19.♗f2 ♖ab8 20.h4 b5 21.♖c1!

A nice move. Besides the defensive idea (against the threat of ...b5-b4), White is also preparing pressure on the c-line.

21...♖fc8

Black could completely close the position

with 21...b4 22.♘d1 a5, but this would give White a very easy game. He simply starts with the idea ♘f2-d3. Even so, after 23.♗f1 ♖fe8 24.♗h3 ♗xh3 25.♖xh3 ♖ec8 26.♗g1 ♕d7 27.♘f2 ♗f8 28.♖h1 ♗d6 29.♘g4 ♕e7 30.h5 g5 31.h6 a4⇄ Black should be able to hold the blockade.

22.♔a1 ♗f8 23.♘d1 a5!?

After a couple of moves which were positional, Carlsen decides to change the nature of the position. Maybe this wasn't the best moment for such a decision.

Black could prepare his idea by playing 23...♕b6 and White can reply 24.b3 with the idea of ♘b2-d3. Of course, the position remains unclear.

24.cxb5 ♗xb5 25.♗xb5 ♖xb5 26.♘c3

White prepares pressure on the c-file; the idea is simply ♖c2 and ♖hc1.

White could play the positional 26.b3!? with the idea of activating the knight via b2.

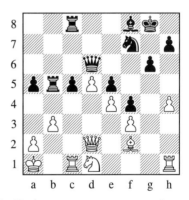

Black's best option seems to be: 26...a4! (26...♕a6 is met by 27.♕d3! ♘d6 28.♘b2 ♕b7 29.♕e2± intending ♘d3 with the better position for White.) 27.♘c3 (27.bxa4 ♖bb8⮌) 27...♖bb8 28.bxa4 (28.♘xa4 c4∞) 28...c4 29.♖b1 ♕a6 This gives Black some compensation; his next move will be ...♗b4.

Still 30.♕c2 ♗b4 31.♘b5 ♕a5 32.♗e1 ♗xe1
33.♖hxe1± should be somewhat better for
White.

26...♖b4

The only move. 26...♖bb8? 27.♘a4± would
be very bad for Black.

27.♖c2 c4 28.♖hc1

After a few forced moves, it may look like
White has the advantage, as he will create
strong pressure on the c-pawn. However, Black
has good practical chances based on his attack
on the white king.

28...a4!

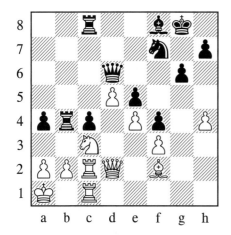

29.a3?

This move is an error. As we will see after a
few moves, Black takes over the initiative.

The alternative was:
29.♘b1!?
    With the idea of ♘a3. Here Black has to
play
29...♕a6! 30.♘a3 ♔g7!
    30...♖xb2 31.♔xb2 ♖b8† 32.♔a1 ♗xa3
33.♖b1 ♖b3! 34.♕e2 ♖xb1† 35.♔xb1 ♘d6
36.♔a1!?± Planning ♗e1-c3.
    30...♖b7!? 31.♘xc4 ♖bc7 32.♘a3 The only
move (a big mistake would be 32.♕d3??

♘d6–+ and White is unable to escape the
pin). 32...♖xc2 33.♘xc2 ♘d6 34.♗e1 ♗e7±
Finally, White has won a pawn, but Black
keeps some chances of surviving.
31.♗e1
White plans ♕e2 (31.h5 g5∞). Black's best
option is:

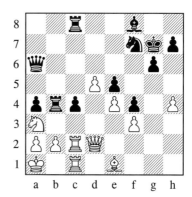

31...♖xb2! 32.♔xb2 ♖b8† 33.♔a1 ♗xa3
34.♖b1 ♖xb1† 35.♔xb1 ♕b6† 36.♔a1 ♗c5
37.♕c1 ♘d6⩲
With good compensation.

29...♖b3

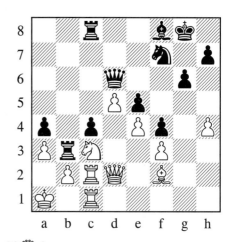

30.♕e2

30.♘xa4?! ♕a6 31.♘c3 ♖a8⩲ would lead to
a dangerous attack on the white king.

30...♕a6! 31.♘b1

This manoeuvre looks very strong and it is very hard to recommend anything else. However, Black has a good reply:

31...♘d6 32.♘d2

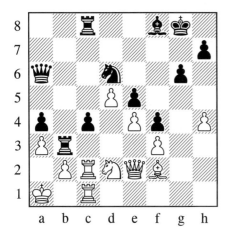

32...♘b5!∓

Now White is fighting for a draw.

33.d6!

33.♘xc4 would lose eventually: 33...♘d6 34.h5 ♖xc4 35.♖xc4 ♘xc4 36.♖xc4 (36.♕xc4 ♕xc4 37.♖xc4 ♖xf3 38.♗b6 gxh5! should be winning for Black.) 36...♗xa3! 37.♖c2 (37.bxa3 ♖xa3† 38.♔b1 ♖c3−+) 37...♕xe2 38.♖xe2 ♗d6−+ Next will be ...♖xf3.

33.♘xb3? axb3 34.♖xc4 ♘d6!

33...♘xd6

On 33...♘xa3 34.bxa3 ♖xa3† White has: 35.♖a2 ♖d3 36.d7! ♖xd7 37.♖ac2∞

34.♕f1

The computer gives 34.h5 as the best defence. After 34...♖b7 35.hxg6 hxg6 36.♖g1 ♔g7∓ Black keeps the advantage.

34...♖b7

This looks passive. 34...♖d3! was most precise, then the only move is 35.♕h3. (35.h5 c3! 36.♖xc3 ♖dxc3 37.♕xa6 ♖xc1†

38.♔a2 ♖d1 39.hxg6 hxg6−+ is lost for White.) But after: 35...♖e8 36.♗e1 (36.h5 c3!) 36...♘b5 37.♖xc4 ♘d4∓ Black is on top.

35.♕h3

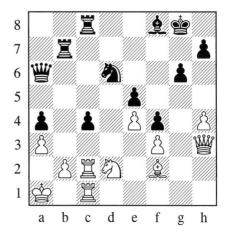

35...♖e8?

This mistake allows White to create counterplay.

This was the last moment for 35...c3! 36.♕e6† ♖f7.

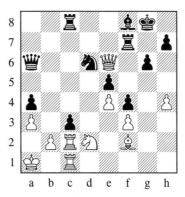

White has to take: 37.bxc3 (37.♖xc3 ♖xc3 38.♖xc3 ♕e2 39.♘c4 ♘xc4 40.♖xc4 ♕d1† 41.♔a2 ♕b3†! 42.♔a1 ♕xf3†) 37...♖e8 38.♕a2 ♘b5 39.♘c4 ♕e6∓ Black still has a huge advantage.

36.h5! g5 37.♗c5 ♖c7

37...c3 38.♖xc3 ♘b5 39.♖c4 ♗xc5 40.♖xc5 ♘d4 41.♖c8 ♖b8 42.♖xe8† ♖xe8 43.♕g4 would also be risky for Black.

38.♗xd6 ♕xd6 39.♖xc4 ♖xc4 40.♘xc4 ♕e6

Now both players had extra time after the 40th move and the game took a normal course. The position is unclear, but White has to be more careful.

41.♕g2 ♗e7 42.♘d2 ♔g7 43.♘b1!

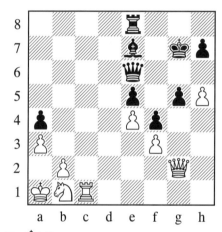

41...♔h6

If instead:

43...♖c8?! 44.♖xc8 ♕xc8 45.♕g4

Now Black should play:

45...♕c6

After 45...♕xg4?! 46.fxg4 Black should be careful. 46...f3 (46...♔f6 47.b4 axb3 48.♔b2 ♔e6 49.♔xb3 f3 50.♘d2↑) 47.b3! ♗xa3 48.♘d2 f2 49.bxa4 ♗b4 50.♘f1± White is better.

46.♘c3 ♔h6=

The game will probably finish as a draw.

44.♖c7 ♖c8 45.♖xc8 ♕xc8 46.♕g4! ♕c4 47.♕f5

47.♕d7= also leads to a draw.

47...♗c5 48.♕xe5 ♗d4 49.♕d6† ♔xh5 50.♕d7!=

The easiest way to secure a draw.

50...♔g6 51.♕f5† ♔h6 52.♕h3† ♔g7 ½–½

GAME 33

▷ **L. Aronian (2805)**
▶ **E. Sutovsky (2700)**
8th World Team Championship, Ningbo
Round 1, 17.07.2011 **[D85]**
Annotated by Borki Predojevic

The first round of the World Team Championship offered us Armenia – Israel, with Aronian playing White against Sutovsky on top board. In the Grünfeld Defence with an early 8.♗e3 (a line which became extremely popular after the 2000 Kasparov – Kramnik match in London), Aronian chose the very rare 9.♘d2!? and Black immediately went for the queen sacrifice with 9...cxd4 and 10...dxe3. But in my opinion, the best option for Black is the solid 9...♘d7 with the threat of ...♕xc3. However, the game was very tricky for both players. After Aronian found the strong idea of 14.♗b5!, Black had to find the right continuation. Unfortunately for Black, at the critical moment he made the mistake 17...♗g4?. White grasped his opportunity and played extremely well right to the end; Black did not have any chances to avoid losing. Instead of 17...♗g4? the best option was 17...♖d7!, which leads to a very complicated game, although the final evaluation is that even after 17...♖d7! White keeps the better chances.

My overall view is that the line with 9.♘d2 is not dangerous for Black. However, players who would like to sacrifice their queen have a clear task facing them – they need to improve on my analysis.

1.d4 ♘f6 2.c4 g6 3.♘f3 ♗g7 4.♘c3 d5 5.cxd5 ♘xd5 6.e4 ♘xc3 7.bxc3 c5 8.♗e3 ♕a5

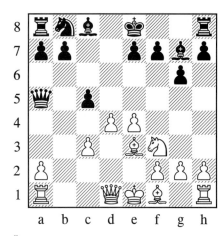

9.♘d2!?

A very rare move. The main line is 9.♕d2.

9...cxd4

In my opinion, the best reaction is 9...♘d7! when Black threatens to take the c3-pawn; White won't have ♖c1xc5 in reply, thanks to knight on d7. White now has four options:

a) 10.♖c1 ♕xa2 11.♗c4 (11.♗e2 0–0 12.0–0 ♕a5 13.d5 b5∓) 11...♕a5 12.0–0 0–0⇄ Black has avoided taking on d4, so it is hard for White to develop an initiative.

b) 10.♗e2 ♕xc3 11.♖c1 ♕a5 12.dxc5 0–0 13.♕b3 ♘e5 14.0–0 ♘c6= leads to a pleasant game for Black.

c) 10.♘b3 ♕xc3† 11.♗d2 ♕b2 12.♗c1 ♕c3†= and White cannot make more than a draw.

d) White can defend his c3-pawn with:
10.♕b3 0–0 11.♖c1
  11.♗e2 cxd4 12.cxd4 ♘c5! 13.♕b5 (13.♕c2 ♘e6 14.e5 ♖d8 15.0–0 ♘xd4 [15...♗d7!?] 16.♗xd4 ♖xd4 17.♘b3 ♕xe5 18.♘xd4 ♕xd4 19.♖ad1 [19.♕c7 ♗e5 20.♕xe7 ♕e4 21.♕d8† ♔g7↑] 19...♕b6 20.♖b1 ♕d6 21.♖fd1 ♗d4 22.♕a4 e5∞) 13...♕xb5 14.♗xb5 a6 15.♗e2 f5 16.exf5 ♗xf5 17.0–0 ♗d3⇄
11...a6

11...♖b8!? intending ...b5.
12.♗e2
  12.♘c4 ♕c7 13.dxc5 ♕c6∞
12...b5⇄
Black has good play.

Black may also try taking a pawn with:
9...0–0 10.♗e2 ♕xc3
  On 10...♖d8 11.0–0 ♕xc3 12.♖c1 ♕a5 (12...♕a3 13.♘c4 ♕a6 14.♘e5 ♕a3 15.♖xc5 ♗e6 16.♕b1↑) 13.♖xc5 (13.d5∞) 13...♕xa2 14.d5∞ White has typical Grünfeld compensation for the pawn.
11.♖c1 ♕a3 12.♖xc5 ♕xa2

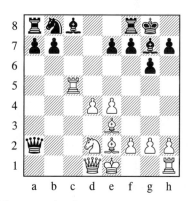

White can develop some initiative with:
13.0–0 ♘c6
  13...♖d8 14.d5∞
14.♖c4
  14.d5 ♘d4↑
14...♕a5 15.d5 ♘e5 16.♖a4 ♕c7
  16...♕d8 17.♖xa7 ♖xa7 18.♗xa7 ♕a5 19.♗e3±
17.f4 b5

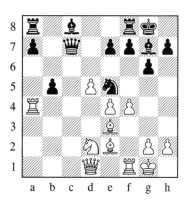

18.罩b4!?N

An improvement on 18.罩a3 ♘c4 19.♕c2 e6! 20.♗xc4 bxc4 21.♕xc4 ♕d8! and White had no advantage. After 22.♗d4 exd5 23.exd5 ♗b7 24.♗xg7 ♔xg7 25.♕d4† ♕f6 26.♕xf6† a draw was agreed in Kasimdzhanov – Navara, Wijk aan Zee 2009.

18...a5 19.罩xb5 ♘d7 20.罩b1↑

White has good chances of achieving an advantage. For example:

20...♗a6 21.♗xa6 罩xa6 22.♕e2 罩aa8

22...罩fa8 23.罩fc1 ♕d8 24.罩b7±

23.罩fc1 ♕d8 24.罩b7±

White maintains pressure on the black position.

10.♘c4

The only logical continuation. 10.cxd4 ♘c6 11.d5 ♘d4 12.罩b1 ♗d7! is good for Black.

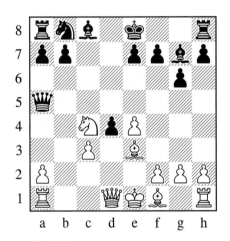

10...dxe3!?N

An interesting, albeit very risky decision by Black. This position may well have been analysed beforehand by both players, since Sutovsky and Aronian are well-known as players who like dynamic and tactical positions.

Of course Black must avoid 10...♕xc3†?? 11.♗d2+−.

Previously Black had played:

10...♕d8 11.cxd4 0–0

11...f5!? should be considered. By delaying castling Black may be able to avoid the complications in the next sub-note.

12.罩b1

A possible improvement for White is 12.罩c1!? but it is very hard to give a clear evaluation after the dynamic 12...f5 13.♕b3 (13.exf5 ♗xf5 14.♕b3 ♗e6 15.♕xb7 ♗d5 16.♕b2 ♘c6⯂) and now:

a) 13...♔h8!? 14.♘e5! (14.exf5 ♘c6 15.fxg6 ♘xd4 16.♕d1 ♗f5 17.♗d3 [17.gxh7!?∞] 17...hxg6 18.♗xd4 ♕xd4 19.♗xf5 ♕xd1† 20.♔xd1 罩xf5⇄) 14...♕xe5 15.dxe5 f4 16.♗c5 ♘c6 17.♕c3 ♗e6 18.♗b5 罩c8 19.0–0 White has the initiative.

b) 13...e6 14.exf5 gxf5 15.g3 (15.♗d3 f4 16.♗d2 ♘c6 17.♗e4 ♘xd4 18.♕d3 f3!∞; 15.f4!? ♘c6 16.罩d1 also looks interesting) 15...♘c6 16.♗g2 ♘xd4 17.♗xd4 ♗xd4 18.0–0 White has good compensation, but that is far from saying that he has an advantage.

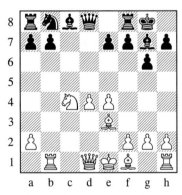

12...f5! 13.exf5 ♗xf5 14.罩xb7 ♘c6 15.d5

On 15.♘e5 ♘xe5 16.dxe5 Black can play: 16...♕c8! 17.罩xe7 (17.♕b3† ♗e6 18.♕b2 罩b8 19.罩xb8 ♕xb8 20.♕xb8 罩xb8 21.♗xa7 罩b1† 22.♔d2 ♗xe5↑) 17...罩b8 18.♕d5† ♔h8 19.f4 ♕c3† 20.♔f2 罩b1 Black's compensation is enough for at least a draw.

15...♗c3†! 16.♗d2 ♘d4 17.♘e3□ ♕a5 18.♗xc3 ♕xc3† 19.♕d2 ♕a1† 20.♕d1 ♕c3†

21.♕d2 ♕a1† 22.♕d1

½–½ Avrukh – Kovchan, France 2011.

11.♘xa5 ♗xc3† 12.♔e2 ♗xa5 13.♔xe3 0–0

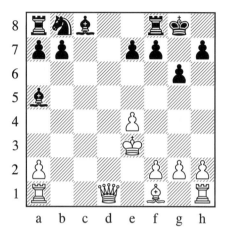

14.♗b5!

The best move. White prevents the fast development with ...♘c6, ...♖d8 and ...♗b6.

Worse is:

14.♗c4 ♘c6 15.♔e2 ♖d8 16.♕c1 ♗g4†!

16...♘e5 leads to a better position for White: 17.♗b3 (17.♗d5 e6 18.♕g5 exd5 19.♕xe5 ♗d7 20.♔f1 ♖ac8⇄) 17...b6 18.♔f1 ♗a6† 19.♔g1 ♘d3 (19...e6 20.h4 ♘d3 21.♕g5 ♗c3 22.♖d1 ♗d4 23.h5!) 20.♕a3 e6 21.♖d1! ♘c5 22.♖xd8† ♖xd8 23.h4 ♖d4 24.h5 ♖xe4 25.hxg6 hxg6 26.♗d1±

17.f3 ♘d4† 18.♔f1 ♗e6 19.♗xe6 ♘xe6 20.♕a3 ♗b6 21.♖b1 ♘f4 22.g3 ♖d3

Black has a strong attack.

14.♗d3 ♘c6 15.♔e2 ♖d8⇄ gives Black reasonable compensation.

14...a6

The only move. 14...♘c6? is just bad. After 15.♗xc6 bxc6 16.♕a4 ♗b6† 17.♔e2 it already looks winning for White.

15.♗a4 b5

15...♖d8 16.♕c1 b5 17.♖d1 ♘d7 18.♗b3 ♗b7 19.♔e2±

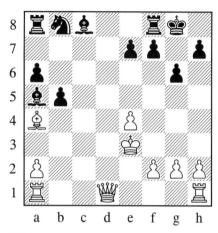

16.♕d5!

Again the best answer by White.

After 16.♗b3 ♗b6† 17.♔e2 ♘c6 Black occupies the d4-square very quickly.

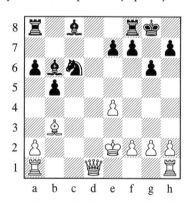

I analysed a couple of options for White:

a) 18.♖e1

This looks logical, but Black has a nice counter:

18...♗g4† 19.f3 ♖fd8 20.♕c1

20.fxg4 ♖xd1 21.♖exd1 ♘d4† 22.♔f1 ♔g7⇄ intending ...♔f6-e5

20.♗d5 ♗e6 21.♖c1 ♗xd5 22.exd5 ♘b4 23.♔f1 ♘xd5⇄ also looks okay for Black.

20...♘d4† 21.♔f1 ♗d7⇄

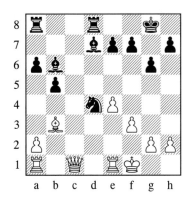

The white rook has avoided being stuck on h1, but the white king on f1 is still not safe.

22.♕f4

22.♕b2 b4! 23.♗c4 (23.♖ed1 ♗b5† 24.♔e1 e5∞) 23...a5 24.♖ac1 ♗a4∞

22...♘xb3 23.axb3 ♗d4 24.♖a2 a5 25.♖d1 e5 26.♕f6 ♖dc8 27.h4!

White must play this in order to attack the black king and secure a draw by perpetual check.

27.♖xd4 exd4 28.♕xd4 ♗e6∓

27...a4 28.h5 gxh5 29.♕g5† ♔f8 30.bxa4 ♗e6 31.♕h6† ♔g8 32.♖aa1 ♖xa4∞

The game will finish in perpetual check.

b) 18.♖c1 ♘d4† 19.♔f1

The white rook on h1 is out of play. Black has several options here, but I suggest:

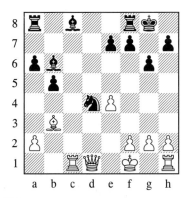

19...♖d8

19...♘xb3 20.axb3 (20.♕xb3 ♗e6 21.♕b2 ♗c4† 22.♖xc4 bxc4 23.g3 ♖ab8 24.♔g2

♖fd8 25.♕e5 ♖b7∞) 20...♖d8 21.♕c2 ♗g4 22.f3 (22.♕a2 ♖d3∞) 22...♖ac8 23.♕b2 ♖xc1† 24.♕xc1 ♗e6∞

20.♗d5

20.h4 ♘xb3 21.♕xb3 ♗e6 22.♕b4 ♖ac8∞ looks good for Black.

20.♕e1 ♘xb3 21.axb3 ♗e6∞

20...♖a7 21.h4

21.a4? bxa4 22.♕xa4 ♗d7 23.♕d1 ♗b5† 24.♗c4 ♘e6! 25.♕e1□ ♗xc4† 26.♖xc4 ♖ad7 27.♖c6 ♗c5! 28.♖xe6 ♖d1 29.♖e5 ♗b4 30.♔e2 ♗xe1 31.♖xe1 ♖1d2† 32.♔f3 ♖a2 33.♖xe7 ♖d3† 34.♖e3 ♖dd2–+

21...h5

21...e6 22.♗b3 ♖ad7 23.h5! and the h1-rook is now well placed, as it supports White's attack on the h-file.

22.a4

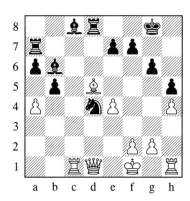

22...bxa4!

22...e6?? 23.a5+–

22...a5 23.axb5

23.♕xa4 ♗d7 24.♕a2

24.♕b4? ♗b5†

24...♗b5† 25.♗c4 ♖c7 26.♔g1 e6

26...♖dc8 27.♗xf7† ♔g7 28.♖xc7 ♖xc7 29.♗xg6!+–

27.♔h2

27.♖h3 ♖dc8 28.♖hc3 a5 29.g3 a4= (intending ...♗a5) 30.♗xb5 ♖xc3 31.♖xc3 ♖xc3 32.♗xa4 (32.♕xa4? ♘f3† 33.♔g2 ♖c2!) 32...♘f3† 33.♔g2 ♘e1† 34.♔f1 ♘d3

35.♕d2 ♖a3 36.♗d1 e5 37.♔g2 ♗d4 38.f3 ♘f2 39.♗e2 ♖b3!=

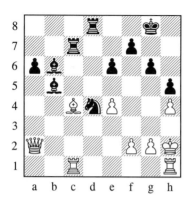

27...♖dc8 28.♗xb5 ♖xc1 29.♕xa6 ♖xh1†
30.♔xh1 ♖c1† 31.♔h2 ♗c7† 32.g3 ♘xb5
   32...♗e5 33.♗f1∞
33.♕xb5 ♗d6 34.f4 ♖c5 35.♕d7 ♗f8=
   The endgame is drawish.

16...♖a7 17.♗b3

The manoeuvre begun with 14.♗b5! has enabled White to develop his bishop and queen. On the other hand, Black has made some gains too; for example, his rook from a8 has come into the game.

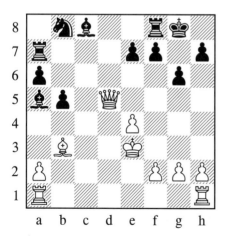

17...♗g4?

This is a crucial mistake. White is now able to keep his rooks connected, and his king will be safe, even on f4.

17...♗b6† 18.♔e2 ♗e6 19.♕g5 ♘c6 looks interesting, but White should get some advantage: 20.♖hb1 ♗d4 21.♗xe6 fxe6 22.f3 ♖c7 23.♖c1 ♗xa1 24.♖xa1±

17...♖d7!

Black had to play this, although it still seems to turn out better for White at the end of an extremely complicated line.

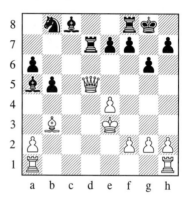

18.♕c5

This looks unnatural, but after 18.♕e5?! ♗b6† 19.♔e2 ♘c6 20.♕f4 ♘d4† 21.♔f1 (21.♔e1 ♗b7⩲) 21...♘xb3 (21...a5!?⩲) 22.axb3 ♖d3⩱ Black has a very nice position.
18...♖d6 19.♔e2

19.♕a3 ♗d2† 20.♔e2 b4 21.♕a5 ♘c6↑
Now Black has a couple of options, but neither of them will offer him a clear path to equality.

19...♖d2†

19...♗b6 20.♕g5 ♘c6 21.♖hd1! (21.♖ad1 ♘d4† 22.♔f1 ♖f6⩲) 21...♖f6! (21...♘d4† 22.♔f1±) 22.f3 (22.f4 ♘d4† 23.♖xd4 ♗xd4 24.♖d1 ♗b6⩲) 22...♘d4† 23.♔f1 ♖xf3† (23...♗h3 24.gxh3 ♘xf3 25.♕g3!+–; 23...a5 24.♖xd4 ♗xd4 25.♖d1 ♗c3 26.e5 ♖f5 27.♕xe7 ♖xe5 28.♕c7 b4 29.♗xf7†±) 24.gxf3 ♗h3† 25.♔f2 ♘e6† 26.♕e3 ♗xe3† 27.♔xe3 ♘c5 28.♖dc1 ♘xb3 29.axb3 ♗e6 30.b4 ♗c4 31.♖d1!± White is much better in this endgame.
20.♔f1 ♘d7

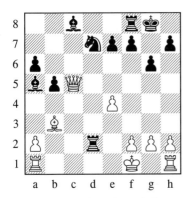

We shall now look at four different squares for the queen:

a) 21.♕g5 ♘f6 22.f3

22.♖e1 ♘g4 23.♖e2 ♖fd8 24.♖xd2 (24.g3 is met by 24...♘e3†! 25.fxe3 ♗h3† 26.♔f2 ♖xe2† 27.♔xe2 ♖d2† 28.♔f3 ♗g2† 29.♔g4 ♗xh1 30.♕xe7 h5† 31.♔f4 [31.♔h4?? ♗d8!] 31...♖f2† 32.♔e5 ♗g2↑ and Black can play for a win) 24...♖xd2 25.♕c5 ♖xf2† 26.♕xf2 ♘xf2 27.♔xf2 e6=/∓ Black has no problems in the endgame.

22...♖fd8⯰ 23.♖c1

After 23.h4 Black has the nice move 23...♘h5!? and now all the squares around the white king are weak. This balances White's material advantage, and the game remains roughly equal:

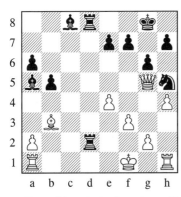

a) 24.♖c1 ♗b6 (24...♗e6!?) 25.♖c6 ♗a7 26.♖xg6†!! (26.♖h2? ♗e6! 27.♖xe6□ fxe6 28.♕e5 [28.♗xe6† ♔f8 29.♗d5 ♖f2†

30.♔e1 ♖c8 31.♔d1 ♖cc2∓] 28...♗d4 29.♗xe6† ♔f8 30.♕c7 ♗e3! 31.♕e5 ♘f6†) 26...hxg6 27.♕xg6† ♘g7 28.♕xf7† ♔h7 29.h5! ♗e6!! (29...♖d1† 30.♗xd1 ♖xd1† 31.♔e2 ♖xh1 32.♕g6† ♔h8 33.h6 ♘e6 34.♕e8† ♔h7 35.♕xe7† ♔xh6 36.♕xa7±) 30.♕g6† ♔h8 31.♕h6† ♔g8 32.♗xe6† ♘xe6 33.♕xe6† ♔f8 and White has nothing better than 34.♕f5† ♔e8 35.♕g6†= with perpetual check.

b) 24.♕xe7! ♘g3† 25.♔g1 ♘e2† 26.♔h2 ♖2d7! 27.♕f6 ♗c7† 28.e5! ♖e8 29.f4 ♘xf4 30.♖he1 ♘h5 31.♕f2 ♗xe5† 32.♔g1 ♗g7 33.♖ad1 ♘f6 34.♖xd7 ♗xd7 35.♖f1 ♗e6! 36.♕c5 ♗xb3 37.axb3 ♖e6⯰ and Black is able to hold this position. The white king is weak and after the exchange of rooks, Black will play ...h5 and either keep his b-pawn or exchange two pawns for one on queenside. The resulting position with pawns on kingside will be a simple draw with a black fortress.

23...♗b7 24.♕e3

24.e5 ♘d5 is okay for Black.

24...e6

It is very hard for White to finish his development and secure his king. Here are some complicated lines which the computer gives:

25.♕a7 ♖8d7 26.h4

26.♔g1 ♘xe4! 27.♕b8† ♗d8 28.fxe4 ♗xe4 29.h4 ♖xg2† 30.♔f1 ♖dd2 31.♖h3 ♖gf2† 32.♔g1 ♖g2†=

26...♔g7 27.♕c5

27.♔g1 ♗c7!

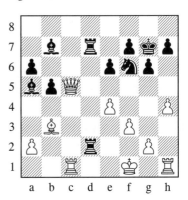

27...h6!

27...♘h5? 28.♕e5† f6 29.♕xe6 ♘g3†
30.♔g1+−

28.♔g1 ♖2d4!

28...♖2d3 29.♔h2 ♗d2 30.♖hd1! ♗f4†
31.♔h1 ♗xc1 32.♖xc1±

29.h5

29.♔h2 ♗b4 30.♕c2 ♖d2 31.♕b1 ♗d6†∓

29...♗d2 30.hxg6 ♗e3† 31.♔h2 ♖xe4 32.♕c3
b4 33.♕a1 ♗d4 34.♕b1 ♘g4†!? 35.fxg4 ♗e5†
36.♔g1 ♗d4†=

It finishes in a draw.

b) 21.♕a3? ♗b6∓

**c) 21.♕e3?! ♘e5 22.f3 (22.♖d1 ♘c4! 23.♕f4
♖b2 24.♔g1 ♗e6⩲) 22...♗e6→**

d) 21.♕xe7!

The strongest move.

21...♗b6

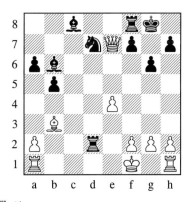

22.♖c1!

Less precise is: 22.♕h4 ♘c5 23.♕f4 ♘xb3
24.axb3 ♖fd8 (24...♖c2 25.h4) 25.h4
(25.♖c1 ♗e6 26.♖c6 ♗xb3∓; 25.♖e1?
♗e6→) 25...♗e6 (25...♗b7 26.h5 ♖xf2†
27.♕xf2 ♗xf2 28.♔xf2 ♖d2† 29.♔e3 ♖b2
30.h6!±) 26.b4 h5 27.g3 ♖xf2† 28.♕xf2
♗xf2 29.♔xf2 ♖d4 30.♖hb1 ♖xe4 31.♖xa6
♖d4 32.♖a5 ♗c4± Black has chances to hold
the draw.

22...♖xf2† 23.♔e1 ♖b2

23...♖xg2 24.♗xf7† ♖xf7 25.♖xc8† ♔g7
26.♕e8 ♘f6 27.♕e6±

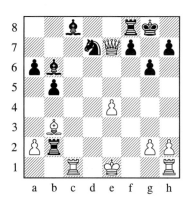

Here White has to play coldbloodedly:
24.h3!!

After this I cannot find equality for Black.

24.h4 ♘c5! 25.♖xc5 ♗xc5 26.♕xc5 ♖b1†
27.♗d1 ♗g4 28.♔f2 ♗xd1 29.♔g3 ♗c2
30.♖xb1 ♗xb1 31.♕a3 (31.♕d6 ♗xa2
32.♕xa6 ♗c4=) 31...♗xe4 32.♕xa6 ♖b8
33.h5 gxh5 34.♔h4 b4! 35.♔xh5 ♗b1
36.♕c4 ♖b6= Black gets a draw.

After 24.♕a3 ♗d4 25.♕d6 ♗c5 26.♖xc5
♘xc5 27.♕xc5 ♖b1† 28.♗d1 ♗g4 29.♔f2
♗xd1 30.♕d4 ♗c2 31.♖xb1 ♗xb1= the
position should be equal.

24...♗a5† 25.♔f1 ♗d8 26.♕a3 ♗f6 27.♖d1

White has consolidated his pieces, and move
by move White increases his advantage.

27...♗e5 28.♕e7 ♔g7

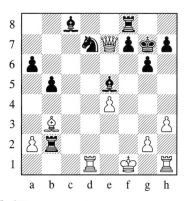

29.♖xd7!

With this move White returns material, but in the ensuing endgame he is clearly better. 29...♗f6 30.♕xf8† ♔xf8 31.♖xf7† ♔e8 32.♖xf6 ♖b1† 33.♔f2 ♖xh1 34.♖f7±

Black is in trouble.

18.♕g5!±

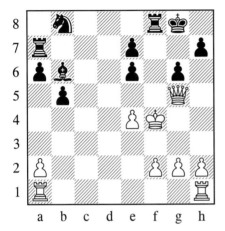

18...♗b6† 19.♔f4 ♗e6

19...♗d7 20.♔g3 ♘c6 21.♖hd1 ♘d4 22.h3± leads to a better position for White.

20.♗xe6 fxe6†

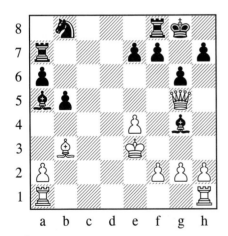

21.♔g3!

The white king is safe on g3. It is clear that Black doesn't have enough compensation for the sacrificed material.

21...♘c6

21...♗xf2† 22.♔h3 ♗d4 23.♖af1+−

22.♔h3 ♘d4 23.♖hd1 ♖c7 24.♖ac1 ♖xc1 25.♖xc1 ♘e2

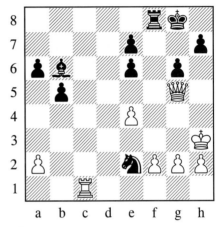

26.♕e5!

An accurate and well calculated move by Aronian. He saw the following line which wins in style.

26...♗d4

After 26...♘xc1 27.♕xe6† ♔g7 28.♕xb6+− Black does not have any real survival chances.

27.♕xe6† ♖f7 28.♖c8† ♔g7 29.g3

The only move, but good enough.

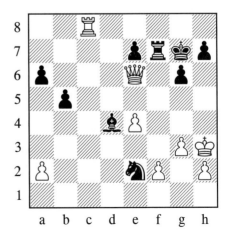

29...♘g1† 30.♔g2 ♖xf2† 31.♔h1+– ♘f3
32.♕xe7† ♔h6 33.♕f8†

The "cool" move, though 33.♖c2 ♖xc2
34.♕f8† ♗g7 35.♕xf3 is winning too.

33...♔h5 34.♖c5†! ♘g5 35.♖xg5† ♗xg5
36.♕d8† ♗f6 37.♕d3 ♔g4

37...♖xa2 38.♕d5†+–

38.♕e3

Black resigned, since he is losing more
material: 38... ♖xa2 39.♕f4† ♔h3 40.♕f1†
♔g4 41.♕xf6+–

1–0

GAME 34

▷ **A. Pashikian (2616)**
▶ **Zhou Jianchao (2636)**
Lake Sevan GM Tournament, Martuni
Round 8, 29.07.2011 **[D85]**
Annotated by Sebastian Maze

In this Grünfeld Defence, Zhou Jianchao
introduced the strong novelty 14...♕a4!N
and succeeded in making a short draw. I
have not managed to find any advantage
for White in this game, so perhaps White
should look to vary earlier, and I recommend
the interesting 14.h4 as worthy of further
investigation.

**1.d4 ♘f6 2.c4 g6 3.♘c3 d5 4.cxd5 ♘xd5
5.e4 ♘xc3 6.bxc3 ♗g7 7.♗e3 c5 8.♕d2 ♕a5
9.♖c1**

9.♖b1 is the other main move, after which the
line 9...cxd4 10.cxd4 ♕xd2† 11.♔xd2 0–0∞
has been played recently by Nepomniachtchi
and Le Quang with good results.

9...0–0

9...cxd4 is also an option, although I prefer
that move when the rook is on b1.

10.♘f3 ♖d8

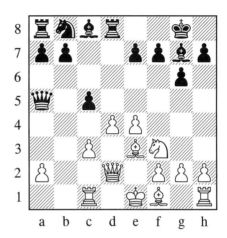

This move has been played in a lot of top
level games in the last few years.

11.d5 e6

Black allowed the pawn to go to d5, but will
now put a lot of pressure on it.

12.♗g5

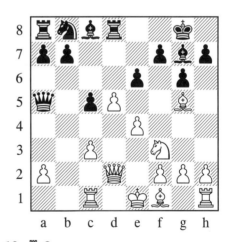

12...♖e8

12...f6 is the main move, with many
interesting games. One recent example
was: 13.♗e3 ♘c6 14.♗d3 exd5 15.exd5 c4
16.♗xc4 ♗e6 17.♖d1 ♘e7 18.dxe6 ♖xd2
19.♖xd2∞ Pashikian – Cornette, European
Championship, Aixs-les-Bains 2011 – see the
May issue of Chess Evolution.

13.d6 ♘d7

A logical answer; the knight has to come to the kingside.

13...b5? is very risky in my opinion. White is ready for an attack, but Black doesn't care and plays on the queenside! 14.h4 ♗b7 15.♗d3 ♘d7 16.h5 e5 17.hxg6 hxg6 18.♗h6 ♗f6 19.♘h2 ♖e6 20.♘g4± Pashikian – Vachier Lagrave, Aeroflot Open, Moscow 2011.

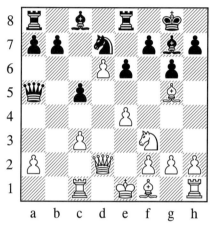

14.♗h6?!

Maybe it is too soon for this move.

I think White should first prepare to open the h-file:

14.h4! h5

This is an interesting attempt to stop the attack.

14...b5 15.♗h6 ♗h8 16.h5 gives White a terrible attack.

14...♕a4 15.♗d3 c4 (15...e5 16.h5 ♘f6 17.hxg6 hxg6 18.♗h6 ♘xe4 19.♗xg7 ♘xd2 20.♗f6+– This important variation should be compared with the game continuation.) 16.♗e2 ♕c6 17.h5 ♕xe4 18.hxg6 hxg6 19.♔f1! White's position is very pleasant: the h-file is open, he has a powerful d6-pawn, and ♗h6 coming. 19...♘b6 (19...b5?! looks too slow) 20.♗h6 ♗f6 21.♘g5 ♕d5 22.♕e3 ♕e5 23.♘e4+–

15.♗h6 ♗h8

It is essential to retain this important bishop.

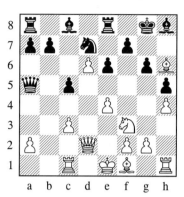

16.♘g5 b5 17.♗e2 b4 18.cxb4 ♕xb4

18...cxb4 19.0–0 ♗c3 20.♕f4 looks dangerous for Black.

19.♕xb4 cxb4 20.♘f3 ♗c3† 21.♗d2 ♗b7 22.♗xc3 bxc3 23.♘g5 f6 24.♗b5 ♖ad8 25.♖xc3 fxg5 26.♖c7 ♗c8 27.0–0

Black can hardly move his pieces.

27...a6 28.♗a4 gxh4 29.♖xc8! ♖xc8 30.♗xd7 ♔f7 31.♗xc8 ♖xc8 32.e5±

The protected passed pawn on d6 assures White of a very pleasant endgame.

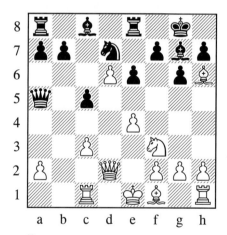

14...♕a4!N

This is a strong novelty by Zhou Jianchao, not only putting pressure on the e4-pawn, but also preventing ♗c4 after a subsequent ...e5.

14...f6? was played in a game last year, but it looks clearly worse: 15.h4 c4 (Here too, Black could try 15...♕a4N 16.♗d3 ♗xh6 17.♕xh6 e5 18.h5 g5 19.♖h3 ♔h8 20.♖g3 ♖g8 21.♘d2 b5 22.♗e2 ♕a6 23.a4 ♕xd6 24.axb5 ♕e7 25.♗c4 ♖g7 26.♖a1. White's position is better, but it's not so easy to play with a queen on h6 which can't move!) 16.♗xg7 ♔xg7 17.♗xc4 ♕c5 18.♗b3+– Lahno – Jerez Perez, Paleochora 2010.

15.♗d3 e5=

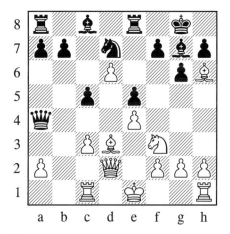

This is an important move, in order to gain some space around the king.

16.h4

Pashikian hopes for a successful attack, but in this case it's hard to believe in it, because Black has many defenders and the e4-pawn is weak.

16.♗c2 ♕a6 17.♗xg7 ♔xg7 18.h4 ♘f6 19.h5 ♗g4□ (19...♘xh5 loses in short order to 20.♖xh5 gxh5 21.♕g5† ♔f8 22.♕f6 ♔g8 23.♘g5 ♗e6 24.♕h6 ♕xd6 25.♘xh7+–) 20.hxg6 fxg6 21.♘h2 ♖ad8 22.♘xg4 ♘xg4 23.♖d1 c4 24.♕g5 ♘f6 25.♕h6† ♔g8 26.g4 ♖d7 27.g5 ♘h5 28.♖xh5 gxh5 29.g6 ♕c6 30.♕xh5 hxg6 31.♕xg6† ♖g7 32.♕f5 ♖g1†= and it will finish in a draw by perpetual check.

16...♘f6 17.♗xg7 ♔xg7 18.h5 ♘xe4 19.♕e3

19.♗xe4 ♕xe4† 20.♔f1 ♕f4 21.♕xf4 exf4 gives Black a considerable advantage.

19...♘xd6 20.hxg6 hxg6 21.♕h6† ♔f6

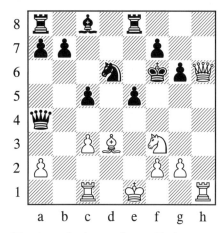

The king looks weak on f6, but it is not actually in danger. White needs more pieces to create a real attack.

22.♕g5†

22.♖h4 ♕xa2 23.♖d1 e4 24.♕g5† ♔g7 25.♕h6† ♔f6=

**22...♔g7 23.♕h6† ♔f6 24.♕g5† ♔g7
½–½**

GAME 35

▷ **Y. Pelletier (2590)**
▶ **M. Carlsen (2821)**
Accentus GM Tournament, Biel
Round 1, 18.07.2011 **[D85]**
Annotated by Borki Predojevic

In the first round of the Super-Tournament in Biel, Carlsen was Black against Pelletier, and he chose the Grünfeld Defence. Against Pelletier's choice of the main line with 8.♖b1 and 9.♗e2, Carlsen opted for the positional 9...b6. Pelletier did not avoid the most dynamic line; he sacrificed a pawn with 11.d5!?. Continuing with 13.♕d3!? White was soon faced with a strong novelty by Carlsen: 15...e6!N. After this improvement Pelletier did not react correctly, and 17.♖bd1 was not the most precise. Black had a pleasant game, and the next imprecise move, 22.♖xd4?!, gave Black a serious advantage. Carlsen then showed his class, and Pelletier wasn't given any chances to save the game.

This is a very important game for the 11.d5!? line, and we shall have to wait to see if White finds a good response to Carlsen's novelty in the future.

1.d4 ♘f6 2.c4 g6 3.♘c3 d5 4.cxd5 ♘xd5 5.e4 ♘xc3 6.bxc3 ♗g7 7.♘f3 c5 8.♖b1 0–0 9.♗e2 b6

In this positional variation, Black develops his pieces to their most solid positions.

A more concrete line is 9...cxd4 10.cxd4 ♕a5† 11.♗d2 ♕xa2 12.0–0 ♗g4∞.

9...♘c6 10.d5 ♘e5 11.♘xe5 ♗xe5 12.♕d2 e6 13.f4 ♗c7 is another option for Black.

10.0–0 ♗b7 11.d5!?

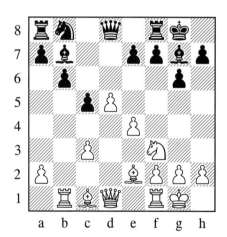

This is the most aggressive approach. White threatens to support the d5-pawn with c3-c4 next move, so Black has no alternative – he has to take the c-pawn.

The main line is 11.♕d3 e6 (11...♗a6 12.♕e3 ♕d7 is another popular choice for Black) 12.♗g5 ♕c7 13.♕e3 ♘d7 14.e5, and here Black can choose from several moves, such as 14...a6, 14...♗d5 or 14... ♖ae8.

11...♗xc3 12.♗c4

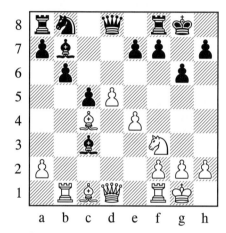

12...♗g7

This is probably the most precise answer. By delaying the development of the b8-knight, Black keeps the possibility of playing ...♗a6.

The alternative is:
12...♘d7 13.♗f4 ♗g7 14.♕b3!?
The white queen is more active here. Another option is 14.♕e2, transposing into the line after 13.♕e2 in the following note.

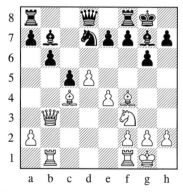

14...♕c8!?N

14...♔h8?! 15.♖fd1 f6 is not the best defence, as it concedes White positional pluses. After 16.a4 a6 17.♕e3 ♘e5 18.♘xe5 fxe5 19.♗g5 ♗f6 20.♗h6 ♗g7 21.♗xg7† ♔xg7 22.♖d3 ♖f6 23.♕g5!± White was better in Dobrov – Turov, Internet 2004.

14...♘f6 15.♖fe1 ♕d7 (15...♘h5 16.♗d2⩲ [intending e4-e5] 16...♘f6 17.h3) 16.♘e5! ♕c8 17.h3⩲

15.e5 ♗a6 16.♖fe1 ♕b7 17.h4!?

White has compensation.

13.♕d3

This move has not been played at a high level recently.

The alternative is:
13.♕e2 ♘d7

13...♕c8 14.e5 ♗a6 is also possible.

14.♗f4

14.e5 e6!

14...♘f6 15.♖fd1 ♕d7

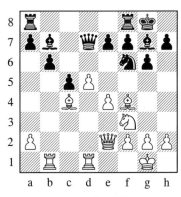

Here the best move for White is:
16.♘e5!

After 16.h3 ♖ad8 17.♘e5 ♕c8 Black has regrouped his pieces with a good game: 18.♗b5 e6 19.♘c6 ♗xc6 20.♗xc6 (20. dxc6 ♖xd1† 21.♖xd1 a6 22.♗xa6 ♕xc6∓) 20...exd5 21.exd5 ♕f5 22.♕f3 (22.♗c7 ♖xd5!∓) 22...♘e4 23.♗c7 ♕xf3 24.gxf3 ♘c3 25.d6 ♖xd6! 26.♖xd6 (26.♗xd6 ♖d8) 26...♘xb1 27.♖d7 ♗f6†/–+ Black went

on to win in Nakamura – Mamedyarov, Dresden (ol) 2008.

16...♕c8 17.h3⩲

White has reasonable compensation.

17...♘e8?! 18.♘c6! ♗xc6 19.dxc6 ♗d4 20.♖bc1 e5 21.♗h6 ♘g7 22.♗d5 ♕c7 23.♖d3!

White had a strong attack in Onischuk – Eljanov, Dresden (ol) 2008.

In a previous game, Carlsen was faced with the move:
13.e5!?

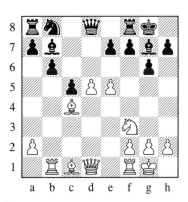

13...♘a6!N

This is an interesting novelty, as the d5-pawn is not secure.

Black has tried 13...♗a6 14.♕d3 and:

a) 14...♗xc4 15.♕xc4 ♘d7 16.♖e1 a6?! 17.♕h4 e6 18.♗g5 ♕c7 19.d6 ♕c6 20.♗h6 f6 21.exf6 ♖xf6 22.♘g5 with the initiative for White. This occurred in Nakamura – Carlsen, Oslo (blitz) 2009. I am sure that Carlsen will have prepared an improvement on this game.

b) 14...♕c8!? 15.♗g5 ♗xc4 16.♕xc4 e6 17.d6 (worse is 17.♖fe1 exd5 18.♕xd5 ♕c6 19.♕c4 ♕e6 20.♕h4 ♘c6 21.♗h6 Komarov – Givon, Petah Tiqwa 2010, and now Black has 21...♗xh6! 22.♕xh6 ♕g4∓) 17...♘d7 18.♖fe1 ♕c6∞

14.♗g5

This is probably White's best try, although it still seems fine for Black.

14.d6 exd6 15.exd6 ♘b4 looks better for Black: 16.a3 (16.♖e1 ♗xf3 17.gxf3 ♕f6 18.♖e4 ♖ad8 19.♗f4 ♘c6 20.♕d3 ♘d4 21.♔g2 ♖xd6 22.♗xd6 ♕xd6∓; 16.♖e1 ♗xf3 17.♕xf3 ♕xd6 18.♗g5 ♘c6∓) 16...♘c6 (16...♗xf3 17.♕xf3 ♘c2 18.♕d5 ♕d7 19.♗b5 ♕e6 is also good for Black) 17.♗d5 ♕d7 18.♗f4 ♘d4 19.♗xb7 ♕xb7 20.♘xd4 ♗xd4 21.♗g5 f6 22.♗e3 ♕d5 Black is clearly better.

On 14.♕b3 ♘b4 15.♖d1, Black has the strong 15...b5! 16.♗xb5 ♗xd5∓ with the better position.

14...h6 15.♗h4 ♘b4 16.d6 g5! 17.♗g3 exd6 18.exd6 ♖e8 19.h4 g4 20.♘d2 ♕d7 21.f3 b5!∓

13.♗f4 can be met by: 13...♗a6! 14.♕e2 (14.♗xa6 ♘xa6) 14...♕c8 15.e5 ♗xc4 16.♕xc4 e6 17.d6 ♘c6 18.♖bd1 ♕d7 19.♖fe1 ♖ae8 Black's position is okay; he is ready for the typical ...f6 break. 20.♗g5 f6 21.exf6 ♗xf6 22.♗xf6 ♖xf6 ½–½ Gelfand – Mikhalchishin, Portoroz 2001. After 23.♖e3 ♗f5= Black has no problems.

White has also tried 13.♗b2, with the idea of exchanging dark-squared bishops and activating the rook along the second rank. Black should offer the exchange of light-squared bishops: 13...♗a6! 14.♕e2 ♕c8 15.♗xg7 ♔xg7 16.e5 e6 17.♖bd1?! (Better was 17.d6 ♗xc4 18.♕xc4 ♘c6 19.♖fe1 ♕d7⇄, although Black has no problems. He will prepare ...f6 as in Gelfand – Mikhalchishin above.) 17...exd5 18.♖xd5 ♗xc4 19.♕xc4 ♘c6 20.♖d6 ♖d8 21.♖fd1 ♕f5!∓ White was unable to hold the position in Onischuk – Kurnosov, Moscow Aeroflot 2009.

13...♕c8

A natural move; Black prepares ...♗a6 to exchange bishops.

In a few games, Black has tried 13...e5. It is important for White to understand the position and avoid taking en passant. In the closed position White has a strong d-pawn and pressure on both wings, which gives him nice, long-term compensation.

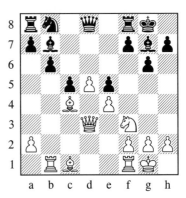

14.dxe6?! ♕xd3 15.exf7† ♖xf7 16.♗xd3 ♗a6 17.♗xa6 ♘xa6∓ Braun – Baramidze, Deizisau 2003.

14.d6?! ♘c6 15.♗g5 ♕d7∓

14.♗e3 ♕d6 15.♘d2 a6 16.a4 ♘d7 17.♕c3 and White intends ♗e2 and ♘c4, with good compensation.

14.h4!?N ♕d6 15.h5 ♘d7 16.h6 ♗f6 17.a4 ♗e7 18.a5 and White has fine compensation for the sacrificed pawn.

14.♗g5

White plays the main theoretical move. Another option for White is:
14.e5

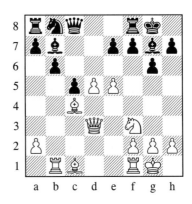

Again Black can try a logical novelty:
14...♘a6!?N

In practice, Black has always played the typical:
14...♗a6 15.♗g5 e6 (worse is 15...♗xc4
16.♕xc4 ♖e8 17.♖fe1 h6 Papenin – Eljanov,
Ukraine 2002, and now White should play
18.e6! with an attack) 16.d6 ♗xc4 17.♕xc4
♘d7 18.♖fe1 ♕c6 19.♕h4 ♕d5 20.♖bd1!?N
(worse is 20.♗h6?! ♘xe5 21.♘xe5 ♗xe5
22.♗xf8 ♖xf8∓ A. Smith – Ostenstad, Norway
[ch] 2011) 20...♕xa2 21.♗h6 f6 (21...♖fe8
22.♘g5 ♗h8 [22...♘f8 23.♗xg7 ♔xg7
24.♕f4+–] 23.♕f4 f5 24.exf6 ♗xf6 25.♘e4∞
leads to an unclear game) 22.♖a1 (22.♗xg7
♔xg7 23.♖a1 ♕d5 24.♖ad1 ♕a2=) 22...♕d5
(22...♕c2 23.♗xg7 ♔xg7 24.exf6† ♖xf6
25.♘g5⩲ with the idea 25...♘f8 26.d7!→)
23.♖ad1 ♕a2= The position is equal.
15.♗g5
15.♕b3 ♘b4 intending ...b5.
15...e6 16.d6 ♘b4

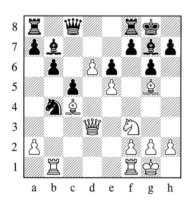

This looks good for Black.
17.♕e2
17.♕e3 ♗xf3 18.gxf3 ♘d5!∓
17...♘d5
17...♗xf3 18.gxf3 ♘d5 (18...♘c6 19.f4
♘d4 20.♕e4 f6 21.exf6 ♗xf6 22.♖fd1↑)
19.♗d2∞
18.♕d3 ♕d7∓
Black can be satisfied with his position.
The next move for him is ...♗c6, followed by
...♖ae8 and ...f6.

14...♖e8 15.e5
This position has occurred twice, and in
both games Black chose 15...♗a6. Here White
should reply 16.♖fe1, when play may transpose
into Papenin – Eljanov, which I analysed above
after 14.e5 ♗a6 15.♗g5. Pelletier was probably
aiming for this transposition, but Black has a
better option.

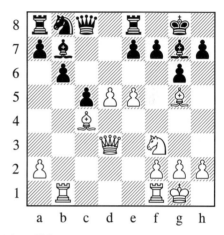

15...e6!N
With this strong novelty, Carlsen
immediately attacks the white centre.

16.dxe6
16.d6? ♘d7∓ is bad for White, since he
cannot defend the e5-pawn.

16...fxe6 17.♖bd1
A critical moment. This logical move gives
Black the chance to sacrifice the exchange and
take over the initiative.

On 17.♖fd1 Black can play the same way as
in the game: 17...♗xf3 18.♕xf3 ♘c6 19.♗b5
♘xe5 20.♕e4 ♘f7! 21.♗h4 ♗d4 22.♗xe8
♕xe8⩱ and it is questionable whether White
benefits from having a rook on b1 rather than
f1.

An important alternative was:
17.♗f6!? ♘c6

Here too, Black can sacrifice the exchange: 17...♗xf3 18.♕xf3 ♘c6 19.♗xg7 ♔xg7 20.♗b5 ♘d4 21.♕f6† ♔g8 22.♗xe8 ♕xe8∞ Black's plan is very straightforward; he will play ...♖d8-d5 or activate his queen with ...♕d8-d5, and then push his queenside pawns. Meanwhile White will try to organize an attack on the black king. The position remains unclear.

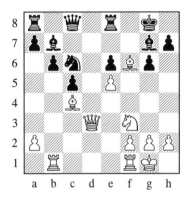

18.♖bd1

A dynamic alternative is: 18.♘g5!? ♘d4□ (18...♘xe5 19.♗xe5 ♗xe5 20.♕h3 h5 21.♖fe1±) 19.♕h3 h6 20.♗d3 ♘f5 (20...hxg5 21.♗xg6 ♕d7 22.♕h7† ♔f8 23.♕h5 g4∞ leads to a very unclear game. The computer gives the advantage to Black, but White's attack shouldn't be underestimated.) 21.♘e4 c4 22.♖fc1 ♗d5 23.♕g4 ♕b7 24.♖xc4 ♗xc4 25.♗xc4∞ White has compensation, but it is doubtful whether it is enough for more than equality.

18...♘a5

18...♘b4 is also playable. White has:

a) The attractive 19.♕d7 ♗h6 20.♘g5 ♕xd7 21.♖xd7 leads to a draw against best play: 21...♗c6! (21...♗d5? 22.♗xd5 ♘xd5 23.f4! ♗xg5 24.fxg5 c4 25.♖g7† ♔h8 26.♖f4!+–; 21...♗xg5? 22.♖xb7 ♗xf6 23.exf6 ♖f8 24.♗xe6† ♔h8 25.♖d1 ♖xf6 26.♗b3± followed by ♖dd7 with a strong attack) 22.♖xh7 ♗xg5 23.♖h8† ♔f7 24.♖h7†= with perpetual check.

b) 19.♕b3 ♗d5 20.♘g5 and:
b1) After 20...h6? 21.♖xd5! White wins in all lines: 21...♘xd5 (21...exd5 22.♗xd5† ♔h8 23.♗xa8 hxg5 24.♕f7+–) 22.♘xe6 ♘xf6 (22...♗xf6 23.exf6 ♘xf6 24.♕f3+–) 23.exf6 b5 24.♗d5 White has a decisive attack.
b2) 20...♕c6 21.♗xg7 ♔xg7 22.a3 b5□ 23.♗xd5 ♘xd5 24.♘xe6† ♔xe6 25.♕xd5 ♕xd5 (25...♕e7 26.♕c6 ♖ad8 27.♕xb5 ♕xe5 28.♖xd8 ♖xd8 29.g3 is slightly better for White. The black pawns are weak and his king is not safe.) 26.♖xd5 ♖ac8⇄ Black has enough counterplay.

19.♗b5

19.♘g5 ♘xc4 20.♕d7! ♕xd7 21.♖xd7 is only enough for a draw: 21...♗h6 22.♖xh7 (22.♖xb7 ♗xg5 23.♗xg5 ♖f8 24.♗f6 ♖f7 25.♖xf7 ♔xf7 26.♖d1 ♔e8!∓ is better for Black) 22...♗xg5 23.♖h8† ♔f7 24.♖h7† ♔g8 25.♖h8†=

19...♗c6 20.♗xc6 ♘xc6 21.♕c4 ♖f8 22.♕h4 ♕c7 23.♘g5 ♗xf6 24.exf6 ♘d4⇄

The position is unclear.

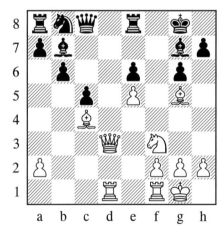

17...♗xf3! 18.♕xf3 ♘c6 19.♗b5 ♘xe5 20.♕e4

20.♕e3 ♘f7 21.♗xe8 ♕xe8 22.♗h4 ♗d4∞

20...♘f7 21.♗h4

21.♗xe8 ♘xg5 22.♕e3 ♕xe8 23.♕xg5 ♗d4 is better for Black.

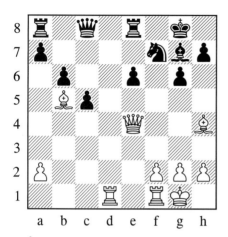

21...♗d4!

Black doesn't care about rook on e8. His idea is to push ...e5.

22.♖xd4?!

After this, Black will have an extra pawn. White was hoping to have compensation due to the weaknesses around the black king. But his problem is the misplaced bishop on h4 – it would have to be on the a1-h8 diagonal to provide counterplay.

22.♗xe8 ♕xe8 23.♖fe1 e5 was a better attempt, although Black's fine compensation for the exchange makes his position preferable. After 24.♕b7 ♕c8 25.♕d5 ♖b8 26.♔h1 ♕f5 27.f3 ♔g7 Black can slowly improve his position, while White has to remain passive.

22...cxd4 23.♗xe8 ♕xe8 24.♕xd4 ♖c8∓/∓

The opening battle has finished with a material plus for Black. In the next part of the game Carlsen shows excellent technical skills.

25.♖e1 e5 26.♕g4 ♖c2 27.h3

27.♗f6 would met by 27...♕c6 28.♕d1 a5!?∓ and White is not able to exploit the active position of his bishop.

27...♕c6 28.♗g3 ♖xa2 29.♗xe5 ♘xe5 30.♖xe5 ♖a4 31.♕d1 ♖f4

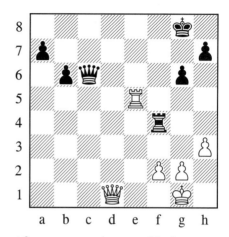

After some exchanges, Black retains his extra pawn and White is faced with a difficult defence.

32.♕b3† ♖f7 33.♖e7 ♕c1† 34.♔h2 ♕f4† 35.♔h1 ♔f8 36.♖e2

36.♖xf7† ♕xf7∓ would increase Black's advantage.

36...♔g7 37.♕d5

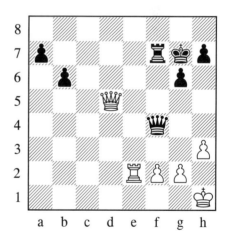

37...a5!

After consolidating his king position, Black is ready to use his queenside pawns.

38.f3

I am not sure that this is the right approach. This pawn move leaves the white king in danger, and Black is able to exchange rooks, increasing his advantage.

**38...♖c7 39.♖e1 ♖c1 40.♖xc1 ♕xc1†
41.♔h2 ♕c7† 42.♔h1 ♘f6! 43.♕d4† ♔e6
44.♕g4† ♔d6 45.♕d4† ♔c6 46.♕e4† ♔b5
47.♕e2† ♕c4 48.♕e8† ♕c6 49.♕e2† ♔c5
50.♕e3† ♔b4 51.♕e1† ♔c4 52.♕e2† ♔c3
53.♕e3† ♔b2! 54.♕d2† ♔b1 55.♕d3† ♕c2
56.♕b5† ♔a1–+**

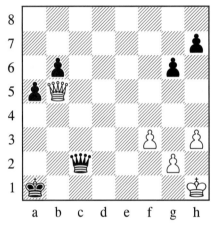

After a large number of checks, the black king has arrived in the right place. Black's passed pawns are supported by both king and queen, and it is clear that the white queen alone is not enough for a successful defence.

57.♔h2
57.♕xb6? ♕b1†–+

**57...♕c7† 58.♔h1 ♕c1† 59.♔h2 ♕f4†
60.♔h1 ♕d4 61.♕f1† ♔b2 62.♕e2† ♔c1
63.♕e4 ♕c3 64.f4 b5**
Finally Black starts to push his queenside pawns.

65.♕e5 ♕c4 66.♕a1† ♔c2 67.♕xa5
This doesn't change anything; the b-pawn will decide the game.

67...b4 68.♕a4† ♔b2 69.f5
What else?

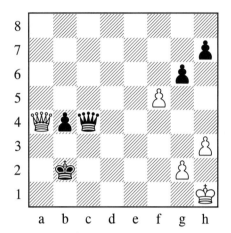

**69...gxf5 70.♔h2 h5 71.♕d7 ♕f4† 72.♔h1
b3**
It has been clear for a long time that White is lost. In the rest of game Carlsen didn't give any chances to Pelletier, and no further comments are necessary.

**73.♕d3 ♕f2 74.♕d5 h4 75.♔h2 ♕f4†
76.♔h1 ♔c2 77.♕c5† ♔b1 78.♕b5 b2
79.♕d3† ♔a2 80.♕a6† ♔b3 81.♕b5†
♔a3 82.♕a5† ♕a4 83.♕c5† ♔a2 84.♕d5†
♔a1 85.♕e5 ♕e4 86.♕a5† ♔b1 87.♕c3 f4
88.♕d2**
White resigned, without waiting for Black to play either 88...f3 or 88...♔a2.
0–1

GAME 36
▷ **A. Timofeev (2665)**
▶ **I. Nepomniachtchi (2711)**
64th Russian Championship, Moscow
Round 3, 10.08.2011 [D85]
Annotated by Borki Predojevic

In this game we shall look at the rare line 7.♗g5 as a possible option for White in Grünfeld Defence. Nepomniachtchi chose to play the endgame after 7...c5 8.♖c1 ♕a5 and he employed the novelty 15...a5!?N. It seems that the previously played 15...♗b7 is good too, as Black's play can be improved later with 18...♗c8!N. Black easily equalized after 15...a5, but he then played a couple of imprecise moves (21...♖ab8?! and 21...♗c8), after which he was faced with problems. Instead, he should have secured the b4-square for his knight with 21...♗f8!. White grasped his opportunity, and with the nice break 26.d5! he went into a technically winning position. But at the critical moment he blundered with 35.♗b5?, allowing Black to consolidate his position. The endgame was slightly better for White, but he wasn't able to win it.

I feel that 7.♗g5 is certainly an interesting line, but Black has several ways to create counterplay. The first is the endgame that Nepomniachtchi played, and the second way is to play the more complicated line 8...0–0 9.♘f3 ♗g4 10.d5 ♕d6, which I also discuss.

1.d4 ♘f6 2.c4 g6 3.♘c3 d5 4.cxd5 ♘xd5 5.e4 ♘xc3 6.bxc3 ♗g7 7.♗g5

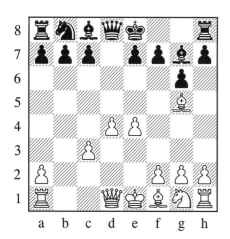

An interesting choice, as Timofeev also plays the Grünfeld Defence with the black pieces. He plays a line which was originally introduced by Yuri Kruppa, and employed at a high level by Ponomariov in 2006. With 7.♗g5 White hopes to gain some pluses in comparison with the line 7.♗e3 c5 8.♕d2 ♕a5 9.♖c1 cxd4 10.cxd4 ♕xd2† 11.♔xd2 0–0 12.♘f3.

7...c5 8.♖c1 ♕a5

Nepomniachtchi decides to go into the endgame. This line hasn't tested at a high level before.

One of the ideas behind White's 7th move can be seen if Black plays: 8...h6 9.♗e3 0–0?! (after 9...cxd4 10.cxd4 ♕a5† 11.♕d2 ♕xd2† 12.♔xd2 0–0, White can go for the interesting 13.♗d3!? ♖d8 14.♘e2) 10.♕d2. Now Black has problems with pawn on h6.

The most popular move is 8...0–0, when Black now threatens to take on d4.

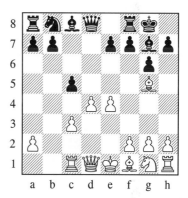

9.♘f3

Another way to protect the d-pawn is 9.d5, but this is less dangerous than the main line. Black has several options here:

a) 9...f5?! is risky: 10.♗c4 ♔h8 11.♕e2 b5!? (11...fxe4 12.♕xe4 ♕a5 13.♘f3 ♗xc3† 14.♔f1⊒) 12.♗xb5 fxe4 13.♕xe4 ♖f5? (better was 13...♗f5! 14.♕e2 ♕xd5 15.♘f3 ♘c6 16.♗c4 ♕e4 17.0–0±) 14.♘f3 ♕a5 Krasenkow – Lavendelis, Warsaw (rapid) 2010. White now missed the strong 15.d6! ♗xc3† 16.♖xc3 ♕xc3† 17.♗d2 ♕a1† 18.♔e2 ♕xh1 19.dxe7+– with decisive threats.

b) 9...♘d7 looks reasonable. After 10.♕d2 ♘f6 11.♗d3 b5 12.♘e2 ♕b6 13.♖b1 a6 14.c4 e6! 15.0–0 exd5 16.exd5 ♗d7 Black was okay in Krasenkow – Timofeev, Dagomys 2008.

c) 9...♕d6!? 10.♗d3 (after 10.♗e2 e6 11.♘f3 exd5 12.exd5 ♗g4 13.0–0 ♘d7⇄ Black had no problems in Bartel – Bobras, Czech Republic 2011; 10.♘f3 ♗g4 transposes to 9.♘f3 ♗g4 10.d5 ♕d6) 10...♘d7 (10...e6!?) 11.♘e2 f5! 12.exf5 ♘e5! 13.0–0 ♘xd3 14.♕xd3 ♖xf5 15.♗e3 ♕xd5 16.♕xd5† ♖xd5∓ Black was clearly better in Housieaux – Vachier Lagrave, France 2011.

9...♗g4

9...cxd4 10.cxd4 ♗g4 11.d5 ♘d7 12.♗e2 ♘f6 13.h3 ♗d7 14.♗d3 gave White the better chances in Nyback – Svidler, Khanty-Mansiysk (1) 2009.

10.d5 ♕d6!?.

The alternative is 10...f5 11.♕b3 ♔h8, and now the best answer is 12.♘d2 fxe4 13.h3 ♗c8 14.♘xe4 ♕c7 15.♗e3 ♘d7 16.♗e2 with the better prospects for White, Prohaszka – Csiba, Budapest 2009.

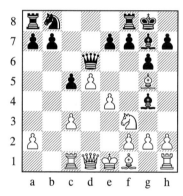

White now has several options:

a) 11.♗e2 ♘d7

Black looks to be fine here.

12.0–0

12.h3 ♗xf3 13.♗xf3 b5 14.c4 b4 15.0–0 a5 16.♗g4 ♗d4 17.♖e1 e5 18.♗xd7 ♕xd7 19.♗e3 ♗xe3 20.♖xe3 a4= Nyback – Svidler, Khanty-Mansiysk (4) 2009.

12...♗xf3 13.♗xf3 b5 14.♗e2

14.a4 a6 15.♗e2 c4 16.f4 f6!↑ is similar, and also gives Black good play.

14...c4 15.f4

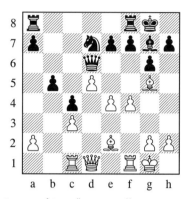

15...f6! 16.♗h4 ♘c5 17.♕d4 e5! 18.dxe6 ♕xd4† 19.cxd4 ♘xe6

Black has good counterplay.

20.♖xc4

20.d5!? ♘xf4 21.♖xf4 g5 22.a4 a6 23.♖f5 gxh4↑

20...f5

20...♘xf4!?

21.e5?

Better was 21.♖b4 ♘xd4 22.♗d3 fxe4 23.♗xe4 ♖ae8∓ and White can still fight for a draw.

21...bxc4 22.♗xc4 ♖fe8 23.d5 g5 24.fxg5 ♘c5 25.d6† ♔h8 26.e6 ♖ad8 27.♖d1 ♖xe6–+

Black had won a piece in Nyback – Kovchan, Aix-les-Bains 2011.

b) 11.♕d2?! was played in one game, but it looks illogical. After 11...♘d7 12.♗e2 ♗xf3 13.gxf3 f5 14.♗f4 ♘e5∓ Black was already better in Eperjesi – Farkas, Hungary 2007.

c) 11.♕b3!?

In my opinion, this is the most dangerous move.

11...♗xf3

11...b6? is wrong. White has 12.♘d2!± followed by h3 and ♗e2 White will finish his development and connect his pawns with c3-c4. Black will not be able to open the game with ...e6 in time, so his position is worse.

12.gxf3

We have arrived at the critical position. Black has managed to destroy the white structure on the kingside, and his plan is simple – to take control over the dark squares and open the position with ...f5 at the right moment. Also, he has the possibility of organizing play on the queenside. On the other hand, White has the bishop pair and a strong centre. It is best for White to keep his king in the centre and try to organize a break in the centre (with f4 and e5) or on the kingside (with h4-h5).

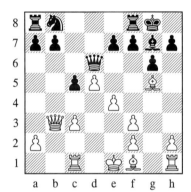

12...♘d7!

The positional 12...b6 looks a bit slow, but may also be playable:

a) On 13.f4?! Black has a miracle reply: 13...h6! (13...♘d7? 14.e5 ♕c7 15.♗b5 ♘f6 16.d6± gave the advantage to White in Sieciechowicz – Shishkin, Baia Sprie 2010) 14.e5 ♕c7 15.♗h4

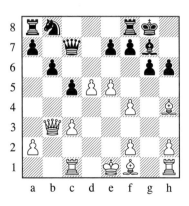

15...♗xe5!! 16.fxe5 ♕xe5† 17.♗e2 (17.♔d1 ♕h5†–+; 17.♔d2 ♕f4†–+) 17...♕f4–+ and White cannot keep his extra material.

b) 13.♗e3 13...♗e5 14.h4 ♘d7 15.h5 ♗f4 16.c4 and the position remains unclear.

Here I suggest:

13.♗e3!?N

Planning to push either h2-h4 or f3-f4.

The risky 13.♕xb7 ♘e5 14.♗e2 ♗f6 15.♗e3 ♖fb8 16.♕a6 ♘xf3†! 17.♔d1 ♖b6 18.♕c4 ♘e5∞ looks fine for Black.

13.h4 ♖ab8 14.a4 (14.c4 ♘f6 15.♕e3 ♘h5↑ and ...♗e5 will give Black control over the f4- and d4-squares) 14...♗e5 15.c4 (15.h5? ♗f4) Here Black should react with 15...♘f6! with the idea of ...♘h5, gaining full control over the dark squares. (Instead 15...f5?! 16.exf5 gxf5 17.♗h3∞ was unclear in Erdos – Tazbir, Bundesliga 2010.)

13...f5 14.h4 ♘e5 15.♗e2 f4 16.♗d2 b6 17.c4∞

White intends ♗f1–h3, and the position remains unclear.

9.♕d2 cxd4 10.cxd4 ♕xd2† 11.♔xd2 0–0 12.♘f3 e6

We can see the difference between the endgames arising after 9.♗g5 and 9.♗e3 if Black tries going for fast development: 12...♘c6? 13.d5 h6 14.♗h4 g5 Necessary to defend the e7-pawn. 15.♗g3 ♖d8 16.♔e3±

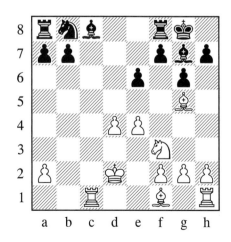

13.♗b5

According to theory, this move is supposed to lead to an advantage for White.

13.♗e7 should not trouble Black: 13...♖e8 (13...♗h6† 14.♔c2 ♖e8 15.♗g5 ♗xg5 16.♘xg5 ♘c6 looks also okay for Black) 14.♖c7 ♘c6 15.♗d6 ♖d8 16.e5 ♗d7 17.♖xd7 ♗xd7 18.♗d3 ♖c8⇄ Black was fine in Prohaszka – Roganovic, Subotica 2007.

13.♖c7

This doesn't give anything to White either. 13...♘c6 14.♗b5

In the first game in this line, White played 14.d5 exd5 15.exd5 ♘b4 16.♗c4 b5 17.♗b3 and now according to Kruppa, Black should play 17...a5! (instead 17...♘a6? 18.♖cc1 ♗f5 19.♖he1 ♖fc8 20.d6± was clearly better for White in Kruppa – Slizhevsky, St Petersburg 2004). This is a typical Grünfeld move. Black doesn't care for the exchange; it is more important to disturb the white pieces and the d5-pawn. Play may continue: 18.♗e7 ♗h6† 19.♔c3 (19.♔d1? a4 20.♗xa4 ♘xd5∓) 19...♘a6! 20.♗xf8 ♗xf8 21.♖c6 a4 22.♗c2 (after 22.♗d1 ♘b4 23.♘e5 ♘xd5†∓ Black has a very strong attack) 22...♘b4 23.♗e4 ♘xc6 24.dxc6 ♗e6∓ Black's position is superior.
14...h6

14...♘xd4 15.♘xd4 ♗xd4 16.♗e7 ♗e5 17.♖c2 a6 18.♗xf8 ♔xf8 19.♗d3±
15.♗xc6

15.♗h4 ♘xd4 16.♘xd4 g5!
15...hxg5 16.♗xb7 ♗xb7 17.♖xb7 ♖fd8

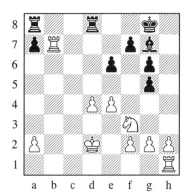

18.♘xg5

After 18.g4 ♗xd4 19.♔e2 ♖ac8 20.♖d1 ♖c2† 21.♖d2 ♖xd2† 22.♔xd2 Black can play 22...f6!? 23.♔e2 e5 and White is not better. For example: 24.♘xd4 (24.h4 gxh4 25.♘xh4 ♖c8†) 24...♗xd4 25.♖xa7 ♖xe4† 26.♔f3 ♖f4† 27.♔g3 ♖c4= leads to a draw.
18...♖xd4† 19.♔e3

19.♔e2 ♗h6! also leads to a draw: 20.♘xf7 (20.f4 ♗xg5 21.fxg5 ♖xe4† 22.♔d3 ♖e5 23.♖f1 ♖d8† 24.♔c3 ♖c5† 25.♔b4 ♗xg5 26.♖fxf7 a5† 27.♔b3 ♗xg2=) 20...♖d2† 21.♔e1 (21.♔f3? ♖f8) 21...♗f4! 22.g3 (22.♘e5 ♖xa2 23.♘xg6 ♖a1† 24.♔e2 ♖xh1↑ would be dangerous for White) 22...♖xa2 23.gxf4 ♖a1† 24.♔e2 ♖xh1 25.♘h6†=
19...♖a4

19...♖ad8!? was possible too.
20.♖d1 ♗h6 21.f4 ♗xg5 22.fxg5 ♖xa2 23.♖dd7 ♖xg2 24.♖xf7 ♖xg5=

A draw was soon agreed in Komarov – Spiridonov, Albena 2009.

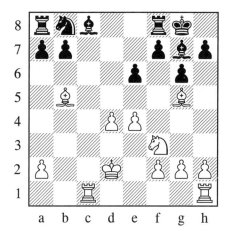

13...a6

The most logical. 13...♘c6?! is dubious: 14.♗xc6 bxc6 15.♔e3 f6 16.♗f4 e5 Black's only shot is to try to solve his problem tactically, since White has a huge positional advantage. 17.dxe5 fxe5 18.♘xe5 ♖xf4 19.♔xf4 g5† 20.♔xg5 ♗xe5 21.♖xc6± Volokitin – Moor, Mainz (rapid) 2007.

14.♗a4 b5

14...♘c6?! 15.♗xc6 bxc6 16.♔e3±/± (16.e5!? also looks interesting) is very similar to 13...♘c6?! above.

15.♗b3

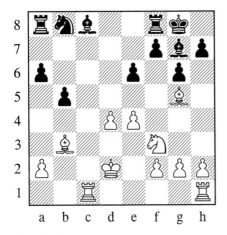

15...a5!?N

This is a novelty. Black advances his queenside pawns in order to disturb the white bishop on b3.

Previously Black had played:
15...♗b7 16.d5
  16.♔e3 ♘c6 17.d5 exd5 18.♗xd5 ♖ac8 19.♖hd1 ♗a8⇄
16...exd5 17.exd5 a5 18.♖c7

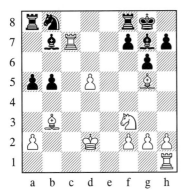

18...♗c8!N
Black intends ...♘a6 next.

This improves on 18...a4? 19.♖xb7 axb3 20.axb3 ♖a2† 21.♔e3 f6 22.♗f4 ♖e8† 23.♔d3 ♘a6 24.♖xb5 ♗f8 25.d6! ♖d8 26.♘d4 ♗xd6 27.♗xd6 ♖xd6 28.♔e3± and White had an extra pawn in Y. Vovk – Bezemer, Dieren 2009.
19.d6 ♘a6 20.♖cc1 ♘b4! 21.a3 a4∞
With a very complicated position.

16.♖c5 a4 17.♗c2 ♗d7

Black prepares ...♘a6. In his notes Kruppa mentioned 17...b4?, but White has the advantage after 18.♖c4±.

18.♖c7

This is the only way to stop the immediate ...♘a6.

18...f6 19.♗e3 ♖d8

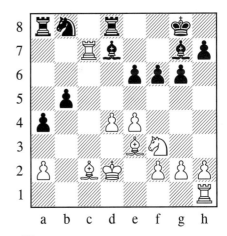

20.♖b1

20.♗d3 ♘a6 21.♖b7 ♖ab8 22.♖xb8 ♖xb8⇄ followed by ...♗f8 or ...♘b4.

20...♘a6

Black has finally managed to develop his knight to a6 with tempo. Also, he has finished his development and he shouldn't have any problems in the future.

21.♖b7 ♖ab8?!

An inaccurate move. Satisfied with his achievements so far, Black now becomes imprudent.

More precise was 21...♗f8! 22.♗d3 (22.e5 ♗c6 23.♖b6 ♗xf3 24.gxf3 fxe5) 22...♖ab8⇄ with a good game for Black. On 23.♖a7 there follows 23...♘b4!.

22.♖a7 ♖a8

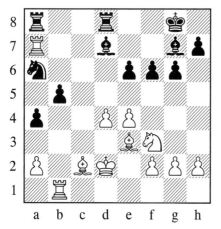

23.♖b7?!

This is not best.

Black would be faced with more problems after:

23.♖xa8! ♖xa8 24.♗d3 ♗c6
24...♘c7? 25.♗f4 ♖a7 26.g4!±
After 24...♖b8 25.♗f4 ♖b7 26.♗d6 ♔f7 27.e5!↑ White would be better. For example: 27...♗h6† 28.♔e2 f5 29.d5! exd5 30.♘d4± with a superior position for White.
25.♘e1
25.d5 is interesting, but White can't improve his position after the forced 25...exd5 26.♘d4 dxe4 27.♘xc6 exd3 28.♖xb5 ♗f8 29.♖a5 a3 30.♗d4 ♔f7⇄. The black d3-pawn is untouchable.
25...♗f8 26.♘c2±/=
White has a small advantage thanks to the black weakness on b5, but Black should be able to hold the position.

23...♖ab8

Again the right move was 23...♗f8!=, as mentioned on move 21.

24.♖a7 ♗c8

Perhaps Black realised that he stood worse after 23...♖a8 and so decided to change decision. Of course this looks risky, but if Black wants to play something else, this is the only possibility.

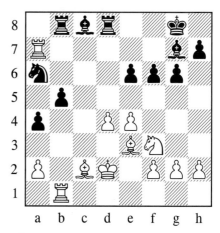

25.♗d3

A serious alternative was: 25.♗f4!? e5 (25...♖b6 26.♗xa4!) 26.♘xe5!? fxe5 27.♖xg7† ♔xg7 28.♗xe5† ♔f7 29.♗xb8 ♘xb8 30.d5! (30.♖xb5 also gives a small plus to White after 30...♗a6□ 31.♖b6 ♖xd4† 32.♔e3 ♖d8 33.♗xa4 ♗c4 34.♖b7† ♔f6 35.h4±) 30...♗a6 31.♗d3 ♘d7 32.♗xb5 ♖b8 (32...♗xb5 33.♖xb5±) 33.♗d3 ♗xd3! (33...♖xb1 34.♗xb1± would give White good chances for win; the white pawns are stronger than the knight) 34.♖xb8 ♗xe4 35.♖b4 (35.♖b7 ♔e7 36.f3 ♗xd5 37.♖a7 ♗xa2=) 35...♗xd5 36.♖xa4 ♗xg2± White has the advantage. His a-pawn is very strong, and it gives him reasonable chances to win the game.

25...♖d7

The only move.

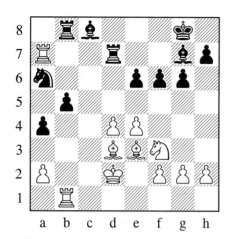

26.d5!

A very nice idea of Timofeev's.

26.Rxd7 Bxd7 27.Bf4± would be just slightly better for White.

26...exd5 27.exd5 f5

This is a questionable decision. Correct is:
27...Rxd5! 28.Nd4 Rd7□
  28...f5 29.Nc6 Bb7 30.Ra8 Rbd7 31.Rxc8†
Kf7 32.Nd8† Rxd8 33.Rxd8 Rxd8
34.Rxb5±

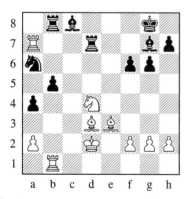

29.Nc6!

This gives White the better prospects.
29.Rxd7 Bxd7 30.Bxb5 Bxb5 31.Rxb5
Rxb5 32.Nxb5 Bf8! (32...Nb4 33.Nc3 a3
34.Bc5 Bf8 35.Bxb4 Bxb4 36.Kd3 Kf7
37.Kc4 Bf8 38.Kd5± gives an advantage
to White) 33.Nc3 Nb4= and White cannot

capture the a4-pawn without losing his own
a-pawn.
29...Rxa7 30.Bxa7 Rb7 31.Rxb5 Rc7 32.Bc4†
Kh8 33.Rb6 Bh6†
  33...Nc5 34.Bb8 Rd7† 35.Ke2↑
34.Ke2 Nc5 35.Bb8 Rd7 36.f4↑
White has the initiative, but Black should be
able to survive.

28.Rxb5 Rxb5 29.Bxb5 Rxd5†

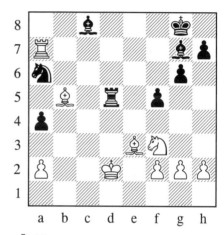

30.Nd4!

The key idea. Now Black is forced to go into
an inferior endgame.

30...Bxd4 31.Bc4 Bxa7† 32.Bxd5† Kf8
33.Bxa7±

The position has calmed down. Black has a
most undesirable task to defend this position.
Technically the position should be winning for
White, because the a4-pawn is weak and the
black knight is badly placed.

33...Ke7 34.Bc4 Kd6 35.Bb5?

A waste of time that helps Black to
consolidate his pieces.

The immediate 35.Kc3± was better, and it is
very difficult for Black. After 35...Bb7 36.g3 I
don't see how he can survive.

35...♗b7 36.g3

White naturally wants to keep all the pawns on the board, and he avoids all possible simplifications.

36...♘b4!

After 36...a3 37.♔c3 ♘c7 38.♗c4 ♗d5 39.♗e3± Black will lose the a-pawn.

37.a3 ♗c6 38.♗c4

38.♗xa4 ♗xa4 39.axb4 ♗b5= leads to draw.

38...♘d5‡

After 35.♗b5? Black was able to improve his position, and now there is no easy win for White, much to Timofeev's disappointment. With last move, Black has prepared an attack on the kingside. White will be able to go a pawn up, but it will not be enough to win.

39.♔d3 ♘f6 40.♔c3 g5!

Forcing exchanges.

41.f4 gxf4 42.gxf4 ♗d5 43.♗d3 ♗e4 44.♗e2 ♗g2! 45.♔d4 ♘g4 46.h4 ♘h2

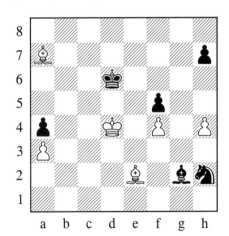

With very good defence, Black has found a way to attack the white kingside pawns.

47.h5?!

47.♗c5† would cause more problems. However, after 47...♔c6 48.♗e7 ♗e4 49.♗d1 ♔b5, Black can hope for a successful defence. For example, 50.♔e5 ♘f3† 51.♗xf3 ♗xf3 52.♔xf5 ♔c6 looks drawish.

47...♗f3=

With this move, Black secures a draw.

48.♗xf3 ♘xf3† 49.♔c4 ♘d2†! 50.♔b4 h6 51.♗f2 ♔c6 52.♔xa4 ♘e4 53.♗d4 ♘g3 54.♗g7 ♘xh5

55.♗xh6 ♘xf4 56.♗xf4 ♔b7= leads to a theoretical draw.

½–½

GAME 37

▷ **M. Vachier Lagrave (2722)**

▶ **A. Morozevich (2694)**

Accentus GM Tournament, Biel
Round 2, 19.07.2011 **[D86]**
Annotated by Borki Predojevic

In the following game Morozevich chose the Grünfeld against a renowned expert on this defence, Vachier Lagrave. The Frenchman chose his pet line with the white pieces, the classical setup with ♗c4, ♘e2 and ♗e3. Morozevich deviated from the main line by playing 11...b6, but this did not confuse Vachier who responded with the strong 15.f4! which led to some advantage for him. Later he went wrong with 27.♖a3? and later 28.♘g5†??, a huge blunder which led to his downfall. The theoretical conclusion is that 15.f4! is the critical test of the 11...b6 line, and it remains to be seen if Black will come up with a satisfactory answer.

1.c4 ♘f6 2.♘c3 d5 3.cxd5 ♘xd5 4.e4 ♘xc3 5.bxc3 g6 6.d4 ♗g7 7.♗c4 c5 8.♘e2 ♘c6 9.♗e3 0–0 10.0–0 ♕c7 11.♖c1

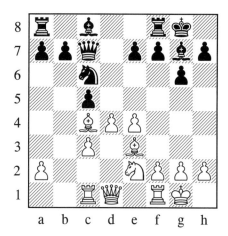

11...b6!?

Over the past few years this move has been tested by Bu Xiangzhi and Caruana, although it is worth mentioning that Vachier also used it to draw with Renet in 2007. According to the database it appeared for the first time in the game Averbakh – Botvinnik, Moscow (training match) 1956. The move has never achieved much popularity at the highest level, although this might be set to change after it received Boris Avrukh's stamp of approval in *Grandmaster Repertoire 9 – The Grünfeld Defence, Volume Two*.

The most popular move has been:
11...Rd8
  From this position, in some recent games White has tried:
12.Bf4
  Other possibilities include 12.f4, 12.h3, 12.Wd2 and 12.Wa4.

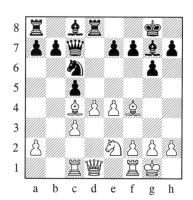

12...Wd7!
  After 12...Bxe5 13.Bxe5 Nxe5 14.Bb3 Ng4 15.Ng3 Wf4 16.We1! Black has some problems; see for instance the game Caruana – Svidler, Amsterdam 2010.
13.dxc5
  13.d5 Na5 14.Bd3 b5 15.Be3 e6 16.Bxc5 exd5 17.e5!? was a pawn sacrifice which gave White reasonable compensation and eventually resulted in a draw in Vachier Lagrave – Nepomniachtchi, Khanty-Mansiysk (ol) 2010.
13...We8 14.Bd5 Ne5 15.Nd4 e6 16.Bb3
Now Black solves his problems with a nice idea.

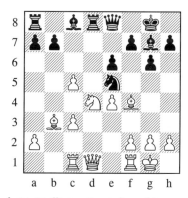

16...Bd7 17.We2 a6! 18.Be3 Bb5! 19.Nxb5 Wxb5 20.Wxb5 axb5 21.Rb1 Bf8 22.Bd4 Nd7 23.Bd1 Ra5 24.Be2
  The players agreed a draw in Gustafsson – Popovic, Bundesliga 2010. It is important to remember Black's plan with ...Bd7, ...a6 and ...Bb5, which can be an important resource after dxc5.

12.Wd2

White wants to exchange the dark-squared bishops and launch an attack against the enemy king.
  12.dxc5 is not good, as after 12...bxc5 13.Nf4 (13.Bxc5 Ne5 14.Bd5 Rb8 15.Bd4 e6 16.Bb3 Ba6∞ gives Black good compensation) 13...e6 14.Nd3 Rd8⇄ Black is doing fine.

12...♗b7 13.♗h6 ♖ad8 14.♗xg7 ♔xg7

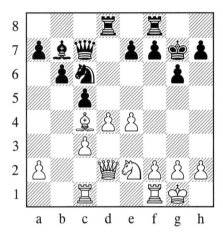

15.f4!

This strong move had not been seen in high-level games before, which is a bit surprising as the plan of attacking on the kingside with f5 is extremely natural.

15.♕e3

This has been the most common choice, but it allows a strong reaction.

15...e5!

After this it seems that Black has a good position.

16.♗b5

16.♗d5 ♘a5 17.♗xb7 ♕xb7 18.♘g3 ♕e7 gives Black a good game for instance: 19.♖fd1 h5 20.dxe5 ♘c4 21.♕e2 ♘xe5 22.f4 ♘g4 23.h3 ♘h6 24.♕f3 ♖xd1† 25.♖xd1 ♖d8= Kindermann – Hort, Germany 1988.

In a more recent game White played 16.d5 but after 16...♘e7 17.♘g3 f6 18.h4 ♘c8 19.♗d3 ♘d6 20.f4 exf4 21.♕xf4 ♕e7 22.♖f2 ♕e5 23.♕xe5 fxe5 24.♘f1 c4 25.♗c2 ♗c8⇄ Black was fine in Fier – Caruana, Gibraltar 2011.

16...♘a5 17.♘g3 ♕e7 18.dxe5 ♕xe5 19.f4?! Too optimistic.

19.♖fd1 was better, for instance 19...♕e7 20.♕f4 ♘c6 21.♗e2 ♖xd1† 22.♖xd1 ♖d8 23.♖xd8 ♕xd8 24.h4 ♕f6 25.♕xf6† ♔xf6=

and a draw was soon agreed in Averbakh – Botvinnik, Moscow 1956.

19...♕d6 20.♖fd1?

Another bad decision, which might have proved costly.

20...♕xd1† 21.♖xd1 ♖xd1† 22.♔f2

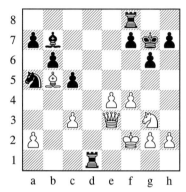

22...♖b1!

In the game Black faltered with 22...♘c6? and allowed his opponent to escape with a draw: 23.♗xc6 ♗xc6 24.f5 ♖fd8 (24...f6 25.e5!⇄) 25.♕g5 ♖1d6 26.♘h5† ♔f8 27.♘f6 ♔g7 28.♘h5† ♔f8 29.♘f6 ♔g7 30.♘h5† ½–½ Renet – Vachier Lagrave, Aix-les-Bains 2007.

23.f5 ♖b2† 24.♔f3 f6!–+

Black is winning.

15...♕d7

15...♕d6!? also looks interesting.

16.♗b5! ♕e6

This move was a novelty, and an improvement over 16...a6?! 17.♗xc6 ♕xc6 18.d5 ♕c7 19.c4 ♔g8 as occurred in Degardin – Giroyan, France 2011. It is clear that White has a nice advantage and he can attack on either side. A logical way to proceed would be 20.a4 ♗c8 (20...e6 21.f5±) 21.♘c3 ♗d7 22.♖b1 ♖b8 23.♖fd1± intending d6, when Black faces difficult problems.

I also analysed:
16...e6?!

But this move looks suspicious.
17.f5! exf5 18.exf5

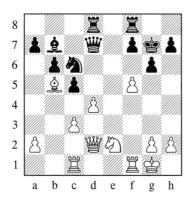

The threat of f6 is troublesome for Black.
18...f6
   18...♔h8 19.♕h6! ♖g8 20.♖f3 gxf5 21.♕f6†
♖g7 22.♖xf5 a6 23.♗xc6 ♗xc6 24.d5+−
   18...a6 19.f6† ♔h8 20.♕h6 ♖g8 21.♖f4+−
   18...cxd4 19.f6† ♔h8 20.♕h6 ♖g8 21.♖f4+−
The text move is more resilient, but now the
e6-square is weakened.
19.♘f4! ♕xf5
   19...gxf5 20.d5! ♕f7 21.♕e2+−
20.♖ce1±
The knight is coming to e6 next, so Black is
in trouble.

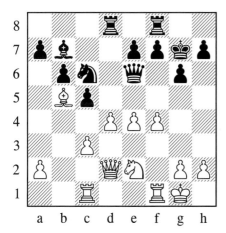

17.f5!
   White continues his attack without regard
for the e4-pawn.

17...♕d6
17...♕xe4!?
   This leads to complications, but White keeps
the upper hand with correct play.
18.♖f4 ♕e5
   The only move, as 18...♕d5 19.♖h4 h5 is
refuted beautifully:

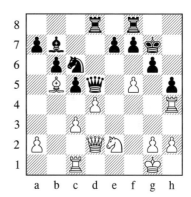

20.♖xh5!! gxh5 21.♕g5† ♔h7 22.♕xh5†
♔g7 23.♕g5† ♔h7 24.♘f4 ♕e4 (or
24...♕d6 25.f6! with mate to follow within
a few moves) 25.♕h4† ♔g8 26.♕g3† ♔h8
27.♗d3+−
19.♘g3!
   19.♖h4 can be met by 19...♔g8 intending
...♕g7.
   19.fxg6 hxg6 20.♖h4 ♔g8!∞

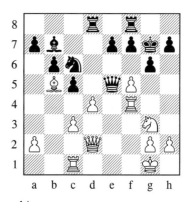

19...cxd4
   19...♔g8 20.♖e1 ♕h8 (20...♕d6 21.♘e4
♕d5 22.f6!+−) 21.♗xc6 ♗xc6 22.♖xe7 cxd4
23.cxd4±

19...♘xd4 20.cxd4 ♖xd4 21.♖xd4 cxd4
22.♗d3 ♖c8 23.♖e1 ♕f6 24.♕e2±

19...♘h8 20.♖e1 ♕f6 (20...♕g7 21.♖xe7!)
21.fxg6 ♕xg6 22.♗xc6 ♗xc6 23.♘f5→

20.♗xc6 ♗xc6

The best chance is probably 20...dxc3!?
21.♕xc3 ♕xc3 22.♖xc3 ♖d1† 23.♔f2 ♖c8
24.♗f3 ♖d2† 25.♔e3 ♖xa2 26.♖xc8 ♗xc8
27.fxg6 hxg6 28.♖c4± when Black has an
inferior ending but he keeps some drawing
chances.

21.cxd4 ♗b7

21...♕d5 22.♖h4 h5 23.♘xh5† ♔g8
24.♖xc6 ♕xc6 25.♕h6 gxh5 26.♕g5†+−
After the text move Black seems to be doing
okay, but White has a subtle and brilliant
move which crushes his dreams.

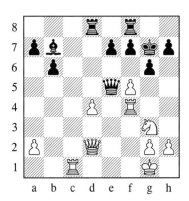

22.♖c2!!

Other moves are not so dangerous for Black:
22.♖h4 ♔g8 23.♖e1 ♕f6 24.♕h6 ♕g7⇄
22.♖e1 ♕a5! 23.♕f2! e6! (23...♕a3 24.♖xe7
♗d5 25.♕e1∞) 24.fxe6 (24.♖e5? ♕a3
25.fxg6 fxg6!−+; 24.fxg6 hxg6 25.♖e5 is
met by 25...♖d5! 26.♖xe6 ♖b5 and the best
for White is 27.♖e1 ♖b2 28.♘f5† with
perpetual check) 24...fxe6 25.♖f1 ♖xf4
26.♕xf4 ♕d5 27.♕f6† ♔g8 28.♕f7† ♔h8
29.♕f6† ♔g8 and the position is equal.

22...♕a5

22...♕d6 23.♖h4 ♖h8 24.♕h6† ♔g8
25.♖g4! ♕b4 26.♖f2+−
22...♕b5 23.♖h4 ♖h8 24.♖c7 ♖d7 25.♕h6†

♔g8 26.♖xd7 ♕xd7 27.fxg6 fxg6 28.♖f4
♕e8 29.♘f5! gxf5 30.♖xf5+−

23.♕e3

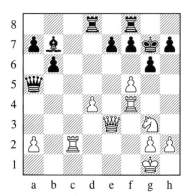

23...♖d7

23...♕b5 24.♖h4 ♖h8 25.♖c7 ♕b1† 26.♘f1
♗a6 27.♕e5† ♔g8 28.♖f4+−

23...♕b4 24.♖h4 ♖h8 (24...h5 25.♘xh5†+−)
25.fxg6 ♕b1† (or 25...hxg6 26.♘f5†!
with an easy mating attack) 26.♖c1 ♕xg6
27.♕xe7+− Black has no good defence
against ♕b7 or ♘h5.

24.♖h4 f6 25.♕h6† ♔f7 26.♕xh7† ♔e8

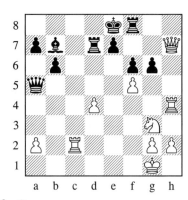

27.fxg6!

More conclusive than 27.♕xg6† ♔d8
28.♕h6 ♖e8 29.♕f4 ♕e1† 30.♘f1 ♖d6
31.♖c1 ♕e2 32.♕f2 ♕xf2† 33.♔xf2 ♖d5
34.♘e3 ♖a5 35.♖c2 ♖a4 36.♖g4± although
White is much better here too.

27...♕e1† 28.♘f1 ♗a6 29.h3! ♕xf1†
30.♔h2 ♕f5 31.g7! ♕xh7 32.gxf8=♕† ♔xf8
33.♖xh7+−

The move played in the game avoids this fate, but it still does not equalize.

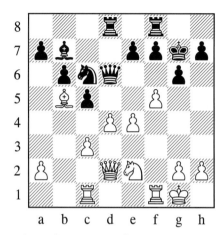

18.♗xc6 ♗xc6 19.d5! ♗d7 20.c4±

White has emerged from the opening with a pleasant advantage. He has more space and the enemy bishop is restricted by the strong pawns on d5 and f5.

20...♕e5

A natural move, as Black certainly did not wish to allow ♕c3†.

21.♖c3 ♖h8 22.♖h3

22.♖a3 ♖a8 23.♖h3!? was another option.

22...f6 23.♕f4 b5!?

Aiming for queenside counterplay was the best practical policy.

23...g5?! 24.♕xe5 fxe5 25.♘c1 leaves Black facing a highly unpleasant endgame.

23...♕xf4

This will bring nothing good for Black.
24.♘xf4 gxf5
24...g5?! 25.♘e6† ♗xe6 26.fxe6 ♖hf8 27.♖a3 ♖a8 28.♖af3± White intends e5 and ♖f7.
25.exf5 ♗xf5 26.♘h5† ♔g6 27.♖g3† ♔xh5 28.♖xf5† ♔h6 29.♖f4 ♔h5

Amazingly Black can avoid being mated, but he is still in trouble if White plays accurately:

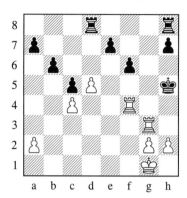

30.♖fg4! e6 31.♔f2! f5 32.♖g5† ♔h6 33.♔f3!
With the deadly threat of ♔f4 and ♖h3 mate.
33.♔e3 is less accurate: 33...♖de8! 34.♔f4 (34.d6? ♖hf8∓; 34.dxe6 ♖xe6† 35.♔f4 ♖g6=) 34...e5† 35.♔xf5 ♖hf8† 36.♔e4 ♖f4† 37.♔d3 ♖d4† 38.♔c3 e4 39.♖5g4 ♔h5 40.♖g7 ♔h6=
33...♖hf8
Now 33...♖de8 34.d6! is winning, as there will not be a threat of ...f4† forking the king and rook.
34.♔f4

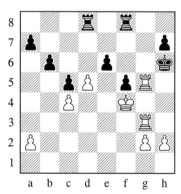

34...e5†! 35.♔xe5 f4 36.♖3g4 b5!
Black is playing 'only moves' but they do not solve his problems fully.
37.♖f5 ♖xf5† 38.♔xf5 bxc4 39.♔e5 ♖f8 40.d6 c3 41.♖h4† ♔g6 42.♖h3

White keeps a clear advantage in the rook endgame.

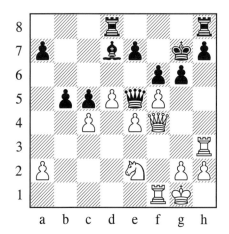

24.Wh6†

White could also have gone for an endgame with 24.Wxe5!? fxe5 25.Ra3 Ra8 26.fxg6 hxg6 27.cxb5 Bxb5 28.Re1 when Black faces a difficult defence.

24...\u00a2f7 25.\u00d8f4 Rdg8

This natural move looks best.

25...Wd4† 26.\u00a2h1 Rdg8 27.\u00d8e6 Wxc4 28.Rhf3 gives White a dangerous attack, for instance:

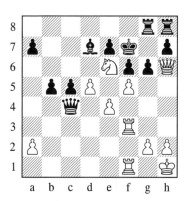

28...b4 (28...\u00a2e8 29.We3! gxf5 30.\u00d8xc5±) 29.R1f2! (29.e5 Wxd5 30.\u00d8g5† fxg5 31.fxg6† \u00a2e8 32.g7 Bb5 33.gxh8=W Rxh8 34.Rg1↑ is also promising for White.) 29...Bc8 30.h3

White can build his attack slowly, as Black has very few active ideas available.

26.\u00d8e6

26.Re3!?, was also possible since 26...bxc4? 27.fxg6† hxg6 28.\u00d8xg6 Rxh6 29.\u00d8xe5† \u00a2e8 30.\u00d8xc4+– gives White a winning position.

26...bxc4

The best chance. Instead 26...Wxe4 27.\u00d8xc5 Wxc4 (27...Wd4† 28.We3 Wxe3† 29.Rxe3 Bxf5 30.Rfe1 Re8 31.cxb5±) 28.\u00d8xd7 Wxd5 29.\u00d8xf6 exf6 30.Rc1± is clearly better for White.

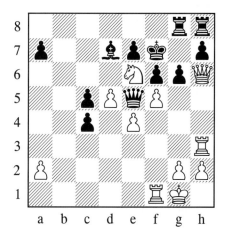

27.Ra3?

A poor choice. Vachier wants to include his rook in the attack from the seventh rank but the idea does not work; presumably he miscalculated something.

27.Rhf3?! was also inaccurate: 27...Wxe4! 28.\u00d8g5† fxg5 29.fxg6† \u00a2e8 30.gxh7 Wxh7 31.Rf8† Rxf8 32.Rxf8† Rxf8 33.Wxh7 Bf5\u221e Black's strong c-pawn gives him enough counterplay, for instance: 34.Wh5† (34.Wg7 Bd3 35.h3 Rf6 36.\u00a2h2 \u00a2d7 37.Wxg5 c3=) 34...\u00a2d7 35.Wf3 g4 36.Wf2 \u00a2d6 37.h3 Rf6 38.hxg4 Be4 39.Wb2 \u00a2xd5 The endgame should be a draw.

The strongest move was:

27.♕d2!

The main point of this subtle retreat is to threaten ♘xc5.

27...♖c8

27...♗xe6?? 28.dxe6† ♔e8 29.♕d7† ♔f8 30.♕d8† ♔g7 31.♕xe7#

27...♕xe4 28.♘xc5 ♕e5 29.♘xd7 ♕d6 30.♘xf6 exf6 31.♖e3± The rook will come to e6 next, causing serious problems for the defence.

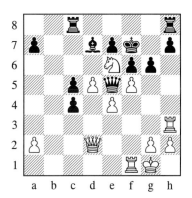

In this position White should once again shift his attention away from the kingside with:

28.♖c3! ♗xe6 29.fxe6† ♔g7 30.♖xc4

White may not be checkmating his opponent now, but he still keeps a considerable advantage.

27...♕xe4!

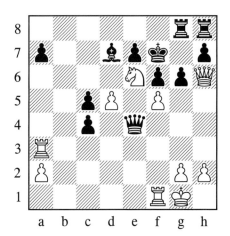

28.♘g5†??

A horrible blunder. The right continuation was 28.fxg6† ♖xg6 (28...hxg6?? 29.♕xh8!+–; 28...♕xg6? 29.♕d2 ♕h5 30.♖e1 a6 31.♘f4 ♕f5 32.♖ae3 ♖e8 33.♖e4±) 29.♘g5† ♖xg5 30.♕xg5 ♖g8 31.♕h5† ♔f8⩱ with a highly unclear position.

By the way, at the end of this line 31...♖g6? would not have been a good idea, as after 32.♕xh7† ♔f8 33.♖g3 ♕d4† 34.♔h1 ♖xg3 35.hxg3 ♕xd5 White has the strong 36.♖b1! ♗e8 37.♖b8± ♕c6 38.♕h3 c3 39.♖c8 ♕b5 40.♔h2 c2 41.♕h8† ♔f7 42.♕h7† with a big advantage.

28...fxg5 29.fxg6† ♔e8 30.♖xa7

Vachier may have overlooked that on 30.g7 Black has 30...♕d4† picking up the pawn.

30...hxg6–+

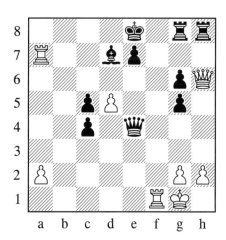

White has no real compensation for the missing piece. He played on for another ten moves in a desperate attempt to confuse his opponent before the time control.

31.♖a8† ♗c8 32.♕xg5 ♔d8 33.d6 ♕d4†
34.♖f2 ♕d1† 35.♖f1 ♕d4† 36.♖f2 ♕d1†
37.♖f1 ♕xd6 38.h3 ♕d4† 39.♔h1 ♖f8
40.♖e1 ♖f6 41.♕g3 ♖hf8
0–1

GAME 38
▷ **A. Salem (2493)**
▶ **I. Cheparinov (2669)**
Biel Open
Round 7, 25.07.2011 **[D90]**
Annotated by Sebastian Maze

In a Grünfeld Defence, Salem tried a novelty with 15.♕c5. In my opinion this move offered White nothing special, and Black equalized easily. In the game Cheparinov played inaccurately and he suffered in the endgame, though he eventually managed to draw. For the readers, I would suggest playing 15.♕h4 or the interesting 15.♖ad1.

1.d4 ♘f6 2.c4 g6 3.♘c3 d5

Cheparinov is a great player and he also plays many openings with Black, so it is quite difficult to prepare against him. In this game he decided to play the Grünfeld, an aggressive opening.

4.♘f3 ♗g7 5.♕a4† ♗d7

5...♘c6 6.♗g5 ♘e4 7.cxd5 ♘xc3 8.bxc3 ♕xd5 9.e3∞ Wojtaszek – Navara, Wijk aan Zee 2011.

6.♕b3 dxc4 7.♕xc4 0–0

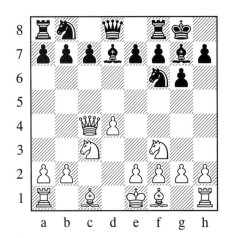

8.♗f4

8.e4 is just about playable, but after the great 8...b5 Black is immediately equal. (8...♘a6!?) 9.♘xb5 ♘xe4 10.♕xc7 ♘c6 11.♗d3 ♘b4 12.♗xe4 ♗xb5= Atalik – Gustafsson, Greece 2003.

8...♘a6 9.e4 c5 10.e5

10.dxc5?! is dubious, as Black gains too much compensation for the pawn with his very active pieces. 10...♖c8 11.e5 ♗e6 12.♕d4 ♕xd4 13.♘xd4 ♘d5 14.♘xd5 ♗xd5 15.♗xa6 bxa6 16.♖c1 f6 Black is fine.

10...♘h5

Inferior is: 10...♗e6?! 11.exf6 ♗xc4 12.fxg7 ♔xg7 13.♗xc4 cxd4 14.♖d1± The three pieces are stronger than the black queen.

11.♗e3 cxd4 12.♕xd4 ♗c6 13.♗e2 ♕a5

13...♗xf3 14.♗xf3 ♕xd4 15.♗xd4 ♘b4 16.0–0–0 White had a small plus in I. Sokolov – Wang Yue, Nakhchivan 2011.

14.0–0 ♘b4

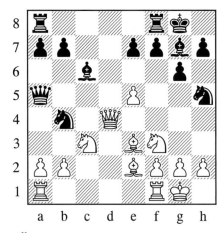

15.♕c5N
And here is the novelty. Well, I'm not sure that Salem prepared this move at home, because it doesn't look so strong and with precise moves, Black's position should be fine.

15.♕h4 ♘c2 16.g4 ♘xe3? (16...♘xa1!?
17.♖xa1 ♕b4∞) 17.fxe3 ♗h6 18.♘d1±
Jakovenko – Topalov, China 2009.

15.♖ad1!? Another novelty. As I see it, this
move needs to be analysed thoroughly.
15...♗xf3 16.♗xf3 ♗xe5 17.♕d7 e6 18.♗xh5
gxh5 19.♕xb7 ♘xa2 20.♘xa2 ♕xa2 21.♗h6
♗g7 22.♗xg7 ♔xg7 23.♕b5±

**15...♕xc5 16.♗xc5 ♘d5 17.♘xd5 ♗xd5
18.♗e3**
18.g3!? was the only way to play for an edge.
18...♖fe8 19.♗e3 f5 20.♖fc1 ♖ec8 21.b3 a6
22.♗d4 ♗h6 Black's position looks OK, but
he will need to play some precise moves to
equalize.

18...f6 19.♖fd1 e6 20.g4 fxe5 21.gxh5
21.♖xd5!? exd5 22.gxh5 gxh5 23.♗d1

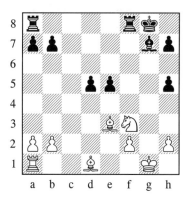

White has two minor pieces against a rook
and one and a half pawns, but Black's strong
centre is enough to secure equality. 23...♔h8
24.♘g5 (24.♔g2 ♖g8 25.♔f1 ♖gf8 26.♔g2=)
24...♖f6 25.♗b3 h6 26.♘h3 ♖d6=

**21...♗xf3 22.♗xf3 ♖xf3 23.hxg6 hxg6
24.♖d7 ♖f7 25.♖ad1 b6 26.♖xf7 ♔xf7
27.♖d7† ♔f6**
So we have an interesting endgame. White is
a pawn down, but has enough compensation
with his very active rook on the seventh rank.

28.h4 ♗f8
Black wants to put his bishop on a better
square. Maybe on c5...

29.♗g5† ♔f5 30.♖f7† ♔e4
The black king is forced away; now the g6-
pawn is weak.

31.♔g2 ♗c5 32.f3†

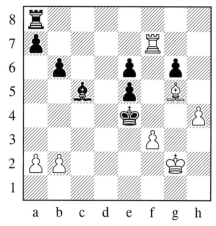

32...♔d5
Black could equalize with: 32...♔d3 33.♖f6
e4 34.fxe4 e5 The point! Now Black's position
is completely fine. 35.♖xg6 ♔xe4 36.h5 ♖h8
37.♖h6 (37.h6 ♔f5 38.♖g7 ♗f8–+) 37...♖g8
38.♖g6 ♖h8 39.♖h6=

**33.♖d7† ♔c4 34.♖g7 ♗d4 35.♖xg6 ♗xb2
36.♗f6**
It was better to push the pawn, and leave
the bishop on g5. After the game move,
Cheparinov will not miss his chance to put
his bishop on the excellent e3-square and then
activate his rook on the second rank.

36.h5 ♖h8 37.h6 ♔d5 38.♖g7 e4 39.♖xa7 ♖f8
40.fxe4† ♔xe4 41.♖a4† ♔d5 42.♗e3±

**36...♗d4 37.♖g4 ♔d5 38.h5 ♗e3 39.♗g7
♖c8**

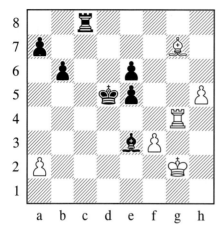

It will be a draw, as the rook will penetrate to c2 and White's king cannot move very far.

40.h6 ♖c2† 41.♔h3 ♖c1 42.♔h2 ♖c2† 43.♖g2 ♗f4† 44.♔h3 ♖xg2 45.♔xg2 ♗xh6 46.♗xh6 e4 47.♔f2

Salem could have tried 47.f4, but Black can draw by force. 47...♔d4 48.♔f1 ♔d3 49.♗g5 e3 50.♔e1 ♔e4 51.♔e2 e5 52.fxe5 ♔xe5 53.♗xe3= The a8-square is white, which we can all see is a different colour from White's bishop!

½–½

GAME 39
▷ **Nguyen Ngoc Truong Son (2637)**
▶ **Li Chao (2669)**
FIDE World Cup 2011, Khanty-Mansiysk
Round 1, Game 2, 29.08.2011 **[D93]**
Annotated by Arkadij Naiditsch

The ♗f4 line against the Grünfeld does not give White any advantage. Even the recent interesting idea with g2-g4 (which is analysed in depth below) does not cause Black any serious problems. Nguyen did manage to get a big advantage after the opening, but only with a lot of help from his opponent; Black could have equalized.

1.d4 ♘f6 2.c4 g6 3.♘c3 d5 4.♗f4 ♗g7

5.e3 c5 6.dxc5 ♕a5 7.♖c1 dxc4 8.♗xc4 0–0 9.♘f3 ♕xc5 10.♗b3 ♘c6 11.0–0 ♕a5

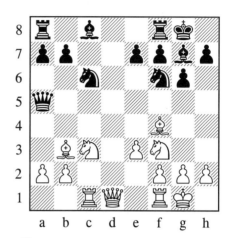

12.♕e2

White's idea in this game is not to lose a tempo by playing the usual h2-h3. So Black switches to a new plan – exchanging the f4-bishop which doesn't have its usual escape square on h2.

12.h3
This is the main move.
12...♗f5 13.♕e2 ♘e4 14.g4
This advance was played recently.
14.♘d5 e5 15.♖xc6 bxc6 16.♘e7† ♔h8
17.♘xc6 ♕b6 18.♘cxe5 ♗e6 is another very old line.
14...♘xc3 15.bxc3 ♗d7
15...♗e4? 16.♘g5 ♗d5 17.c4±
16.♖fd1

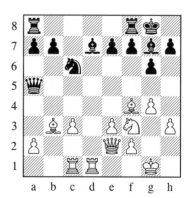

a) 16...♗e8N

Black has the better structure on the queenside. The pawn on g4 is at least not a plus for White and more a potential weakness on the kingside. Black's plan is to improve the position of his pieces with ideas such as ...♕a3, ...♞a5, ...♖c8 and ...♗c6. White has to try to make use of his short-term initiative to create some threats very quickly.

17.♖d5

17.♘d2 ♞e5 18.♘c4 ♞xc4 19.♕xc4 ♗c6 20.♕b4 ♕xb4 21.cxb4=

17.e4 ♖c8 18.♖d5 (18.♕e3 ♕b6 19.♕xb6 axb6 20.♗e3 ♞a5 21.♗xb6 ♞xb3 22.axb3 ♖xc3 23.♖xc3 ♗xc3=; 18.e5 ♞d8 19.♘d4 ♞c6 20.e6 f5∞) 18...♕b6 19.♖b1 ♞a5 (19...a6 transposes to the 17.♖d5 line) 20.♗c2 ♕c6 21.♖xa5 ♕xc3 22.♖xa7 ♕xc2 23.♕xc2 ♖xc2 24.♖bxb7 ♗c6 25.♖xe7 ♗f6 26.♖ec7 ♗xe4 27.♖xc2 ♗xc2 28.a4±

17...♕a3

17...♕b6 18.♖b1 (18.e4 ♞a5 19.♗c2 ♗c6 20.♖b1 ♗xd5 21.♖xb6 ♗c4∞; 18.♖b5 ♕a6 19.♗c4 ♞a5∓) 18...a6 After this move Black keeps the possibility of playing ...♕a7 or ...♗b5 at certain moments. (18...♞d8 19.♞e5↑) 19.e4 (19.♖d7 ♕c5 [19...♔h8 20.♖dd1 ♕c5 21.♗d5 ♖d8 22.c4 b5 23.♖bc1 b4∞] 20.♖xb7 e5 21.♗g3 ♞a5 22.♖b4 ♗b5∞; 19.♘d2 e6 20.♞c4 ♕a7 21.♖dd1 b5 22.♞d6 ♞e5=) 19...♖c8 (19...♗xc3? 20.♖d3 ♕a5 21.e5↑ Black's bishop can get into big trouble on c3) 20.♖d7 e6 (20...♕a7 21.♖xb7 ♕xb7 22.♗xf7† ♖xf7 23.♖xb7 ♖xf4 24.♞g5 h6 25.♞e6 ♖f6 26.♞xg7 ♔xg7 27.♕xa6±) 21.♗e3 (21.♖dd1 ♞a5 22.c4 [22.♗d6 ♗b5 23.c4 ♖fd8 24.cxb5 ♖xd6 25.♖xd6 ♕xd6=; 22.♗a4 ♕c5 23.♗d6 ♕c4 24.♕xc4 ♞xc4 25.♗xf8 ♗xa4 26.♗xg7 ♗xd1 27.♖xd1 ♔xg7 28.♖d7 ♖c5=] 22...♞xb3 23.axb3 ♗c6 24.♗e5 White's idea should be to put pressure on the dark squares, or to provoke a weakness in Black's structure. 24...f6 25.♗d6± White has a great bishop on d6,

and soon c4-c5 and ♞d4 will follow, which will guarantee White some advantage.) 21...♕b5 22.c4 (22.♕xb5 axb5 23.♖xb7 ♞a5 24.♖a7 ♞xb3 25.♖xb3 ♗c6=) 22...♕b4 23.a3 ♕xa3 24.♖xb7 ♞a5 25.♖b6 ♞xb3 26.♖6xb3 ♕a4∞

18.♖b1

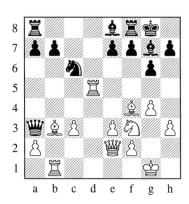

a1) 18...♖c8 19.♞e1 e5 (19...♗xc3 20.♞c2 ♕a6 21.♕xa6 bxa6 22.♖c5 transposes to line a2 18...♗xc3) 20.♗g5 h6 21.♖h4 g5 The e7-square is needed for the black queen. 22.♞c2 ♕e7 23.♗g3 b6 24.e4↑ The white knight is on its way to the d5- or f5-square, which gives White a big advantage.

a2) 18...♗xc3 19.♞e1!?

19.e4 e6 20.♕e3 (20.♗d6 ♗b4 21.♗xf8 ♗xf8 22.♖dd1 ♖c8 Black probably has good compensation for being the exchange down. The bishop pair is going to be strong in the future plus he has an extra pawn and the super-strong dark-squared bishop should make Black feel quite confident about the future. 20.♖d3 ♕a6 21.♕e3 ♗g7 22.♗d6 ♖d8 23.♖bd1 ♖xd6 24.♖xd6 ♕a5∞) 20...exd5 21.♕xc3 ♕b4 22.♕f6 ♕e7 23.♕xe7 ♞xe7 24.exd5∞

19...♖c8

19...♞b4 20.♞c2 ♞xc2 21.♕xc2 ♗g7 22.♕c7 ♕a6 23.♖a5 ♖c8 24.♕xc8 ♕xa5 25.♕xb7 ♕c5 26.e4±

20.♘c2 ♕a6 21.♕xa6

   21.♗c4 b5 22.♖bxb5 ♘e5 23.♖xe5 ♖xc4 24.♕xc4 ♗xe5 25.♖c5 ♕xc4 26.♖xc4 ♗b5=

21...bxa6 22.♖c5 ♗f6 23.♘b4 ♗d7

   23...e5 24.♗h6 ♗e7 25.♖bc1 ♖xc5 26.♖xc5 ♗d7 27.♘d5 ♖fd8 28.♘f6† ♚h8 29.♗xf7± 24.♘d5↑

a3) 18...♘a5 19.♘d4 ♘xb3 20.♖xb3 ♕c1† 21.♔h2

White is playing to trap the black queen.

21...♖c8

   21...♗a4 22.♖xb7 ♗xd4 23.♖xd4 ♗c6 24.♖d1 ♕a3 (24...♕xd1? 25.♕xd1 ♗xb7 26.♕d7+−) 25.♖c7 ♖fc8 26.♖c4±

   21...a6 This keeps open the possibility of ...♗b5 at any moment. 22.♖xb7 ♗xd4 23.♖xd4 ♗c6 24.♖d1 ♕a3 25.♖c7±

22.♘f5

   22.♘e6 fxe6 23.♖d1 ♕xd1 24.♕xd1 ♗a4 25.♕b1 ♗xb3 26.♕xb3 ♖xc3 27.♕xb7 ♔f7=

22...gxf5

   22...♖xc3 23.♖d1 ♖c2 24.♖xc1 ♖xe2 25.♘xe7† ♔h8 26.♖xb7 ♖xf2† 27.♔g3 ♖xa2 28.♖c8+−

23.♖d1 ♕xd1 24.♕xd1 ♗a4 25.gxf5 ♗xb3 26.♕xb3 b6 27.♕a3 ♖c5 28.♕xa7 ♖xf5 29.♕xe7 ♗xc3∞

b) 16...♖ad8 17.♖d5

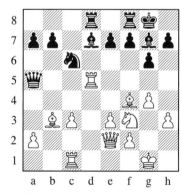

b1) 17...♕b6 18.♖b1

Now Postny – Caruana, European Championship, Aix-les-Bains 2011, continued 18...♗c8 19.♖g5 ♗e6 20.♖b5 ♕a6 21.♗xe6 fxe6 22.♘g5±.

Instead Black should look at:

18...e6!? 19.♖dd1

   19.♗c2 ♕xb1† 20.♗xb1 exd5∞

19...♘a5

   19...♘e7 20.♗g5 ♖fe8 21.♗d5±

   19...♕a5 20.♗g5±

20.♗c2 ♕c6 21.♗d6 ♖fe8 22.♘e5

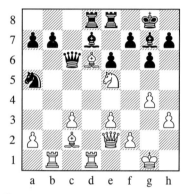

22...♕xc3

   22...♖xe5 23.♗xe5 ♘c4 24.♗f6 ♖c8 25.♗d3±

23.f4

   23.♘xd7 ♖xd7 24.♗a4 ♘c6 25.♖dc1 ♕a5 26.♗xc6 bxc6 27.♖xc6 ♗f8=

23...♖c8

   23...♕c8 24.♖bc1 ♗c6 25.h4 ♗f8 (25...♖xe5 26.fxe5 b6 27.♗d3↑) 26.♗xf8 ♖xf8 27.g5↑

24.♖d2

   24.♗e4 ♗a4 25.♖d3 ♕c2 26.♕e1 ♘c4 27.♖d4 ♕xa2 28.♖a1 ♕b3 29.♖b1 ♕a2=

24...♘c4 25.♘xc4

   25.♖d3 ♕xc2 26.♕xc2 ♘xe5 27.♗c5 ♘xd3 28.♕xd3 ♗a4 29.♕a3 ♗c6=

25...♖xc4 26.♖xb7 ♗c6 27.♖b3 ♕a5 28.♖a3

   28.♕xc4 ♕xd2 29.♕xc6 ♕e1† 30.♔h2 ♕d2† 31.♔g3 ♕e1†=

28...♕b5 29.♔f2 ♖xc2 30.♖xc2 ♕d5 31.♔g3 e5 32.♖d3 exf4† 33.♗xf4 ♕e4 34.♖d6

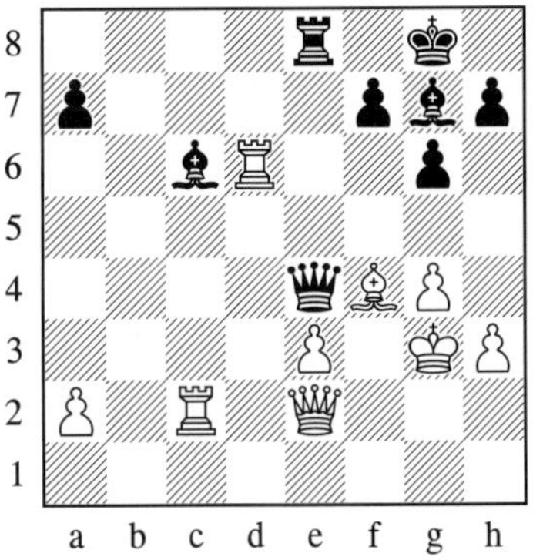

34...g5

34...♗e5 35.♖dxc6 ♗xf4† 36.exf4 ♕xe2 37.♖xe2 ♖xe2 38.♖a6±

35.♖dxc6 gxf4† 36.♔f2 fxe3† 37.♔g1∞

b2) 17...♕a3

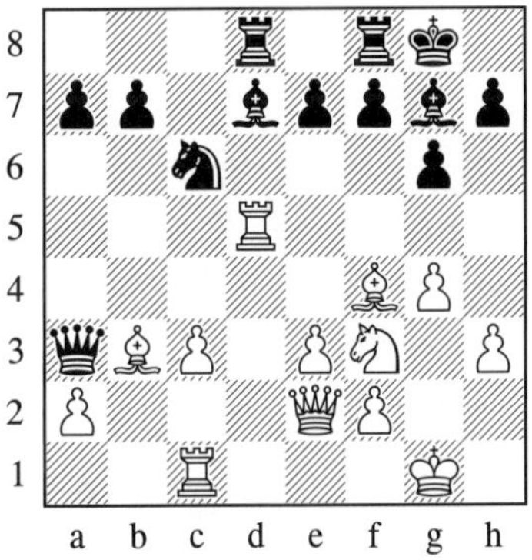

18.♖cd1

18.e4?! e6 (18...♗e6 19.♖xd8 ♘xd8 20.♕b5 ♗xb3 21.axb3 ♘e6 22.♗e3 b6 23.e5 ♖c8∞) 19.♖dd1 ♗c8 20.♘d4 ♘xd4 21.cxd4 ♖xd4 22.♖xd4 ♗xd4 23.♕c4 ♕b2 (23...♖d8 24.♔g2 ♗f6 25.g5 ♗g7 26.♕c7 ♕f8 27.♗e3↑) 24.♖c2 ♕a1† 25.♖c1 ♕b2 26.♖c2 ♕a1†= After 27.♔g2 Black can play on, if he wants, with 27...b6∞.

18...♗e6 19.♖xd8 ♘xd8 20.♕b5 ♗xb3

20...a6 21.♕b6 ♗xb3 22.axb3 is a more accurate move order.

20...b6?! 21.♗e5 ♗xb3 22.axb3 ♘e6 23.♖d7 ♖c8 24.♕b4 ♕xb4 25.cxb4 ♘g5 26.♘xg5 ♗xe5 27.♖xa7 ♗d6 28.♖b7 ♖c6 29.♘f3 ♗xb4 30.♘e5 ♖e6 31.♘d3 ♗c3 32.♘f4 ♖d6 33.♖xe7 ♖d1† 34.♔g2 ♖b1 35.♖b7 ♖xb3 36.♘d5 b5 37.♘xc3 ♖xc3 38.♖xb5± Fridman – Lupulescu, Novi Sad 2009.

21.axb3 a6

21...♗xc3 22.♗h6 (22.♖d7 ♕b4 23.♘d4 ♘c6 24.♕xb4 [24.♖xb7 ♘xd4 25.♕xb4 ♗xb4 26.exd4 a5=] 24...♗xb4 25.♘xc6 bxc6 26.♖xa7 ♗d6 27.♗xd6 exd6 28.♖d7 d5 29.♖c7 ♖b8 30.♖xc6 ♖xb3 31.♖d6 ♖d3 32.♔f1 ♖d1† 33.♔e2 ♖h1=) 22...♗g7 23.♗xg7 ♔xg7 24.♖d7 (24.♕e5† ♔g8 25.♕c7 ♘e6 26.♕xb7 ♖d8 27.♖xd8† ♘xd8 28.♕a8 ♕c1† 29.♔g2 ♕c7 30.♘d4 ♔g7=) 24...♕c1† (24...♕a1† 25.♔g2 ♕f6 26.♕c5 ♘c6 27.♖xb7 ♕d6 28.♕xd6 exd6 29.♖c7 ♘e5 30.♘g5± 1–0 M. Andersen – Wieczorek, Krakow 2011) 25.♔g2 ♕c6 26.♕xc6 (26.♕e5† f6 27.♕d4 ♘e6 28.♕a4 ♔f7 29.♕xc6 bxc6 30.♖xa7=) 26...♘xc6 27.♖xb7 ♖b8 28.♖c7 ♖b6 29.♘d2 (29.♘g5 h6 30.♘e4 ♔f8 31.♘c5 ♔e8 32.♖c8† ♘d8 33.♖a8 ♖b5=) 29...♔f8 30.♘c4 ♖a6 31.g5 ♘a5 32.♘e5 ♘xb3 33.♖c8† ♔g7 34.♘g4 f6 35.♖c7 ♔f8 36.gxf6 exf6 37.♖xh7 ♘c5=

22.♕b6 ♘e6

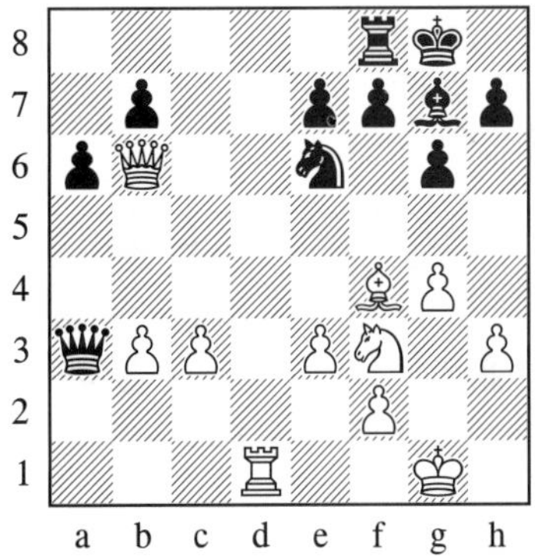

23.c4!?

An interesting try for the advantage, but Black can hold.

23.♗e5 ♗xe5 (23...♕c5?! 24.♕xc5 ♘xc5 25.♗xg7 ♔xg7 26.b4 ♘e4 27.♖d7 ♖b8 28.♖xe7 ♘xc3 29.♖d7 ♔f6 30.♘d4 b6

31.♘c6 ♖f8 32.♖b7 ♘a4 33.♘b8 ♖d8 34.♘xa6 ♔e6 35.♔g2± Dreev – Delchev, Cento 2011.) 24.♘xe5 ♕c5 (24...♕b2 25.♕xb7 ♕c2 26.♖f1 [26.♖d5 ♘g5 27.♕xe7 ♘xh3† 28.♔g2 ♕xf2† 29.♔xh3 ♕xe3† 30.♔h2 ♕f2†=] 26...♕xc3 27.♘c6± Targeting a6 and e7.) 25.♕xc5 (25.♘d7 ♕xb6 26.♘xb6 ♖d8 27.♖xd8† ♘xd8=) 25...♘xc5 26.b4 ♘e4 27.♖d7 Here, Tomashevsky and Svidler agreed a draw; it looks as though Svidler showed how to equalize in this line. 27...f6 28.♘d3 ♔f7 29.c4 (29.♖xb7 ♘xc3 30.♘c5 ♖a8=) 29...♖c8 30.c5 ♖b8 31.♘f4 a5=

23...a5

23...♘c5 24.♖d5 (24.b4 ♘d3 25.♕xb7 ♕b3 26.♖xd3 ♕xd3 27.c5 ♕b1† 28.♔g2 a5∓) 24...♘xb3 25.♖d3 ♕a1† 26.♔g2 ♘a5 27.♕c7 ♕a4 (27...♕b1 28.♖d7 ♘c6 29.♘d2 ♕b4 30.♕xb7 ♕xb7 31.♖xb7 ♖c8 32.c5) 28.♖d7 (28.c5 ♕b5 29.♖d7 ♘c6 30.♕xb7 ♕xb7 31.♖xb7 ♖c8 32.♘d2 This transposes to the 27...♕b1 line.) 28...♘xc4 29.♖xe7 b5 (29...♕c6 30.♕xb7 ♕xb7 31.♖xb7 ♖a8 32.♘g5 h6 33.♘xf7 g5 34.♗g3 a5 35.♘d6 ♘xd6 36.♗xd6 a4 37.♗a3 ♗f8 38.♗b2 a3 39.♗a1 ♖c8 40.♖a7∞) 30.♘g5 ♕a5 (30...♕a2 31.♖e8 ♘d6 32.♖xf8† ♗xf8 33.♗xd6 ♕d5† 34.e4 ♕xg5 35.♕b8 ♕h6 36.e5↑

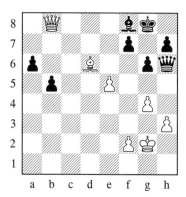

Black can't move, but it is also hard to find a winning plan for White. Probably White

could try to play for a win by bringing his king to the queenside, while carefully avoiding the black queen.) 31.♕a7 ♕b6 32.♖xf7 ♕xa7 33.♖xa7 ♖e8 34.♖xa6 b4 35.♖c6 ♘d2 36.♖b6 b3 37.e4

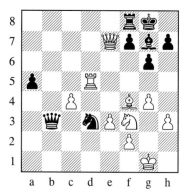

37...b2! 38.♗xd2 ♗e5!= Black will play ...♖b8, forcing White to sac on b2.

24.♕xb7 ♘c5

24...♕b2 creates two ideas: ...a5-a4 and ...♕e2. 25.♕b5 ♕e2 26.♕d5 ♕c2 27.♖d3 ♕b1† 28.♔g2 ♘c5 29.♖d4 ♘xb3 (29...♕xd4 30.exd4 ♘d3 31.♗h6∞) 30.♘d2 25.♕xe7 ♕xb3 26.♖d5 ♘d3

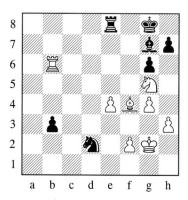

27.♗g3

White had a good chance: 27.♗d6! And now 27...♕b1† 28.♔g2 ♕c2 29.♖xd3 ♕xd3 30.♕c7 ♕e4 31.♗xf8 ♗xf8 32.♕xa5 ♕xc4 33.♘d4± or 27...♕xc4 28.♕b7 ♕c2 29.♖xd3 ♕xd3 30.♗xf8 ♗xf8 31.♘e5 ♕d1† 32.♔g2 ♕d8 33.♕xf7† ♔h8 34.♕e6±.

27...a4 28.♖d8 h6 29.♘e5 ♕b1† 30.♔g2
♘e1† 31.♔h2 ♖xd8 32.♕xd8† ♔h7 33.♕d5
a3 34.♘d7 a2 35.♗e5 ♗xe5† 36.♘xe5 ♕b8
37.♕xf7† ♔h8 38.♕f6† ♔g8 39.♕xg6† ♔h8
40.♕xh6† ♔g8 41.♕g6† ♔h8 42.♕f6† ♔g8
43.f4 ♕b7=

Mamedyarov – Sutovsky, Bursa 2010.

12...♘h5

12...♗f5 is another option.

13.♗g5

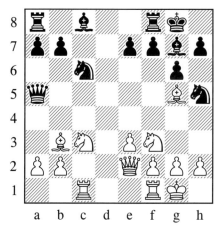

13...♗g4

This clearly looks more solid than the
plan with ...h6 and ...g5, which creates huge
weaknesses on the kingside.

13...h6 14.♗h4 g5

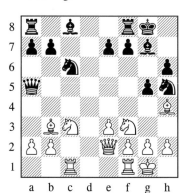

15.♖fd1!

Black will eventually exchange the white
bishop, but after ...h6 and ...g5 the black
king feels a bit unsafe. The knight on h5 is
currently out of play and Black still needs to
finish developing his queenside.

15.♘xg5? looks nice, but it doesn't work:
15...hxg5 16.♕xh5 gxh4 17.♘d5 ♕d8
18.♖c4 (18.♖fd1 e6∓; 18.♘f4 ♕d7 with
the idea of ...♕g4) 18...♗f5 19.♘f6† ♗xf6
20.♕xf5 e6 21.♕h5 ♘e5 22.♖e4 ♘g6
23.♗xe6 ♔g7∓

15...♗g4!?

15...e6 16.♗g3 ♘xg3 17.hxg3±

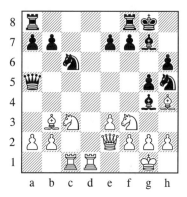

16.♖d5

16.h3 ♗e6 By provoking h2-h3, Black takes
away from White the normal possibility
after ♗g3 ...♘xg3 of taking with the h-pawn
on g3. 17.♗xe6 fxe6 18.♗g3 (18.♕c4
♕f5 19.♗g3 ♘xg3 20.fxg3 ♘e5 21.♘xe5
♕xe5=) 18...♘xg3 19.fxg3 ♖ac8∞) 16...♕b4
17.♗xg5 hxg5 18.♖b5 (18.♖xg5 ♘f6 19.h3
♗xf3 20.♕xf3 ♕h4∓) 18...♕d6 18...♗xf3
19.♕xf3 ♕h4 20.g3 ♕h3 21.♖xg5 ♘f6
22.♘e4 ♘xe4 23.♕xe4 ♖ad8 24.♖cc5→

19.♖xg5 ♘f6

19...♘e5 20.♘e4 ♕d3 21.♕xd3 ♘xd3
22.♖d1 ♘e5 23.♘xe5 ♗xd1 24.♗xd1 ♘f6
25.♘c3∞

20.h3 ♗xf3 21.♕xf3

In this very interesting position White is
probably better.

14.♗h4

14.♘d5 e6 15.♘e7† ♔h8 16.♘xc6 ♕xg5=

14...♕b4

Black is still playing for his basic idea – to exchange White's h4-bishop for a knight.

14...g5!? was also an option.

14...♖ad8 15.h3 (15.♘e4) 15...♗xf3 16.♕xf3 ♗f6 17.♗xf6 ♘xf6 18.♖fd1 ♔g7 19.♘d5∞

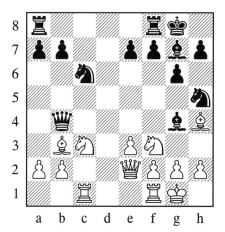

15.♕c4

White can use the same square for a different piece:
15.♗c4 ♖ad8
15...♘e5 16.♘d5±
16.a3
16.♘d5 ♖xd5 17.♗xd5 ♗xf3 18.♗xf3 ♕xh4 19.♕b5∞ Another very interesting position. Black has two pieces against the rook, but the pawns on a7 and b7 are under pressure, as the black queen and knight are far from the queenside and unable to help them.
16...♕a5 17.b4 ♕xa3
17...♕f5 18.h3 ♗xf3 19.♕xf3 ♕xf3 20.gxf3 ♗f6 21.♗xf6 ♘xf6 22.f4 With a small advantage for White. White's next idea to improve his position could be to transfer the bishop to the long diagonal h1-a8.
18.♘d5 ♖fe8

18...e6 19.♘e7†±
19.♘c7 ♖f8
19...♘e5 20.♘xe8 ♗xf3 21.gxf3 ♖d2 22.♘xg7 ♖xe2 23.♗xe2 ♔xg7 24.♗xe7±
20.♘d5 ♖fe8 21.♖c2 ♘xb4 22.♘xe7†
22.♘xb4 ♕xb4 23.♗xf7† ♔xf7 24.♖c4 ♕b3 25.♘g5† ♔g8 26.♕xg4 ♖d6∞
22...♔h8 23.♖d2 ♗f6 24.♗xf7 ♗xh4 25.♗xe8 ♖xe8 26.♘xg6† hxg6 27.♕b5 ♗f2† 28.♖dxf2 ♘c6∞

15...♗xf3?!

Better was the simple:
15...♕xc4
It is hard to see where White planned to find an advantage in this endgame, as it looks very equal.
16.♗xc4 ♖fd8
16...♗xf3 17.gxf3 ♗f6 18.♗xf6 ♘xf6 19.♘d5 ♖fd8 20.♘xf6† exf6 21.♖fd1 ♖ac8 22.♗d5 ♔f8 23.♗xc6 ♖xd1† 24.♖xd1 ♖xc6 25.♖d7 ♖b6 26.b3 ♖a6 ½–½ Yusupov – Leko, Essen 2002.
16...♖ad8 17.♗b5 ♗xf3 18.gxf3 ♗f6 19.♗xf6 ♘xf6 20.♗xc6 bxc6 21.♖c2±
17.♘g5 ♘e5 18.♘d5
18.♗b3 h6 19.♘ge4 ♘d3 20.♗xe7 ♖d7∓

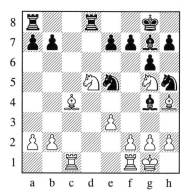

18...♗f8
18...♘f6 19.♘xe7† ♔f8 20.f3 ♘xc4 (20...♘h5 21.♗b3 ♔xe7 22.g4↑) 21.fxg4 ♘xe3 22.♖xf6 ♗xf6 23.♘xh7† ♔e7 24.♗xf6† ♔e6 25.♗xd8 ♖xd8 26.♘g5† ♔f6 27.h4±

18...罝d7 19.桌b3 桌e2 20.罝fe1 ⑤d3 21.罝c7 罝xc7 22.⑤xc7 ⑤xe1 23.桌xf7† 含h8 24.⑤xa8 桌xb2 25.桌b3± There are still many pieces on the board, so the black king will continue worrying about his health.

19.桌b3 h6 20.f3 hxg5

20...桌f5 21.⑤xf7 ⑤xf7 22.g4 g5 23.gxf5 gxh4 24.罝c7 含h8 25.⑤xe7 桌xe7 26.罝xe7∞

21.fxg4 gxh4 22.gxh5 罝ac8

22...e6 23.⑤f6† 含g7 24.桌xe6↑

23.罝xc8 罝xc8 24.hxg6 ⑤xg6 25.罝xf7 含xf7 26.⑤b6† e6 27.⑤xc8 桌c5 28.含f2 ⑤e7=

16.營xb4 ⑤xb4 17.桌xe7 ⑤xa2?

This is a mistake. Black was already worse but much stronger was:

17...桌xc3

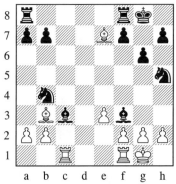

a) 18.罝xc3 ⑤d5 19.桌xf8 (19.桌xd5 桌xd5 20.桌xf8 含xf8 21.罝d1 桌c6 22.f3 White's idea is to play f3 and e4 to reduce the activity of the black bishop and improve his king by playing 含f2-e3. This position is close to equal.) 19...⑤xc3 20.桌h6 ⑤e2† 21.含h1 桌g4 22.罝e1 罝c8 23.h3 ⑤f6 24.f3 桌xf3 25.gxf3 ⑤c1 26.罝d1 ⑤xb3 27.axb3 With an advantage to White because of the unsafe position of the black king on the 8th rank, which is not an easy trap to get out of. White has many different ways to improve his position. For example, e4 and 含g2-f2-e3 after which Black would be close to lost.

b) 18.gxf3 罝fe8 (18...桌xb2 19.桌xf8 罝xf8

20.罝c7 ⑤a6 21.罝xb7 ⑤c5 22.罝xa7 ⑤xb3 23.axb3 罝b8 24.罝d1 ⑤f6 25.罝d3±) 19.桌d6 罝ad8 20.罝fd1 桌xb2 21.罝c7 罝xd6 22.桌xf7† 含f8 23.罝xd6 桌e5 24.桌b3 桌xd6 25.罝f7† 含g8 26.罝e7† 含f8=

c) 18.桌xf8 含xf8 19.bxc3 (19.gxf3 桌e5 20.罝fd1 ⑤c6 21.罝d7 ⑤d8 The knight on d8 is very strong because it protects both of the weak pawns on f7 and b7. 22.f4 桌xb2 23.罝cc7 ⑤f6 24.罝d2 桌a1 25.罝d1 桌b2=) 19...⑤d3 20.gxf3 ⑤xc1 21.罝xc1 罝c8 22.含f1 White has a clear extra pawn, but it is not easy to win this position. Black's idea is to play ...含e7, ...⑤f6-d7 and typically ...罝c5. The rook will go along the fifth rank with ...罝h5 and press against the h2-pawn or perhaps ...罝a5 and ...⑤c5 playing against the pawns on a2 and c3. Black will always have some counterplay.

18.桌xa2

18.⑤xa2 罝fe8 19.罝c7 桌g4 (19...桌e5 20.桌d6 桌xd6 21.桌xf7 桌e2 22.罝e1 桌g4 23.罝f6† 桌e6 24.罝xe6 罝xe6 25.桌xe6†±) 20.桌a3 桌e6 21.罝xb7 罝eb8 22.罝xb8† 罝xb8 23.桌xe6 fxe6 24.罝b1± White's plan is ⑤c1-d3 and 含f1-e2.

18...罝fe8 19.桌a3 桌xc3

19...桌c6 20.⑤d5 罝ac8 21.⑤e7† 罝xe7 22.桌xe7 桌xb2 23.罝c2±

20.gxf3 桌a5 21.桌d5 罝ab8 22.罝fd1±

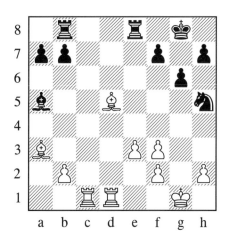

White has a big advantage due to his bishop pair and excellent centralization.

22...♗b6 23.♔f1

23.♗d6 ♖bd8 24.♗xb7? ♖xe3=

23...♖ed8

23...♘g7 24.♗d6 ♖bd8 25.♗xb7 ♘f5 26.♗f4± This last move stops Black gaining any extra chances with a sacrifice on e3.

24.♗e7 ♖dc8 25.f4

Already White could win a pawn, but exact calculation was needed: 25.♖xc8† ♖xc8 26.♗xb7 ♖c2 (26...♖c7 27.♖d8† ♔g7 28.♗f8† ♔f6 29.♖d6† ♔g5 30.♗c6+–) 27.♖d7 (27.b4±) 27...♖xb2 28.♗d5 ♖b1† 29.♔e2 ♖b2† 30.♔d3 ♖xf2 31.♖b7+– Black cannot avoid disaster on the 7th rank.

25...♖xc1 26.♖xc1 ♔g7 27.♗f3 ♘f6 28.♗b4

After 28.♗d6 ♖d8 29.♗e5 ♖d7 30.♖c8 the b7-pawn is falling.

28...♖d8

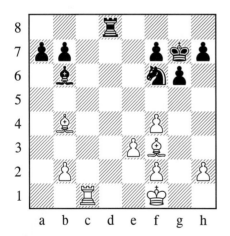

29.♗xb7!

A good move by White! Nice concrete play. 29.♗c3 ♖d7 Finally Black manages to put his rook on the 7th rank. 30.♗e5 ♗d8 (30...♖e7 31.♖c8 g5 32.♖b8 gxf4 33.♗xf4 ♘e4

34.♗xe4 ♖xe4 35.♖xb7±) 31.♖c8 ♗e7 32.♖a8 ♗c5 33.b4 ♗xb4 34.♖xa7 ♗c5 35.♖xb7 ♖xb7 36.♗xb7±

29...♖b8 30.♗f3 ♖xe3 31.♖c4 ♗b6 32.♗c3 ♖d8 33.b4

33.♖c6? ♗d4=

33...♖d6 34.♗e5 ♖d2 35.♗e2 h5 36.♖c6

Black is helpless against the pin, especially after the exchange of the pawns on b7 and e3, which gave White an extra attacking square for the rook on c6.

36...♗d8 37.b5 ♖d7 38.h3

Black's position is hopeless. Only the black rook can move, which of course leads nowhere.

38...♖d5 39.♗c4 ♖d7 40.♔e2 h4 41.♔e3 ♗b6† 42.♔f3 ♗d8 43.♔e2 ♗e7 44.♗b3 ♗d8 45.♗c2 ♖d5 46.♗d3+–

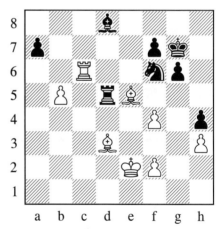

White has no reason to hurry. He can enjoy his domination for a while and try to put all his pieces on their perfect squares before the final action.

46...♗e7 47.♔d2 g5 48.♔c3 gxf4 49.♗d4 ♖d7 50.♔c4 ♗d6 51.♗f5 ♖c7 52.♖xc7 ♗xc7 53.♗xa7 ♔h6 54.b6 ♗e5 55.b7 ♔g5 56.♗c8 f3 57.♔d3
1–0

GAME 40
▷ **A. Morozevich (2694)**
▶ **M. Vachier Lagrave (2722)**
Accentus GM Tournament, Biel
Round 7, 26.07.2011 **[D97]**
Annotated by Sebastian Maze

Here the two players do battle in a Grünfeld Defence, from opposite sides of the board compared with the earlier D86 encounter. Morozevich shows his patriotism by opting for the Russian System, and Vachier-Lagrave responds with the rare 8...e5. A few moves later White opted for 12.d6, but I believe that 12.♕c4 would have been more challenging. In the game Black played a novelty in 12...♖e8 which gave him a satisfactory position, but two moves later the French player made a strategic error and Morozevich never let him back into the game.

1.d4 ♘f6 2.c4 g6 3.♘c3 d5
The Grünfeld is Vachier-Lagrave's favourite opening against 1.d4.

4.♘f3 ♗g7 5.♕b3 dxc4
5...c6?! is passive and White easily obtains a pleasant position. 6.cxd5 cxd5 (6...♘xd5 7.e4 ♘xc3 8.bxc3 0–0 9.♗e2±) 7.♗g5 e6 8.e3± Black's bishop does not belong on g7 in positions with this central structure.

6.♕xc4 0–0 7.e4

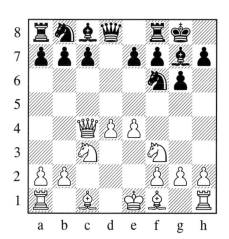

7...♘c6
One of the main alternatives is:
7...a6
7...♘a6 and 7...♗g4 are also popular.
8.e5 b5 9.♕b3 ♘g4
I am not a big fan of this move, as the knight might find itself in trouble on h6.
Best is 9...♘fd7, which can be found in the next game (Morozevich – Svidler).
10.h3 ♘h6 11.♗f4 c5

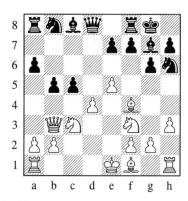

12.dxc5!
Better than 12.♖d1 cxd4 13.♘xd4 ♖a7!N (13...♕a5 14.♗d3 ♗b7 15.0–0±) 14.♘c6 ♘xc6 15.♖xd8 ♖xd8 16.♗e3 ♗e6 17.♕c2 ♘d4 18.♗xd4 ♖xd4 with a complicated position where it seems to me that Black is perfectly fine.
12...♗e6 13.♕c2±
Zakhartsov – Stambulian, Krasnodar 2001.

8.♗e2
8.♗f4 is less accurate: 8...♘d7 (8...♘h5?! 9.♗e3 ♗g4 10.0–0–0 gave White a good initiative in Markus – Lupulescu, Subotica 2009) 9.♘d5 ♘b6 10.♘xb6 axb6 11.d5 ♘a5 12.♕xc7 ♕xc7 13.♗xc7 ♗xb2=

8...e5!?
This move has been a rare guest at high levels, but this might change in the future as it seems to offer Black interesting counterplay.
The main line is 8...♗g4 when one recent

game continued: 9.d5 ♘a5 10.♕b4 ♗xf3
11.♗xf3 c6 12.0–0 ♕b6 13.♕a4∞ Giri –
Swinkels, Netherlands 2011.

9.d5

A logical answer. Instead 9.dxe5 ♘g4
10.♘d5 ♗e6 11.0–0 ♘gxe5 12.♘xe5 ♘xe5
13.♕xc7 ♗xd5 14.♕xd8 ♖axd8 15.exd5 ♖xd5
16.♗e3 is equal.

9...♘d4

This pawn sacrifice was the idea behind
Black's eighth move. The point is to open the
centre and of course the long diagonal.

10.♘xd4 exd4 11.♕xd4 c6

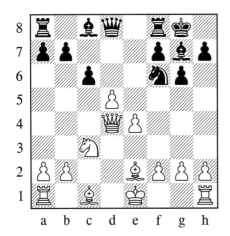

12.d6

A natural reply, but it does not seem to
bring White any advantage against correct
play. Therefore I propose the following
improvement:
12.♕c4!

Removing the queen from the long diagonal
while maintaining the pawn on d5, in order
to prevent the black bishop from coming to
e6.
12...cxd5 13.exd5 ♗f5 14.0–0 ♖c8 15.♕b3
♘e4 16.♘xe4 ♗xe4 17.♗f3 ♗xf3 18.♕xf3
♕d7
18...♕f6 19.♕xf6 ♗xf6 20.♖d1 ♖c2 21.♖b1

a6 22.a4 ♖d8 23.b3±
18...♖e8 19.♖d1 ♖c2 20.♕d3 ♖ce2 21.♗e3
♖xb2 22.d6±
19.♖b1 a6 20.♗f4±
White keeps an extra pawn and can play for
a win without taking any risks.

12...♖e8!

A logical and promising novelty. Apart from
threatening to take on e4 with the knight,
Black also prepares to put his rook on e6 to
capture the d-pawn.

Previously Black had tried 12...♘d5?! but
after 13.♕d3 ♘xc3 14.bxc3 ♕f6 15.♗b2 ♖d8
16.♖d1 White kept his extra pawn and a clear
advantage in Carlsen – Dominguez, Sofia
2009.

13.♕d3 b5 14.f3

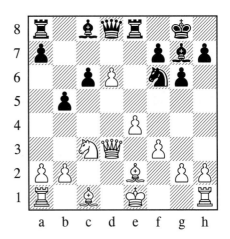

14...b4?

An important strategic error. The knight
on c3 has no future, so Black should be in no
hurry to drive it away. His last move also gives
the white pieces an excellent outpost on c4.

14...♖e6 was better, for instance 15.0–0
(15.d7 ♕xd7 16.♕xd7 ♘xd7 17.♗e3 ♖e8
18.0–0 a5=) 15...♖xd6 16.♕c2 ♕b6† 17.♔h1
♕c5 18.a3 a5= and Black equalizes easily.

15.♘d1 ♖e6 16.♕c2 ♘h5

16...♖xd6 17.♗f4 ♖d7 18.♗e3 ♗b7 19.0–0
♘e8 20.♘f2 ♘c7 21.♖fd1 ♘e6 22.♖xd7 ♕xd7
23.♖d1 ♘d4 24.♗c4 c5 25.♕d2±

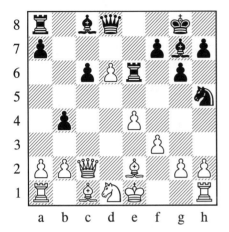

17.♗e3±

There was no sense in risking 17.♕xc6? ♗d7
18.♕c7 ♕e8 19.♗e3 ♗e5 20.g3 ♗xd6 21.♕a5
♖e5 when Black has strong counterplay and
the white queen is uncomfortable.

After the text move White has a pleasant
advantage, as Black's queenside is weak and the
knight on h5 is not doing much.

17...♗e5 18.g3 ♖xd6 19.♕c5

19.♗c5?! allows 19...♗d4! 20.♗xd6 ♕xd6
21.♘f2 c5 with good compensation for Black.

19...♗d4 20.♗xd4

20.♕xb4! c5 21.♕a3 ♕f6 22.0–0 ♗h3
23.♖f2 ♖ad8 24.f4 would have given White a
larger advantage.

20...♖xd4 21.♘e3 ♗e6?

A bad decision from Maxime. Instead the
e6-square should have been reserved for the
knight.

21...♘g7!

This was the only way to stay in the game.

22.♕xc6 ♗d7 23.♕b7!

Alternatives are less challenging:

23.♕a6? ♘e6 24.♘d5 (24.♖c1 ♕g5 25.♔f2
♘c5 26.h4 ♕e5∓) 24...♖c8 25.♕b5 a6
26.♕c6 ♖b8 27.♗xa6 ♖xd5 28.exd5 ♘d4∓
After 23.♕c2 ♖c8 24.♗c4 ♗h3 Black's well-
coordinated pieces will give White some
problems.

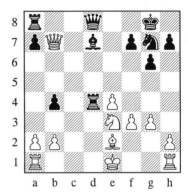

23...♘e6 24.♘d5 ♘c5 25.♕c7 ♕xc7 26.♘xc7
♖c8

Black's activity gives him decent practical
compensation, notwithstanding the queen
exchange.

27.♘d5 ♔g7 28.♖d1

28.♔f2 ♖d2 29.♔e3 ♖xb2 30.♖hb1 ♖xb1
31.♖xb1 a5=

28...♖xd1† 29.♔xd1 f5 30.exf5 ♗xf5 31.♘e3
♗e6 32.b3 ♖d8† 33.♔e1 a5

Black is still worse, but he has good drawing
chances.

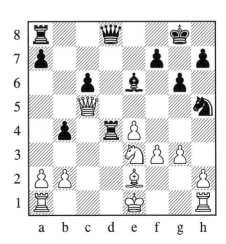

22.♘c2! ♖d2

22...♖d7 23.♘xb4 ♕f6 24.♕c3 ♕xc3†
25.bxc3 c5 26.♘d3± and 22...♖d6 23.♘xb4
♕f8 24.♖c1 a5 25.e5 ♖d7 26.♘xc6± are both
excellent for White.

23.♘xb4 ♖xb2 24.♕c3 ♖xb4 25.♕xb4±

Black has sacrificed an exchange with some
vague hopes of impeding White's castling, but
the idea is woefully inadequate and Morozevich
easily solves the problem of coordinating his
pieces.

**25...♖b8 26.♕c3 ♕b6 27.a3 ♗h3 28.♗f1
♗e6 29.♖d1 ♕c7 30.♔f2 ♖b3 31.♕d4 ♖xa3
32.♕d8†**

After the queen exchange the game will be
over as a contest. Black struggles on for a few
more moves before resigning.

**32...♕xd8 33.♖xd8† ♔g7 34.♗e2 ♘f6
35.♖c1 ♖a2 36.♗e3 a5 37.♖d2 ♖a3† 38.♖d3
♖a2 39.♖xc6 a4 40.♖cc3 ♘d7 41.♖a3 ♖b2
42.♖d2 ♖b4 43.♖d4**
1–0

GAME 41
▷ **A. Morozevich (2694)**
▶ **P. Svidler (2739)**
64th Russian Championship, Moscow
Round 7, 15.08.2011 **[D97]**
Annotated by Kamil Miton

In recent years the biggest challenge for White
in the ♕b3 Grünfeld has been the plan with
7...a6 followed by ...b5 and later ...c5.
Morozevich decided to try an unusual
approach with 10.♗e2. I don't know if it came
as a surprise for Svidler, but his reaction was
correct and he obtained a decent position.
Later he blundered and lost the game, but in
my opinion it was the first and the last time
that Moro used this option on move 10.

**1.d4 ♘f6 2.c4 g6 3.♘c3 d5 4.♘f3 ♗g7
5.♕b3 dxc4 6.♕xc4 0–0 7.e4 a6 8.e5 b5
9.♕b3 ♘fd7 10.♗e2!?**

The overwhelming majority of games have
featured one of the three main lines of 10.♗e3,
10.e6 and 10.h4.

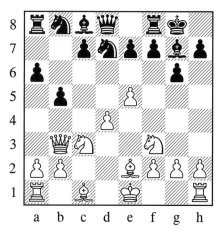

10...c5 11.e6 fxe6

Apart from this move Black had two other
interesting options:

11...c4 12.exf7† ♖xf7 13.♕d1
After 13.♕c2 ♘b6 14.♕e4 ♗f5 15.♕h4
the white queen has arrived at a good
square, but the manoeuvre has cost several
tempos. 15...♘c6! 16.♘g5 h5 17.♘xf7
♔xf7 18.0–0 ♘xd4 Black has carried out
a typical exchange sacrifice, obtaining fine
compensation in the form of his extra pawn
and active pieces.
13...♘b6
One of the main theoretical variations of the
Russian System features the move h2-h4 in
this position instead of ♗f1-e2.
14.a4!?
Undermining the c4-pawn is a logical idea.
14.h4?! is of course too slow now: 14...♘c6
15.h5 ♘xd4 16.♘xd4 ♕xd4 17.♗e3 ♕xd1†
18.♖xd1 ♖b8 19.♖d8† ♖f8∓
14.0–0 is possible, although after 14...♘c6
15.♘g5 ♖f8 16.♗f3 ♘xd4 17.♗xa8 ♘xa8

18.♗e3 ♗f5 Black has good play for the exchange.

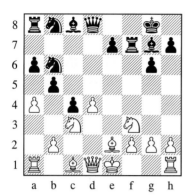

14...b4

14...♘c6 15.axb5 ♘xd4 16.♘xd4 ♗xd4 17.♗f3±

15.a5 bxc3

After 15...♘d5 16.♘e4 ♗f5 17.♘c5± the c4-pawn is weak.

16.axb6 cxb2 17.♗xb2 ♕xb6 18.♗c3±

11...cxd4!?

With this interesting move Black sacrifices a piece in return for two central pawns and the initiative.

12.exd7

After 12.exf7† ♔h8 13.♘e4 ♘c6 14.h4 h6 15.h5 g5 16.♗xg5 ♘de5 Black should be fine, as pointed out by Maze.

12...♘xd7 13.♘e4 ♗b7

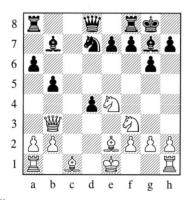

14.♕d3

14.♗d3 ♖c8 15.0-0 ♗xe4 16.♗xe4 ♘c5 17.♕d5 e6 18.♕xd8 ♖fxd8⊒

14.♘fd2 ♘e5 15.0-0 d3 16.♗d1 ♖c8∞

14...d5!

Taking control of the a2-g8 diagonal in preparation for ...f5 and ...e5.

15.♗d1

15.♘xd4? ♗xe4 16.♕xe4 ♘c5-+

15...f5!? 16.♗b3 e6 17.♗xd5 exd5

Black retains adequate compensation even with damaged pawns.

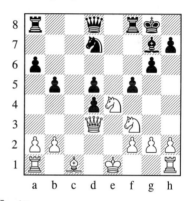

18.♘ed2

18.♘eg5 ♘c5 19.♕d1 h6 20.♘h3 ♕e7† 21.♔f1 g5 22.♘xd4 ♖ae8 23.♘b3 f4→

18.♘g3 ♘c5 19.♕c2 ♕e7† 20.♔f1 d3 21.♕d1 ♖ae8 22.♘b3

22.g3 f4 23.g4 ♘e4↑

22...♕e2† 23.♕xe2 dxe2† 24.♔e1 ♘d3† 25.♔d2 ♘xf2 26.♖e1

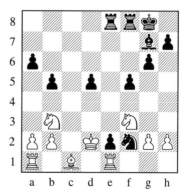

26...♗h6†! 27.♔c2 ♗g7!

Threatening ...♖e4 followed by ...d4-d3, so White has nothing better than...

28.♔d2=

Repeating the position.

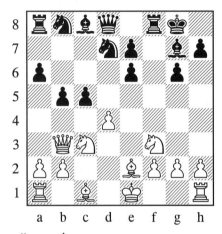

12.♕xe6† ♔h8 13.dxc5

13.♕d5 cxd4 14.♘xd4 ♘b6 15.♕xd8 ♖xd8=

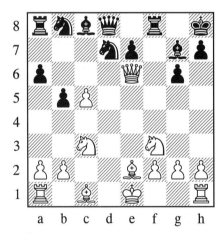

13...♘e5

13...b4?! does not really work for Black: 14.♘e4 ♘xc5?! (14...♘e5 15.♕b3 ♘xf3† 16.♗xf3 ♘c6 17.♗e3 ♘d4 18.♗xd4 ♕xd4 19.0-0 ♕xb2 20.♖xb2 ♗xb2 21.♖ab1 ♗a3 22.♘d2±) 15.♕c4 ♘xe4 16.♕xe4 ♖a7 17.0-0±

13...♘xc5!?

An interesting and complicated possibility.

14.♕e3 ♘bd7 15.0-0

15.h4!? ♗b7 16.h5 ♕b6 17.hxg6 ♕xg6 18.♔f1∞

15...♗b7

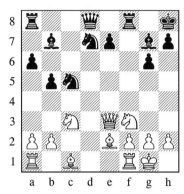

White's trumps include a better pawn structure and attacking ideas based on ♘g5, as Black's e6-, f7- and h7-squares are all a bit vulnerable. On the other hand Black has an open f-file and his minor pieces are very active.

White has two main candidate moves which we will consider in turn.

a) 16.♖d1 e6!

Simple and strong. Black is preparing the ...b4 advance.

The immediate 16...b4 is met by 17.♘d5±.

16...♕c7 is possible, but after 17.b4! ♘a4 (17...♘e4 18.♘xe4 ♗xa1 19.♘eg5→) 18.♘xa4 ♗xa1 19.♘g5 White has good attacking chances.

17.b4

17.♘g5 ♕f6=

17...♘a4

Now the critical continuation is:

18.♘xa4!

18.♗d2 ♘b2! gives Black excellent play.

18...♗xa1 19.♘c5 ♗d5 20.♘xe6 ♗xe6 21.♕xe6 ♖e8 22.♕d5 ♖xe2 23.♘g5

White has sacrificed a rook for a dangerous attack, but Black can obtain a safe position by returning the material.

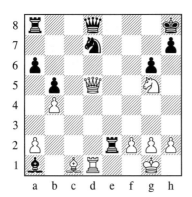

23...♘e5! 24.♕xd8† ♖xd8 25.♖xd8† ♔g7 26.♔f1 ♖xa2=

b) 16.♘g5

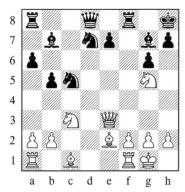

From this point, aside from the weak 16...♖c8? 17.b4±, Black has three notable options.

b1) 16...b4 17.♘ce4 ♘xe4 18.♘xe4 ♘e5!

Black has a dubious pawn structure and numerous weak squares, but these negatives are balanced by his active pieces and better development.

Playable but uninspiring is: 18...♕b6 19.♕xb6 ♘xb6 20.♘c5 ♗d5 21.♘xa6 b3! (21...♗c4 22.♗xc4 ♘xc4 23.♘xb4 ♘xb2 24.♗g5±) 22.axb3 ♗xb3 23.♗g5 ♖f5 24.♗xe7 ♖e8 25.♗c5 ♖xe2 26.♗xb6 ♗xb2 27.♖ab1 ♔g8 28.♗e3± Black's bishop pair, combined with the limited material remaining on the board, should enable him

to draw the endgame a pawn down, although it will not be much fun for him.

19.♘c5

Also possible is: 19.♘g5 h6 20.♕h3 (20.♖d1 ♕c8 20.♘e6?? ♕d5–+) 20...♕c8! It is useful for Black to exchange his opponent's active queen. 21.♕xc8 (21.♘e6 ♖f6 22.♘xg7 ♕xh3 23.gxh3 ♗f3=) 21...♖fxc8 22.♘e6 ♗f6 23.♗xh6

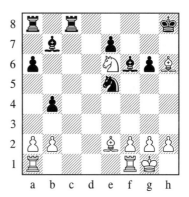

23...♗d5! (23...♖c2?! 24.♗d1! ♖xb2 25.♗c1±) 24.♘d4 (24.♘f4 ♗f7 leaves the bishop on h6 in danger) 24...g5! (24...♘c4 25.♘c2 a5 26.♖ad1 ♗e4 27.♘e3 ♘xb2∞) 25.♗xg5 ♗xg5 26.f4 ♗h6 27.♘f5 ♘f7 28.♘xe7 ♖c2 29.♘xd5 ♖xe2 30.♖f2 ♖xf2 31.♔xf2 ♖d8 It is White who will have to play accurately to draw.

19...♗d5 20.♖d1 ♕d6

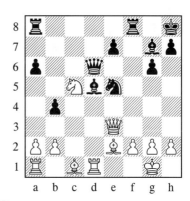

21.f4

21.♗d2 and 21.a3 should both be met by 21...♕c6.

21.♘xa6 e6 22.♘c5 ♕c6 is fine for Black, as
23.f3? runs in to 23...♗xf3!.

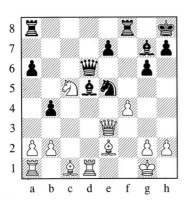

21...♘d7

21...♖ac8 22.fxe5 ♕xc5 23.♗xa6 ♖c7
24.♕xc5 ♖xc5 reaches an endgame in which
Black's active pieces give him good chances
to hold the position a pawn down.
22.♗f3 ♘f6 23.a3 a5 24.axb4 axb4 25.♖xa8
♖xa8 26.♘e6 ♖c8

26...♖a1 27.♘xg7 ♔xg7 28.g4±

27.f5 gxf5 28.♘xg7 f4 29.♘f5 fxe3 30.♘xd6
exd6 31.♗xe3 ♗xf3 32.gxf3 d5

White has the more pleasant side of this
endgame, but the reduced material makes a
draw the most likely outcome.

b2) 16...h6

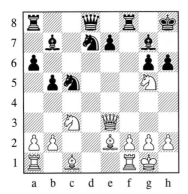

17.b4!?

Plunging the game into complications.
17.♘e6 is playable but Black little to fear.
17...♘xe6 18.♕xe6 ♘f6 White has two ideas:

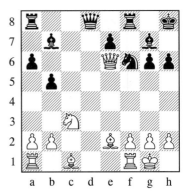

i) 19.♗e3 ♕d7! (19...b4 20.♘a4 ♕d5
21.♕h3) 20.♕xd7 ♘xd7 21.♖fd1 ♘f6 Black
has a worse structure but his bishops are
excellent, and overall the position is equal.

ii) 19.♖d1 ♕c7 20.♗e3 b4! Normally, this
type of pawn lunge would merely weaken
Black's queenside, but here it is played with
a specific purpose in mind. 21.♘a4 ♕c2!
22.♘c5 ♕xe2 23.♘xb7 ♖ac8 (23...♕xb2?
24.♗d4 ♕c2 25.♕xe7 a5 26.♘d6±) 24.♖d2
♕b5 25.♕xe7 ♖ce8 26.♕c7 ♖c8 27.♕e7
♖fe8 28.♕f7 ♖f8=

17...hxg5 18.bxc5

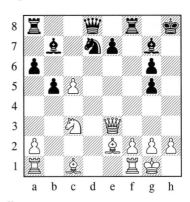

18...♕c7!

18...b4? 19.♕h3† ♔g8 20.♗c4†+−

18...♘xc5!? 19.♕xc5 ♕c8 is a cute tactic,
which nevertheless does not equalize:
20.♕xg5 ♕xc3 21.♗e3 (21.♕xg6 ♖xf2
22.♖xf2 ♕xa1 23.♖f1 ♖f8 24.♖xf8†
♗xf8 25.♕h5† ♔g8 26.♕g6†=) 21...♕f6
(21...♕c2 22.♗g4±) 22.♕g3± The black

king is a bit vulnerable.

19.♕h3†

19.♗a3 ♗e5 20.g3 ♕c6 21.f3 ♕f6 22.♖ad1 ♗xc3 23.♖xd7 ♖ad8 24.♖fd1 ♖xd7 25.♖xd7 ♗c6 26.♖d1 b4 27.♗c1=

19.a4 b4 20.♕h3† ♔g8 21.♗c4† ♖f7 22.♘d5 ♗xd5 23.♗xd5 ♗xa1 24.♗xa8 ♘xc5 25.♗d5 e6 26.♗xe6 ♘xe6 27.♕xe6 ♔g7 28.♗xg5 ♗d4⩱ White has an extra pawn, but f2 is weak and the passed b-pawn is a major asset for Black.

19...♔g8 20.♗d3

20.♗xg5 ♖f5 21.♗xe7 ♘xc5 22.♖ae1 ♗e5 23.♗xc5 (23.f4 ♗d4† 24.♔h1 ♘e6 25.♗d3 ♘xf4 26.♖xf4 ♕xf4 27.♗xf5 ♕xf5 28.♕xf5 gxf5⩱) 23...♕xc5 24.♗g4 ♗xc3 25.♗xf5 gxf5 26.♖c1 b4 27.♖fd1∞ Black has two strong bishops for a rook and a pawn, but his exposed king renders the position unclear.

20...♘e5!

20...♘f6 21.♗xg6 ♕xc5 22.♕e6† ♔h8 23.♗b2±

21.♕e6† ♔h7 22.♗e4 ♗c8 23.♕b6

After 23.♘d5 ♕xc5 24.♕xe7 ♕d4 this complex position should eventually peter out to equality:

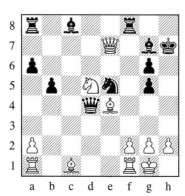

25.♗xg5 (25.♘f6† ♖xf6 26.♗xa8 ♖xf2 27.♖xf2 ♘g4 28.♗e3 ♘xe3 29.♖c1 ♘g4 30.♕e2 ♘xf2 31.♕xf2 ♗e6=) 25...♕xe4 26.♘f6† ♖xf6 27.♗xf6 ♘f3† 28.gxf3 ♕xe7 29.♗xe7 ♗xa1 30.♖xa1=

23...♕xb6 24.cxb6 ♖b8 25.♗xg5 ♘c4

Black's active pieces should make up for his slight material deficit.

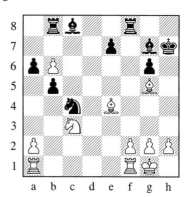

26.♖ac1 ♖xb6 27.♗xe7 ♖e8 28.♗c5 ♖be6 29.♗d5 ♖e5 30.♗xc4 ♖xc5 31.♗f7 ♖f8 32.♘e4 ♖e5 33.♖fe1 ♔h6

Black's bishop pair provides ongoing compensation.

b3) 16...♕c7 17.♕h3 h6 18.♖d1

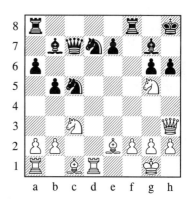

18...♘e5

18...♘b6? meets with a strong counter: 19.b4! ♕e5 20.bxc5 ♕xc3 21.♗e3 ♘d5 22.♖ac1 ♕f6 23.♘e6 ♗c8 24.♗g4 ♗xe6 25.♗xe6 ♘f4 26.♗xf4 ♕xf4 27.♖c2± Black will not stop the c-pawn.

19.b4 ♔g8!?

19...♘cd3 20.♘e6 ♘xf2 21.♘xc7 ♘xh3† 22.gxh3 ♘f3† 23.♗xf3 ♗xf3 24.♗b2 ♗xd1 25.♖xd1 ♖ac8 26.♘e6±

19...♗c8 20.♘d5! reaches a funny situation where both queens and knights are hanging.

20...♕c6 21.♕h4 ♘cd3 22.♗xd3 (22.♘xe7!
should give White some advantage)
22...♘xd3 23.♖xd3 ♕c4 24.♘e4 ♕xd3
25.♗b2 ♖f7 26.♘xe7 ♖xe7 27.♕xe7 ♗xb2
28.♘f6 ♗xf6 29.♕xf6† ♔h7 30.♕f7† ♔h8
31.♕f8† ♔h7 32.♖e1 ♖a7 33.♕xc8 ♕d2=
20.bxc5 hxg5 21.♕e6† ♘f7

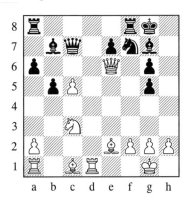

The position remains double-edged, for
instance:
22.♕xg6 ♕c6 23.♕xc6 ♗xc6 24.♗b2 b4
25.♘d5 ♗xb2 26.♘xe7† ♔g7 27.♘xc6 ♗xa1
28.♖xa1∞

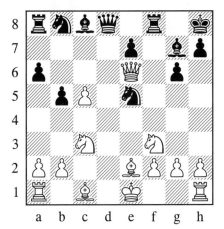

14.♕d5 ♕xd5 15.♘xd5 ♗b7 16.♘c7
  16.♘xe5 ♗xd5 17.♗f3 ♖f5 18.♘f7† ♔g8
19.♘h6† ♗xh6 20.♗xd5† ♖xd5 21.♗xh6
♖xc5=

16...♘xf3† 17.gxf3

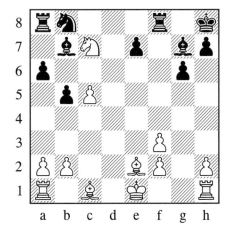

17...♗xf3?
  A terrible mistake for a player of Svidler's
calibre.

17...♖a7 would have maintained approximate
equality: 18.♘e6 (18.a4 b4) 18...♗xf3
19.♘xf8 (19.♗xf3 ♖xf3 20.♔e2 ♖f5 21.♗e3
♘c6=) 19...♗xh1 20.♘e6 ♗d5 (20...♗f6 21.f3
leaves the bishop on h1 in trouble) 21.♘xg7
♔xg7 22.♗f4 ♘c6 23.0–0–0 e6 Black's solid
light-squared setup does not allow White to
exploit his two bishops and passed c-pawn.

18.♗xf3 ♖a7 19.♘xb5!
  Maybe Svidler forgot about this move.

19...axb5 20.♔e2±
  With an extra pawn and two bishops, White
has a technically winning position.

20...♖a6
  20...♘d7 is most convincingly met by:
21.♖d1! (21.♗e3 ♘e5 is still favourable for
White, but ultimately less clear) 21...♘xc5
22.♗e3 ♖c7 23.♖ac1 ♘e6 24.♖xc7 ♘xc7
25.♖d7 ♘e6 26.b3± Black regained his pawn,
but White has a dominating position and will
soon create a passed a-pawn which will decide
game.

21.♗b7 ♖e6† 22.♗e3 ♗xb2 23.♖ab1 ♗d4

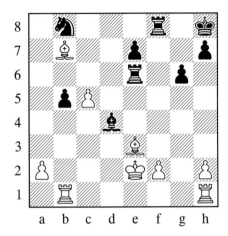

24.罝xb5+−

Since his slip on move 17 Svidler has failed to offer much resistance. This may have had something to do with the fact that he had performed superbly in the preceding part of the tournament and secured sole first place before the present game (the final round of the tournament) even started.

24...包a6 25.c6 包c7 26.罝b3 罝f4 27.罝d1 當g7 28.a4 皀c5 29.罝d7 皀d6 30.罝d3 包e8 31.a5

The a-pawn is unstoppable, so Black resigned.

1−0

GAME 42

▷ **A. Onischuk (2675)**

▶ **D. Navara (2722)**

FIDE World Cup 2011, Khanty-Mansiysk Round 2, Game 1, 31.08.2011 **[D98]**

Annotated by Arkadij Naiditsch

This game features the 8...皀g4 branch of the Russian System against the Grünfeld, which I can recall David using often in his junior years. Onischuk is a great technical player but he failed to achieve anything and soon found himself in a difficult position, although accurate defence enabled him to hold it. The game and accompanying notes show that it is hard for White to obtain any advantage in this line.

1.d4 包f6 2.c4 g6 3.包c3 d5 4.包f3 皀g7 5.豐b3 dxc4 6.豐xc4 0–0 7.e4 包c6 8.皀e2

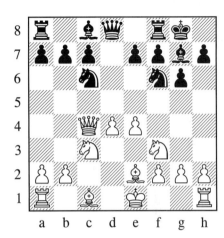

8...皀g4

8...e5!? is featured in Game 40 (Morozevich – Vachier Lagrave).

9.d5

9.皀e3 is an older variation which has scored lower for White than the text move. The main line continues 9...皀xf3 10.皀xf3 (After 10.gxf3 e5 11.dxe5 包xe5 12.豐b3 包h5! Black takes control over the dark squares with ...豐h4 coming soon.) 10...e5 11.d5 包d4 12.皀d1 as in Karpov – Kamsky, Elista (1) 1996.

9...包a5 10.豐a4

White's other possibility is:

10.豐b4 皀xf3 11.皀xf3 c6 12.0–0 豐b6

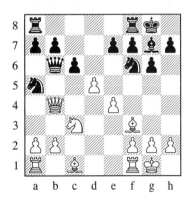

Now there are two main branches.

a) 13.♕xe7 ♘c4 14.♗f4

14.a3 a5 15.♘a4 ♕b5 16.♘c3 ♕b6=
14...♖fe8

14...g5 15.♘a4 ♕b5 16.♗xg5 ♖fe8 17.♕c7
♘e5 18.♘c3 ♕xb2 19.♖ac1±
15.♕c7

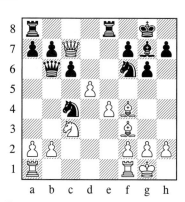

15...♕xb2

15...♕xc7 16.♗xc7 ♘d7 17.♖ab1 ♖ac8
18.d6 ♘d2 19.♗g4 f5 20.exf5 h5 21.♗h3
g5 22.g4 hxg4 23.♗xg4 ♗f6∞
15...♘h5!?
16.♖ab1

16.dxc6 bxc6 17.♖ac1 ♕b6=
16...♕xc3 17.♖fc1 ♕d4

17...♕d3 18.♖b3
18.♖xb7 ♖f8 19.♖b4

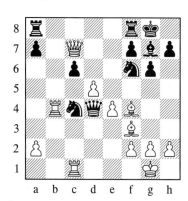

19...♘xe4!

19...cxd5 20.♗e3 ♕e5 21.♖cxc4 ♘xe4
22.♕xe5 ♗xe5 23.♗xe4 dxe4 24.♖xe4±

20.♗e3 ♕e5 21.♕xe5 ♘xe5 22.♗xe4 cxd5
23.♗xd5 ♘d3 24.♗xa8 ♖xb4 25.♗f3 ♘xa2
26.♖c7 a5 27.♗d5 ♘c3 28.♗c4 a4 29.♗c5 ♖a8
30.♖xf7 ♔h8 31.♗a3 ♘b1∓

b) 13.♕a4 ♘d7

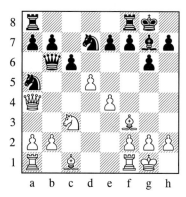

Now White has three worthy continuations:

b1) 14.♖d1 ♘c5 15.♕c2 ♘c4 16.♗e2

16.b3 ♕b4 17.bxc4 ♕xc3 18.♕xc3 ♗xc3
19.♖b1 cxd5 20.cxd5 ♗e5 21.♗e3 b6 is solid
enough for Black.
16...♕b4 17.a3 ♕b3 18.♕xb3 ♘xb3 19.♖b1
♘b6 20.♗e3 ♖fd8 21.♔f1 ♔f8 22.f3 e6
23.dxc6 bxc6

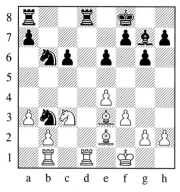

Despite having the bishop pair and a better
pawn structure, White has no advantage
here. Black's knights are quite disruptive in
the queenside, and the bishop on g7 is a
fantastic piece.

24.♗a6 ♗e5 25.f4 ♗d4∞

Jovanic – Avrukh, Zurich 2009.

b2) 14.♗e3 ♕xb2

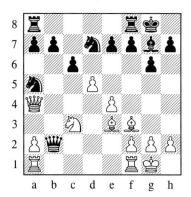

15.♖fc1

15.♕xa5 ♕xc3 16.♕xc3 ♗xc3 17.♖ac1 ♗a5
18.dxc6 bxc6 19.♖xc6 ♘e5 20.♖a6 ♗b6=

15...♗xc3 16.♖ab1 ♘b6

16...b5!? 17.♖xb2 bxa4 18.♖xc3 cxd5
19.exd5 ♖ac8 deserves attention.

17.♗xb6 axb6 18.♖xb2 ♗xb2

This position been already played several
times. Black has good drawing chances, but
objectively White should be a little better.

b3) 14.♗e2

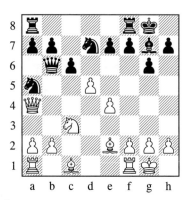

14...♘c5

14...♖ac8?! 15.♖d1 ♘c5 (15...♖fd8 16.♗d2±)
16.♕a3 ♗xc3 17.♕xc3 ♘xe4 18.♕f3 cxd5
19.♖xd5 f5 20.♖b5 ♕c6 21.♗h6±

15.♕c2

15.♕a3!? has not yet been tested. I analysed
the following line: 15...♗xc3 16.bxc3
(16.♕xc3 ♘xe4 17.♕e5 cxd5 18.♗h6 ♘f6
19.♗xf8 ♘c6 20.♕c3 ♔xf8∞) 16...♘xe4
17.♗e3 ♕c7 18.c4 b6 (18...cxd5 19.cxd5
♘c4 20.♗xc4 ♕xc4 21.♕xe7 ♕xd5 22.♖fd1
♕c6 23.♖ac1 ♘c3 24.♕e5 ♘e2† 25.♔h1 f6
26.♖xc6 fxe5 27.♖c7±) 19.♗h6 (19.♕b2!?
♖fd8 20.♗h6 ♘f6 21.♖ac1 ♘b7 22.♗f3
♘c5 23.♖cd1 cxd5 24.♗xd5 ♖ac8 25.♖fe1
♖e8 26.h3 e5 27.f4→) 19...♖fd8 20.♕b2
♘f6 21.♖fe1 ♖ac8 22.♖ac1 cxd5 23.cxd5
♕d7! 24.♖cd1 ♘c4 25.♗xc4 (25.♕d4
♘d6) 25...♖xc4 26.d6 ♖c6 27.dxe7 ♕xd1
28.exd8=♕† ♕xd8 29.h3 ♖d6

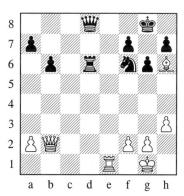

We have ended up with a strange situation
resembling a double zugzwang, in which
neither side can improve their position
much and so a draw is the most likely result.

15...♕b4

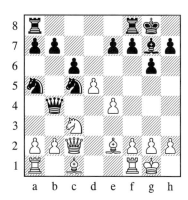

16.♗e3

16.♗d2 ♘c4 17.♗xc4 (17.♗g5 ♘xb2 18.♗xe7 ♖fe8 19.♗xc5 ♕xc5 20.♖ac1 ♕xc3 21.♕xc3 ♗xc3 22.♖xc3 cxd5=) 17...♕xc4 18.b3 ♕d3 19.♕xd3 ♘xd3 20.dxc6 bxc6 21.♖ad1 ♖fd8 22.♘a4 f5!?= Normally a position with this pawn structure should give White a clear advantage, but here Black's super-strong knight on d3 gives him sufficient play.

16...♗xc3 17.bxc3!?N

This new idea deserves serious attention. White sacrifices a pawn in return for a strong initiative.

17.♖ac1 ♗d4 18.♗xd4 ♕xd4 19.♕xc5 ♕xb2 20.♗f3 b6 21.♕xe7 ♖fe8 22.♕g5 (22.♕d7 ♕e5 23.dxc6 ♖ed8 24.♕g4 ♖ac8 25.♖fd1 ♘xc6 26.♖d5 ♕e8=) 22...♕e5 23.♕d2 ♖ad8 24.g3 cxd5 25.exd5 ♘b7 26.♖fe1 ♕f6 27.♔g2 ♖xe1 28.♕xe1 ♘c5 29.♕e3 ♗f8 30.♖e1 ♗g7 31.h4 h6 32.♖d1 ♖d7 33.♖e1 ½–½ Babula – Ruck, Novi Sad 2009.

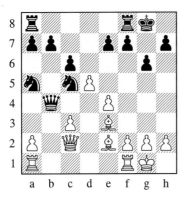

17...♕xe4

17...♕a4 18.♕xa4 ♘xa4 19.c4±

18.♕d1 b6

18...♘a6 19.♖e1 ♘c7 (19...♕xd5 20.♕a4±) 20.♗f3 ♕c4 21.d6 exd6 22.♕xd6 ♘e6 23.♕e5 ♕b5 24.♕f6 ♕f5 Black should try to exchange queens at any costs. 25.♕xf5 gxf5 26.♗h6 ♖fe8 27.♖e5 ♘c4 28.♖xf5±

19.♗f3 ♕c4

19...♕d3 20.♗xc5 ♕xd1 21.♖axd1 bxc5 22.♖fe1 ♖fe8 23.dxc6 ♖ac8 24.♖d7 ♘xc6 25.♗xc6 ♖xc6 26.♖xa7 e6 27.♖b1±

19...♕e5 20.♖e1 ♘c7 21.♕d4 e5 22.♕h4 cxd5 23.♗xd5 ♕d8 24.♕xd8 ♖axd8 25.♗xc5 ♖fe8 26.c4 bxc5 27.♗e3± White keeps some advantage thanks to the dominant bishop on d5.

20.♕d4

20.♗d4 cxd5 21.♗e2 ♕a4 22.♗xc5 ♕xd1 23.♖axd1 bxc5 24.♖xd5 ♖fc8 25.♖d7 e6=

20...cxd5

20...♕xd4? 21.cxd4 ♘d3 22.dxc6 ♖ac8 23.♖ab1±

20...♖fd8 21.♕e5 ♘d3 22.♕xe7 cxd5 23.♗h6 ♕xc3 24.♖ad1 ♖ac8 25.♕h4↑

20...♖fe8 21.♗h6 f6 (21...e5 22.dxe6 ♕xd4 23.exf7† ♔xf7 24.cxd4±) 22.♖fd1 e5 23.dxe6 ♕xe6 24.h4∞

21.♗h6

21.♕xc4 ♘xc4 22.♗xc5 bxc5 23.♗xd5 ♘d2 24.♖fd1 ♖ad8 25.♖xd2 e6 26.♖ad1 exd5 27.♖xd5 ♖xd5 28.♖xd5 ♖b8=

21...♕xd4 22.cxd4 ♘e6 23.♗xd5 ♘xd4 24.♖fd1 e5 25.♗xa8 ♖xa8 26.♔f1 ♘ac6 27.♖ac1 ♖d8

Even with two pawns for the exchange Black cannot equalize.

28.♗e3 ♖d6 29.♗xd4 exd4±

Black faces a tough battle for a draw.

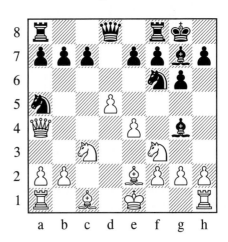

10...♗xf3

10...c6?? is a blunder due to 11.e5!+–.

11.♗xf3 c6 12.0–0

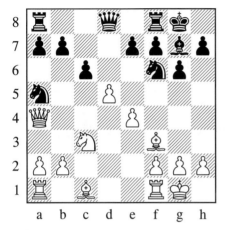

12...b5

The most principled continuation, although a couple of other moves deserve attention.

12...cxd5 13.♖d1 ♘c6

13...♘c4 14.♘xd5 ♘xd5 15.♕xc4 ♘b6 16.♕b4 ♕c7 17.♗g5 e6 18.♖ac1 ♕e5 19.♗e7 ♖fc8 20.♖xc8† ♖xc8 21.b3±

13...♖c8!? 14.e5 ♘d7 15.♘xd5 ♘c6 (15...♖c4 16.♕a3) 16.♗g5 ♘b6 17.♕xc6 bxc6 18.♘xe7† ♔h8 19.♖xd8 ♖cxd8 20.♘xc6 ♖d7∞

14.exd5 ♘e5 15.♗e2 ♘e8

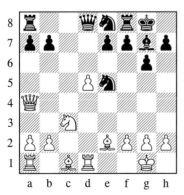

16.♗f4

16.♘e4 ♘d6 17.♘xd6 ♕xd6 18.♕b3 ♘d7 19.♕xb7 ♖ab8 20.♕xa7 ♗xb2 21.♗xb2 ♖xb2 22.♗f1 ♖fb8 23.a4 ♘f6 24.h3 ♘e4 25.♕e3 ♘xf2 26.♖d4∞

16.♗e3 ♘d6∞

16...♘d6 17.♖ac1 a6 18.♕b4 b5 19.a4 a5 20.♕b3 bxa4 21.♘xa4 ♖b8 22.♕a2 ♘f5 23.b3 ♕d6 24.g3 ♖fc8∞

12...♖c8!?N

This interesting move has not yet been tested.

13.dxc6

This leads to complex positions that are interesting to analyse, but the strongest continuation is probably: 13.♖d1! b5 14.♕b4 a6 15.e5 ♘xd5 16.♗xd5 cxd5 17.♘xd5 ♘c6 18.♕a3 ♗xe5 19.♗h6 ♖e8 20.♘f6† ♗xf6 21.♖xd8 ♖exd8 22.♖c1±

13...♘xc6 14.♗e3

14.♖d1 ♕b6 15.♕a3 ♘d4 (15...♘e5!?) 16.e5 ♘c2 17.♕xe7 ♖fe8 18.♕xb7 ♘xa1 19.♕xb6 axb6 20.exf6 ♗xf6 21.♘d5 ♗g7 22.♗g5 ♘c2 23.♘e7† ♖xe7 24.♗xe7 ♗xb2=

14...e6 15.♖fd1

15.♗c5 ♖e8 16.♖fd1 (16.♘b5 ♘e5 17.♗a3 ♘xf3† 18.gxf3 ♘d7→) 16...♘d7 17.♗e3 ♕e7 18.♖ac1 a6 19.♗e2 ♖ed8 20.f4 ♘c5 21.♕c4 ♗f8

15...♕e7

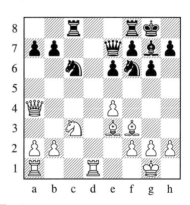

16.♖ac1

16.♕b5 a6! (16...♖fd8 17.e5! ♘d7 18.♕xb7
♘dxe5 [18...♘cxe5 19.♗e2 ♖b8 20.♕xa7
♖xb2 21.♖ab1 ♖c2 22.♖bc1 ♖xc1 23.♖xc1
♘c6 24.♕a4±] 19.♗xc6 ♘xc6 20.♕xe7
[20.♖xd8† ♕xd8 21.♖d1 ♕c7 22.♖d7
♕xb7 23.♖xb7±] 20...♘xe7 21.♖xd8† ♖xd8
22.♗xa7 ♖d2 23.♘d1) 17.♕b6 (17.♕c5
♕xc5 18.♗xc5 ♖fd8 19.♗b6 ♖xd1†
20.♖xd1 ♘e5 21.♗e2 ♗f8) 17...♘e5 18.♗e2
♘c4 19.♗xc4 ♖xc4 20.f3 ♖fc8 (20...♖b4
21.♕c5±) 21.♖ac1 ♘e8 22.♘e2 ♖xc1
23.♖xc1 ♖xc1† 24.♘xc1 ♕c7=

16...♖fd8

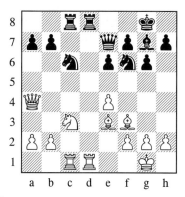

17.♗e2

17.e5 ♘xe5 18.♖xd8† ♖xd8 19.♕xa7 ♘xf3†
20.gxf3 ♘d5∓

17.♗xa7?! ♖xd1† 18.♖xd1 b5 19.♘xb5
♖a8 20.♖d6 (20.e5 ♘d5 21.♘c3 ♘xa7
22.♘xd5 exd5 23.♗xd5 ♖b8 24.♗b3 ♖b7∓)
20...♘xa7 21.g3 ♕b7 22.♖a6 ♘d7 23.♖xa7
♖xa7 24.♘xa7 ♘c5 25.♕a3 (25.♕e8† ♗f8
26.♘c6 ♕xb2 27.♘d8 ♕f6∓) 25...♗d4
26.e5 ♘e4 27.♘c8 ♕xc8 28.♗xe4 ♕c1†
29.♔g2 ♕d2 30.♕f3 ♕xb2 31.a4 ♗xe5=

17.♘b5 a6 18.♗c5 ♖xd1† 19.♕xd1 ♕d7
20.♘d6 ♖b8 21.♘c4 b5 22.♘b6 ♕xd1†
23.♖xd1 ♗f8 24.♗e3 ♘e5∞

17.♕b5 ♘e8! (17...a6 18.♕b6 ♘e5
[18...♕b4 19.♕xb4 ♘xb4 20.e5 ♘fd5
21.♘xd5 ♘xd5 22.♖xc8 ♖xc8 23.♗xd5
exd5 24.♖xd5 ♖e8 25.♗d4 f6 26.♖d7 fxe5
27.♗c3±] 19.♗e2 ♖xd1† 20.♖xd1 ♘e8

21.f4 ♘c4 22.♗xc4 ♖xc4 23.e5 f6) 18.♗c5
♕g5 19.h4 ♕xh4 20.♕xb7 ♗e5 21.g3 ♗xg3
22.fxg3 ♕xg3† 23.♗g2 ♘e5=

17...♘d7 18.f4

18.♘b5 ♘b6 19.♗a3 ♕xa3 20.bxa3 ♖xd1†
21.♖xd1 ♘a4 22.♖d7 a6 23.♖xb7 axb5
24.♗xb5 ♘c5 25.♗xc5 ♘a5 26.♖a7 ♖xc5
27.♖a8† ♗f8 28.♖xa5 ♖c1† 29.♗f1 ♗c5=

18...♘b6 19.♗xb6 axb6 20.e5 g5⇄

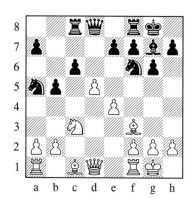

13.♕b4

13.♕d1 ♖c8!?

I believe this move to be more promising
than the fashionable 13...b4.

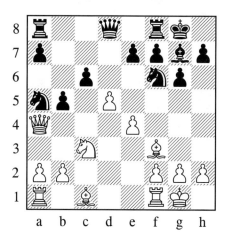

14.dxc6

14.♗f4 cxd5 15.exd5 (15.e5 ♘d7 16.♕xd5
b4 17.e6 ♘c5 18.exf7† ♖xf7 19.♕xd8†
♖xd8 20.♗c7 bxc3 21.♗xd8 cxb2 22.♖ab1
♘ab7∞) 15...♘c4 16.♘xb5 (16.♕b3 a6

17.a4 ♞a5 18.♕d1 b4↑) 16...♕d7 17.b3
♕xb5 18.bxc4 ♕xc4 19.g3 ♖fd8=

14.♖e1 should be met by 14...a6, stabilizing
the queenside.

14...b4 15.e5

15.♞b5 ♞xc6 16.♕a4 ♞e5 17.♗e2 ♞d3
(17...a6 18.♕xa6 ♖c2 19.♗d1 ♖c6 20.♕a7
♞xe4∞) 18.♖d1 ♞xc1 19.♖xd8 ♞xe2†
20.♔f1 ♖fxd8 21.♔xe2 ♞xe4⩱

15.♞d5 ♞xc6 16.♗g5 e6 17.♞xf6† ♗xf6
18.♕xd8 ♗xd8 19.♗h6 ♖e8 20.♖fc1 ♗b6=

15...bxc3 16.exf6 ♗xf6 17.bxc3 ♞xc6 18.♗h6
♗g7 19.♗xg7 ♔xg7 20.♖e1

20.♕a4 ♞e5

20...e6 21.♕a4 ♕b6 22.♖ab1 ♕c5 23.♕b5
♕xb5 24.♖xb5 ♖c7 25.♗xc6 ♖xc6 26.♖a5
♖xc3 27.♖xa7=

Vallejo Pons – Roiz, Dresden (ol) 2008.

13...a6

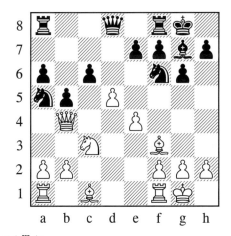

14.♖d1

14.♗g5 h6!

14...♖c8? 15.e5

14...cxd5 15.exd5 ♖c8 16.d6 exd6 17.♖ad1
♞c4 18.♗b7 ♖c5 19.♕xc5 (19.♞e4 ♖xg5
20.♞xg5 ♕b6 21.♗f3 h6 22.♞e4 ♞xe4
23.♗xe4 ♗xb2 24.♗d3 ♕c5) 19...dxc5
20.♖xd8 ♖xd8 21.♗xa6 h6 22.♗xb5 ♞xb2
23.♗c1 ♞d5 24.♞xd5 ♖xd5 25.a4 ♞d1
(25...c4 26.♗xb2 ♗xb2 27.♗xc4 ♖d2 28.a5

♗d4 29.a6 ♔g7 30.g3 h5 31.♖b1±) 26.a5
♞c3 27.♗c6 ♖d6 28.♗b7±

15.♗e3

15.♗h4?! ♖c8 16.e5 c5 17.♕f4 ♞d7∓

15.♗xf6 ♗xf6 16.e5 ♗xe5 17.dxc6 ♖c8
18.♖fe1 ♗d6 19.♕h4 ♔g7 20.♖ac1 ♞xc6
21.♞xb5 axb5 22.♗xc6 b4=

15...cxd5

15...♞c4 16.dxc6!

16.exd5 ♞c4 17.d6 a5 18.♕xb5 ♞xe3 19.fxe3
♖b8 20.dxe7 ♕xe7 21.♕e2 ♖fe8 22.♖fe1 h5∞

14...♞d7 15.♗e3

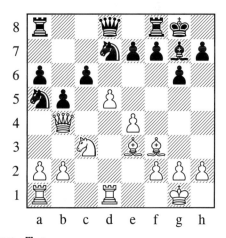

15...♖c8

I find it strange that almost nobody has
played 15...c5! 16.♗xc5 ♞xc5 17.♕xc5 as in
the game Krivousas – Borisek, Balatonlelle
2001. At this point after 17...♞c4!N Black has
excellent play on the dark squares.

16.dxc6 ♞xc6 17.♕b3 e6

Having exchanged off his bishop, Black
sensibly uses his pawns to control the light
squares. He will look for opportunities to
utilize dark squares such as c5, d4 and e5 for
his minor pieces. Establishing a knight on c4
would also be a major achievement for him.
On the other hand, Black's queenside pawns
are a bit vulnerable, and White's main plan will
be to attack them as on the next move.

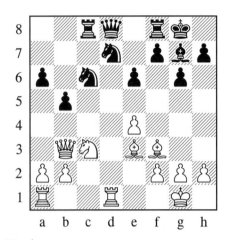

18.a4

18.♗e2 is a bit slow and after 18...♕e7∞ Black is ready for ...♘c5, which means that White does not have time for the desirable plans of a2-a4 and f2-f4 followed by e4-e5.

18...b4

Another recent game continued:
18...♘a5 19.♕b4 ♘c4

Black should also consider 19...♘c6!? 20.♕d6 ♘de5 21.♗e2 b4 22.♕xd8 ♖fxd8 23.♘a2 ♖xd1† 24.♖xd1 b3 with promising counterplay as the b2-pawn is weak.
20.♗c1

20.axb5 ♘xb2 21.♕xb2 ♗xc3 22.♕a3 ♗xa1 23.♕xa1 axb5 24.♗h6 ♕f6∓
20...♕c7 21.axb5 axb5

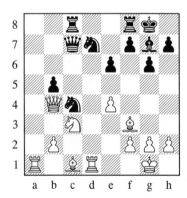

22.♗e2!?

An interesting alternative to 22.♘xb5 ♕c5 23.♕xc5 ♘xc5 24.♖a7 ♘xb2 25.♗xb2 ♗xb2 26.♖a2 ♗e5 27.g3 which led to equality and a subsequent draw in B. Lalic – Delchev, Cappelle la Grande 2011.
22...♘de5

22...♕c5 23.♕xb5 ♗xc3 24.♕xc5 ♘xc5 25.♗xc4 (25.bxc3 ♘xe4 26.♖d4 ♘cd6 27.♗d3 ♖fd8 28.♗f4 g5 [28...♘c5 29.♗xd6 ♘b3 30.♖aa4 ♖xc3 31.♗f1 ♘xd4 32.♖xd4±] 29.♗e3 f5 30.f3 e5 31.♖b4 ♖xc3 32.fxe4 ♖xd3 33.♗xg5 ♖e8 34.exf5 ♘xf5=) 25...♗g7 26.f3 ♖b8 (26...♘xe4 27.♗a6±) 27.♗e3 ♖fc8 28.♗a5 ♘b3 29.♖a3 ♘c5 (29...♖xc4 30.♖xb3 ♖cc8 31.♖xb8 ♖xb8 32.♗f4 e5 33.♗c1±) 30.b3 ♗f8 31.♖da1 ♘xb3 32.♖xb3 ♖xb3 33.♗xb3 ♖c3 34.♔f2 ♖xb3 35.♖a8 ♔g7 36.♗d4† f6 37.♗xf6†±
23.♘xb5

23.♖b1 ♘c6 24.♕xb5 ♘d4 25.♕xc4 ♕xc4 26.♗xc4 ♖xc4 27.♔f1 ♖b8∞
23...♕b6

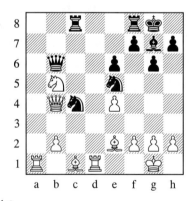

24.b3

24.♕a4 ♖c5 25.b3 ♕xb5 26.♕xb5 ♖xb5 27.bxc4 ♘xc4=
24.♗f4 ♖c5 25.♗xe5 ♘xe5 26.♖a6 ♘f3† 27.♗xf3 ♕xb5 28.♖b6 ♕xb4 29.♖xb4 ♖c2 30.b3 ♖fc8=
24...♘c6 25.♕xc4 ♗xa1 26.♗e3 ♕a5

26...♕a6 27.♘d6 ♕xc4 28.bxc4 ♖a8 29.c5∞
27.♘d6 ♖c7 28.♘b5 ♖cc8 29.♘d6

White has nothing better than repeating moves, but Black could consider playing on. 29...♘e5!? 30.♕a6 ♖a8 31.♕xa5 ♖xa5 32.b4 ♖a3 33.b5 ♖b8∞

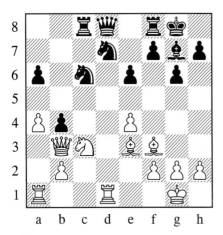

19.♘e2?!

Onischuk avoids decentralizing his knight, but it was more important to keep the e2-square free for the bishop.

The correct move was 19.♘a2, when Black has two options.

a) 19...♕e7 20.♖ac1 a5 21.♗e2

White's only problem is the knight on a2. If he succeeds in manoeuvring it to d3, he should be able to claim a solid advantage.

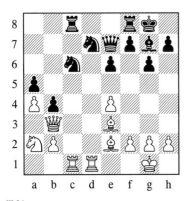

21...♖fd8

21...e5!? 22.♕d5 ♘f6 23.♕b5 ♘d4 24.♗xd4

exd4 25.♕xa5 b3 26.♖xc8 ♖xc8 27.♘b4 ♘xe4 28.♕a6 ♖e8 29.♗b5 ♘xf2 30.♖f1 d3 31.♗xe8 ♘h3† 32.♔h1 ♘f2†=

22.♗a6 ♖c7

22...♘d4? 23.♗xd4 (23.♖xd4?! ♖xc1† 24.♘xc1 ♗xd4 25.♗xd4 ♘b8 26.♗b6 ♖d6 27.♗c5 ♘xa6 28.♗xd6 ♕xd6 29.♕d3=) 23...♖xc1 24.♘xc1 ♗xd4 25.♖xd4 ♘c5 26.♖xd8† ♕xd8 27.♕c4 ♕d1† 28.♕f1 ♕xa4 29.♗d3 (29.♗c4 ♕c2 30.b3 a4 31.bxa4 ♕xa4 32.♗e2 b3 [32...♘xe4 33.♗d1±] 33.♗d1 ♕b4 34.♘d3 ♘xd3 35.♕xd3 b2 36.♗c2 ♕e1† 37.♕f1 ♕c1 38.♗b1±) 29...b3 30.♗c4 ♕b4 31.♕e2 a4 32.g3 a3 33.bxa3 ♕xa3 34.♘d3 ♘a4 35.♔g2 b2 36.♕c2 ♕a1 37.♘xb2 ♘xb2 38.♗b3±

23.♗b5 ♖dc8

23...♘de5? 24.♖xd8† ♘xd8 25.♕d1 ♖xc1 26.♘xc1±

23...♘db8? 24.♖xd8† ♘xd8 25.♖d1 ♘dc6 26.♘c1 ♘d4 27.♕d3 ♘bc6 28.♘b3 ♘e5 29.♕xd4 ♘f3† 30.gxf3 ♗xd4 31.♘xd4+−

24.♖d2

After 24.f4?! ♗d4 25.♗xd4 ♘xd4 26.♖xc7 ♘xb3 27.♖xc8† ♘f8 28.♖dd8 ♕a7† 29.♔h1 ♗g7 30.♖xf8 ♕f2∓ Black is better; once again the knight on a2 is the problem. 24...♘a7 25.♖xc7 ♖xc7 26.♕d1 ♘xb5 27.axb5 ♗f6 28.♘c1 a4 29.b6 ♖b7 30.♕xa4 ♘xb6 31.♕b3∞

b) 19...♘a5!

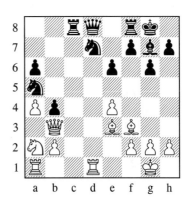

In my opinion this is the better practical decision. Black tries to exploit the badly-placed knight on a2 by sacrificing a pawn for immediate counterplay.

20.♕xb4

20.♕d3 b3 (20...♗xb2 21.♖ab1 b3 22.♖xb2 bxa2 23.♖xa2 ♘e5 24.♕xd8 ♖fxd8 25.♖xd8† ♖xd8 26.♗e2 ♘ec4 27.♗g5±) 21.♘c3 ♗xc3 (21...♘e5 22.♕xa6 ♘xf3† 23.gxf3 ♖a8 24.♕e2 ♕h4∞) 22.bxc3 ♘e5 23.♕xa6 ♘xf3† 24.gxf3 ♖a8 25.♖xd8 ♖xa6 26.♖xf8† ♗xf8 27.♗c5† ♔e8 28.♖b1 ♔d7∞

20...♘c4 21.♗c1

21.♗d4 ♘ce5 22.♕a3 ♘xf3† 23.♕xf3 ♗xd4 24.♖xd4 ♘e5 25.♕d1 ♕b6∞

21...♕c7 22.♗e2 ♘de5

Black has promising compensation for a pawn, as the following lines demonstrate.

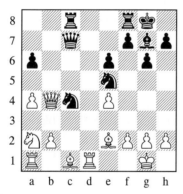

23.♗f4

After 23.b3?! ♖b8 24.♕c3 ♕b7 25.bxc4 ♘c6 26.♕e1 ♗xa1 27.♗a3 ♗g7 28.♗xf8 ♗xf8 Black is better thanks to his domination over the dark squares.

23.f4 ♕a7† 24.♔h1 ♘e3 25.♗xe3 ♕xe3 26.♕d2 ♕xd2 27.♖xd2 ♘c4=

23.♕e1 ♖b8 24.f4 (24.♘b4 ♕b7 25.♗xc4 ♘xc4 26.♘d3 ♖fd8 27.♗f4 ♖bc8 28.♕e2 ♕b3∞) 24...♘xb2 25.♗xb2 ♖xb2 26.fxe5 ♗xe5 27.♔h1 (27.♘c1 ♗xh2† 28.♔h1 ♗g3 29.♕f1 ♕e7 30.♗g4 ♖f2 31.♕g1 ♕h4† 32.♗h3 g5∓) 27...♗xh2 28.♖d3 ♗e5 29.♘c3 ♖d8↑

23...♘f3†!?

Sacrificing a piece for an attack.

23...♕a7 is a safe alternative: 24.♖dc1 (24. b3 ♘b2 25.♗e3 ♕a8 26.♖d6 ♘ed3∞) 24...♘xb2 25.♖xc8 ♖xc8 26.♖c1 ♕a8 27.♖xc8† ♕xc8=

24.gxf3 ♕xf4 25.♗xc4 ♗e5

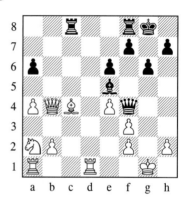

26.♖ac1

26.♖ab1 ♖fd8 27.♘c3 ♕xh2† 28.♔f1 ♗d4 29.♖d2 ♗e3 30.♖c2 ♖d4 31.fxe3 ♕h1† 32.♔f2 ♕h2†=

26...♖b8 27.♕d2 ♕xh2† 28.♔f1 ♖xb2 29.♖c2 ♖fb8 30.♘c3 ♗f4

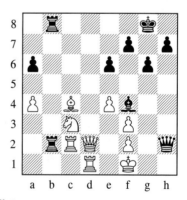

31.♕d3

31.♕d8† ♖xd8 32.♖xd8† ♔g7 33.♖xb2 ♕h1† 34.♔e2 ♕c1 35.♖b3 h5↑

31...♗e3!

Black keeps enough of an attack to maintain the balance, and the most likely outcome is a perpetual check.

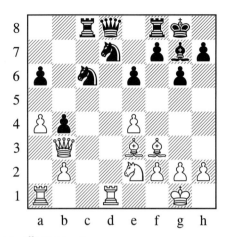

19...♕e7 20.a5

White continues with his plan, fixing weaknesses in the enemy queenside to attack later. The only problem is that his bishop has no time to retreat to e2, which gives Black enough time to equalize and even to take over the initiative.

20...♘de5 21.♘d4

21.♘c1?! ♘xf3† 22.gxf3 ♕f6∓

21...♘xd4 22.♗xd4 ♘xf3† 23.♕xf3 ♗xd4 24.♖xd4 ♖c2∓

Black's pieces are becoming active.

25.♕b3

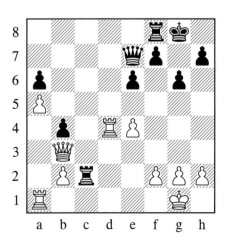

25...♕c5

A slightly better way to fight for a win would have been:

25...♖fc8! 26.♖ad1

26.h3?! ♕f6∓

26...♖e2

After 26...♕f6 27.♕e3 ♖xb2 28.e5 ♕e7 (28...♕f5 29.g4 ♕c2 30.♖d8† ♖xd8 31.♖xd8† ♔g7 32.♕f4 ♖b1† 33.♔g2 ♕c6† 34.f3 ♕c1 35.♕f6† ♔h6 36.♕h4† ♔g7=) 29.g3 White has good drawing chances thanks to Black's weakened kingside.

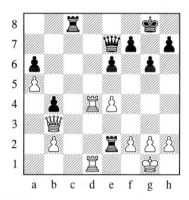

27.♖xb4

27.♕xb4 ♕f6 28.♖f1 ♖xf2 29.♖dd1 ♖xb2 30.♕a3 ♕e5∓

27.♖c4 ♖xc4 28.♕xc4 ♖xb2 29.♕xa6 ♕c5 30.♕b6 ♖d2 31.♖b1 ♕xb6 32.axb6 ♖d6∓

27...♖cc2 28.♖b8† ♔g7 29.♕b6

29.♖f1? ♖xf2–+

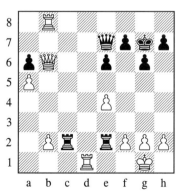

29...♖xf2 30.♕d4† e5 31.♕xf2 ♖xf2 32.♔xf2

♕h4† 33.♔g1 ♕xe4∓

Black keeps some winning chances in this endgame.

26.♖ad1 e5 27.♖4d2 ♖xd2 28.♖xd2 ♕xa5 29.g3 ♕b6 30.♖d7

Black is a clear pawn up, but he has few winning chances as White's pieces are so active.

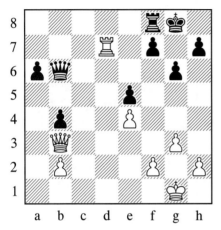

30...a5 31.♕d5 a4 32.♖b7 ♕f6 33.♖xb4 ♖d8

Black has returned the extra pawn in order to get some attacking chances, but Onischuk defends coolly and the game is soon drawn.

34.♕a5 ♖d1† 35.♔g2 ♖d3 36.♔g1 h5 37.♖xa4 h4 38.♕e1 ♕f3 39.♖a3 hxg3 40.hxg3 ♖xa3

½–½

E

GAME 43
▷ **L. Fressinet (2698)**
▶ **E. Bacrot (2710)**
86th French Championship, Caen
Round 3, 16.08.2011 **[E03]**
Annotated by Ivan Sokolov

The players debated a line of the Catalan which arose through an English/Reti move order. Bacrot unveiled an interesting novelty in 10...♘b4!?, instead of the usual 10...♗b7 as featured in the 2006 Kramnik – Fritz match, or the rare but interesting 10...♘e5!?. In the game White was unable to find anything convincing against his opponent's new tenth move. The critical direction looks to be 11.♕e4!? but according to my analysis Black is doing well there too.

1.♘f3 d5 2.c4 e6 3.g3 ♘f6 4.♗g2 dxc4 5.♕a4† ♘bd7 6.♕xc4
6.0–0 a6 7.♕xc4 b5 8.♕c2 ♗b7 gives Black easy play.

6...a6

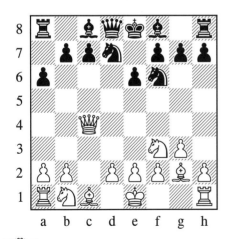

7.♕c2
Another option is 7.♕b3 although Black should be okay here: 7...♖b8 (But not 7...c5?! 8.a4! ♖b8 9.a5 when Black's queenside is fixed and sooner or later he will have to

damage his pawn structure, for instance: 9...♗d6 10.d3 0–0 11.0–0 h6 12.♗d2 ♖e8 13.♘a3 e5 14.♘c4 ♗c7 15.♖fd1 ♕e7 16.♘h4 b5 17.axb6 ♘xb6 18.♘a5 ♘bd5 19.♕c2± Lputian – Piket, Sarajevo 1998.) 8.d4 b5 9.0–0 ♗b7 10.♗f4 ♗d6 11.♖c1 ♗xf4 12.gxf4 ♘d5 13.e3 c5 14.dxc5 ♖c8 15.c6 ♗xc6 16.♕a3 ♗b7= Ivanchuk – Naiditsch, Warsaw 2005.

7...c5 8.d4
This seems to be the most testing approach. Other moves are not dangerous for Black:

8.a4 works less well than in the analogous position after 7.♕b3 c5?! 8.a4! as noted above. The point is that with the queen on c2 instead of b3, Black can safely play 8...b6! as 9.♘e5?! can be met by 9...♘d5.

8.0–0 b6 (8...b5 9.a4 ♗b7 10.axb5 axb5 11.♖xa8 ♕xa8 12.♘a3 ♗c6 13.d3 ♗e7 14.♘e1 ♘d5 15.f4 0–0 16.f5 exf5 17.♖xf5 g6 18.♖f1 ♕b7= Zaichik – Beliavsky, Yaroslavl 1982) 9.b4 ♗b7 10.bxc5 ♖c8 11.♘c3 ♗xc5 12.♕b3 0–0 13.a4 ♕c7 14.♗b2 ♗xf3 15.♗xf3 ♘e5 16.♘e4 ♘xf3† 17.♖xf3 ♘xe4 18.♕xe4 ♖fd8 19.♗c3 ♖d5 20.♖fb1 ♕d7∓ Akopian – Piket, Madrid 1997.

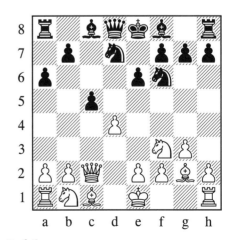

8...b6

After 8...cxd4?! 9.♘xd4 Black has problems developing his queenside, and his problems were demonstrated as far back as six decades ago: 9...♘c5 (9...♗c5 10.♘b3 ♗a7 11.0–0 0–0 12.♗d2 ♕e7 13.a3 ♖e8 14.♗b4 ♕d8 15.♘c3 ♕c7 16.♖ac1 ♕e5 17.♕d1 ♕g5 18.♘d2 ♕h6 19.♘de4↑ Smyslov – Kan, Leningrad 1947.) 10.♘b3 ♘xb3 11.♕xb3 ♕c7 12.0–0 ♗c5 13.♗f4 e5 14.♗g5 ♗e6 15.♕xb7 ♕xb7 16.♗xb7 ♖b8 17.♗xf6 gxf6 18.♗xa6 ♖xb2 19.♖c1 ♗b6 20.♘c3 ♗a5 21.♘d1 ♖d2 22.♘e3 ♔e7 23.♘c4 ♖d5 24.a4± Smyslov – Botvinnik, Moscow 1951.

On the other hand 8...b5!? deserves attention: 9.dxc5 ♗xc5 10.♘d4 (10.♘e5 ♖b8 11.♘c6 ♕c7 12.♔f1 ♖b6 13.♗f4 e5 14.♘xe5 ♘xe5 15.♘d2 ♗b7 16.♘f3 ♗xf3 17.♗xf3 ♕e7–+ Alburt – Speelman, Hastings 1983) 10...♘d5 11.♘b3 ♗b7 12.♘xc5 ♘xc5 13.0–0 ♖c8 14.♖d1 0–0 15.♘c3 ♘d7 16.♗xd5 ♗xd5 17.♕d3 ♗c6 18.♗f4 e5 19.♗e3 f5 20.f3 ♕e8= ½–½ Andersson – Korchnoi, Johannesburg 1981.

9.♘e5 ♘d5

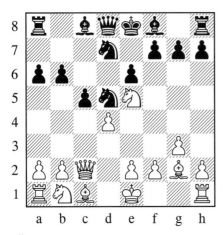

10.♘c3

10.♘c6 is not dangerous for Black: 10...♕c7 11.e4 ♘5f6! (After 11...♘e7?! 12.♘xe7 ♗xe7 13.♗f4 ♕a7 14.d5 e5 15.♗e3 0–0 16.♘d2

♕b8 17.a4 ♘f6 18.h3 b5 19.0–0 c4 20.b3 cxb3 21.♘xb3 ♗d7 22.♘a5↑ bxa4 23.♘c6 ♗xc6 24.dxc6± White's passed c-pawn went on to decide the battle in Tkachiev – A. Sokolov, Belfort 2010.) 12.d5 ♗b7 13.0–0 ♗d6 14.♘d2 0–0= 15.♘c4 exd5 16.exd5 ♘xd5 17.♗xd5 ♗xc6 18.♖d1 ♗xd5 19.♖xd5 ♗e7 20.♖xd7 ♕xd7 21.♘xb6 ♕e6 22.♘xa8 ♖xa8 23.♗e3 ♖c8 24.a3 ½–½ Landa – Meier, Copenhagen 2010.

10.♘xd7 ♗xd7! (10...♕xd7 11.dxc5 ♗xc5 12.0–0 ♗b7 13.♖d1 ♕c8 14.♘c3 ♘xc3 15.♕xc3 0–0 16.♗f4 ♗xg2 17.♔xg2 ♖d8 18.♕f3 ♖a7 19.♖ac1 ♖ad7 20.♖xd7 ♕xd7 21.♖c3± White had a microscopic advantage in Andersson – Lombard, Biel 1977) 11.dxc5 ♖c8 12.0–0 ♗xc5 13.♕b3 0–0 14.♘d2 ♗b5 15.♗f3 ♘b4 16.a4 ♘c2 17.♕xc2 ♗xf2† 18.♔xf2 ♖xc2 19.axb5 ♕d4† 20.♔g2 axb5 21.♘e4 f5 In this unbalanced position Black's chances were slightly higher in Postny – Naiditsch, Moscow 2005.

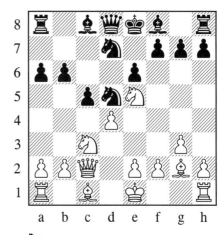

10...♘b4!?
Bacrot's novelty, and it seems to be a good one.

The most natural and common continuation has been 10...♗b7 11.♘xd5 when both candidate moves have been tried.

a) 11...exd5 does not equalize, although in the following game Black got the upper hand: 12.0–0 ♗e7 13.♖d1 0–0 14.♕f5 (14.♗f4!?± deserves attention) 14...♘xe5! 15.dxe5 ♖a7! 16.e6 d4 17.♗xb7 ♖xb7 18.e3 ♗f6 19.exd4 ♖e7 20.♗e3 fxe6 21.♕g4 h5 22.♕xh5 (22.♕e4 cxd4 23.♗xd4? loses to 23...♖d7 as the rook on d1 is no longer protected) 22...cxd4 23.♕e2 ♕d5 Black had the initiative and went on to win in Hübner – Smyslov, Tilburg 1982.

b) 11...♗xd5!
   Exchanging the light-squared bishops is a more reliable approach for Black.
12.♗xd5 exd5 13.0–0
   13.♘xd7 ♕xd7 14.dxc5 ♗xc5 15.0–0 0–0 16.♕d3 ♖fe8 17.♗d2 ♕g4 18.e3 h5 19.♔g2 ♖ad8 20.♖ae1 h4∓ Rustemov – Landa, Germany 2006.
13...♘xe5 14.dxe5 ♕c8 15.♖d1 ♕e6 16.♕d3 ♗e7 17.♕xd5 ♖d8 18.♕b3 ♖xd1† 19.♕xd1 0–0 20.♕b3 c4 21.♕c3 f6

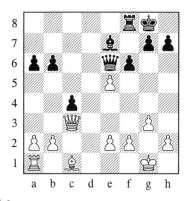

22.b3
   A possible improvement for white is 22.♗f4!? b5 (after 22...♖d8 23.exf6 ♗xf6 24.♕c2 Black's compensation is rather questionable) 23.♖d1 b4 (23...g5 24.♗e3 fxe5 regains the pawn, but Black's loose kingside means he is not yet out of the woods) 24.♕e3 ♖c8 It is not easy to say if Black has enough compensation for the missing pawn.
22...♖c8 23.♗b2 b5 24.♕e3 fxe5 25.bxc4

♖xc4 26.♗xe5 h6
   Black had enough counterplay and game was eventually drawn in Kramnik – Fritz 10, Bonn (3) 2006.

Before moving on, let us note that the rare 10...♘xe5!? deserves attention, for instance 11.dxe5 ♗b7 12.0–0 ♕c7 13.♘xd5 ♗xd5 14.♗xd5 exd5 15.♗f4 ♕c6 16.♖fd1 ♗e7 17.♕d3 d4 18.♖ac1 ♕e6 and Black was at least okay in Burmakin – Heinz, Bad Wiessee 2009.

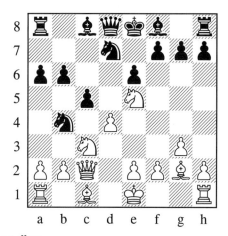

11.♕d1
   Faced with a prepared novelty over the board, Fressinet goes for a safe reply. Two other moves deserve consideration.

Firstly, it should be noted that 11.♕b3 cxd4! 12.♗xa8 ♘xe5 13.a3 ♘bc6 is a promising exchange sacrifice for Black.

11.♕e4!?
   It seems to me that this must be the critical path, although it is far from clear if White can make it work.
11...♖a7!
   The safest continuation.
   11...♘xe5 is playable although it enables White to develop a dangerous initiative:

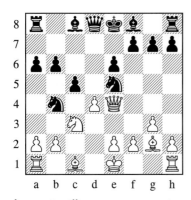

12.♗g5!? (12.♕xa8? is a mistake due to 12...cxd4 or 12...♘c2†; 12.dxe5 ♖a7 is approximately equal) 12...f6 (12...♕xg5 13.♕xa8 ♕d8 14.dxe5 ♘c2† 15.♔f1 ♘xa1 16.♗c6†! [16.♗e4 ♗e7 17.♗g2 0–0 is roughly equal] 16...♗d7 17.♗xd7† ♔xd7 18.♕xa6 looks rather dangerous for Black.) 13.dxe5 fxg5 14.♖d1 ♘d5 The resulting position is messy; the computer prefers Black, although in practice his position would not be easy to play.

12.0–0

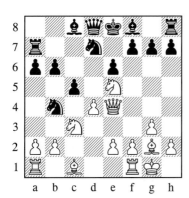

12...f5!

Black's position may look compromised, but White's pieces in the centre are unstable and his temporary initiative is about to evaporate.

13.♕f4 cxd4

Another reliable option is 13...♗d6 14.♖d1 ♘c2 15.♘c6 ♗xf4 16.♘xd8 ♔xd8 (also possible for Black is 16...♖xc1 17.♖axc1 ♘xd4) 17.♗xf4 ♘xa1 18.dxc5 bxc5 19.♖xa1

♗b7 20.e4 when White's compensation should be enough for a draw at best.

14.a3

14.♕xd4 ♗c5 is clearly better for Black.

14...♘xe5 15.axb4 ♘g6 16.♕b8 ♕c7

White faces an uphill struggle to demonstrate compensation.

11...♘xe5 12.dxe5 ♕xd1† 13.♔xd1 ♖a7!

This standard manoeuvre solves all of Black's problems.

14.a3 ♖d7† 15.♗d2 ♘d5 16.♘xd5 exd5 17.b4

White tries to undermine his opponent's pawn centre, but maybe he should have been less ambitious as later in the game Black's c-pawn becomes dangerous. In any case, the opening can be counted as a success for Black, and in the game he soon takes over the initiative.

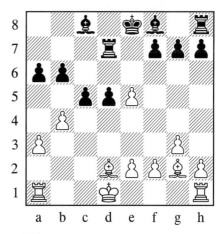

17...♖d8!

Well played. The rook steps back to allow the bishop to join the action along the c8-h3 diagonal.

18.♗g5

It is not easy to give advice to White, but the ensuing bishop exchange does not seem to help him, as it speeds up Black's development while his king remains safe in the centre.

18...♗e7 19.♗xe7 ♔xe7 20.bxc5 bxc5 21.♖b1 ♗f5

22.♖b7†

22.♖b6 ♖b8 is also good for Black.

22...♔e6 23.f4 ♖b8 24.♖a7 ♖a8 25.♖b7 ♖hb8 26.♖c7 ♖c8 27.♖b7 ♖ab8 28.♖a7 ♖a8 29.♖b7 ♖ab8 30.♖a7 c4!

After repeating for a few moves, Black correctly decides to play on. The other way was 30...♖c6!?.

31.♔d2 c3† 32.♔e3

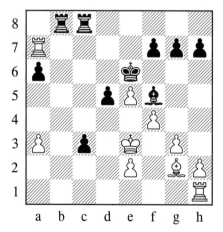

32...c2!

Black goes for the direct approach and refuses to waste time defending the a6-pawn.

33.♖c1!

33.♖xa6†? may look logical, but it is crucial for White's defence that the black king remains on e6, so that in certain variations the move exf5 can be played with check. 33...♔e7 34.♖a7† ♔e8! 35.♖c1 ♖b1 36.♔d2 ♖c4! White's situation is becoming perilous, for instance 37.♖a8† (or 37.e3 d4) 37...♔e7 38.♖a7† ♔d8 39.e3 d4 40.e4 ♖xc1 41.♔xc1 d3 and Black wins.

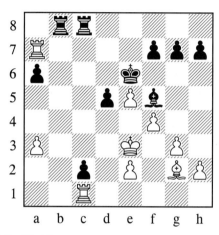

33...♖b3†

Compared with the previous note, 33...♖b1 is less convincing as after 34.♔d2 ♖c4 35.e3 d4 36.e4! White threatens to take on f5 with check. Play continues 36...♗g4 37.♗f1 ♖c3 38.♖xa6† ♔e7 39.♖a7† (39.♖d6? ♖f3) 39...♔d8 40.♖a8† (40.♖a4 ♖f3 41.♖xd4† ♔e7∓) 40...♔c7 when Black is likely to win a piece, but in return White will obtain three pawns and good drawing chances.

34.♔d2 ♖xa3 35.♗f3 g6 36.♖b7 ♖c5

Black could also have considered 36...♖c6 protecting the sixth rank, or 36...♖a4 taking control of the fourth.

37.♖b6† ♔e7 38.♖d6?!

38.♖b7† ♔f8 39.g4 looks better.

38...♖a4 39.♔e3 ♗e6 40.g4

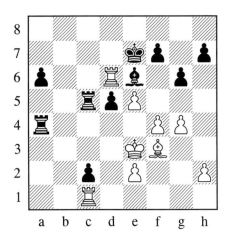

40...a5

40...f6! followed by ...fxe5 would have damaged the enemy pawn structure and should eventually win for Black.

41.♖a6 ♖c7 42.h3 h5 43.gxh5 gxh5 44.♗xh5 ♖e4† 45.♔d3 ♖xf4 46.♗g4 ♗xg4 47.hxg4 ♖xg4?!

It was necessary to play 47...♖fc4! keeping the c2-pawn.

48.♖xa5 ♔e6 49.♖xc2 ♖g3† 50.♔d2 ♖xc2† 51.♔xc2 ♔xe5

White has survived and the resulting endgame is easy to hold. Bacrot plays on for a while, but is eventually forced to accept the inevitable.

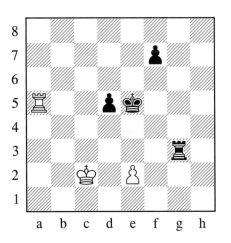

52.♔d2 f5 53.♖a8 ♖g6 54.♔d3 f4 55.♖e8† ♔f5 56.♖d8 ♖g3† 57.♔d2 ♔e4 58.♖e8† ♔d4 59.♖f8 ♖g4 60.♖xf4† ♖xf4 61.e3† ♔e4 62.exf4 d4 63.f5 ♔xf5 64.♔d3 ♔e5 65.♔d2 ♔e4 66.♔e2 d3† 67.♔d2 ♔d4 68.♔d1 ♔e3 69.♔e1 d2† 70.♔d1 ♔d3

½–½

GAME 44

▷ **G. Meier (2656)**
▶ **A. Giri (2701)**
39th Dortmund GM Tournament
Round 8, 29.07.2011 **[E04]**
Annotated by Sebastian Maze

Giri played a rare line in the Catalan with 7...♖b8 and Meier reacted with the classic plan of 9.b3, opening the c-file. The Dutch player found a novelty with 10...♘b4, which in fact is dubious; the simple 12.♖d1 would have given White a strong advantage. In the game, the German player chose the wrong plan with 12.♘c6 and had to play an unpleasant endgame. He finally managed to draw after a long fight.

1.♘f3 d5 2.d4 ♘f6 3.c4 e6 4.g3 dxc4 5.♗g2 a6 6.0–0 ♘c6 7.e3

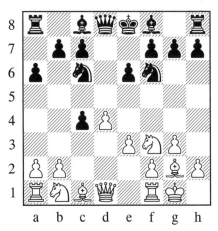

7...♖b8

In my opinion, this move is too passive and it is rarely seen at the top level.

7...♗d7 is more popular and active. 8.♘c3 ♘d5 9.♘d2 ♘b6 10.♕e2 ♘a5∞ This was played during the summer in Caruana – Morozevich, Biel 2011. The position is really unclear; Black is a pawn up but White has good compensation with a strong centre and also because the black knights are a little passive on the edge.

8.♕e2?!

8.♘fd2 is preferable. 8...e5 9.♗xc6† bxc6 10.dxe5 ♘g4 11.♘xc4 ♕xd1 12.♖xd1 ♗e6 13.♘bd2± White has a pleasant endgame.

8...b5 9.b3

9.♗d2 and 9.♖d1 are good alternatives, but I like the idea of breaking up Black's pawn structure and opening the c-file.

9...cxb3 10.axb3

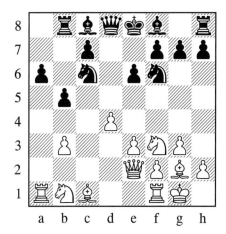

10...♘b4?N

A highly dubious novelty.

10...♗e7 was clearly stronger: 11.♗b2 0–0 12.♖c1 ♗b7 13.♘bd2∞ Black is a pawn up but White has good compensations with his powerful rooks on the a- and c-files plus his strong centre.

11.♘e5 ♘d7

11...♗d6 12.♗d2 ♖b6 13.♗xb4 ♗xb4

14.♘c6 ♕d6 15.♖c1 0–0 16.♘xb4 ♕xb4 17.♕c2 ♘e8 18.♘d2 ♕e7 19.♕c5± All White's pieces are working, while Black's pieces are completely uncoordinated. I like White's position very much; it's easy to play and Black will suffer a lot.

11...♗e7 12.♗a3±

12.♘c6?

What a bad move! It's really weird to exchange this strong knight for the bad knight on b4 – a significant strategic mistake.

12.♖d1

Of course! It is logical to put the rook on the same file as the black queen. Also, the b4-knight is still in a dubious situation with no future!

12...♕f6

12...♗d6? 13.♗a3 ♖b6 14.♗xb4 ♗xb4 15.♘c6 ♖xc6 16.♗xc6 0–0 17.♕c2±

12...♘xe5 13.dxe5 ♗d7 14.♘c3 ♗e7 15.♗a3 0–0 16.♖ac1± White's pieces are well placed, while the black pieces lack coordination.

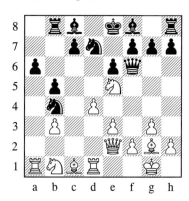

13.f4 h5

13...♗e7 14.♗d2 ♘xe5 15.dxe5 ♕f5 16.♗xb4 ♗xb4 17.♗c6† ♔e7 18.♕b2 ♖b6 19.♕d4 ♖xc6 20.♕xb4† ♔e8 21.♕d4 ♗e7 22.♖xa6 ♖xa6 23.♕b4† ♔e8 24.♕xb5† ♔e7 25.♕b4† ♔e8 26.♕b8+–

14.♗d2 ♘xe5 15.dxe5 ♕f5 16.♗xb4 ♗xb4

17.♗c6† ♔e7 18.♕b2

With the idea of moving to d4.

18...a5 19.♘a3±

Now if 19...h4 then 20.♕d4 and White has a winning position.

12...♘xc6 13.♗xc6 ♖b6 14.♕f3 ♗b4

Now Black is completely back in business! The position is still unclear, but Giri must have been quite satisfied to reach this situation after such a dubious novelty...

15.♗d2 ♗xd2 16.♘xd2 0–0

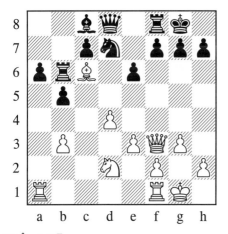

17.♗xd7?!∓

The German player wants to play with his knight against the bishop. He hopes to take control of the dark squares and put his knight on c5.

17.♖fc1 ♘b8 18.♗e4 e5 gives Black a comfortable position.

17...♕xd7 18.♘e4 ♕d5 19.♕f4

19.♘d2 ♕d8 (19...♕xf3 20.♘xf3 f6 21.b4 ♗b7 22.♘d2 e5 23.dxe5 fxe5 24.♖fc1=) 20.♕d1 ♗b7 21.f3 e5 22.♘e4 ♗xe4 23.fxe4 exd4 24.exd4 ♖d6∓

19...f6 20.♘c5 e5

Opening the position for the bishop.

21.♕h4 exd4 22.exd4

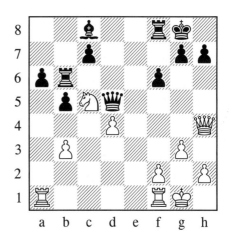

22...g5

22...h5 was the best move, with the idea of playing ...♗g4 to trap the queen. 23.♕e4 (23.♖fe1? ♗g4∓) 23...♕xe4 24.♘xe4 Compared to the game, the f6-pawn is still protected by the g7-pawn. 24...♖d8 25.♖fd1 ♖c6∓

23.♕e4 ♕xe4 24.♘xe4 ♖e8

24...♖d8 25.♖fd1 ♖c6 26.d5 This is the difference between 22...g5 and 22...h5. White should be able to hold the position.

25.f3 h6 26.♖fe1 ♔f7 27.♔f2

Let's analyse this endgame. Black has a pawn more on the queenside but the knight on e4 is strong and White is controlling two important squares in c5 and a5. In my opinion, with precise defence White has good drawing chances.

27...f5 28.♘c5 ♖d8 29.♔e3 ♖bd6 30.♖ed1 f4†

Giri tried to make something happen with this move. Unfortunately, it draws immediately.

30...♖e8† was better, but after 31.♔f2 ♔g6 32.♖d2 it is still really difficult to find a way to win for Black.

31.gxf4 gxf4† 32.♔xf4 ♖xd4† 33.♖xd4 ♖xd4† 34.♔e5= ♖d6 35.b4

The position is a dead draw; White's pieces are too active and there is no constructive plan for the Dutch player.

35...♔e7 36.♖g1 ♔f7 37.♖c1 ♔e7 38.♖g1 ♔f7 39.♖c1 ♖c6 40.f4 ♖f6 41.♖a1 ♔e7 42.♖g1 ♔f7 43.♖a1 ♖d6 44.♖c1 ♖d8

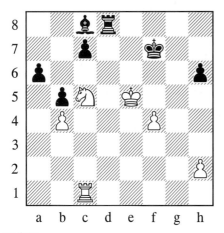

45.f5?!

Better was: 45.♘e4 ♖e8† 46.♔d4 ♖e7 47.h4 ♔g6 48.♖c6† ♔h5 49.♘c5=

45...c6 46.♘e6 ♖d5† 47.♔e4 ♗xe6 48.fxe6† ♔xe6 49.♖xc6† ♖d6 50.♖c7

With the idea of playing ♖h7.

50...♔f6 51.h4 ♔g6 52.♖c5 ♖d1 53.♖c6† ♔h5 54.♖xa6 ♖b1 55.♖b6 ♖xb4† 56.♔f3

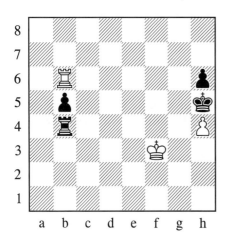

Black's king cannot move because h6 would be hanging; the position should be a draw and indeed Meier holds it easily.

56...♖b3† 57.♔e2 ♖b2† 58.♔e3 ♖b1 59.♔e2 b4

The last trick! Meier just has to put his king on g2 when the b-pawn reaches b2.

60.♔f2 b3 61.♔g3 ♖b2 62.♔h3 ♖b1 63.♔g3 b2 64.♖b5† ♔g6 65.h5† ♔f6 66.♔g2 ♔e6 67.♔h2 ♔f6 68.♔g2 ♔e6 69.♔h2 ♔f6

½–½

GAME 45

▷ **G. Meier (2656)**
▶ **V. Kramnik (2781)**
39th Dortmund GM Tournament
Round 2, 22.07.2011 **[E15]**
Annotated by Kamil Miton

This was a very interesting game between two solid players. After choosing a rare continuation, Kramnik tried hard to complicate the game and was pressing the whole time. However, at certain points Meier had good chances to grab the advantage, but towards the end (probably in time trouble) he made three weak moves and finally lost.

1.d4 ♘f6 2.c4 e6 3.♘f3 b6 4.g3 ♗a6 5.b3 ♗b4† 6.♗d2 ♗e7 7.♗g2 0–0

The main line of 7...c6 has been very popular in recent years.

8.♘c3 d5 9.cxd5 exd5 10.0–0 ♖e8 11.♖c1 ♗b7 12.♘e5 ♘a6

In my opinion, the plan with ...♘bd7-f8 looks more solid, but the idea is the same as in the game; at some point Black will bring the knight to the e6-square.

12...♘bd7

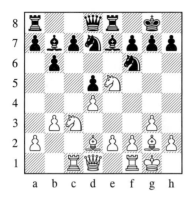

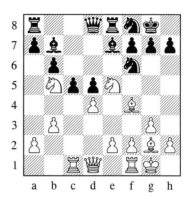

13.♘b5!?

I think this rare move is very interesting.

The normal choice is: 13.♗f4 c6 (13...♘f8) 14.e4 ♘f8 (14...dxe4?! 15.♘xe4 ♘xe5 16.dxe5 ♘d5 [16...♕xd1 17.♖fxd1 ♘d5 18.♘d6 ♗xd6 19.exd6 ♘xf4 20.gxf4±] 17.♕h5 g6 18.♕f3 ♕d7 19.♖fe1 ♖ad8 20.♗h6↑) 15.exd5 cxd5 16.♗h3 (16.♘b5 ♘e6 17.♗h3 ♘xf4 18.gxf4 ♗d6 19.♔h1∞) 16...a6 17.♘e2 ♗d6 18.♘c6 ♗xc6 19.♖xc6 ♗xf4 20.♘xf4 ♘g6 21.♘xg6 hxg6 22.♖e1 ♖xe1† 23.♕xe1 b5 24.a3± Epishin – Spraggett, Coria del Rio 2007.

13.♘d3!? is also worth considering.

13...c5 14.♗f4

14.♘c4?! ♗a6=

14.♗g5 h6=

14...♘f8!

Black has to play this to gain chances for equality.

14...♘xe5 15.dxe5 ♘e4 16.f3 a6 17.fxe4 axb5 18.exd5 ♖xa2 19.♕c2 ♖xc2 20.♕xc2±

14...a6 15.♘xd7 axb5 (15...♘xd7 16.♘c7 g5 17.♘xe8 gxf4 18.dxc5 ♘xc5 19.♘c7 ♕xc7 20.b4±) 16.♘xf6† ♗xf6 17.dxc5 bxc5 18.♖xc5 ♖xa2 19.♗xd5 ♗xd5 20.♖xd5±

14...♘h5 15.dxc5!?N (15.♗h3 ♘xe5 16.♗xe5 ♗f8 17.♗g4 ♘f6 18.♗c7 ♕e7 19.♗d6 ♕d8 20.♗c7 ♕e7 21.♗d6 ½–½ A. Maric – Chiburdanidze, Groningen [16] 1997) 15...♘xc5 (15...bxc5 16.♘xf7!+–) 16.♗e3 ♘f6 17.b4 ♘e6 18.♕b3±

15.dxc5

15.♗h3 a6 (15...♘e6 16.♗xe6 fxe6 17.♘f3 ♘d7 18.♘d6 ♗xd6 19.♗xd6±) 16.♘xf7 ♔xf7 17.♗c7 axb5 18.♗xd8 ♖exd8∓ The engines like this idea for White, but I prefer the black position.

15...bxc5 16.♘c4 ♘e6

This leads to a lot of sharp lines.

The alternative is 16...♘g6 and now:

a) 17.♘bd6 ♘xf4 transposes to the sub-note after 17.♗e5 below.

b) 17.♕d2 dxc4 18.♗xb7 ♕xd2 19.♗xd2 ♖ab8 20.♗a6 ♗f8 21.♘c3 cxb3 22.axb3 ♖xb3 23.♗g5=

c) 17.♗g5 ♖b8 (17...♗a6 18.♗xf6 gxf6 19.♕xd5 ♕xd5 20.♗xd5 ♗xb5 21.♗xa8 ♖xa8 22.f4∞) 18.♗xf6 dxc4 19.♕xd8 (19.♗xe7 ♕xe7 20.♗xb7 ♖xb7 21.bxc4 ♖d7 22.♕a4 ♕xe2 23.♘c3 ♕g4∞) 19...♗xd8 20.♗xd8 ♗xg2 21.♔xg2 ♖xb5 22.bxc4 ♖b2 23.♗c7 ♖exe2 24.♗d6 ♘e5 25.♗xc5 ♖xa2=

17.♗e5

17.♘bd6 ♘xf4 18.♘xb7 (18.♘xe8 ♘xg2 19.♗xf6† ♗xf6 20.♘d2 ♘e3 21.fxe3 ♗g5∓) 18...♕c7 19.gxf4 dxc4 (19...♕xb7 20.e3 ♖ad8 21.♘e5 ♗d6 22.♕c2±) 20.♖xc4 ♖ab8 21.♘xc5 ♗xc5 22.♕c2 ♘d7 (22...♗xf2† 23.♖xf2 ♕b6 24.♗f3±; 22...♖bc8 23.e3±) 23.e3 a5 24.♗h3 ♕a7 25.♗xd7 ♕xd7 26.♖xc5 ♕g4† 27.♔h1 ♕f3† 28.♔g1 ♕g4†=

17...♘g4

17...♗a6 18.♘cd6 ♘g4 (18...♖f8 19.h3

[19.♗xf6 ♗xf6 20.♗xd5 ♕b6 21.a4 ♖ad8 22.♘c4 ♕b8 23.e4 ♗xb5 24.axb5 ♕xb5 25.e5 ♘d4! 26.♘d6 ♖xd6 27.exd6 ♘e2† 28.♔g2 ♘xc1 29.♕xc1 ♗e5 30.♖d1 ♗xd6 31.♗xf7† ♔xf7 32.♖xd6 ♕xb3 33.♕xc5 ♕b7†=] 19...♕b8 20.a4 ♗xb5 21.♘f5 ♕xe5 22.♘xe7† ♔h8 23.axb5±) 19.♘xe8 ♗xb5 20.♘xg7 ♘xe5 21.♕xd5 ♕xd5 22.♗xd5 ♘d4 23.♘f5 ♖e8 24.♘xe7† ♖xe7 25.♖xc5 ♗xe2 26.♖fc1 ♗f3 27.♗xf3 ♘exf3† 28.♔g2 ♘e1† 29.♔h3∞

18.♗a1

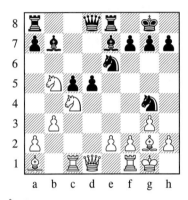

18...♗a6
18...♖b8 19.♘e5 a6 20.♘d4 ♘xe5 (20...cxd4 21.♘xg4 ♗a3 22.♖c2 ♕g5 23.h3± followed by ♘h2-f3) 21.♘xe6 fxe6 22.♗xe5 ♗d6 23.♗xd6 ♕xd6 24.♕d2±
18...♕d7 19.e4 d4 20.♘xg4 ♕xb5 21.f4↑
19.♘ca3 ♗g5
19...d4 20.e3 ♘f6 21.exd4 cxd4 22.♖c6 ♗b7 23.♖xe6 (23.♘c4!? ♗xc6 24.♘xc6 ♗c5∞) 23...♗xg2 24.♖xe7 ♕xe7 25.♔xg2 a6 26.♘xd4 ♕xa3 27.♘f5 ♕b4= intending ...♕e4†.
19...♖b8 20.e4 ♘xh2 21.♔xh2 d4 22.e5 ♗xb5 23.♘xb5 ♖xb5 24.♗c6 ♖b6 25.♗xe8 ♕xe8 26.f4±
20.♖c2
20.e3 ♘xe3!
20...♖b8 21.♗xd5 ♗xb5 22.♘xb5 ♖xb5 23.♗c6 ♖b6 24.♗xe8 ♕xe8 25.e4 h5 26.h3 ♗f6 27.hxg4 ♗xa1 28.♕xa1 ♘d4⇄

The position remains most unclear, with chances for both sides.

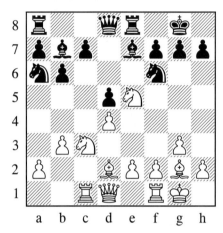

13.♗f4
White may also try:
13.♘b5 c6
We shall see this tricky move again in some similar positions. 13...♗f8 14.♗g5 c6 15.♘xc6 ♗xc6 16.♖xc6 ♕d7 17.♕c1 ♘e4 18.♗xe4 ♖xe4 19.a4 ♖xe2∞
14.♘xc6
14.♖xc6!?
14...♗xc6 15.♖xc6 ♕d7 16.♕c1 ♘b8
16...♘c5 17.♖c7 ♕xb5 18.dxc5 ♗xc5 19.♗c3±
17.♖xf6 ♗xf6 18.♘c7 ♖c8 19.♘xd5 ♖xc1 20.♘xf6† gxf6 21.♖xc1 ♕xd4 22.♗e3 ♕b2 23.♗xa8∞

13...h6
Kramnik doesn't hurry to advance his c-pawn. It appears he did not want to play the structure with an isolated pawn which would arise after:
13...c5 14.dxc5
14.♘b5 ♘e4 15.dxc5 ♗xc5 16.♘d3 ♕d7 17.a4 d4 18.b4 ♘xb4 19.♘xb4 ♗xb4 20.♖c7 ♕d5 21.♕xd4 ♕xd4 22.♘xd4 ♗a6 23.♘b5 ♗c5 24.♖xc5 ♘xc5 25.♗xa8 ♖xa8 26.♘c7 ♖d8 27.♘xa6 ½–½ Fridman – Miroshnichenko, Eforie 2009.

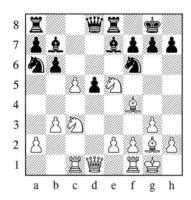

14...♘xc5

14...bxc5 15.♘c4 followed by ♘e3 targets the weak d5-pawn.

15.♘b5 ♗f8 16.♘d3 ♖c8

16...♘e6   17.♘c7   ♘xc7   18.♖xc7   ♗a6 19.♕c2±

17.♘xa7 ♖a8 18.♘b5 ♖xa2 19.♘c3 ♖a7! 20.♘xc5 bxc5 21.♗g5 d4=

14.♘b5 ♗f8

14...c6 15.♘xc6 ♗xc6 16.♖xc6 ♕d7 17.♖xf6 ♗xf6 18.♘d6±

15.♗h3?!

Other options were better:

15.a3 c6 (after 15...c5 White can sacrifice a pawn with the interesting 16.b4 cxb4 17.axb4 ♗xb4 18.♕a4 ♗f8 19.♗h3⯅) 16.♘xc6 ♕d7 17.♘cxa7 ♖xa7 18.♘xa7 ♖a8 19.b4 ♖xa7∞

15.♕c2!? c5

15...c6 16.♘xc6 ♗xc6 17.♕xc6 ♘b4 18.♕b7 ♖xe2 19.♗e5!? ♖xa2 20.♗h3!? (intending ♗c8!) 20...♘d3 21.♗xf6 (21.♖cd1 ♘xe5 22.dxe5 ♖b8 23.♕c6 ♕e8 24.♕xe8 ♘xe8 25.♖xd5 a6 26.♘d4 ♖d2⇄) 21...♕xf6 22.♖c3 ♖e8 23.♖xd3 ♖e1 24.f4 ♕g6 25.♖xe1 ♕xd3 26.♘d6 ♕xd4† (26...♗xd6 27.♕xd5 g6 28.♕xd6 ♕d2 29.♖e8† ♔h7 30.♖h8† ♔xh8 31.♕f8† ♔h7 32.♖xf7†=) 27.♔h1 ♕f6 28.♘xf7 ♕c3 29.♘xh6† ♔h8 30.♘f7† ♔g8 31.♖g1 ♕f3† 32.♗g2 ♖xg2 33.♖xg2 ♕f1† 34.♖g1 ♕f3†=

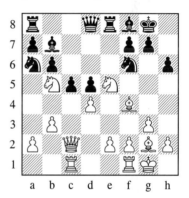

16.♕b2!

An accurate move. White avoids ...♘b4 coming with tempo, and improves the support of the e5-knight, because one of Black's ideas is to take on d4 and play ...g5.

16.♖fd1   ♘b4   (16...cxd4   17.♘f3   ♘b4 18.♕b2 d3=) 17.♕b2 a6 18.♘xf7 ♔xf7 19.♘c7 ♖c8 20.♘xe8 ♕xe8 21.a3 ♘c6 22.dxc5 bxc5 23.♖xd5 ♘d4 24.♖xd4 ♗xg2 25.♖dd1 ♗d5 26.f3∞

16...♕e7

16...♘e4 17.dxc5 ♘axc5 18.♗xe4 dxe4 19.♘c4± and White will occupy the weak d6-square.

16...g6 17.b4 ♘xb4 18.dxc5 bxc5 19.♘c7 ♕xc7 20.♘g4 ♕xf4 21.gxf4 ♘xg4 22.a3 a5 23.axb4 axb4 24.h3±

17.♖fd1

17.♖fe1!?

17...cxd4
  17...g5 18.♗e3 ♗g7 19.♕b1±
  17...g6 18.dxc5 bxc5 19.♘d6 g5 20.♘exf7
gxf4 21.♕c2 ♗g7 22.♕g6 ♔f8 23.gxf4±
18.♘xd4 g5 19.♘ec6
  19.♘f5 ♕e6 20.♘d4 ♕e7=
19...♕d7 20.♗e5 ♘g4
  20...♘h5 21.b4 f6 22.b5 ♘c5 (22...fxe5
23.bxa6 ♗xa6 24.♘c2 e4 25.♘2b4↑)

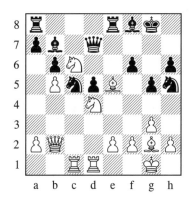

23.♗b8! ♖axb8 24.♘xb8 ♖xb8 25.♘c6±
21.♗h3 ♗c5
  21...f5 22.b4 (or 22.f4) and:
  a) 22...♘xe5 23.♘xf5 ♗xc6 (23...g4
24.♘xe5 ♖xe5 25.♕xe5 ♖e8 [25...gxh3
26.♖c4→] 26.♕f4 gxh3 27.♘xh6† ♗xh6
28.♕xh6±) 24.♘xh6† ♗xh6 25.♗xd7 ♗xd7
26.♖xd5 ♗g7 27.♕a3 ♗e6 28.♖dd1 ♘b8
29.♖c7∞
  b) 22...♖ac8 23.b5 ♘c5 24.♘xf5 ♕xf5
25.♗d4±
  c) 22...♘xb4 23.♘xb4 ♘xe5 24.♗xf5 ♕f7∞

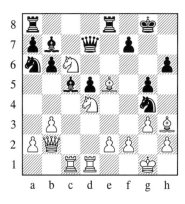

22.b4
  22.a3 ♗xc6 23.♗xg4 ♕xg4 24.♘xc6 ♖ac8
(24...♕e6 25.b4 ♕xc6 26.bxc5 bxc5 27.e4
d4 28.♗xd4 ♕b6 29.♗g7 ♕xb2 30.♗xb2
♖xe4 31.♖d7∞; 24...♕f5 25.♘d4±) 25.♘xa7
♗xf2† 26.♔xf2 ♖xc1 27.♖xc1 ♕f5† 28.♔g1
♕xe5 29.♕xe5 ♖xe5 30.♔f2 ♘c5 31.♘c6±
  22.e3 f5∞
22...♘xb4 23.♘xb4 ♖xe5 24.♖xc5 bxc5
25.♘d3 ♕a4 26.♘b3
  26.♖b1 ♕xd4 27.♕xd4 cxd4 28.♖xb7 ♖xe2
29.♗xg4 ♖xa2 30.♗h5↑
  26...♖ae8 27.♘dxc5 ♕c4 28.e3 ♖f5 29.♘a5
  29.♖d2!?
  29...♕xc5 30.♗xg4 ♗c8 31.♗xf5 ♗xf5
32.♘b3∞

White will have a strong knight on d4,
but the weak light squares give Black enough
counterplay.

15...c5 16.a3 ♘e4

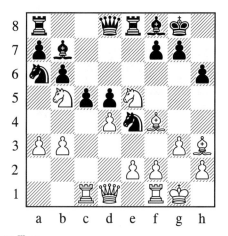

17.♖c2

An interesting option was the pawn sacrifice
with 17.b4!?. In return for the pawn, the
black pieces stay passive and the pressure on
the centre is removed. With ...cxd4 no longer
threatened, White's e5-knight would be more
comfortable.

17...g6

17...cxd4 18.♘c6 ♗xc6 19.♖xc6 ♘c3 20.♘xc3 dxc3 21.b4 d4 22.♖c4± and the knight on a6 is out of play.

18.♕c1

An alternative is 18.♗g2, but that would admit that White's plan with 15.♗h3 was just a waste of time.

18...g5

18...cxd4 19.♘c6 ♗xc6 20.♖xc6 g5 21.♗c7 (or 21.♗d2) 21...♘xc7 22.♘xc7 ♘c3 23.♕c2 ♖xe2 24.♕d3 ♖b8 25.♘a6 ♖b7 26.♖xc3 dxc3 27.♕xe2 ♗xa3 28.b4± would be more pleasant for White.

19.♗e3

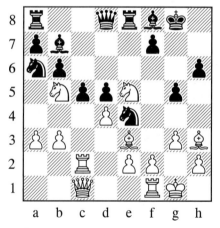

19...♗g7

The immediate sacrifice on e5 does not work: 19...♖xe5? 20.dxe5 ♕e8 21.f3 ♘xg3 22.♖f2 ♕xb5 23.♗xg5 hxg5 24.♕xg5† ♗g7 25.♖g2+−

However, it is interesting if Black plays a different version of the sacrifice:
19...cxd4!? 20.♗xd4 ♖xe5 21.♗xe5 ♕e8 22.♗a1
    22.♘c7 ♕xe5 23.♘xa8 ♗xa8 24.b4∞
22...♕xb5 23.♕b2 f6 24.f3 ♗c5† 25.♔h1
    25.♖xc5 ♕xc5† 26.♔h1 ♘f2† 27.♖xf2 ♕xf2 28.♗e6† ♔h7 29.♗f5†=

25...♗e3 26.fxe4 d4!
    Black has nice compensation for the sacrificed material.
27.♗g2 ♕e5 28.♖c4 ♘c5 29.♖xd4 ♗xd4 30.♕xd4 ♕xd4 31.♗xd4 ♘xb3 32.♗xf6 ♘d2 33.♖d1 ♘xe4 34.♖d7 ♘xf6 35.♖xb7 ♖e8 36.♖xa7 ♖xe2=
    The game is equal.

20.♘f3

White decides to go back with knight, thereby removing the threat of ...cxd4.

20.f4 f6 21.♘g6 ♔h7 22.f5 Generally, this kind of structure is bad for White, because the g6-knight, h3-bishop and e3-bishop have all stopped playing. 22...♕d7∓

Black has no problems after:
20.f3 ♘d6 21.♘xd6 ♕xd6 22.f4 f6

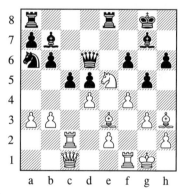

23.♘g6 c4!?
This is a logical solution, hoping to connect the pawns with ...b5 soon.
    23...g4?! 24.♗g2 (24.♗xg4 f5 25.♗xf5 ♖xe3–+) 24...♕e6 25.♖c3 ♕f5 26.♘h4±
    23...♗c8 24.f5 ♗b7∞
    23...♖ad8 24.♖f2 cxd4 25.♗xd4 ♘c5 26.♗xc5 bxc5 27.♖xc5 f5 28.♘e5 g4 29.♗g2 ♗xe5 30.fxe5 ♖xe5 31.b4±
24.♖c3 ♘c7 25.bxc4 dxc4 26.♖xc4 ♘d5
    26...♕d5 27.♖xc7 ♕h1† 28.♔f2 ♕xh2† 29.♔e1 ♗a6 30.♖f2 ♕xh3 31.♕c6±

27.♗f2 ♖xe2 28.♗c8 ♖xc8 29.♖xc8† ♔h7

Black has the better chances.

20...♕e7 21.♖d1 ♖ad8

An interesting approach; Black sacrifices a pawn for the initiative. Other moves are possible, but clearly Kramnik was feeling ambitious.

22.♘xa7 ♘d6

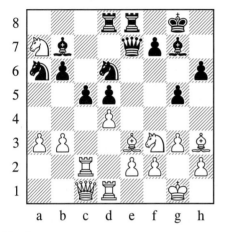

23.a4

White can initiate a forced line with:

23.dxc5 bxc5 24.♗xc5 ♘xc5 25.♖xc5 ♘c4
  25...♕xe2 26.♘d4 ♗xd4 27.♖xd4 ♕e5 28.♕d1 (28.♖d1 ♘e4 29.♖c7 ♕f6 30.♕c2 d4! 31.♗f1 ♗d5∓) 28...♖a8 29.♘c6 ♕e1† 30.♗f1 ♖ac8 (30...♖xa3=) 31.♖dxd5 ♖xc6 32.♖xc6 ♗xc6 33.♖xd6 ♗b5 34.♖d3 ♔g7 35.b4 ♗xd3 36.♕xd3 ♕a1 37.b5∞
26.♘c6 ♕xc5
  26...♗xc6 27.♖xc6 ♕b7 28.♖xh6 (28.♖xc4 dxc4 29.♖xd8 ♖xd8 30.♕xc4∞) 28...♗xh6 29.bxc4 ♕a6 30.e3 dxc4 31.♖xd8 ♖xd8 32.♗f1 ♕f6 33.♘d2 c3 34.♘e4 ♕e5 35.♕xc3 ♕xe4 36.♕f6 ♖d2 37.♕xh6 ♕f5 38.f4 gxf4 39.♕xf4 ♕xf4 40.exf4 ♖a2=
27.♘xd8 ♖xe2

The game is very unclear. White has a material plus, but it does not look like this is enough for an advantage.

28.♖f1 ♗a6 29.bxc4 ♗f6 30.♕d1 ♗xc4 31.♘d2 ♗xd8 32.♘xc4 ♕xc4 33.♗g2 ♗b6 34.♗xd5 ♕c2=

The position is equal.

23...♘b4

23...♖a8!? is an interesting idea, albeit not a human one. After 24.♘b5 (24.dxc5 bxc5 25.♘b5 d4↑) 24...♘xb5 25.axb5 ♘b4 26.♖cd2 ♖a5 27.♗f5 ♕c7 (27...♖xb5 28.h4→) 28.dxc5 ♖xe3 29.fxe3 bxc5 Black has compensation for the sacrificed exchange.

24.dxc5 bxc5 25.♖xc5 ♘a2

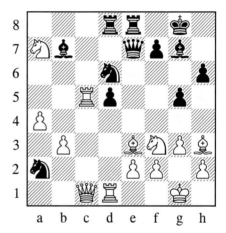

26.♕c2

White could also consider:
26.♕b1 ♘e4 27.♘b5
  27.♕xa2 d4! (27...♘xc5 28.♘d4±) We shall see this strong idea of advancing the d-pawn in several sharp variations. Black gets super-active play, because both the d-file and the a8-h1 diagonal are opened. 28.♘c6 ♕xc5 (28...♗xc6 29.♖xc6 dxe3 30.♖xd8 ♖xd8 31.♕c2 ♘xf2 32.♗f1 ♖d1∞) 29.♘xd8 ♖xd8 30.b4 (30.♗d2 d3–+) 30...♕e7 31.♖xd4 ♗xd4 32.♗xd4 h5∓
  27.♘c6 ♗xc6 28.♖xc6 ♘ec3 29.♕d3 ♘xd1 30.♕xd1 ♘c3 31.♕d3 d4 32.♗d2 ♕e2 33.♕xe2 ♖xe2∞
27...♘xc5 28.♕xa2 d4

Typical! Otherwise White blockades on the d4-square, and the black rook and b7-bishop will be out of play.

29.♘bxd4 ♗xd4

29...♘e6!?

30.♖xd4 ♖xd4 31.♘xd4 ♕e4 32.♘f3 g4 33.♗xg4 ♕xg4 34.♗xc5 ♗xf3 35.exf3 ♕xf3 36.♕d2 ♖e5 37.♕d8† ♔h7 38.♗b4∞

26...♘b4 27.♕c1

After 27.♕b1 ♘e4 28.♖dc1 (28.♖cc1 d4 29.♖xd4 (29.♘xd4 ♗xd4 30.♖xd4 ♖xd4 31.♗xd4 ♘d2–+) 29...♗xd4 30.♗xd4 ♖xd4 31.♘xd4 ♘xf2 32.♔xf2 ♕e3† 33.♔f1 ♖xd4 34.♘b5 ♕d2–+) Black has 28...d4 29.♖c7 dxe3 30.♖xe7 exf2† 31.♔f1 ♖xe7 Black has good compensation for the queen.

Another alternative was:
27.♕d2

But it is always hard to decide to allow a fork.
27...♘e4

27...d4 28.♘xd4 ♗xd4 29.♗xd4 ♘e4 30.♕xb4 ♘xf2 31.♗g2 ♘xd1 32.♕xb7 ♕xb7 33.♗xb7 ♖xd4∞
28.♕xb4 d4

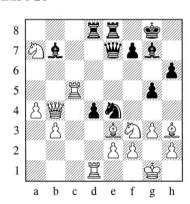

29.♖xd4

There is a long line which ends in Black's favour after: 29.♘xd4 ♘xc5 30.♗g4 ♗xd4 31.♖xd4 ♖xd4 32.♗xd4 ♕e4 33.♗f3 ♕b1† 34.♔g2 ♗xf3† 35.exf3 ♘d3 36.♕b5 ♘e1†

37.♔h3 ♖d8 38.♕e5 ♖xd4 39.♕xd4 ♘xf3 40.♕c4

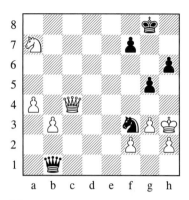

40...h5–+

29...♗xd4 30.♘xd4

30.♗xd4 ♘xc5 31.♗f1 ♘e4 32.♕xe7 ♖xe7∓
30...♘xc5 31.♘ac6 ♕e4 32.♕xc5 ♗xc6 33.♕xc6 ♖xd4 34.♕xe4 ♖d1† 35.♔g2 ♖xe4 36.♗f5 ♖b4 37.♗c2∞

We have reached a very interesting position. White has two bishops and three pawns for two rooks. The position is probably equal, since Black can sacrifice a rook for the light-squared bishop and the b-pawn.

27...♘c4?

A risky move. Kramnik didn't want a draw, but objectively speaking that was the correct choice for Black. 27...♘a2= repeats.

28.bxc4 d4

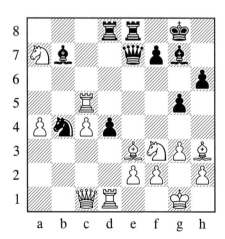

29.♗xg5??

A huge mistake. It is not easy to understand why White chose this move.

29.♘xd4 ♕xc5 30.♘f5 ♖xd1† 31.♕xd1 ♕xc4 32.♕d7 ♖b8 33.♘e7† ♔h8 34.♘ac8 ♖xc8 35.♕xb7 ♖d8 36.a5± would have given White an easy game. On the other hand, Black has some problems since the squares around his king are weak and his counterplay is limited.

Another good option was 29.♖xd4 ♖xd4 30.♘xd4 ♕xc5 31.♘ab5± with the better prospects for White.

29...♕xc5

Natural and best.

Black could play 29...hxg5, but this would give him only a draw after 30.♖xg5 ♗xf3 31.exf3 ♕xa7 32.♖xg7† ♔xg7 33.♕g5† ♔f8 34.♕h6† ♔g8. White can try 35.♗f5 f6 36.♕xf6, but after 36...♕g7 37.♗e6† ♔h8 there is nothing better than 38.♕h4† ♕h7 39.♕f6† with a draw by perpetual check.

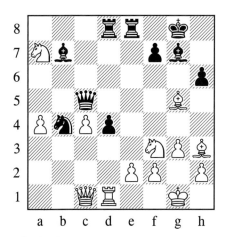

30.♗xd8 d3!

White has a piece and three pawns more, but all the black pieces are included in the attack. Black is attacking with five pieces plus the d3-pawn, while White's defence consists of the queen, rook, f3-knight and h3-bishop. If we look at the position in this way, Black has an extra piece!

31.♘e1?

The final mistake, but the white position was already worse.

The forced line after 31.e4 ♕xa7 32.♕a3 ♕c5 33.♖b1 ♖xd8 34.♕xb4 ♕xb4 35.♖xb4 ♗xe4 36.♘d2 ♗c3 37.♘xe4 ♗xb4 38.♘f6† ♔g7 39.♘d5 ♗c5∓ is in Black's favour.

31.♖d2 was a better option than the game move, but the white position remains critical: 31...♕xa7 32.♘e1 ♗d4

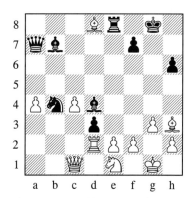

33.e3 ♗xe3 34.fxe3 ♕xe3† 35.♔f1 ♖xd8 Black has a very strong attack, and he is only a pawn down.

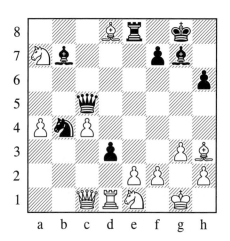

31...♖xe2 32.♕f4 ♖xf2
0–1

GAME 46
▷ **J. Hammer (2610)**
▶ **A. Naiditsch (2706)**
Greek Team Championship, Eretria
07.07.2011 **[E20]**
Annotated by Kamil Miton

This is an interesting game in the 4.f3 line against the Nimzo-Indian, which is becoming fashionable again. Black chose a rare and aggressive line with 4...c5 and 8...b5 and it seems he managed to equalize after the opening. Probably 12...♗xc3!? would have led to an equal position. In a very sharp middlegame and after mistakes by both sides, Black reached an almost-winning position, but eventually it slipped away to a draw.

1.d4 ♘f6 2.c4 e6 3.♘c3 ♗b4 4.f3 c5 5.d5 0–0 6.e4 ♖e8 7.♘ge2 d6 8.♘g3 b5
Black's idea is to sacrifice a pawn for the initiative. White has not finished his development yet and Black can try to use the e-file and the g1-a7 diagonal to create active play.

9.dxe6 ♗xe6

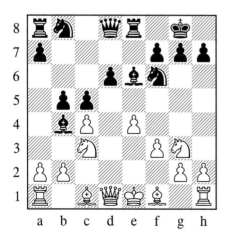

10.cxb5
10.♗f4 ♕a5 (10...bxc4 11.♕xd6 ♕a5 12.♕d2 ♘c6 13.♗e2 ♖ad8 14.♕c1 ♘d4 15.0–0 h6 16.♖f2∞; 10...♘c6 11.cxb5 ♘d4 12.♗e2 d5 13.0–0 ♘xe2† 14.♕xe2 d4 15.♖fd1∞) 11.cxb5 ♗xc3† (11...d5 12.♗e2 d4 13.a3 ♗xc3† 14.bxc3 ♕xc3† 15.♗d2 ♕b2 16.♖b1 ♕xa3 17.♖a1 ♕b2=) 12.bxc3 ♕xc3† 13.♗d2 ♕a3 14.♗e2 ♘bd7 15.0–0∞

10...d5 11.♗d2
11.♔f2 ♕b6↑

11.a3 ♗a5 12.b4 cxb4 13.axb4 ♗xb4 14.♕d4 ♗a5 15.e5 ♗b6† The king is a target on e1.

11...♘bd7
11...dxe4 12.♘cxe4 ♘xe4 13.♘xe4 ♘d7 14.♗e2

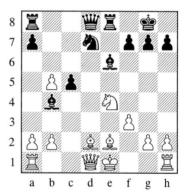

14...♕h4† (14...♘e5 15.♗xb4 [15.0–0 ♕d4† 16.♖f2 ♕xb2 17.♗xb4 ♕xb4=] 15...cxb4 16.♕xd8 ♖axd8 17.b3 f5 18.♘g5 ♘d3† 19.♗xd3 ♖xd3 20.0–0 ♗d7=) 15.g3 ♕h3 16.♔f2 ♖ad8 17.♗xb4 cxb4 18.♕d4 ♘f6 (18...♘b6 19.♕xb4 ♗d5 20.♖ad1±) 19.♘xf6† gxf6 20.♕xb4 ♗xa2 21.♖ad1 ♗d5 22.♖d2 ♔g7∞

11...d4?! 12.♘ce2 ♗xd2† 13.♕xd2 ♘bd7 (13...a6 14.bxa6 ♘xa6 15.♘f4 ♘b4 16.♘xe6 fxe6 17.♗c4 ♘fd5 18.0–0 ♘e3 19.♖fc1±) 14.♘f4 ♘e5 15.b3±

12.exd5 ♘xd5

An interesting option was:
12...♗xc3!?

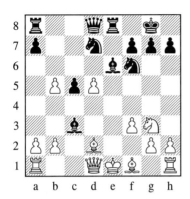

a) 13.♗xc3 ♘xd5 14.♗e2 ♘e3
 14...♕b6 15.0–0 ♘e3 16.♕d2 ♘xf1 17.♖xf1
 c4† 18.♔h1 ♕xb5 19.♘e4⩲
15.♕d2 ♗c4
 15...♘xg2† 16.♔f2 ♘h4 17.♖ad1↑ A typical
 situation. Sometimes it is better to give back
 the pawn in order to improve one's position
 and gain the initiative rather than defend
 passively all the time.
16.♔f2 ♗xe2 17.♘xe2
 17.♖he1 ♘d1† 18.♖axd1 ♗xd1 19.♖xd1
 ♘b6 20.♕c1 ♕h4∓
 17...♕g5 18.♘g3 ♘f6 19.♖he1 ♖ad8 20.♕c1
 ♖d3 21.♔g1 ♘fd5 22.♗d2 h5↑

b) 13.bxc3 ♗xd5† 14.♗e2 ♗c4 15.0–0 ♗xe2
16.♘xe2 ♕b6 17.c4 ♖ad8

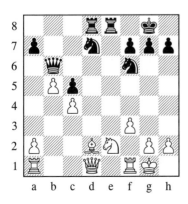

White has an extra pawn but Black's rooks
are very active and after ...♘e5 it will be very
hard to defend the c4-pawn.
18.♗c3
 18.♘g3 ♘e5 19.♕c1 ♘xc4 20.♕xc4 ♖xd2=
 18.♗g5 ♕e6 19.♘g3 ♕xc4 20.♘e4 ♘e5
 21.♕b3 ♘xe4 22.♕xc4 ♘xc4 23.♗xd8
 ♘ed2 24.♗g5 ♘xf1 25.♔xf1 f6=
 18.♕a4 ♖xe2 19.♗a5

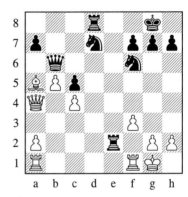

19...♘e5! Nice move! 20.♖fe1 (20.♗xb6
 ♖dd2–+) 20...♖xe1† 21.♖xe1 ♕d6 22.♗xd8
 ♕d4† 23.♔h1 ♘d3–+
18.♖c1 ♘e5 19.♘g3 ♘d3 20.♖c2 ♘b4
 21.♖b2 ♘d3=
18...♕e6 19.♖e1 ♕e3†
 19...♕xc4 20.♕b3
20.♔f1 ♘e5 21.♕c1 ♘xc4
 21...♘xf3 22.♕xe3 ♘xh2† 23.♔g1 ♖xe3
 24.♔xh2 ♖de8 25.♗xf6 gxf6 26.a4 ♖xe2
 27.♖xe2 ♖xe2 28.a5±
22.♘f4 ♘d5 23.♘xd5
 23.♖xe3 ♘cxe3† 24.♔g1 ♘xf4 25.♕a3 ♘c2
 26.♕a4 ♘e2† 27.♔f2 ♘xa1 28.♗xa1 ♘d4∓
23...♕d3† 24.♔g1 ♕xd5=

13.♗e2

Sharp play also results after:
13.♘xd5 ♗xd5† 14.♗e2 ♗c4
 14...♘e5 15.0–0 ♕b6 (15...♘c4 16.♗c1±)
 16.♗e3 ♖ad8 17.♕c1±
15.0–0 ♗xe2 16.♘xe2 ♕b6 17.♘c3 ♘e5
 17...♖ad8 18.♘d5 ♕b7 19.♘xb4 cxb4

20.♗xb4 ♕xb5 21.♗c3 ♘e5 22.♕c2 ♘d3 23.♔h1 ♕c5∞ An interesting position. White is a pawn up, without any weaknesses, and has a strong bishop on c3. White's problem is how to improve his position, because the knight on d3 totally paralyses the white rooks; after ♖ad1 then ...♘f2 always works.

18.♘d5 ♕xb5 19.♘c7 ♕d7 20.♘xe8 ♗xd2 21.♖f2

21.♕e2 ♕d4† 22.♔h1 ♖xe8 23.♖ad1 ♖d8 24.♖xd2 ♕xd2 25.♕xe5 ♕f2∓

21...♖d8 22.♕e2 ♕xe8 23.f4 ♘c4 24.♕xc4 ♗e3 25.♖e1 ♗xf2† 26.♔xf2 ♕c6=

13...♘7b6

13...♗xc3 14.bxc3 (14.♗xc3 ♘e3 transposes to the 12...♗xc3 line considered above) 14...c4 15.0-0 (15.♗xc4 ♕c8 16.♗e2 ♘xc3 17.♕c2 ♘xe2 18.♕xc8 ♖axc8 19.♔xe2 ♘c5↑) 15...♕b6† 16.♔h1 ♕xb5 17.♘e4 ♕c6∓

14.0-0

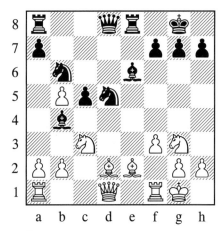

14...♕f6

The last two black pieces are coming into the game.

14...c4 15.♘ce4

15.♔h1!?

15.♘xd5 ♘xd5 16.♗xc4 ♗xd2 (16...♕b6†

17.♔h1 ♖ad8 18.♗g5 f6 19.♗c1±) 17.♕xd2 ♘e3 18.♕xd8 ♖exd8 19.♗xe6 ♘xf1 20.♗xf7† ♔xf7 21.♔xf1 ♖d2 22.b3 ♖b2 23.♘e4 ♔e7∞ Black's idea is ...♖c8 then doubling on the 7th rank.

15...♗xd2

15...♗e7 16.f4 ♕c7 17.f5 ♗d7 18.a4 ♖ad8 19.♔h1±

16.♕xd2 ♕c7 17.♖fd1±

15.♕c1

Preparing the idea of ♗g5 to discourage ...♖d8.

15.♕c2

This move, with the idea of ♖d1, looks more natural.

15...♖ad8

15...♕d4† 16.♔h1 ♘e3 17.♗xe3 ♕xe3 18.♖ad1±

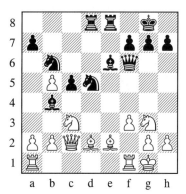

a) 16.♘ge4 ♕d4† 17.♔h1 f5 18.♖ad1
18.♘g5 ♘e3 19.♗xe3 ♕xe3 20.♘xe6 ♖d2 21.♕xf5 g6 (21...♗xc3 22.bxc3 ♖xe6 23.♗d1 c4 24.f4 ♘d5 25.♗f3 ♘xc3 26.♖ac1∞) 22.♕e4 ♖xe6 23.♗c4 ♕xe4 24.♘xe4 ♘xc4 25.♘xd2 ♗xd2 26.♖f2∞
18...fxe4 19.♗g5 ♗xc3
19...♕e5 20.♗xd8 ♗xc3 21.♗xb6 axb6 22.bxc3 ♘e3 23.♕xe4 ♕xe4 24.fxe4 ♘xd1 25.♖xd1 ♗a2 26.♔g1 ♖xe4 27.♗f3 ♖e6 28.♖a1 ♗c4 29.♗c6±
20.♖xd4 ♗xd4 21.♗xd8 exf3 22.♗xf3 ♖xd8∞

Usually, from a practical point of view, three pieces are much better than a queen.

b) 16.♖ad1 ♘xc3 17.♗xc3
   17.bxc3 ♖xd2 18.♖xd2 ♗xc3 19.♘e4 ♗d4†
   20.♔h1 ♕e7⩲ The d4-bishop is not worse than a rook.
17...♗xc3 18.♖xd8 ♖xd8 19.bxc3
   19.♕xc3 ♕xc3 20.bxc3 ♖d2=
19...♕e5 20.♖d1
   20.♘e4 f5∞
20...♕e3† 21.♔f1 ♖xd1† 22.♕xd1 f5⩲
The g3-knight is out of play.

15...♕d4†

Less appealing is:
15...♖ad8 16.♗g5 ♕d4† 17.♔h1 f6
   17...♖d7 18.♖d1 ♕e5 19.f4 ♕c7 20.f5
   ♗xf5 21.♘xf5 ♗xc3 22.bxc3 ♖xe2 23.c4 h6
   (23...♘b4 24.♗f6!+−) 24.cxd5 hxg5 25.d6±
18.♖d1 ♕e5 19.♗d2 ♘xc3 20.bxc3
   20.♗xc3 ♖xd1† 21.♗xd1 ♗xc3 22.♕xc3
   ♗xa2=
20...♖xd2 21.♕xd2 ♗xc3 22.f4 ♗xd2 23.fxe5
♗c3 24.♖ac1 ♗xe5 25.♖xc5 ♗xa2 26.♗f3±

For the exchange, Black has a pawn and a strong bishop, but White has chances of winning the a7-pawn.

16.♔h1 ♘a4

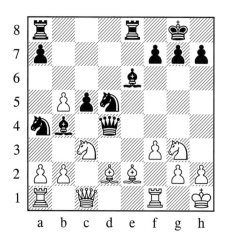

17.♘ge4

Also complicated is:
17.♘xd5 ♗xd2
   17...♖xd5 18.♗xb4 ♕xb4 19.b3 ♘c3
   20.♗d3 ♖ad8 21.♕c2±
18.♕c2 ♕xd5
   18...♕xb2 19.♕xb2 ♘xb2 20.♘c7 c4
   21.♘xa8 ♖xa8 22.♘e4 c3 23.a4 ♗f5
   24.♘xd2 cxd2 25.♔g1 ♖e8 26.♔f2±
19.♖fd1 ♖ad8 20.♕xa4 ♕d4 21.♕c2
   21.♕xd4 ♖xd4 22.♘e4 ♗d5 23.♖xd2 ♖xd2
   24.♘xd2 ♖xe2 25.♖d1 ♗xa2=
21...♕b4
And now in both the lines White can choose, Black's bishops give him good compensation for the pawn.
22.♗d3
   22.b3 ♗c3 23.♖xd8 ♖xd8 24.♖d1 ♖xd1†
   25.♕xd1 ♗d4⩲
22...♗f4 23.♗xh7† ♔h8 24.♗e4 ♕xb5 25.♘e2
♗e5⩲

17...f5

Another possibility for Black was:
17...♘xb2
But during the game it would be hard to calculate all the lines.
18.♕xb2 f5

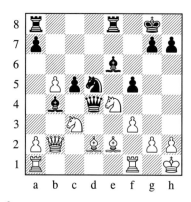

19.a3
   19.♘d6 ♖ed8 20.♘xf5 ♗xf5 21.♖ac1 ♔h8
   22.♖fd1 c4 23.♗e1 ♗d3 24.♗xd3 cxd3
   25.♕b3 ♘f4 26.♗g3 ♖ac8 27.♘e4 ♖xc1

28.♖xc1 ♘e2 29.♖d1 ♘xg3† 30.hxg3 h6∞
The strong d3-pawn should prevent White from winning this position.

19.♕c2 fxe4 20.♘xd5 ♗xd5 21.♗xb4 exf3 22.♗xf3 ♗xf3 23.♗xc5 ♗xg2† 24.♔xg2 ♕d5† 25.♖f3 ♖ac8 26.♖c1 ♖e5=

19.♖ab1 fxe4 20.♘xd5 ♗xd2 (20...♕xb2 21.♖xb2 ♗xd5 22.♗xb4 cxb4 23.fxe4 ♖xe4 24.♗f3 ♖e5 25.♗xd5† ♖xd5 26.♖xb4±) 21.♘c7 e3 22.♕c2 ♕d6 23.♘xa8 ♖xa8 24.a4∞

19...fxe4 20.axb4 e3 21.♗e1 cxb4 22.♘d1 ♕xb2 23.♘xb2 ♘f4 24.♗c4 ♗xc4 25.♘xc4 e2 26.♖g1 ♘d3 27.♖b1±

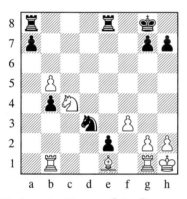

27...♖ed8 28.h3 ♖ac8 29.♘b2 ♘xe1 30.♖gxe1 ♖c2 31.♔g1 b3 32.♔f2 ♖dd2⇄

Probably White will have to give back a knight for two pawns (on e2 and b3). Then Black will reach a rook endgame a pawn down, but with good drawing chances.

18.♘xa4

We also have to consider the following lines:

18.a3 fxe4 19.axb4 e3 20.♗e1 ♘axc3 21.♗xc3 21.bxc3 ♕f6 leaves White with 22.f4!?, 22.♗d3!?, 22.bxc5 ♘f4 23.♕b2 ♕g5 24.♗g3 ♘xe2 25.♕xe2 ♕xc5= and 22.♖a6 ♘f4 23.♗c4 ♕g5 24.♗xe6† ♖xe6 25.♗g3 ♖xa6 26.bxa6 ♘d3 27.♕d1 c4 28.♕e2 ♖e8⇄.
21...♘xc3 22.♕xc3
22.bxc3 ♕d2 23.♕xd2 exd2 24.bxc5 ♗b3

25.♗d1 ♗c4 26.♖g1 ♗xb5=
22...♕d2 23.♕xd2 exd2 24.bxc5 ♗b3 25.♗d1 ♗c4 26.♖g1 ♗xb5=

18.♘xd5 ♗xd2 19.♕xd2 (19.♘xd2 ♗xd5 20.♗c4 ♖ad8⇄) 19...♗xd5 20.♖ad1 fxe4 21.♕c1 ♕xb2 22.♕xb2 ♘xb2 23.♖xd5 ♖ad8 24.♖xd8 ♖xd8 25.fxe4 ♖d4 26.♖b1 ♘c4

18...fxe4

19.♗xb4?!

After this move White still has the advantage, but Hammer missed a better way to exchange pieces.

19.♗c3! Now White forces the exchange of more pieces and is a safe pawn up. 19...♗xc3 (19...♕e3 20.fxe4 ♕xe4 21.♗f3+−) 20.♘xc3 ♘e3 (20...♖ad8 21.fxe4 ♘xc3 22.♕xc3 ♕xc3 23.bxc3 ♖d2 24.♖fe1 ♖c2 25.♖ac1 ♖xa2 26.♖a1±) 21.♖e1 exf3 22.♗xf3 ♘g4 23.♗xg4 ♗xg4 24.♕g5±

19...cxb4 20.fxe4

20.♕c5 leads to equality: 20...♕d2 21.fxe4 (21.♖ad1 ♕xe2 22.♖fe1 exf3 23.♖xe2 fxe2 24.♖e1 ♖f8 25.♔g1 ♖ad8↑) 21...♕e3 22.♖fe1 ♖ac8 23.♕g5 h6 24.♕g3 ♖f8 25.b6 (25.♗f3? ♘c2 26.♖ad1 ♘xe1 27.♖xd2 ♖c1−+) 25...axb6 26.♘xb6 ♖c6 27.♘d5 ♘xd5 28.exd5 ♗xd5=

But good enough for an edge was 20.♘c5. Simple and logical; White gets the knight into the game before Black can play ...♖c8 at some moment and prevent it. 20...♘e3 21.♘xe6 (21.♖e1 ♗f7 22.♘xe4 [22.fxe4 ♖ac8 23.♗f3 ♘xg2∓] 22...♖ac8 23.♕b1 ♘c2 24.♖d1 ♕e5 25.♗d3 ♘xa1 26.♘d6

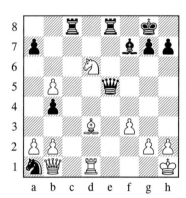

26...♘c2 27.♘xc8 ♘e3 28.♗xh7† ♔f8∓) 21...♖xe6 22.♖e1 (22.fxe4±) 22...exf3 23.♗xf3 ♖d8 24.♕c7±

20...♘e3
20...♖ac8 21.♕g5 ♘e3
  21...♕xe4 22.♗h5±
22.♖f3 ♘g4 23.♖af1 h6
  23...♕xe4 24.♗d3 ♕d5 25.♗f5 ♘e5
24.♕f4 g5
  This idea is very risky for Black because it makes his king weak.
  24...♖f8 25.♕xf8† ♖xf8 26.♖xf8† ♔h7 27.♗xg4 ♗xg4∞
25.♕g3 ♕xe4 26.♗d3
  26.h3 ♕xe2 27.hxg4 ♖c2↑
26...♕d4
  26...♕e5!?
27.h3 ♘e5 28.♖e3 ♘xd3 29.♖xd3 ♕c4 30.b6 ♕b5 31.♖df3 ♕xa4 32.♖f6 ♕b5 33.bxa7→

21.♖f3 ♘g4 22.♕g1
  22.h3 ♘f2† 23.♔h2 ♘xe4 24.♕e3 ♕d6† 25.♕f4±

22...♕d2

White is two pawns up, but his pieces have no coordination.

22...♕xe4 23.♗d3 ♕e5 24.h3 ♘f6 25.♕c5±

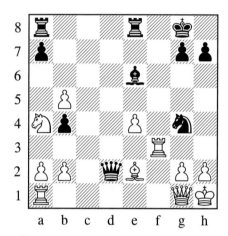

23.♕e1
  Another possibility was 23.♖e1 with the idea of b2-b3 at some point. 23...♗xa2 (23...♘e5 24.♖g3 ♗xa2 25.b3 The bishop is not happy on a2.) 24.♖d3 (24.b3 ♖xe4 25.♗c4† ♖xc4 26.bxc4 ♗xc4 27.♖e4 ♗xb5 28.♖xg4 ♗xa4 29.♖fg3 g6 30.♕a1 ♕d1† 31.♕xd1 ♗xd1 32.♖xb4±) 24...♕c2 25.♖d4 ♕xa4 26.♗xg4 ♗e6 27.♗h5 ♖e7 28.♖ed1 g6 29.♗e2±

23...♕c2
  23...♖ad8 24.♘c5 ♘e5 25.♘xe6 ♖xe6 26.♖b3 ♕xe1† 27.♖xe1 ♖d4 28.♗f1±

24.♗d1
  All the time White's pieces are looking for cooperation, and Black's pieces are disrupting them.

24...♕c7
  24...♕c4 25.♖f5 ♖ad8 26.♗xg4 ♗xf5 27.♗xf5 g6 28.b3 ♕d4 29.♗h3 ♖xe4 30.♕g1±

25.♖g3 ♘f6 26.♖e3
  White could have played 26.♕xb4 ♘xe4 and now best is 27.♖f3± planning ♗b3. Less

convinging is 27.♕xe4 ♗f7 28.♖xg7† ♔xg7
29.♕g4† ♗g6 30.♗f3 ♖ad8∞.

26...♖ad8

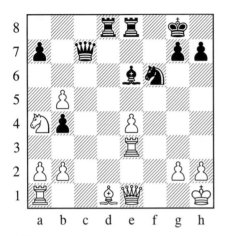

27.♗f3

27.♕xb4? ♖xd1† 28.♖xd1 ♘g4∓

27.a3 ♖xd1 28.♖xd1 ♘g4 29.♖g3 ♕c2 30.♖d4
♕xa4 31.h3 ♘f6 32.♖xb4 ♕a5 33.♕f2± The
material situation has changed a bit, but finally
White's pieces are on useful squares; White has
a significant advantage.

27...♕c4 28.♖c1 ♕xb5

This is an important psychological moment.
White gave back one pawn and we can see that
the white pieces are starting to cooperate, so
now White can give back the second pawn to
activate the knight. However, during a game it
is not easy to make such a decision because of
our materialistic instincts.

29.b3

29.♘c5! ♗xa2 (29...♖c8 30.♘xe6 ♖xc1
31.♕xc1 ♖xe6 32.e5 ♖xe5 33.♖xe5 ♕xe5
34.♕c4† ♔h8 35.♕xb4±) 30.e5 ♘d5 31.♖d3
♗c4 32.♖d4 ♕xc5 33.♖cxc4 ♕a5 34.h3 ♘b6
35.♖xd8 ♖xd8 36.♖f4± The e-pawn is very
strong while b4 is weak.

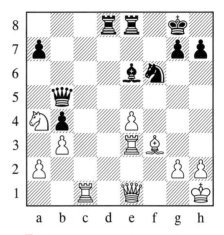

29...♖c8!

A strong move. Black plays against the
knight on a4; the position is now unclear.

30.h3 ♖xc1 31.♕xc1 ♖c8 32.♕d2 h5

Black plans to create pressure with ...h5,
...g5 and ...g4, but first it was obligatory to
blockade the e5-square.

32...♕e5 33.♕xb4

33.♘b2 a5 34.♘d3 ♕d4⇄

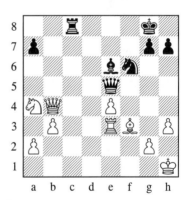

33...♘d5

Better is 33...♖c2 34.♗d1 ♖xa2 35.♘c5 ♗f7
36.♘d3±.

34.♕a5 ♕g3 35.♖d3

Or 35.♖e1 ♘f4 and ...♗xh3 is on the way.

35...♘e3

35...♖c1† 36.♖d1 ♖xd1† 37.♗xd1 ♘f4
38.♕d8† ♔f7 39.♕d2 ♗xh3 40.gxh3 ♘d3

41.♕g2 ♕e1† 42.♕g1 ♘f2† 43.♔g2 ♕xg1†
44.♔xg1 ♘xd1 45.♔g2±

36.♘b2 ♗xh3 37.♖d8† ♔f7

37...♖xd8 38.♕xd8† ♔f7 39.♕d2±

38.♕h5† ♔f6

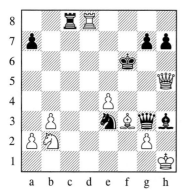

39.e5† ♕xe5 40.♕h4† ♔f7 41.♘d3 ♕a1†
42.♔h2 ♖xd8 43.♕xd8 ♗f5 44.♕c7† ♔e6
45.♕c6† ♔f7 46.♗d5† ♘xd5 47.♕xd5† ♗e6
48.♕b7† ♔f6 49.♕xa7±

33.♖e1

Missing his chance to play the strong 33.e5±.

33...♕e5 34.♕xb4

34.♘b2! The most important thing is
to improve the prospects of the a4-knight.
34...♕g3 (34...♖c3 35.♘d1±) 35.♖f1 a5
36.♘d3 ♖d8 37.♕f4 ♕xf4 38.♘xf4 ♗f7
39.♘d5±

34...g5

34...♗xh3 35.♕d2 (35.gxh3 ♕g3∓)
35...♗g4 36.b4 (36.♖c1 ♖xc1† 37.♕xc1
♕g3⇄; 36.♗xg4 hxg4∓ The white king is in
trouble.) 36...♖c4 37.♘c5 ♗xf3 38.gxf3 ♕g3
39.♖f1 ♖xb4 40.♕xb4 ♕h3† 41.♔g1 ♕g3†=

35.♔g1

35.♕d2 g4↑ is too risky for White, but
possible was 35.♗e2 with the idea of ♕b5.
35...♘xe4 36.♗a6 ♘f2† 37.♔g1 ♘xh3†
38.♔h1 ♘f2† 39.♔g1=

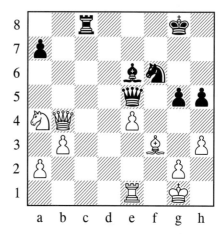

35...g4

The immediate piece sac was only enough
for a draw:

35...♗xh3 36.♖d1 g4

36...♗e6 37.♕d6 ♕xd6 38.♖xd6 ♔f7 39.e5
♖c1† 40.♔h2 g4 41.exf6 gxf3 42.gxf3 h4=

37.♗e2

37.♕d4 ♕xd4† 38.♖xd4 gxf3 39.gxh3 ♖c2
40.e5 ♘h7 41.♖d8† ♔g7 42.♖d7† ♔g6
43.h4 ♖xa2 44.♖xa7 ♖g2† 45.♔f1 ♖h2∞

37...♖c2 38.♗f1

38.♖d2 ♖c1† 39.♗d1 (39.♗f1 ♗xg2–+)
39...♕g3 40.♘b2 ♖c3 41.♔f1 ♖e3 42.♖d8†=
Again, it is a perpetual check.

38...♗xg2 39.♗xg2 ♕g3 40.♖d8† ♔g7

40...♔f7 41.♖f8† ♔g6 42.♖xf6† ♔xf6
43.♕f8†=

41.♕e7† ♔g6 42.♖g8† ♘xg8 43.♕e8† ♔h6
44.♕f8† ♔h7 45.♕f7† ♔h8 46.♕xh5† ♔g7
47.♕g5†=

36.hxg4 hxg4 37.♗e2

The white king is not safe because the a4-
knight and the queen are too far away to help.
Black has good compensation for two pawns.

If instead 37.♗d1 then 37...♖c7 with the idea
of ...♖h7.

37...♖c2

Other options include:

37...♖c7 38.♖d1± With the idea of ♕d6.

37...g3 38.♕d2
   38.♗f3 ♖c2↑
38...♘xe4 39.♕d3 ♕h8 40.♗f3 ♕h2† 41.♔f1
♗g4 42.♕d5† ♔g7 43.♕d4† ♔g8 44.♕xe4
   44.♗xg4 ♕h1† 45.♕g1

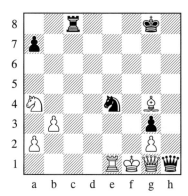

45...♖e8 46.♔e2 ♕h4 47.♗d7 ♕h5†
48.♔d3 ♕d5† 49.♕d4 ♘f2† 50.♔c3
♕xd4† 51.♔xd4 ♖xe1∓
44...♕h1† 45.♔e2 ♕xg2† 46.♔e3 ♗xf3
47.♕e6† ♔g7 48.♕e5†=

38.♗d3

The position is very unclear. Black has good pressure against the white king, but in many forcing lines we shall see that White's most effective counterplay is to look for perpetual check.

38...a5

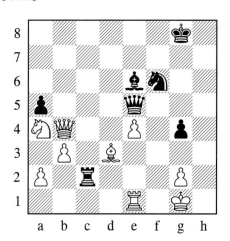

39.♕e7

39.♕b6 ♕g3 (39...♖xa2!?∞) 40.♕xe6† ♔g7
41.♕e7† ♔g8 42.♗c4† ♖xc4 43.♕d8† ♔f7
44.♕d1
   44.♕d2 ♖c2 45.♖e3 ♕c7 46.♖c3 ♕a7†
47.♕e3 ♖c1† 48.♔h2 ♕b8† 49.e5

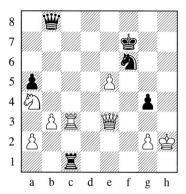

49...g3† 50.♕xg3 ♕h8† 51.♕h3 ♘g4†
52.♔g3 ♕xe5† 53.♔xg4 ♕d4† 54.♔h5
♕e5† 55.♔h4 ♕f6†=
44...♖c8 45.e5
   45.♘b6 ♖h8 46.♘d5 ♕h2† 47.♔f1 ♕g3
48.♘e3 ♘xe4 49.♕d5† ♔f8 50.♕f5† ♔g7
51.♕xg4† ♕xg4 52.♘xg4 ♖h1† 53.♔e2
♘c3† 54.♔d2 ♘b1† 55.♔e2 ♘c3† 56.♔f2
♘d1†=
45...♖h8 46.exf6 ♕h2† 47.♔f1 ♕f4† 48.♔g1=

39...♖c7

Correctly, Black did not want a draw and played for a win; in practice it is much harder to play this position for White.
   39...♕d4† 40.♔h1 ♕f2 41.♕xe6† ♔h8
42.♗xc2 ♕xe1† 43.♔h2 ♕h4†=

40.♕d8† ♔g7 41.♗e2 ♔g6 42.♖f1

Instead 42.♖d1, planning ♕d6, is well met by 42...♗d7!↑ (less strong are: 42...♖c2 43.♗d3 ♖xa2 44.♗b1 ♖a1⩲; 42...♖h7 43.♕d6†; 42...♘xe4 43.♕d4 ♕xd4† 44.♖xd4 ♖c1† 45.♖d1 ♖xd1† 46.♗xd1±).

42...♖h7 43.♗d3

With the idea of ♖xf6.

43...♘d7 44.♔f2

44.♕e8† ♔g7 (44...♔g5 45.♕d8† ♔g6=) 45.♗c4 (45.♕e7† ♔h6–+) 45...♕h2† (45...♕d4† 46.♖f2 g3 47.♕e7† ♔h8 48.♕d8† ♔g7=) 46.♔f2 ♕f4† 47.♔e2 ♕xe4† 48.♔d2 ♕xg2† 49.♔c1 ♖h1 50.♕e7† ♔h8 51.♕e8†=

44...♖h2

44...♖f7† 45.♔e2 ♖xf1 46.♔xf1 ♕a1† 47.♔f2 ♕xa2† 48.♔g3 ♕xb3 49.♕e8† ♔f6 50.♘c3∞

45.♕e8† ♔g7 46.♕e7† ♔g6 47.♕e8† ♔h6

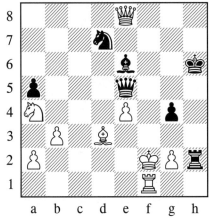

48.♔e3

It is impossible to avoid perpetual check. The knight stayed on a4 till the end; White did not manage to get it into play and that was the main reason White could not convert his two extra pawns into a win.

48...♕g3† 49.♔d4 ♕e5† 50.♔e3 ♕g3† 51.♔d4

51.♖f3 ♕e1† (51...gxf3 52.♕xe6† ♕g6 53.♕xg6† ♔xg6 54.gxf3 ♖xa2 55.f4±; 51...♕e5 52.♖f2 ♕g3† 53.♔e2 ♕e5∞) 52.♗e2 (52.♔d4 ♕b4† 53.♔e3 ♕e1† 54.♔f4 ♕d2† 55.♖e3 ♕f2† 56.♖f3=) 52...gxf3 53.♕xe6† ♔g5 54.♕f5† ♔h6 55.♔xf3 ♕g1 56.♕f4† ♔g6=

51...♕e5†
½–½

GAME 47
▷ **S. Mamedyarov (2765)**
▶ **S. Ganguly (2627)**
8th World Team Championship, Ningbo
Round 2, 18.07.2011 **[E32]**
Annotated by Borki Predojevic

Mamedyarov is well-known as a player who likes dynamic chess. In this game he chose the dynamic and modern 5.e4 line in the 4.♕c2 Nimzo-Indian. Ganguly followed the main line with 10...♘dc5 and 15...♗b7 then played a novelty 18...♕a4!? that improves on the game Krush – Van den Doel, Wijk aan Zee 2008. Mamedyarov had also analysed this line and found a great resource for White with the positional pawn sacrifice 19.♗g5! and 20.♘e2!. Despite this, Ganguly defended well until the 21st move when he should have played 21...♖fc8! keeping defensive chances. Instead he played 21...♖ac8? after which White went on to win.

The whole line is very interesting and I give plenty of new ideas for both sides starting with 10...♕h4!? as an alternative to the main line, or 15.c4!? which leads to a small advantage for White in an endgame.

1.d4 ♘f6 2.c4 e6 3.♘c3 ♗b4 4.♕c2 0–0 5.e4 d5 6.e5 ♘e4 7.♗d3 c5

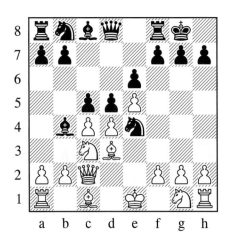

8.♘f3

After 8.a3 ♗xc3† 9.bxc3 cxd4 10.cxd4 ♕a5†
11.♔f1 ♘c6 12.♘e2 f6 Black has a good game.

8...cxd4 9.♘xd4 ♘d7 10.♗f4

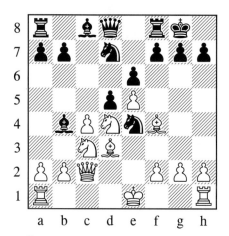

10...♘dc5

A rare but modern alternative is:
10...♕h4

Here White is forced to play:
11.g3

After which I propose:
11...♕h3!?

11...♕h5 is another option for Black.
12.0–0–0

12.cxd5 exd5 13.f3 ♘xc3 14.bxc3 ♗c5
(Krasenkow) 15.♗f5 (15.♔f2 ♘b6⇄;
15.0–0–0?! ♘b6 16.♘b3 ♗a3† 17.♔b1
♗d7∓) 15...♕h5 16.♗g4 ♕g6 17.♗f5
(17.♕xg6 hxg6⇄) 17...♕h5 18.♗g4 ♕g6=
This leads to a draw.

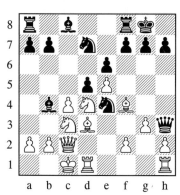

12...♗xc3!

The main move is 12...♘xc3 but after
13.bxc3 ♗a3† 14.♔b1↑ White looks better.
13.bxc3

13.♗f1 ♕h5 14.bxc3 ♘b6 transposes to
13.bxc3 ♘b6 14.♗f1 ♕h5.
13...♘b6

Now White has a few options, but it seems
that Black always has counterplay.
14.♗f1

Worse is 14.♘f3? which was played in Krush
– Koneru, Moscow (blitz) 2010.

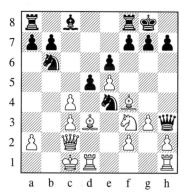

Now the best option is 14...♗d7!N and Black
is already better. 15.♗xe4 dxe4 16.♘g5 ♕h5
17.♖d4 ♗a4 18.♕d2 ♖ac8∓ Black has a
huge attack.
After the forcing line: 14.cxd5 exd5 15.f3
♘c5 16.♗f5 ♗xf5 17.♕xf5 (17.♘xf5 ♘ca4!
creates a strong attack on the queenside)
17...♕g2! This leads to an equal game:
18.♕c2 (18.♕b1 ♘e6↑) 18...♕h3 19.♕f5
(19.♘f5 ♘e6↑ looks nice for Black)
19...♕g2= With a draw.
14...♕h5 15.cxd5

15.h4 f5 16.f3 ♘c5 17.cxd5 ♘xd5 18.♗c4
♘b6 19.♗b3 a5∓
15.♗e2 ♕h3 16.cxd5 exd5 17.f3 ♘c5∞
15...exd5 16.f3 ♘c5

White needs to react very fast to stop
attacking ideas with ...♗d7 and ...♖ac8. He
can exchange queens by playing:
17.g4

17.h4 ♗d7 18.g4 ♕g6 19.h5 (19.♕xg6
fxg6∓) 19...♕xc2† 20.♔xc2 ♗a4† 21.♘b3
f6↑ Black has the better prospects.

17...♕g6 18.♕xg6 fxg6 19.♗g3

There is no advantage for White after:

19...♗d7 20.♔d2 ♘c4† 21.♗xc4 dxc4 22.♔e3
♘d3∞

With an unclear position.

11.0–0 ♘xd3 12.♕xd3 ♗xc3 13.bxc3 b6

The main move and Black's best option.

13...♕h4?!

This is much worse. White should continue
with the normal:

14.♕e3 b6

14...h6 15.cxd5 exd5 16.c4±

White now has a strong reply:

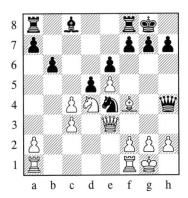

15.cxd5!N

15.f3 ♘c5 16.♗g5 ♕h5 17.♗e7 ♖e8
18.♗xc5 bxc5 19.♘b5 ♖d8 20.♖ae1? (better
was: 20.♖fb1! [planning ♘c7] 20...♗d7
21.♘d6 ♖db8 22.♖b3±) 20...♗a6 21.♕xc5
♖dc8 22.♕a3 ♗xb5 23.cxb5 ♕h4∞ Rezan –
Zelcic, Zadar 2010.

15...exd5 16.c4 ♗a6

16...♗e6 17.cxd5 ♗xd5 18.♘f5±

17.♖fc1

Also good is: 17.♘f5 ♕g4 18.♘e7† ♔h8
19.♘xd5 ♘c5 (19...♗xc4 20.f3+−) 20.♖ac1±

17...♗xc4 18.♖xc4 dxc4 19.♕xe4±

With an almost decisive advantage.

14.cxd5 ♕xd5

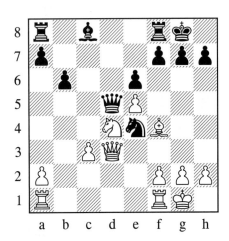

15.♖fd1

Less precise is 15.♖fe1 ♗b7 16.f3 ♘c5
17.♕e3 when Black has: 17...♕c4! (planning
...♕d3) 18.♖ad1 ♖ac8 19.♗g5?! (19.♗h6
gxh6 20.♕xh6 ♘d7 21.♘b3 ♕xc3 22.♖e3
♕c6 23.♖xd7 ♕xd7 24.♕g5†=) 19...♔h8!↑
Planning ...♘a4 hitting c3. Black had a good
position, but he eventually lost in Karpov –
Mamedyarov, Moscow (blitz) 2008.

An interesting option for White is to go into
an endgame after:

15.c4!? ♘c5

15...♕b7?! does not look good. White
can continue with 16.♖fe1 ♘c5 17.♕g3
♔h8 18.♖e3 ♕e7 19.♖ae1↑ with better
coordination than in the main line and a
serious initiative.

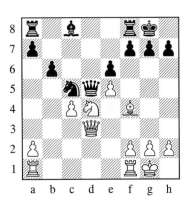

16.♕xh7†

16.♕c3 ♕e4⇄

16...♚xh7 17.cxd5 exd5

And after the normal:

18.♖fd1

18.♗e3 ♖e8 19.f4 f6 20.♘f3 ♗a6 21.♖fc1 fxe5⇄

White's position is slightly better, but it is very hard to say if it will be enough to win. Black can choose many moves and here I give some of them:

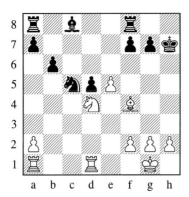

18...♘e6

18...♗a6 19.a4± Intending to meet 19...♘d3 with: 20.♗g3 ♖fe8 21.♘b5! ♗xb5 22.axb5 ♘xe5 23.♖xd5±

18...♗d7 19.♘e2 ♗e6 20.♘c3 ♖fd8 21.♗e3± White retains some pressure.

19.♗e3 ♘xd4 20.♖xd4 ♗e6 21.a4 ♖fc8 22.a5 bxa5

22...b5 23.a6±

22...♚g6 23.h3±

23.♖xa5 a6

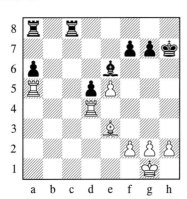

24.h3±

Despite White's advantage, Black should be able to hold the draw.

15...♗b7

An interesting option is:

15...♖d8!?

15...♘c5 is passive: 16.♕g3 ♕e4 17.♘b3 ♗b7 (17...♗a6 18.♖d4 ♕g6 19.♘xc5 bxc5 20.♖a4 ♗d3 21.♗e3 ♕xg3 22.hxg3 ♖fc8 23.♖a5 a6 24.♗xc5± Cmilyte – N. Kosintseva, Tbilisi 2011; 17...♘xb3 18.axb3 ♗b7 19.f3 ♕c2 20.♗h6 ♕g6 21.♕xg6 fxg6 22.♗e3±/±) 18.f3 ♕f5 19.♗h6 ♕g6 20.♕xg6 hxg6 21.♘xc5 bxc5 22.♗e3 ♖fc8 23.♖ab1 ♗d5 24.♖d2 ♖c7 25.♖b5 ♖ac8 26.♖a5± Black is fighting for a draw, Ushenina – N. Kosintseva, Ohrid 2009.

15...♗d7?! looks very passive: 16.♕e3 (16.c4 ♕b7 17.♘b3 ♗a4 18.♗e3↑ also looks better for White) 16...♕b7 17.♘b3 ♗c6 18.f3 ♘c5 19.♘xc5 bxc5 20.♕xc5± White was clearly better in Issing – Fish, Germany 2010.

16.c4 ♕b7

Best for White is to continue similarly as in the main line:

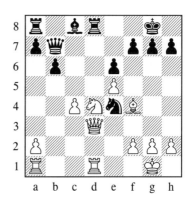

17.♕e3!

17.♕c2 ♗d7 18.f3 ♘c5 19.♘b5 ♗xb5 20.cxb5 a6 21.bxa6 ♕xa6⇄ Inarkiev – Gashimov, Poikovsky 2009.

17...♗d7 18.f3 ♘c5 19.♗g5 ♖dc8 20.♘e2↑

After a few more or less forced moves we have reached a similar set-up for White as in the main line. White will transfer his knight to h5 to increase the pressure on the kingside. Black's pieces are very passive and he does not have real counterplay.

20...♗a4 21.♖d4 ♘d7

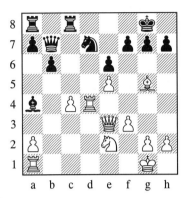

22.♘g3!N

White was also better after: 22.♘c3 ♗c6 23.h4 ♕c7 24.♖e1 h5 25.♖d6 ♘f8 26.♖ed1 ♗b7 27.♖1d4 ♕c5 28.♗e7 ♖e8 29.♗xf8 ♖xf8 30.♘e2 ♕b4 31.♘f4 ♕b1† 32.♔h2 ♕f5 33.♘d3± Holt – Rensch, Berkeley (op) 2011. However, 22.♘g3!N is sounder and better.

22...♖c5

After 22...♕a6 White has a nice resource: 23.♗h6! Black is in big trouble. 23...♔h8 (23...♖xc4 24.♕g5 g6 25.♖xd7+–; 23...♕a5 24.♖xd7 gxh6 25.♖d4±) 24.♘h5 gxh6 (24...♔g8 25.♖xd7 ♗xd7 26.♕g5+–) 25.♖xd7 (25.♕xh6 ♖g8 26.♖xd7?? ♖g6!–+) 25...♕xc4 26.♖xf7 ♕c5 27.♕xc5 ♖xc5 28.♘f6 ♗c2 29.♖d1!+– Black is lost.

23.f4

Here I will give a few more lines that prove the position favours White.

23...♕a6!

23...♗c6 24.♘h5→ ♘f8 (24...♗xg2 25.♘xg7 ♖c7 26.♘h5 ♕f3 27.♕xf3 ♗xf3 28.♖xd7+–) 25.♘xg7! ♗xg2 (25...♔xg7 26.♗f6† ♔g8 27.♕h3+–) 26.♘h5 ♘g6 27.♕g3+–

23...h6 24.♗xh6! gxh6 25.f5+– With a decisive attack.

24.♕d3

After 24.♘e4 ♖xc4 25.♖xd7 ♗xd7 26.♘f6† gxf6 27.♗xf6 ♔f8 28.♕g3 Black has a strong reply: 28...♗a4! 29.♕g7† ♔e8 30.♕g8† ♔d7 31.♕xa8 ♖c8 32.♕xa7† ♕c7⇄ With excellent drawing chances.

24.♕a3!?

24...♖ac8 25.♖c1

Preparing ♘e4 or ♘h5.

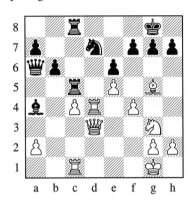

25...♗b5

The only move, but sufficient to survive.

25...♖5c7 26.♘h5 ♘f8 27.♘xg7! A typical sacrifice which we have seen before. 27...♔xg7 28.♗f6† ♔g8 29.♕h3 ♖xc4 30.♖cxc4 ♖xc4 31.♕g4†+–

25...h6 26.♗e7 ♖5c7 27.♗d6 ♘c5 28.♕e3 ♖d7 29.f5+–

26.♘e4

26.♘h5 ♗xc4 27.♕g3 ♗d5–+

26...♗xc4 27.♕d2 ♗d5

27...♖d5 28.♘d6 ♖xd6 29.♖xd6±

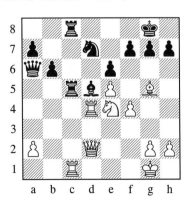

28.♘xc5 bxc5 29.♖d3 c4 30.♖g3 ♛b6†
31.♛f2±

White has the advantage, but Black is still in the game. The long line I have shown after 15...♖d8 looks very dangerous for Black.

16.c4

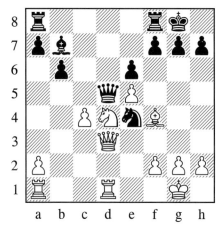

16...♛a5

After 16...♛d7 White can choose 17.f3 ♘c5 18.♛e3 when there is no better move than 18...♛a4, which transposes to the game.

16...♛d8 does not look logical. After 17.f3 ♘c5 18.♛e3↑ the black queen will be threatened and it has no active square, while White can prepare a similar attack as in the game or just transfer the knight to d6 via b5.

17.f3

Less ambitious is: 17.♘b5 ♗c6 18.a4 ♛b4 19.♗e3 (19.♘d6 ♖ad8 20.f3 ♘xd6 21.exd6 This is Javakhishvili – T. Kosintseva, Dresden [ol] 2008, and now 21...♖fe8∞ intending ...e5-e4.) 19...♖fc8 20.♖db1 ♛e7 21.♘d6 ♘xd6 22.exd6 ♛b7 23.f3 e5 24.♛d2 e4 25.f4 ♛a6 26.a5 bxa5 27.♖xa5 Kasimdzhanov – Efimenko, Wijk aan Zee 2009, was agreed drawn here.

17...♘c5 18.♛e3

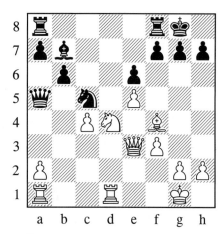

18...♛a4!?N

A novelty which was probably analysed by GM Ganguly at home.

The previously played alternative looks worse: 18...♖fc8 19.♘b5 ♗c6 20.♘d6 ♖c7 21.h4!?
 On 21.♖d4 Black can try: 21...♘b7 22.♖ad1 (22.♗h6 ♛c5! 23.♖e1) 22...♘xd6 23.exd6 ♖d7 Despite Black's passive pieces, White does not have a direct attack. For example: 24.c5 (24.♗e5 f6 25.♗xf6 gxf6 26.♛xe6† ♖f7∞) 24...bxc5 25.♖c4 ♗d5 26.♖xc5 ♛xa2 27.♛d4 ♛b3! (27...♛b7 28.♖c7±) 28.♖c7 ♖dd8⇄ Black intends ...♛b6.
21...♘d7
 21...♘b7!? 22.h5↑ h6 (22...♗a4 23.♖d4 ♘xd6 24.exd6 ♗c5 25.♛d3 ♖xh5 [25...e5 26.♗d2 ♛a6 27.♖h4] 26.♛e4! ♖d8 27.c5± White exploits the loose bishop on a4.) 23.♖d4 ♘xd6 24.exd6 ♖b7 25.♗e5 (25.c5 e5!) 25...f6 26.♗xf6 gxf6 27.d7 ♗xd7 28.♛e4 ♛c5 29.♛xb7
22.♔h2 ♛c5 23.♛e1! h5 24.♛g3±

White was obviously better in I. Krush – Van der Wiel, Wijk aan Zee 2008.

19.♗g5!

A surprising and very strong move by Mamedyarov! He prepares an attack on the black king with a very nice positional manoeuvre.

19...♕xc4

An interesting and provocative idea is:
19...h6!?

In my opinion White should play the calm:
19...♖fe8? 20.♘b5! ♖ec8 21.♘d6 ♖c7
22.♖d4± Planning to meet 22...♕c2 with
23.♗h6! gxh6 24.♖g4† ♔h8 25.♕xh6+–.

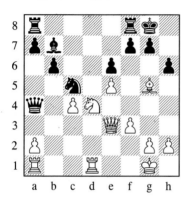

20.♗e7

Avoiding the tempting sacrifices on h6 or f6,
which do not lead to a win:
20.♗xh6 gxh6 21.♕xh6 (21.♘b5? ♔h7
22.♘d6 ♕c2–+ The black queen comes
to the defence.) 21...♖fd8□ (21...♕xc4?
22.♖ac1 ♕xa2 23.♘b5! ♕b2 24.♕g5†
♔h8 25.♘d6+– Black is helpless.) 22.♕g5†
(22.♕f4 ♕e8=) 22...♔f8= White is forced
to take a draw with 23.♕h6† because
advancing the h-pawn is too slow: 23.h4
♕xc4 24.h5? (24.♕h6† still leads to a draw)
24...♖xd4 25.h6 ♔e8 26.h7 ♔d7 27.♕f6
♘d3–+ Black has too much material.
20.♗f6!? gxf6 21.♕xh6 fxe5! (21...f5 22.♘b5
Planning ♖d4-h4.) 22.♕g5† (22.♖e1 f5=)
22...♔h7 23.♘f5 exf5 24.♕xf5† ♔h8
25.♕h5† ♔g7 26.♕g5† ♔h7=

If Black reacts with:
20...♖fc8

20...♖fe8 21.♗xc5 bxc5 22.♘b5 ♗c6
23.♘d6±

21.♘b5 ♗a6 22.♘d6 ♖c7

Then it is finally time to sacrifice:

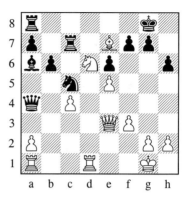

23.♗f6!

23.♗h4 ♗xc4 24.♖d4 ♘b3 25.♖g4 ♘xa1
26.♗f6 ♕d1† (26...♔f8 27.♖xg7) 27.♔f2
♕c2† 28.♔g3 ♕h7!⇄

23...gxf6

23...♘b7 24.♕f4! ♘xd6 25.exd6 ♖d7
26.♕g3 is clearly in White's favour.

24.♕xh6 fxe5 25.♕g5† ♔h7

25...♔f8 26.♕xe5 leads to a strong attack.

26.♕xe5

White has a powerful attack. After the best
possible defence with:

26...f6 27.♕h5† ♔g8

27...♔g7 28.♖d4+–

28.♖d4 ♖d8

28...♖g7 29.♖h4+–

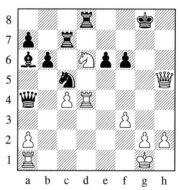

**29.♖h4 ♔f8!! 30.♕h8† ♔e7 31.♘f5† exf5
32.♕g7† ♔d6 33.♕xf6† ♔d7 34.♖d4† ♔c8
35.♕xd8† ♔b7±**

Black survives the immediate attack, but his
position remains critical.

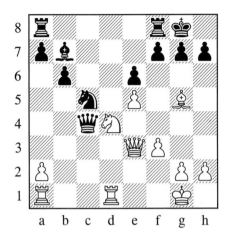

20.♘e2!

White's last two moves present a completely new concept in this variation. The positional pawn sacrifice does not look dangerous at first sight, but just in the next few moves Black will lose the game.

20...♗a6!

Worse is: 20...h6?! 21.♗xh6 gxh6 22.♖d4 ♕c2 23.♕xh6 ♘e4 24.♖e1 ♖ad8 25.fxe4 ♖xd4 26.♘xd4 ♕c5 27.♕g5† ♔h8 28.♖d1 ♗xe4□ 29.♕h4† ♔h7 30.♕f4 ♕e7 31.♖c1 ♖g8 32.h4± With advantage to White.

An interesting alternative was to play the immediate:
20...♖fc8!?
Here White can continue with:
21.♖d4
The plausible 21.♗f6!? is not enough for a win: 21...gxf6 (21...♕c2 22.♖ac1 ♕g6 23.♘f4 ♕h6 24.♗e7 ♖c7 25.♗d6 ♖cc8 26.♖d4 ♗a6 27.♖cd1⩲) 22.♖d4 ♕c2 23.♖g4† ♔f8 24.♘d4 ♕d3 25.♕h6† ♔e8 26.♕xf6 ♘d7!? (Black can force a draw with: 26...♖d8 27.♖g8† ♔d7 28.♕xf7† ♔c8 29.♖xd8† ♔xd8 30.♕f8† ♔c7 31.♕d6† ♔c8 32.♕f8†=) 27.♖g8† ♘f8 28.♖xf8† ♔xf8 29.♘xe6† ♔e8 30.♘g7† ♔d7 31.e6† ♔c6 32.a4!?∞ With a very unclear position. The computer says White is better, but the

position is double-edged with chances for both sides.
21...♕c2 22.♗e7!?
And now if:
22...♗a6
White has a nice move:

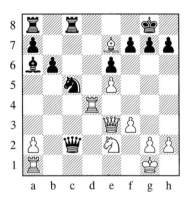

23.♘g3!⩱

This secures compensation. This is a good square for the knight because the white rook can go to g4 immediately. Note that ♘g3 wasn't possible in the game because Black played 20...♗a6.
If Black plays:
23...h6
Then White replies:
24.♗f6! ♗d3
24...♕b2 25.♖ad1 ♘d3 26.♖g4±
25.♖h4 ♘d7□
25...♗h7 26.♗xg7±
26.♗xg7 ♕c5 27.♕xc5 ♖xc5 28.♗xh6 ♘xe5 29.♘h5↑
White has the initiative.

21.♘f4

On 21.♗f6 Black has the clever defensive move 21...h6!. Now it is best for White to force a draw with: 22.♖d4! (22.♘g3 ♘d3 23.♘h5 gxf6∓ and there is no mate) 22...♕xe2 23.♕xh6 gxh6 24.♖g4† ♔h7 25.♖g7†

21.♘g3? gives Black a chance to play 21...♘d3∓.

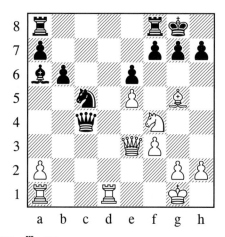

21...Rac8?

Also bad is:

21...Rfe8? 22.Rd4 Qc2 23.Nh5 Qe2□

White has a strong punch:

24.Rg4!

With the advantage.

24...Nd7!?

24...Kf8 25.Nxg7 Qxe3† 26.Bxe3 Rec8 27.Nh5 Nd7 28.Rg7± also looks bad for Black.

If 24...Kh8 then White has 25.Qf4!+– with a decisive attack.

24...Qxe3† 25.Bxe3 Kh8 26.Rxg7 Bd3 27.Bh6±

25.Qf4!

25.Nxg7 Nxe5 26.Qxe2 Bxe2 27.Nxe8 Nxg4 28.Re1 Rxe8 29.Rxe2 f6 30.Bh4 Ne5 31.Bxf6±

25...Nxe5

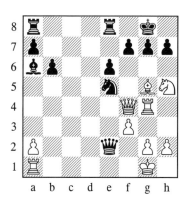

26.Qd4!!

Now Black is forced to play:

26...f6

26...f5 27.Rg3 Kf7 28.Be3!+–

26...Bd3 27.Re4! Qxf3 28.Rxe5 Qxh5 29.Qxd3±

27.Bh6 Re7 28.Nxf6† Kh8 29.Bxg7† Rxg7 30.Rxg7 Kxg7 31.Ng4 Qb5! 32.Nxe5 Qc5 33.Qxc5 bxc5 34.Rc1 c4 35.Rc3±

White is much better in the endgame.

Black's best defence and the critical line is:

21...Rfc8! 22.Rd4

22.Nh5 Nd3∓

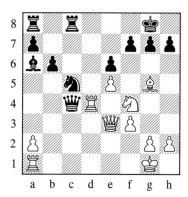

22...Qc2!

22...Qb5? looks bad because Black doesn't have any threats. Now White plays the simple 23.Rad1! with increasing pressure. (23.Nh5 Qe2!) 23...Na4 (23...Nb7 24.Nh5 Qe2 25.Qxe2 Bxe2 26.R1d2 Rc4 27.Rd7 Rc1† 28.Kf2 Ba6 29.Rxf7! Rf1† [29...Kxf7 30.Rd7† Ke8 31.Re7† Kf8 32.Rxg7] 30.Kg3 Kxf7 31.Rd7† Black is lost after either 31...Ke8 32.Rxg7+– or 31...Kg6 32.Kg4+–.) 24.Nh5!± Qe2 25.Qxe2 Bxe2 26.R1d2 Bb5 27.Nxg7! Black's position is bad: 27...Kxg7 (27...Nc3 28.Nh5 Nd5 29.Nf6† Nxf6 30.Bxf6+–; 27...h6 28.Bf6+–) 28.Bf6† Kf8 29.Rh4 Kg8 30.Rg4† Kf8 31.Rg7+– White wins.

After the main move I was unable to find anything better than:

23.Rd2

23.♘h5 is not so strong as in the game. After 23...♕e2! Black is better. For example: 24.♖g4 ♕xe3† 25.♗xe3 g6 26.♗h6 f5!? 27.♘f6† (27.exf6 ♔f7∓) 27...♔f7 28.♖d4 ♖d8 29.♖h4 ♖h8∓/∞

23.♖ad1?! ♕xa2 This secures the b3-square for the black queen, while 24.♘h5 still doesn't work in view of 24...♕e2!∓.

23...♕c4!?

23...♕a4 24.♖ad1⩲̲

23...♕f5 24.♗e7 h6 25.♖ad1 ♘b7∞ is also very unclear.

24.♖d4

24.♗f6? gxf6 25.♘h5 ♘d3!

24.♘h5 ♘d3 25.♖ad1 ♕c5 26.♖xd3 ♗xd3 27.♖xd3 h6! 28.♗f4 ♕xe3† 29.♗xe3 ♖c2∓

24.♗e7 ♖e8 25.♗f6 gxf6 26.♘h5 ♘d3 27.♖ad1 ♕c5 28.♘xf6† ♔g7 29.♘xe8† ♖xe8 30.♖xd3 ♗xd3 31.♕xc5 bxc5 32.♖xd3 ♖b8 33.♖c3 ♖b1† 34.♔f2 ♖b2† 35.♔g3 ♖xa2 36.♖xc5=

24...♕c2=

With a draw.

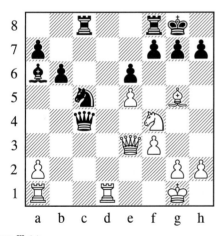

22.♖d4+–

Suddenly, Black is lost!

22...♕c2

22...♕b5 doesn't help. White continues as in the game: 23.♘h5 ♘d3 (23...♘d7 24.♖ad1+–; 23...♕b2 24.♖e1+–) 24.♘f6† ♔h8 (24...gxf6

25.♗xf6+–) 25.♖h4+– Black cannot escape mate.

23.♘h5 ♕e2

This is not good, but what else? 23...♕b2 24.♖e1

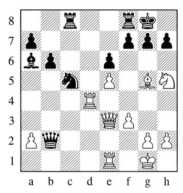

And now 24...♗d3 25.♘xg7 ♗g6 26.♗f6+– or 24...♕c2 25.♗h6!+–.

24.♕xe2 ♗xe2

25.♗e7!

After this move Black is losing the exchange.

25...f5

25...♖fe8 26.♘f6† ♔h8 (26...gxf6 27.♖g4†) 27.♘xe8 ♖xe8 28.♗xc5 bxc5 29.♖d7+–

26.exf6 ♖f7 27.♘xg7

1–0

GAME 48

▷ **Y. Seirawan (2635)**
▶ **J. Polgar (2699)**
8th World Team Championship, Ningbo
Round 6, 23.07.2011 **[E32]**
Annotated by Borki Predojevic

The main line with 4.♕c2 against the Nimzo-Indian is very popular nowadays. In this game Black avoided playing the early development ...b7-b6 and ...♗b7. Thanks to this, Judit Polgar could develop the c8-bishop to a6 creating immediate pressure on the c4-pawn. White employed an original plan with an early 11.dxc5!? and 13.0–0–0 and then the strong novelty 15.♖d2!N. Black did not realise the danger of White's plan and after the positional mistake 16...♖fc8? her position was very passive.

Overall, the theoretical fight gave White an edge and he convincingly won the game. My advice for Black is either to deviate with 10...♕c8, as played by Leko and Milov who are both experts in this line, or choose 13...♖ab8! as a better reaction to White's 13.0–0–0.

**1.d4 ♘f6 2.c4 e6 3.♘c3 ♗b4 4.♕c2 0–0
5.a3 ♗xc3† 6.♕xc3**

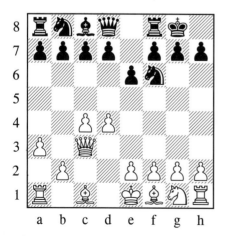

6...d6!?
This modern approach recently became popular with the new generation of world-class Russians (Vitiugov, Tomashevsky, Alekseev, etc.).

The classical line is 6...b6 7.♗g5 ♗b7:

Previously theory considered the main line to be the endgame which arises after: 8.f3 h6 9.♗h4 d5 10.e3 ♘bd7 11.cxd5 ♘xd5 12.♗xd8 ♘xc3 13.♗h4 ♘d5 14.♗f2 c5 There were plenty of high-level games, as especially Kramnik liked to play this endgame with White. This was the fashion until 2007 when Peter Leko showed new ideas for Black in his match against Mikhail Gurevich. He won two games in this line after: 15.e4 ♘e7 16.♘e2 (16.0–0–0 ♖ac8 17.♔b1

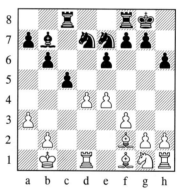

17...c4! 18.♘e2 f5 19.exf5 ♘xf5 20.♘c3 ♘f6 21.♗e2 ♘d5 22.♘xd5 ♗xd5 23.h4 b5∓ M. Gurevich – Leko, Elista [2] 2007) 16...f5! 17.♘g3 fxe4 18.fxe4 cxd4 19.♗xd4 ♖ac8 Preventing queenside castling. 20.♖d1 ♖fd8 21.♗c3 ♘g6 22.♗b5 ♘c5 23.0–0 ♗a6 24.♗xa6 ♘xa6= Black had equalized easily and after a few mistakes by White he won in M. Gurevich – Leko, Elista (4) 2007.

Now many prefer to play: 8.e3 d6 9.♘e2 ♘bd7 And now White has a few options: 10. ♕d3 (the main line), 10.♕c2, 10.♖d1 or 10.♕d2. In all of them, White's moves are easier and Black needs to play very accurately to equalize.

7.♗g5

White is aiming for the main line which arises after 6...b6. As we will see, Black has other options and she is not obliged to transpose to the main line.

White can play 7.♘f3, but after 7...b6 8.e3 ♗b7 9.♗e2 ♘bd7 10.0–0 ♘e4 11.♕c2 f5⇄ Black has good counterplay.

An interesting option is:
7.g3
When Black reacts with:

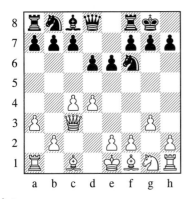

7...♗d7!

7...b6?! is now imprecise, since White has 8.♗g2± and Black can't play ...♗b7.
8.♗g2 ♗c6 9.♘f3
As an example of how Black should play this type of position, I suggest the following game:
9...♘bd7 10.0–0 ♗e4 11.b3 ♕e7 12.a4 a5 13.♖e1 b6 14.♗h3 c5 15.♘d2 ♗b7 16.e4 cxd4 17.♕xd4 ♘c5=
Black has already equalized. The way he now accelerated from equality to a better position is very instructive:
18.f3 ♘fd7 19.♗b2 ♘e5 20.♖e3 f6! 21.♕c3 ♕f7 22.♕c2 ♖ad8 23.♖f1 ♘c6 24.♗c3 f5!∓

Black had the initiative in Kulaots – Eljanov, Turkey 2011.

7...♘bd7 8.e3 b6 9.♘e2 ♗a6

One of the big ideas behind 6...d6 is this possibility. 9...♗b7 would transpose to the main line.

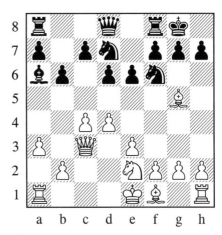

10.♕c2

A normal move which prepares further development with ♘c3. The position after 10.♕c2 can be considered the tabiya for the 9...♗a6 line.

Premature is: 10.b4?! c5 11.b5 ♗b7 12.♕d3 ♖c8 13.♘c3 cxd4 14.exd4 (14.♕xd4 h6 15.♗h4 ♕c7∓ is simply better for Black) Now Black can react better than in the game Grigorov – Brkic, Belfort 2005, by playing: 14...h6! 15.♗e3 d5∓ With a clear advantage, Alonso Rosell – Pinto Munoz, Spain 2008.

10...c5

The most common move in this position, but in my opinion the following move also deserves serious attention:

10...♕c8!?

10...h6 11.♗h4 c5 12.dxc5 bxc5 13.♘c3 would lead to a similar position as in the main line.
Now the main move is:
11.♘c3
On 11.0–0–0 Black can react with the interesting: 11...d5!? (11...c5 12.♘c3

cxd4 13.♖xd4 ♕c5∞ is another possibility)
12.cxd5 exd5 13.♘c3 ♗xf1 14.♖hxf1 ♖e8⇄
With an unclear position, Ekstroem –
Psakhis, Elista (ol) 1998.
11.b4 c5 12.dxc5 (12.b5 ♗b7) 12...bxc5
13.b5 ♗b7 14.a4 (In the game Krush
– Psakhis, Internet [blitz] 2000, White
played 14.f3 h6 15.♗h4 d5 16.♗f2 ♕c7
17.♘g3 ♘e5 18.♗e2 and here Black missed
18...♘xc4 19.♗xc4 dxc4 20.♕xc4 a6!∓ with
the initiative, as suggested by GM Mihail
Marin.) 14...d5 15.a5 ♖b8 16.♘g3 ♕c7
17.♗e2 ♕e5 18.♗xf6 ♘xf6 19.0–0 h5 20.h4
♖fd8 21.♖ad1 g6= Black was OK in Bareev
– Leko, Elista (4) 2007.

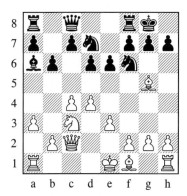

11...c5

11...d5 12.cxd5 exd5 (12...♗xf1 13.dxe6
♗xg2 14.exd7 ♘xd7 15.♖g1 ♕b7 16.♕f5!?±)
13.♘b5! (13.♖xa6 ♕xa6 14.0–0–0 ♖ac8⇄
is suggested by Psakhis) 13...♗xb5 (13...c5
14.♘d6 ♕c7 15.♗xa6 ♕xd6 16.0–0± White
is better thanks to the bishop pair) 14.♗xb5
c5 15.dxc5 bxc5 16.0–0± White has pressure.
12.♖d1!
If 12.dxc5?! then Black has 12...♕xc5!∓ and
now we can see the idea behind 10...♕c8!?.
12.0–0–0 cxd4 13.♖xd4 ♕c5 14.♗xf6 ♘xf6
15.♗e2 ♖ac8= Kacheishvili – V. Milov,
Batumi 1999.
12.♘e4?! ♘xe4 13.♕xe4 ♖e8 14.♖d1 h6
15.♗h4 ♗b7↑ Lapcevic – Vratonjic, Serbia
2010.

12.d5 exd5 13.cxd5 ♗xf1 14.♔xf1 ♕b7↑
looks good for Black.

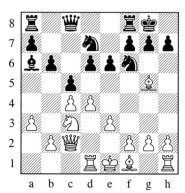

And here I suggest a novelty:
12...d5!?N 13.cxd5 ♗xf1 14.♖xf1
    14.♔xf1 ♘xd5 15.♘xd5 exd5 16.dxc5 ♕c6⇄
14...♘xd5 15.♘xd5 exd5⇄
Black has a good game.

11.dxc5!?

White's whole idea in this game is connected
with this move (instead 11.♖d1 is the main
line). Now Black has three ways to take on c5:

11...bxc5

In Agrest – Korchnoi, Malmo 1996, Black
played:
11...♘xc5 12.♘c3 ♖c8 13.♖d1 h6
    After 13...♕e7 14.♗e2 ♘cd7 White has
    15.♕d2 ♗xc4 16.♕xd6± ♕e8 17.♗xc4 ♖xc4
    18.0–0± and his position remains better.
14.♗xf6 ♕xf6 15.♖xd6
15.b4!? also deserves attention.
15...♘b7

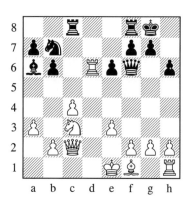

Here White missed:

16.♘d5! ♕g5

16...♕e5 17.♘e7† ♔h8 18.♘xc8 ♘xd6 19.♘xd6 ♕xd6 20.♗e2±

17.f4 ♕h4† 18.g3 ♘xd6 19.gxh4 exd5 20.♖g1±

11...dxc5 12.♘c3± leads to typical small but long-term advantage for White.

12.♘c3 ♕b6 13.0–0–0

Another plan is possible, based on castling short:

13.♗e2

The best option for Black is to immediately play:

13...h6 14.♗h4

14.♗f4 d5 15.cxd5 ♘xd5 16.♘xd5 exd5 17.♖d1 ♗xe2 18.♕xe2 ♕e6 19.0–0 ♘f6 20.♕b5 A draw was agreed in Dreev – Kunte, Gibraltar 2004.

14...d5 15.0–0

15.cxd5 exd5 16.0–0 ♗xe2 17.♕xe2 d4⇄ is good for Black, Petrik – Berescu, Hungary 2009.

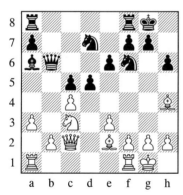

15...♗xc4!N 16.♗xc4 dxc4

Now White doesn't have anything better than:

17.♗xf6 ♘xf6 18.♘a4 ♕b5 19.♖ac1 ♘d5 20.♕xc4 ♕xc4 21.♖xc4 ♘b6 22.♖e4 ♘xa4 23.♖xa4 ♖fb8=

With a drawish position.

13...♗b7

Maybe this is premature. On a6 the black bishop was putting pressure on c4, so an idea with ...♘e5-c6 and ...d5-d4 would be faster as the c4-pawn remains weak.

Better is:

13...♖ab8!

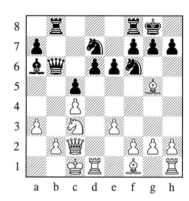

Saving ...♗b7 for later and preparing the d5-break.

14.♖d2

This was played twice by Irina Krush; Black's best reaction is:

14...♖fe8!

Waiting for the right moment to push ...d6-d5.

Worse is: 14...♖fd8 15.♗e2 ♘e5 16.♗xf6 gxf6 17.♘e4 f5 18.♘f6† ♔g7 19.♘h5† ♔f8 (19...♔h6 20.f4!→ The black king is in danger on h6.) 20.f4 ♘c6 21.♕c3 e5 22.♖hd1 ♔e7 23.♘g3 ♗c8 All this was played in I. Krush – Yudasin, New York (rapid) 2003, and here White missed: 24.fxe5 ♘xe5□ 25.♖xd6! ♕xd6 (25...♖xd6 26.♕xe5† ♔d7 27.♘xf5 ♖d1† 28.♗xd1+–) 26.♖xd6 ♔xd6 27.♕d2†! ♔e7 28.♕a5+– Winning more material.

15.♗e2

If 15.e4 then Black can play 15...♘e5! 16.♗xf6 gxf6 17.f4 ♘c6 18.♖xd6 ♖ed8 19.♖xd8† ♖xd8∞ with good compensation for the pawn.

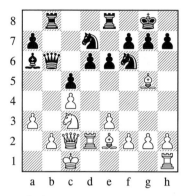

Now Black can try:

15...d5!N

Krush – Medvegy, China (rapid) 2008, continued: 15...h6 16.♗h4 ♗b7 (16...d5 17.♖hd1 ♕b7 18.cxd5 ♗xe2 19.♘xe2 exd5 20.♘c3 d4 21.exd4 cxd4 22.♖xd4 ♕xg2 23.♗g3 ♖b7 24.♔b1↑) Now White should play the same plan as Seirawan:

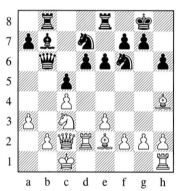

17.e4!N   e5   (17...♘e5   18.♖hd1   ♘c6 19.♖xd6±) 18.♖hd1 ♖e6 19.f3 ♘f8 (The plan of transferring the knight to d4 is impossible. For example: 19...♖d8 20.♗f1 ♘b8 21.♘d5± Planning to meet 21...♕a5 with 22.♘xf6† gxf6 23.♕b3 ♕c7 24.f4! exf4 25.e5!+– with a crushing attack.) 20.♗f1± White is better; he can play ♗f2 with the idea of b4-b5, or g2-g3 planning ♗h3.

16.♖hd1 ♕b7 17.cxd5 ♗xe2 18.♘xe2 ♘xd5 18...exd5 19.♘c3 d4 20.exd4 cxd4 21.♖xd4 ♕xg2 22.♗f4 ♖b7 23.♔b1↑

19.e4 ♘5b6∞

Black has a good game. For example: 20.♗f4?! e5 21.♗e3 ♘f8!

Planning ...♘e6-d4; Black is already attacking.

14.e4 ♖ab8

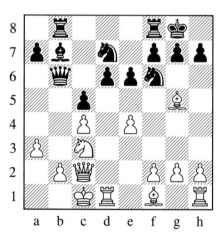

15.♖d2!N

This is an improvement. We have already seen the same plan after 13...♖ab8!.

In Sasikiran – Ghaem Maghami, Asian Championship, Esfahan 2005, White played 15.f3 but after: 15...♖fd8 16.♗e2 ♘e5 17.♗f4 ♘g6 (17...♘e8!? intending ...♘c6-d4) 18.♗e3 ♗a6 19.♖d2 ♘e5 20.♘a4 ♕c7 21.♖hd1 ♘c6⇄ Black had a nice game.

15...♖fc8?

A serious mistake. Judit wants to play ...♘e8 and ...♘e5-c6 but as we shall see, this is too slow.

This was the last chance to transfer the knight to c6 with the risky but justified:
15...♘e5! 16.♗xf6

On 16.♗e2 Black has 16...♗a6!.
16...gxf6 17.♗e2

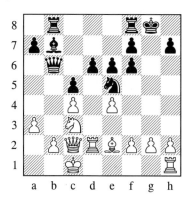

17...♗a6

17...♖fd8 18.♖hd1 ♗a6 19.♘b5! ♗xb5 20.cxb5 c4 21.f4 ♘d3† 22.♗xd3 cxd3 23.♕xd3 ♕c5† 24.♔b1 ♖xb5 25.♖c2↑ This should lead to a small advantage for White.
18.f4

After 18.♘b5 Black has: 18...♘xc4 19.♕xc4 (19.♗xc4 ♗xb5 20.♗xb5 ♕xb5 21.♖xd6 c4→) 19...♗xb5 20.♕xb5 ♕xb5 21.♗xb5 ♖xb5 22.♖xd6 ♖fb8 23.♖d2 c4 24.♖hd1 ♔g7= And next will be ...c3.
18...♘c6 19.♖xd6 ♕c7 20.♕d3

Interesting is the forcing line 20.e5 ♘d4 21.♖xd4 cxd4 22.♘e4 fxe5 23.♘f6† ♔g7 24.♕xh7† ♔xf6 25.♕h4† ♔g7 26.♕g5† ♔h8 27.♕h6†= with perpetual check.
20...♘d4 21.♕g3†

21.♖xa6 ♕b7 22.♘b5 ♕xa6 23.♘xd4 cxd4 24.♕xd4 ♕c6 25.♖xf6 ♕xe4 26.♕g5† ♔h8 27.♕f6† ♔g8= With a draw.
21...♔h8

Now White has to play:
22.♕h4

In order to save the game after:
22...♘xe2† 23.♘xe2 ♕xd6 24.♕xf6† ♔g8 25.♕g5† ♔h8 26.♕f6†=

16.♗e2 ♘e8 17.f4!±

White is taking control over the e5-square. This stops the plan with ...♘c6-e5 and gives White the advantage; Black has problems finding any kind of counterplay.

17...♘f8 18.♖hd1

18.f5 f6 19.♗f4 e5 20.♗e3± also looks better for White.

18...f6 19.♗h4 ♘g6

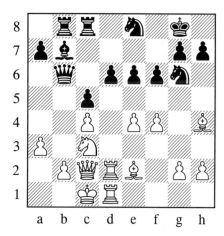

20.g3!

An interesting approach; White wants to keep the position dynamic.

An alternative is 20.♗g3 e5 (20...♘e7 21.♗g4±) 21.f5 ♘h8 22.♗f2 ♘f7± and White has the advantage. Now he can even try: 23.b4!? a6 (23...♕a6 24.♔b2 ♗a8 25.b5↑) 24.b5 ♕a5 25.a4↑ With the initiative.

20...♖d8 21.♗g4 e5

On 21...♗c8 White has the strong retort: 22.e5! ♘xh4 23.gxh4 f5 (or 23...g6 24.h5 f5 25.hxg6 hxg6 26.♗f3 with a strong attack) 24.♖h5!? Provoking more weaknesses in Black's position after: 24...g6 25.♗f3 ♗b7 26.♗xb7 ♖xb7 27.h5 ♖bd7 28.hxg6 hxg6 29.♖g1± White is on top.

22.♗e6† ♔f8?!

A risky decision. Safer was 22...♔h8 23.f5 ♘xh4 24.gxh4 ♘c7 25.h5±.

23.f5 ♘e7

After this Black is too passive; the plan with ...♘c6-d4 is not enough for equality due to her king not being safe on f8 from White's attack.

Better was:
23...♘xh4 24.gxh4 ♘c7
But even so, White's attack on the g-file is fast:
25.♖g2 ♖e8 26.♖dg1 ♖e7
26...♘xe6 27.fxe6 g6 (27...♖e7 28.♕f2! planning ♕xf6) 28.h5+–
27.♕d2!
Now the idea is ♕h6 and Black has to sacrifice a pawn to stop the mate threats with:
27...♘xe6 28.fxe6 ♔g8 29.♕h6 ♕c7 30.♕xf6 ♖f8 31.♕g5±
White is better.

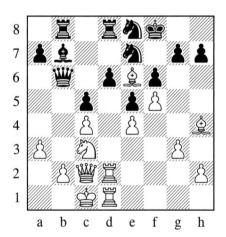

24.g4± h6

This is the only way to stop the immediate break with g4-g5.

25.♗f2 ♘c6 26.♘d5 ♕a5 27.h4 ♘d4 28.♗xd4 cxd4 29.g5

After a few more or less forced moves, White has finally made real threats against the black king. Now it is very difficult for Black to defend.

29...♗xd5 30.exd5

A natural decision, but maybe not the best one.

The inaccurate 30.gxh6? would give Black the opportunity to play: 30...♗xe6!? 31.h7 ♔e7 32.h8=♕ ♗f7!⚐ Black has fine compensation (but not 32...♗xc4 33.♕xc4 ♖dc8 34.♕xc8 ♖xc8† 35.♔b1±). 33.♕d3 ♕a4 34.♖c2 ♖dc8→ Black takes over the initiative.

Paradoxically, the best move was:
30.♗xd5!

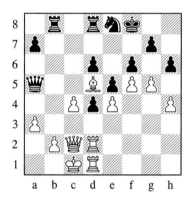

Black's position remains critical. For example:
30...h5
30...hxg5 31.hxg5 fxg5 32.♖g2 ♕b6 33.♕d2 ♕b3 34.♕xg5 ♕e3† 35.♕xe3 dxe3 36.♖h1+–
30...♘c7 31.gxh6 gxh6 32.♖g1 ♘xd5 33.exd5 ♔f7 34.♖dg2 ♖g8 35.♕e2 ♖xg2 36.♕xg2 ♖f8 37.♕g7† ♔e8 38.♕b7+–
31.♖g2 fxg5 32.♖xg5 ♘f6 33.♖dg1 ♖d7 34.♕e2 ♕b6 35.b4 ♕a6 36.♔b2 ♕a4 37.♖1g3±

30...hxg5?

Judit is trying to find practical chances by opening the position. As usual, this helps White.

A better defence was:

30...♖b7! 31.gxh6 gxh6

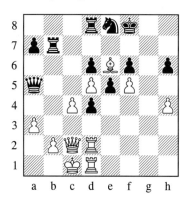

Despite the fact that White is clearly better, it is not so easy to convert it into a win.

32.♖d3

32.♖g1 ♖db8 33.♖g8† ♔e7 34.♖h8 ♔d8⇄

32...♖db8 33.b4 ♕a6 34.♖g1 ♖c7 35.c5

35.♖g8† ♔e7 36.c5 dxc5 37.bxc5 ♕a5 transposes to 35.c5.

35...dxc5 36.bxc5 ♕a5! 37.c6!

37.d6 ♘xd6 38.♖g8† (38.♖dg3 ♘e8!) 38...♔e7 39.♖g7† ♔d8 40.♖xc7 ♔xc7 41.cxd6† ♔xd6⯧ Black has compensation.

37...♔e7 38.♖b3 ♖xb3 39.♕xb3 ♔d6 40.♗d7 ♖xd7 41.cxd7 ♔xd7 42.♗d1!?±

White has kept the advantage, but Black has more practical chances than she would have had after 30.♗d5!.

31.hxg5 fxg5

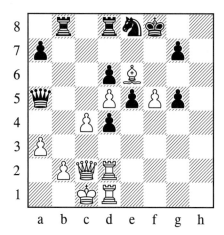

32.f6!+−

Sacrificing a pawn to open the diagonal for the queen. Black cannot stop ♕g6 without sacrificing on b2, but after that everything is clear.

32.♖g2 ♕b6 33.f6! was also good enough.

32...♖xb2 33.♔xb2 ♘xf6 34.♔a2

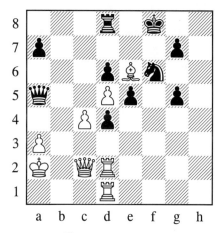

Judit could have resigned, but she kept playing for a few more moves; I assume because Seirawan was in time trouble.

34...♕c7 35.♖g2 ♖c8 36.♗xc8 ♕xc8 37.♖xg5 ♘d5 38.♕f5† ♕xf5 39.♖xf5† ♘f6 40.c5 ♔e7 41.c6 ♘d5 42.♖g1 d3 43.♔b3 ♔e6 44.♖fg5

1–0

GAME 49
▷ **V. Kramnik (2781)**
▶ **R. Ponomariov (2764)**
39th Dortmund GM Tournament
Round 1, 21.07.2011 **[E94]**
Annotated by Kamil Miton

As a player, Ponomariov is a fighter and he is not afraid to employ rare, unclear continuations. Although Black missed a chance at one point, in general I believe that with accurate play White should be better off in this line. This game will demonstrate to us how many complications can arise in structures with pawns on e4-c4 against d6-c6.

1.d4 ♘f6 2.c4 g6 3.♘c3 ♗g7 4.e4 d6 5.♗e2 0–0 6.♘f3 e5 7.0–0 exd4 8.♘xd4 ♖e8 9.f3 c6 10.♔h1 ♘bd7 11.♗e3

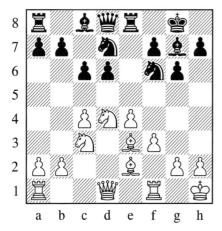

11...a6
The central break is wrong here:
11...d5? 12.cxd5 cxd5
    12...♘xd5 13.exd5 ♖xe3 14.dxc6 bxc6
    15.♘xc6 ♕f8 16.♘d5 ♖e6 17.♘c7 ♖xc6
    18.♘xa8±
13.♘db5 ♘e5
    13...dxe4 14.♗f4± ♘h5 15.♗d6±
    13...♘b6 14.a4 ♗e6 15.e5 ♘fd7 16.f4 f6
    17.a5 ♘c4 18.♘xd5 ♘xe3 19.♘xe3 fxe5
    20.f5 gxf5 21.♘xf5 ♘f6 22.♕xd8 ♖axd8
    23.♘c7 ♗xf5 24.♘xe8 ♘xe8 25.♖xf5+–
    Petkov – Gajewski, Plovdiv 2008.
14.♘xa7 ♗e6 15.♘ab5±
White has an extra pawn and the better position.

12.♘c2
12.♕d2?! is met by 12...d5. This is now correct because the b5-square is under control. 13.exd5 cxd5 14.♖ad1 (14.cxd5 ♘b6=) 14...dxc4 15.♗xc4 b5 16.♗b3 ♗b7= Black is okay.

12...♘e5
Let's say a few things about this position. The main ideas for Black are to get active play after ...d5 or ...b5. White usually makes a couple of consolidating moves, such as ♕d2 and ♖d1, while the plan of chasing the knight from e5 at the right moment may allow him to take control of the situation. Both sides have to play very accurately, because it is very easy to fall into a worse position.

13.f4
Kramnik takes the decision to advance the f-pawn immediately. He had other playable moves too:

a) 13.♕d2
This is a bit slow.
13...♗e6 14.b3 d5 15.cxd5
    15.f4 ♘eg4 16.e5 dxc4 17.bxc4 ♘xe3
    18.♕xe3 ♘g4 19.♕g3 ♘h6= and Black will
    play ...f6 at some point.
15...cxd5 16.f4 ♘c6
    16...♘eg4 17.e5 ♘e4 18.♘xe4 dxe4 19.♘d4
    ♘xe3 20.♕xe3 ♗d5 21.♖ad1 ♕b6 22.♘f5
    ♕xe3 23.♘xe3 ♗c6 24.♗c4 ♖ac8=

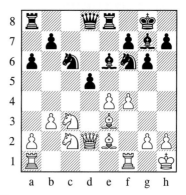

17.f5
17.e5 ♘e4 18.♘xe4 dxe4 19.♘d4 ♘xd4
20.♗xd4 f5 21.exf6 ♗xf6 22.♖ad1 ♗xd4
23.♕xd4 ♕xd4 24.♖xd4 ♖ad8 25.♖fd1
(25.♖xe4 ♗xb3) 25...♖xd4 26.♖xd4 ♖c8!=
It is important for Black to play actively, otherwise when the white king comes to

the centre, the e4-pawn could become really weak.

17...♘xe4 18.♘xe4 ♗xf5 19.♗g5 f6 20.♘xf6† ♗xf6 21.♗xf6 ♕xf6 22.♗d3 ♖ad8 23.♖ad1 ♕e6 24.♗xf5 gxf5

The weakness of the black king gives White compensation, but only enough for equality.

b) 13.b3 b5 14.c5 d5

14...dxc5 15.f4 ♘eg4 16.♕xd8 ♖xd8 17.♗xc5± 15.♗g5

15.exd5 ♘xd5 16.♘xd5 ♕xd5 17.♕xd5 cxd5 18.♖ae1 ♘c6 19.♗d3 ♗e6=

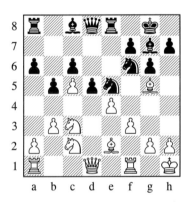

15...h6

15...♕c7 16.exd5 ♘xd5 17.♘xd5 cxd5 18.♖c1 ♕xc5?! (better is 18...♘c6∞) 19.♘e3 ♘c4 (19...♕a3 20.♘xd5 h6 21.♘c7 ♗e6 22.♘xa8 ♖xa8 23.♗f4 ♕xa2 24.♖a1 ♕xb3 25.♕xb3 ♗xb3 26.♗xb5±) 20.♘xd5 ♖xe2 21.bxc4 (21.♕xe2 ♕xd5 22.♕e8† ♗f8 23.bxc4 ♕xg5 24.♕c6 ♖b8 25.♕c7 ♖a8 26.♕c6=) 21...♖e5 22.♗f6 ♗e6 23.♗xe5 ♗xe5 24.cxb5 ♕xd5 25.♕xd5 ♗xd5 26.♖c5± 16.♗xf6 ♗xf6 17.exd5

17.f4 ♘g4 18.e5 ♘xe5 19.fxe5 ♗xe5 20.♘d4 ♗d7∞

17...♘d7

17...♘g4 18.fxg4 ♗xc3 19.♗f3 ♗xa1 20.♕xa1 cxd5 21.♕d4 ♗e6 22.♘b4⩱ 18.♘d4 ♘xc5

18...cxd5 19.b4±

19.♘xc6 ♕d6 20.♖c1 ♗d7=

c) 13.♗g1!?

A very interesting idea. White does not hurry with f3-f4, but makes a prophylactic move first.

13...♗e6

13...b5 14.c5 dxc5 15.♗xc5±

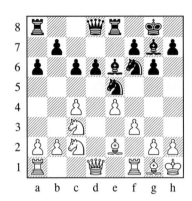

14.b3

14.f4 ♘xc4 15.♘d4 (15.f5 gxf5 16.exf5 ♘xb2 17.♕d2 ♗c4 18.♘e3 ♗xe2 19.♕xe2 d5 20.♕xb2 d4 21.♖ad1 dxc3 22.♕xb7 ♕c8‡) 15...♘b6 (15...b5 16.b3 ♘b6 17.♗f3 ♖c8 18.♘xe6 ♖xe6 19.e5 ♘fd5 20.♘xd5 ♘xd5 21.♗g4 ♖e8 22.♗xc8 ♕xc8 23.♗d4 dxe5 24.fxe5 ♗xe5 25.♖e1 ♗xd4 26.♕xd4±; 15...♘xb2 16.♕c2±) 16.♘xe6 ♖xe6 17.♕b3 ♘bd7 (17...c5 18.♗f3⩲) 18.♕xb7 ♖b8 19.♕xc6 d5 20.♕a4 ♘xe4 21.♘xe4 ♖xe4 22.♕xa6 ♗xb2 23.♖ab1=

14.♘e3 b5 15.c5 (15.cxb5 axb5 16.f4 ♘c4 17.♗xc4 ♗xc4 18.♘xc4 bxc4 19.♕f3 ♖b8 20.e5 dxe5 21.fxe5 ♖xe5 22.♕xc6 ♖xb2 23.♖ad1 ♕e7=; 15.b3=) 15...dxc5 16.f4 ♕xd1 17.♖axd1 ♘eg4 18.♘xg4 ♗xg4=

14...♕a5

14...b5?! 15.f4 ♘eg4 and now:

a) 16.h3 ♘h5 17.♖f3 (17.♕e1 ♗xc3 18.♕xc3 ♕h4 19.♗xg4 [19.♖f3!?∞] 19...♘g3† 20.♔h2 ♘xf1† 21.♖xf1 ♗xg4 22.♗f2 ♕h6 23.♔g1⩲) 17...♕h4 18.♕e1 ♕xe1 19.♖xe1 ♘xf4 (19...♘h6±) 20.hxg4 ♘xe2 21.♘xe2 ♗xg4 22.♖f4±

b) 16.f5 ♗c8 17.♗xg4 ♘xg4 18.♕xg4 ♗xc3

19.♖ad1 and White has strong pressure on the dark squares.

15.♕d2

15.♘a4 ♗xc4 16.♗xc4 ♘xc4 17.♗f2 b5∓

15.b4 ♕c7 leaves the c4-pawn weak: 16.f4 ♘xc4 17.f5 gxf5 18.exf5 ♗d5 19.♗d4∞

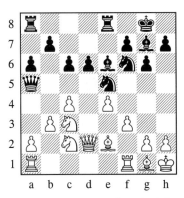

I looked at two options for Black here:

c1) 15...♖ad8 16.f4 ♘eg4 17.b4

17.h3 ♘h5 (17...d5 18.e5 [18.cxd5? ♘xd5] 18...dxc4 19.♕e1 ♘xe5 20.fxe5 [20.b4 ♘d3 21.♗xd3 ♕h5 22.♗e2 ♗g4∓] 20...♕xe5 21.♗xc4 ♘h5 22.♖f3 ♗xc4 23.♖e3 ♖d3 24.♖xe5 ♖xe5 25.♕h4 ♖xc3 26.♕d8† ♗f8 27.bxc4 ♖xc2 28.♗h2 ♖e6∞) 18.♖f3

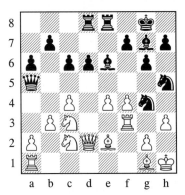

18...♗xc3 (18...♘xf4 19.♕xf4 ♗xc3 20.hxg4±) 19.♕xc3 ♕xc3 20.♖xc3 ♘gf6 21.♗xh5 ♘xh5 22.♗b6 ♖d7 23.♖f3 f5=

17...♕h5

17...♕c7 18.h3 ♘h5 19.♗xg4 White can

play this now that the c3-knight is not hanging. 19...♘g3† 20.♔h2 ♘xf1† 21.♖xf1 ♗xc4 22.♖e1±

18.h3

The black pieces are strangely placed, and the position is not easy for a human to play.

18...♕h6 19.♗b6 ♘h5

19...♖c8!? 20.♔g1 ♘e5 21.♘e3 ♘ed7 22.♗d4 c5 23.bxc5 dxc5 24.♗xf6 ♗xf6∞ 25.e5?! ♘xe5 26.fxe5 ♗xe5∓

20.♔g1 ♘g3 21.♗xg4 ♗xg4 22.♖fe1 ♖c8 23.hxg4 ♕h1† 24.♔f2 ♕h4 25.♔f3

25.♔g1 leads to a draw by repetition.

25...h5 26.gxh5 ♗xc3 27.♕xc3 g5 28.fxg5 ♘xe4 29.♖xe4 ♖xe4 30.♗e3 ♖xc4 31.♕d3 ♕xh5† 32.♔f2 ♕h4† 33.♔g1 ♕e4 34.♕xe4 ♖xe4 35.♔f2∞

c2) 15...b5 16.♖ad1!?

16.f4 b4! (16...♘eg4 is also possible) 17.♘a4 (17.♘xb4 ♕xb4 18.fxe5 dxe5=) 17...♘xe4 18.♕e3 (18.♕xb4 ♕xb4 19.♘xb4 a5∞) 18...♘xc4 19.♕xe4 ♘d2 20.♕d3 ♘xf1 21.♖xf1 ♗f5 22.♕d1∞

16.c5 dxc5 17.♗xc5 ♖ad8 and Black will play ...♘fd7 next, with a pleasant position.

16...bxc4

16...♘h5 17.♘d4 ♗d7 18.f4 ♘g4 19.f5 ♘hf6 20.♗xg4 ♘xg4 21.♘de2± The black position has several weaknesses: the d7-bishop, the d6-pawn and the dark squares in general.

16...♖ad8 17.f4±

17.f4

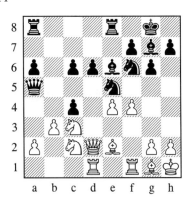

17...cxb3

17...♘eg4 18.b4 ♕h5 19.♕e1 ♖ad8 20.h3±
17...♘d3 18.f5 (18.♗xd3 cxd3 19.♕xd3
♘xe4!∓; 18.♘d4!?) 18...gxf5 19.exf5 ♗xf5
20.bxc4 (20.♘e3 ♗e6 21.♘xc4 ♗xc4
22.♗xd3 ♗xd3 23.♕xd3 ♖e6∓) 20...♘b2
21.♖xf5 ♕xf5 22.♘d4 ♕d7 23.♖f1
(23.♕xb2 c5!) 23...♘e4 24.♘xe4 (24.♕xb2
c5 25.♗h5 ♖ab8 26.♕c2 ♘xc3 27.♗xf7†
♕xf7 28.♖xf7 ♔xf7 29.♘f5 ♖e1∓) 24...♖xe4
25.♘f5 ♘xc4 26.♗xc4 ♖xc4 27.♘xg7 ♔xg7
28.♗d4† ♖xd4 29.♕xd4† ♔g8 30.♖f3 ♖e8
31.♖g3† ♔f8 32.♕g7† ♔e7 33.♕g5† ♔f8=
18.axb3 ♘ed7

18...♘eg4 19.h3 (19.b4 ♕h5 20.♕xd6?

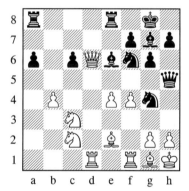

20...♗c4! 21.♗xc4 ♘xh2−+) 19...♘h5
20.♖f3 ♗xc3 21.♕xc3 ♕xc3 22.♖xc3 ♘gf6
23.♗xh5 ♘xh5 24.♖xd6 ♘xf4=
19.b4

19.♘d4 ♘c5 20.♘xc6 ♕c7 21.♗xc5 ♕xc6
22.♕xd6 ♕xd6 23.♗xd6 ♗xb3 24.♖c1 ♗f8
25.♗xf8 ♖xf8 26.e5 ♘d7=

19...♕c7 20.♕xd6 ♕xd6 21.♖xd6 ♗f8
22.♖xc6 ♘xe4!

22...♖ac8 23.b5±
23.♘xe4 ♗d5 24.♖xa6 ♗xe4 25.♖xa8 ♖xa8
26.♗f3 ♗xf3 27.gxf3 ♖a2=

13...♘eg4

13...♘ed7 14.♗f3±

14.♗g1 h5

14...♘h6 15.♗f3±

15.♗f3

15.h3

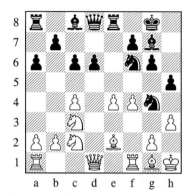

15...♘xe4! 16.♘xe4 ♖xe4 17.hxg4 (17.♗d3
♘f6 18.♗xe4 ♘xe4∞) 17...♕h4† 18.♗h2
♗xg4 19.♗xg4 hxg4 20.g3 ♕h5 21.♖f2 ♖ae8
22.♕xd6 ♗xb2 23.♖af1 ♕f5∞

After 15.♗d3 Black has 15...h4 (15...b5
16.cxb5 axb5 17.h3 ♘h6 is another option)
16.h3 ♘h6 17.♕f3 ♘h5 18.♘e2 f5 with
typical active play.

15...♗e6

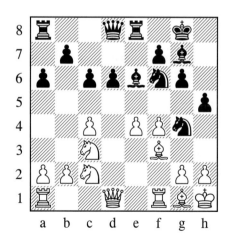

16.b3

The alternative was:
16.♕d3!? b5

16...♘d7 17.♕xd6 ♗xc4 18.♖fd1 ♗e6 19.♘d4±

17.cxb5

17.♖fd1 would be met by: 17...♗h6 18.♕xd6 (18.e5!?∞; 18.g3 ♗f8∞) 18...♕xd6 19.♖xd6 ♗xf4 20.♖xc6 bxc4 White must be careful here. For example, 21.♘d5 ♗e5 22.h3 ♖ab8 23.hxg4 ♗xd5 24.exd5 hxg4 25.♗d1 ♔g7 gives Black a strong initiative.

17...axb5

17...cxb5 18.♖fd1 ♗h6 19.g3±

18.♖fd1

White has pressure on the d-pawn.

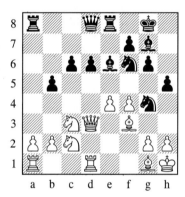

18...d5

18...♗f8 19.h3±

18...♗h6 19.♕xd6 ♕xd6 20.♖xd6 ♗xf4 21.♖xc6±

19.e5 ♘d7 20.♘d4 ♘gxe5 21.fxe5 ♘xe5

Black has some compensation, but White is certainly better.

16...♕a5 17.♕e1 b5

If Black does not play actively, the position is pleasant for White: 17...♘d7 18.♘d4±

18.c5

18.h3 b4 (18...bxc4 19.b4 ♕c7 20.hxg4 hxg4 21.♗e2 ♘xe4 22.♘xe4 ♗f5 23.♘xd6 ♕xd6 24.♖d1±) 19.♘a4 ♗xc4 (19...♖ab8 20.a3±) 20.♗b6 ♕b5 21.♘d4 ♗xf1 22.♘xb5 ♗xb5 23.♖c1 (23.hxg4 hxg4 24.♗d1 ♘xe4 25.♖c1 c5∞) 23...♘h6 24.♕xb4 c5 Black has

some compensation for the queen, but I don't believe that it is enough.

18...b4

18...dxc5 19.♗xc5 ♘d7 20.♗d4±

19.♘a4

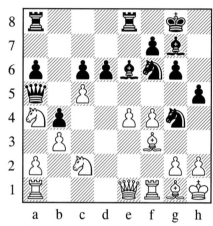

19...♗c4?

A mistake. Ponomariov missed the chance to play the strong:

19...♘xe4! 20.♕xb4

20.♗xe4 ♗d5 (20...♗f5 21.♗xf5 ♖xe1 22.♖axe1 gxf5 23.cxd6±) 21.♕xb4 ♕xb4 22.♘xb4 ♗xe4 23.♖ae1 a5 24.♘b6 axb4 25.♘xa8 d5 26.♘b6 h4 27.h3 ♘h6∓ with fine play for Black

20.♕xe4!? ♗xb3 21.axb3 ♖xe4 22.♗xe4 ♗xa1 23.♖xa1 Maybe White can claim some advantage in this very unclear position.

20...♕xb4 21.♘xb4

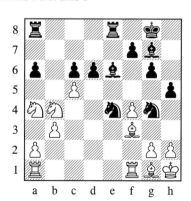

21...♘ef2†

21...♘xc5!? is also interesting.

22.♗xf2 ♘xf2† 23.♔g1

23.♖xf2 ♗xa1 24.♖f1 ♗d4 25.cxd6 ♖ad8 26.♗xc6 ♗d7∓

23...dxc5 24.♘xc5 ♗d4 25.♘xe6 ♖xe6 26.♘xc6 ♘h3† 27.♔h1 ♗xa1 28.gxh3 ♗f6 29.♘e7† ♖xe7 30.♗xa8 ♖e2=

White doesn't have any chances for a win in this endgame, because the black rook is active and the white kingside pawns are very weak.

20.♕xb4

This is the human move. The computer line is:

20.e5!? ♗xf1 21.♕xf1 dxe5

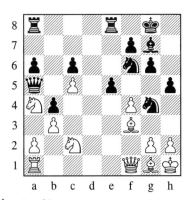

22.♗xc6 exf4

22...♖ad8 23.♗xe8 ♖xe8 24.♖e1 e4 25.h3 ♘h6 26.♘e3 also gives some advantage to White.

23.♕xf4 ♖ad8 24.♗xe8 ♖xe8 25.♖e1 ♖xe1 26.♘xe1 ♕b5 27.♘b2 ♘d7

27...♘d5 28.♕f3 ♕c6 29.♘c4 ♘e5 30.♘xe5 ♗xe5 31.♘d3±

28.♘c4 ♘xc5 29.♘d6 ♕e2 30.♕xf7† ♔h7 31.♘e8 ♘f2† 32.♕xf2 ♕xe8 33.♘f3 ♘d3 34.♕a7±

The weakness of the a6-pawn gives Black some problems.

20...♕xb4 21.♘xb4 ♗xf1 22.♖xf1 ♘xe4

22...♖xe4 23.♗xe4 ♘xe4 24.♘xc6 dxc5 25.♘xc5 ♘xc5 26.♗xc5+−

22...dxc5 23.♘xc5 ♗f8 24.♘xc6 ♗xc5 25.♗xc5 ♘xe4 26.♘e7† ♖xe7 27.♗xe7±

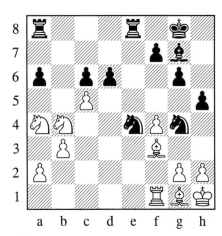

23.♘b6±

White's position is much better. Kramnik now plays very accurately and wins easily.

23...♖a7

23...♘d2 24.♖d1 ♘xf3 25.gxf3 dxc5 26.♘xc6 ♘h6 27.♘xa8 ♖xa8 28.♗xc5 ♘f5 29.b4±

24.cxd6 ♘xd6 25.♗xc6 ♖e2

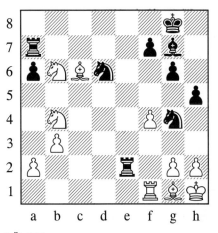

26.♘6d5

White is the exchange down, but the black rook on a7 is trapped.

26...♘c8 27.h3 ♘h6 28.♖c1

White doesn't rush to take on a7, instead preparing an attack on another black piece, the knight on c8.

28...♘f5 29.♗b5 ♘g3†

29...♖c7 30.♘xc7 axb5 31.♘xb5+–

30.♔h2 ♘f1† 31.♖xf1 axb5 32.♗xa7 ♘xa7 33.♔g3±

The last ten moves from White have been played at the highest level. He exchanged a few pieces, while keeping his knights very active. Now his king will be activated too. Black's chances of survival are minimal.

33...♘c8 34.♖d1 ♗f8 35.♔f3 ♖b2 36.g4 ♔g7 37.gxh5 ♘d6

37...gxh5 loses to 38.♖g1†.

38.hxg6 fxg6 39.♘c7 ♔f7

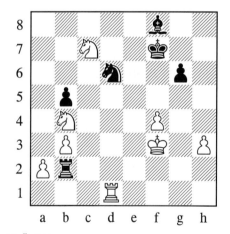

40.♘d3!

The final touch. Black will lose more material after ♘e5†.

40...♖xa2 41.♘e5† ♔f6

41...♔g8 42.♘xg6+–

42.♘d7†

1–0

GAME 50

▷ **V. Kramnik (2781)**

▶ **H. Nakamura (2770)**

39th Dortmund GM Tournament

Round 10, 31.07.2011 **[E97]**

Annotated by Sebastian Maze

In a King's Indian, Kramnik played an early novelty with 11.a4N. The position is very complicated, and in my opinion White should be slightly better. Perhaps it would be possible for White to try a plan with 18.♖c3, aiming to open the c-file. In the game the Russian went for a crazy line with 23.♘fxg5. After this dubious sacrifice Black was better, but an inaccuracy gave White the chance to draw. However, Kramnik missed this opportunity and Nakamura managed to win.

1.d4 ♘f6 2.c4 g6 3.♘c3 ♗g7 4.e4 d6 5.♘f3 0–0

Nakamura's decision to play the King's Indian could be considered a risky choice, because Kramnik has a huge score against this opening.

6.♗e2 e5 7.0–0 ♘c6 8.d5 ♘e7

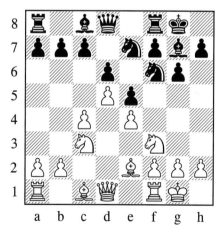

9.b4 ♘h5 10.c5

10.g3 f5 11.♘g5 ♘f6 12.f3!? is one of Van Wely's favourites lines.

10.♖e1 f5 11.♘g5 ♘f6 12.♗f3∞ has been played in a lot of high level games.

10...♘f4

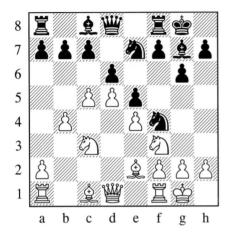

11.a4N

Amazingly, we already have a novelty! Kramnik wants to attack quickly on the queenside. But that is not the only point of the move; White may also put his rook on a3 to protect the f3-knight.

11.♗xf4 exf4 12.♖c1 h6 13.♘d4 a6 14.h3∞ Ivanchuk – Grischuk, Nalchik 2009.

11...f5

11...a5 12.cxd6 cxd6 13.bxa5 f5 14.♘g5 ♗f6 15.h4 ♕xa5 16.♘b5±

12.♗c4 fxe4 13.♘xe4 h6

13...♗g4 14.♖a3 a5 (14...♘f5 15.♗xf4 exf4 16.♕d2 ♗xf3 17.♖xf3 b6 18.♖e1± and the weakness of the light squares will cause Black problems) 15.bxa5 ♖xa5 16.♗d2 ♖a8 17.h3±

This position was reached via a different move order in a previous game, meaning that Kramnik's next move is his second novelty of the game!

14.♖e1N

A logical move. The rook is placed on an important file, at the same time offering some fresh air to the king.

14.g3?! ♘h3† (14...♘h5?! 15.♘fd2 ♔h8 16.♖a3 a6 17.cxd6 cxd6 18.b5± Bareev – Amonatov, Dagomys 2009) 15.♔g2 ♗g4 and Black is fine.

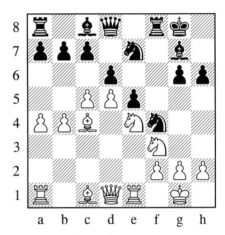

14...♗g4 15.♖a3 g5

A strong move from Nakamura, giving him the possibility of using the g6-square.

16.h3 ♗h5 17.♗xf4

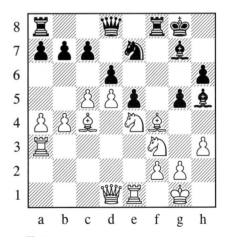

17...♖xf4

The other captures are:

17...exf4?! is simply bad. The e-file is opened and White gets a pleasant position: 18.cxd6 cxd6 19.♘c5 dxc5 20.d6† ♗f7 21.dxe7 ♕xd1 22.exf8=♕† ♔xf8 23.♖xd1 ♗xc4 24.♖b1±

17...gxf4!? 18.♕d3 ♘f5 19.♖c3 ♔h8 20.a5 Of course, White controls the light squares in the centre, but at some point an attack down the g-file may be possible for Black.

18.g3
18.♖c3 is an interesting possibility: 18...b6 (18...a5 19.bxa5 ♖xa5 20.♕b3 ♔h8 21.♘fd2±) 19.g3 ♖f8 20.cxd6 cxd6 21.♗a6± The bishop is strong on a6, securing the c-file for White by controlling the c8-square.

18...♖f8 19.a5 ♔h8 20.♔g2 ♖b8 21.♕d2 b6 22.axb6 axb6

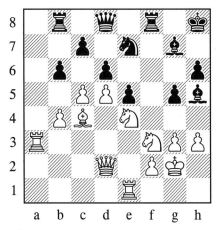

23.♘fxg5
What a surprising move, especially coming from Kramnik! While I was following the game, I was sceptical about this sacrifice. And later, with the help of the silicon machine, we can say confidently that this move was too optimistic.

23.cxd6 cxd6 24.♗b5 ♖c8∞ and the position is about equal.

23...hxg5 24.♕xg5 ♗g6

24...♖f5 25.♕h4 ♗f6 26.♘xf6 ♘g6 27.♕xh5† ♖xh5 28.♘xh5 ♕g5 29.cxd6 cxd6 30.♗e2 ♕d2∓ also gives Black the better position.

25.cxd6 cxd6 26.♖a7

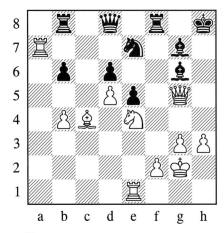

26...♖c8?!
26...♖f7 27.♕g4 ♘g8 28.♕xg6 ♖xa7 29.♘xd6 ♕f6 30.♕h5† ♘h6 31.♘e4 ♕f7∓ In this odd position White is a rook down, but can claim some compensation from the good coordination of his pieces and his three extra pawns!

27.♖xe7
Now Kramnik is right back in the game!

27...♖xc4 28.f3

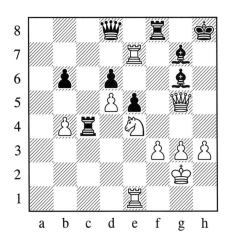

28...♖c2†

28...♖xb4 29.h4 b5 30.♖e2 ♖f6 31.♖a7∞ leads to a completely unclear position. The e4-knight is very strong, whereas the two bishops do not have great prospects.

29.♔g1 ♖c8 30.♖a1

30.h4! leads to a forced draw:

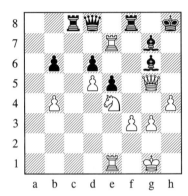

30...♖f7 31.♕xg6 ♕xe7 (31...♖xe7 32.♘g5 ♗f8 33.♕h5† ♔g8 34.♕g6† ♖g7 35.♕e6† ♔h8 36.♕h6†=) 32.♘g5 ♔g8 33.h5 ♕f6 34.♘xf7 ♕xf7 35.♕g4 ♖c3 36.h6 ♕f6 37.hxg7 ♕xf3 38.♕e6† ♔xg7 39.♕e7†=

30...♖f7 31.♕xg6

After 31.♖aa7 ♖xe7 32.♖xe7 ♖c1† 33.♔g2 ♖c2† 34.♔g1 ♖c1† it seems that neither player can avoid the draw. 35.♔f2 ♖c2† 36.♔e3?! b5 looks too dangerous for White.

31...♕xe7

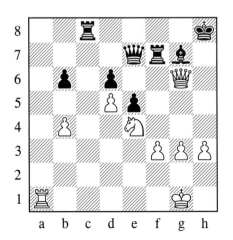

32.♘g5?

This move is too optimistic.

32.♘xd6 was the only move to stay in the game: 32...♖cf8 33.♘xf7† ♕xf7 34.♕xf7 ♖xf7 35.♖a8† ♔h7 36.♔g2 ♖d7 Black is a piece up, but White has very good chances of holding the position.

32...♔g8 33.♕h7† ♔f8 34.♘e6† ♔e8 35.♕h5 ♗f6 36.g4?

After this, the white position collapses immediately.

36.♕g6∞ had to be tried. Although Black has a rook more, the position is not easy for him to play, and the bishop on f6 looks like a pawn!

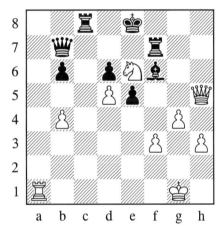

36...♕b7∓

Not bad, but even better was: 36...e4! 37.♖f1 exf3 38.g5 ♗e5 39.g6 ♖f6 40.g7† ♔d7–+

37.♖d1 ♕a6

Now the queen will be able to harass the white king.

38.♕g6 ♔e7 39.g5 ♗h8 40.♖e1 ♕a3 41.♘d4 ♕xb4 42.♘f5† ♔f8 43.♖d1

43.♕h6† ♗g7 44.♕xd6† ♕xd6 45.♘xd6 ♖d8 46.♘xf7 ♔xf7 47.h4 ♖xd5 48.h5 ♗f8 and the endgame is an easy win for Black.

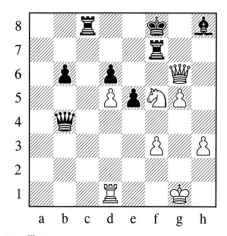

43...罝c2

The game is over.

44.包d4 exd4 45.豐xc2 豐c3 46.豐e4 豐e3†
47.豐xe3 dxe3 48.當g2 皇c3 49.當f1 罝xf3†
50.當e2 罝xh3
0–1

Miraculous Rook Endgames

by GM Konstantin Landa

We are fortunate that chess requires not only good opening play and sharp tactical skills in the middlegame, but also knowledge of the final stage of chess – the endgame. In recent times many young players have not bothered to read any endgame books – the opening stage is taking too much of their time, in particular the search for deep novelties. The games of such players rarely reach an endgame; instead they end in a sharp tactical middlegame. When an endgame does appear, it is hard to watch without shedding a tear over how these youngsters are playing it – of course with the exception of a few top class players.

When the editors of *Chess Evolution* asked me to write a section about the endgame, for a long time I could not find the right topic. To cover elementary endgames, as provided by many other chess publications, would of course be sensible – refreshing our knowledge of rook endgame theory is always healthy, but this can easily be done by the dear reader himself by opening any endgame book.

I came up with the idea of my current endgame topic by remembering when I was watching live the last round of the French league, where the outcome of the following game decided the result of a match.

M. Choisy (2207) – A. Muller (2152)
Mulhouse 2011, French League

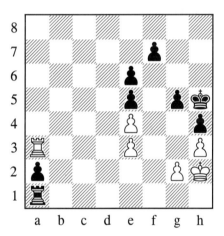

55...f5 56.罝a5 g4

A good move, but to be honest almost any move should also lead to a win. Black played a great game and managed to get an absolutely winning position.

57.hxg4† fxg4 58.g3

If 58.罝xe5† then White is not in time to take the black pawns: 58...含g6 59.罝xe6† 含f7 60.罝a6 g3† 61.含h3 罝h1† 62.含g4 a1=營

58...hxg3† 59.含g2

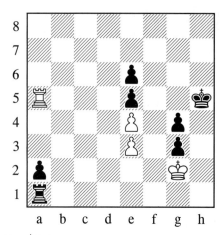

59...♔h4

The first step in the wrong direction. Instead after 59...♔g6 it is obvious that the white rook will not be in time to stop the black king from eating the tasty pawns on e3 and e4. The easiest way to win would be: 60.♖a6 ♔f7 61.♖a7† ♔f6 The rook is now obliged to let the black king go around: 62.♖a8 ♔e7 63.♖a6 ♔d7 64.♖a8 ♔c6 65.♖a6† ♔c5 66.♖a5† ♔c4 67.♖a8 ♔d3 68.♖a3† ♔xe4 69.♖a4† ♔xe3 Now Black's e-pawn is going forward and White can resign.

60.♖a7 ♖e1

Black decides not to bother with the long king march to win the sweet white pawns – a mistaken decision.

61.♖xa2 ♖xe3 62.♖a8 ♖e2† 63.♔g1 ♖xe4 64.♖h8† ♔g5 65.♔g2 ♖e3

It is hard to imagine that this game can end in anything other than victory for Black.

66.♖g8† ♔f4

Another winning line was: 66...♔f6 67.♖xg4 e4 68.♖g8 ♖f3 69.♖f8† ♔e5 70.♖g8 ♔f4 71.♖f8† ♔e3 72.♖e8 e5 73.♖xe5 ♔f4 74.♖e8 ♖f2† 75.♔g1 e3–+

67.♖f8† ♔e4 68.♖e8 ♖a3 69.♖xe6 ♔f5 70.♖e8 ♖f3 71.♖f8† ♔e4 72.♖a8 ♔f4

73.♖f8† ♔e3 74.♖g8 e4 75.♖xg4

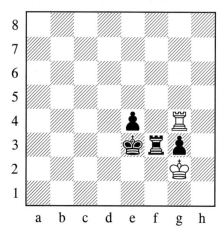

75...♔d3

Another winner was: 75...♖f2† 76.♔xg3 ♖a2! 77.♖g8 ♖a1! 78.♔g2! ♔e2 79.♖b8 e3 80.♖b2† ♔d3 81.♖b3† ♔d2 82.♖b2† ♔c3 83.♖e2 ♔d3–+

76.♖g8 ♔e2?

Allowing a draw, as would 76...♔e3? 77.♖a8! ♖f2† 78.♔xg3 ♖b2 79.♖a3†=.

The correct and winning path was:
76...♖f2†

Winning involves an old but pleasing rook manoeuvre to the a-file.
77.♔xg3 ♖a2

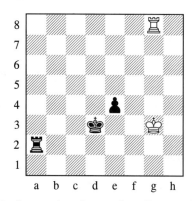

Not letting the white rook go far enough away to have checking distance from the long side.

78.♖b8 ♔e2□

78...e3 79.♔f3 ♖f2† 80.♔g3 ♖f7 81.♖a8 e2
82.♖a3†=

79.♔g2

79.♖h8 ♖a3† 80.♔g2 ♖a7–+

79...e3 80.♖b1 ♔d3† 81.♔f3 ♔d2

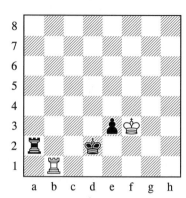

82.♖b8 e2 83.♖d8† ♔e1 84.♔g2 ♖a5–+

77.♖e8 ♔d3

Also drawing was: 77...e3 78.♖a8 ♖f7
79.♖a2† ♔d3 80.♔xg3 e2 81.♖a3† ♔d4
82.♖a4† ♔e5 83.♖a5† ♔e6 84.♖a6† ♔d7
85.♖a7† ♔c6 86.♖a6† ♔d7 87.♖a7† ♔e8
88.♖a8† ♔e7 89.♖a7† ♔f8 90.♖xf7† ♔xf7
91.♔f2=

**78.♖d8† ♔c2 79.♖e8 ♔d3 80.♖d8† ♔e2
81.♖e8**
½–½

If you think that only women players fail to
win such crushing endgames, then you are
sexist and mistaken. The following endgame
appeared in the same tournament and White,
who is rated over 2600, was totally winning.
Is it possible to imagine that such a position
could end in a draw?

F. Peralta (2608) – J.R. Koch (2476)
Mulhouse 2011, French League

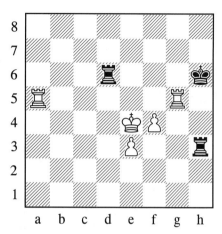

77.♖gd5

The start of the trouble. Why did White let
the black king out of h6?

77.♖a8 was winning by force: 77...♔h7
78.♖a7† ♔h6 (78...♔h8 79.♖e5+–) 79.♖gg7
♖e6† 80.♔f5+–

**77...♖b6 78.♖ab5 ♖a6 79.♖a5 ♖b6 80.♖ab5
♖a6**

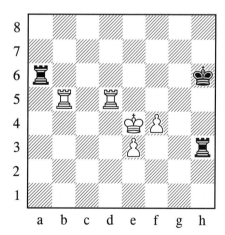

81.♖d4?

After having had enough of chasing the
black rook, White decides to take a rest and
give Black a turn.

After the calm 81.♖b3 ♔g6 82.♖db5 ♖e6†
83.♔d4 ♖f3 84.♖e5 ♖a6 85.♖c3 ♖f2 86.♖ec5
White should win.

Even stronger was: 81.♖g5! ♖a3 82.♔f5 ♖hxe3
83.♖b6† ♔h7 84.♖b7† ♔h8 85.♔g6 ♖a6†
86.♔f7+−

81...♖e6†! 82.♔f5
No better was: 82.♖e5 ♖xe5† 83.♔xe5 (83.
fxe5 ♔g7! 84.♖d7† ♔f8 85.♔d4 ♔e8 86.♖g7
♖h6 87.♔d5 ♖a6 88.e4 ♖b6 89.e6 ♖b1=)
83...♖xe3† 84.♔f6 ♖a3 85.♖e4 ♖a1 86.f5
♔h7=

**82...♖hxe3 83.♖e5 ♖6xe5† 84.fxe5 ♔g7
85.♔e6 ♖e1 86.♖d7† ♔f8 87.♖d8† ♔g7
88.♖e8 ♖a1**
Black knows how to defend such endgames!
Rook to the long side.

89.♖e7† ♔f8 90.♖d7 ♔e8 91.♖d6 ♖h1
½–½

In my opinion, these two examples are enough
to show that huge gaps in endgame education
exist not only with average chess players, but
also grandmasters. A reader could ask: "This
is France – could the same thing happen in
Russia?" After all, the Russian chess school is
famous for its fundamental knowledge. So,
especially for the readers, I looked at the games
of the 2011 Russian individual championship
in Taganroge, in which I also participated.
In 330 games, I found more than 33 rook
endgames, which a crazy statistician would
claim means every participant had a rook
endgame at least once during the tournament!
Anyway, it shows it is worth being reminded of
how to play them.

I will use the good old rules that were first
recommended to me by my chess coach
Jakov Rusakov. In rook endgames the most
important factors are:

1. Active rook
2. Passed pawns
3. Active king
4. Material advantage
5. Pawn structure

These are the five "Golden Rules". For me it
is not important who found them, what is
important is that they work!

So let's see some rook endings from the 2011
Russian championship. First, a typical mistake
made by a famous GM in his game against a
little known IM:

A. Danin (2534) – A. Lastin (2617)
Russian Championship 2011

There are equal pawns on the board, but
the position of the black pieces is terrible.
Alexander makes the right decision – to give
up a pawn to activate his rook.

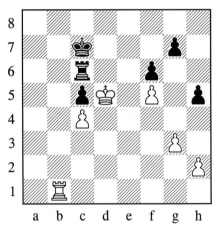

38...♖d6†! 39.♔xc5 ♖d2?
Too early! Maybe Lastin did not have enough
time to think deeply about his move.

The right way was 39...♖c6†!. Black should
force the active white king as far away as
possible. 40.♔d4 ♖d6†! 41.♔c3 ♖a6 42.♖e1
♔d7=

40.罩a1

White quickly makes use of the mistake and the game ends suddenly.

40...罩xh2

Also hopeless was 40...堂b7 41.罩e1+−.

41.罩a7† 堂d8 42.罩xg7 罩g2 43.堂d6 1–0

Active versus passive rook

T. Kosintseva (2559) – E. Alekseev (2673)
Russian Championship 2011

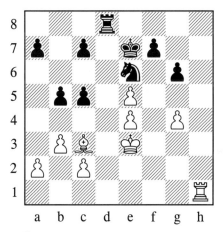

35...包d4?

A bad attempt to win immediately.

36.盒xd4! cxd4† 37.堂f4?

Kosintseva makes absolutely the wrong decision about how to place her pieces in this rook endgame.

37.堂d3!

The white king has to control Black's passed pawn and the rook has to be active. When you look at the diagram you understand that the square from which the white rook can enter Black's position is f6! The conclusion is easy – don't close the f-file.

37...堂e6 38.罩f1 罩d7 39.罩f6†!

The weak pawn on e5 should not play any role in the game. It is much more important for the rook to be active!

39...堂xe5 40.g5

White is not worse.

40...c5 41.罩c6=

37...c5 38.罩h3 c4 39.bxc4 bxc4

White is completely lost; just three moves earlier it was an easy draw! Chess is a hard game.

40.罩h1 d3 41.cxd3 cxd3 42.堂e3 d2 43.罩d1 堂e6

White resigned, as the pawn endgame is simply lost.

0–1

T. Kosintseva (2559) – A. Shimanov (2583)
Russian Championship 2011

Tatiana also has nice memories of rook endgames.

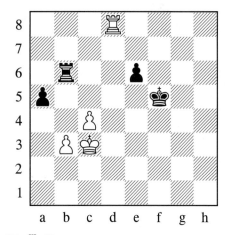

67...罩a6?

Now the rook is passive. Black would have had more drawing chances after:

67...e5 68.罩a8 罩h6 69.罩xa5 罩h3†

An important move, forcing White's king away from the passed e-pawn.

70.堂b4

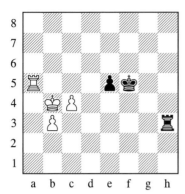

70...♖h8!

Now both variations lead to a winning queen endgame for White according to the Nalimov tablebase, but it's not so easy to find a 60-move long win!

71.c5

71.♖a7 ♔e6 72.♖a6† ♔f5 73.c5 e4 74.c6 e3 75.♔c5 ♖h1 76.♖a4 e2 77.c7 ♖c1† 78.♖c4 ♖xc4† 79.bxc4 e1=♕ 80.c8=♕†+−

71...e4 72.c6† ♔e6 73.♔c5 ♖h5† 74.♔b6 ♖xa5 75.♔xa5 e3 76.♔b6 e2 77.c7 e1=♕ 78.c8=♕†+−

68.c5

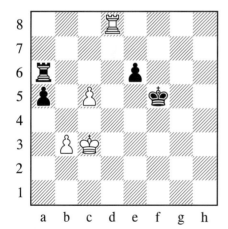

68...♔f6

68...a4 also loses: 69.b4 a3 70.♖d1!.

69.♔c4 ♔e7 70.♖h8 e5 71.♔b5 ♖e6 72.c6 ♔d6 73.♔b6
1–0

I. Bukavshin (2502) – I. Khairullin (2649)
Russian Championship 2011

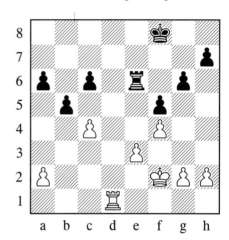

27.♔f3?!

The right way was: 27.♖d7! Active rook! 27...♖e4 28.cxb5 cxb5 29.♖xh7 ♖a4 30.a3!! ♖xa3 31.♖b7 ♖a4 32.♔g3 ♖e4 33.♔f3 ♖e6 34.h3 ♔e8 35.g4 ♔d8 36.♔e2 ♔c8 37.gxf5 gxf5 38.♖f7=

27...♔e7 28.c5!?

Also murky was: 28.cxb5 axb5 29.♖d4 ♖d6 (29...c5 30.♖d5 ♖c6 31.a3 ♔e6 32.e4=) 30.♖b4 ♖d2 31.a4 ♔d6 32.axb5 ♔c5 33.♖b1 cxb5 34.♖c1† ♔b6 35.g4 b4 36.gxf5 gxf5 37.♖c8∞

28...♖e4 29.♖d6 ♖a4 30.♖xc6 ♖xa2

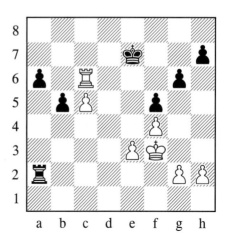

31.罝c7†??

Amazing greed! White should draw simply with: 31.罝b6 罝a4 32.g4 b4 33.gxf5 gxf5 34.e4=

31...堂e6 32.罝xh7 堂d5 33.g4 b4

The black pawns decide the outcome of the game.

34.gxf5 gxf5 35.罝h5 b3 36.罝xf5† 堂c6 37.罝f8 罝a5

0–1

Activating the king; passed pawns

I. Kurnosov (2633) – M. Kobalia (2679)
Russian Championship 2011

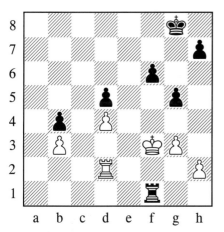

White is a pawn down and has a passive rook. The only chance to fight for a draw is to activate the king!

37.堂g4! 37...堂f7!

Black has to very careful! Getting greedy with 37...罝b1 would have given White great chances of escaping: 38.罝a2! Active rook! 38...罝xb3 39.堂f5 罝f3† 40.堂e6

38.堂h5 罝f3 39.罝a2 罝xb3 40.罝a7† 堂e6 41.罝xh7 罝d3 42.堂g6! 罝xd4 43.罝f7 g4!

An important move! One pawn on g4 is fixing two – h2 and g3.

44.罝xf6† 堂e5 45.堂g5 堂e4! 46.罝b6

White cannot take on g4 and that means he is going to lose. Let's see why he can't take it: 46.堂xg4 堂e5†! 47.堂g5 罝g4† 48.堂xg4 堂xf6 49.堂f3 b3–+

46...堂d3 47.堂f5 堂c3 48.堂e5 罝c4 49.堂xd5 b3

0–1

A. Galkin (2598) – Arty. Timofeev (2665)
Russian Championship 2011

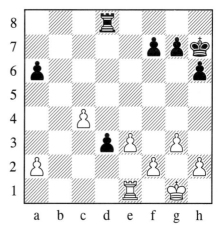

32...堂g6!

Here we have an example of successful activation of the king by the defending side. Black is a pawn down, but has a passed pawn on d3. Timofeev shows the right way to play rook endgames, as he decides to activate his king!

32...罝c8 is a bit too early: 33.罝d1 罝xc4 34.罝xd3 罝a4 35.a3 Probably the position is still a draw, but Black would have a very hard fight ahead of him.

33.罝d1 堂f5 34.f3 g5

The black king needs to get to e4 to defend

the passed pawn and free the rook for active service.

35.g4†! ♔e5 36.♔f2 f5 37.gxf5

Also level is: 37.h3 f4! 38.c5 ♖d5 39.♖c1 d2 40.♖d1 fxe3† 41.♔xe3 ♖xc5 42.♖xd2 ♖c3† 43.♔f2 ♖a3=

37...♔xf5 38.c5

38.♔e1 ♖c8 39.♖c1 g4!

38...g4 39.c6

39.fxg4† ♔e4

39...gxf3 40.c7 ♖c8 41.♖xd3 ♖xc7 42.♔xf3 ♖c2=

The game ends with a lot of pawn-munching by both sides.

43.♖d5† ♔e6 44.♖a5 ♖xh2 45.♖xa6† ♔e5 46.♖a5† ♔e6 47.a4 h5 48.♖a6† ♔e5 49.a5 h4 50.♖a8 h3 51.♔g3 ♖e2 52.♖e8† ♔d6 53.♔xh3 ♔d7 54.♖e4 ♖a2 55.♖e5 ♔d6 56.♖g5 ♖a3 57.a6 ♖xe3† 58.♖g3 ♖xg3† 59.♔xg3 ♔c6
½–½

K. Landa (2613) – E. Romanov (2624)
Russian Championship 2011

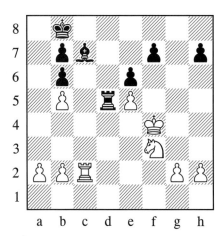

27.♔g5!

The black king is out of the game, so White decides to sacrifice his "proud" e5-pawn, and after that the pawn on b5, for the one on h7.

27...♗xe5 28.♘xe5 ♖xe5† 29.♔h6

White's passed pawn on the kingside decides the game.

29...♖xb5 30.♔xh7 ♖c5

No better is: 30...♖h5† 31.♔g7 ♖xh2 32.♔xf7 e5 33.♔f6 e4 34.♔f5 e3 35.♔f4+–

31.♖xc5! bxc5 32.♔h6 ♔c7 33.h4 ♔d7 34.h5 e5 35.♔g5 ♔e7 36.h6 ♔f8 37.♔f6!
1–0

Material advantage

A. Shomoev (2566) – Y. Balashov (2426)
Russian Championship 2011

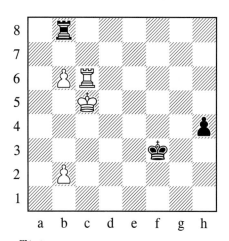

55.♖h6

Black resigned. The reason is simple – White has a reserve pawn on b2. Material plays one of the most important roles in rook endgames!
1–0

Some more typical examples of rook endings:

Cutting off the king

B. Grachev (2669) – V. Papin (2565)
Russian Championship 2011

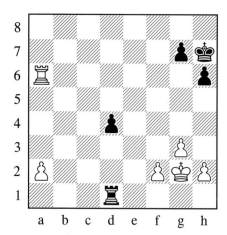

39...d3 40.♔f3 ♖e1!

Another very important manoeuvre, cutting the king off from the passed pawn – this helps Black to reach a drawn endgame.

The clumsy 40...d2? leaves Black in trouble after 41.♔e2 ♖h1 42.♔xd2 ♖xh2 43.♔e3±.

41.♖d6 ♖a1 42.♖xd3 ♖xa2 43.g4 ♖a5! 44.h4 h5!

The most precise continuation.

45.g5 ♖a4 46.♔g3 ♖g4† 47.♔h3 ♔g6 48.f3 ♖g1 49.♔h2 ♖a1 50.♖d5 ♖b1 51.♔g3 ♖a1 52.♖e5 ♖h1 53.♖e7 ♖a1 54.♔f4 ♖h1 55.♔g3 ♖a1 56.♖e4 ♔f5 57.♖f4† ♔g6 58.♖b4 ♔f5=

Black cannot achieve anything in this endgame.

59.♖b5† ♔g6 60.♖e5 ♖h1 61.f4 ♖f1 62.♖e6† ♔f5 63.♖e5† ♔g6 64.♖d5 ♖g1† 65.♔f3 ♖g4 66.♔e4 ♖xh4 67.♖d6† ♔f7 68.♔f5 g6† 69.♔e5 ♖g4 70.♖d7† ♔g8 71.♖d4 ♔f7 72.♖d7† ♔g8 73.♖a7

♖h4 74.f5 ♖b4 75.f6 ♔f8 76.♖a8† ♔f7 77.♖a7† ♔f8 78.♖h7 ♖b1 79.♖h8† ♔f7 80.♖h7† ♔f8 81.♖g7 ♖b5† 82.♔e6 ♖b6† 83.♔d5 ♖b5† 84.♔d6 ♖xg5 85.♔e6 ♖g1 86.♖f7† ♔e8 87.♖e7† ♔f8 88.♖f7† ♔e8 89.♖e7†
½–½

Perpetual attack

N. Vitiugov (2733) – V. Zvjaginsev (2659)
Russian Championship 2011

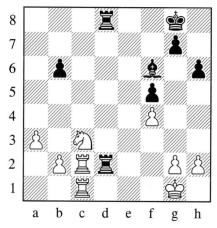

White is a pawn up, but Black can force a rook endgame where White cannot find any good way to defend his queenside pawns.

28...♗xc3 29.bxc3 ♖xc2 30.♖xc2 ♖a8 31.♖a2 ♖c8 32.♖c2

Also level is 32.♖b2 ♖xc3 33.♖xb6 ♖xa3=.

32...♖a8 33.♖a2 ♖c8 34.♖c2

It's just a draw.
½–½

Freaky chess!

T. Kosintseva (2559) – V. Papin (2565)
Russian Championship 2011

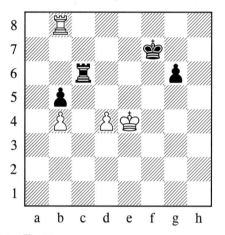

70...Re6†!

In rook endgames it is always good to force the opponent's king to a more passive position.

70...g5

This leads to amazing complications:
71.Rxb5 Rg6 72.Kf5

In this main line Black reaches a draw in an incredible way which definitely deserves attention.

72.Rb7† Ke8 73.Kf5 Rd6 74.Ke5 Rg6!
72...Rd6!

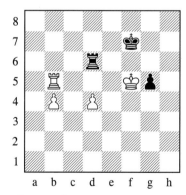

73.d5 Ke7 74.Kxg5

74.Ke5 Rg6!
74...Rd7!! 75.Kf4 Kd6

One vital point of Black's defence is: 76.Ke4 Rb7!! 77.Rxb7 Stalemate!

Thus the best try is:
76.Ke3

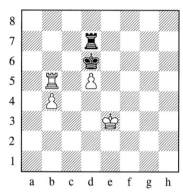

Now there is a split: A) 76...Rh7 and B) 76...Ke5!

A) 76...Rh7 77.Kd3

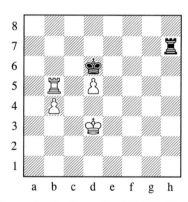

We need a further split: A1) 77...Rh3†? and A2) 77...Rh4□:

A1) 77...Rh3†? 78.Kc4 Rh4† 79.Kb3 Kc7
  79...Rd4? 80.Rc5+–
80.Ka4 Rd4 81.Ka5! Rd1 82.Rc5† Kb7
  82...Kd6 83.Kb6+–
83.b5!

83.Kb5 Rd4 doesn't bring anything for White.

83...Rd2

83...Rd4 84.b6 Rd1 85.Rc7† Kb8 86.Rd7+–
84.Kb4 Rd1 85.Kc4 Rc1† 86.Kd4 Rd1†
87.Ke5 Kb6

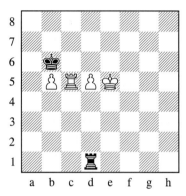

88.Rc8!

88.Rc6† doesn't win due to: 88...Kxb5
89.Kd6 Rh1= Flank attack!

88...Rh1

There is no time to take the pawn: 88...Kxb5
89.d6 Kb6 90.Ke6 Re1† 91.Kf7 Rf1†
92.Ke7 Re1† 93.Kd8 Rh1 94.d7 White is
winning.

89.d6

White makes progress: the d-pawn moves
forward!

89...Rh5† 90.Ke6 Rh6† 91.Kd5 Rh5†
92.Kc4 Rh4† 93.Kc3 Rh3† 94.Kb4 Rd3
95.Rc6† Kb7 96.Kc5

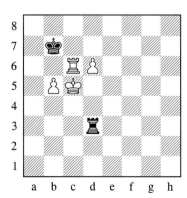

96...Rc3†

96...Rd1 97.Rc7† Kb8 98.b6+–

97.Kd5 Rd3† 98.Ke6 Re3† 99.Kf7 Rf3†
100.Ke8 Re3† 101.Kd8 Rh3 102.Rc7† Kb8
103.Re7 Rh8† 104.Re8 Rh7 105.d7 Kb7
106.Re6+–

A2) 77...Rh4□

The white king should not be allowed to
reach the b-pawn.

78.Kc3 Kc7□ 79.Rc5† Kb6 80.Rc4 Rh3†
81.Kd4 Rh4† 82.Kc3 Rh3† 83.Kb2 Rh2†
84.Kb3 Rh3† 85.Ka4

85.Rc3 Rh4 86.Rd3 Kb5 87.d6 Rxb4†
88.Kc2 Rc4† 89.Kd2 Rc8=

85...Rd3 86.Rc5 Rd1 87.Kb3 Rd4! 88.Kc3
Rh4□

A miracle draw!

B) 76...Ke5! The easiest way – cutting the king
off from the pawns. 77.Kd3 Rc7 (77...Rxd5†
78.Kc4+–) 78.Ra5 Rc8! White cannot achieve
any advantage.

71.Kd3 g5 72.Rxb5 Rg6

With White's king on d3, Black has no
problems at all!

73.Ke4 g4

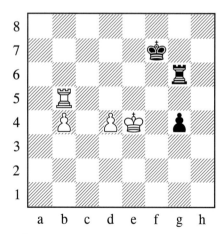

74.Kf5??

A terrible blunder. 74.Rf5† Ke7 75.Rf1=
was a simple draw.

74...g3 75.罩b7† 堂e8 76.堂xg6 g2 77.堂f6
g1=豐 78.d5 堂d8 79.b5 堂c8 80.罩e7 豐b6†
81.堂e5 豐xb5 82.堂e6 豐c4 83.堂d6 豐a6†
84.堂e5 豐a1† 85.堂e6 豐e1† 86.堂d6 豐b4†
87.堂e6

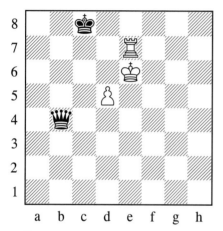

87...豐g4†

The fastest winning path started with
87...豐f4!–+. For example: 88.d6 豐e4† 89.堂f6
豐d5 90.d7† 堂c7 91.罩f7 豐h5 92.堂e6 豐g6†
93.堂e7 豐d6† 94.堂e8 豐e6† 95.堂f8 豐e5!
96.堂g8 豐g5† 97.堂h7 堂d6 98.罩g7 豐h4†
99.堂g8 豐d8† 100.堂h7 堂e6 101.堂g6 豐h4

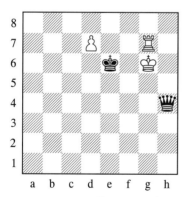

And now 102.罩h7 豐f6† 103.堂h5 堂f5 or
102.罩f7 豐g4† 103.堂h7 堂xf7 104.d8=豐
豐g7#.

88.堂e5 堂d8??

Black could still win with various checks
including 88...豐e2†–+.

89.d6=

With the pawn on d6, White is safe. Black
kept trying to win, but didn't manage.

89...豐f3 90.罩c7 豐h5† 91.堂e6 豐e2†
92.堂d5 豐b5† 93.堂e6 豐a4 94.堂d5 豐a8†
95.堂e5 豐f3 96.罩e7 豐e3† 97.堂d5 豐d3†
98.堂e5 豐b5† 99.堂e6 豐c6 100.堂e5 豐c5†
101.堂e6 豐d4 102.罩d7† 堂c8 103.罩c7†
堂d8 104.罩d7† 堂c8 105.罩c7† 堂b8
106.罩e7 豐e4† 107.堂d7 豐d5† 108.罩e1
豐b5† 109.堂e7 豐g5† 110.堂d7 豐g4†
111.罩e6 堂b7 112.堂e7 豐g5† 113.堂e8
豐h5† 114.堂e7 豐h4† 115.堂e8 豐h8†
116.堂e7 豐g7† 117.堂d8 豐f8† 118.堂d7
堂b6 119.罩e7 豐f6 120.罩e6 豐f7† 121.罩e7
豐d5 122.罩e6 堂c5 123.堂e7 豐g5† 124.罩f6
豐g7† 125.堂e6 堂c6 126.堂e5 豐a7 127.堂e6
豐e3† 128.堂f7 堂d7 129.罩g6 豐e5 130.堂g7
豐h5 131.罩h6 豐e5† 132.罩f6 豐e8 133.罩f8
豐e4 134.罩f6 豐d4 135.堂f7 豐e5 136.堂g7
堂e8 137.堂g6 堂d7 138.堂g7 豐xf6†
139.堂xf6 堂xd6
½–½

How interesting and challenging endgames
can be is illustrated by the fact that the
Kosintseva – Papin game was the last to finish
in the tournament.

Good luck to the readers in their self-education!

12 Puzzles

by GM Jacob Aagaard

In previous versions of *Chess Evolution* the puzzle section has been a repetition of positions that could be found elsewhere in the book. When we decided to make some small changes to the layout and structure of *Chess Evolution*, it was natural to stop this practice and have a small section with 12 combinations from the last two months.

Of the twelve positions I have selected, most of them could be said to be difficult. The first six positions are probably within reach of most readers without too much effort, some more than others. But don't get too cocky; some top class players managed to misplay a majority of these positions!

The next six positions are harder. Even though Hou Yifan did manage to win one of them, she did not manage to do so in the most direct way. The other five positions all include mistakes and failures for the grandmasters included; not because they are not great players, but because chess is a brutally difficult game.

Still, our sympathy and respect for these players should not ruin the enjoyment of succeeding where they failed. It might be a cheap pleasure, but why pay overprice for happiness?

My own preference when it comes to combinations is a blend of logic and classical beauty. I like the surprise, but I also like the detail quite a lot. I have tried to annotate these positions based on their core ideas, the points you have to discover to solve the positions. But at the same time, combinations are as concrete as you get in chess; so there are plenty of variations to prove my point.

Finally, before we begin, here is a little warm-up position:

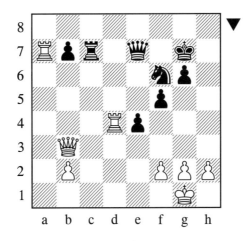

1. Bologan - Ragger

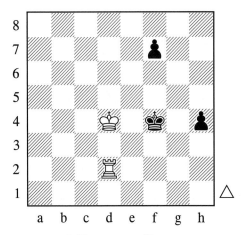

4. Vachier Lagrave – Pelletier

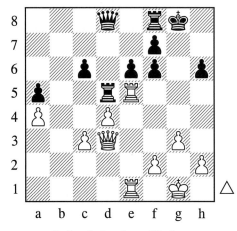

2. Romanov – Dreev

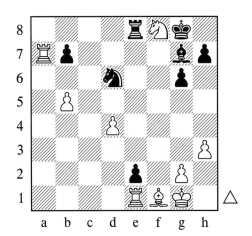

5. Areshchenko – Shoker

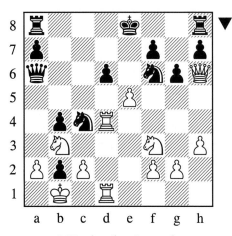

3. Safarli – Kovchan

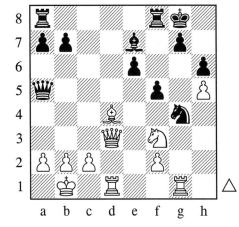

6. Naiditsch – Laznicka

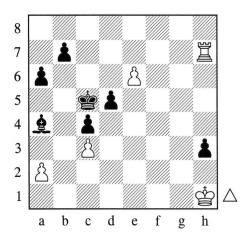

7. Timofeev – Svidler

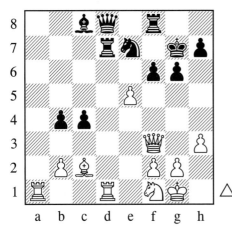

10. Hou Yifan – Sebag

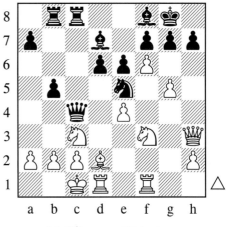

8. Adams – Paragua

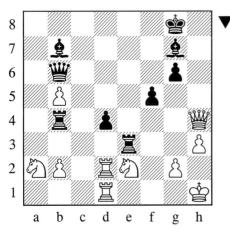

11. Eljanov – Nisipeanu

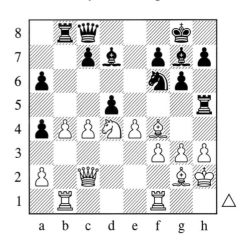

9. Jobava – Wojtaszek

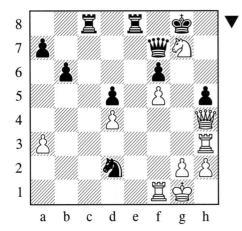

12. Hou Yifan – Movsesian

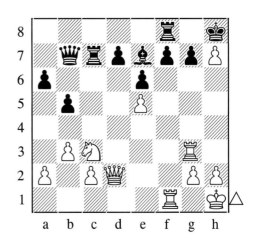

1. Bologan - Ragger, Greece 05.07.2011

White wins by delaying the advance of the h-pawn, forcing Black to lose enough time for the rook to make it to the 8th rank and decide the game from behind. **69.♖d3!!** Instead the game ended with: 69.♖f2+? ♔g3 70.♔e3 h3 71.♖xf7 ♔g2! (71...h2?? 72.♖g7+ ♔h3 73.♔f2! was seen in the recent World Cup in the game Bacrot-Robson (1.5), with the exception that the rook was on h6 instead of f7 to start with.) 72.♖g7+ ♔f1 73.♖h7 ♔g2 74.♔e2 h2 75.♖g7+ ♔h1 76.♔f2 and Black was stalemated. **69...f5** 69...g4 70.♔e3! ♔g3 71.♖d8 also wins easily. **70.♖a3 ♔g4 71.♔e3! ♔g3 72.♔e2+ ♔g2 73.♖a8** White wins. Black can delay matters with 73...♔g3 according to the tablebases, but obviously there is no hope there. **73...h3 74.♖g8+ ♔h1 75.♔f2 f4** Or 75...h2 76.♖a8 with mate on the next move. **76.♖g7 f3 77.♖d7 ♔h2 78.♖h7 ♔h1 79.♖xh3#**

2. Romanov – Dreev, Baku 08.08.2011

31.♘e6!! A nice zwischenzug, allowing White to remain an exchange up. 31.♗xe2 ♗xd4† 32.♔h2 ♗a7= **31...♖xe6** 31...exf1=♕† 32.♔xf1+− **32.♖a8† ♔f7 33.♖xe2+− ♗xd4† 34.♔h2 ♗e5† 35.♔h1 ♘f5 36.♖f2 ♔g7 37.g4 ♘e3 38.♖d8 ♖e7 39.♖d3 ♗c7 40.♖e2 ♗f4 41.♗g2 ♖c7 42.♖e1 ♘c4 43.♖ed1 ♘b6 44.h4 ♖c5 45.♖f1 g5 46.hxg5 ♗xg5 47.♖f5 ♖c1† 48.♔h2 h6 49.♗xb7 ♖c2† 50.♔g3 ♗e7 51.♗c6 ♘c4 52.♖d7 ♖e2 53.♗d5 ♘d6 54.♔f3 1–0**

3. Safarli – Kovchan, Konya 10.07.2011

21.♗xg7! White initiates a typical attack. Black presumably hoped it was only going to lead to a perpetual check. **21...♔xg7** 21...♖fd8 22.♗d4 ♔f8 23.♖xg4! fxg4 24.♕h7! wins quickly. **22.♖xg4† fxg4 23.♕g6† ♔h8 24.♕xh6† ♔g8 25.♕xe6† ♖f7?!** The toughest defence was: 25...♔h8 26.♘e5! ♗f6 (26...♕b6 27.♘g6† ♔g7 28.♕xg4+−) 27.♘g6† ♔g7 28.♖d7† ♔h6 29.♘xf8 ♖xf8 (29...♕e5 30.♕xe5 ♗xe5 31.♖h7† ♔g5 32.♘e6† ♔f5 33.♘c5+−) 30.♕e4!+− The double threat of ♕g6† and ♕h7† forces Black to play 30...♔xh5 when the computer recommends 31.c4 and 31.f3 as the best options, since Black cannot prevent ♖d5† winning the queen anyway. **26.♘e5 ♖af8 27.h6!** 27.♖g1!?+− **27...♕a6 28.h7† ♔xh7** 28...♔g7 29.♕xg4† **29.♖h1† ♗h4 30.♖xh4† ♔g7 31.♖xg4† ♔h7 32.♕xa6 bxa6 33.♘xf7 ♖xf7 34.f4 ♔h6 35.b3 ♔h5 36.♖g5† ♔h4 37.♖g6 1–0**

4. Vachier Lagrave – Pelletier, Biel 27.07.2011

23.♖xe6! Not a difficult first move. But as we shall see, it is hard to find the winning follow-up even if you are up close and personal. **23...fxe6 24.♕g6† ♔h8 25.♕xh6† ♔g8 26.♕g6† ♔h8 27.♖e4!** Forcing a clearance of the sixth rank. **27...f5 28.♕h6† ♔g8 29.♖xe6 ♖d7** The only defensive try. **30.♖g6† ♔f7** This position was probably already in Vachier-Lagrave's mind when he took on e6. But he did not solve the last remaining problem then, nor did he do it once he reached the position over the board. **31.♖xc6??** 31.♕h5! wins easily; Black's best defence loses the queen for the rook, and if 31...♔e7 32.♕e2†! mate is very near. Technically speaking 31.d5 also wins, but only because of 31...cxd5 32.♕h5!, so the queen move is the crucial detail that White must find. **31...♔e8 32.d5 ♖e7 33.c4⩱ f4 34.♕h5† ♖ff7 35.♔g2 f3† 36.♔h3 ♕d7† 37.g4 ♔d8 38.♕g5 ♖g7?!** 38...♕e8!= **39.♕f4± ♔e8 40.♔g3 ♕b7?** 40...♕d8± **41.♕f5± ♖c7? 42.♖h6 ♖h7 43.♖e6† 1–0**

5. Areshchenko – Shoker, Ningbo 17.07.2011

23...♖c8!! 23...♘a3† 24.♔xb2 ♖c8 is an inferior move order. After 25.♖c1 the position is quite unclear. **24.exf6** 24.♖xc4 ♕xc4 25.♘fd4 dxe5 26.♕g7 exd4 27.♘xd4 ♔e7 28.♖e1† ♔d7 29.♕xf6 ♖he8–+ Black is in control. **24...♘a3† 25.♔xb2 ♖xc2† 26.♔a1 ♘c4 27.♖e4†** 27.♘c1 ♕a3–+ **27...♔d8 28.♘c1 ♕a3 0–1**

6. Naiditsch – Laznicka, Valjevo 30.08.2011

White missed the winning move: **42.♖d7!!** Preventing ...d5-d4 and keeping the king away from the e-pawn at the same time. The game went: 42.♖xb7? Black now gets sufficient counterplay with the passed c-pawn. 42...d4 43.cxd4† ♔xd4 44.♔h2 ♔d3 45.♖b4 ♗e8 46.♖b2 ♗a4 47.♖b8 ♔e3 48.♖c8 ♔d3 49.♖d8† ♔e3 50.♖c8 ♔d3 51.♖d8† ½–½ **42...♗c6 43.♔h2 b5 44.♖d8!** An important finesse. 44.a3? a5 45.♖d8 is the computer's preference, but exchanging the a-pawn leads to a draw: 45...b4 46.axb4† axb4 47.cxb4† ♔xb4 48.e7 ♔b3! It is nice that there is no pawn on a2! (48...♔c5 49.♖c8!) 49.♖xd5 c3 50.♖c5 ♗d7 51.♖c7 ♗e8 52.♖c8 ♗d7= **44...b4!** The only try. 44...a5 45.e7 b4 46.♖c8!+– **45.cxb4† ♔d4** 45...♔xb4 46.e7 White is threatening ♖xd5. In this line Black does not have ...♔b3 to support the pawn, and after 46...c3 White has 47.♖b8†! followed by ♖c8 winning. **46.e7 c3 47.♖c8 ♗b5 48.e8=♕** 48.♖c5 also wins, but the text is simple. **48...♗xe8 49.♖xe8 ♔c4 50.♖c8† ♔xb4 51.♔xh3 d4 52.♔g3 d3 53.♔f3 d2 54.♔e2+–**

7. Timofeev – Svidler, Moscow 13.08.2011

White missed his big moment to impress. **28.♖a7!!** Instead White played: 28.♘e3? b3 29.♗e4 (29.♖xd7 ♕xd7 30.♗d1±) 29...♕c7 (29...f5!?=) 30.♖dc1?! (30.♖xd7 ♗xd7 31.exf6† ♖xf6 32.♕d1 ♖d6 33.♕c1±) 30...♖d4 31.♕g3? f5!–+ 32.♗f3 f4 33.♕h4 h6! 34.♘g4 ♘f5 0–1. **28...♖xd1** 28...♖xa7 29.♖xd8 ♖xd8 30.exf6†+–; 28...b3 29.♗xb3 cxb3 30.♖axd7 ♗xd7 31.♕b7 leads to a losing ending as well: 31...♗c8 32.♖xd8 ♗xb7 33.♖d7 fxe5 34.♖xb7 ♔f6 35.♖xb3+– Some technical issues remain, but White should win. **29.♕xd1 b3** The only try. **30.exf6†!** A very important point. 30.♕xd8? ♖xd8 31.♗xb3 cxb3 32.♖xe7† is close to winning according to the computer, but my analysis indicate that the weakness of the b2-pawn gives Black enough counterplay to draw. 32...♔f8 33.♖xh7 ♗e6 34.♖h8† ♗g8 35.exf6 ♖d1 36.g4 ♖b1 37.g5 ♖xb2 Even if White has a study-like win here, it is terribly impractical to end up having to find it. **30...♔xf6 31.♕f3† ♔g7 32.♕c3† ♔f7** 32...♖f6 33.♗e4+– Despite the equal material, it is obvious that Black is toast. **33.♕xc4† ♗e6 34.♕f4† ♔g8 35.♕e3 bxc2 36.♕xe6† ♔h8 37.♕e5† ♔g8 38.♕c5 ♕d1 39.♕c4†!** White is winning, for instance: **39...♔h8** 39...♘d5 40.♖c7+– **40.♕c3† ♔g8 41.♖xe7 ♖f7 42.♖e8† ♔f8 43.♕b3† ♔g7 44.♖e7† ♔f6 45.♕e6† ♔g5 46.♕e3† ♖f4 47.h4† ♔g4 48.♕h3† ♔h5 49.♖xh7#**

8. Adams – Paragua, Khanty-Mansiysk (1.2) 29.08.2011

Black is much better, and could simply take on b5 and rely on technique. What he played was not bad, but slowly White was able to get back in to the game and hold. The chance to decide the game immediately was based on the following trick: **36...♗f6!** The game continued 36...♖bb3? 37.♘g1 (37.♘ac3!∓) 37...♖xb5 when Black was winning, but went on to misplay his position. The game was drawn on move 114 and Paragua was eliminated. **37.♕h6** 37.♕f2 ♖xh3† 38.♔g1 ♗h4!–+ is an important point. White cannot defend the b6-g1 diagonal. **37...♗g5!!** A standard deflection, but devilishly hard to see. White is just lost. **38.♕xg5 ♖xh3† 39.♔g1 d3† 40.♘d4 ♖xd4!!** Very likely this is what Paragua missed. The immediate 40...♕xd4† leads to a perpetual, as the rook cannot join the attack: 41.♖f2 ♖xb2 42.♕xg6†= **41.♖f2 ♖g4–+** The g2-pawn falls and White collapses.

9. Jobava – Wojtaszek, Khanty-Mansiysk (2.1), 31.08.2011

Black missed a great shot and a chance to take the lead in this mini-match: **27...♘xf1!** The game ended with 27...♔xg7? 28.♖g3† ♔f8 29.♕f4! ♘xf1 30.♕h6† ♔e7 31.♖g7 ♘e3 32.♖xf7† ♔xf7 33.♕h7† ♔f8 34.♕h6† ♔f7 35.♕h7† ♔f8 36.♕h6† ♔f7 when a draw was agreed. **28.♘xe8** 28.♘xh5 ♖c1! is the same thing with an extra rook for Black. **28...♖c1!!** This is the trick shot. The f6-square is indirectly defended. **29.♘xf6† ♕xf6!** 29...♔f8?? 30.♕g5!+– **30.♕xf6 ♘g3† 31.♔f2 ♘e4†–+**

10. Hou Yifan – Sebag, Hangzhou 15.07.2011

I have always had a fascination with this kind of combination. **21.g6!!** Clearance! The knight comes to g5 with decisive effect. **21...fxg6** 21...hxg6 22.♘g5 is simple. 21...♘xg6 22.♘g5 h6 is less so, but Black is just busted after 23.♘xf7! . After 23...♔xg7 24.fxg7† ♔xg7 25.♖g1, the attack is obviously decisive. And the attempt 23...e5 is met with either 24.♘xh6† first, or simply 24.♕xd7 ♕xf7 25.♕h3! with a winning attack. The d5-square comes in handy: 25...gxf6 26.♘d5 ♘f4 27.♗xf4 exf4 28.♖xf4 ♗g7 29.♖g1 ♔h8 30.♖xf6!+– is a good example of what could happen. **22.♘xe5 dxe5 23.f7† ♔h8 24.♖f3!** Threatening ♕xh7†!. **24...h6** 24...g5 was possible, but White has enough time: 25.♕g4 ♗c6 26.♖h3 h6 27.♕xg5 and mate is near. **25.♗xh6!** Many moves win, but this is nice and direct. 25.♖g1 ♔h7 26.♕g4 g5 27.♗xg5 would have been the way I would have done it. **25...gxh6 26.♕g4?!** To me this is poor attacking technique. Bring in the last rook please! 26.♖g1! ♔h7 27.♖xg6! runs straight through without the need of calculation. **26...g5?!** This makes White's job easier. 26...♔g7! was critical. White is still winning with 27.♖g1 g5 28.♕h5 ♗e7 29.h4! with a decisive attack, but to me this is not efficient technique. The continuation might be 29...♕d4! 30.♖gf1!! ♔f8 31.♖g3! ♔h7 32.♖ff3! when Black is forced to play something silly like 32...♖g8 to avoid immediate mate. (32.hxg5 ♗xg5† 33.♔b1 ♕d2 34.♖h1 also wins.) **27.♕h5 ♔g7 28.♖h3** 28.♖g1 ♗e7 29.h4 also wins. **28...♔f6 29.♖xd7 b4 30.♕xh6† ♗xh6 31.♖xh6† ♔g7 32.f8=♕† 1–0**

11. Eljanov – Nisipeanu, Konya 05.07.2011

White had a great chance to take the full point with: **21.g4!** Instead he played 21.e5?, allowing Black to gain real counterplay: 21...♗xh3! 22.♔g1 dxc4 23.exf6 (23.♘c6!? ♘d5! 24.♕xc4 ♗xg2 25.♕xd5 ♕h3 26.g4 ♗xf1 27.♖xf1 ♗h6!! 28.♘xb8 ♗xf4 29.♕d8†=) 23...♗xf6 24.♗e3 c5 25.bxc5 ♖xb1 26.♖xb1 ♗xd4 27.♗xd4 ♗f5 28.♕b2 ♗xb1 29.♕xb1 c3 30.♕c2 ♖xc5 31.♗xc5 ♕xc5† 32.♔f1 ♕e3 33.♕e2 ♕c5 34.♕c2 ♕e3 35.♕e2 ♕g5 36.♕c2 ♕e3 At this point a draw was agreed. **21...♘xg4† 22.fxg4 ♗xg4** This was certainly Black's idea, but here White had a chance to throw a curve-ball (to go all-American) with **23.♘c6!!**, winning an important tempo. After **23...♔h8 24.♘xb8 ♗xh3 25.♘c6** White has simply too much material: **25...♗xg2† 26.♔xg2 ♕g4† 27.♗g3 dxe4 28.♖xf7+–**

12. Hou Yifan – Movsesian, Khanty-Mansiysk (1.2), 29.08.2011
White could have equalized the match with a double sacrifice, of her rook and her passed
pawn on the 7th rank. **30.♖xg7!!** The game continued: 30.♕d4? f5? (30...♖c5 31.♖xg7 ♔xg7
32.♕g4† ♔xh7=) 31.♘e2? (31.exf6 ♖xf6 32.♖ff3!?±) 31...g5 32.♘f4?? gxf4 33.♕xf4 ♕e4 By
now Black is winning, and the contest was soon over. 34.♕xe4 fxe4 35.♖xf8† ♗xf8 36.♖g8†
♔xh7 37.♖xf8 ♖xc2 38.♔g1 ♖xa2 39.h4 e3 40.♔f1 a5 41.♖f7† ♔g6 42.♖xd7 ♖f2† 43.♔e1 ♖xg2
44.♖d3 ♖g3 45.♖d6 ♔f5 46.♖a6 ♔xe5 47.♖xa5 ♔e4 48.♖a6 ♔f3 0–1. **30...♔xg7 31.h8=♕†!!**
♖xh8 31...♔xh8 32.♕h6† ♔g8 33.♖f6!! is an important point, and might be what Hou Yifan
missed. Black is mated after 33...♖e8 34.♕g5† ♔f8 35.♕h5! ♗xf6 36.exf6 when all the kings,
rooks and queens can't put his kingside together again. **32.♕f4! ♗d8!** The best defence. 32...♖f8
33.♕g4† ♔h6 34.♘e4 also gives White a winning attack. Black should maybe give up the queen,
but the prospects would then look very grim. And after the natural try 34...♖xc2 White mates
with: 35.♖f6†! ♗xf6 36.♕f4†! ♔g6 (36...♔h5 37.♘xf6† ♔g6 38.♕g4† is mate in a few moves
too.) 37.♕xf6† ♔h7 38.♕h4†! ♔g7 39.♕g5† ♔h8 40.♕h6† ♔g8 41.♘f6# **33.♕xf7† ♔h6**
34.♖f3! ♗xf3! 35.♕xf3+– This ending is winning for White, although there will be a few more
complications in the proof of this statement.

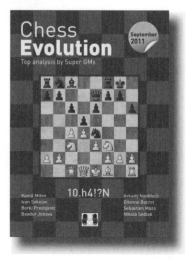